THE TRUST

THE TRUST

The Private and Powerful Family
Behind *The New York Times*

SUSAN E. TIFFT
ALEX S. JONES

**LITTLE, BROWN
AND COMPANY**
Boston New York
London

FIRST EDITION

Library of Congress Cataloging-in-Publication Data
Tifft, Susan E.
The trust : the private and powerful family behind the New York Times /
Susan E. Tifft and Alex S. Jones. — 1st ed.
p.   cm.
Includes index.
ISBN 0-316-84546-9
1. New York Times Company — History   2. Newspaper publishing —
New York (State) — New York — History — 20th century.   3. Newspaper
publishing — New York (State) — New York — History — 19th century.
4. Ochs, Adolph S. (Adolph Simon), 1858–1935 — Family.   5. New York
Times — History.   6. Ochs family.   7. Sulzberger family.
I. Jones, Alex S.   II. Title.
Z473.N44T54   1999
071'.471 — dc21   99-18937

10 9 8 7 6 5 4 3 2 1

MV-NY

Designed by Steve Dyer
Printed in the United States of America

For Rosa, Will, Eliana, and Andres
&
Annie, Marshall, John Mason,
Alex, and Will

CONTENTS

PART THREE

The Inheritor

PART FOUR

The Next Generation

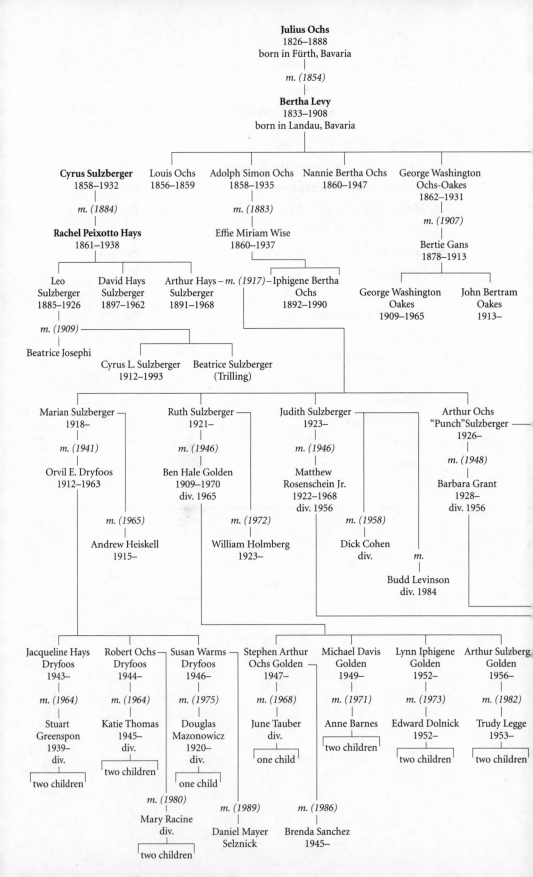

Julius Ochs
1826–1888
born in Fürth, Bavaria

m. (1854)

Bertha Levy
1833–1908
born in Landau, Bavaria

Cyrus Sulzberger 1858–1932 — Louis Ochs 1856–1859 — Adolph Simon Ochs 1858–1935 — Nannie Bertha Ochs 1860–1947 — George Washington Ochs-Oakes 1862–1931

m. (1884) — *m. (1883)* — *m. (1907)*

Rachel Peixotto Hays 1861–1938 — Effie Miriam Wise 1860–1937 — Bertie Gans 1878–1913

Leo Sulzberger 1885–1926 — David Hays Sulzberger 1897–1962 — Arthur Hays Sulzberger 1891–1968 – *m. (1917)* – Iphigene Bertha Ochs 1892–1990 — George Washington Oakes 1909–1965 — John Bertram Oakes 1913–

m. (1909) — Beatrice Josephi

Cyrus L. Sulzberger 1912–1993 — Beatrice Sulzberger (Trilling)

Marian Sulzberger 1918– — Ruth Sulzberger 1921– — Judith Sulzberger 1923– — Arthur Ochs "Punch" Sulzberger 1926–

m. (1941) — *m. (1946)* — *m. (1946)* — *m. (1948)*

Orvil E. Dryfoos 1912–1963 — Ben Hale Golden 1909–1970 div. 1965 — Matthew Rosenschein Jr. 1922–1968 div. 1956 — Barbara Grant 1928– div. 1956

m. (1965) — *m. (1972)* — *m. (1958)*

Andrew Heiskell 1915– — William Holmberg 1923– — Dick Cohen div.

m. — Budd Levinson div. 1984

Jacqueline Hays Dryfoos 1943– — Robert Ochs Dryfoos 1944– — Susan Warms Dryfoos 1946– — Stephen Arthur Ochs Golden 1947– — Michael Davis Golden 1949– — Lynn Iphigene Golden 1952– — Arthur Sulzberg Golden 1956–

m. (1964) — *m. (1964)* — *m. (1975)* — *m. (1968)* — *m. (1971)* — *m. (1973)* — *m. (1982)*

Stuart Greenspon 1939– div. — Katie Thomas 1945– div. — Douglas Mazonowicz 1920– div. — June Tauber div. — Anne Barnes — Edward Dolnick 1952– — Trudy Legge 1953–

two children — two children — one child — one child — two children — two children — two children

m. (1980) — Mary Racine div. — two children

m. (1989) — Daniel Mayer Selznick

m. (1986) — Brenda Sanchez 1945–

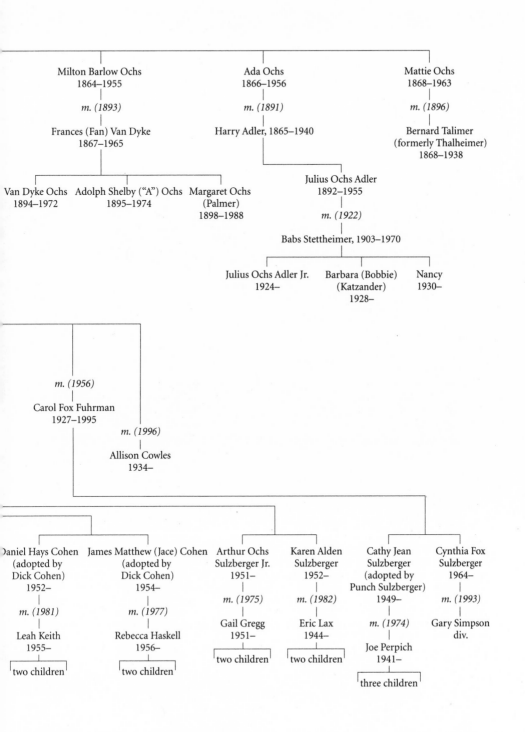

Milton Barlow Ochs
1864–1955

m. (1893)

Frances (Fan) Van Dyke
1867–1965

Ada Ochs
1866–1956

m. (1891)

Harry Adler, 1865–1940

Mattie Ochs
1868–1963

m. (1896)

Bernard Talimer
(formerly Thalheimer)
1868–1938

Van Dyke Ochs
1894–1972

Adolph Shelby ("A") Ochs
1895–1974

Margaret Ochs
(Palmer)
1898–1988

Julius Ochs Adler
1892–1955

m. (1922)

Babs Stettheimer, 1903–1970

Julius Ochs Adler Jr.
1924–

Barbara (Bobbie)
(Katzander)
1928–

Nancy
1930–

m. (1956)

Carol Fox Fuhrman
1927–1995

m. (1996)

Allison Cowles
1934–

Daniel Hays Cohen
(adopted by
Dick Cohen)
1952–

m. (1981)

Leah Keith
1955–

two children

James Matthew (Jace) Cohen
(adopted by
Dick Cohen)
1954–

m. (1977)

Rebecca Haskell
1956–

two children

Arthur Ochs
Sulzberger Jr.
1951–

m. (1975)

Gail Gregg
1951–

two children

Karen Alden
Sulzberger
1952–

m. (1982)

Eric Lax
1944–

two children

Cathy Jean
Sulzberger
(adopted by
Punch Sulzberger)
1949–

m. (1974)

Joe Perpich
1941–

three children

Cynthia Fox
Sulzberger
1964–

m. (1993)

Gary Simpson
div.

JUNE 26, 1996

I N THE COPPER TWILIGHT OF EARLY SUMMER, Arthur Ochs Sulzberger Jr. bounded up the granite steps of New York City's Metropolitan Museum of Art with the self-assured air of royalty. At the top he greeted Ted Koppel, host of ABC's *Nightline,* and NBC news anchor Tom Brokaw, then plunged into the throng, a mixture of business magnates, society mavens, artists, politicians, television anchors, and the seniormost executives and editors of his family's newspaper, *The New York Times.* Lean as a whippet in an elegantly tailored tuxedo, he air-kissed the women and clapped the men on the back, exchanging wisecracks, his signature way of dealing with people. Since becoming publisher of the *Times* in 1992 at the age of forty, he had tried to curb his lifelong habit of shooting verbal darts, but under stress he often forgot himself.

Arthur Jr.'s wife, Gail Gregg, mounted the stairs at her own gait, looking chic if slightly uncomfortable in a black sheath dress cut high up her thigh. She had been raised in Kansas and was detached in a sensible Midwestern way from the role expected of the spouse of a *Times* publisher. In the world she came from, there were no words for the haute couture dress she was wearing. "In Topeka," she observed wryly, "there were only two categories of clothes: church clothes and nonchurch clothes." For Gail, who had given up her own promising career as a journalist rather than cause problems for her husband, marrying into the Sulzberger family had been a mixed blessing. "The family," as the clan called itself, provided warmth, wealth, and opportunity, but for the in-laws — "the real heroes of this family," as one of Arthur Jr.'s cousins remarked — its demands had occasionally fostered frustration.

But this was a night for family unity, not division. It was the evening on which the direct descendants of Adolph S. Ochs, Arthur Jr.'s

xiii

great-grandfather, had gathered to salute the moment one hundred years earlier when his destiny and that of the nation had abruptly collided.

In the summer of 1896 Adolph Ochs had become the proprietor of a famous but bankrupt newspaper known then, with a quaint hyphen, as *The New-York Times.* Adolph had been, in fact, a recent arrival in New York. The barely educated son of German Jewish immigrants, he had grown up in Ohio and Tennessee, still spoke with a slight twang, and was himself deeply in debt. Despite these handicaps, he had managed to take the once mighty *New-York Times,* which through misfortune and mismanagement had been reduced to printing cheap fiction and partisan bluster, and build it into the most influential newspaper in the world.

In the process, Adolph had also created "the family," an extended group of Ochses and Sulzbergers that was arguably the most powerful blood-related dynasty in twentieth-century America. The family not only had owned *The New York Times* but had actively run it for a century, nearly half of the nation's history. The position of publisher had always been a family preserve, an office tantamount to a permanent, inherited cabinet post that passed from generation to generation, as unquestioned a divine right as the crown resting on the head of a Tudor or a Windsor. Presidents might come and go, but the *Times* was a constant, and its voice in the affairs of the United States had always been ultimately that of an Ochs or a Sulzberger, whether by birth or by marriage.

Yet the family had remained fiercely private. Ostentation and self-promotion were frowned upon; to be accused of having a "big head" was a stinging rebuke. Glory was reserved for *The New York Times,* and the family was content to bask in its brilliant reflection. Over the years modesty had become something of a genetic trait, a quirk of nature passed down from one generation to the next, like dyslexia or depression, which were also in the mix. "We are not the sort of people who feel we must have yachts," said Iphigene Ochs Sulzberger, Adolph's daughter and only child, who during her ninety-seven-year-long life had profoundly shaped the family and the *Times* and continued to influence both long after her death.

So it was all the more extraordinary that, contrary to custom, this self-consciously reserved clan had made itself the centerpiece of the most elaborate, expensive, and opulent extravaganza *The New York Times* had ever sponsored. With its monumental scale and air of unassailable permanence, the Metropolitan Museum of Art was an ideal venue for the occasion. Arthur Ochs "Punch" Sulzberger, Arthur Jr.'s father and the chairman and CEO of The New York Times Company, headed the museum's board; Arthur Hays Sulzberger, Punch's late father and a former *Times* publisher, had served as a director. During his often lonely childhood, Punch had spent many hours wandering the Met's arms and armor exhibit, a collection he still found fascinating as an adult.

The fact that the newspaper had endured for one hundred years under the same owners was highly improbable. Family companies of any sort that survive into a second generation, much less a third, are rare. Almost all the families that owned papers in 1896 had long since sold out to chains, relinquished day-to-day management to professional retainers, or seen their papers disappear altogether.

Arthur Jr. was a member of the fourth generation of the Ochs-Sulzberger family to own and run *The New York Times.* Unlike his father, who had been the sole male in his generation, Arthur Jr. faced competition for the ultimate prize — power over The New York Times Company — from several of his cousins as well as from one of the company's professional managers. As Arthur Jr. worked the crowd, there was whispered speculation as to whether he would eventually win his father's titles of chairman and CEO to go along with the publisher's mantle Punch had already bestowed.

In a visual effect straight out of a Busby Berkeley musical, one hundred tuxedoed violinists — one for each year of the family's ownership — stood on the Met's Grand Staircase playing selections from Cole Porter, Jerome Kern, and Lerner and Loewe. To their left and right, at either end of the Great Hall, the deep, sad eyes of a man with an unusually large head stared down at the revelers. The face was that of a young Adolph Ochs, emblazoned on banners that fluttered from the Met's second-floor balconies.

With "Begin the Beguine" and "On the Street Where You Live" playing in the background, guests queued up in a receiving line to be greeted by Punch Sulzberger and his third wife, Allison Cowles. Punch had married Allison only seven months after his wife of thirty-nine years, Carol, died of cancer. Long before she had become ill, the once congenial union had turned sour, and Punch, seventy, had made little effort to conceal his happiness at finding Allison, prompting the city's gossip columnists to make tart comments about the haste of his remarriage.

So it was all the more startling when family friends glimpsed what appeared to be Carol's ghost gracefully navigating the cool marble floor of the Great Hall. The figure was, in fact, Cynthia Sulzberger, thirty-two, the only child of Punch and Carol's marriage, who had purposely chosen to wear her mother's signature gown, a deep brown dress with a hand-painted butterfly fluttering on its diaphanous train. The subtly defiant gesture seemed to make Carol a presence at the party her husband and his new wife were hosting.

Punch, who normally favored conservative suits bought off the rack at Paul Stuart, was dressed on this night in a stylish tuxedo with a rich brocade vest of red and blue paisley. As each guest approached the receiving line, he shook hands and introduced his bride, then passed the person on to his three sisters, who stood in order of age, just as they had in family photos dating back to the 1920s: Marian, the oldest, then Ruth, then Judy. Punch was the youngest of the four, but as head of The New York Times Company, he had long been the first among equals. Whether the issue was the publication of the Pentagon Papers or jobs for their children at the *Times,* Punch's sisters had given him their unwavering support, and he was careful never to abuse their trust. Family solidarity was a legacy of their mother, Iphigene, who had inculcated in all of them the importance of unity, so much so that Punch had once warned his late wife, "Don't ever try to come between me and my sisters."

Despite their wealth and position, Punch and his siblings were remarkably unaffected. To outsiders, they seemed content to live in their own self-referential world, a charming trait that under certain conditions could also make them appear vague and oblivious to social realities. The evening's guest list was a perfect example. Apart from family members, many of those invited to the centennial dinner barely knew the Sulzbergers; a professional party planner had assembled the list with little input from Punch and none from his sisters. The result was a hodgepodge that was heavy on glitter and light on representatives of print journalism, especially newspapers. The three network news anchors were there, along with *20/20*'s Barbara Walters and *60 Minutes*' Mike Wallace, while the publishers and editors of *The Wall Street Journal,* the *New York Post,* the *Daily News, The Washington Post, Time,* and *Newsweek* were not in evidence. Brooke Astor mingled with songwriter Stephen Sondheim, *überhausfrau* Martha Stewart, and Joseph Heller, author of *Catch-22,* but Gay Talese, a former *New York Times* reporter whose book *The Kingdom and the Power* remained the defining account of the paper's news operation, had inexplicably not been included.

Among the *Times'* executives, conversation centered on one conspicuous absence among their ranks: Lance Primis, the New York Times Company president and top nonfamily executive in the organization. Primis had decided to leave town a day early for a meeting of the board of directors of the *International Herald Tribune,* the Paris-based newspaper published jointly by *The New York Times* and *The Washington Post.* He wanted to play golf with the *IHT*'s publisher, he had told Punch, and, following the meeting, to take a vacation in France with his family.

In an uncharacteristically direct way, Punch had told Primis that it was important for him to be present at the centennial dinner, but Lance had chosen not to understand. Since becoming president in 1992, he had increasingly irritated the Sulzbergers by suggesting that the time had come for *The New York Times* to abandon its "candy store" approach to running the company, derisive code words that in Primis's vocabulary signaled his desire to end day-to-day family management at the top.

If Primis had insulted the family with his absence, the family had been equally insensitive to what Punch dismissively called the "peripherals," the plentiful Ochs relatives who claimed their own strong ties to the *Times* but were not direct descendants of Adolph Ochs. These men and women were livid at having been excluded from a celebration of what they considered to be "their" family, too. "It was deliberate," fumed Bobbie Adler Katzander, Ochs's grandniece, whose father, Julius Ochs Adler, had once been general manager of the *Times* and as close as a son to Adolph. "I can't tell you how angry and bitter I am."

The composition of the centennial party guest list underscored a harsh truth: the descendants of Adolph through his daughter, Iphigene, had become the family of *The New York Times* while the other branches had been slowly but inexorably cut away. This distinction applied as well to a less numerous but equally ardent collection of Sulzbergers, none of whom had been invited to the festivities, despite the fact that Cyrus L. Sulzberger, Punch's recently deceased second cousin, had been a celebrated foreign correspondent and columnist at the *Times* for nearly forty years. While she was alive, Iphigene had paid careful attention to the peripherals; she understood their yearning to claim kinship to *The New York Times.* Had she been involved in the party planning, they would not have been overlooked.

After an hour of cocktails and canapés, a dramatic fanfare from long trumpets summoned the nearly five hundred guests into the soaring gallery that housed the Temple of Dendur, the only complete Egyptian temple in the Western Hemisphere, which had been transformed for the evening into a turn-of-the-century dining room, complete with globed candelabra and tablecloths printed with old *Times* headlines.

As the crowd settled down to a first course of lobster tarragon over artichoke bottoms, Barbara Walters eyed the head table, visibly seething. There, to Punch's right, in the seat of honor, sat Diane Sawyer, the cohost of ABC-TV's *PrimeTime Live* and Walters's network rival, looking soigné in a single-shouldered black dress. Walters was an old friend of the Sulzbergers, so close that she had been one of two nonfamily members to deliver a tribute to Carol Sulzberger at her memorial service. By all rights she felt *she* should have been in Sawyer's place, and made no secret of her displeasure to her dinner companions.

Like so many aspects of the party, however, Punch's choice of dinner partner was another curious accident. Punch hardly knew Diane Sawyer; she had not even been on the original guest list. She was included only after her husband, playwright and director Mike Nichols — a favorite of the *Times* — had been invited in an attempt to increase representation from the arts. Nichols had sent his regrets, saying that he was scheduled to be out of the country, but Sawyer had accepted. It was Susan Dryfoos, Punch's niece and a key organizer of the party, who had placed Sawyer next to the chairman to symbolize youth and vigor, words not usually associated with an institution known for decades as the Good Gray Lady.

In her role as the family's historian and guardian of its public face, Susan had overseen the planning of all centennial observances. Earlier in the year she had commissioned and then abruptly rejected a brief documentary about Adolph's life that had been intended to serve as entertainment at the Met party. The filmmaker she had hired — a celebrated documentarian — had tried to puncture the stiff iconic legend of Adolph Ochs and portray him as a human figure. When Susan screened the final product, however, she cringed at references to Adolph's battles with depression and immediately canceled the project. The filmmaker was paid, but only after agreeing never to make a copy of the film or to show it to anyone. Not even Punch had had a chance to see the tape before Susan placed it under lock and key.

The situation had set off a panicked rush for substitute entertainment. The Pulitzer Prize–winning playwright Wendy Wasserstein and Frank Rich, a *Times* columnist and former theater critic, agreed to fill the void, coauthoring an imaginary dialogue based on letters between Adolph and his wife, Effie, during the days leading up to his acquisition of *The New York Times*. When the moment came for the performance, Sam Waterston played Adolph with the slightest hint of a hayseed accent, while Kate Nelligan portrayed Effie as a loving, commonsensical spouse.

Although the party was in honor of his grandfather, the night belonged to Punch Sulzberger, who stepped to the lectern to welcome everyone on behalf of the Ochs-Sulzberger clan. He described the four centennial exhibits at the New York Public Library, the Pierpont Morgan Library, the Museum of Modern Art, and the Museum of Natural History. He spoke of a special centennial project at the Adolph S. Ochs Middle School in Brooklyn. Finally, he quoted Adolph Ochs's most famous line — the credo of *The New York Times* — which had appeared in the first editorial written under his management: "to give the news impartially, without fear or favor, regardless of any party, sect or interest involved."

The pledge, the soul of *The New York Times,* appeared in bronze under a bust of Adolph on the *Times'* executive floor, in two official histories of the newspaper, and countless times in the paper itself. The standards it embodied had inspired journalists everywhere. Like a commandment chiseled in stone and passed down from the *Times'* own Moses, the words amounted to a living covenant between the Ochs-Sulzberger family and the singular institution they had nurtured.

But almost from the moment that Adolph's famous phrase had first appeared in the paper, the *Times* had been misquoting it. Even Punch, who recited the words so reverentially at the centennial dinner, did not realize he was misstating what his grandfather had written. Since 1896, it seemed, no one had gone back to verify what the *Times'* patriarch had actually said.

Adolph had composed the "without fear or favor" editorial during a period when the *Times* was considered an organ of the Democratic Party. His aim was to reassure Republicans of the paper's political objectivity. The *Times,* he wrote, would "give the news impartially, without fear or favor, regardless of *party,* sect or *interests* involved." Punch, like legions of speakers and authors before him, had injected the word *any* before *party* and made *interests* singular, unwittingly stripping the phrase of its political point and changing the meaning to a more general disavowal of prejudice.

The gaffe was emblematic, for even as they celebrated their rich and worthy past, the fact was that the Ochs-Sulzberger family knew little more about their own history, or that of *The New York Times,* than the myths and legends that had grown up around both. The truth, as it turned out, would prove to be more complicated — and much more interesting.

THE TRUST

PART ONE

The Paterfamilias

1

The Boy with No Childhood

S ITTING IN HIS CRAMPED OFFICE JUST INSIDE
the gates of Temple Israel Cemetery, Fred Maier, the superintendent, heard the familiar sound of an idling Packard limousine. He
immediately abandoned his paperwork to greet his illustrious visitor
and emerged from the stone-and-stucco building just in time to see a
small, roundish man in a glossy fur coat alight from the car's rear door.
"Mr. Ochs," said Maier, referring to the owner and publisher of *The New
York Times* in the formal manner that he preferred. "How nice to see you
again."

Adolph S. Ochs's gait was unsteady, his face impassive, and his blue
eyes slightly lopsided, as though he had had a stroke. Since Hitler's rise
to power the previous year, Ochs had been in the grip of a deep depression that had changed him from an exuberant, energetic, even lusty figure into a despairing old man. As the son of German Jewish immigrants,
Adolph feared that the Nazis' virulent brand of anti-Semitism might
take root in America, toppling him from what he viewed as his fragile
pedestal of success and respectability. Normally a sentimental, almost
naive optimist, he was now, in the winter of 1934, a gloomy man,
obsessed with his own mortality and beset by a near hysterical anxiety
about which family member should follow him as steward of the most
powerful newspaper in the world.

Ochs extended his hand warmly to Maier and exchanged a few pleasantries before asking for the key to his unfinished mausoleum. Since
purchasing the gravesite in January 1933 — the largest in the cemetery,
with room for six aboveground coffins and twelve more to be buried —
Adolph had been a regular visitor, taking a keen interest in the construction of his final resting place.

For decades he had planned to be buried in Chattanooga, Tennessee,
the hardscrabble town where he had first triumphed as the youthful

proprietor of *The Chattanooga Times*. Even now, after nearly forty years of living in New York City, Adolph referred to Chattanooga as "home." But when he discovered that his son-in-law's family, the Sulzbergers, were interred at Temple Israel, only fifteen minutes from Hillandale, his estate in White Plains, Adolph abandoned his Chattanooga shrine. Instead, he erected a tomb in New York so that his cherished only child, Iphigene, could more easily visit the grave, along with her husband, Arthur Hays Sulzberger, their four children, and the clamorous extended clan of New York–based Ochs siblings, in-laws, nephews, and nieces whose fortunes had long been linked to that of Adolph and *The New York Times*.

Adolph's mausoleum would be the final magisterial gesture of his life. He had never shied away from P. T. Barnum–like pomp and swagger, and in contemplation of death he was no different. To ensure that his resting place made the appropriate statement, he hired as its architects the New York firm that had designed the Empire State Building. The result was a stately stone sepulchre with an imposing bronze door, glass windows crisscrossed with iron bars to discourage vandals, and a foundation covered with two coats of tar to keep out moisture.

Adolph had located his tomb within sight of the more modest Sulzberger graves and those of their Sephardic relatives, the Hayses and Peixottos. As a German Jew, he was all too aware of the Jewish pecking order that placed his background a firm notch below that of the Sephardim, who had been driven from the Iberian Peninsula by the Inquisition and had arrived on American shores early enough to fight in the Revolution. To lie in splendor mere feet from these Jewish aristocrats was both a fitting culmination of Adolph's ambitions and a mild rebuke to the old-line Jewish establishment that he felt had never fully embraced him.

For all his love of spectacle, Adolph Ochs was at heart a man with simple tastes, virtues, and vices. He was unschooled and, even after reaching near iconic status, was disarmingly — even shockingly — modest. "A plain man," said Maier, who had carefully observed that, unlike his more status-conscious son-in-law, Adolph always exited his limousine himself rather than ostentatiously waiting for the chauffeur to assist him.

As he had grown ever more despondent, Adolph had spoken with increasing urgency of returning to Chattanooga. Out of affection and nostalgia, he had instructed the New York architects to build his crypt from white Tennessee marble and to landscape the grounds with Tennessee flora — mountain laurel, dogwood, hemlock, pine trees, and pin oaks.

Adolph enjoyed money and fame and had worked hard to acquire both during his nearly seventy-six years, yet riches, renown, and power had never been central concerns. As the end of his life drew near, he found himself recalling his earliest ambitions, ones forged in deprivation, the humiliation of being the son of an honorable but ineffectual father, and the tenuousness of being Jewish in an overwhelmingly gentile world.

His mausoleum was almost complete. As Adolph trudged the grounds, eyeing the work approvingly, his mind turned to his epitaph. He had decided years before on the words he wanted inscribed on his sarcophagus: just two lines, a fragment of a Fitz-Greene Halleck poem he had chanced to see on the tombstone of a now forgotten poet in Brooklyn in 1903:

> None knew thee but to love thee,
> None named thee but to praise.*

Love and praise. Affection and reputation. Simple goals, unsuitable for the voracious appetites of a Hearst or a Pulitzer, but not for Adolph Ochs, who had long ago yearned for both, making them the North Star in the black sky that was his childhood.

§

Adolph's father, Julius, was born in 1826 in Fürth, Bavaria, to Lazarus Ochsenhorn, a prosperous diamond merchant and talmudic scholar. He attended college in Cologne, displaying a talent for scholarship, especially in music and languages.

When Lazarus died in 1840, Julius's oldest brother became the head of the family, as was the custom, and promptly ordered Julius to abandon his studies and apprentice himself to a bookbinder. Finding the life of a tradesman dull, and the laws restricting work and marriage for Jews oppressive, Julius emigrated to America in 1845, joining several older

---

*These are the lines as they appear on Ochs's grave, but they misquote Halleck, who actually wrote: "None knew thee but to love thee / Nor named thee but to praise."

siblings in Louisville, Kentucky. With his command of English, he had hoped to reenter college, but his family again dissuaded him; using the shortened name of Ochs, he compliantly followed the path of so many of the German Jewish immigrants who fled to America about the time of the revolutions of 1848: he became an itinerant peddler.

Before the Civil War Julius wandered widely throughout the South, taking a variety of jobs: a teacher in a small Kentucky girls' school, a watch merchant in Cincinnati, and a clerk in his brother's Louisville dry goods store. Because of his religious training and fluency in Hebrew, he was often called upon to conduct services for the tiny Jewish congregations in the communities where he lived. Soon he assumed the position of lay rabbi.

In 1855 Julius married Bertha Levy, the plain-faced daughter of a merchant and tailor from Landau, Bavaria. Bertha was as determined and inflexible as Julius was dreamy and accommodating. As a fifteen-year-old student at Heidelberg Seminary during the revolutionary movement of 1848, she had defiantly dipped her handkerchief in the blood of an executed comrade to show her sympathy for the cause. To escape arrest, she fled to Natchez, Mississippi, to live with an uncle. Her parents soon followed, and by 1854 the family had settled in Nashville, Tennessee. It was there that Julius, then working for a cousin, became engaged to Bertha on the evening of Yom Kippur.

Bertha's youthful liberalism proved to be deceptive. In Natchez she had embraced a contemptuous antebellum view of blacks, and for the rest of her life was dogmatically conservative, even reactionary. Julius, on the other hand, recoiled at the sight of slave auctions in Mississippi and Louisiana, where he worked briefly during the early 1850s. Declaring slavery a "villainous relic of barbarism," he became as determined to abolish the South's "peculiar institution" as Bertha was to preserve it.

It was into this fractious household that Adolph Simon Ochs was born on March 12, 1858, on the eve of the Civil War. Although the Ochses by then were living north of the Mason-Dixon line — Julius had moved to Cincinnati soon after his marriage — Bertha remained a Confederate to the last, even insisting that she be buried with the Stars and Bars. Adolph grew up hearing "mother [give] father a lot of trouble" about the war and saw neighbors lose husbands and sons on both sides. Those experiences contributed to a distrust of rigid ideology and an affinity for compromise that would later shape his newspaper career.

The critical event of Adolph's childhood was the death of his older brother, the Ochses' firstborn, Louis, who succumbed to scarlet fever in 1859 at the age of two. "The blow almost prostrated me," Julius wrote years later, "for my very soul was wrapped up with that child." Bertha's response was to pour her furious energy and ambition into Adolph, and he reacted by trying to be both the son she had lost and the provider his father could never be. Even as a very young boy, he was the source of income and manly strength for his parents and for the five siblings who eventually joined him in the Ochs household: Nannie, George, Milton, Ada, and Mattie. "All I have accomplished in life I owe to her," Adolph later said of his mother. She "is my inspiration, my comfort and the creator of all that gives me self-respect."

The bond between mother and son was fortified by Julius's frequent financial reversals and his many absences during the Civil War. After the fall of Fort Sumter in April 1861, Julius organized a company of Ohio volunteers, taking the title of captain. He was as much a misfit at soldiering as he was at business, and served only six months. He had hoped to join the regular military service, but the vocally Confederate Bertha discouraged the idea. Instead, Julius peddled necessities to Tennessee Unionists, crisscrossing the countryside in rude covered wagons.

It didn't help Julius's business — or his peace of mind — that his wife freely trumpeted her Southern sympathies. In the fall of 1861, soon after the arrival of the couple's third son, Bertha was arrested for smuggling quinine to rebel forces across the Ohio River. The drugs were hidden in the bottom of a baby carriage that held the newborn, whom Julius had patriotically named George Washington Ochs. Only her marriage to a Union loyalist saved Bertha from incarceration.

In 1864 Julius moved his family to Knoxville, then under Federal control, and briefly served as an officer in a regiment organized to protect the city. After Appomattox he capitalized on the region's pent-up appetite for merchandise by buying dry goods and quickly reselling them at a handsome profit. Intoxicated by the artificial boom, Julius borrowed wildly, acquiring a house in Knoxville and an eighty-one-acre estate in the country, which he grandly dubbed Ochsenburg. For a brief moment the Ochses were prosperous, reveling in the luxury of carriages, horses, and servants.

Their Arcadia was short-lived. In 1867, a year of economic panic in the South, creditors began knocking on Julius's door. Hopelessly overextended, he declared personal bankruptcy and sold his home, farm, and business to pay his debts. The family moved into an unpainted rented house east of town. At the suggestion of some kindly friends who realized he could never succeed as a merchant, Julius became a justice of the peace and a member of the county court, later adding notary public to his list of fee-producing titles. Nevertheless, the Ochses were soon forced to take in boarders to make ends meet.

In the late 1860s and early 1870s, Knoxville was an up-and-coming, class-conscious city of 8,700 still bitterly divided by the war. Families had buried rebels and Unionists alike, and the town teemed with hate-filled partisans on both sides. Anti-Jewish feeling, which crested during the war, continued to thrive in the overheated atmosphere of the city. Although fifteen thousand Jews had fought for the Union, almost as many had served the Southern cause, and rumors persisted that Jewish bankers had secretly financed the Confederacy. As the oldest son of a nearly impoverished Jew with a distinct German accent, Adolph, with his black curls and "round Jewish face," learned to value compromise, work harder than anyone else, and seek harmony whenever possible. At an early age he was convinced — as much by pragmatic necessity as by principle — that "there was much to be said on both sides of most questions."

To boost the family's finances, Adolph got a job when he was eleven as a carrier boy for the *Knoxville Chronicle*. He arrived at the *Chronicle* office every morning at 5:00 A.M. to fold the fifty papers on his route. He then walked four miles delivering them, went home for a brief breakfast, and by 7:00 A.M. was seated in his desk at school. For his labor, Adolph earned twenty-five cents a day. He was soon joined at the paper by his younger brothers, George and Milton. In a show of solidarity, Julius arose with his sons and accompanied them to the *Chronicle* every morning in the predawn darkness.

Adolph made brief detours into the grocery business and drugstore trade, but it was newspapers that gave him the opportunity to cultivate the approving older men who would prove critical to his success. Over the next six years he worked for both the *Knoxville Chronicle* and the *Knoxville Tribune*, advancing rapidly from office boy to printer's devil to apprentice to journeyman printer. When he was fourteen, Adolph left school to devote himself full-time to supporting his family. For the rest of his life, "Muley" Ochs, as he was nicknamed (a lame joke on his last name, which was pronounced "ox" and actually meant that in German), had an awestruck reverence for people with formal education. As a young man he wrote letters riddled with bumpkinish mistakes such as "it ain't" and "it don't." Although he later learned to write and speak properly, in distinguished groups he would often listen in respectful silence rather than risk making a grammatical error. But Adolph had qualities that would prove to be just as important as education: boundless energy, an ingratiating personality, and a mature self-confidence, nurtured by Bertha, that struck contemporaries as almost comical. "I laughed immoderately at your letter," a Louisville cousin told fifteen-year-old Adolph. "It contained such high style."

In August 1875 President Andrew Johnson died, and Adolph proposed to the Louisville *Courier-Journal* that he cover the funeral in nearby Greeneville, Tennessee. The resulting article was so heavily edited that Adolph could "hardly recognize it as my work." Nevertheless, the experience whetted his appetite for the wider world, and two months later he left Knoxville for Louisville, where he hoped to amass enough cash to press on to his ultimate destination: California.

On Adolph's last night in Knoxville, his fellow *Chronicle* compositors threw a farewell banquet of steamed oysters and beer. Their parting gift was a book of poetry by Thomas Hood, a former engraver, in which they inscribed their names. Adolph, though just seventeen, had impressed them all with his diligence and good humor. In the dedication at the front of the book, the men grandly predicted that he would eventually be counted "among the nation's honored sons."

Adolph knew how to put such sentiments to practical use. In preparation for his departure, he had bought a bound leather autograph book in which he had carefully collected the job references and testimonials he hoped would help catapult him to fortune and glory. Captain William Rule, the *Chronicle*'s editor, had made a lengthy entry, as had Henry Collins, the head of the composing room, who declared his enterprising apprentice "a necessity, hard to part with."

But it was Adolph's own inscription that would prove to be the most telling. On the first page, in his plump, almost feminine hand, he had copied from memory — and thus slightly incorrectly — a famous quotation from *Othello:*

Who steals my purse steals trash;
Twas mine, 'tis his, and has been slave to thousands;
But he who filches from me my good name
Robs me of that which not enriches him,
and makes me poor indeed.

2

Chattanooga Days

I N LOUISVILLE ADOLPH BOARDED WITH COUSINS, worked as a typesetter at Henry Watterson's *Courier-Journal,* and in the hope of preparing himself for an editorial position, studied syntax and spelling. In his leisure hours he indulged in parties, danced till dawn, and romanced girls, a form of adolescent rebellion that — as far as Julius was concerned — threatened to sully the "good name" his son sought to burnish.

From a distance Julius sternly asserted his parental authority. The Ochs household, like that of many German Jews, was *streng und gerecht* — strict and righteous. No matter how mean their circumstances, Julius and Bertha expected obedience and respect from their children and did not take kindly to the supercilious tone of Adolph's infrequent letters home. When, after three months in Louisville, Adolph sent his father fifty dollars, Julius accepted it only because he had no choice; the youngest children were without decent shoes or stockings. But he scolded his son for giving the sum in a manner "calculated to wound my pride." As for the frivolous "nonsense" that took up disproportionate space in Adolph's letters, Julius was brutally frank. "You are getting to be a great Ladies man," he wrote. "Remember, no *great Ladies man* ever made a great statesman, a great politician, a great merchant. In fact, no great Ladies man ever made anything else *great.*"

Julius needn't have worried. Adolph was flirtatious and would go on to pursue women all his life, but he was also steady, reliable, and single-minded about bettering himself. His great hero was Horace Greeley, the rural New Hampshire printer who had struggled up from poverty to become owner of the influential *New York Tribune.*

By the spring of 1876, when it was clear he could not advance at *The Courier-Journal,* Adolph gave up his dream of reaching the Pacific and returned home, lured by the prospect of working as assistant to the composing-room foreman at the *Knoxville Tribune*. There, his "grim application to business" caught the eye of Colonel J. E. MacGowan, the paper's scholarly editor, and its raffish business manager, Franc S. Paul.

Adolph had been back in Knoxville less than a year when his father suffered a business reversal that pushed the struggling Ochses further into poverty. In his capacity as agent for the Phoenix Insurance Company, Julius was unable to account for $345.53 in insurance premiums he had collected for his employer, prompting two friends who held mortgages on the family's personal property and a performance bond on Julius to reluctantly liquidate the Ochs household in order to pay the debt. It was difficult to say which was worse: Julius's shame at being assumed to be an embezzler or his horror at watching everything the family owned sold at public auction. In a matter of days, the Ochses saw the accumulated possessions of a lifetime pass out of their hands: Julius's beloved piano, on which he had composed comedic operettas; the family's lace curtains; parlor chairs; clocks; carpets; mattresses and pillows. Even the Ochs chamber pot was put up for sale.

The trauma caused Julius, fifty-one, to experience chest pains and the nervous exhaustion of a mind "strained beyond almost human capacity." Fearing he might have "an accident," he wrote an anguished letter to his children instructing them what to do in the event of his death. He berated himself as a "professional borrower," a man who had foolishly lived beyond his means and whose honor was now besmirched because people "took me to be a swindler." Having known the sting of being smugly pitied, he admonished his children always to practice charity with humility, "so as not to hurt the feelings of the person you wish to relieve." "My life has been misspent," he wrote balefully. "I have often wished for death and a great boon it would be to me and a relief to my family."

His father's disgrace had a transformative effect on Adolph. Determined to rescue his family's fortunes and reputation, Adolph agreed to join MacGowan and Paul in the publication of a new newspaper in Chattanooga, 114 miles to the south, where Paul had once edited *The Rebel*. MacGowan and Paul put up several hundred dollars; Adolph pledged sweat equity. By April 1877 the trio had produced the first issue of *The Chattanooga Daily Dispatch*, with Adolph as business solicitor.

The *Dispatch*, "so poorly printed as to be almost unreadable," was ill-fated from the outset. The deceptively quiet Paul turned out to be an alcoholic and opium addict who paid people only when they forced his hand by quitting. Adolph, too, had to resign in order to get what was due him. When he showed up to collect, he found Paul in a pitiful state. "I just can't get along without you," he wailed. "No business [can] succeed without an Irishman or a Jew." The backhanded compliment proved effective. Adolph resumed work, telling Bertha in December 1877 that he soon hoped to "be able to make you all a comfortable home where want is unknown and send my brothers and sisters on their different roads rejoicing."

That day was yet far off. The *Dispatch* soon collapsed under a mountain of unpaid bills. Still smarting from his family's recent humiliation in Knoxville, Adolph resolved to settle the debt. Though only nineteen years old, he so impressed the paper's creditors that they appointed him receiver. Their trust was well placed: he paid back every cent. His main means of recovery was the failed paper's job-printing plant. One day, while cranking out flyers on an old Gordon handpress, Adolph hit upon the idea of producing Chattanooga's first city directory. With David Harris, a former *Dispatch* printer, he canvassed door-to-door, visiting every bank, store, house, and hotel, carefully recording the location, number, race, occupation, and place of origin of the town's inhabitants. In the spring of 1878 the Chattanooga *City Directory and Business Gazetteer* made its debut, with Adolph S. Ochs as publisher. Although it listed only 2,981 people (2,196 whites, 785 colored) out of a total population of 11,488, the booklet made enough money to permit Adolph to send two dollars a week back to his family.

Despite his disheartening experience as cofounder of the *Dispatch*, Adolph remained enthralled with the idea of owning a newspaper in Chattanooga. He was now in a favorable position to do so, for in the course of gathering material for the directory, he had met nearly every banker and businessman in town. By honorably settling the *Dispatch* debt, he had also established himself as a worthy credit risk. So when S. A. Cunningham, proprietor of the near moribund *Chattanooga Daily Times*, inquired whether he was interested in buying the nine-year-old paper, Adolph scrambled to put together a staff and financing. Colonel MacGowan, whom Adolph regarded as "my generous foster-father [and] . . . greatest helpmeet," said he would serve as editor for $1.50 a day. Four journeymen printers — casualties of the *Dispatch* disaster — agreed to work for short wages.

Cunningham demanded $1,500 for a half interest, with $250 as a down payment and the balance in monthly installments of $100. Despite the modest success of the directory, Ochs was virtually destitute, unable even to pay his board bill, and MacGowan's finances had been decimated by the bankruptcy of the *Dispatch*. But Adolph, who had grown a thick mustache in an effort to look older, possessed persuasive powers beyond his years. He managed to borrow the down payment from a cousin in Louisville and convinced Elbert A. James, a struggling local businessman and former Democratic state senator, to co-sign a $300 banknote for working capital.

In early July the deal was concluded, with the added stipulation, demanded by Adolph, that he have the right to buy the remaining half of the paper in two years. Because Adolph, then twenty, was not legally of age, it was Julius who had to sign the ownership papers, a responsibility that must have been intensely uncomfortable. Earlier, fearful that his son would follow his own example and spiral into debt, he had urged Adolph to abandon the venture. Now, worn down by the young man's persistence, and having no promising prospects of his own, he reluctantly agreed to sign a contract that made him — Julius — legally responsible if the newspaper failed.

On July 2, 1878, the first issue of *The Chattanooga Daily Times* appeared under the proprietorship of Adolph S. Ochs. After the down payment, office rent, a short week's salaries, and a subscription to the Associated Press, Adolph was left with just $12.50 with which to run his publication. The staff, consisting of five "executives," eight printers, and two black press operators, worked in a dark, twenty-by-forty-foot, one-story brick shed at the corner of Eighth and Cherry Streets. Circulation was unpromising; under Cunningham it had plummeted to 250.

The paper's fragile condition was not apparent in the statement of new ownership, signed by Adolph, that appeared inside the four-page paper. Politically, he explained, *The Chattanooga Daily Times* would be "in line with the Conservative Democrats of the South" and would devote itself to the "material, educational, and moral growth of our progressive city and its surrounding territory." To the creditors who had hounded the previous management, he sent a reassuring message: "we shall conduct our business on business principles."

Despite his high-minded tone, Adolph's "business principles" were not entirely orthodox. Because he intuitively understood the importance of appearances, he made a show of being prosperous despite the grim reality. One of his first acquisitions was a finely tooled leather checkbook with checks so beautifully printed that some recipients kept them as keepsakes. When a bill was presented for payment, Adolph ceremoniously pulled out the leather book, but instead of writing a check, he asked for a day to "audit" the account, a request that most creditors considered reasonable. He then hustled to shift funds from one bank to another or collected debts from friends to cover the bill.

Ochs's perseverance was put to the test within weeks of acquiring the paper. In late August 1878 Chattanooga suffered an epidemic of yellow fever that depopulated the city and brought commerce, including newspaper advertising, to a near standstill. Adolph, in Cincinnati on business, was prevented by a quarantine from coming home and had to secure new loans to keep the paper afloat. By the time the plague abated in November, 366 people, including a *Times* printer, had died, but the *Times,* reduced at one point to a single sheet, never missed an issue.

Chattanooga was an unusually congenial place for a man with Adolph's temperament. The Civil War had ravaged the city, reducing its population to just 3,500 by 1865. But rebels and Yankees alike had battled to hold the town and recognized the commercial potential in its once great railroads and strategic location on the Tennessee River. After Appomattox they flocked to Chattanooga and formed a city that was neither northern nor southern but distinctly American. While other southern towns tarred and feathered carpetbaggers, Chattanooga enthusiastically courted them in the hope that their capital and expertise would enrich the city. The result was a remarkable melting pot of nearly 12,000 people in 1878, of whom only 773 were native-born. For Adolph, born in the North and raised in the South, Chattanooga's seeming indifference to parentage, religion, or economic circumstance was a welcome relief from the humiliations, anti-Semitism, and factional backbiting of Knoxville. Here, at last, he had a clear shot at making it on his talent and hard work.

For all its rapid growth, Chattanooga remained little more than a frontier outpost in the late 1870s. There were no paved streets, cattle wandered at will, and hogs rooted in the gutter. Gun- and knife-toting mountaineers, rivermen, and loggers routinely staggered out of the city's saloons, and it was common for readers to physically threaten newspapermen for publishing unpopular stories. By nature a peaceful, even timid man, Adolph soon acquired a massive dog to protect him from the robbers and roughhousers who roamed the town at night.

He saw beyond the deep mudholes and grimy iron and metal plants, and became a feverish booster of Chattanooga. His newspaper pushed for better sanitation, a nonpartisan municipal government, river improvements and road works, and adopted a dim view of nay-saying "croakers." He acted as the city's chief advocate and unofficial greeting committee, painting a rosy vision of what the town eventually would become: the Dynamo of Dixie.

The first three years in Chattanooga were bitterly hard, but under Adolph's adroit management, *The Chattanooga Times* (*Daily* would eventually disappear from the title) advanced steadily. By 1880 S. A. Cunningham's half interest had appreciated so much that he was reluctant to part with it. Ochs ultimately had to pay $5,500 — nearly four times the value of his initial purchase — to ensure his unencumbered ownership. By then the paper had relocated to more spacious quarters on Market Street, the main thoroughfare, and although conditions were still shabby — desks consisted of poplar boards thrown across two sawhorses — Adolph brightened his bottom line by producing *The Tradesman, The Baptist Reflector,* and other small publications.

When Adolph turned twenty-one, he ran a birthday notice entitled "A Specimen of a Newspaper Man's Cheek Blowing His Own Horn." In it he declared that whereas a "boy" had been publisher of the *Times* only the day before, the paper could now proudly proclaim that it was run by "a man" and a "citizen." The self-mocking tone was deceptive. Adolph sincerely believed the transition to be pivotal. "I feel that I am no longer a boy," he solemnly told a cousin a few weeks later. "My ambition has taken possession of me. I see myself living in luxury, honored and respected by all; the mantle of fame and position rests on my shoulders; my parents, sisters and brothers around me sharing the fruits of my success."

Adolph was already well on his way to making himself the emotional and economic fulcrum of his family. Less than six months after acquiring the *Times,* he hired his father as bookkeeper and his brother George as a reporter. Milton helped out in between stints at Cincinnati's Chickering Institute and the University of Tennessee, and later joined the staff full-time. Soon Adolph acquired a rambling twelve-room Georgian-style redbrick house with a white-columned portico at the corner of Fifth and Cedar in a part of town called Cameron Hill. There he installed his parents, siblings, and his profoundly deaf maternal grandfather, Joseph Levy. If Julius resented his son's benefaction, he gave no sign. "Adolph [was] the salvation in retrieving our condition in life," he wrote with considerable feeling years later.

That was Adolph's grand plan: to provide security and employment for every member of the extended Ochs clan. The arrangement created predictable tensions, but it also brought him gratitude, devotion, and love. When a bespectacled Chattanooga clothing-store clerk named Harry Adler proposed to the Ochses' daughter Ada, Adolph wasted no time offering him a position as head of the *Times'* job-printing plant. Harry would go on to spend the rest of his professional life in his brother-in-law's employ, gratefully accepting gifts of stock at Christmas and eventually becoming general manager of *The Chattanooga Times*. To Harry, Adolph was "Prince Big-Heart." To Adolph's sister Mattie, he was her "Christ" and her "God," and to Nannie, another sister, he was "our father-brother." Adolph's generosity did not come without strings, of course. Years later an Ochs descendant who otherwise admired Adolph would fault him for his "imperial domination" of his family. A *New York Times* executive would be less generous: "He treated his family as though he were an emperor in a castle with everybody else on a little plot of ground below."

§

With his many responsibilities, Adolph had little time to indulge in the sort of social life he had enjoyed during his brief Louisville fling. His chief pleasure was visiting lady friends on baking day to sample their cakes. Though trim for a man only five foot seven inches tall, he ate prodigiously. His favorite Sunday dinner consisted of soup, two portions of fish, cucumbers and radishes, a pound of beef and onions, parsnips and cauliflower, half a fried chicken, tomatoes and peas, pudding, pie, ice cream, nuts, coffee, and cheese. "If my purse was as strong as my digestion . . . I should be very comfortable," he joked with a friend after a particularly Falstaffian repast.

Adolph danced and rode horses with Sarah Loveman, Jean Gillespie, Emma Kay, and several other Chattanooga belles, but he was equally content to share the company of older couples, whose approval he sought with a childlike eagerness. When visiting his neighbors, the

Goodmans, he never failed to pull from his pocket a letter of praise from a friend or a business acquaintance and then bask in the approving words. "It was as though he could be Adolph Ochs and be an outside admirer at the same time," recalled Mrs. Goodman, who felt (as did others) that Adolph was an unusually serious young man, more concerned with getting ahead than with finding a wife.

That changed when Adolph met Iphigenia Miriam Wise, known as Effie. During his many newsprint-buying trips to Cincinnati, Adolph had struck up a friendship with Effie's brother Leo, editor of *The American Israelite*. In 1881 Leo invited him to dine at the Wise home, where Adolph found himself seated next to a slender, raven-haired girl of twenty-one. Though romantically linked to another, Effie instantly captivated him with her carefree vivacity. Unskilled at small talk, Adolph fumblingly tried to engage her interest by recounting a race he had just seen between two famous horses, Longfellow and Harry Bassett. He ended by triumphantly telling her that he owned a shoe Harry Bassett had thrown in a recent competition. The next day, clearly smitten, Adolph sent Effie the horseshoe, and their love affair was launched. By July 1882 they were engaged.

Effie was an odd match for Adolph. Ethereal and fey, she was a stark contrast to the command-and-control model of womanhood embodied by his mother. Adolph's nickname for her was Peter Pan. She called him Boy, and through her he seemed to experience the childhood he never had. At the same time, she had an earthiness that appealed to Adolph's libidinous side. In 1891, eight years after their marriage, Effie filled out a questionnaire that asked what she considered the "sublimest passion of which human nature is capable." "Honest, hearty love," she wrote, adding that her personal motto was "Women, lager, pretzels, wine."

Effie's upbringing had been both more distinguished and less regimented than Adolph's. Her father, Isaac Mayer Wise, was a celebrated rabbi, the moving force behind the formation of the Union of American Hebrew Congregations and Hebrew Union College, and the man generally considered to be the founder of Reform Judaism in America. An émigré from Bohemia, now part of the Czech Republic, Wise scandalized his American "coreligionists" by discontinuing many Orthodox traditions, such as covering one's head and the separation of the sexes in synagogue. His aim was to modernize Jewish tradition — to emphasize the core beliefs instead of the practices that appeared suspiciously foreign and even medieval to American eyes.

At home, Wise was a disorderly intellectual with an inflexible will who kept his Bohemian-born wife, Therese Bloch, continually pregnant. In addition to her parental responsibilities, Therese served as hostess to the hordes of guests who descended on an almost daily basis to talk to the great rabbi. She organized her forgetful husband's wardrobe and kept track of the family finances. As a result, said a granddaughter, the Wise offspring "grew up wild, [they] used to torture their tutors . . . and were not very disciplined." After bearing ten children, of which Effie was the seventh, the exhausted Therese died in 1874.

A year later Wise married Selma Bondi, a Dresden native, who produced four more children. Cheerless, homely, and dour by nature, Selma was disinclined to lavish affection on her unruly stepchildren. Effie, fifteen, felt unwelcome and underfoot and soon effectively left home, living for months at a time with her married sisters. Years later Effie's daughter, Iphigene, would say that Selma, whom Effie coolly referred to as Mrs. Wise, was "the only person I ever knew that my mother disliked."

There is little doubt that Effie was attracted to Adolph in part because he offered her an escape from her troubled household. In a letter written on the eve of their wedding, Adolph promised to provide her with a home where she would "never more feel that those about you wish you were out of the way." Adolph, in turn, would be marrying up in a stunning manner, acquiring ties to one of the country's most prominent rabbis and a wife with refinement and education — albeit an untraditional one for a Jew. Dissatisfied with the local girls' academy, Rabbi Wise had sent Effie to a Catholic convent school.

The Ochses were delighted with the match. Julius was in complete accord with Rabbi Wise's liberal brand of Judaism, although he disagreed with Wise's rejection of abolitionism before the war. He gloried in the association when, soon after the engagement was announced, Wise dedicated Chattanooga's first temple. As for Wise, he did not actively oppose the union but was skeptical about the suitability of an alliance between his daughter and an "obscure printer."

The wedding, held on February 28, 1883, in Cincinnati's Plum Street Synagogue, was an opulent affair. Adolph chartered a special Pullman car to transport himself and his guests to the festivities. Fifty *Times* employees whooped and cheered as the train pulled out of Chattanooga in a showy send-off more fitting for a presidential candidate than a prospective bridegroom. *The Chattanooga Times* described the departure in great detail and slyly headlined the story ANOTHER CONVERT.

Rabbi Wise had no official role in the ceremony, but as part of the congregation he observed as Effie, barely five feet tall and nearly obscured in swaths of Ottoman silk and Spanish lace, entered the synagogue on the arm of her uncle. Afterward, the bridal couple and 150 guests repaired to Hexter's Hotel, the social hub of Cincinnati's German community, where they feasted on bluepoint oysters and Roederer champagne. At 7:00 P.M. the new Mr. and Mrs. Ochs caught a train to Washington, D.C., where Adolph had arranged an impressive surprise for his wife: tea with President Chester A. Arthur, whom he knew slightly through newspaper connections.

Effie was in for a rude awakening when they returned to Chattanooga to set up housekeeping. Bertha made it clear that she, and she alone, ruled the Ochses' congested Fifth and Cedar home. Rather than battle such a formidable matriarch, Effie adopted the role of guest in her own house, gradually becoming a pampered recluse. Most days she slept till noon, descending only when Adolph came home for the midday meal. At table she rarely said a word, preferring instead to listen to the contentious Ochs clan argue about everything from the meaning of a certain phrase in Longfellow's "The Song of Hiawatha" to the Civil War — a topic Effie considered unbearably boring. "Having discovered many years ago that the war was over, I grow a little weary of those who have not yet found it out," she told her husband in private. She would then disappear into her room to read or paint. In time, her absence in Chattanooga society became so conspicuous that the Ochses began telling people she was an invalid.

Blinded by loyalty to his mother, Adolph was oblivious to the eccentric nature of this arrangement. He didn't socialize much himself, and except for occasional trips to Atlantic City, Lookout Mountain, and nearby Tate Springs, he and Effie rarely took vacations. Their life together revolved almost exclusively around *The Chattanooga Times*. Adolph worked late each evening at the paper, and Effie often joined him there, writing book reviews while she waited for him to finish. He seemed unperturbed by his wife's sequestered habits and lack of social ambition, and insisted that he was happy to have more time to work.

Effie's failed attempts to have children only served to drive her more deeply into herself. Her first child, a daughter, was stillborn. She was soon pregnant again and in the summer of 1888 successfully produced a healthy baby girl, but after two and a half months the child died suddenly of a urinary blockage. Doctors in Cincinnati, where Effie and the baby were staying, had foolishly prescribed a hot bath, and the infant expired in fifteen minutes. Grief-stricken, Adolph rushed to the scene. He carried the tiny body to a friend's house for embalming and lovingly laid it in a flower-strewn casket so that Effie, who had not yet learned of the death, could see it before burial. "[The baby] looked very beautiful . . . like a wax doll," he wrote his family back in Chattanooga.

But Effie was in no condition to absorb the shock. She had been able to endure labor and delivery only through liberal applications of morphine, and now she was thoroughly addicted. For days Adolph could not bring himself to tell his wife the sad truth. Instead, he said their child was severely ill and had been taken to College Hill, Rabbi Wise's country home. In her drug-induced haze, Effie listened to the news impassively, absentmindedly arranging flowers as Adolph spoke.

When Adolph finally revealed that their daughter had died, Effie cried a little but asked no further. She reacted in the same way she had earlier to the deaths of her first child and her own mother — by burying her emotions. "Not to speak of her grief is certainly a peculiarity of hers," Adolph wrote at the time. "I think she feels the death of the baby keenly, but will not show it, never now, never will."

Effie's difficult delivery had resulted in an abscess that caused temporary paralysis in her feet, and for a time she could not walk. The more pressing problem, though, was her morphine addiction, which Adolph took it upon himself to cure. For two consecutive days he stayed with her as she endured the painful withdrawal process, screaming and swearing and begging for relief. By mid-October Effie had recovered sufficiently to return to Chattanooga.

Within days the Ochs family suffered a new calamity: Julius, sixty-two, died of a bronchial ailment in his room at the Fifth and Cedar house. Gripped by a hacking cough and unable to swallow, he had dwindled to ninety-eight pounds. At the interment in Chattanooga's Jewish cemetery,

Rabbi Wise summed up his life in a simple phrase that, for Adolph, reverberated with meaning: "Here lies a good man."

§

On September 19, 1892, Effie bore her third child, the only one to survive — a nine-and-a-half-pound girl whom Adolph described as having "much dark hair, a nose that inclined to be puggy, [a] double chin [and] the cutest of hands and nails." To avoid another medical bungle, he had installed Effie in Cincinnati's Hotel Alms well in advance of the delivery. He chose the location because the hotel, named after Frederick Alms, a local department-store owner, was next door to a physician he considered competent. Years later Iphigene, as the girl was named in honor of Effie, told people with a deadpan expression that she had been born in an almshouse.

Adolph was in New York City attending a meeting of the Associated Press on the day his daughter was born. Unable to leave until the following morning, he stayed up all night sending excited wires and drinking champagne with the hotel's desk clerk, bellboy, and telegraph operator. When he finally arrived bleary-eyed in Cincinnati, he presented a diamond brooch to Effie and, declaring Iphigene the "sweetest, brightest, dearest chunk of humanity ever seen," raced out to buy her a cloak and two pairs of shoes, and then "drank enough to drown the whole family." Adolph's sister Nannie, who had come to help Effie, stood on a chair and hoisted the infant aloft — a variation of the German Jewish custom of *Hollakreishe* — in the hope that she would always "live high."

Adolph was absolutely besotted with his daughter, whom he called Baby. After so much death and disappointment, here at last was a plunge into pure love and unrestrained joy. "You should have been named Sunshine," he wrote in a letter to the infant two days before her first birthday. "The thought of you makes me happy."

Iphigene's arrival coincided with a period of expansion in the Ochs household. In 1893 Adolph's handsome younger brother Milton, whom Adolph had made managing editor of the *Times*, wed Fanny Van Dyke, one of the city's most eligible ingenues. The marriage of a Jew and the son of a Union officer to the daughter of a Confederate captain and a "first-pew Presbyterian" shocked many hidebound Chattanoogans. Although Miss Fan, as she was known, held fast to her Christian beliefs, she refused to tolerate the slightest whisper of anti-Semitism. "These are my people," she said fiercely whenever anyone disparaged Jews.

Like Effie, Adolph's sister Ada had difficulty producing children. Her first attempt, eight months after her marriage to Harry Adler, nearly killed her; the forceps-aided delivery was so violent that the child, a daughter, emerged in pieces. But in December 1892, three months after Iphigene's arrival, Ada successfully bore a son. She named him Julius Ochs Adler, after her father, and the two cousins — Iphigene and Julie — played together as closely as brother and sister in the crammed Fifth and Cedar house. Surrounded by a loving hodgepodge of grandparents, aunts, uncles, and black servants, Iphigene and Julie belonged as much to "the family" as to their own biological parents. As the only boy, Julie came to be known universally as Son.

In 1896, at the marriage of Adolph's sweet and rather homely sister Mattie to Bernie Talimer, a Philadelphia lawyer and Harry Adler's first cousin, the Ochses dressed up three-and-a-half-year-old Iphigene and Julie as a miniature bride and groom. Guests stood on the pews in the crowded synagogue to watch the twosome awkwardly precede their aunt down the aisle. Outfitted in a high-necked white lace dress and veil, and tiny satin knee breeches with a frilly lace jacket, Iphigene and Julie looked like oversize dolls.

The costumes had an element of seriousness, however. Years later some family members would look back on the occasion and wistfully voice their wish that the cousins' portrayal as a married couple had been prophetic.

§

Unlike most of his fellow publishers, Adolph sought to make his newspaper impartial rather than a party organ or a shill for business interests. To modern readers, the paper's prose seems flowery and overheated, but for its era *The Chattanooga Times* was remarkably evenhanded, at various times offending and pleasing both Democrats and Republicans. As a product of Yankee and rebel parents, Adolph had a kneejerk aversion to vitriolic argument; as a Jew, political visibility was a luxury he could not afford. "We should live quietly, happily, unostentatiously," Adolph once advised the Jews of Chattanooga's Mizpah congregation. "Don't be too smart. Don't know too much."

When Chattanooga was the subject, however, Adolph remained an unabashed propagandist. In 1886 he organized the first news train in Tennessee. The specially hired cars, filled with Chattanooga dignitaries, chugged through east Tennessee as onboard newsboys threw copies of the *Times* at every depot and farmhouse. Using the *Times* offices as headquarters, Adolph mounted extravagant Fourth of July celebrations featuring floats, electric illumination, and elegant balls. He was the inspiration for the so-called steel banquet — a coming-together of northern and southern industry that brought to Chattanooga the largest number of U.S. congressmen and senators ever assembled outside of Washington.

Adolph had a talent for the excessive gesture, believing that "it requires no more energy to do a big thing than to do a little thing." He loved circuses, amusement parks, fireworks, the razzle-dazzle of the big show. In 1891 his instincts found a gratifying outlet in the erection of an impressive new building for the *Times* and its subsidiaries. Declaring the project his "greatest undertaking" to date, he laid the cornerstone on May 7, Effie's birthday, on a small hill at the corner of Georgia and Eighth Streets.

Nineteen months later, on December 8, 1892, ten thousand people — a third of Chattanooga's growing population — flocked to the dedication of Ochs's six-story wonder, a granite building of Italian Renaissance design with arched windows and a cupola surmounted by a gleaming gold dome. Inside was an efficient, modern newspaper plant with elevators and recently introduced Mergenthaler typesetting equipment. While not exactly "one of the most notable buildings of the continent," as the *Times* described it, the Ochs Building was certainly the tallest in Chattanooga. In gratitude for all that Adolph had done for the city, a group of local citizens used the occasion to present him with an eight-foot-high grandfather clock made in Geneva out of quartered oak with a silver dial and figures in raised gold. At the clock's unveiling in the lobby of the new building, Adolph, flanked by Effie and Bertha, listened solemnly as Mayor D. M. Key, a former postmaster general, predicted that even "grander heights . . . broader fields . . . and brighter victories" awaited him.

The words rang with majesty but, appearances notwithstanding, Adolph's situation didn't warrant them. He was hopelessly in debt, a fact he had managed to hide from all but his closest friends and business associates. Since taking charge of *The Chattanooga Times* in 1878, the paper had made money every year; in 1891 it had cleared $25,000. But Adolph's ambitions had outpaced the *Times'* profits. By the time he broke ground for the $182,000 Ochs Building — financed with $150,000 in borrowed funds — he owed so much money that critics later speculated he had erected the structure to quiet local gossip about the true nature of his affairs.

The chief cause of his distress was a real estate boom that in the late 1880s and early 1890s gripped Chattanooga with the ferocity of a cult. The craze for acquiring property, which swept other areas of the South as well, came at a time when many local businessmen felt brashly certain that Chattanooga, rich in iron ore and virgin forest, was destined to become another Pittsburgh. Land prices skyrocketed beyond all reason. A tract bought for $800 in 1885 sold for $1,900 the following year and for $30,000 in 1887. Fortunes were made overnight. Near the height of the madness, Chattanooga had one hundred real estate agents, and Adolph had to publish a twelve-page paper every day just to accommodate the ads for land.

Driven by civic ambition as much as by the desire to make a quick buck, Ochs had plunged into the game with ill-considered optimism. Though he later chided himself for his "insanity," at the time he was as cocky and self-assured as a riverboat gambler. "Gold-mine stock may be good, but I prefer Chattanooga real estate," Adolph haughtily told a Louisville relative who disapproved of his "speculative tendencies."

With several partners, including his cousin Ben Franck, Adolph had formed the Chattanooga Land, Coal, Iron and Railway Company, which acquired forty thousand acres of iron- and coal-rich land in adjacent Red Bank and Signal Mountain. (The syndicate was known locally as the Over-the-River Company because the envisioned development stretched across the Tennessee River and up into the hill country on the other side.) The plan was to construct mines and sawmills and develop a summer residence and resort reachable from downtown by a private railroad. Adolph, ever the huckster, had dubbed one of the lots Timesville. He laid out the streets himself, naming them after relatives, and gave away one lot with each year's subscription to *The Chattanooga Times*. By the time the property was paid for, however, there was no money left for development, and the partners had been forced to scour Boston and other northern cities for loans.

That would have been bad enough, but Adolph had made an even more critical error. When the Over-the-River Company was buying up land, one key seller had shrewdly insisted on making a deal with an individual rather than a faceless corporation. Confident that the syndicate would back him, Adolph had agreed to sign for the debt, which was then transferred to the corporation, and the land was acquired. The struggling Over-the-River Company soon fell behind in its payments, a lawsuit ensued, and Adolph had been forced to give the landowner a personal check for $103,000. From that point on, his finances spiraled downward as the land boom fizzled in the early 1890s and the country struggled with a national economic panic in 1893. When he finally summoned the courage to total up the cost of his folly, Adolph discovered to his horror that he had lost nearly $500,000, a figure that resurrected terrifying memories of Julius's desperate straits twenty years earlier.

Adolph's borrowing to finance the Ochs Building further compounded his dilemma. At first he had put up the structure itself as collateral. Then, as his real estate obligations multiplied, he had formed The Chattanooga Times Printing Company, which issued $300,000 in bonds secured by the building, the press equipment, franchises, and goodwill. In short, despite his apparent prosperity, by the time the Ochs Building was completed, Adolph had mortgaged everything he owned and was practically a pauper.

Between 1891 and 1895 he traveled with increasing frequency to New York in a frantic attempt to arrange loans and juggle debt, always staying in second-rate hotels and walking to save carriage fare. By then he had little hope of reducing his liability; he was barely able to meet interest payments. Even so, concerned about appearing too anxious, Adolph refused to accept loans for less than $1,000. As he explained to his brother George, "It looks bad." The logic may have been wise, but it would have been of little consolation to the staff at *The Chattanooga Times*. Conditions were so mean that reporters wrapped copy paper around pencil stubs to form holders, thereby eking out the last half inch of lead.

Adolph refused to follow his father's example and declare personal bankruptcy. Instead, with the help of a friend, New York lawyer Leopold Wallach, he tried to persuade Manhattan banks and insurance companies to take Chattanooga Times Printing Company bonds. The task was fruitless; no one outside the region was interested in securities that were "new and unknown." Scrounging for funds "is the meanest business a man can undertake," Adolph wrote Effie despairingly.

Although he had a wide acquaintance in the newspaper business, Adolph still felt like a shambling greenhorn in the presence of big-city editors. So it was all the more remarkable that as his situation became more and more desperate, Adolph decided to dig himself out of debt not only by acquiring another newspaper in order to generate income but by acquiring a newspaper in New York. With his back against the wall — a position that always invigorated him — he set his sights on securing a paper in the biggest, most competitive and sophisticated market in the country. Surely an "industrious, energetic and practical worker" could succeed there, Adolph wrote a Cincinnati banker, adding that he possessed "special capabilities in this direction."

His first chance came in May 1895, when Wallach informed him that *The New York Mercury* was for sale. Ochs was interested but wary. The paper was small and unimpressive, trafficking mostly in sports and theater news. More troubling was its flirtation with free-silver Democrats, who sought an end to the gold standard and the adoption of unrestricted silver coinage. Adolph would have benefited greatly from the adoption of "soft money"; overnight his debt could conceivably have been cut in half. But he feared that silver would promote "fictitious prosperity" and perhaps even incite revolution. Although *The Chattanooga Times* had long advocated the gold standard, Adolph now wrestled with the question anew, discussing with Effie "the morals at stake" as well as the monetary issues, which he freely admitted were "beyond my comprehension." In the end he remained faithful to hard money, deciding that he would acquire the *Mercury* only if he could be assured the complete editorial and business control that would permit him to change its policy on the issue.

Negotiations on this point, as well as on the asking price — $160,000, far more than the $100,000 Adolph felt he could borrow — continued throughout the summer and fall. The *Mercury* deal would finally collapse in early April 1896, following Adolph's discovery that the paper's owners were not in a position to transfer their United Press franchise to a new publisher. Adolph knew that without the vital contributions of a wire service, he didn't stand a chance of making the *Mercury* a success. "I am ashamed I ever thought of it," he later remarked of his quest for the paper.

If the *Mercury* experience would ultimately prove to be a disappointment, it nonetheless turned Adolph's dream of owning a New York newspaper into a passion. On March 17, 1896, five days after his thirty-eighth birthday, Adolph received a telegram from Harry Alloway, a Wall Street reporter for *The New-York Times* whom he had first met in Chattanooga in 1890, when Alloway was covering southern industry. At the time, Adolph had casually told Alloway that he thought *The New-York Times,* then in the beginning of a slide toward bankruptcy, offered "the greatest opportunity in American journalism." Alloway, "a schemer from way back yonder," knew of Adolph's New York ambitions and his troubled negotiations for the *Mercury.* His message, therefore, was brief and to the point:

Would New-York Times proposition be attractive now?
Answer confidential. H. Alloway.

3

A Jay Comes to Town

A T THE TIME OF ALLOWAY'S TELEGRAM, *THE New-York Times'* circulation had shrunk to nine thousand and the paper was losing $1,000 a day, making it even more insolvent than the *Mercury,* which was losing a mere $1,000 a week. Yet among the journalistic cognoscenti, the *Times* was still admiringly referred to, in terms suggestive of a great actress grown old, as "the most picturesque old ruin among newspapers in America."

Founded in 1851 by two disgruntled Republicans, Henry J. Raymond, Speaker of the New York State Assembly, and George Jones, a banker, *The New-York Daily Times,* as it was briefly known, began life as a conservative counterpoint to Horace Greeley's *Tribune,* which advocated abolition and the free-soil movement. After Raymond's shocking death in 1869 — he expired of a heart attack in the apartment of his lover, an actress named Rose Eytinge — Jones took over as publisher and quickly brought acclaim to the *Times* by courageously exposing the corruption of William M. "Boss" Tweed and the Tammany machine in the face of Tweed's demands that he stop and the specter of financial ruin.

Under Jones, *The New-York Times* gradually turned away from Republican orthodoxy. In 1884 it refused to support James G. Blaine, the party's scandal-ridden presidential nominee, and went on to endorse the Democrat, Grover Cleveland, prompting Republican readers and advertisers to flee the *Times.* By 1891, the year Jones died, annual profits, which had stood at $188,000 prior to Cleveland's election, had plummeted to an anemic $15,000.

The *Times* passed to Jones's heirs, who had no interest in owning the paper. They found an eager buyer in the *Times'* heavyset, balding editor, Charles R. Miller, who sank all his available funds into the purchase and obtained the balance from wealthy New York friends of President Cleveland, a former governor of the state. The list of investors in The

New-York Times Publishing Company, as the syndicate was called, read like a who's who of America's business plutocracy: among its roughly sixty-two members were James J. Hill, who ran the Great Northern and Northern Pacific Railways, and banking luminaries J. P. Morgan, Jacob Schiff, and August Belmont.

By 1893 Miller was president as well as editor, in full operational control of *The New-York Times*. A native New Englander and lifelong Democrat, he took pleasure in gentlemanly pursuits such as literature, billiards, and chatty repartee at New York's elite Century Association, but as a businessman he was a disaster. While raising money to buy the *Times*, he had skimped on working capital, a fact that became all too apparent when the panic of 1893 dried up financial advertising, the paper's mainstay. With few resources available for newsgathering, the *Times* staked its journalistic reputation on a strong editorial voice, and its ledgers went from barely black to deep red. Soon Miller and his family were forced to leave their fine Brooklyn home and take in lodgers in a more modest dwelling on West Fifty-fifth Street.

In 1896, with the *Times* rumored to be weeks away from extinction, a populist gale from the South and West began to blow through the Democratic Party, making it critical to members of the party's conservative wing that *The New-York Times* be kept afloat to represent their advocacy of sound money. Of this group, no one was more concerned about the fate of the dollar than the Equitable Life Assurance Society, the largest insurer in the world and one of the most powerful "combines of capital" in the country, with diverse holdings in banks, trust companies, real estate, railroads, and syndicates. Equitable had $50,000 invested in New-York Times Publishing Company stock, and several of its directors, including Belmont, Hill, Marcellus Hartley, and Jacob Schiff, either owned *Times* shares themselves or controlled shares through others. Still, neither they nor the other New-York Times Publishing Company stockholders relished throwing good money after bad.

The shareholders scrambled furiously to find new investors and a better manager, but every man they approached turned them down, judging the business to be beyond redemption. It was at this juncture that Adolph received Alloway's urgent message, which fired his desire to take control of what he considered to be "the ideal newspaper of every publisher in America" — a stunning prize with a distinguished history, despite its bedraggled appearance. Adolph, who had built his life on the importance of reputation, understood that the "good name" of *The New-York Times* was "its greatest value" and "all that I cared to purchase." If he could somehow manage to possess *that,* he would own the essence of the enterprise. He was certain that with "intelligent and prudent management" he could then transform the paper into a going concern. That he was drowning in debt and a southern rube — a "jay come to town," as he said — didn't faze him. On the contrary, it redoubled his resolve to "overcome all difficulties and obstacles . . . at all hazard." Like Houdini, Adolph delighted in making breathtaking escapes from seemingly doomed situations. "I am of a queer make-up," he told Effie, in a rare moment of self-reflection. "I am at my best in adversity."

§

Adolph arrived in New York City on Thursday, March 26, on the 8:30 P.M. train from Chicago, where he had rushed in the wake of Alloway's telegram to secure funds and references. His meeting with John Walsh, president of the Chicago National Bank, had been disappointing — a "cold bath" — but he had managed to get letters of introduction from Melville Stone, the manager of the Associated Press, and H. H. Kohlsaat, editor and publisher of the *Chicago Times-Herald* and *Evening Post,* addressed to Charles R. Flint, an influential *New-York Times* shareholder and member of the committee charged with finding a solution to the paper's financial crisis.

The next day, after dining with Alloway, Ochs settled into his quarters at the Fifth Avenue Hotel, near Madison Square, and reviewed his strategy. Privately, he nursed doubts about whether he was equipped for the job, but he was determined to take the advice Kohlsaat had given him over lunch in Chicago: "Don't tell anybody and they will never find it out." Appearances would be paramount. To capture his prey, he knew he would have to exploit every aspect of his character, from the noble to the dark, ingratiating himself with those in power, bluffing about the true nature of his finances, shading the truth and inflating his successes, all the while fending off a herd of howling creditors. Adolph's plan was as simple as it was improbable: he must convince the stockholders of The New-York Times Publishing Company that he had the funds to warrant eventual ownership and that he was capable of resuscitating the paper. "Now for the supremacy of gall for a country newspaper man burdened with debt!" he crowed to Effie.

Adolph's first move was to make an ally of Charles R. Miller, the *Times'* president and editor, whom he had never met. Miller was certain that a small-town southern publisher was an unlikely contender, but at Alloway's insistence he made time to see Ochs one evening before going to the theater. When Adolph was ushered into Miller's parlor, he summoned all the intense sincerity he could to make his case. Short and stocky, he was self-conscious speaking to large groups but had a quietly commanding voice and a rare talent for seducing individuals on whom he focused his full attention. After years of extracting loans from skeptical bankers, he knew just what to say to convince his listener that he was honorable and trustworthy. So spellbinding was his power of persuasion that witnesses likened it to being hypnotized.

Miller proved to be equally susceptible, and forgetting entirely about his theater engagement, he stayed up well past midnight listening to Adolph's plan to revive *The New-York Times* as an independent Democratic paper, "decent, dignified [and] . . . devoted to the general welfare . . . [and] free from all ulterior influences." Adolph's conquest was so complete that Miller offered to introduce him to Charles R. Flint the following morning.

Adolph had meticulously prepared for his encounter with Flint, the gruff organizer of the U.S. Rubber Company who commanded outsize influence with *The New-York Times'* other shareholders through the sheer force of his personality and his life-sustaining infusions of cash. Aware that the magnate was a supporter of Grover Cleveland, Adolph had, with characteristic brashness, contacted the president (whom he had entertained several years earlier in Chattanooga) and solicited a letter attesting to his "faithful adherence to Democratic principles" and support of the "ideas and policies which tend to the safety of our country as well as our party." Like Flint, Cleveland wanted a *New-York Times* proprietor dedicated to the Democratic Party. Adolph's daring maneuver reassured both men he could be trusted to be exactly that.

Satisfied with Adolph's political credentials, Flint invited him to "take a large interest" in the *Times* "for easy terms" and sign on as its manager for a salary he intimated might reach as high as $50,000 a year. Adolph refused. He was "hardly prepared on such short notice to make as large an investment," he told Flint, betraying no hint that he was awash in debt. Later Adolph admitted that in his strapped state, the prospect of a five-figure income was "most seductive," but at the time, he imperiously insisted that he "would not care to go into any property that I did not control."

Though flabbergasted at Ochs's hubris, Flint was sufficiently impressed to introduce him to Spencer Trask, the head of the committee searching for a way out of the *Times'* financial troubles. During the meeting that ensued in Trask's Pine Street office, the banking baron proved to be more flexible than Flint. Perhaps a solution could yet be found that would be "satisfactory" to Adolph, he said; the first step was to demonstrate to the committee that Adolph was a "reputable man," in possession of both the character and the funds to acquire control of *The New-York Times.*

Adolph, who rarely left home without admiring testimonials in his pockets, needed no further encouragement. In a single day he dashed off solicitation letters to fifty-five bankers, publishers, cabinet members, religious leaders, and businessmen, including the president of the Louisville & Nashville Railroad, whom he had met just two weeks earlier on the train from Chicago to New York. In modest yet confident prose, he urged them to elaborate on his "public spirit and progressive ideas," with particular attention to his stand on "the money question" (meaning free silver). Dodging the unpleasant truth, he assured them that he possessed the financial wherewithal to "handle" *The New-York Times.* Enclosed in each envelope was a copy of President Cleveland's letter. These efforts generated a flood of mail in Trask's office and helped convince the banker, and other members of the committee, that Adolph was a man of honor. Now his task was to persuade them he was also a man of means.

In Chattanooga Adolph had created an aura of prosperity with a fancy leather checkbook and artfully delayed checks. In New York he produced a similar effect with a phony bank account. Before going to New York, Adolph had asked Citizens' Savings Bank of Chattanooga, one of his friendlier creditors, to place funds in his name in a New York bank. "I want some money to carry with me so that those people will think that I have it," he explained. He promised never to actually use the account, and gave Citizens' Savings a check for the full amount, drawn on the New York account, to cash whenever it liked. But his hope was that the bank would simply let the funds sit idle so that he "could have the appearance of money behind him." The deception worked: though Ochs was virtually penniless, he appeared respectably solvent to Miller, Flint, and Trask.

Naively certain of the new friends and favorable impression he had made, Adolph presented Trask and his committee with a proposal that would eventually put him in charge of the *Times* in return for $50,000 cash, provided that he put the paper on sound footing. With his history of lining up loans, the sum, to Adolph's mind, presented no obstacle, and the idea that he was close to becoming publisher and general manager of the *Times* made him as giddily boastful as he had been during the first days of the Chattanooga land boom. "I am succeeding beyond my wildest flights of imagination," he wrote a cousin before leaving New York for a brief visit home. Typesetting companies, eager to sell new equipment, sent him obsequious letters of congratulations. *The Fourth Estate*, a newspaper trade journal, reported rumors that "Colonel [sic] Adolph Ochs" had secured an option to buy *The New-York Times.*

The celebration turned out to be premature. Toward the end of April Adolph learned that Flint, determined to maintain his power at the paper, had persuaded a group of prominent stockholders to adopt an alternative plan to merge *The New-York Times* with *The New York Recorder,* another weak daily, and install Charles Emory Smith, editor of the *Philadelphia Press* and former ambassador to Russia, as editor of the consolidated publication. Incorporation papers for the Times-Recorder Company were filed in Albany just a few days after Adolph rushed back to New York.

Adolph wasn't the only one dismayed by the merger. Charles R. Miller stood to lose his job. He had a three-year contract to continue as editor of *The New-York Times* at an annual salary of $15,000, but if the *Times* died or mated with another paper, the agreement would mean nothing. At least Adolph had given him the impression that he could remain editor in an Ochs regime. The prospect of personal ruin roused Miller and caused him to lock arms with Adolph in a desperate gambit to scuttle the *Times-Recorder* union, which by then had the blessing of nearly 90 percent of the *Times'* weary shareholders.

In a last-minute effort Miller persuaded two of his five fellow directors in The New-York Times Publishing Company to put the paper into receivership. With that, the merger ground to a halt and the *Times* was legally bankrupt, its business conducted by a court-appointed receiver while a reorganization committee headed by Trask, who had opposed the *Times-Recorder* deal, tried to figure out what to do next.

Trask attempted to sell Adolph's earlier proposal to the paper's creditors, but several judged the terms unacceptable and Trask abandoned the scheme, telling Adolph he was free to do what he could to secure the property. Over the next several weeks Ochs furiously courted Trask and George Foster Peabody, Trask's business partner, convincing them he was the "one person who can put the *Times* on its feet as a sound Democratic newspaper." Trask helped Adolph reconstitute the reorganization committee with sympathetic men, and on June 9 the revamped proposal was approved. The plan created a new entity — The New-York Times Company — with $1 million in stock and $500,000 in bonds backed by a mortgage on everything the *Times* owned, from broken-down chairs to its name. Adolph's aim was to induce the paper's disgruntled creditors to accept bonds as payment, a strategy that in the near term would limit his cash outlay to the 5 percent interest on the bonds, and to convince the owners of worthless New-York Times Publishing Company shares to exchange their old stock for stock in the new company on a five-for-one basis. If the Ochs plan succeeded, it would satisfy the paper's creditors and shareholders, raise new working capital, assure Adolph operational control, and — key to the strategy — award him a majority of the stock when the company under his management had shown a profit for three consecutive years.

With the committee's approval in hand, Adolph shrewdly targeted the most influential stockholders first, despite the fact that he was frankly cowed by several of them. The most intimidating was J. Pierpont Morgan, who met Adolph in his regal offices at 23 Wall Street and, to Adolph's astonishment, signed the papers converting his $25,000 in old *Times* stock in just fifteen minutes. Jacob Schiff, the diminutive head of Kuhn, Loeb, simply made a present of his shares, telling Adolph in his heavily accented English that it was a "personal endorsement" of him and that he "could do with it whatever [he] wanted." He had decided to become a Republican, Schiff said offhandedly, and wanted nothing more to do with a Democratic newspaper.

Schiff's vote of confidence was particularly meaningful to Adolph, who had earlier entreated his Wise relatives and business associates in Cincinnati to write the financier on his behalf. The banker's personal history as a self-made man had special resonance, of course, but just as important, Schiff and other prominent Jews like Isidor Straus, coowner of R. H. Macy & Company, had made it clear they wanted Adolph to succeed because they believed he "could be of great service to the Jews generally." Much later, when the *Times* was under attack as a "Jewish newspaper," Adolph would insist that "no Jew, except myself . . . played any part in my acquiring the ownership of the *Times.*" Although the vast majority of his backers were non-Jews, the support of powerful Jewish financiers and businessmen was, in fact, critical.

§

With frenetic determination, Adolph eventually won the cooperation of the *Times'* creditors and the signatures of 95 percent of the old stockholders. On a single day in mid-June, he kept fourteen appointments in various locations around Manhattan, including an hour with Wall Street tycoon August Belmont and an hour with Western Union, to which the paper was heavily in debt, while still allotting forty-five minutes for lunch and three hours for writing letters.

Adding to Adolph's frantic state was concern about Effie's health. In early June, the day before he presented the Ochs plan to the reorganization committee, Effie had informed him that she was pregnant. Theoretically, the news should have been welcome; Adolph certainly wanted more children. But Effie's previous deliveries had been so hellish that she was disinclined to endure another. Her intention, she told Adolph, was to ask Dr. Stark, the Cincinnati physician who had delivered Iphigene, to perform an "operation." "If he does nothing," she wrote, "why I will have to go on to term and stand my chances of getting through alive." By early July the "operation" — which Adolph described as "a close call" that gave him "a day of anxiety" he wished never to repeat — was over. By mid-August her "delayed visitor," as Effie coyly called her period, had arrived, and her recovery was complete.

As the summer wore on and his successes mounted, Adolph put into motion the next phase of the Ochs plan. Having persuaded the *Times'* creditors to accept $275,000 worth of New-York Times Company bonds as payment, he now had to sell the remaining $225,000 of the issue in order to raise the working capital he would need to restore the paper to its former glory. As an inducement to new investors, he agreed to offer fifteen shares of New-York Times Company stock with each $1,000 bond bought, and to purchase $75,000 worth himself.

This was a rash promise indeed for a man who had barely $750 in ready cash (much less $75,000) and who was spending every spare moment fending off impatient creditors, many of them friends and kinsmen. To make matters worse, the political climate that had made a conservative, gold-standard Democrat like Adolph attractive to Trask, Flint, Belmont, and other businessmen among the *New-York Times* stockholders now threatened to be his undoing.

During the spring of 1896 William Jennings Bryan, the cyclone from Nebraska, the "boy orator of the Platte," had emerged as the champion of poor farmers and other prairie populists who saw in the free coinage of silver a salvation from debt. In mid-July the Democratic Convention in Chicago nominated Bryan for president and adopted a populist platform that *The New-York Times* judged to be as "complete in its wickedness as in its absurdity." If anything, Bryan's nomination made Adolph more politically appealing to the *Times'* stockholders, but financially it was a disaster. The prospect of Bryan in the White House suddenly made it impossible for anyone to borrow money. Banks were reluctant to make loans in gold-backed dollars, knowing that if Bryan had his way, they would be repaid later in devalued silver-backed currency. The situation became so dire that less than two weeks after the Democratic Convention, George Ochs, who was running *The Chattanooga Times* in his brother's absence, wasn't sure he had enough money to meet the payroll. "I look with horror on . . . using any of that special loan you have in New York," he wrote Adolph, alluding to the phony bank account arranged through Citizens' Savings.

In this unpromising environment, Adolph somehow managed to come up with $75,000. To the end of his life, he never revealed how he did so, and it remains a mystery. Several *Times* histories suggest that he tapped banks in Chattanooga, but given the panic of 1893, the local real estate bust, and his own overextended credit, that seems unlikely. Instead, evidence suggests that he got part of it in the form of a bank loan arranged by an executive with Walter Scott & Company, a firm that brokered newspaper presses, in return for Adolph's promise to buy new equipment; part as gifts from female relatives; and part from Henry B. Hyde, the founder and president of the Equitable Life Assurance Society, who gave him the critical final sum a mere twenty-four hours before the date the court had set to sell *The New-York Times* at auction.

The sale took place on August 13 at noon in the New York Real Estate Exchange across from Trinity Church and went off quietly. As a legal formality, Spencer, Trask, as head of the reorganization committee, made a $75,000 bid for the old *Times,* and it was knocked down to him. There were no other bidders. Three weeks earlier, when things were at their bleakest, Adolph had assured Effie, *"I will win."* Now that he had actually done so, he seemed a little stunned. The yokel from Tennessee had accomplished the impossible: he had bought *The New-York Times* using none of his own money. And if he kept his part of the agreement and put the paper on a paying basis for three successive years, he would effectively gain control of the *Times* for no personal stake except his hard work.

After dashing off fifteen ebullient telegrams, Adolph adjourned with friends to Cafe Savarin in the basement of the Equitable Building for a celebratory feast of champagne and English mutton chops. When George Ochs received word that Adolph had won his great battle, he broke down and wept. In a letter composed that day, he offered his brother "a million masseltovs" and extravagantly compared him to "Napoleon after Austerlitz . . . Washington after Yorktown, Wellington after Waterloo." Effie, more subdued, reminded her husband how far he had come from "the little boy who tramped the streets of Knoxville . . . delivering papers," and then apologized for her understated reaction. "I am not good at rhapsodizing," she told him. "So if I say little, do not imagine I am not in sympathy with your heart and soul."

Adolph claimed he did not feel "in any way exalted" by the purchase and was capable of occupying "this great position without having my head turned." But on Monday, August 17, 1896, exactly five months after receiving the Alloway telegram, as he sat at the publisher's desk in the sweltering Park Row offices of *The New-York Times* for the first time, he picked up one of the paper's two telephones and called Effie, who was vacationing in nearby Atlantic City with Iphigene and several Ochs relations. "The publisher of *The New-York Times* greets you!" he exclaimed.

In his new acquisition, Adolph felt confident he had a gold mine, albeit one that needed a strong hand and a thorough sweeping out. "If I am nearly as successful in handling the *Times* as I have been with the creditors," he told Effie, "I should make a great fortune quickly." As Adolph was about to discover, his prediction was premature.

4

"A Stroke of Genius"

NEW YORK CITY IN 1896 WAS WELL ON ITS WAY TO becoming the second-largest metropolis in the world, exceeded by only London. Lured by jobs in offices and factories, small-town Americans streamed into the city after the Civil War, followed by thousands of immigrants, many of them Eastern European Jews who crowded into grimy two-room tenements on the Lower East Side. On Fifth Avenue, known as "the Fifth," massive mansions stood as a testament to the excesses of the Gilded Age. Delmonico's remained the quintessence of fine dining, with multipage menus, elaborate sautéed specialties, and *pièces montées* (ornate sugar confections), while among the poor malnutrition was rampant.

Saloons, bordellos, and gambling dens flourished despite a recent campaign by the Presbyterian pastor Charles H. Parkhurst to root out the corrupt officials who winked at it. Cocaine fortified over-the-counter medications, yet the sin that offended New Yorkers most was spitting in public — "our loathsome vice," as *Harper's Weekly* called it — a habit indulged in by men of high and low birth alike. The Brooklyn Bridge, a marvel of technology completed in 1883, was still being crossed by horse-drawn buses and streetcars that left the stench of manure in their wake, adding the clatter of hooves to the rumble of elevated trains. In two years an invention called the automobile, which had just been unveiled in Detroit, would make its debut in New York.

The city's newspapers were as varied, competitive, and colorful as its restless population. William Randolph Hearst, who had recently arrived from California to take over the *New York Journal,* was in a fierce battle for readers with Joseph Pulitzer, a self-styled champion of the common man and owner of the scandal-mongering New York *World.* As practitioners of "yellow journalism" — so called because both papers published a color comic featuring a street urchin named the Yellow

Kid — Hearst and Pulitzer trafficked in tales of sex, crime, the wealthy, and the offbeat. The formula was not high-minded, but it sold newspapers and provided funds to hire some of the best reporters of the day, including Nellie Bly and Stephen Crane.

By 1896 the circulations of the *Journal* and *The World* dwarfed that of the city's so-called quality press, and their success had already forced two of its representatives, Charles A. Dana's *Sun* and James Gordon Bennett Jr.'s *Herald,* to lower their standards in order to compete. On August 18, 1896, the day Adolph was formally installed as publisher of *The New-York Times, The Sun* featured "Body Sent to Morgue," the story of a man who barely escaped being embalmed alive, along with a straight-faced news report headlined A FISH THAT PLAYS THE PIANO. The *Herald,* not to be outdone, led with "Wife Uses a Whip," the tale of an adulterous millionaire who had been thrashed by his spouse in Atlantic City. Even the *New York Tribune,* known for its sober emphasis on financial news, gave a nod to sensationalism with coverage of an explosion that had demolished a hotel, killing several people.

In this combative atmosphere, Adolph assumed his place at the helm of the least viable of the city's four serious papers. *The New-York Times'* anemia was embarrassingly apparent to even the most casual reader. Photographs rarely graced its pages; the paper was simply too poor to afford them. The type was tiny and blurred, the consequence of presses so battered that they would soon be sold for scrap iron, and its design, a forbidding series of unbroken columns, was primitive and uninviting. In the desperation of recent days, Charles R. Miller had resorted to publishing fiction, a practice he had once held in contempt, and accepted advertising for patent medicines and other questionable products.

Rival publishers gloated that the *Times* was "dull," "hopeless," and "inconsequential," its future under the "greenie" from Tennessee "experimental" at best. Adolph paid no attention to the criticism, for he now occupied the chair that had once belonged to Henry J. Raymond, "the most illustrious newspaper publisher in America." To him, *The New-York Times* was like a solid but dilapidated house: its foundation "is all right," he assured Effie. "It is the superstructure that needs straightening out."

The first *Times* listing Adolph Ochs as publisher appeared on August 19, the day after he had officially taken possession of his eight-by-ten-foot office on the ground floor of 41 Park Row, a crowded nook that looked out on Printing House Square. In an article blandly headlined

BUSINESS ANNOUNCEMENT, Adolph proclaimed the journalistic principles under which *The New-York Times* would henceforth be run. He had composed the salutatory himself, borrowing heavily from a speech he had given five years earlier in Saint Paul, Minnesota, on how to manage a country newspaper. The previous Sunday in Atlantic City, Effie had read the draft and diplomatically suggested shortening it and dispensing with "the pyrotechnics."

What remained was a straightforward contract between a publisher and his readers. Adolph promised to produce a "clean, dignified and trustworthy" publication with news presented in "a concise and attractive form . . . as early, if not earlier, than other papers." Then, in a burst of lyricism, he delivered the phrase that would become his legacy, the enduring definition of journalistic integrity for newspapers everywhere. It was his "earnest aim," he said, "to give the news impartially, without fear or favor, regardless of party, sect or interests involved." Newspapers across the country reprinted the statement in full, a fact, Adolph said, that "did me great honor." If the concept of a paper that published news instead of partisan diatribes or "planted" stories was hardly original — other newspaper proprietors had expressed similar sentiments — the difference, Adolph would explain years later, long after *The New-York Times* had become the most influential paper in the world, was that he actually believed what he wrote.

Adolph wanted to demonstrate quickly that the *Times* was under new management, and like the former printer he was, his first instinct was to give the paper a face-lift. He threw out the standing announcements on the editorial page, did away with eye-straining agate type, and ordered technical changes that forced the best performance from the paper's creaking presses. The improvement was immediate and dramatic. Just nine days after Adolph took control, *The Fourth Estate* heralded *The New-York Times* as a "typographical beauty . . . a gleam of sunshine on a cloudy day."

Adolph's next step went far beyond the cosmetic. While negotiating for the *Times,* he had discovered that a major reason for the paper's distress was its undisciplined management. Miller showed up whenever he felt like it, disappearing into the cigar smoke and sherry glasses of his club most evenings, and the staff had as many secretaries as it did editors — a luxury even in good times. "There is going to be a cyclone in this office when I am blown in!" Adolph had vowed to Effie at the time.

The "cyclone," when it arrived, drove a devastating path through every inch of *The New-York Times* except the news department. Much later Adolph would brag that he had transformed the *Times* without hiring new staff; what he neglected to add was that he mercilessly slashed the staff he had inherited. With the cooperation of the president of the printers union, to whom he opened the *Times'* books, Adolph shaved $1,000 a week off the payroll of the "ruinously overmanned" composing room and discharged the foreman. Letting people go was "an awful nasty job," he admitted, unsuited to his temperament, and he tried to do so without making enemies. Indeed, the advertising manager felt so warmly toward Adolph after being fired that he agreed to dine with him that evening. "[That] was the refinement of cruelty," an associate joked to Adolph upon hearing about it.

But Adolph knew that cost cutting alone would not make a success of the *Times,* whose future would depend on generating new advertising and attracting more readers. At the suggestion of Henry Loewenthal, the city editor, Adolph resisted the temptation to produce another sheet of mass appeal like the *Herald* or *The Sun.* Instead, he geared the paper toward the city's merchants and financiers. His initial vehicle was a daily column reporting the names of out-of-town buyers who had just arrived in New York; lists of real estate transactions and fires soon followed. These innovations, coupled with market reports and more vigorous Wall Street coverage, brought a substantial number of new subscribers to the *Times.* Before long, men of affairs began referring to *The New-York Times* as their "business bible."

Other newspapers viewed Ochs's emphasis on financial news with bemusement, smugly certain that readers would find the "new" *New-York Times* even more tedious than the old one. When *The Sun* ran a story about a water main break that flooded the *Times'* pressroom, it ended by reassuring readers that the crisis was over. "The *Times* will come out tomorrow as dry as ever," it said. Adolph was unperturbed, content to have the niche of factual, nonsensational reporting all to himself; it suited his conservative tastes as well as his business interests.

Another change was the launch of an eight-page Saturday supplement called the *Review of Books and Art,* which drew women to the paper, underscored its refinement, and incidentally brought in book ads. His new *Illustrated Sunday Magazine* section, a halftone tabloid, stressed current events over the fluff and filler favored by his competitors. Adolph made certain that whatever was newsworthy that week, whether it was a horse show or the opening of the opera, got into the magazine. Gratified readers began flocking to the *Times*, pulling more advertisers with them.

Editorially, Adolph charted a careful middle course. With some reluctance, he retained Miller as editor, reasoning that he represented continuity and, as a Dartmouth graduate, personified the kind of educated man who would be an appropriate helmsman for a paper of the *Times'* eminence. Miller had balked at Adolph's salary offer of $150 a week, half what he wanted, but eventually capitulated. Even at that price, Adolph told Effie, "He has to prove himself worth it."

Miller's position put him in charge of the *Times'* editorial page, a section that Adolph, in his quest to create an impartial newspaper, had seriously considered dropping. Crusading editorials only alienated readers and advertisers, he believed, and the faltering *Times* could afford to lose neither. His compromise was to run editorials largely drained of vehemence and advocacy, except on important questions such as the choice of a president.

Adolph chaired the daily editorial council, occasionally suggesting topics of a positive or sentimental nature, and considered himself the final word if there was a disagreement. In the fall of 1896, just before the presidential election, he insisted on two columns, "Better Times Near at Hand" and "The Usefulness of Bryan," that credited the Democratic nominee, "this facile and hare-brained youth," with unintentionally unifying the country behind "an honest-money standard." To underscore the paper's evenhandedness, Adolph published entire pages of letters to the editor, regardless of whether the writer agreed with the *Times'* point of view — a revolutionary act in an era of polemical press lords.

Adolph promoted the *Times* with every gimmick he could think of. Advertisers received daily mailings highlighting positive aspects of the paper. Nonsubscribers in the city's upscale neighborhoods were bombarded with flyers touting a new feature, passing on praise, or calling attention to the *Times'* probity. Cable-car transfers bore the prim legend NO WOMAN IS EVER ASHAMED TO BE SEEN READING THE NEW-YORK TIMES IN PUBLIC PLACES.

In late October 1896 Adolph came up with the idea of a contest to find a slogan for the paper. He had already created his own — "All the News That's Fit to Print" — and earlier in the month, as a publicity stunt, the words had appeared in colored lights on the wall of the Cumberland Hotel overlooking Madison Square. Now he offered a prize for a better motto of not more than ten words, asking Richard Watson Gilder, the distinguished editor of *Century Magazine,* to serve as judge.

The reaction was overwhelming, and Adolph mined it for all it was worth. Every day for weeks the *Times* printed a column of entries, ranging from "News for the Millions, Scandal for None" to "Free from Filth, Full of News." (*The Sun*'s offering was typically insulting: "Why Is *The New-York Times* Published? God Only Knows.") Newspapers around the country chronicled the excitement with editorials praising the *Times* for its renunciation of the "sewer and morgue fields" wallowed in by *The World* and the *Journal.*

The winning slogan, "All the World's News, But Not a School for Scandal," put $100 in the pocket of D. M. Redfield, the New Haven man who wrote it, but it brought him no lasting fame. In the end Adolph decided he liked his own invention best and decided to keep it. In early February 1897 "All the News That's Fit to Print" appeared for the first time in the upper-left-hand corner of the front page, where it remains today.

§

Adolph didn't disappoint the plutocrats who had supported his quest to acquire *The New-York Times.* When 110,000 businessmen staged a sound-money parade through the streets of Manhattan four days before the election, he was at the head of the newspaper's fifty-man delegation, marching as a "private" rather than riding in the carriage to which his position entitled him. Although it was raining, and the silk banners bearing the words THE NEW-YORK TIMES were soon soaked and drooping, Adolph took heart from the men, women, and children who lined the route and yelled, "All the news that's fit to print," and "Hurrah for *The New-York Times!*" He was a superstitious man, ever mindful of auguries, and it did not escape his notice that this stirring affirmation of his efforts had taken place on the eighth anniversary of his father's death. That night he lit a yahrzeit candle in memory of Julius and the following Friday said Kaddish during services at the Fifth Avenue Temple.

In its news columns, *The New-York Times* treated both Bryan and his Republican opponent, William McKinley, with such balance and fairness that the managers of the national committees of both parties later wrote letters of thanks, even though the *Times* did not ultimately endorse either man. Bryan, though a Democrat, stood on the loathsome platform of free silver; McKinley, despite his embrace of gold, was a Republican. It was John M. Palmer, the nominee of the National Democracy Party, a breakaway faction of the sound-money Democrats, who got the paper's official backing. Although Palmer had no chance of winning — he would receive only 133,000 votes — his endorsement was a fence-straddling exercise that kept the *Times* firmly in the Democratic column even as it prayed for a McKinley victory.

A Bryan presidency was a palpable threat to Ochs's precariously lever-aged finances. "I doubt very much whether there [are] many men in the United States whose future [is] so largely dependent on the result [of the election] as mine," Adolph wrote Effie. His Chattanooga real estate debts continued to dog him, even though he considered them a blessing of sorts: if he hadn't been in such dire circumstances, he would later say, "it would never have occurred to me to try to get *The New-York Times*." In addition to these obligations, he had a sheaf of short- and long-term notes outstanding on the *Times*. That fall several lenders began pester-ing him for repayment. With his usual deftness, he put them off by writ-ing checks for interest.

On election night Adolph stood in his tiny office and watched a crowd of fifty thousand revelers shouting and singing in City Hall Park. He had to concede that *The New-York Times*' tally of returns, displayed on the face of the building at 41 Park Row as well as on a stereopticon screen at Madison Square, was inferior to that of *The World*. But the election went as he had hoped; McKinley won with just 51 percent of the vote. "Hurrah for Weuns'es!!!" Adolph exulted to Effie, adding that now his "fixed pur-pose" was to be "freed from the thraldom of my creditors."

If McKinley's election allayed some of Adolph's problems, it wors-ened others. As long as the occupant of the White House was in ques-tion, Adolph and the powerful financiers, bankers, and insurers behind him were united in a common cause: to elect a man sympathetic to sound money. But as soon as the political crisis had passed, Adolph quickly moved to assert the *Times*' independence and make it clear that he intended to run the paper with "almost autocratic power."

The first signal came shortly after election day, when *The New-York Times* turned down $33,600 in city advertising, the paper's share of a $200,000 contract the board of aldermen had voted for six newspapers

to print a complete canvass of the results. Initially Adolph had welcomed the money, writing his mother that it was "our good fortune" to
get it, but a day later he changed his mind and instructed Miller to write
an editorial attacking the contract as a waste of public funds. For
Adolph, the praise heaped on him by readers and staff was far more
valuable than any money the paper stood to make. "[This] is my opportunity . . . to show that I cannot be bribed from doing my duty to the
community," he told Effie the day the editorial appeared.

Taking on *The New-York Times'* shareholders was a more dangerous
proposition. Although Adolph had operational control of *The New-York
Times,* absolute control rested with the reorganization committee and
would continue to do so until he satisfied the three-year profitability
requirement and took possession of the stock held for him in escrow.
Under certain conditions, the committee could even fire him. Therefore,
it was no surprise that the most meddlesome shareholder was Spencer
Trask, chairman of the committee and president of The New-York
Times Company, who felt that both his position and his past support of
the Ochs plan entitled him to issue orders about stories.

Trask was particularly unhappy with Harry Alloway, the *New-York
Times* financial reporter whose telegram had played a pivotal role in
Adolph's acquisition of the paper. Alloway's coverage showcased corporate shortcomings and impropriety far too often for Trask's taste. He
menacingly informed Adolph that if Alloway "is not amenable to suggestions, [he] will have to go." The reporter stayed.

Ochs was a pragmatist and could bend when he had to, but it was not
long before Trask pushed him too far. The precipitating incident concerned Cosmopolitan University, a mail-order institution in Saratoga
Springs that *The New-York Times* considered suspect but Trask supported. The paper's first editorial on the subject was "rather sneering," in
Trask's view, and he warned Adolph that he wanted no more mention of
the school, positive or negative. When a second "sarcastic" editorial
appeared, he demanded that Adolph instruct the editors never to refer
to Cosmopolitan "without consulting me or submitting any proposed
mention of me and having my O.K."

Adolph knew that the moment had come to assert his authority, but
with typical tact he chose to characterize Trask's attitude as a "misun-
derstanding" rather than a personal affront. "I am very sorry that you
believe you can write such a letter to me," he replied to Trask. "I cannot

enter an order such as you seem to demand. I do not recognize that you have any right to expect me to comply with such a request. I do not understand that you have any control whatsoever of the editorial conduct of *The New-York Times.*"

To reinforce his point, an editorial appeared three days later disparaging Cosmopolitan University as "a long-distance dispensary of advice." The article inflamed Trask anew. "If a request of mine about an indifferent matter can carry no more weight than this," he told Adolph in a furious letter, "I shall see either that it does, or the *Times* management will see if my influence is of value."

The threat proved hollow. Ochs's independence had been a major reason Trask had been attracted to him in the first place, and he was generally pleased with Adolph's performance. From that point on, he ranted about Alloway from time to time, but his manner was solicitous, not demanding. "I do not expect that I or any of the directors have the right to insist that any of our views should influence the course of the *Times*," he said in a letter requesting the "courtesy" of favorable coverage on an issue of no "special importance." Adolph's firmness and diplomacy, coupled with his bedrock self-assurance, had produced the desired result while still enabling him to keep a valuable ally. "When you entered the newspaper business," George later told his brother, "the world lost a promising lawyer."

§

During those first frantic months, Adolph slept just five hours a night, shuttling between 41 Park Row and the "lonely room" he came to "heartily despise" in the nearby Astor House, a five-story hotel favored by businessmen. As the new proprietor of *The New-York Times,* he was deluged with invitations to dine in the city's most coveted salons, but he quickly decided that social events interfered with his business hours and entailed too much personal expense. To save time and money, he rarely went out, choosing instead to work late each evening and "leave nothing undone at the office."

In late October 1896 he broke with his monastic routine to celebrate the thirtieth birthday of Ben Franck, his cousin and Chattanooga real estate partner, who had joined *The New-York Times* as his assistant. Several weeks earlier Bertha and Nannie had come for a visit and Adolph, eager to show off, had hosted a lunch at Delmonico's and taken them to the theater every night. "Adolph looks like another man, fat as a pig, prosperous . . . and full of energy and confidence," George reported to the family after seeing his brother for the first time in his New York incarnation.

Effie and four-year-old Iphigene joined Adolph in December. After two weeks at the Gerald, a second-rate hotel that catered to vaudeville people, the Ochses and their black nurse moved to a rented town house on East Thirty-ninth Street near Lexington Avenue. The Third Avenue el made it easy to commute to the *Times,* and the house was large enough to accommodate Effie's brother Isidor Wise, who worked briefly at the paper until his drinking forced Adolph to fire him.

When their lease expired in the fall of 1897, the family lived for several months in the Majestic, a recently constructed apartment-hotel on West Seventy-second Street that featured bowling alleys, a ballroom, and a roof garden, while Adolph scouted more permanent quarters. He found them just down the street, on the second floor of a brownstone owned by Thomas Read, an English teataster. The Read home had many advantages: proximity to Central Park, a board bill of just $37.50 a week, and the Reads' six children as playmates for Iphigene. The arrangement proved so agreeable that when the Reads moved to a house in the next block in 1899, the Ochses followed them.

As publisher of *The New-York Times,* Adolph earned $10,000 a year, a sum sufficient to allow him to live in better circumstances than a boardinghouse. But his debts had made him cautious. As he wrote his mother, "I think for a couple of years it will be nice to live natural and modest." Buying a suit was an occasion for rejoicing. "I look spick and span," he told Effie with pride after acquiring new trousers and a jacket. "Even Ben has no fault to find."

Adolph's dream of bringing his large extended family to New York within two years of his arrival proved impossible. George and Milton Ochs and their brother-in-law Harry Adler stayed in Tennessee to run *The Chattanooga Times,* and Bertha was too much an unreconstructed southerner to feel comfortable in Manhattan. Instead, the clan gathered every summer in Atlantic City, where they lived and took meals en masse in a large wooden house Adolph rented not far from the ocean.

For Adolph the trip was a three-hour undertaking. Every Saturday morning he boarded a train in New York, his arms laden with toys and boxes of candy for Iphigene and his nephew Julius. The following night, after a twenty-four-hour whirl of minstrel shows, boardwalk shooting galleries, fishing, and band concerts on the Steel Pier, Adolph returned to New York and the comparatively calm life of a summer bachelor.

At the shore Effie again found herself under her mother-in-law's despotic rule and reflexively resumed her Chattanooga habits: sleeping late, taking a swim before lunch, shopping, reading and going to the theater in the evening. Heavy five-course meals were the order of the day, regardless of the heat, and were occasions for the ear-piercing arguments typical of the Ochs brood. "I should not like to be here all summer," Effie told Adolph wearily one day in late June. "I have grown [tired] of all the bickering and squabbling and talk about people I neither know nor care for."

Dressed in black with a bonnet and veil, Bertha was still hale enough to do the daily marketing and terrorize the servants, whom she regularly accused of stealing. In the afternoons she took a chair ride on the boardwalk or played flinch, a card game, with Iphigene and Julius, who knew that their grandmother hated to lose and became masters at cheating to let her win. Every Saturday, before Adolph's arrival, the Ochs women went to temple, where Iphigene, bored and perspiring, sat crammed between her well-padded aunts, trying to avoid contact with the sharp edges of their steel-boned corsets.

Iphigene and Julius were constant companions. They roamed the boardwalk for hours, visiting the Turkish palm reader, ogling the freaks, eating ice cream, and steering clear of Julius's dour and unbending mother, Ada, whose strict child-rearing philosophy called for liberal application of the rod. When Iphigene's Swiss governess and her boyfriend took the children to a striptease show, the unorthodox afternoon cost the woman her job. A favorite game was competing for hotels. "This hotel is mine," Iphigene would say, pointing to a rambling wooden structure in sight of the boardwalk. "This hotel is *mine,*" Julius would counter, pointing to a slightly grander specimen. It wasn't until later that Iphigene discovered that the nicest hotels in Atlantic City didn't accept Jews, a restriction she found baffling.

Being Jewish had meant little in Chattanooga, where the need to build and boost the town had transcended ethnic and religious divisions. There, Adolph had succeeded on the strength of his energy, professionalism, and goodwill; his Jewishness rarely came in for comment. New York was a different story. Although Jews traveled easily in the uppermost reaches of merchandising and finance, the world of debutante balls and private clubs was a barrier breached by only a token few. German Jewish families with names like Straus, Schiff, Loeb, and Guggenheim reacted by forming their own social elite, a group so tight-knit and self-sustaining that it came to be called *Unser Kreis* — Our Crowd.

The unspoken rules of his new home bewildered Adolph at first. "I have met more Jews in the past two months than I ever knew in my life," he told Effie soon after acquiring *The New-York Times*. Despite his father's role as a lay rabbi, Adolph was largely unobservant. He fasted on Yom Kippur and occasionally attended services, but like most Reform Jews he worked on the Sabbath and ignored the dietary laws. In 1896, after dining at the Lawyers' Club as the guest of Spencer Trask and discovering that "only a few members . . . are Jews," he declared that henceforth he would not "join any club where Jews are prohibited even though I can myself be admitted." Within a year Adolph's desire for status and business contacts had worn down his resolve. He joined not only the Lawyers' Club, located in the Equitable Building and decorated with animal heads and hides provided by Equitable founder Henry B. Hyde, but the Hardware Club, a downtown merchants organization with just a handful of Jews.

§

With its clean appearance, new features, and elevated tone, *The New York Times* was again a paragon of respectability by the end of Ochs's first full year of management.* President McKinley read only three newspapers closely; one of them was the *Times*. But with an annual loss of $68,000, the paper had yet to turn a profit. When rumors of war with Spain began to circulate, fanned by Hearst and Pulitzer, any hope of emerging from the red was abruptly abandoned. Wall Street became paralyzed, and the *Times'* biggest moneymaker — financial announcements — completely disappeared.

Adolph supported the Cuban rebels, and the *Times* cheered when the United States declared war against Spain in April 1898, but there was no money to spend on war coverage. While Bennett's *Herald* sent four boatloads of correspondents to the conflict and Hearst's *Journal* dis-

---

*The hyphen in *New-York Times* was dropped in December 1896.

patched its finest swashbuckler, Richard Harding Davis, the artist Frederic Remington, and eventually Hearst himself, *The New York Times* had to rely on the colorless accounts of the Associated Press.

The atmosphere at 41 Park Row came to resemble a death watch. Before long, stories appeared asserting that William Waldorf Astor was about to buy *The New York Times* — gossip that Adolph quickly squelched by claiming, falsely, that the paper was "not running behind but on the contrary [is] prosperous." Within the Times Building, Adolph made every effort to appear hopeful. "If you feel things are particularly bad," he later told a friend, "that is the time you must not show it and take other men's courage away." He dressed in his best clothes, put a flower in his lapel, and strode through the plant, smiling at everyone "as though he were living on the crest of a wave." But as spring gave way to summer and business worsened, Adolph found his formidable optimism severely tested by another crisis, this one from an unlikely quarter: a vindictive, anti-Semitic former bookkeeper in *The New York Times* circulation department named W. L. Woolnough.

Woolnough, an eleven-year veteran of the *Times,* felt he had good reason to be disgruntled. As part of Adolph's crusade to cut costs, Louis Wiley, the *Times'* new circulation manager, had recently fired him. To get even, in early August Woolnough sent a whistle-blowing circular to the only major revenue source *The New York Times* had left: department stores and dry goods merchants. It was their advertising, pegged to circulation figures, that in the fragile financial climate of the Spanish-American War kept the paper from tumbling over the precipice into bankruptcy.

During his years as a bookkeeper, Woolnough had had access to the precise number of papers sold each day. He knew that, desperate to woo advertisers, Adolph had been artfully vague about circulation, suggesting to stores such as Wanamaker's and Bloomingdale's that as many as 25,000 people bought the *Times* each day. The truth was starkly different. In the last week of July 1898, the *Times* was, in fact, *printing* 25,000 papers a day but selling only, on average, fewer than 10,000 copies in Manhattan, and a small number in outlying areas. Woolnough's anonymous handbill exposed the discrepancy and, in the strongest possible language, accused *The New York Times* of deceit and dishonesty.

Deeply worried, Ochs deputized Wiley to prevent any further damage. Tipped off that Woolnough was the likely instigator, Wiley hired a

Pinkerton detective, who convinced the bookkeeper to talk to him by posing as a merchant interested in ascertaining the truthfulness of his allegations. Woolnough, "defiant and vengeful," told the gumshoe he was so sure his figures were accurate that he was prepared to sign an affidavit. A week later, when the detective, accompanied by a lawyer, revealed his true identity to Woolnough and threatened him with legal action, the accountant only became more belligerent.

Adolph, certain he could work his magic on an inconsequential clerk, invited the bookkeeper for a private audience. He trotted out all his usual tricks, but Woolnough would have none of it. "We have got you where we want you," he wrote Adolph afterward. "You have no circulation and never will . . . and advertisers will not keep on waisting [sic] their money." His tirade became so blistering and anti-Semitic that several of his former coworkers later reprimanded him for insulting the boss.

In September Woolnough stepped up his campaign. "You have been fleeced by *The New York Times* long enough," he wrote the owner of O. H. Neill & Company, a large advertiser, adding that other merchants, including Bloomingdale's and Best & Co., had canceled their contracts with the *Times* after discovering the paper's real circulation. In a last-ditch attempt to trump his tormentor, Ochs threatened to sue Woolnough for the "very large discrepancy" he claimed to have found while reviewing his work at the *Times*. The bookkeeper remained unbowed. If Adolph took him to court, he replied, "I will have the great pleasure of seeing your books placed before the public."

By early October Adolph was in a quandary. Woolnough showed no signs of being intimidated, and a lawsuit was unthinkable. Revealing the truth about the *Times'* actual circulation would be a catastrophe. The paper would lose the only advertisers that separated it from insolvency, and, far more important, Adolph would be denounced as a liar. Adolph had always before felt that "the closer quarters I get into, the calmer and cooler I become," but now he had to accept that few options remained to him.

It was at this moment that Adolph made one of the most risky — and ultimately, most brilliant — business decisions of his life: he slashed the price of *The New York Times*. On October 11, 1898 — a week after Woolnough's final threat — readers awoke to a ten-page paper with ONE CENT! proclaimed in heavy black letters on either side of the Gothic script of *The New York Times'* name. The maneuver shocked the city; for the past two years the paper had charged three cents, and the loss of revenue represented by a two-thirds cut was bound to hurt in the short term. More to the point, at one cent, *The New York Times* would cost the same as the unsavory "penny press." Even Adolph's own staff grumbled that the *Times* was now on a doomed slide into the sewer of sensationalism.

But Adolph had given the move careful thought. By pricing the *Times* at a penny, he undercut the *Herald* and the *Tribune*, his chief competitors in the quality press, which charged three cents, and matched *The World* and the *Journal*. Bargain hunters would switch to the *Times*, he reasoned, quickly boosting circulation and rendering Woolnough's claims obsolete. If his strategy worked, he would keep his prized advertisers and add many more.

None of his underlying reasons were apparent in the story announcing the *Times'* new pricing policy. Instead, Adolph explained that the change to one cent was motivated by high-minded principle. Circulation increases since 1896 had been "steady and substantial" but "too slow," said the *Times;* management was convinced that "educated, intelligent, refined" people now subject to the "vulgarity and madhouse methods" of the yellow press would prefer a paper of "high and honorable aims," but at three cents, the price was simply too high.

That afternoon Spencer Trask, in Washington for an Episcopal convention, wrote Adolph a chilly letter. "I am surprised a step so important should have been taken and I have known nothing of it," he told him. "What fresh money . . . have [you] got to warrant this 'cut'?" So hasty was the decision — and so potentially unpopular with the reorganization committee — that Adolph had made it without consulting anyone. But his high-wire act proved a success. Predatory pricing, as it is called today, guaranteed new readers and ensured the future of *The New York Times*. By December 1898 daily circulation had jumped to more than 60,000; at the beginning of the new century, it stood at nearly 91,000, with commensurate gains in revenue.

Subsequent histories of *The New York Times* would characterize the one-cent gambit as Adolph's "greatest inspiration" and "a stroke of genius," and his insight that people would rush from the scandal sheets to the *Times* if the price was right, "pure clairvoyance." Adolph himself encouraged this view, but the truth is that *The New York Times* did *not* lure *World* and *Journal* readers by reducing the price. They were a lost cause, perfectly content to go on consuming titillating entertainment for a penny, and Adolph knew it. The readers he wanted were the men and women who patronized the city's other quality papers — the *Herald, The Sun,* and the *Tribune.* Indeed, soon after *The New York Times* dropped to one cent, it overtook the *Tribune* in circulation, and within a few years bested the other two.

The fact that a former bookkeeper's hate campaign against Adolph played a critical role in the financial salvation of *The New York Times* never came to light. As for Woolnough, he had taught Adolph a valuable lesson. From that point on, Ochs never lied about his circulation; he simply provided no numbers at all. It was the "character" of *New York Times* readers that mattered, he assured advertisers, not how many of them there were.

§

In 1899 Commodore George Dewey made a triumphal procession through the streets of Manhattan to commemorate his victory over Spanish forces in Manila. As the parade approached West Seventy-second Street, Effie and Iphigene waited on the bunting-bedecked reviewing stand that Adolph had erected over the front stoop of the Reads' brownstone, poised to hand sandwiches and fruit to the marching soldiers. As New York's most distinguished citizens rode by in horse-drawn landaus, Iphigene stood on tiptoe and peered closely at each carriage, searching for her father. Finally Adolph appeared, looking awkward in a cutaway and high silk hat and waving to the crowd with the solemn bearing of a potentate. "He had arrived," she said later. "It was a great thrill for a child."

Indeed, by 1899 Adolph did seem to have arrived. The price drop to one cent had turned out to be a great revenue-enhancer, edging *The New York Times* into the black for the first time under his management. The paper was "enjoying quite a 'boom' in circulation and advertising," Adolph told a Cincinnati newspaper broker proudly. "I believe we are now on the high road to great success." He felt so flush that he paid for the train fare for an elderly Knoxville printer to come to New York City, and for two weeks gave his former coworker "the time of his life."

Adolph's high spirits were in part a reflection of his relief. After nearly a year of searching for more working capital, the Equitable Life Assurance

Society had recently agreed to loan *The New York Times* $150,000, taking as security the controlling stock in the company. Under the terms of the original purchase agreement, those shares were destined for Adolph, provided he put the paper on a paying basis for three consecutive years. In the best of all worlds, he would have preferred that his escrowed shares not be used as collateral for a loan, but he had had little choice.

With his capital problems solved, Adolph was consumed with a new worry: how to convince the reorganization committee that he had earned the legal right to the shares. In July 1900 he applied to the committee for the stock, using an arithmetic that was inventive, to say the least, and not exactly what the authors of the purchase agreement had contemplated when they required a profit for three consecutive years. By the calendar, the *Times* had not begun to make money until 1899. But Adolph asserted that because the paper's total profits for the preceding thirty-six months were greater than its total losses over the same period, he had made good on his part of the contract. The committee thought otherwise and in mid-July denied his request.

The rejection startled Adolph, who launched a furious campaign to change the minds of Trask and the others. At home Iphigene listened to heated debate about *escrow,* an unfamiliar word that sounded to her like *escarole.* "Why they put the stock in a salad I never could quite figure out," she recalled. The mortified Adolph later destroyed all correspondence with Trask about the disagreement and asked his brother George to do the same with family letters.

By the time the committee reconvened in early August, Adolph had succeeded in persuading three of its four members to reconsider. On August 14, 1900, almost exactly four years to the day since Adolph had acquired *The New York Times* at auction, the committee voted to award him the stock that legally established his control. John G. Agar, a lawyer and the single negative vote, was resolute in his conviction that Adolph had not earned it. He endorsed the certificates, he said, only because the majority had voted affirmatively; by law, that was sufficient.

For Adolph, it was a tarnished victory, but he had accomplished his mission: *The New York Times* was finally his. "I congratulate you and Baby, who share my all and find happiness in my achievements," he wrote Effie. "I believe we can now consider ourselves as rich as we ever expected to become." He was, he said, the "monarch of all I survey and none my rights to dispute."

Technically, of course, he was not an unfettered monarch; his sovereignty had a lien against it. If he defaulted on Equitable's $150,000 loan, the company could take over *The New York Times*. But Adolph was certain he had nothing to fear. The men who owned and ran the insurance giant were his friends, admirers, and supporters, gentlemen of reason and honor. As events would soon prove, however, Adolph's appraisal of their character was disastrously off the mark.

5

The *Times'* Mystique

A DOLPH DELIGHTED IN SQUIRING IPHIGENE around the *Times,* introducing her to his editors and reporters and gently instructing her in the business of the newspaper. As a former printer, he was especially proprietary about the composing room, where during one visit Iphigene was presented with her name set in lead type. On New Year's Eve 1900 he decided that the inauguration of a new century was sufficiently exceptional to allow his eight-year-old daughter to stay up and watch it from the New York Times Building.

That night the Ochses dined in the ten-room apartment they had been renting since the previous fall, not far from the Reads' boarding-house. Iphigene changed into warm clothing, and father and daughter ventured out, arriving at 41 Park Row a little before 10:00 P.M. Adolph had recently vacated his cramped cubbyhole on the ground floor and moved into a larger eighth-floor office more befitting the publisher of *The New York Times* and president of The New York Times Company — a title that had come with his majority interest in the paper. From this height, Adolph and Iphigene had a commanding view of City Hall, which was trimmed in red, white, and blue electric lights for the occasion. In the surrounding park a noisy throng had gathered, blowing small tin horns and ringing cowbells. A band played martial airs, and local choruses sang sentimental German ballads as the crowd waited for the new century to begin.

At one minute to midnight, the thousands in the park suddenly fell silent and the lights on City Hall blinked out. For a moment Adolph and Iphigene were engulfed in the black stillness of the cold winter night. Then, precisely at midnight, the bells of nearby Trinity Church began to peal. Boats in the harbor erupted in a dissonant symphony of toots and bells. Lyddite bombs reverberated throughout the city. The lights decorating City Hall flashed on again, and across the front of the building a sign appeared in large electric letters: WELCOME TWENTIETH CENTURY. *Times* printers, who had climbed to the roof to mark the moment, sent Roman candles and bright skyrockets sailing into the streets below. The fiery glitter drifted by Adolph's window as Iphigene watched the spectacle, wide-eyed.

The next day's *Times* captured the excitement: TWENTIETH CENTURY'S TRIUMPHAL ENTRY/WELCOMED BY NEW YORK WITH TUMULTUOUS REJOICING. Adolph, who dutifully wrote his mother every Sunday, composed an eight-page letter that gloried in the possibilities of the coming era. "How do you like the new century?" he asked Bertha. "It certainly opens auspiciously for us."

§

With the incorporation of the five boroughs two years earlier, New York in 1900 was a city of 3.4 million people, more than a third of them foreign-born, sprawled over three hundred square miles. Imposing steel-and-concrete structures called skyscrapers housed the headquarters of the nation's leading corporations. Public works projects flourished as the first subway was dug, the Williamsburg and Manhattan Bridges were planned, new docks were installed, and cobblestones were replaced with smooth pavement to accommodate the automobiles that parried horse-drawn carriages on the city's broad avenues.

Nationally, too, the mood was upbeat. Business was booming, and burgeoning technology promised to make life longer, healthier, easier, sweeter. The open wounds of the Civil War and Reconstruction had become merely visible scars, and for the first time in decades the United States, advantageously situated as Cuba's trading partner after the Spanish-American War, began to look outward rather than inward. On the threshold of the modern age, New York and the nation were buoyant and open, as cocksure of their success as a strutting adolescent.

After four years of struggle and anxiety, *The New York Times* entered the new century with yearly revenues of $917,000 — although Adolph, as usual, rounded the figure upward for the audience he wanted most to impress: his family. "*The New York Times* is now doing an annual business of more than a million dollars," he boasted in a letter to "Mama and All" shortly after the New Year's Eve festivities in City Hall Park.

During his thirty-nine-year tenure as publisher of *The New York Times*, Adolph would never draw a salary of more than $25,000; in 1900 his household budget was less than half that amount. Now that the worst of his money problems seemed to be over, he began to take pleasure in the fruits of his labors. With his disproportionately large head, short stature, and bushy eyebrows, he was incapable of cutting a truly stylish figure, but he took a new interest in his appearance, buying tailored suits from Rock's fashionable Fifth Avenue shop. He was now forty-two, and years of hearty eating had left him with a distinct embonpoint, which he vowed to reduce through regular horseback riding. "I am getting fat and I don't want to be a little fat fellow," he said. "My face seems to be getting bigger and rounder every day."

Except for the family's weekends in Atlantic City, Adolph had never taken a proper vacation or traveled widely. Now he was as open to the world as the newly awakened America. In August 1901 he organized a two-month grand tour of Europe, booking passage for Effie, Iphigene, her governess, and assorted relatives on the *Deutschland,* the fastest passenger ship in the world.

Adolph was afraid of the water and never learned to swim, but he felt safe on an ocean liner and was in high spirits on the voyage over. He quaffed champagne, twirled nightly on the dance floor, and one evening became so tipsy that he got into a loud argument with Effie about the wisdom of taking a late-night promenade around the deck dressed in his silk top hat and opera cloak. Effie thought the hour too late and the outfit ridiculous; Adolph went anyway.

The trip included England, Germany, France, Belgium, and Switzerland and challenged even Adolph's indefatigable energy. He was curious about everything, voracious in his desire to see the cathedrals, tombs, paintings, and castles that he had read and heard about as a boy. Just keeping up with him as he scaled towers and prowled dungeons left the rest of the Ochs party exhausted. With Iphigene, he was relentlessly didactic, insisting that she memorize each day's itinerary, reciting aloud the names of the towns they stopped in, how they got there, what they ate, every monument they saw and its significance. "I wouldn't be surprised if I could remember it fairly accurately now," she said more than seventy years later.

While returning home on the *Fürst Bismarck,* Iphigene got a lesson of another sort. Each night in the first-class dining room, the Ochses were served gargantuan multicourse dinners while the steerage-class passengers, many of them Eastern Europeans, hovered on the deck outside, clutching babies and staring through the portholes at the tables heaped with food. Troubled by the inequity, Iphigene surreptitiously handed rolls out the window. Later she and several other children and adults wrapped candy and sandwiches and threw them from the first-class deck down to the eager hands in steerage, "as if we were dropping food into a bear pit."

After that first voyage Adolph made Europe a regular part of the Ochses' life. Except for occasional trips to the American West or Alaska, he took his family abroad nearly every year, never missing an opportunity to broaden Iphigene's horizons. In Europe, he would awaken his daughter at 7:00 A.M. — too early for the late-rising Effie — and the two of them would walk together for several miles, ending up at a local bakery where he would insist that Iphigene use her halting French or German to buy pastries for breakfast. "Iphigene is quite at home talking French," he wrote his mother. "She attracts much attention."

In 1904 Adolph's new sense of prosperity led him to purchase a secondhand Mercedes from William Reick, president of *The New York Herald.* Several months earlier a Packard called *Old Pacific* had crossed the country from San Francisco to New York in fifty-two days, and Adolph, like most Americans, had caught car fever. True to form, Effie was unimpressed with the new acquisition. For years she had happily rented carriages and later owned her own coach-and-four. When Adolph presented her with the Mercedes, she shrugged and said little. "That's the way!" he later told a friend. "Just so accustomed to luxuries, you can't get a rise out of her!"

In keeping with his age and station, Adolph never learned to drive. Instead, he hired a German mechanic who had worked at the Mercedes factory to be the family chauffeur. Iphigene considered him "the most disagreeable person that ever lived," but there was no denying the wisdom of having someone along who could repair the engine and change tires when they blew out — which was often.

The first summer he owned the car, Adolph took Effie, Iphigene, and Julius on a tour of New England that started in Manhattan and ended in Halifax, Nova Scotia, with intermediate stops to see Yale University and New Hampshire's White Mountains. The trip required the fortitude of a pioneer — many roads were little more than rutted trails — and the Mercedes, although elegant for its day, was an open-air vehicle, without top or windshield, and provided no shelter from the rain and wind.

Outfitted in goggles, dusters, and raincoats, their luggage lashed to the back with rubber sheets over it, the Ochses looked more like British explorers setting out to conquer Tibet than tourists from New York. Country horses were so undone by the sight and sound of the car and its passengers that farmers unhitched their teams and hid them in the woods.

During the New England trip twelve-year-old Iphigene came face-to-face with the anti-Semitism she had first heard about in Atlantic City. While staying at the Bretton Woods Hotel in the White Mountains, a friend of Effie's came to call. "How can you stay here?" the woman inquired indignantly. "Don't you know they don't take Jews?" Stunned, Adolph hurried to the front desk to retrieve a brochure, and sure enough, at the bottom it said, NO HEBREWS ADMITTED. Were they exceptions because of his position at the *Times*? Did *Ochs* sound less obviously Jewish than *Levy* or *Rosenbaum*? He did not want to find out and immediately moved the family to the nearby Fabian House, a less commodious hotel that was almost entirely Jewish. At the time, the experience was merely "unpleasant," but later Iphigene felt "enraged [and] angry" at such blatant discrimination, observing that "it's always easier to hate than to understand, you don't need to use your brains."

§

Publications such as *Printer's Ink* downplayed Ochs's transformative effect on *The New York Times,* claiming that he merely "re-awoke a sleeping Minerva," but there was no denying that by the turn of the century, Adolph had fostered a mystique about the *Times* that had many people convinced the paper was well on its way to becoming the greatest in the nation, if not the world. His technique was to create the appearance of sweep and majesty, then to work relentlessly to make it a reality. Letters to the editor almost always included one or more tributes to the *Times,* usually from another newspaper, that were not unlike the scribbled compliments Adolph had pulled from his pockets as a young man. He especially liked to publish testimonials from people whose political views differed from those of the paper but who nevertheless lauded its willingness to report all sides of an issue.

The *Times* wasn't the only paper that was self-promoting, of course, but what differentiated it from its competitors was Adolph's willingness — indeed, his eagerness — to plow back profits so that the *Times* could actually live up to its carefully cultivated image of reliability, comprehensiveness, and objectivity. Keeping the price of the paper at a penny (it went to two cents only in 1918) caused circulation to grow, and with it, advertising revenues, which Adolph used to add more bureaus and buy bigger presses — improvements that, in turn, increased circulation even more and kept the juggernaut going. New York City, with its power centers in business, the arts, and retail, provided the engine for further growth, and the *Times* soon became an information titan, a newspaper bulging with facts, lists, and official pronouncements. Libraries across the country considered it indispensable; editors treated it as a news utility. In 1913 it would become the first paper to publish an ongoing index to itself, leading to a moniker that remains to this day: the Newspaper of Record.

If any one appointment could be said to have helped Adolph realize his far-reaching ambitions, it was that of Carr Van Anda as managing editor in 1904. Ochs lured Van Anda away from his position as night editor of the New York *Sun* with a handsome salary, the promise of a free hand, and an option to buy *New York Times* stock. (The latter was a great boon to Van Anda, who owned shares worth $500,000 by the time he died in 1945.) With his high forehead, wire-rim glasses, resolute mouth, and direct blue eyes, Van Anda gave the impression of a serious scholar — and, at heart, he was. At sixteen, he had studied math, Greek, and physics at Ohio University and was considered something of a mathematical prodigy. "He was not an amateur in any of his pursuits," said Iphigene, who regarded Mr. Van Anda — as he was called by everyone, including the impeccably formal Adolph — as "tough [and] a bit of a cold fish." In the newsroom his reproving glare was known as "the death ray."

Adolph was in awe of the man's intelligence, although he subsequently came to resent the suggestion that it was Van Anda, not Adolph, who had "created" *The New York Times*. Three decades later, when an admiring book about the editor was published, Ochs wrote Louis Wiley a wounded seven-page letter complaining that his own contributions had been overlooked. Van Anda, he said, was an "important cog in a big machine, but not the whole machine." Still, he was genuinely grateful to have a managing editor in sympathy with his philosophy of presenting the news impartially. Here at last was a man who understood Adolph's vision and could make it a reality on deadline every day.

Van Anda had little interest in partisan politics. What charged his imagination was science, a fortuitous passion, given that the early decades of the century were a remarkably fertile period for discovery and cultural change. Van Anda even made news himself, personally correcting one of Einstein's equations and exposing a hieroglyphic forgery on the wall of King Tutankhamen's tomb.

Adolph knew virtually nothing about science but recognized a promotional opportunity when he saw one. To boost circulation, he offered prizes to inventors and adventurers along with fees for exclusive rights to their stories. The danger in such arrangements was that *Times* sponsorship put the paper in the position of violating its own vaunted impartiality, which is precisely what happened in the case of Commander (later Rear Admiral) Robert E. Peary. In 1908, after several failed attempts to reach the North Pole, the shaggy-haired explorer signed a contract with *The New York Times* paying him $4,000 for the New York rights to the story of his next expedition, with the *Times* as his agent worldwide. On July 6 he set out for the Pole.

Fourteen months later, when Dr. Frederick A. Cook, a surgeon who had accompanied Peary on two earlier trips, emerged from the frozen wilderness to report that he had reached the North Pole on April 21, 1908, *The New York Herald,* which had paid Cook $25,000 for the rights to his story, ballyhooed his feat in banner headlines, while *The New York Times,* urged on by a skeptical Van Anda, questioned whether Cook had actually done what he claimed. Two days later a telegram from Peary, who had just docked in Labrador, was delivered to the *Times* newsroom indicating that he, too, had arrived at the Pole. Based on that report, and several other brief messages to the paper, the *Times* ran five triumphant pages on Peary, who announced that he had reached his destination on April 6, 1909 — a full year after Cook alleged to have done so.

When Peary learned of Cook's claim, he angrily disputed it, and every major scientist and newspaper in the world took sides. The story that had begun as a tale of scientific exploration turned into a melodrama of jealousy, alleged dishonesty, and mammoth egos. Adolph, his competitive instincts aroused, was largely uninterested in finding out whether Peary's account was true. "Every newspaper in New York is in a panic about our tremendous scoop," he told Effie exuberantly. "There is little doubt now that Cook is a faker." Indeed, *The New York Times* actively encouraged that impression when, three months later, it published a blockbuster story based on the testimony of two men — paid for in part by the *Times* — who said they had helped Cook fabricate evidence of his polar observations.

Later the U.S. Congress and several worldwide scientific bodies officially recognized Peary's discovery, vindicating Adolph's faith in the explorer — or so it seemed. In recent years no fewer than six books have cast doubt on both Peary's and Cook's claims, including one which concludes that Peary didn't reach within one hundred miles of the North Pole. The *Times* duly reported the debunking on page one.

§

Adolph's campaign to build the *Times'* prestige was not confined to the United States. Early in 1900 he dispatched his brother George, general manager of *The Chattanooga Times,* to Paris to oversee the printing and distribution of *The New York Times* at the International Universal Exposition. Adolph never expected to make money on the venture, but he wanted wider visibility in Europe.

With 1,500 square feet of space in the American Publishers' Building on the exposition grounds and $50,000 worth of Linotype machines, a Goss press, and stereotyping equipment, the Paris edition of *The New York Times* was a modern-day marvel. Each day for five months, crowds gathered outside the large plate-glass windows of the Publishers' Building at 4:00 P.M. to watch the ten- to fourteen-page paper roll off the presses, full of slightly dated news sent from the *Times* in New York and original stories reported and written on site in Paris.

Its success notwithstanding, the Paris edition strained relations between Adolph and George, who went to France with no knowledge of the language and a decided taste for the high life. Taking rooms at 107 rue de l'Université, George — still a bachelor at thirty-nine — gaily reported that "champagne drinking has become such a matter of fact affair with me that the only way I can quench my thirst now is with Heidseick [sic] brut or Carteblanche." When he did work, conditions were far from ideal; power outages, equipment breakdowns, and personnel problems were daily occurrences. The Paris *Herald,* owned by *The New York Herald,* refused to run an ad for its rival's Paris edition, relenting only in the face of George's irate protests. It hardly mattered: the ad, when it finally appeared, was buried on the sports page.

Back in New York Adolph grew increasingly impatient with his younger brother, who, he was convinced, kept the worst of the Paris edition's fiascos from him. The first issue was such a "sorry-looking paper" that George had tried to prevent it from being mailed to Adolph, fearing he would be ordered home at once. Far more disturbing, from Adolph's point of view, was the fact that George had had the audacity to list himself as "publisher" in the paper.

Adolph had an ironclad policy on who got individual credit at *The New York Times*, insisting that "the business of the paper must be absolutely impersonal." Bylines on stories were virtually nonexistent, and no editor, reporter, or business manager was permitted to have stationery with his name on it. Even Adolph's letterhead featured nothing more than OFFICE OF THE PUBLISHER at the top, although of course his name appeared under his title on the *Times'* editorial page.

So he was galled beyond belief when he examined the first issue of the Paris edition and spied on its title page "George W. Ochs, Director and Publisher." He immediately fired off a sharp letter to his brother. "I cannot begin to tell you how embarrassed I felt when the people in the office saw your name conspicuously displayed," he wrote. Not only would it lead European readers to assume that George was publisher of *The New York Times* as well as the Paris edition, but it undermined Adolph with his employees, who now felt, understandably, that there was one policy for them and another for members of the Ochs family.

Stung by the criticism, George moved his name from the title page to a less obvious spot, protesting in rather pedantic language that he in no way sought "self-glorification" but was merely complying with French law, which required that the name of director or publisher be clearly indicated in the paper. As the only one in the Ochs clan with a college degree, he had no lack of ambition of his own. His sister Ada was constantly reminding the family that George never got his due. "George is the real intellectual," she would insist. "*He* is the one who has the core of what our father had." Not surprisingly, George took umbrage at being ordered to disappear into the large gray shadow of *The New York Times*, which was, after all, the shadow of Adolph himself.

But soon George got some of his own back. After returning home in January 1901, he was awarded the French Legion of Honor for his work in connection with the Paris edition. At the time, Adolph gave every appearance of being thrilled for his brother. "Just think of it — an Ochs, a Jew, an American decorated by the French Government," he wrote his mother. "You have cause to be proud." But the truth was that he was crushed that he himself had not received the award. "I only learned thirty years later that he was deeply hurt by this slight," recalled Iphigene.

Despite its many problems, the Paris edition whetted Adolph's appetite for a permanent overseas presence as well as for increased coverage of international news in *The New York Times*. Looking to the future, he predicted that American and European business interests would draw closer together and that prohibitively high cable rates would come down, making a European version of *The New York Times* financially feasible. While George was still in Paris, he authorized him to explore joint publication with *The Times* of London, then the most respected paper in the world, with a reputation for conservatism and vast news-gathering resources.

George, the obvious choice for editor, was eager to make the deal; Spencer Trask volunteered to invest $10,000. Had the two papers joined forces, their international edition would likely have trounced James Gordon Bennett Jr.'s Paris *Herald*. But Adolph soon cooled to the proposition, fearing a London link would saddle *The New York Times* with accusations of a pro-British bias. More important, he was concerned that a Paris paper would overburden him financially at a time when he was pursuing plans — which later proved fruitless — to acquire an evening paper in New York.

To placate George, Adolph reluctantly sent him back to Paris in March 1901 with orders to make preliminary arrangements. But by May plans for an international edition were dropped. In Chattanooga local gossips had long predicted that George would "become so intoxicated with life abroad [he] never can come down to life" in Tennessee. But by the summer of 1901 that was precisely and most unhappily where he was.

6

Sidestepping a Scandal

A S THE *TIMES* GREW IN STATURE AND REACH, SO did its need for space. Forty-one Park Row was seriously over-crowded, and Adolph, as usual, had grand plans for relocation that were as much about theatrics as the physical needs of the paper. For its new home he envisioned an eye-arresting skyscraper that would, he said, "wake up the nation."

His initial plan was to build nearby, on the site of what is now the Woolworth Building. But when several of the property's owners raised the price, he, like the rest of the swelling metropolis, shifted his gaze northward. In July 1902 he settled on a quirky, trapezoidal island of land between Forty-second and Forty-third Streets that was only twenty feet wide facing north and slightly less than sixty feet wide facing south. To the east was Broadway, to the west Seventh Avenue. A rundown hotel called the Pabst occupied most of the space.

The neighborhood, known as Long Acre Square, was in a state of transition. A decade earlier it had been the province of buggy manufac-turers and blacksmiths, who borrowed the name Long Acre from the London street on which many of England's finest carriage makers were located. By the turn of the century, its shabby rooming houses and brownstones had begun to disappear, replaced by the theaters, "silk hat" brothels, and sparkling lights that would eventually transform the district into the Great White Way. Soon it would claim upscale hotels such as the Astor and the Knickerbocker; swank nearby restaurants such as Delmonico's, Sherry's, and Shanley's; and stately neighbors such as the New York Public Library. With several surface-car lines already in place, and the opening of two subway lines eagerly anticipated, the site was an ideal transportation and distribution hub.

Adolph may have picked the right neighborhood for *The New York Times,* but his selection of site and building design was decidedly eccentric, totally unsuited for the production of a newspaper. At Adolph's insistence, the architects C. L. W. Eidlitz and Andrew C. MacKenzie drew up plans inspired by Giotto's campanile in Florence, which the publisher had admired during one of his European trips. The narrow twenty-five-story structure consisted of three floors of Indiana limestone surmounted by sixteen stories of white brick decorated with elaborate ornamental balconies and cornices cast from terra-cotta in a Gothic style. The final six stories rose as a thin office tower and observatory topped by a lantern and flagpole that made the nearly 363-foot New York Times Building the second-tallest structure in the city, visible from a distance of twelve miles. Adolph never got over the building's number-two status, always hastening to explain that, when measured from the floor of its second subbasement, sixty-one feet below the street, to the top of the flagpole, the Times Tower, as it came to be called, was in fact the *tallest* in town.

The peculiar design, however, posed a number of problems for the people who actually put out the paper. Beneath the building, where four new seventy-five-ton presses were housed, there was no room for expansion. The reason was simple: the presses shared space with a permanent roommate in the form of the new Interborough Rapid Transit (IRT) subway, which rumbled through a tunnel occupying a fifty-foot-wide right-of-way in the upper portions of the basement. To protect the building's aboveground tenants from rattles and tremors, a cushion of sand had to be laid between the first and second levels. Additionally, there was only one small elevator to transport rolls of newsprint from the street to the presses and then convey finished newspapers back to waiting carriages and delivery trucks. Adolph, unperturbed by such impracticalities, valued his edifice of "architectural beauty" for the worldwide attention and new sense of "place" it would bring *The New York Times*.

There were few dignitaries present at 3:00 P.M. on January 18, 1904, when eleven-year-old Iphigene took up an ivory-handled silver trowel and, with Adolph and *Times* editor Charles R. Miller looking on, laid the cornerstone of the new Times Tower. The day was simply too cold for the ceremony to draw a crowd, with a biting wind that made Iphigene grateful her mother had insisted on her wearing heavy black tights under her dress. Adolph had composed a grandiloquent dedication for the event, which Iphigene dutifully memorized and recited without error until she came to the awkward word *plumb*. When the cornerstone was lowered into place, Iphigene patted it with her trowel and solemnly proclaimed, "I declare this stone to be *plump*, level, and square."

The Times Tower was only a steel skeleton on April 8, 1904, when the New York City Board of Aldermen passed an ordinance renaming Long Acre Square "Times Square." The change greatly pleased Adolph, who thought it appropriate to have his own geographical signature to rival James Gordon Bennett Jr.'s Herald Square eight blocks to the south. He was especially gratified, he said, that the step was taken "without any effort or suggestion on the part of the *Times*." The statement was technically true, but Adolph was also well aware that there was a man closely connected with *The New York Times* who had been instrumental in the naming of Times Square: August Belmont.

Because of the role that monied interests had played in helping Ochs acquire the *Times*, rumors persisted that Belmont and other Wall Street tycoons actually controlled *The New York Times*. Belmont never owned stock in the paper, although he controlled blocks of shares through E. Mora Davison, his longtime business associate and a former member of Adolph's handpicked reorganization committee, and through Julien Davies, counsel for the elevated railroads in New York City. Still, it was Belmont's Subway Realty Company that had sold Adolph the land for the Times Building, and Belmont himself who, as president of the IRT Company, had personally promoted the rechristening of the square, arguing that the new subway station beneath the Times Tower needed a name more memorable than "Forty-second Street" or "Broadway."

A day before Times Square got its name, William Randolph Hearst revived the old gossip about Belmont's influence over *The New York Times*, a charge with thinly veiled anti-Semitic tones because Belmont, who was raised as an Episcopalian, had Jewish ancestry. The attack, signed by Hearst and published in his morning *American* and evening *Journal*, was so viciously personal that Adolph would soon sue him for libel. In the column, headlined MR. AUGUST BELMONT AND HIS TAME OCHS, Hearst described Adolph as an "uneducated . . . oily little commercial gentleman with . . . obsequiously curved shoulders" who took orders from Belmont and then passed them along to his editor. Adolph was so rattled by this Shylock-like portrait of himself that two days later the news about the birth of Times Square failed to appear on *The New York Times*' front page, instead running inconspicuously on page two.

Adolph had reason to be careful. In addition to his many other roles, Belmont was a director of the Equitable Life Assurance Society, which still held the controlling stock of *The New York Times* as security for a five-year-old, $150,000 loan and had also recently made a first mortgage on the new Times Tower for roughly $1.1 million. Hearst had no way of knowing that Ochs was so heavily indebted to Equitable — and therefore indirectly to Belmont — and Adolph certainly had no desire to draw attention to the relationship.

Moreover, Hearst's attack came just two weeks after Adolph had unsuccessfully petitioned Equitable for additional funds. Cost overruns had plagued the building project from the start, sending the initial estimate of $1.1 million closer to $1.3 million. (When finally completed, the actual cost was closer to $1.7 million.) The original plan had been to rent out thirteen floors to commercial tenants, including Equitable. Indeed, so eager had Equitable been to occupy the building that in the original loan agreement, it insisted on "substantially greater sign privileges than . . . any other tenant" and forbade Adolph from leasing space to competing insurance companies. But as time wore on, high rents necessitated by rising construction costs discouraged Equitable and other major businesses from signing leases.

To reduce expenses, Equitable suggested that Adolph scale back his plans and dispense with the building's crowning glory — its six-story tower. Adolph refused, arguing that the tower was a necessity Equitable should underwrite. "The tower makes the building monumental and . . . differentiates it from the usual skyscraper type and avoids it being termed 'The Little Flat Iron,' a term that I think would be harmful," Adolph wrote to Equitable vice president James Hazen Hyde, the son of the company's late founder, Henry B. Hyde.

James Hazen Hyde had submitted Adolph's request for more money to the society's executive committee, but its members had turned him down. Dismayed but undaunted, Adolph went ahead and built the tower anyway. It is unclear where he got the funds; as usual, Adolph's early financial records are incomplete or nonexistent. A likely candidate is Daniel Guggenheim, the mining magnate, who appears to have given Adolph a personal loan for $250,000 — approximately the cost of the tower — at roughly this juncture.

On New Year's Eve 1904, one day before the *Times* moved into its new home, thousands of bell-ringing, horn-honking New Yorkers gathered at the base of the "Monarch of Times Square" to watch a fireworks display launched from the still-unfinished tower. It would be two years before Adolph came up with one of his greatest publicity stunts: lowering a large illuminated globe down the flagpole to inaugurate the New Year, a tradition that survives to this day. But even at this early stage at its new address, the *Times* had scored a coup. Never again was City Hall Park the place to be on New Year's Eve. Times Square, the Times Tower, and the *Times* itself now stood at the center of the city's attention — just as Adolph had always dreamed.

§

Adolph's euphoria over the inauguration of the new building was short-lived, for within six weeks one of the biggest financial scandals in American history erupted, with the *Times'* principal creditor — Equitable — and its young vice president and designated heir, James Hazen Hyde, at the center. Before the uproar died down, nearly every major insurance company in the country was investigated and found guilty of self-dealing, corruption, and improper speculation with policyholders' money. What the probe failed to unearth, however, were the certificates for the controlling stock of *The New York Times* held by Equitable. Had their existence come to light, Hearst's *Journal,* Pulitzer's *World,* and other papers would have gleefully ridiculed Adolph's journalistic rectitude, destroying his reputation and, along with it, the *Times'* credibility.

Since 1896, the year Equitable helped Adolph purchase *The New York Times,* relations between the publisher and the insurance behemoth had been unusually close. Because of his late father, James Hazen Hyde was favorably predisposed toward Adolph, although in style the two men could not have been more different. A dedicated Francophile with a home in Paris, the younger Hyde was a tall, overbearing playboy. Outfitted in his trademark French-cut coat with a boutonniere of fresh violets and patent-leather pumps with bright red heels, he was frequently seen careening down Broadway in a beflagged coach-and-four, blowing a bugle as though out for an afternoon of foxhunting. A cultured aristocrat and one of New York City's most eligible bachelors, Hyde was reputed to have declared, with characteristic immodesty, "I have wealth, beauty, and intellect; what more could I wish?"

Hyde and his Equitable associates brought much of the adverse attention upon themselves through an unseemly quarrel over power and succession. After the death of his father in 1899, the twenty-three-year-old Hyde inherited a majority interest in the company under a trust arrangement set to expire on his thirtieth birthday, when he would personally take control of the shares. In the meantime, he was made an officer of Equitable, serving as understudy to president James W. Alexander, for whom he harbored an ill-concealed "ambivalence and, sometimes, contempt." Alexander, meanwhile, was disgusted by his charge's boulevardier lifestyle and worried about his involvement in strategies that personally enriched Hyde and others at Equitable.

In 1904 Theodore Roosevelt, campaigning for president as a reformer, had included life-insurance companies on his list of "malefactors of wealth," and rumors had begun to swirl that Equitable, with returns of only 4 percent, might soon find itself the target of a hostile takeover. While Hyde looked forward to his thirtieth birthday in 1906, when he would finally become the unencumbered head of the company, Alexander and his partisans schemed to ensure Hyde's removal.

The poisonous atmosphere became public in February 1905, soon after Hyde threw an extravagant debutante ball for six hundred guests at Louis Sherry's. To bolster his position within Equitable, Alexander leaked fabricated and lurid accounts of the party to the city's sensation-hungry journals. Led by Pulitzer's *World*, the row at Equitable gradually grew into an exposé of the company's freewheeling practices. When readers learned that Hyde and other Equitable officers treated the company as their own personal checking account — padding salaries, paying off politicians, helping friends through interlocking directorates — confidence in the industry was severely shaken.

Throughout 1905 *The New York Times* closely covered the unfolding drama, publishing 115 front-page articles, just seven fewer than *The World*, which approached the story with the tenacity of a bloodhound and a pronounced bias against Hyde and Equitable. If *The World*'s position was clear, so was that of *The New York Times*. During the early months of the scandal, the paper treated the company and the beleaguered Hyde gingerly, encouraging a restoration of amicable relations among Equitable's officers and directors and praising their "open-minded wisdom and sound judgment."

In an effort to mollify his critics, Hyde offered to keep his controlling shares in trust for another five years and on March 15 wrote Adolph to tell him what a *New York Times* editorial should say on the subject. Several years later, in an unrelated libel trial, Adolph would be asked whether he had ever taken editorial "directions" from James Hazen Hyde. His reply, under oath: "Never in the remotest degree." While the letter may not literally have constituted "direction," an examination of the *Times* editorial of March 16 — the day after Hyde's letter — shows that much of the language was lifted directly from Hyde.

In April New York governor Frank Higgins asked state insurance superintendent Francis C. Hendricks to make a report on the entire insurance industry. Two months later, in response to Equitable directors' demands that he divest himself of his shares, Hyde resigned his vice presidency and sold his controlling stock for $2.5 million to Thomas Fortune Ryan, a transit magnate and principal in the National Bank of Commerce, a trust company with strong ties to Equitable. *The New York Times* commended Hyde for his "sacrifice."

But once Hendricks's preliminary conclusions were released in June, the paper could no longer continue its policy of excuse and deny. It published the full text of the report and in an editorial censured the "misconduct" of Equitable officers, describing their behavior as "lamentable and deserving of the severest sanction." For Adolph, the moment was fraught with terror, for buried deep in the Hendricks documents was a list of Equitable stockholders who, the report suggested, had profited from a scheme that promoted their private interests over the welfare of the company — and Adolph's name was on it. If a "preliminary" report had come so close to Adolph's doorstep, what would happen if a full-blown investigation were launched and Equitable's outstanding loans, and those of its officers and directors, exposed? What if it were revealed that Equitable held the controlling stock in *The New York Times* as security for a loan? Hearst and Pulitzer would feast on Ochs's shame and misery.

Adolph was not worried about whether Equitable's $1.1 million building loan was discovered; that was a straightforward business deal. But he was desperate to get out from under the agreement that gave the insurer a call on the majority interest in *The New York Times.* In a state of extreme agitation, he approached Marcellus Hartley Dodge, the twenty-four-year-old grandson of Marcellus Hartley, the late munitions millionaire who had initially introduced him to Henry B. Hyde and sat on

Adolph's handpicked reorganization committee as Equitable's representative. As a small boy, Dodge had visited Adolph many times in the company of his grandfather; he had complete faith in the *Times* publisher
and could be counted on to be discreet. As important, from Adolph's
point of view, Dodge had no potentially embarrassing political or financial entanglements.

On his visit to Dodge, Adolph explained in vague terms that he had
borrowed money from Equitable for the benefit of the *Times,* and in the
current climate of inquiry and scandal, "it would be serious for the
paper if this fact came out." Dodge asked how he could help. "I want you
to take up the loan from Equitable," Adolph told him, "and I would like
[in addition] to borrow from you $300,000 and I will put up for it stock
in *The New York Times*." After consulting with the executor of his grandfather's estate, Dodge asked for the controlling interest in the paper as
security. Adolph accepted the terms, and the majority stock of *The New
York Times* was transferred from Equitable to Dodge's safe, "one [credi-
tor] replacing the other."

The transaction came none too soon. Almost immediately after the
switch, Governor Higgins formed a legislative commission to investigate the state's insurance companies. With Adolph free of his potentially
embarrassing connection to Equitable, the *Times'* coverage of the
inquiry became more detached and professional. In 1906 the commission made its findings public, including recommendations that eventually led to sweeping reforms in the insurance industry.

As for the controlling stock in *The New York Times,* it remained with
its new caretaker for eleven years, unknown to anyone at the paper
except Adolph. Dodge, who succeeded his grandfather as president of
the Remington Arms Company, never asked for repayment of the loan,
but in 1916, when the company became overextended because of the collapse of the Russian government, to which it had sold rifles and ammunition, Mrs. Dodge mentioned her husband's distress to Adolph. The
loan was soon repaid in full, and Adolph claimed possession of the
majority interest in *The New York Times.*

It was not until then, two decades after he had acquired the paper,
that Adolph obtained free and clear title to the controlling stock in his
enterprise. For nearly half that time, it had been in the hands of two of
the most powerful representatives of big business in the United States.
Yet during all those years, and forever afterward, Adolph staunchly

maintained that *The New York Times* was completely independent of outside influences. Physical possession of the shares had mattered little to him; what had counted was his confidence in his own ability to resist outside demands. As he told *Forbes* magazine, "There has never been anyone who had any control of or voice in my affairs or who in any form could affect my entire freedom of action."

7

"My Ownest Daughter and Onliest Son"

GIVEN HIS SHAME ABOUT HIS OWN LACK OF EDU-
cation, Adolph might have been expected to be intently interested in the academic preparation of his daughter, but while he
expected great things of her, he was oddly indifferent to her formal
instruction, content to leave Iphigene's schooling to his wife. Effie
tutored her at home until she was eight, reading aloud from the Bible,
history books, and Greek myths until the girl knew the Trojan War and
Bulfinch's *Age of Fable* by heart. To supplement this classical fare, Effie
took her daughter to a light musical or theatrical matinee every Saturday, varying the routine occasionally with an evening at the Metropolitan Opera, to which she held season tickets. The experience made a
lifelong opera-hater out of Iphigene, who as an adult compared the
"shriek" of sopranos to women "being burned at the stake." On Mondays the two wandered through the Metropolitan Museum of Art,
watching young artists copy paintings in the silent galleries before walking back through Central Park to the family's apartment at Broadway
and West Seventieth Street. "I practically grew up at the Metropolitan
Museum," recalled Iphigene. "I knew every statue in the place."

Because of Effie's highly selective — and completely oral — tutoring
methods, Iphigene was unable to read or perform simple arithmetic
when she enrolled at Dr. Sachs's School for Girls on West Fifty-ninth
Street, run by a member of the Goldman Sachs banking family. Her lack
of preparation was apparent; the teachers considered her intelligent but
indolent about learning fundamental skills. The truth was that Iphigene
suffered from an inherited learning disability, a form of dyslexia, that
caused her to reverse numbers and letters, making reading difficult and
spelling nearly impossible. Moreover, the poor lighting at the school
gave Iphigene headaches. When the Ochses' doctor suggested eyeglasses,
Effie refused, pulled Iphigene out of classes, and resumed teaching at

home, insisting that her daughter need not return until she was twelve years old.

Adolph, worried that she would become "fat and lazy" at home, strongly disagreed. During a visit with Theodore Roosevelt at Oyster Bay in the summer of 1902, he asked the president to send an autographed photo of himself to Iphigene. When it arrived, he used the honor of the occasion to stress to his wife the need to prepare their daughter for the elevated role she was one day certain to assume. "Perhaps this incident will impress you with the importance of the training she should have," he wrote Effie, "for she will have entre [sic] into the society of the best of the land. She will be much courted and her good will placed at a high value. . . . There is nothing beyond her reach."

Such arguments carried little weight with Effie; she was blithely unconcerned with social status and cared more for the Ochses' pet canary (with whom Adolph regularly had conversations) than she did for presidents of the United States. Nevertheless, she permitted Iphigene to reenter Dr. Sachs's, where the child continued to flounder. One day the school's founding headmaster, convinced that Iphigene had laughed during one of his lectures, demanded that she come to his office after school. At the appointed hour Iphigene arrived and for several minutes stared blankly at Dr. Sachs as he ranted about her impertinence. Discomfited by her impassive expression, he stopped suddenly and asked, "What are you thinking about?" "I think you have no business talking to me the way you are," she replied.

For this breach of discipline, she was promptly expelled. Adolph managed to get her reinstated long enough to finish out the year, but he was so busy with his affairs at the paper that he had little time to focus further on the details of his daughter's education. "I don't think my parents ever followed what I was doing in school," remarked Iphigene years later. "My father thought I was brilliant, and my mother thought that whatever I did was all right. She just assumed you can learn anywhere."

In fact, Iphigene was something of a poor little rich girl, spoiled and indulged yet slightly neglected, too, with a cool, cerebral air disconcerting in one so young. Brown-eyed, with an abundance of dark hair, she was attractive, but her features were too strong to be considered classically beautiful. As an adored and sheltered only child, she spent an inordinate amount of time with adults. Her best "friend" was an imaginary dog. "Growing up in that kind of atmosphere, she was always lonely, I think," said Sally Reston, widow of *New York Times* correspondent and columnist James "Scotty" Reston. "Lonely from the beginning."

Effie's lack of discipline and her otherworldly personality made her more of a fellow child to her daughter than a nurturing mother or wise adviser. Hers was a curiously self-centered and cocooned world that revolved almost exclusively around her husband, daughter, and close relatives. Effie invariably charmed anyone who happened to enter the Ochs home, but she had no interest in entertaining people or participating in the wider world of New York. On the rare occasions when Adolph invited guests home to a formal meal, he had to arrange the place cards himself.

Her one domestic interest was interior design, and her taste tended toward the exotic: the apartment featured a "Turkish corner" complete with a couch covered by a tentlike canopy festooned with fake pistols and swords. Otherwise, Effie abdicated most adult responsibility. She expected relatives, visiting friends, and maids to fulfill the duties normally performed by a wife. For many years Blanche Aaron, a cousin of Harry Adler's who lived on West Sixty-sixth Street, planned the Ochses' meals and ordered provisions. "Everybody who came to the house was always so busy taking care of her, they never had time to do much of anything else," remembered Iphigene. As she got older, Iphigene, too, began to take care of her mother and, like the others, accepted the task with bemused resignation. She considered Effie a "free-thinker" and "an original character." Only years later did she confide to a close friend that her aunt Nannie "brought me up more than my mother did in many ways."

Occasionally, Effie took Iphigene shopping at Stern's on Twenty-third Street or Wanamaker's on lower Broadway. When Iphigene tired of looking at ready-to-wear clothing, then a novelty, Effie would drop her off at the nearby Eden Musée waxworks, where the dimly lit chamber of horrors in the basement provided hours of repulsive fascination.

Her excursions with her father were more wide-ranging and educational. On Sundays the two took long walks in Central Park, Adolph dressed in the extravagant weekend couture of the era — a high silk hat, stiff collar, and cutaway — and Iphigene in a black velvet coat and a hat trimmed with ostrich feathers. Thus attired, father and daughter would call on Daniel Guggenheim, Jacob Schiff, or Andrew Carnegie, whose sixty-four-room mansion had recently been completed at Fifth Avenue and Ninety-first Street. The men talked about politics, finance, newspaper publishing, and world affairs, hardly subjects of great interest to a young girl. But Iphigene listened with genuine attentiveness, grateful that her father wanted to include her in his world and, at the same time, eager to prove she was deserving of the honor. "I used to follow him around at his heels," she said of their Sunday outings. "I was more faithful than my dog is to me."

Adolph was delighted with Iphigene in every respect except one: she was a girl, and therefore inconceivable as someone who could succeed him as publisher of *The New York Times*. Nevertheless, his dynastic impulses were so strong that he couldn't help grafting the aspirations normally associated with a son onto his daughter. When she was an infant, he referred to her as "the heir apparent to it all," yet like many doting fathers, he didn't want his little girl to grow up. He called her Baby until, at the age of eight, she demanded that he stop; even in his seventies, he carried a gold pocket watch with her likeness as a child emblazoned on its face. At the same time, he treated Iphigene with a rationality and a sense of partnership more appropriate to an oldest son and made no secret of his dual expectations. In a 1902 letter he greeted her as "My Ownest Daughter and Onliest Son." The conflicting hopes, emotions, and expectations made for a complex relationship that transcended traditional gender roles.

Iphigene thus found herself in an impossible dilemma, yearning for her father's approval but always feeling slightly imperfect because of the accident of her sex. Effie, with her own childlike needs, was incapable of providing comfort or even an acceptable model of feminine behavior. These elements, coupled with Iphigene's learning disability, made her susceptible to Adolph's natural domination and unusually lacking in self-confidence. Years later, when she was in college, her freshman English teacher astutely observed that Iphigene "had a father who was a great man and nothing she did must be unworthy of him. . . . Very early she felt the responsibilities of being her father's child. Her inability to be what a son would have been to him made her inclined to underestimate herself."

Culturally, Adolph had little to teach Iphigene. He rarely read the classics, preferring melodramatic sagas of damsels in distress or moral tales with simple sampler wisdom. For entertainment, he sought out light comedy or burlesque reviews like the Floradora chorus. His primary contribution to Iphigene's education was a curriculum of his own cherished

values: charity, curiosity, love of family, and the importance of protecting his prized jewel, *The New York Times*. He took her to homes for the
aged to underscore the fact that she, too, would be old someday and so
should treat the elderly with respect, and to factories to show her how
working people lived. On their Sunday strolls through Central Park, he
spoke rhapsodically about nature and open spaces, making her a proselytizing advocate of municipal parks for the rest of her life.

By his own life and example, Adolph taught his daughter the importance of staying slightly in the background, of not drawing too much
attention to oneself. The blank impersonality of *The New York Times*
conformed to his philosophy of good journalism; it also gave him a cur-
tain behind which he could labor in relative safety. What Hearst,
Pulitzer, and Bennett sought was money, political power, and notoriety;
what Adolph sought was admiration. His reticence was due in part to
insecurity about his social skills and public speaking, but it also had to
do with his feelings about being Jewish. "My father always said that if he
hadn't been a Jew, he'd have had more difficulty making a success in
life," said Iphigene.

When Iphigene was nine, the country was in an uproar over the
fact that Theodore Roosevelt had invited a black man — Booker T.
Washington, founder of Tuskegee Institute, one of the leading black
educational institutions in the country — to lunch with him at the
White House. On the subject of race, Adolph was a man of his era and
region, and hardly the "early liberal" Iphigene later portrayed him to be.
He relished telling off-color jokes in Negro dialect, loathed miscegena-
tion, did not think twice about using the word *nigger* or *darkie,* and permitted stories in *The New York Times* describing blacks' "unremitting
and never-satiated appetite" for chicken and watermelon.

Washington's unthreatening brand of social activism pleased many
whites, including Spencer Trask, who had joined the board of Tuskegee
and told Adolph good things about its founder. When Adolph learned
that Washington was coming to Carnegie Hall with the Tuskegee
Singers, he saw yet another chance to prepare Iphigene for the world in
which she would one day play a part. Over the protests of the visiting
Bertha — still a vocal Confederate at sixty-eight — he took Iphigene to
hear Washington speak. The lecture made little impression on her; she
was deeply disappointed that Washington was light-skinned rather than
really *black*. However, the evening was salvaged when Adolph spied a

familiar face in the crowd and rushed up to greet him. "Mr. Twain," said Adolph, employing the pen name of the author of *Tom Sawyer* and *Huckleberry Finn*, "I would like you to meet my daughter, Iphigene, the future publisher of *The New York Times*." Years later Iphigene dismissed the comment as mere "levity," but she never forgot it. To the ears of a nine-year-old, it sounded like a harbinger of her destiny.

§

After Iphigene's ignominious ouster from Dr. Sachs's school, Adolph and Effie enrolled her as a day student at a nearby boarding school run by the Misses Ely. When the two sisters moved to the suburbs, Iphigene transferred to the Benjamin-Deane school on Riverside Drive, not far from the Ochses' new rental apartment at West End Avenue and West Eighty-third Street. There were far better private schools in New York City, but many declined to take Jews, and Adolph refused to "grovel . . . and pull strings" to get Iphigene in. At Benjamin-Deane she spent what she described as four "pretty much wasted" years.

Her education might have ended there had it not been for a new governess, Miss Henrietta MacDonnell, who arrived at the Ochs home in 1904, when Iphigene was twelve. A handsome woman in her fifties, with blond hair, blue eyes, and a turned-up nose, Miss MacDonnell was Irish Catholic, fluent in French, and until recently had been employed in the household of the French minister to Persia. Iphigene, on the brink of adolescence, considered herself too old for a minder and did her best to discourage the new addition from staying. Miss MacDonnell, perhaps perceiving Iphigene's deep need for a mother, played to her sympathy. "I've never been in America before," she confided one day when Iphigene was particularly disagreeable. "I've left all my family in England. I'd hoped you'd take the place of my favorite niece."

With that, Iphigene's resistance melted, and soon the two became great friends. In the ensuing years Miss MacDonnell became Iphigene's big sister, mother substitute, teacher, and role model, guiding her through the mysteries of young womanhood. With her strict moral code, advanced education, and sense of propriety, Miss MacDonnell was just the kind of surefooted confidante and counselor Iphigene craved.

Shocked by her charge's poor reading skills, Miss MacDonnell launched an intensive tutoring program. She sat Iphigene down and recited one paragraph, then listened patiently while Iphigene struggled through the next. In this manner, Iphigene gradually learned to read. "It was Miss MacDonnell's encouragement that kept me from turning my back on education altogether," she explained. Thereafter, she was rarely without a book. Even at night, while sitting in front of her bedroom mirror, Iphigene would dreamily brush her long dark hair with one hand and turn the pages of Dickens or Thackeray with the other. Books became her passport to a wider world and a substitute for friends her own age. "She was so alone and traveling so much with her parents and all these older people that a book was her companion," her daughter Marian said years later.

Miss MacDonnell was equally appalled to discover how little Iphigene knew about Judaism. Like many assimilationist German Jews of the day, the Ochses practiced their faith in selective ways. They celebrated Christmas with a decorated tree and a festive bowl of eggnog but never held a Passover seder. Effie, perhaps overwhelmed with religion as the daughter of a great rabbi, took Iphigene to temple only on Friday nights, when she knew the service would consist mostly of music and she could avoid the tedium of a sermon. As a mark of their emerging status, the Ochses quickly abandoned the Fifth Avenue Temple for the more prestigious Temple Emanu-El, the first avowedly Reform congregation in New York, where Effie worked with the Emanuel Sisterhood, a charity group headed by Mrs. Jacob Schiff.

Like most children, Iphigene was curious about religion. When she was eight, she asked her father whether Jesus Christ was the son of God. "Do you believe if I had the power to do any and everything, that I would allow my only child to be killed?" he asked. "Of course not," she replied. "That's the reason we don't believe Christ was the son of God," said Adolph. "I don't, either," Iphigene agreed, adding for the record that she already knew that the Jews had not killed Christ.

Adolph and Effie were as lackadaisical about their daughter's religious training as they had been about her math and reading. They sent her to Sunday school to learn Hebrew and Jewish history, but when she decided she didn't like it, they did not insist she persevere. "My parents were both devoted to Liberal Judaism and wanted me to be a good Jewess," said Iphigene, "but I was an only child and much indulged."

Miss MacDonnell took it upon herself to inculcate Iphigene in the rudiments of her religion. Not being Jewish herself, she ended up essentially teaching a version of Catholicism without Jesus. Iphigene eventually rejected this unnatural hybrid and, at fifteen, after reading Thomas Paine's *Age of Reason,* declared that she was, in fact, not a Jew but a Deist — a person who believes that God made the world and thereafter assumed no control over his creation. Alarmed, Adolph arranged private lessons with Hyman Enelow, the rabbi at Temple Emanu-El. After two years under his tutelage, Iphigene returned to the fold, even commenting that a Yom Kippur service made her feel appropriately "like dust," but she was not a particularly observant or devoted Jew. Her faith was more intellectual than emotional, more rational than impassioned.

Miss MacDonnell arrived in the Ochs home at a delicate moment: Iphigene was on the cusp of adolescence, with all the tantalizing and terrifying sexual longings made even more confusing by the double standards of the Victorian era. Effie was hardly equipped to counsel her daughter, so it was left to Miss MacDonnell, with her rigid code of female behavior, to steer Iphigene through the shoals of incipient womanhood.

Iphigene was an awkward teenager, with fallen arches so severe that she had to wear Ground Grippers — hideous square-toed shoes with metal plates inside. Adding to her discomfort was Miss MacDonnell's clear message that the female body was shameful. As a young girl in a Catholic convent school, Miss MacDonnell had been made to bathe fully clothed in her nightgown. She did not impose such hysterical modesty on Iphigene, but neither did she allow her to soak long and luxuriously in the tub, as she liked, because that was "indulging the flesh."

While other girls dressed in bright dresses that called attention to their features, Iphigene chose dull colors and boxy designs more suitable to an older woman. By her own description, she was "rather a pretty girl," but she disliked lace and frilly feminine accoutrements. It was as if, like her father, she was trying to be inconspicuous, to blend in with the background — a habit that persisted throughout her life. "I don't think I ever saw her in a red dress or a red jacket," said Sally Reston. "Her clothes were always very subdued in color. Almost Quakerish."

Like many young girls, Iphigene went through a romantic phase with her father, addressing him in one letter as "the handsomest, the bestest, the sweetest, the cleverest, the most adorable, the most generous, the grandest, the most remarkable, the most lovable, the greatest of beaux among men." Two weeks after her sixteenth birthday, she decided to rearrange her schedule in order to spend more time with him. "I am going to do all my lessons in the afternoon so that my evenings will be free to be with you," she informed Adolph.

But as Iphigene grew from child to ingenue, one aspect of her father's behavior mortified her: the physical affection he showered on females. Adolph's penchant for kissing women was a standing joke in the family. "He was always kissing you and pawing you, always had his arms around you when he could," said Jean Steinhardt, a distant relative by marriage. As a teenager, Iphigene came to dread her birthday parties because Adolph would enter the room with great fanfare and proceed to scoop up her friends one by one and squeeze them. "When he kissed the girls, it embarrassed me," she said. "I didn't think it was proper."

Iphigene herself did not like to be hugged or kissed by her father, and even as a young child wriggled out of his embrace. "I think she probably had a sense of not wanting her father to be too cozy with her," said her daughter Judy. "Maybe because she was an only child. Maybe she felt something that just wasn't right." Her aversion to physical contact — with anyone — became a permanent part of her personality. "Even when she was older, if you tried to take her arm, she would tell you she did not like to be physically touched," said her granddaughter Jackie Dryfoos.

Except for members of her wide-ranging family, Iphigene had almost no experience with boys. In 1908 her cousin Julius Ochs Adler came up from Chattanooga and enrolled at Lawrenceville, a boarding school in New Jersey that prepared young men for Princeton, visiting the Ochs home on weekends and during vacations. The arrangement was more than a logistical convenience; it was the beginning of his apprenticeship as a surrogate son. By shipping their son off to Adolph, the Adlers hoped that Julius, the only suitable male in the next generation, would be in a position to eventually succeed Adolph as publisher of *The New York Times*. When speaking to Adolph, they pointedly referred to Julius as "our boy," as though they and Adolph shared a kind of joint parentage. "His parents were fantastically ambitious for him and not altogether too bright in that respect, because they sort of counted me out," said Iphigene. "They pretty nearly handed Julius to my father on a silver platter as his heir."

Adolph, though, was entirely complicit in these plans. He could not imagine his daughter as publisher. She was a woman, after all, and Julie was everything one could wish in a protégé: athletic, serious, outstanding academically, and appropriately worshipful of his successful uncle. Strangely enough, it did not seem to occur to Adolph that his daughter might one day have a role in *The New York Times* through a husband — at least a husband from outside the family. Among members of the extended Ochs clan, the unspoken expectation, encouraged no doubt by the Adlers, was that Julius and Iphigene would someday marry. The practice of first cousins' marrying to consolidate business interests was not uncommon among German Jews; indeed, it had already united two branches of the family that owned Lehman Brothers. If Iphigene was aware that her marital future had been predetermined, she did not let on. Her feelings for Julie were hardly romantic; to her, he was a "dear brother."

When Iphigene was eighteen, she had her debut. At the same time, Adolph had a coming-out of his own — in the *Social Register of New York,* a mark of distinction bestowed on only a few Jews at the time. Listed under her father's name as a "junior" in the 1910 edition, Iphigene was now secure in a social milieu Adolph could barely have imagined at her birth. In May of that same year she was invited to celebrate the twenty-first birthday of Nathan Straus Jr., son of the owner of Macy's, at the Harmonie, a private Jewish club so exclusive and so thoroughly German that until World War I a portrait of the kaiser hung on the wall. Between dances, Iphigene and her partners walked out to the adjacent roof garden and watched Halley's comet streak across the sky. Subsequently, the diminutive Nathan Jr., whom Iphigene considered "very bright [and] amusing [but] not . . . good looking . . . at all," became her frequent escort.

The arrangement pleased Adolph — as long as nothing serious developed. He wanted to remain the only man in his daughter's life. For Iphigene, breaking free of her domineering father would prove extraordinarily difficult. Luckily, she had a determined aide-de-camp: Miss MacDonnell. "It was [her] support that helped me gain my independence from my father," she said. "That was a struggle, because my father didn't want me to grow up. I was his little girl."

§

Nineteen hundred and twelve was a banner year for Adolph and *The New York Times.* Daily circulation stood at 248,170, a jump of about 44,000 from the previous year, and advertising volume was the most robust in the paper's history. Total receipts had shot up to an all-time high of $3.15 million. Adolph was so pleased that he ran a box on the front page of the paper on New Year's Day 1913 with the boasting headline THE TIMES' BEST YEAR.

Adding to Adolph's sanguinity was the sale of his Philadelphia newspaper, *The Public Ledger,* for $2 million to Cyrus Curtis, publisher of *The Saturday Evening Post* and *Ladies' Home Journal.* Adolph had bought *The Philadelphia Times* in 1901 and *The Public Ledger* in 1902, merged them under the *Ledger's* name and made his brother George publisher. It was in Philadelphia that George had finally ended his bachelorhood at age forty-six, marrying Bertie Gans, the daughter of a wealthy local merchant, in 1907.

Adolph had originally bought the Philadelphia properties with an eye toward amassing a national newspaper chain, but by 1912 he seemed ready to abandon the idea. Recently he had incurred heavy expenses to erect yet another new building for *The New York Times.* The paper had rapidly outgrown its improbable tower in the middle of Times Square, and a twelve-story annex on West Forty-third Street was already under way, its design inspired by the castle of Chambord in France.

George had lobbied for the *Ledger's* sale, arguing that it would benefit him because, under Curtis's proposal, he, George, would receive an infusion of cash while retaining "absolute and complete control" as the paper's salaried publisher. Unspoken but clearly understood was George's real aim: to run a newspaper free of Adolph's hovering presence. Therefore, when the transaction was consummated, Adolph outwardly agreed that the deal was "a fine trade from every point of view." Privately, though, he patted himself on the back for being so generous to his younger brother and speculated that George might soon find life outside Adolph's orbit unappealing.

On the news side of *The New York Times,* the year was also memorable because of the sinking of the *Titanic.* Thanks to Carr Van Anda's confident deductions, the *Times* ignored the White Star Line's insistence on the integrity of its ship, and for a full day was the only paper carrying the correct story of the doomed liner's icy end. Days later, when the rescue ship *Carpathia* docked in New York, the *Times* scored another coup by obtaining an exclusive account of the *Titanic's* last hours as related by a young wireless operator who survived the calamity. Several books about the *Times* credit Van Anda and his brilliant planning for the achievement. The truth was that luck and an enterprising reporter played a far greater role than Van Anda, who was known to indulge occasionally in self-glorification.

As for Adolph, he experienced "the capstone of my career" in 1912: hosting a lunch for President William Howard Taft at home. He would have preferred to hold the event at the paper, but the Times Tower did not have a dining room. Effie, of course, had no desire to organize such an affair, but luckily Miss MacDonnell had stayed on to run the Ochs household after Iphigene outgrew the need for a governess. The efficiency she brought to the task enabled Adolph and Effie to entertain occasionally.

Adolph's willingness to play host may have been appropriate in the case of a president, but it was also highly unusual. Normally he left the newspaper's social duties to Louis Wiley, whom he had promoted from head of circulation to business manager in 1906. Indeed, Wiley became so omnipresent on the New York "celery circuit" that many people thought he was the publisher. A Republican and lifelong bachelor, Wiley stood just four foot seven inches tall. Smart and witty, he made a point of collecting contacts, dispensing compliments, and congratulating people when they received awards, no matter how small. As a consequence, he knew virtually everyone in New York, and served the *Times* well as both its most visible social lion and inside source of news tips. At the office Wiley was a loyal lieutenant, treating Adolph with the obsequious deference of a Uriah Heep and running his staff with the exaggerated efficiency of a martinet.

By making the charming Wiley the face of the *Times* in New York's salons and banquet halls, and the intellectual Carr Van Anda its face on the news side, Ochs had created a comfortable wall between himself and the vaguely frightening world of well-educated, socially adept Gentiles around him. These two men spoke for the newspaper, and yet the newspaper also spoke for itself, without the distracting — and potentially dangerous — element of Adolph's background intruding.

When it came to ceremonial occasions with powerful figures, however, Adolph sought center stage, and by the time President Taft arrived at the Ochs home, he finally had a residence worthy of the role. In 1909, after thirteen years of living in boardinghouses and rented apartments, Adolph had bought a twenty-seven-room town house at 308 West Seventy-fifth Street for $106,000. The five-story brick building was not particularly distinguished-looking, but its bowed front was graceful, and it featured both an impressive oak-paneled library and a large glassed-in conservatory in the rear that looked out onto a small garden. The neighborhood was fittingly prosperous, with the Hotel Esplanade and the $5 million French-style château built by steel tycoon Charles Schwab nearby. Regrettably, Effie had filled the rooms with heavy, dark furniture of an early Victorian vintage, much of it bought at auction, and the effect was cluttered and gloomy. But the house was certainly adequate for a visiting president, a man whom the *Times* had endorsed in the previous election.

Adolph was "quite nervous" at one o'clock on Sunday afternoon, January 28, 1912, when his brothers, George and Milton, and his brother-in-law Harry Adler gathered at the Ochs home along with Charles Miller, Carr Van Anda, Louis Wiley, and fifteen others from the *Times*. At 1:30 P.M. the president arrived with his entourage, pushing through the curious crowd of onlookers who hovered around the Ochs doorstep. Adolph greeted Taft and escorted him to the landing, proudly introducing his distinguished guest to Effie, Miss MacDonnell, and Iphigene, who was fascinated and somewhat horrified by Taft's enormous girth. Iphigene had bought a special dress for the occasion, although she was not invited to lunch; in keeping with the prevailing custom, the meal was strictly stag. "Those were the male chauvinist pig days," she remarked later.

After a few pleasantries the women demurely excused themselves and the men adjourned to the conservatory, where a table for twenty-six had been elaborately set by Louis Sherry's. For the next two and a half hours, the president, flanked by Adolph and Miller, ate his way through an elaborate seven-course meal that began with caviar; proceeded to terrapin Baltimore, saddle of mutton, breast of chicken, and Virginia ham; and ended with glacé Emile, cheeses, and coffee. The bill came to nearly $1,000, including $250 for flowers and potted plants.

Adolph was radiant and relieved when the event was over. The next morning a small item about it appeared on page two of the *Times*. Then, at the first available moment, on Wednesday night, January 31, he sat down and wrote a long letter to his "Dear Ones All" describing every delicious detail. For years Adolph had bragged about his accomplishments to his mother, and she had passed the letters on to his siblings, in-laws, cousins, and far-flung relations. Now, following Bertha's death four years earlier, Adolph continued the tradition of omnibus letters, which circulated among the extended family, knitting them together, as Adolph always intended, as a kind of closed corporation with him at the head, the paterfamilias of a clan that now, surely *now*, had finally arrived. After all, wasn't *his* success *their* success? "I am as proud as Lucifer," Adolph boasted to his brothers and sisters about the Taft lunch. "It was a red letter day for us."

8

A Non-Jewish Jew

A DOLPH RARELY USED *THE NEW YORK TIMES*
to advance a cause, especially one associated with Jews. But in
1914, when Louis Marshall, president of the American Jewish
Committee, asked him to help rally support for Leo Frank, the Brooklyn-
reared Jewish manager of the National Pencil Company in Atlanta,
Georgia, Ochs threw himself into the task.

Frank had been found guilty of the April 26, 1913, murder of Mary
Phagan, a thirteen-year-old worker in his factory, whose battered and
sexually violated body was discovered facedown on a slag heap in the
plant's basement. The trial became a lightning rod for southern resentment of northern capitalists and exposed ugly veins of anti-Semitism;
vicious screeds in Georgia's populist *Jeffersonian Magazine* demanded
the swift execution of the "filthy, perverted Jew of New York." Alarmed,
Jewish leaders across the country banded together to fight a verdict they
thought unfair, a trial they considered a mockery, and a climate of bigotry they feared might spread.

Ochs was not immediately certain that Frank was innocent, but after
Marshall persuaded him that a "horrible miscarriage of justice" had
been committed, he lobbied his journalistic colleagues to editorialize in
favor of Frank and published story after story about developments in
the case. Nationally, *The New York Times* led the crusade for a new trial
and then, when that effort failed, for a commutation of the death sentence. It was the first time Adolph had gotten so emotionally involved in
a story. Privately, many in the newsroom deplored the publisher's "campaign of righteous publicity" and worried that the *Times* had "slopped
over about Frank."

What drove Adolph to so public a stand was not Leo Frank himself,
whom he personally considered an egotist and a man who actually
enjoyed his doomed celebrity. "I think he would be delighted to make a

dramatic speech from the gallows," Adolph told members of the *Times* editorial council. What impelled him, rather, was a sentimental belief that in America an innocent man could not be hanged. In Adolph's civics-lesson view of the world, people had only to be apprised of the true facts to enable them to make the "right" decision. He certainly did not think that Frank had been persecuted because he was a Jew, and as a southerner, Adolph felt he knew what Georgians were like — and they were not anti-Semites. In Chattanooga being Jewish had never been a handicap; his brother George had even been elected mayor twice.

But in his eagerness to dismiss "racial prejudice" as a factor in the Frank case, Adolph failed to take into account that by 1914 feelings toward Jews in all regions of the country had hardened. Vast numbers of Jewish immigrants, fleeing Russia and Eastern Europe, had arrived in the United States in the early part of the century, taxing the nation's ability to absorb them. In 1906, at the peak of the influx, a national economic panic made jobs scarce for everyone, heightening ethnic resentments. And unlike the assimilationist German Jews who preceded them, the Eastern Europeans, though hardworking, were poorer, not as well educated, and more inclined to preserve their suspiciously foreign habits of language, dress, and diet, making them easy targets for ridicule and ostracization. Adolph himself had little tolerance for Jews who wore unclipped beards and long black frock coats, feeling it was unfair of them to set themselves "apart from other men, and then complain that [they are] treated differently from other men."

To blunt the charge that the new arrivals would become a public burden, Jews everywhere contributed money to help them and by 1910 were raising $10 million annually for philanthropy. Adolph did his part, giving small donations to organizations such as the Hebrew Sheltering and Immigrant Aid Society, but he disliked singling out Jews under any circumstances, even for charity. As an alternative, he established the Hundred Neediest Cases Fund to solicit money for what the *Times* described, with Dickensian hyperbole, as "the uttermost dregs of the city's poor." Touched by *Times* stories about blind widows and helpless cripples, New Yorkers gave $3,630 to the fund in 1912, the first year of its existence; by the time of Adolph's death, the sum had swelled to well over one hundred times that amount.

Adolph considered Judaism a religion, like Methodism or Lutheranism, and nothing more. "Mr. Ochs is a non-Jewish Jew," Garet Garrett, a young member of the *Times'* editorial council, wrote in his diary in 1915. "He will have nothing to do with any Jewish movement." In 1903 and again in 1905, bloody massacres of Jews at Kishinev in Bessarabia, then part of Russia, prompted Adolph to give money to a national refugee-relief effort and to permit his name to be published on a list of general committee members. He joined the Wanderers, an informal Saturday supper club formed by Jacob Schiff, Louis Marshall, and others, where the conversation often turned to human-rights abuses against Jews. But in 1906, when Marshall organized the American Jewish Committee to attack these problems publicly, Adolph declined to serve on its advisory board, insisting that Jewish matters should be handled through temples and synagogues.

Adolph was certainly no stranger to anti-Semitism. His own top editors, Charles R. Miller and Carr Van Anda, enjoyed membership in the Century Association — the "exclusive of the exclusives," as Adolph wistfully called it — which admitted men of arts and letters and was within easy walking distance of the office. Although the *Times'* founders, Henry J. Raymond and George Jones, had both been Centurians, Ochs dared not allow his name to be put forward, for fear of rejection. "My father was terribly hurt [by that]," Iphigene said. "It was the only thing I'd ever heard him express that he wanted to join."

Adolph's reluctance probably sprang as much from his sense of educational inferiority as his fears of anti-Semitism. Although the Century accepted few Jews, it was no more restrictive than the elite businessmen's clubs in which he already had membership. Men such as Felix Adler, founder of the New York Society for Ethical Culture, and Leopold Eidlitz, the renowned architect, had long enjoyed lunch and dinner in the Century's imposing quarters on West Forty-third Street. But a businessman's club was one thing; a club that "put a premium on sobersided intellectual qualities" was another.

On the pages of *The New York Times,* Jews were rarely visible, even when by rights they should have been. Until 1912, when Adolph, at the request of the newly formed Anti-Defamation League, commissioned and circulated a suggested policy for the proper use of the word *Jew,* newspapers across the country — including occasionally the *Times* itself — freely used expressions such as *Jew boy, Jew store,* and *Jew down.* During the celebrated Dreyfus affair in the late 1890s, Adolph had refused to permit the *Times* to take the lead in freeing the Jewish French army captain, who had been wrongly court-martialed and imprisoned on Devil's Island. "I thought it would be unwise for *The New York Times* to begin the campaign, as it would be at once attributed to a Jewish interest," he explained later. When other papers took up Dreyfus's plight, the *Times* followed suit, carefully avoiding the use of words such as *Jew, Jewish,* or *anti-Semitism* in headlines. Adolph was determined not to have the *Times* ever appear to be a "Jewish newspaper."

So it was all the more remarkable that Adolph championed Leo Frank. Always before, he had resolutely refused to flex his muscle, or that of *The New York Times,* in the service of any highly charged cause, however worthy. What emboldened him to act now was the perceived security of his position. Financially, *The New York Times* was an unquestioned success; in 1914 it led every New York City newspaper in advertising volume. Journalistically, its preeminence was unassailable. As for Adolph, at the age of fifty-six, he was a near iconic figure in the American press.

For months *The New York Times* worked on Frank's behalf, decrying his trial as a "veritable thicket of perjuries" and endorsing an appeal effort, led by Louis Marshall, that went all the way to the U.S. Supreme Court. When the appeal was denied and Frank's execution set for June 1915, the *Times* launched a feverish campaign to persuade Georgia governor John Slaton to commute the sentence to life imprisonment. Five days before leaving office, in a move that ruined his political career, Slaton did just that. But Frank's victory, and that of the *Times,* was short-lived. Two months later, on August 16, 1915, a band of angry men dragged Frank from the state prison farm at Milledgeville, Georgia, drove him to a field about a hundred miles away, and hanged him.

The lynching devastated Adolph, who nevertheless continued to cling to his belief that "race hatred" played no part in the killing. The *Times* immediately sent one of its best reporters, Charles Willis Thompson, to Georgia to investigate. His stories, which Adolph reluctantly published, left no doubt that anti-Semitism had been a deciding factor in Frank's death and that most Georgians approved of it. One detail particularly shocked Adolph: Thompson alleged that Robert E. Lee Howell, a cousin of Clark Howell, editor of *The Atlanta Constitution* and a close friend of Adolph's, had viciously stomped on the face of the corpse.

In a final attempt to redeem the southerners he felt he knew so well, Adolph beseeched Georgia newspapers to reprint a *New York Times* editorial calling on justice-minded residents of the state to prove Frank's innocence posthumously. Most papers declined. *The Macon* (Ga.) *Telegraph* sent an angry wire to Adolph, contending that it was "outside interference of the Jews," especially the "offensive propaganda" printed in *The New York Times,* that had "made it necessary to lynch Frank."

The message sent Adolph reeling. Now he could no longer avoid the raw truth about the anti-Semitism inherent in the affair. At an editorial-council meeting, he was in a "gloomy state of mind." Not only had the influence of *The New York Times* been found to be "as a straw upon the tides of human wrath," but Adolph had unwittingly encouraged a perception of the paper as "Jewish" — something he had vowed never to do. Far from feeling the potency of his position as the most prominent publisher in the United States, he again experienced the frightening marginality of being Jewish. Hate mail began to arrive, most of it addressed personally to Adolph, who felt sufficiently threatened to post a guard in the corridor leading to his office and plainclothesmen in the lobby of the Times Building.

Soon after the lynching, Adolph disappeared from the office. He returned in a few days, but by September he was clearly in a "nervous state." The following month the *Times'* city editor, Arthur Greaves, died, and as an outlet for his agitation over the Frank case, Adolph arranged a spectacular funeral procession that served to remind the public — and perhaps even himself — that *The New York Times* was still "the greatest newspaper in the world." All work stopped for half an hour, and employees were made to stand bareheaded outside the annex on West Forty-third Street as Greaves's hearse and the attendant cars passed by en route to Grand Central Station. When Adolph's cab approached the row of mourners, he shook the arm of the editorial writer sitting next to him. "See, we're coming to it," he said. "Isn't it nice?" He repeated the phrase as they passed: "Isn't it nice?" When they drew away, he could not bear to part with the theatrical image and twisted around in his seat to look back one more time. He shook Charles R. Miller. "Isn't it nice?" he said again.

By February 1916 Adolph's nerves were completely shattered. He went to Atlantic City for a rest, but it did no good. He was so jittery that he came back after only a few days, confessing to Garet Garrett that he "had been for some time in a state of depression." What he needed, Adolph said, was a total change of scene. He departed for California, where he stayed at the Hotel del Coronado in San Diego and spent long hours on the beach trying to lose his ghostlike pallor. By late April he was back at work, looking fit and much revived. "I am in good spirits and feel like my self again," he wrote a relative in Cincinnati. "I now realize that it was highly important that I get away from my grind and take a good rest. I was perilously near a general breakdown."

Never again did Adolph publicly support a cause, certainly not one involving Jews. When Russia refused to honor the passports of American citizens who were Jews, *The New York Times* did not protest. News stories about the issue omitted the word *Jew;* editorials blandly stated that Russia should not discriminate against Americans of any race, origin, or religion. The sanitized coverage so infuriated Jacob Schiff that in August 1916 he accused Ochs of actively "strengthening the hands of [your brethren's] unmerciful oppressors."

That same year President Woodrow Wilson nominated Louis Brandeis to the U.S. Supreme Court, prompting strong opposition from *The New York Times*. Privately, Adolph derided Brandeis as a "professional Jew," rejected his embrace of Zionism, and considered his liberal views on labor and his reformist attitude toward big business too radical. The *Times*' conservative editor, Charles R. Miller, was in complete accord. Iphigene, however, was beginning to have a mind of her own. "I disagreed with my father on this appointment," she said. "I thought Brandeis's radicalism was great."

§

By the time she was sixteen, Iphigene dreamed of attending Bryn Mawr, even going so far as to suggest to Adolph that she apply two years in advance to secure a place. But as the time for her matriculation drew near, she became reluctant to go to college at all. Her unhappy experience at the Benjamin-Deane school had soured her on formal education, and she feared competing with better-prepared girls. But Adolph had his heart set on Iphigene's getting the education he had been denied, although he did not want her to go *away* to school. Like many prosperous New York parents of the era, he decreed that she should live at home and commute to Barnard College, the women's division of Columbia University.

In the fall of 1910 Iphigene entered Barnard as a "special student," in a two-year nondegree program that permitted her to bypass the usual admissions requirements and design her own course of study. To her amazement, she found that she loved the school — the classes, the professors, the students, and most of all, the intoxicating atmosphere of free inquiry that was such a liberating counterpoint to the suffocating Victorianism of the Ochs household.

She soon made up her mind to enroll as a regular student, which meant she had to pass the freshman entrance exams she had recently avoided. Adolph hired tutors in math and Latin, her two weakest subjects, and though it took until her junior year, Iphigene finally succeeded in becoming a full-fledged member of her class. Her reward was to go back and take all the freshman courses she had missed, including trigonometry and solid geometry, both of which she managed to conquer only because of her near photographic memory. While her reading was slow, information on a page could be recalled in detail once it was digested. "I got through with a B, I don't know why or how," she remarked. "I never understood a single concept."

At the time, the Barnard campus consisted of two buildings set on a plot of urban acreage that ran from West 116th Street to West 119th Street. There was an inadequate library and no gymnasium; Barnard students used the gym and pool at Teachers College. In this spartan setting Iphigene stood out, not only because she had successfully overcome her scholastic handicaps but because, compared with her peers, she was, as her freshman English instructor, Clare Howard, put it, "singularly worldly." Years of European travel and mingling with accomplished people had given her a certain savoir faire, as well as an air of patrician entitlement. When Howard assigned "weekend guests" as her class's first essay topic, Iphigene submitted a blunt primer of do's and don'ts. "Always ask a guest for a definite short time," she wrote, "so if he is a disappointment you will not have to endure him long. On the other hand, if he is a success, you can ask him to stay for some days more." She also advised to "see that your guest has plenty of bedcovers."

At Barnard Iphigene for the first time struggled to liberate herself from the intellectual domination of her father. A key figure in this passage was the prominent historian James Harvey Robinson, a graduate of Harvard and the University of Freiberg, who delighted in attacking *The New York Times* for its conservative opinions. "I am now going to show you a perfect example of the workings of the medieval mind," he would say sarcastically, waving the newspaper aloft as he stood at the lectern. He would then proceed to read aloud from one of Charles R. Miller's stuffy editorials while Iphigene cringed in her seat.

The *Times'* opposition to women's suffrage was a particular embarrassment to Iphigene, who soon joined the Barnard chapter of the Equal Suffrage League of New York State (Professor Robinson was also a member) and supported it liberally with her allowance money. Most Reform Jews advocated the vote for women, but Adolph, perhaps because of his southern heritage, did not. At a meeting of the Southern States Women's Suffrage Conference, he politely told the ladies he would do his "utmost to delay the coming of [the female vote]," which he feared would make women more like men, take them out of the home, and demean motherhood.

At 308 West Seventy-fifth Street Adolph was alone in his unenlightened notion of women's place. Around the dinner table Iphigene sparred with her father about the paper's suffrage editorials while Effie and Miss MacDonnell cheered from the sidelines. Even her cousin Julius, despite being raised largely in the South, took issue with his uncle. In a debate between Harvard and Princeton, the school Julius entered the same year Iphigene went to Barnard, he defended the suffragette side. None of this had any effect on Adolph, who took great satisfaction in the defeat of the suffrage amendment in New York State in November 1915.

The New York Times was equally "medieval" about contraception and "sex hygiene," two other crusades Iphigene embraced. When John D. Rockefeller Jr., an early supporter of birth-control activist Margaret Sanger, submitted an article in favor of sex education and implored Adolph to run it to balance a "narrow and one-sided" column that had appeared in a recent Sunday edition, he received a polite but firm refusal. While admitting that *The New York Times* might be a "little too conservative and old-fashioned in some of [its] views," Adolph told Rockefeller that such an article would "severely strain" the *Times'* motto, All the News That's Fit to Print. His rigid sense of propriety did not stop Iphigene from volunteering at a home for unwed mothers, something George Ochs and other members of the family found shocking.

It was at Barnard that Iphigene became enthralled with the egalitarian political movements then roiling Russia and other parts of Europe.

One of her favorite teachers was Professor Vladimir Simkhovitch, an economist who taught a course called "Radicalism and Social Reform as Reflected in the Literature of the Nineteenth Century." Exposure to his lectures and seminars "turned me into an early socialist," said Iphigene. "I never quite lost my leftist leanings."

To avoid embarrassing her father, she declined to join the Intercollegiate Socialist Society, which included members such as Freda Kirchwey, later to become the editor and publisher of *The Nation*. Instead, like many daughters of well-to-do German Jewish families, she worked at the Henry Street settlement house on the Lower East Side, helping Eastern European immigrants find their footing in America. In her senior year she became a Jewish Big Sister and also worked at Cedar Knolls School, an institution for emotionally disturbed children run by the Jewish Protectory and Aid Society.

Adolph sympathized with Iphigene's altruistic inclinations, but he was disturbed by the dogmatic tone with which she expressed her beliefs. One of his greatest gifts was the ability to see an issue from all sides, to disassociate himself from the passion surrounding a subject and, instead, examine it as though it were a specimen under a microscope. To temper his daughter's assertiveness, Adolph insisted that she commit to memory page ninety-five of Benjamin Franklin's autobiography, a section in which Franklin resolves to forswear all "overbearing" argument, exchanging words such as *certainly* and *undoubtedly* for more tentative phrases such as *I imagine* or *it so appears to me at present*. Whenever Iphigene got carried away with fervor, Adolph would sternly exclaim, "Page ninety-five, Iphigene!" If she persisted with her unqualified statements, he would make her recite the entire passage.

By her junior year Iphigene was sufficiently steadied academically to earn an A on an economics paper impressively titled "Constitutionality of Protective Labor Legislation as Determined by the Decision of the United States Supreme Court." An attractive, studious girl who wore glasses for reading, she had a spontaneous side that showed itself in an enthusiasm for the theater. She played a Gypsy maiden in the sophomore show, *The Road to Yesterday*, assembling her costume out of peasant clothes her parents had brought back from Europe. On the little stage in Brinckerhoff Hall, "Iphigene was romantic, released, and rapturous — something she never allowed herself to be in her self-imposed code of good manners," recalled Clare Howard. The Gypsy garb came in handy later that year when, to help raise money for the Building Fund, Barnard students held an Oriental bazaar. Iphigene, dressed in her Slovak finery and stationed in a tent, drew throngs as a palm reader.

Sororities were abolished while Iphigene was at Barnard, to which she had no objection since none of them accepted Jews, but she soon discovered that she had prejudices of her own to overcome. Late one night, while studying in the library at Kent Hall, she looked up from her books and discovered that she was alone except for a black man and a Chinese man. Immediately she thought: *Chinese — white slavery! Negroes assault white women!* Then she stopped and realized with a blush of shame that the two young men were just students like herself; they hadn't even noticed her. "I learned a lesson there very quickly: This is just idiocy," she recalled.

On June 2, 1914, Iphigene graduated from Barnard with a bachelor of arts degree and the following night attended the senior dance in Earl Hall. In the class yearbook she was dubbed "the Talker," a reference, no doubt, to her love of spirited debate. Two weeks later Julius Adler gave the opening oration at Princeton's Class Day, the precursor to graduation. His speech, which predicted that the "dream of universal peace" would soon be realized, was reported at length in *The New York Times*. The coverage was not unusual; Julius was a prize debater, and his college successes had been faithfully chronicled in his uncle's paper. Julius had made it clear to Princeton classmates that his future lay in journalism; he planned to start work at *The New York Times* in the fall. As Iphigene and Julius doffed their mortarboards, the future seemed serene and full of promise. Within weeks that optimistic vision would prove to be an illusion. The sheltered life the two Ochs cousins had known was about to be changed forever, swallowed up by a global cataclysm. "All my school years were in a different world," said Iphigene much, much later.

§

For the Ochses, the summer of 1914 held the tantalizing prospect of yet another grand tour of Europe. By late July Effie, Iphigene, Julius, Miss MacDonnell, and the family's French maid, Henriette, were happily ensconced at the Oberhof Resort in Germany's Thuringian Forest. Julius's mother, Ada, was in Munich with Mattie and her husband, Bernie Talimer. Adolph was scheduled to rendezvous with the family in

Hamburg in early August after crossing the Atlantic on the *Vaterland,* later renamed the *Leviathan.* But world events soon altered his plans.

On July 31 Effie received an urgent telegram from Adolph: COME HOME IMMEDIATELY. EUROPE IS ON THE BRINK OF WAR. The next day, as the Ochs party hurried to nearby Erfurt to catch a train to Holland, Germany declared war on Russia. Adolph, as usual, tried to manage the situation from afar. Although he had complete confidence in Julius's ability to guide the Ochs party to safety in neutral Britain, he did not consider Bernie physically capable of performing the same function in Munich, so he advised them to stay where they were until the foreign exodus calmed down and "travel resumes regularly."

The trip to Amsterdam, which normally took two hours, dragged on for seven because the cars had to crawl carefully over the bridges and trestles, which were rumored to be mined. At 1:30 A.M. on Monday, August 3, the Ochses finally straggled into the Dutch capital, bleary-eyed and eager to get some rest at the Amstel Hotel. The war had thrown the city into chaos; paper money was worthless. While Julius scoured the streets for food, returning with five small ham sandwiches, Effie retrieved the hundred dollars' worth of gold coins she kept hidden in her clothes for just such emergencies. Their rooms thus secured, the exhausted group fell asleep, only to awaken later that day to the news that Germany had declared war on France.

In the early-morning hours of August 4, the Ochses managed to clamber aboard a ship bound for Britain. Built to accommodate three hundred, the boat carried more than twice that number and lay so perilously low in the water that Julius refused to undress or sleep because "the danger of an accident was too great." As the vessel pulled into Harwich, it passed forty-five British torpedo boats steaming in the other direction. While the family had been en route, Britain had declared war on Germany.

With the help of *The New York Times'* London bureau chief, the Ochses took rooms at Claridge's, but Effie declared the accommodations too expensive, and the next day the group decamped to the Rubens Hotel opposite Buckingham Palace. "Here at last are the poor refugees safe and sound in London," Iphigene wrote her relieved father. His shepherding duties done, Julius immediately turned around and returned to Germany to rescue his mother, aunt, and uncle, who were waiting nervously in Munich's Russischer Hof Hotel.

A little more than a week later, the Adler party limped into London to find that Effie, Iphigene, and Henriette had already departed for New York, arranging passage on a British ship that had been condemned for scrap. On September 12 Julius and his charges followed them on the Cunard liner *Lusitania*. By the end of the month, Julius, lionized as a hero by the grateful Ochs clan, was comfortably installed in his new office on the eleventh floor of *The New York Times*, not far from Adolph. Whenever the subject of his summer adventure arose, he modestly played down the danger. "It was a great experience, and I shall never forget it," he said enthusiastically.

§

World War I gave Adolph the opportunity to demonstrate on an international stage that *The New York Times* deserved its description as the Paper of Record. On August 23, 1914, the *Times* published in its entirety the British white paper, a compilation of official correspondence leading up to Britain's decision to enter the conflict. The next day it featured Germany's version of events. The German letters, written by the kaiser's diplomatic aides, ran, like their British equivalent, uncut and unaltered. As the war progressed, the *Times* printed official documents from all combatants, something no other newspaper did, often recirculating them in widely disseminated pamphlets.

Four months into the war, Adolph launched a new vehicle for chronicling the conflict: *Current History,* a monthly magazine designed to record "impartially and without editorial comment, the social, economic, political and military developments . . . growing out of the world convulsion." The magazine absorbed the overflow of official information that the *Times* could not publish because of its limited press capacity, and also provided a job for Adolph's brother George, who came to New York early in 1915 to take over as editor.

Since selling his shares in Philadelphia's *Public Ledger* to Cyrus Curtis and assuming the position of salaried publisher, George had been dogged by personal tragedy and professional misfortune. In May 1913 his wife, Bertie, died of an infection seven days after giving birth to their second son, John. "The circumstances of her death were never spoken of," John recalled. "I don't remember asking about her. My father would get all teary." George's sister Nannie, who had never married, immediately moved into the Ochs home in Elkins Park, a Philadelphia suburb.

She became a surrogate mother to John and his older brother; the two boys called her Auntie.

In the weeks following Bertie's death, George did not come into the office, which gave Curtis an opportunity to move his son-in-law into the paper's business department and other of his loyalists into positions of power. In this environment it was only a matter of time before George decided to resign, charging that Curtis not only had breached their original management agreement but had turned a highly profitable newspaper into a losing one. On December 31, 1914, George's last day as publisher, Curtis put out a perfunctory statement citing their "entirely amicable but irreconcilable difference of views."

George had battled all his life to break free of the magnetic field that pulled members of the Ochs clan irresistibly toward Adolph. In many respects he had succeeded, earning a reputation as the family maverick. Now, bereft and weary, he accepted Adolph's paternal embrace, moving Nannie and his sons into a cluttered apartment in the Ansonia on New York's Upper West Side, two blocks from his brother's stately town house.

As editor of *Current History* and a rotogravure supplement called *Mid-Week Pictorial,* George, owlishly outfitted with a monocle, settled into quarters on the tenth floor of the Times Annex, one floor below Adolph. Relations between the brothers were correct and friendly, but never intimate. Away from the office George was determined to preserve what little independence remained to him. Occasionally he would go to Adolph's home for dinner, and three or four Sundays a year Adolph would return the favor by dropping in on the Ansonia ménage to perform coin tricks for his nephews. But these visits, said John, were "really to see Auntie."

§

In the early months of the war, when the United States was not yet involved, the *Times* gave nearly as much coverage to the arguments of the Germans as to those of the British, a practice that angered many readers. While dining with several of her father's friends, Iphigene was astonished to hear that two of them had stopped reading the *Times* because they felt "German news was always given such prominence and the pictorial was full of German pictures." Ironically, on the editorial page the *Times* laid the blame for the war squarely at the feet of Germany and Austria. As it would so often under Adolph's management, *The New York Times* was bitterly attacked by one faction or another merely for presenting both sides of an issue.

On December 15, 1914, a two-column editorial, written by Charles R. Miller and titled "For the German People, Peace with Freedom," forcefully stated the *Times'* position. "Germany is doomed to defeat," it began, going on to argue that, on moral grounds, "the world cannot, will not, let Germany win this war." In its vision of a nation "bled to exhaustion, drained of her resources," Miller shrewdly anticipated the punitive tone of the Versailles treaty five years later. But at the time, the editorial served only to reinforce suspicions among German sympathizers that *The New York Times* was controlled by the British. Anonymous letters poured in to the *Times* asking Adolph why he didn't change his name to John Bull and sarcastically inquiring of Iphigene how she liked living off British blood money.

Three months later Miller and Carr Van Anda were summoned before a U.S. Senate investigating committee, ostensibly to explain the *Times'* opposition to the Wilson administration's proposal for the purchase of interned shipping. The real reason, though, was to confront the two men with a letter insinuating that the *Times* was indebted to unspecified "British interests" and that Lord Northcliffe, proprietor of *The Times* of London, had a hand in the paper's policy. Miller and Van Anda ably deflected every attack and, after inspecting the letter, declared its signature to be identical to that attached to a number of calumnious missives recently received at the *Times*. Officially, that put an end to rumors of foreign influence at the paper.

However, perhaps because of his brush with the Equitable scandal ten years earlier, Adolph felt unusually sensitive about questions concerning his ownership. Following the Senate hearings, he ran a brief item on the editorial page under the headline ADOLPH S. OCHS AND THE NEW YORK TIMES. The item consisted of a short excerpt of Miller's testimony and an unqualified statement of his own, written in the third person:

> Mr. Ochs wishes to make the assertion . . . that he is in possession, free and unencumbered, of the controlling and majority interest of the stock of The New York Times Company, and has no associates in that possession, and is not beholden or

accountable to any person or interest in England or anywhere else in the world, nor had he ever been beholden or accountable, in any shape, form or fashion, financial or otherwise, for the conduct of *The New York Times* except to his own conscience and to the respect and confidence of the newspaper reading public.

Everything Adolph said was technically true. But the stock was not quite as "free and unencumbered" as he made out. At that very moment, Adolph's controlling shares in *The New York Times* still sat in the safe of Marcellus Hartley Dodge.

9

War, Worry, and a Wedding

O N MAY 7, 1915, THE *LUSITANIA*, THE SAME SHIP
that had ferried the Adlers and the Talimers back from Britain
eight months earlier, was sunk by a German submarine off the
Irish coast. Carr Van Anda hurriedly put out an extra edition of *The New
York Times* at 5:30 A.M. The final phrase of the eight-column headline
presciently summed up the fatal blow to American neutrality that had
just occurred: WASHINGTON BELIEVES THAT A GRAVE CRISIS IS AT
HAND.

By midsummer President Woodrow Wilson had made it clear that he
was not yet prepared to mobilize U.S. troops. In response, a group of
about twelve hundred war-minded volunteers took matters into their
own hands and organized an officers' training camp at Plattsburgh, New
York, to prepare themselves for what they predicted would be America's
inevitable entry into the conflict. Julius immediately signed up, backed
by his uncle Adolph, who favored the move primarily because he
thought it would "bring him in contact with a lot of nice young men."
The camp was such a success that it was repeated the following summer.
Julius attended that session, too, advancing rapidly from private to corporal to sergeant. Soon a number of Plattsburghs sprang up around the
country.

Julius was now a permanent member of the Adolph Ochs household,
and on weekends off from Plattsburgh, he often invited his camp friends
home for visits. One such guest in the summer of 1916 was a dark-
haired, blue-eyed businessman named Arthur Hays Sulzberger, who,
since graduating from Columbia in 1913, had been working in his
father's cotton-goods business, N. Erlanger, Blumgart & Company. Over
his father's protests, he had taken a leave of absence to enlist.

Iphigene knew Arthur slightly; they had met while she was at Barnard
and he at Columbia, and had left little impression on each other. This

encounter was different, and romance blossomed quickly. She began seeing him whenever he could get leave, usually meeting at Abenia, a rambling Victorian estate on Lake George in upstate New York that her father had rented for the summer from his friend George Foster Peabody. On the weekends that he was confined to base, she traveled to Plattsburgh with a chaperone and stayed at the nearby Lake Champlain Hotel.

At the time, Iphigene, like many of her Barnard classmates, was half-heartedly pursuing professional training while simultaneously preparing to abandon her plans the moment marriage came along. Adolph had a high regard for his daughter's intelligence and industry; he would soon put her on *The New York Times'* board of directors, which at the time consisted almost entirely of family members. But he had no intention of allowing her to work, certainly not at the newspaper. Iphigene had taken several journalism classes in college and shortly before graduation, with the clandestine help of Carr Van Anda, had secured an entry-level reporter's job on the paper. She thought her father would be pleased. Instead, "he was enraged and nearly murdered both of us." Iphigene's journalistic ambitions died at that moment.

Prevented from fulfilling the destiny Adolph himself had dangled in front of her as a child — to be the publisher of *The New York Times* — Iphigene set her sights on becoming a professor. To that end, she began work toward a master's degree in history at Columbia in the fall of 1915. Six months later Adolph intervened again, pulling her out of school in order to break up an infatuation with a young German man, Baron George von Seebeck, whom she had met the previous summer during her voyage home from Britain. Von Seebeck had been studying banking in London when war broke out and, to prevent being interned, had hastily moved to the United States. Adolph disliked his daughter's titled beau. To cool Iphigene's ardor, he sent her to celebrate Mardi Gras with friends in New Orleans, hoping she would soon forget von Seebeck. She did, but returned to be immediately sought after by a series of new suitors.

Adolph had exacting standards for any gentleman who sought to court Iphigene. When one unfortunate young man announced that he was studying to be a dentist, Adolph wailed privately to Iphigene, "A dentist! My God, that's worse than being a butcher!" In truth, he did not want his daughter to marry anyone — unless, of course, she wed Julius, his nephew and her cousin. "He was possessive about me ... because he had an only child who happened to be a daughter, and he didn't like the idea of losing me to another man," said Iphigene. "He never interfered with my having dates or going to parties, but he cast a jaundiced eye at [sic] anyone who looked seriously at me."

In the case of Arthur Hays Sulzberger, he had little to worry about, at least at first. On August 12, 1916, after a whirlwind courtship, Arthur proposed to Iphigene under a spruce tree on the grounds of Abenia. As he would later describe it, she fell into his arms and said no. In the becalmed months before America's entry into the war, Iphigene was lighthearted, carefree, and not ready to settle down. Besides, she was enamored of another man at the moment, an intellectual of the radical persuasion who did not reciprocate her sentiments. "I got to know him very well later, and he was a stuffy bore," she admitted.

Her rejection did not discourage Arthur, who quietly continued to press his suit after returning in the fall to his father's cotton-goods firm. He was in China on a textile-buying trip with his older brother Leo in February 1917, when President Wilson severed diplomatic relations with Germany. Arthur hurried home to enlist, but his return route was torturously long, and he arrived one week too late to get his commission without going through the training program at Plattsburgh again. On April 6 the United States entered the war.

By then Iphigene had gotten herself engaged and disengaged twice. The emotional tumult, coupled with the suddenly sober mood of wartime, caused her to make a more serious appraisal of Arthur. Born in 1891 in a redbrick town house opposite Mount Morris Park, an area of northern Manhattan considered almost rural at the time, Arthur was the fourth child and third son of Cyrus L. Sulzberger, a Philadelphia native who had joined Erlanger, Blumgart as a bookkeeper in 1877 and by 1902 had risen to be its president. Like Iphigene, Arthur had traveled widely in his youth, a fact that, he noted later, helped make him a dedicated internationalist. He took his first overseas trip at the age of four and a half and learned table manners in the dining rooms of posh hotels such as the Savoy in London. Under the tutelage of a German governess, he spoke German fluently.

With the arrival of his younger brother, David, in 1897, the Mount Morris house became cramped, and the Sulzbergers moved, first to West Eighty-seventh Street and later to West End Avenue, ten blocks north of the Ochs home. In contrast to Adolph's educational traditionalism, Cyrus Sulzberger made a point of sending his sons to Horace Mann School, a private, co-ed institution so progressive that the boys were taught to sew and the girls tended the garden on the school's West 120th Street campus. Arthur, "slim . . . modest and unassuming," went on to Columbia, where despite a lack of focused ambition and a self-avowed tendency to be lazy, he excelled at math and decided to pursue engineering. But he wanted to be economically independent sooner than engineering would allow, so, following graduation, he did what was easy and expected of him: he joined his father's firm on Fourth Avenue, in what is now SoHo, where his brother Leo already had a position as a merchandiser.

In the pyramid of American Jewish bona-fides, Arthur's family occupied a tier above that of the Ochses. To be sure, his Sulzberger ancestors were Ashkenazic — German Jews who immigrated to the United States about the time of the revolutions of 1848 from Sulzbürg in the Bavarian Palatinate. But his mother, Rachel Hays Sulzberger, was a descendant of the Sephardim, Jews who consider themselves to be — as Stephen Birmingham would flippantly characterize it years later in *Our Crowd* — "the most noble of all Jews because, as a culture, they claim the longest unbroken history of unity and suffering."

After fleeing Spain and Portugal in 1492 in the wake of the Spanish Inquisition, Rachel's paternal forebears, the Hayses, lived some two hundred years in Holland before arriving in the New World in the first quarter of the eighteenth century. They acquired farmland in Westchester County, New York, and fought in the American Revolution, a distinction of which Rachel was inordinately proud. To demonstrate that Jews had done their part to win the War for Independence, she joined the Daughters of the American Revolution and insisted that Arthur become a member of the male counterpart.

Her maternal ancestors, the Seixases and the Peixottos, were as platinum-plated as the Hayses. Benjamin Seixas, Rachel's great-grandfather, was one of the founders of the New York Stock Exchange; her grandfather, Daniel Levy Maduro Peixotto, was a physician and president of the New York Medical Society in the early nineteenth century. Compared with the eminence of these bloodlines, Cyrus Sulzberger's genealogy was positively anemic, and his wife's family never let him forget it. "[Rachel] told me her father could never master the name *Sulzberger*," said Iphigene. Arthur had adopted some of his mother's Sephardic pride. When he discovered that another Arthur Sulzberger lived in New York — a member of a meatpacking clan — he insisted on using his full name: Arthur Hays Sulzberger.

Arthur was never particularly close to his father, perhaps because Cyrus was preoccupied with work, politics, and Jewish causes during his sons' childhood years. A handsome man with an "illuminating smile . . . [and] understanding, powerful eyes," he served as president of United Hebrew Charities and was an organizer of the Industrial Removal Office, which sought to relieve the congestion of Jewish immigrants in New York at the turn of the century by relocating them to other cities. In 1903 he ran for president of the borough of Manhattan on an anti-Tammany fusion ticket and received the endorsement of *The New York Times,* which saluted his "probity." He lost the election but not his sense of humor. His wife presented him with what had been intended as a victory cake, on which appeared the words "President of the Borough of Manhattan." When his defeat was certain, Cyrus picked up a knife and swirled out the *P* so that the message read: "*resident* of the Borough of Manhattan."

Though they agreed on little regarding Jewish issues, Cyrus Sulzberger and Adolph Ochs had crossed paths many times. The two first met in the fall of 1896, shortly after Adolph bought *The New York Times,* at a private (and kosher) dinner at Delmonico's in honor of Joseph Jacobs, a Jewish author and critic from England. In his capacity as an advocate for Jewish refugees, Cyrus corresponded with Adolph about the *Times'* coverage of immigration legislation and related issues. After the Kishinev pogrom of 1903, he embraced Zionism, a movement Adolph unequivocally opposed, and for a time was the vice president of the American Zionist Federation, even taking young Arthur with him to Zionist congresses.

If Arthur got his public-spiritedness from his father, he got his intellectual curiosity from his mother, who attended what is now Hunter College and taught in the public schools before her marriage. Rachel did not overflow with maternal warmth. She shunned outward displays of emotion and evidenced what Arthur described as "austere Sephardic blood." In 1894, when she lost a son, five-year-old Cyrus L. Sulzberger Jr., she told a friend that she no longer believed in a God of mercy, only in an indifferent, all-pervading power that "for my pain . . . cares nothing."

In Arthur, Iphigene saw a man whose background was, in essential respects, similar to her own. He knew what it was like to have a father consumed by public life and a mother emotionally removed from the household. Witty, charming, and very handsome, Arthur was at ease in a variety of social settings and not the least bit cowed in the company of important people. They both shared a love of the theater; Arthur had participated in several plays at Horace Mann and even appeared as a chorus girl in a Columbia musical. Temperamentally, they complemented each other. Iphigene was sober and earnest; Arthur was breezy and debonair. He hummed while he worked at Erlanger, Blumgart, made puns, wrote funny poems, and drew cartoons of near professional quality. As important, he had been vetted by Julius and, like Adolph, was supremely self-confident, even domineering, a trait that made Iphigene feel secure and oddly at home. Best of all, he possessed the strength to hold his own with her authoritarian father, a significant plus in Iphigene's book.

For Arthur, Iphigene was an unusual combination of feminine submission and masculine seriousness of purpose. She was self-contained, dutiful, and rational, yet also a daddy's girl with a Victorian deference to men. In her subdued and classically poised company, Arthur could shine, freely exhibiting his love of fine clothing, art, strong drink, and spirited conversation. Iphigene had a certain dark Hebraic beauty, but physically he was the more arresting presence. And although he had the advantage of aristocratic Jewish ancestry, Iphigene, as Adolph Ochs's sole descendant, had the alluring dowry of *The New York Times.*

Arthur spent the summer of 1917 training at Plattsburgh, seeing Iphigene as often as his responsibilities allowed. In mid-August he was commissioned as a second lieutenant in the 322nd U.S. Field Artillery and assigned to Camp Wadsworth in Spartanburg, South Carolina. After settling in, he got a weekend pass to visit Iphigene at her father's Lake George estate, which Adolph had recently decided to acquire as a substitute for the grand European trips he could no longer take because of the war. It was there that Iphigene abruptly announced she was ready to accept his marriage proposal of the previous year. Later Arthur would jokingly celebrate the day she had turned him down rather than the day she agreed to be his wife, explaining to his children that the date was a memorial to the "virtue of persistence." At the time, he told his mother in a letter written en route back to Spartanburg that Iphigene's assent was "nothing new. Merely the culmination of something which I had decided a year ago and which makes me extremely happy now."

Adolph, predictably, was distressed by Iphigene's news. "He really liked Arthur very much until I fell in love with him," she said. He could not explain, even to himself, the complicated emotional and practical reasons he wanted Iphigene to remain single, so instead he asked her, in disingenuous perplexity: "Why do you want to get married? You've got a good home." Adolph was especially troubled by the fact that, given the war, the betrothal promised to be a long one. He didn't like the idea that Iphigene would be bound for months or even years to a man who might not survive combat. He urged the young couple to view their status merely as an "understanding," not a formal engagement.

Undaunted by his future father-in-law's resistance, Arthur lobbied to announce an engagement, and in September Adolph reluctantly agreed, protesting to Iphigene even as she packed for Spartanburg to accept the ring. Arthur had scoured the town for an appropriately romantic spot for the presentation, finally settling on a lovely park with a small garden. Once the ring was on her finger and they were leaving the property, Iphigene noticed a sign indicating that, his meticulous planning notwithstanding, Arthur had formally asked her to marry him on the grounds of the local lunatic asylum.

Despite their formal engagement, no announcement appeared in *The New York Times*. Soon Iphigene began to worry that the passage of time only played into Adolph's hands, giving him the chance yet again to manipulate her romantic life. Moreover, once Arthur was assigned to troops, he would have difficulty getting a furlough to come home for a wedding. Taking action to protect her interests, on October 1 Iphigene wrote an urgent letter to Arthur suggesting that he obtain a leave of absence for early November so they could arrange to be married then. "This thing was every bit as much of a surprise to me as it must have been to you," Arthur informed his startled parents. "I hadn't urged marriage or even been speaking of it."

Within the week, Arthur wrote Adolph a letter so deft, diplomatic, and subtly flattering that it could have been written by Adolph himself. The idea of an "early marriage," he said, was completely Iphigene's, not his. Like Adolph, he wanted only Iphigene's happiness: "You and I should understand each other. That which I know lies closest to your heart, you know equally well is ever in mine." With the arrival of

Arthur's "splendid and manly" letter, Adolph relented a bit, even volunteering to use his influence to help Arthur get a leave.

But soon a crisis over money brought new conflicts. Adolph offered to help support the newlyweds with a monthly allowance of $1,000, which, after discussing it with Iphigene, Arthur politely but firmly refused. His income at Erlanger, Blumgart was $5,000 a year, he told Adolph, and that sum would be increased substantially when he returned from the war. "Thank you for your offer but thank you still more for your kindness in withdrawing it," he wrote, adding that he hoped Adolph would understand that "only by working out things for ourselves can we find real happiness, the happiness that grows from entire independence."

Entire independence was a phrase that in Adolph's vocabulary applied only to himself, certainly not to his daughter. Moreover, he worried about what would happen if Iphigene spent her time, energy, and the wealth he would one day bequeath her on the promotion of another man's enterprise. Being a southern male of his generation, he could not conceive that a woman could ever truly have any interest separate from her husband's. Adolph had raised Julius as his heir apparent, but Iphigene was his heir by blood. He would not allow one of the central pillars of the empire he had so painstakingly constructed to be toppled and carried away. He told Arthur that before he would give his final blessing to the marriage, Arthur must agree to leave his father's firm and come work for *The New York Times* — "if and when I survived the war," as Arthur dryly put it later.

For Arthur, the decision was simple. The cotton-goods trade was not particularly engaging, and he had grown impatient serving as an apprentice to his older brother, Leo, whom he considered bossy and difficult. *The New York Times*, on the other hand, was an exciting, glamorous enterprise; even before his courtship of Iphigene, he had toyed with the idea of talking to Julius about a job there. So in late October Arthur, Iphigene, and their parents convened in Washington, D.C., and Arthur formally agreed to join *The New York Times*. On October 30 a small engagement announcement appeared on page fifteen of the newspaper, although it included no date for a wedding.

By now Arthur shared Iphigene's urgent desire to marry at the earliest possible moment. He had become convinced that given the opportunity, Adolph would continue to stall for time, creating obstacle after obstacle in the hope that Arthur would be shipped safely overseas before a ceremony could take place. When Arthur got ten days' leave and the couple settled on November 17 for the wedding, Adolph, invoking vague reasons, insisted that the date be changed to a time when he knew it would be impossible for Arthur to get away. "To say that I am fighting mad is to express with a considerable degree of mildness my actual state of mind," Arthur wrote his parents. "I still question the wisdom [of an imminent marriage] . . . but there is no more doubt in my mind that it's going to be done. I want it — it's my fight — and I'm going to see that it's put through without any more procrastination on the part of a certain party. He's 'played wolf' once too often and I'm taking no more chances."

Adolph was no match for Arthur and Iphigene's resolve and, at 5:00 P.M. on Saturday, November 17, the couple was married in the conservatory of the Ochs home on West Seventy-fifth Street. Rabbi Joseph Silverman of Temple Emanu-El performed the service in what *The New York Times* characterized as a "quiet home wedding." Carrying a bouquet of orchids and lilies of the valley and wearing a gown of ivory satin and silver brocade, Iphigene looked serene and far younger than her years, although, at twenty-five, she was hardly a child. Arthur, resplendent in his uniform, nearly missed the ceremony because of the foot-dragging of Julius, his best man and a captain of the cavalry. To make up for his poor performance, Julius dramatically unsheathed a saber to cut the wedding cake, but the affair was hardly a joyful celebration. "My father seemed resigned to the inevitable," recalled Iphigene. "He grumbled up until the moment Arthur and I were pronounced man and wife." In the official wedding photograph, taken against a lush backdrop of potted palms, no one is smiling, not even the newlyweds.

Iphigene departed for a weeklong honeymoon — a trip south en route to Camp Wadsworth in Spartanburg — in a gown of military blue duvetyn trimmed with seal and a toque and muff to match. When Arthur and Iphigene reached Washington, Adolph insisted that they meet privately with the president, as he had done on his own wedding trip thirty-four years earlier. The new Mr. and Mrs. Sulzberger were not keen on the idea, but in his daily phone calls to their suite at the Shoreham Hotel, Adolph was unrelenting.

The Washington bureau of *The New York Times* made the arrangements, and at the appointed hour, the couple was ushered into a waiting area at the White House. After what seemed hours, they were summoned into an adjoining room, only to find themselves not at a private audience but in a long line of well-wishers. When their turn came to greet President Wilson, Iphigene, unsure of what to say, blurted out, "My father sends his regards." Looking confused, Wilson murmured a polite thank you, shook her hand, and moved on to the next person. "He didn't have the remotest idea who my father was," she said.

At the time, the marriage was the only happy spot in Arthur's life. His military experience had consisted of one disappointment after another. Though trained in the artillery, he had been placed, inexplicably, in the National Guard unit at Camp Wadsworth. When he and Iphigene arrived back in Spartanburg in late November and took up residence in the Hotel Cleveland, he found that his unit was to be stuck indefinitely in the field, awaiting orders. Bored, he requested reassignment, and was placed temporarily in the Quartermaster Corps, overseeing accounts and supplies for the officers' mess. That Christmas he contributed generously out of his own pocket to help buy a holiday dinner for the enlisted men. His performance was so outstanding that when his National Guard unit finally arrived, his commanding officer would not release him.

Finally, early in 1918 orders came through assigning him to a unit in Chillicothe, Ohio. There he was led to believe that by the summer he and other attached officers would be sent overseas. The Ohio winter was so bitterly cold that "we nearly froze to death," remembered Iphigene. But the hours spent huddling indoors had a salutary effect, at least as far as the future of the Ochs and Sulzberger dynasty was concerned. By early April 1918 Iphigene was pregnant.

§

The New York Times was careful not to inflame war hysteria in the months following the sinking of the *Lusitania*. Believing that the country was unprepared psychologically and militarily for armed conflict, it supported President Wilson's efforts to preserve peace as long as was honorably possible. But when the moment arrived, the *Times* backed intervention wholeheartedly, even with its own blood. More than 185 *Times*men went into the service; five died.

In New York and Chattanooga members of the Ochs family eagerly signed up to help the cause. Well prepared by his Plattsburgh training,

Julius enlisted as soon as war was declared, and he advanced rapidly. In Chattanooga his father, Harry Adler, served on the draft board for the Eastern District of Tennessee; Adolph's youngest brother, Milton, fifty-three, was given a commission as captain of the Fourth Tennessee Infantry; and Milton's son, Van Dyke Ochs, was made a first lieutenant in the cavalry.

Despite their ancestry, several members of the Ochs family became violently anti-German. They are "savages at heart," declared Adolph's sister Ada. The national mood took a similar turn. In Cincinnati, which had a sizable German population, the city council changed Berlin and Bremen Streets to Republic and Taft. German-language newspapers were banned, and efforts were made to eliminate German from schools.

In this highly charged atmosphere, George made a decision guaranteed to infuriate his brother Adolph: he altered his own last name and changed entirely that of his two sons. He did not want his boys to be burdened, he explained, with "an alien appellation . . . one that will be anathema" in the future. So in the fall of 1917 he legally changed his sons' names from Ochs to the less-German-sounding Oakes and added the same name to his own, making him George Washington Ochs Oakes. Later, he placed a hyphen between the *Ochs* and the *Oakes.*

George tried to persuade Nannie and his brothers to follow his example, with no success. Instead, they were insulted by his presumption. Others close to the family suspected he was trying to hide that he was Jewish. True, George was not above making insensitive remarks about Jews. He once publicly suggested that American Jews should call themselves *monotheists* instead of *Jews*. The connotation of the word *Jew*, he said, was simply too derogatory to continue in use.

Nonetheless, the charge that he was trying to pass as a Gentile stung. To prove that the change to Oakes had nothing to do with masking his Jewish roots, George insisted that his children get a formal Jewish education, making them the only family members of their generation to be schooled in Jewish history and theology. Young George and John attended Sunday school at Temple Emanu-El and were "confirmed" — the term many Reform Jews preferred at the time to *bar mitzvahed*, which was considered vaguely Eastern European. Adolph was so pleased with John's performance that he offered the boy a bribe — a gift of $10,000 a year — if he would agree to become a rabbi. (John declined.)

Given the gravity of world events, however, George's idiosyncratic behavior was a minor irritant to Adolph, who had far more serious matters to think about. Like everyone in the family, he feared for the safety of his nephew Julius, who, after working three months as a senior instructor at Camp Upton on Long Island, was sent to France in April 1918 as a company commander in the Seventy-seventh Division, the so-called Statue of Liberty Division. And he fretted that his new son-in-law, Arthur, would soon follow, leaving behind a pregnant Iphigene.

Despite these worries, Adolph had abundant reason to be optimistic. *The New York Times* was unrivaled in its coverage of the war, an event made to order for the tactical brilliance of Carr Van Anda, who, by studying military maps and movements, was able to anticipate campaigns far enough in advance to dispatch reporters to the battlefronts long before competing papers. Daily circulation had risen accordingly — from 230,000 just before the outbreak of hostilities to 368,492 in 1918. So remarkable was the *Times'* performance, particularly its publication of the official speeches and reports of all parties, that in June 1918 the paper won the Pulitzer Prize for disinterested and meritorious public service, journalism's highest honor. Financially, the paper was flourishing, in spite of wartime cable bills that soared to $750,000 a year.

Even as he basked in these accolades and achievements, Adolph was on the brink of one of the most devastating personal and professional crises of his life, a trauma that would demonstrate the fragility of his position. It all began innocuously enough on Sunday afternoon, September 15, 1918, with a startling Austrian offer for a tentative and nonbinding discussion of peace terms. By then Germany and its allies were near defeat, desperately hoping to secure peace through negotiation rather than surrender in humiliation. Within hours the U.S. State Department rejected the proposal, and the next day both stories — the Austrian bid and Washington's refusal to entertain it — appeared on the front page of *The New York Times.*

Carr Van Anda and Charles R. Miller both interpreted the Austrian maneuver as an offer to surrender. Van Anda was particularly eager for a cessation of hostilities; his son, Paul, had just completed training for the Air Corps and would soon be shipped out. When the managing editor telephoned Adolph on Sunday night to relay the news, he exulted, "This is the beginning of the end!"

Adolph was at Abenia, his Lake George estate, at the time of Van Anda's call, sitting in the mansion's red-carpeted third-floor library, with Iphigene at his side. Three months away from giving birth, she spent as much time as she could in the countryside to escape the Spanish influenza epidemic, then raging, that would eventually claim the lives of half a million Americans.

Adolph was as hopeful as Van Anda that peace was at hand, but he was also characteristically cautious. "Better go easy on it," he advised. Van Anda agreed and, to reassure the publisher, went on to inform Adolph that Miller was personally writing the editorial. "Well, then," said Adolph, "I'm sure it will be all right." He had complete confidence in both men, especially Miller, who shared his conservative beliefs and patriotic sympathy for the Allied cause.

Miller was at his summer home in Great Neck, Long Island, and had not seen the Austrian dispatch, which had been read to him. He subsequently dictated his editorial over the phone, forgoing the usual formality of reviewing galley proofs. That night Adolph called Miller to ask his views of the Vienna initiative, but the telephone connection was so poor that the two men could not carry on a conversation.

Under the headline THE AUSTRIAN PEACE OVERTURE, Miller's editorial appeared on Monday, September 16, suggesting that peace discussions should be pursued seriously. "We cannot imagine that the invitation will be declined," it stated, possibly reflecting Miller's ignorance, due to his absence from the office, that Washington had already done exactly that. Although the *Times* had long insisted on "no peace without victory," the editorial went on to endorse the prospect of a negotiated settlement. "When we consider the deluge of blood that has been poured out in this war, the incalculable waste of treasure, the ruin it has wrought, the grief that wrings millions of hearts because of it, we must conclude that only the madness or the soulless depravity of someone of the belligerent powers could obstruct or defeat the purpose of this conference."

To modern eyes, the piece hardly seems incendiary. But at the time, the country was consumed with such bloodlust for Germany's unconditional surrender that many readers felt that the *Times'* position bordered on treason. Adolph did not even read the editorial until late Monday afternoon, when a paper was delivered to Abenia. He immediately rushed back to New York; by the time he arrived at the Times Annex, his desk was piled high with hundreds of angry telegrams and telephone messages denouncing the newspaper, and Adolph personally, for "running up the white flag." Readers canceled their subscriptions; advertisers pulled business out of the paper. President Wilson was reportedly in a fury and asked his aides to find out whether the damaging editorial had been cabled to Europe; it had.

Throughout the war, other New York newspapers had watched with alarm as *The New York Times* gained in readership and respect. Now they descended on their chief competitor, as Adolph said later, "like a pack of hounds." The *Herald* launched a circulation drive with the pointed slogan "Read an American Newspaper," and other papers characterized the *Times'* owner and editors as traitors. The only local journal that supported the *Times* was the New York *Sun,* which published an editorial saying that the paper's patriotic credentials were beyond question.

Members of New York's Union League Club, a prestigious Republican bastion, petitioned for a special meeting to consider public denunciation of *The New York Times,* prompting Adolph to dispatch his well-connected business manager, Louis Wiley, to lobby several of the club's most prominent members on his behalf. As a result, the diplomat Elihu Root, the five-and-dime-store magnate Frank W. Woolworth, and Chauncey M. Depew, president of the New York Central Railroad, declined to attend and, in letters to the club secretary, described the Austrian editorial as an "unfortunate" but forgivable mistake in an otherwise "great journal."

Adolph was hurt and bewildered by the hostility he faced. One visitor to his office found him sitting at his desk in a daze. Later he was seen wandering disconsolately through the pressroom. He felt as if his precious creation — *The New York Times* — and his precious reputation were on the verge of destruction simultaneously.

His loyalty as an American had been questioned. Jingoistic suspicions about his German origins and Jewish background had been raised, reviving the helplessness and anxiety he had felt during the worst days of the Leo Frank case. *The Manufacturer's Record* of Baltimore perniciously theorized that Jewish banking interests had pressured him to preach for peace in an effort to "save them from the losses which they will inevitably have to face if Germany is compelled to assume the entire cost of the war incurred by the Allies." To counteract rumors of a Jewish conspiracy, Adolph drafted a boilerplate letter to readers who wrote the *Times* to complain; in it he described Charles R. Miller, the editorial's author, as "American in every fibre and tissue, a New Hampshire Yankee of Puritan stock."

In the face of this brutal assault, Adolph stood by his editors. Privately he told Julius that the editorial was "a mistake, a grievous mistake." Yet he never publicly blamed Van Anda or Miller, to whom he pledged to "stick . . . though the heavens fall." To mollify Woodrow Wilson, who had been frequently unhappy with the *Times* despite its general support of his policies, Adolph asked Henry Morgenthau Sr., a friend and former Wilson appointee, to arrange a meeting with the president's chief adviser, Colonel Edward M. House, not so much to defend the editorial as to proclaim his patriotism and point out that the *Times* had consistently been pro-Allies.

The worst of the firestorm was over by early October. By then Adolph was so shaken that he told Morgenthau he was considering retiring from active involvement in *The New York Times* and transferring management to a trustee. Morgenthau talked him out of the idea, but within two weeks Adolph was forced to confront a new crisis, one that concerned the health and well-being of his nephew and surrogate son, Julius, who had been in France since the spring serving as a captain in the Seventy-seventh Division, 306th Infantry.

§

On the afternoon of October 14, 1918, as part of the 306th's advance on the Argonne Forest, Julius and his men took part in the capture of the hamlet of Saint Juvin. Broad-shouldered and barrel-chested, Julius was a cynosure of physical bravery: at eight he had endured an unanesthetized tooth-pulling without wincing. That quality was never more on display than at Saint Juvin, where he and another officer charged into a nest of 150 Germans, pistols blazing, calling on them to surrender. After the capture of the town and nearby Hill 182 — a critical German stronghold — Julius and his men repulsed eight counterattacks, holding on through the night until reinforcements arrived. At the conclusion of the campaign, General Pershing himself came to the 306th's headquarters to commend the Seventy-seventh Division's commander. Julius was awarded top honors for his courage, including the Distinguished Service Cross, the Silver Star with Oakleaf Cluster, and the Purple Heart. During the battle Julius had been gassed, and he spent several weeks in the hospital before returning to the 306th with the new rank of major.

Even as Adolph worried about his injured nephew, he was relieved that, despite his son-in-law's hopes for an overseas assignment, Arthur remained safely at home. For Arthur, however, waiting out the war stateside was humiliating. He never rose above the rank at which he entered, despite personal pleas from Adolph to friends with contacts in the War Department. By the time of the Armistice in November 1918, he was stationed at Fort Jackson near Columbia, South Carolina. Given the job of drawing up the discharge list for his unit, he put his name first, an act of which he was ashamed for the rest of his life. Once he returned to civilian life, he washed his hands of the army, refusing to remain in the reserves or join the American Legion. "He never got over his disappointment of not being a hero in the First World War," said Iphigene.

After moving in with Iphigene and the senior Ochses at 308 West Seventy-fifth Street, Arthur reported for work on the eleventh floor of the New York Times Building on Saturday, December 7, still wearing the boots, spurs, and uniform of a second lieutenant. He was given an office, a part-time secretary, and nothing definite to do. "My father had a very peculiar way of starting him," observed Iphigene. "Perhaps the intention was to determine whether he would float or sink." Just as likely, Adolph did not want to spell out Arthur's responsibilities too clearly before Julius returned to the *Times*.

Officially, Arthur's title was assistant to the executive manager, George McAneny, who had worked in New York City politics and had overseen Cyrus Sulzberger's unsuccessful 1903 campaign for president of the borough of Manhattan. McAneny was bright but lazy, and Arthur soon busied himself taking on whatever his boss did not feel like doing. Because it was so close to Christmas, his first project was the Hundred Neediest Cases Fund, but when that was over, Arthur was at loose ends, reading rejected letters to the editor and wandering through the *Times* plant, affable and a little lonely. "He wanted to prove himself to my father," said Iphigene. "He nearly went frantic for a while."

His anxiety was eased momentarily by the arrival of his first child, a daughter, on New Year's Eve 1918. He and Iphigene called her Marian Effie. Adolph was thrilled with his new grandchild and greatly relieved that Iphigene had come through her pregnancy and delivery without the physical impairment Effie had suffered thirty years earlier. His brother's loss of his wife in childbirth was never far from his mind, and he had worried inordinately about Iphigene's safety. After the horror of Julius's gassing, he could not bear the thought of any harm coming to his beloved only child.

Julius was officially demobilized in the spring of 1919 and joined the ever expanding group living in the Ochs town house. In May he resumed his position at *The New York Times*. According to family lore, the first day he reported back to the eleventh floor, he found Arthur sitting in what had been his office before the war. Despite their past friendship and new ties through marriage, Julius could not contain himself. "Get the hell out of my office!" he stormed. "I won't stand for this!" Arthur obediently moved. Whether or not the confrontation actually occurred, the two men ended up working in offices nearly side by side and quickly settled into a cordial, though tense, competition. Within months both were made vice presidents; Julius got the additional title of treasurer. But their duties remained largely unspecified. "I think [my father] wanted to see which of the boys turned out better," said Iphigene.

Even though he had effectively orchestrated it, Adolph was deeply distressed by the simmering rivalry between his nephew and his son-in-law. The mere anticipation of a battle over succession, and thus over the future of his family and of *The New York Times*, troubled him enormously. The month before Julius's return, Adolph was so nervous that he went to Atlantic City for several weeks, staying at the Hotel Traymore. By May he was spiraling downward into a full-blown depression. "I . . . really think it is going to take all summer to get him back into good shape," Julius's father, Harry Adler, wrote Adolph's secretary, Kate Stone.

The cause of Adolph's "nervous breakdown," as it was called, was not just the anticipation of tension between two family members, although that probably was the final, precipitating event. The momentum had been building since the Leo Frank lynching. The wartime attacks on the *Times* for being simultaneously British-controlled and treasonously sympathetic to the Germans also took their toll, as did the loss of his daughter to marriage, his subsequent worry over her pregnancy, and the fact that his nephew Julius almost died in France. "He had enough to drive anybody into a nervous breakdown," said John Oakes.

Though *Times* profits continued to increase steadily after the war, Adolph also became obsessed with the idea that he was insolvent. When Carr Van Anda, Charles R. Miller, and Louis Wiley each demanded $25,000 as postwar bonuses, he was paralyzed with anxiety about his finances, certain he had filed false income-tax forms and would be asked to pay huge penalties to the government. He destroyed many of his financial records and had trouble sleeping.

Alarmed, the Ochs family put Adolph under the care of Dr. Frederick Tilney, a Yale-trained neurologist and former reporter for the New York *Sun.* Tilney prescribed complete rest — with no work of any sort — and placed Adolph on a regimen that included regular exercise, reading, hot baths, a sedative at bedtime, and enemas twice a week. Closely observing him, Tilney noticed that Adolph followed a cycle of elation and depression, energy and despondency — the classic symptoms of manic-depression.

The family's hope was that Adolph would be cured after a summer's relaxation at Lake George. But it was not until November that he managed even to visit the *Times,* and within weeks it became clear that he was not yet ready to sustain regular work. At Tilney's suggestion, he checked into Dr. Andrew Green Foord's Nonkanahwa Sanitarium at Kerhonkson, New York, in the Catskills, returning to the city only for meetings of the Associated Press, where he was a director. For the Ochs clan, the abrupt change in their patriarch's personality was terrifying. "We didn't know whether he had lost his mind or not because he admitted he was acting irrationally," said Iphigene. "There was something like hysteria in the whole family. He had been such a strong man, such a strong leader, and everybody's livelihood was tied up with *The Chattanooga Times* or *The New York Times.*"

As Adolph rode the ups and downs of his illness, the question arose whether he should be relieved of his position as publisher of *The New York Times,* even if only temporarily. The matter came up before the five-member board of directors, which until that point had been so much a rubber stamp that it almost never held meetings; Adolph made all the important decisions. Now a crisis was at hand that required firm action.

Harry Adler, general manager of *The Chattanooga Times,* put himself forward as a candidate to assume control. He was pleasant and fun-loving but high-strung and largely ineffectual — hardly the steady hand the *Times* required; Adolph's brother George also volunteered. For Iphigene, a director of *The New York Times* since 1917, the dilemma was the first real test of her power and values. Bound by love and loyalty to her father, she had to consider what was best for the institution that would one day be hers. At the board meeting she spoke in the confident tones of an inheritor. "The *Times* staff is an extraordinarily capable group," she said. "For the time being they don't need leadership. They'll produce a quality paper on their own momentum." Charles R. Miller, the paper's editor and only nonfamily director, backed her up. Eventually the rest of the board came around to agreeing that nothing should be done. For at least a year, *The New York Times* sailed on like the *Flying Dutchman,* no skipper at her helm.

Adolph spent his time shuttling between New York City, Lake George, and Dr. Foord's sanitarium, and by the spring of 1920 the danger seemed to have passed. He returned to the office "feeling better than I have in months." To friends who inquired after his health, he characterized his ordeal as a blessing in disguise, one that reminded him that "I am not as young as I used to be." He agreed with his Chattanooga editor, Lapsley Walker, who told him, "You have won the right to enjoy the balance of your days. . . . Find the man whom you can trust, arrange it so you will be spared the heaviest part of the strain and above all . . . don't worry!!!" But deciding which man he could trust — Julius or Arthur — was a strain he could not delegate. In the coming years it would again bring Adolph to the snapping point.

10

The Great Man

ADOLPH PULLED OUT OF HIS DEPRESSION JUST in time to see flags, bunting, and glittering electric lights go up on the tower and annex to mark the twenty-fifth anniversary of his acquisition of *The New York Times*. At a silver anniversary dinner on August 18, 1921, in the annex's assembly room, the benevolence that characterized his leadership of the family as well as of the newspaper was on full display. To accommodate all 1,150 employees, the meal was served in five shifts from 11:45 A.M. until 10:00 P.M. After Adolph's remarks — identical at each sitting — an orchestra played "The Sidewalks of New York," "Sweet Rosie O'Grady," and other songs from the 1890s while diners perused the party favors arranged at each place: a souvenir menu; a clothbound copy of a commissioned history of *The New York Times* from 1896 to 1921 by Elmer Davis, a *Times* editorial writer; and an announcement that, to commemorate his anniversary, Adolph had inaugurated a generous employee-benefit package, including pensions and health and disability insurance.

Off to one side, for all to see, was a memorial volume of testimonials, telegrams, and congratulatory messages seven inches thick, bound — appropriately — in silver. Conspicuously missing was a tribute from Woodrow Wilson, whose unpopular League of Nations the *Times* had championed. The former president had been asked to contribute something but had churlishly refused on the grounds that he was "entirely unfamiliar" with Adolph's role in shaping the *Times* and considered the paper unprogressive and slavish to Wall Street. Even a personal entreaty from Bernard Baruch had failed to move him.

Adolph had ample reason to feel self-satisfied. In his twenty-fifth-anniversary message, published in the paper and widely reprinted elsewhere, Adolph took special pride in the fact that of the $100 million in gross revenue earned by the *Times* over the period of his ownership, only 3 percent had been distributed to the shareholders; the rest had gone back into the paper, making it bigger, better, ever more glorious. *Time* magazine put Adolph on its cover, declaring, "If there is a national newspaper in the U.S., it is the *Times.*"

Reviewing his achievements should have made Adolph feel secure and given him the freedom to do what he claimed he wanted most at this stage in his life: to risk, to experiment, to "indulge some pet ideas and theories." Instead, it made him even more cautious and a little melancholy. No longer was he the struggling outsider, a role that had always energized him. Now he was fully established, with a position to maintain — a challenge not nearly as much fun. At sixty-three, he realized that his days of impassioned creation were largely behind him, replaced by the burden of leaving an enduring legacy. "A perfect issue of the *Times,* if that were conceivable to your restless spirit, would give you but a moment's happiness," former editorial writer Garet Garrett said knowingly in his anniversary tribute. "For perfection is of this instant, tomorrow is a new time, and tomorrow is where you live."

With one eye on his place in history, and the memory of Leo Frank and the Austrian peace bid debacle never far from his mind, Adolph entered the 1920s with an even greater reluctance to challenge authority, a timidity that led to some lamentable journalistic lapses. Reporters at the *Times* watched as other papers bested them on several of the most important stories of the era, including the Sacco-Vanzetti case and the Scopes monkey trial. The most glaring example was the *Times'* coverage of the Teapot Dome incident. In June 1921 President Warren G. Harding had transferred control of the naval oil reserves at Teapot Dome in Wyoming from the Navy Department to the Interior Department. The oil was intended to fuel military ships in a crisis, but Albert B. Fall, the secretary of the interior, leased the land to private interests. When several New York papers revealed that he had received a $100,000 loan from oilman Harry F. Sinclair in an apparent bribe, a full-blown scandal was afoot.

The *Times* had editorialized against Harding in the previous election, describing him rather harshly as "a very respectable Ohio gentleman of the second class." Nonetheless, the president had vigorously courted Ochs, offering him a place on the board of visitors of the U.S. Naval Academy (which he declined) and making him feel so much at ease during a White House lunch that Adolph had told the First Lady a joke about a woman who on the witness stand had confused her age with her bust size. "I was very fond of [Harding] and I think he fully reciprocated the feeling," he said.

By the time Fall's "loan" was made public, the *Times* had known for months about improprieties involved with Teapot Dome. The paper had "early information concerning the oil scandals," Adolph later told the *Brooklyn Eagle*, "but we would not print one word about them until the reports were confirmed in Washington. . . . [A] responsible newspaper is always very careful to see that the news it publishes is true." Even when a Senate committee launched an investigation that eventually led to the White House, the *Times* saved its wrath for the accusers. "They profess to be engaged in the laudable effort to uncover corruption . . . but they make it seem that their real purpose is to paralyze the Administration, to terrorize members of the Cabinet, to break down the efficiency of the Government." The *Times* was not alone in its dilatoriness on Teapot Dome; *The Wall Street Journal* and *The New York Herald* were also quick to err on the side of business and government. But the *Times'* performance was seized upon by its critics to reinforce the opinion, colorfully stated by *Nation* proprietor Oswald Garrison Villard, that the secret to Adolph's success was "his unending devotion to the God of things as they are."

The paper's conservatism was also reflected in its coverage of race, sex, and radicalism — salient issues in the rich social stew of the twenties. After a race riot in Washington, a *Times* editorial analyzed the problem from the perspective of a reactionary newspaper in the Deep South. "The majority of Negroes in Washington before the Great War were well behaved," it said, adding that in those happier times, "most of them admitted the superiority of the white race and troubles between the two races were unheard of." The *Times'* treatment of the American socialist movement was similarly punitive in tone. When the U.S. Department of Justice, under the demagogic attorney general A. Mitchell Palmer, suggested building concentration camps for "Reds," the *Times* applauded the idea and urged the department to continue its policy of harassing and arresting "the conspirators against our government" — anarchists, pacifists, Bolsheviks, and political dissenters. As for the new sexual freedom, Adolph predictably recoiled in disgust. When Arthur urged him to permit a review of *The Well of Loneliness,* a highly admired book with a lesbian theme, he adamantly refused. After the issue was settled, he confessed to some curiosity. "Now tell me," he asked his son-in-law, "just what the hell *is* a lesbian?"

The trappings of personal power, which had mattered little to Adolph in the early years, began to take on new importance. When the annex added three stories and a tower in the mid-1920s, he designated the fourteenth floor the executive wing and built a mahogany-paneled office for himself calculated to convey magisterial authority. To reach Adolph's enormous desk, which stood before a green marble fireplace, visitors had to cross nearly thirty feet of carpeted floor and pass walls dense with signed photographs of presidents, prime ministers, and other notables. Next door he constructed a private and more informal refuge in the style of an English library, with walnut side tables, chairs of blue Moroccan leather, and a tapestry-upholstered wing chair.

Every day at 12:30 P.M., in the annex's private dining room, Adolph presided over the Publisher's Luncheon, which featured a guest newsmaker and a brace of *Times* editors and business managers. To put outsiders at ease, he pointed at the rose in the center of the dining-room ceiling. "Whatever is said today will be strictly 'sub rosa,'" he assured them. He also inaugurated the tradition of asking each visitor to sign a brown leather volume with THE NEW YORK TIMES GUESTS' BOOK stamped in gold on its front.

Adolph's new fascination with luxury was most ostentatiously on display during a four-month grand tour of the Middle East, northern Africa, and Europe in 1922. With Effie; his sister-in-law Fanny; Fanny's daughter, Margaret; Jules, his prickly Swiss valet; and Rose, Effie's temperamental Irish maid, he set out on the SS *Adriatic,* making friends en route with fellow passengers H. G. Wells and the actress Marie Dressler. In Gibraltar the Ochs entourage toured the city pasha-style in sedan chairs; in Cairo they rode camels to the Pyramids and had an audience with the sultan, a man who had been accidentally shot as a child and still carried the bullet in his neck, causing him to emit violent hiccups that, to Adolph's ear, sounded disconcertingly like a dog's barking. By the time the party arrived in Paris in April, the rich living had begun to tell. After an evening on the town with Edwin L. James, the *Times'* Paris correspondent, Adolph returned to his suite at the Hôtel de Crillon, took a double dose of castor oil, had a massive bowel movement, and promptly fainted dead away. Effie revived him with whiskey and summoned a doctor, who diagnosed his condition as "auto-intoxication."

For the rest of the twenties, Adolph trekked to Europe each year in similar style. Effie gradually became less enthusiastic about trips of any sort and, except on rare occasions, stayed home, while Adolph became, by his own description, a "Wandering Minstrel, an old and creaky frame enclosing a youthful spirit out on a spree." In the dozens of letters recounting his adventures, there is not a mean or sarcastic word about anyone, only delight — especially at being recognized and sought out. He was enormously puffed up when Douglas Fairbanks, whom he barely knew, greeted him in Paris like an old friend and the next morning over breakfast poured out his business woes in Adolph's room.

One element of foreign travel gave Adolph particular pleasure: pursuing young women, an activity he engaged in whether Effie was along or not, and about which he freely boasted in omnibus letters home. "A woman is only as old as she looks, and a man is only old when he stops looking," he was fond of saying. In Paris he escorted the screen actress Madge Bellamy — that "bewitching little creature" — to a "very naked show" and later accepted her gift of a miniature of herself painted on ivory.

The Ochs family was alternately amused and appalled by these antics, which only increased as he got older. Once, as a joke during a transatlantic crossing, Adolph's sister-in-law Fanny arranged to have a gardenia at his place each evening with a card from a different woman. Finally, on the last night, there was a gardenia and message from Effie. "You've been getting flowers from your 'once-in-a-whiles,'" the card said, "but this is from your 'steady.'"

At *The New York Times,* employees cringed at Adolph's habit of half-embracing women he barely knew. His favorite technique was to escort female visitors through the newspaper plant, then pin them against the walls of the narrow corridors in a feigned attempt to shield them from the passing parade of inky pressmen. Still, few people other than family members and close friends knew anything of his amatory escapades; in New York Adolph's image was that of a man above reproach.

That is, until Andrée Clerc, a French woman he had met in Paris, came perilously close to unmasking him. In letters marked "personal" and sent to him in America, she told "dearest Mr. Ochs" of her desire to come to New York to see him. "I shall be so happy if you would think of me a little," she wrote. Less than four months later, Andrée had some-how managed the trip and was living in an apartment on West Seventy-first Street. "I have in my possession your dear picture . . . but I want to see the original," she told Adolph. "I have been thinking of you all the time." Horrified, Adolph agreed to meet her just once but, as he carefully noted later in a handwritten addendum on her letters, "only at the office and in the presence of Ben [Franck]."

In 1927, when Josephine Baker, the legendary black star of the Folies-Bergère, singled out Adolph as her dancing partner at 2:00 A.M. in a Montmartre nightclub, the normally unflappable Ochses were taken aback. What offended them was not that he actively pursued what he described as a "real riotous Paris life" but that he had associated closely with a black woman. His letter about the incident, carefully marked CONFIDENTIAL — FOR THE FAMILY ONLY — TO BE RETURNED, raced through the appalled Ochs clan. "The idea of dancing or sharing a glass of champagne with Josephine Baker, a black woman and nightclub host-ess!" said John Oakes. "This was the most shocking thing any of us had ever heard about Adolph."

§

The struggle between Arthur and Julius over who would be Adolph's successor quickly became a matter of quiet debate within both the *Times* and the family. Julius's mother, Ada, often compared her situation to the Old Testament story of Hannah, who was barren and made a pact with God: if he would give her a son, she would dedicate him to God's ser-vice. Just as Hannah indentured Samuel to the temple, Ada said, she had indentured Julius to *The New York Times.* The other Ochses thought Ada a trifle melodramatic, but they certainly agreed that Julius, by training and by right, was Adolph's natural inheritor. He had been a star student at Princeton and a decorated war hero, and temperamentally he was very much like his uncle: modest, energetic, good-natured. Indeed, friends often told Adolph that his nephew resembled him more closely in personality than did his own daughter, whom they considered admirable but "too sedate." Most important, Julius was one of "the tribe," a blood relative, with Ochs as his middle name. "Julius was the obvious successor, the Prince of Wales," said John Oakes. By compari-son, Arthur was a mere pretender. The only thing that entitled him to be in the running at all was his marriage to Iphigene.

But at least Arthur *was* married and producing children. Julius, nearing thirty, had yet to find a mate. It was in this competitive atmosphere that Julius met a visiting Stanford University freshman, Barbara Stettheimer, at a New York dinner party. With her fashionably short dress, lipstick, red high heels, and expertly handled cigarette, Babs, as she was known, appeared to be the very essence of a modern woman, a flapper straight out of *Smart Set* magazine. To the balding, much older Julius, she was both chic and unspoiled, a girl from the San Francisco suburbs refreshingly free of the sharp-elbowed sophistication he had come to associate with New York women. "He may have felt he could deal with her," said his daughter Bobbie. "I suspect my father was rather shy with women."

Julius was instantly smitten and, in the courtly manner of a southern gentleman, pursued Babs intently. Soon the Stettheimers' Spanish-style home in Atherton, California, was deluged with flowers, letters, and daily phone calls. Though flattered by the attention, Babs thought Julius a bit stiff and old-fashioned. He had a nervous habit of tugging his left earlobe whenever anyone told a risqué joke in mixed company, and he loved horseback riding, a sport she loathed. Still, Julius had made it clear in so many words that he was likely to succeed his uncle at the paper one day. A future as "Mrs. New York Times," with all the wealth and glamour that implied, was tantalizing to contemplate. Besides, Babs longed to escape the emotional frigidity of the Stettheimer household; putting an entire continent between herself and her parents was appealing indeed.

Initially Babs found the clannish warmth of the Ochses attractive, but steeped as they were in strict Victorianism, they were not quite prepared for her. Privately George complained that her lipstick was unseemly. The others thought Babs judgmental and excessively social. "She was the new wave in our family," said John Oakes. When Julius announced that he intended to marry her, however, they closed ranks and in late August 1922 trooped to California for the wedding. Effie, as usual, begged off, but her half brother Rabbi Jonah Wise performed the ceremony, which took place in the Stettheimers' garden in front of a fountain. Arthur was Julius's best man, just as Julius had been for him; Iphigene was an attendant.

The newlyweds honeymooned in Europe, and when they returned, Adolph insisted they live with him and Effie in the West Seventy-fifth

Street town house. Babs quickly discovered why Adolph had made such a generous gesture. "After the second time he chased her through the house in her nightie, she finally persuaded my father to move out," explained Bobbie. The Adlers took an apartment around the corner on West End Avenue, and Julius rode to the *Times* each morning with his uncle.

Babs was genuinely unhappy with many aspects of her new life. Compared with California, Jewish society in New York was rigid and unforgiving, and the gemütlichkeit of the Ochses quickly became oppressive. Adolph expected Julius and Babs for dinner once a week, as well as for every family birthday and anniversary. "The family" was to come first in their lives, as it did for everyone else, and Julius, raised with a strong sense of duty, never questioned the premise. "She had to do this, she had to do that," said her future daughter-in-law, Anne Freeman. "Babs was frustrated from the very beginning."

Whether Babs knew when she married Julius that he faced a succession battle with Arthur is unclear, but she undoubtedly realized it soon after they settled in New York. Adolph was noticeably more equivocal than Julius had portrayed him, making it clear that a male grandchild to carry on the line mattered a great deal. For years Iphigene and Arthur had been trying to present him with precisely that.

The Sulzbergers' second child, Ruth Rachel, had been born on an auspicious date — March 12, 1921, Adolph's birthday — but she was, of course, a girl. Six months after Julius and Babs married, Iphigene became pregnant again, and on December 27, 1923, she produced a third child — another daughter, Judith Peixotto. Arthur claimed to be overjoyed and, with Adolph clearly in mind, drew a cartoon that showed himself dreaming of a *New York Times* with the headline THIRD GRANDDAUGHTER BORN TO PUBLISHER CAUSES GREAT CONSTERNATION/ CHILD'S FATHER ONLY ONE THAT REMAINS SANE.

Babs later said that she never wanted children at all, male or female, but the strategic advantage of having a son was obvious, especially in light of Iphigene and Arthur's failure. Julius would then represent not just a second generation of Ochses running the *Times*, but a third as well, establishing a male bloodline. Seventeen months after their wedding, Babs became pregnant. On November 24, 1924, to great family rejoicing, Julius Ochs Adler Jr. came into the world.

§

As Arthur and Iphigene produced girl after girl, Adolph's disappointment had become increasingly apparent. He had greeted Marian with joy; she was his first grandchild and unusually pretty. Ruth was less attractive, and Adolph, according to a doggerel verse Arthur composed for her second birthday, claimed he saw no beauty "in eyes or nose or yet in mouth or chin." By the time Judith Peixotto was on the way, his yearning for a boy had become explicit. The night Iphigene entered Sloane Hospital for Women, Arthur instructed Marian and Ruth to put a lump of sugar on the windowsill to entice the stork to bring a brother. When the bribe didn't work, they shared their parents' sense of defeat.

After Julie Jr., as the Adlers called their son, was born the following year, Arthur and Iphigene redoubled their efforts. On February 5, 1926, all three Sulzberger daughters put sugar lumps on the sill, and this time the bird took the bait. Adolph sent telegrams and cables all over the world proclaiming the arrival of his eagerly sought grandson. Effie's brother Isidor Wise was aboard the SS *Scythia* in the Mediterranean when he heard the news, and could not resist sharing it with Julius Rosenwald, a fellow passenger and owner of Sears, Roebuck. "His face shown [sic] like an electric globe," he reported to Adolph. "The arrival of the boy has caused commotion and rejoicing over thousands of miles."

In New York the celebration of the baby's arrival was quickly marred by a disagreement over what to name him. Arthur lobbied for Robert Ochs Sulzberger because it successfully combined an all-American first name with honor for Adolph in the middle. Iphigene was agreeable until her father came to see her in the hospital. Adolph took one look at the wrinkled infant and pronounced him unacceptable. "The poor child hasn't a chance," he exclaimed. "He can't possibly turn out well."

The comment was probably meant to be humorous, but to Iphigene, who had tried so hard to please her father, it had a cruel and wounding ring. It reminded her of the moment she had succeeded in getting hired as a reporter at the *Times,* thinking Adolph would be proud, only to be rebuffed. Iphigene retaliated with a weapon she knew was bound to find its mark: she declared that the child would be called Arthur Hays Sulzberger Jr., with no recognition of Adolph at all. Arthur was unenthusiastic — he didn't like "juniors" — but Iphigene was in no mood to discuss it. The name was inscribed on the birth certificate, and on February 24 Iphigene came home from the hospital. When Adolph realized what had happened, he was immediately contrite and within a few months became a "slave of the baby." After she felt she had punished her father enough, Iphigene relented and legally changed Arthur Hays Sulzberger Jr. to Arthur Ochs Sulzberger. But by then the boy already had the nickname he would be known by for the rest of his life: Punch.

. The name had its origin in the elaborately illustrated book Arthur created for his new son, which he impishly called *Idles of the King or the Story of King Arthur and His Nights & Days*. Just as Arthur had pulled the sword from the stone and proved his right to be king, the book said, so this newest Sulzberger had a destiny to "wield a pen more mighty than the famed Excalibur." The baby had been born into a "brood of Amazons," it went on. Like the henpecked seventeenth-century English puppet of the same name, he had come to "play the Punch to Judy's endless show."

Several months before Punch was born, the Sulzbergers moved into an enormous five-story town house at 5 East Eightieth Street, half a block from Fifth Avenue and the Metropolitan Museum of Art. The residence, previously occupied by a member of the Rothschild family, was a giant step up from the eight-room West Side apartment they had rented in the early years of their marriage. Adolph chose the $180,000 house, made a gift of it, and put the deed in Iphigene's name, reinforcing the point, as if it needed to be emphasized, that his concern was for his daughter, not Arthur.

Fifth Avenue and the streets directly off it had long been the preserve of wealthy merchants and millionaires, gentile and Jewish alike. Iphigene had no idea what to do with a house so immense that it came with its own elevator. She was ignorant about decorating; her only desire was to avoid the dark, cluttered look she had grown up with. Soon the Sulzberger home began to fill up with bright chintz and classic Chippendale, colonial desks, rose taffeta curtains, and colorful Bokhara rugs, much of it purchased from Charles of London, an antiques dealer and decorator on East Fifty-sixth Street. Arthur indulged his domestic flair by rearranging the furniture with maddening frequency and buying up handpainted screens, chandeliers, and objets d'art on trips overseas. "He had much better taste than Mother, and a wonderful sense of color," said Ruth, who as she got older was pressed into service as a furniture mover.

In the formal rooms Arthur, with obsessive neatness, realigned knick-knacks, straightened pictures, and shifted cigarette lighters on tabletops to achieve what he considered to be the perfect effect.

The aura created by these largely English furnishings was warm but surprisingly formal, a fitting reflection of the household itself. The Sulzbergers employed ten servants, including a live-in cook, a laundress who lived out, a chauffeur, and a parlor maid. Marian and Ruth each had her own room on the fourth floor, while Punch and Judy shared a room with Nana, their Irish nurse, who slept in a bed between them. Arthur and Iphigene occupied separate quarters one floor below — his a starkly modern room that looked out on the back courtyard, hers a traditional American space with a skirted canopy bed that faced the street.

The younger Sulzbergers rarely ate with their parents. Every morning the children took breakfast in a small dining room near the first-floor solarium, and before leaving for school mounted the gracefully curved staircase to say good-bye to their parents, who were served on trays in their rooms. At 6:30 P.M. they gathered again for a separate children's dinner. Sometimes they listened to radio programs as they ate, but more often Iphigene read aloud to them from Greek mythology, just as her own mother had done when she was young.

On Friday nights Arthur, Iphigene, and the two older children were expected at the West End Avenue home of the senior Sulzbergers for a traditional Sabbath-night dinner. Cyrus Sulzberger, immobile from gout, had aged into a dyspeptic old man whose recitation of Hebrew prayers as he broke the bread and drank the wine made him a rather frightening figure to his grandchildren. Rachel, her posture patrician-perfect and her attendance interrupted by short sessions of smoking behind the dining-room screen, oversaw the meal with the meticulousness of a kashruth rabbi. Dinner was invariably fish, not because it was a Jewish custom but because it had been the Friday-night tradition in her own family.

In contrast, Sunday lunch with Adolph and Effie was an unbridled affair. In good weather Arthur and Iphigene promenaded their brood across Central Park to the Ochses' West Seventy-fifth Street town house for a long afternoon of roast beef, Yorkshire pudding, storytelling, and cards. Never having had much of a childhood himself, Adolph delighted in playing with his grandchildren. If there was a birthday to celebrate, he insisted they make a racket with party horns, whistles, and cowbells or take part in a squealing contest with Marian and Ruth on one side and Punch and Judy on the other. Effie's parlor trick was to recite Gilbert and Sullivan librettos from memory. As she had gotten older and indulged her fondness for sweets, her figure had expanded accordingly. With her white hair and ample bosom, she resembled an amusing and approachable Queen Victoria. "Granny was just ebullient," said Punch. "You ran and jumped in her arms whenever you saw her."

Arthur and Iphigene's love of the theater had drawn them together early in their marriage. During the Broadway season they went at least once a week, preferring the lighthearted musicals of Cole Porter and Rodgers and Hart to heavy drama. Iphigene had few social outlets of her own and used what spare time she had to work for the Girl Scouts, the New York Child Adoption League, and the Society for the Prevention of Cruelty to Children. Arthur was a founding member of the Once-a-Year Poker and Pretzel Club, a group of friends who had played poker together as teenagers and continued the practice as adults. The bets were small — twenty-five cents — and the company distinguished: Henry Morgenthau Jr., who would one day serve as Franklin Roosevelt's secretary of the treasury; Harold K. Hochschild, the future CEO of American Metal Climax; Alfred Jaretski Jr., a lawyer with Sullivan & Cromwell; and Eddie Greenbaum, Arthur's personal lawyer and oldest friend. As the two "junior" members, David Sulzberger, Arthur's younger brother, and Walter Hochschild, Harold's younger brother, received invitations with little pink bows.

The Roaring Twenties never really penetrated the Sulzbergers' lives. Like Adolph, Arthur observed the letter of the law by refusing to serve liquor at home, though he gratefully accepted a drink if it was offered to him. But toward the end of the decade, when the corrupting influence of Prohibition had become clear, he and Iphigene made some "pretty awful" bathtub gin using a quart of pure alcohol given them as a gift by *The New York Times* doctor. Whereas Arthur loved to drink, Iphigene was moderate by nature; she rarely imbibed more than a single whiskey sour, and then only to be polite. Still, when Rachel expressed curiosity about speakeasies, Iphigene took her to dinner at Jack and Charlie's 21, the haunt of Robert Benchley, Dorothy Parker, Alexander Woollcott, and other literary figures, and detected her mother-in-law's discernible disappointment when the place failed to get raided.

Prohibition made home entertaining preferable to restaurants, and costume and theme parties were all the rage. Iphigene once attended a party dressed in nothing but a black slip because that was what she was wearing when she got the call inviting her to a "Come as You Were When the Phone Rang" party. Every New Year's Eve the Sulzbergers went to a dinner dance at the Fifth Avenue mansion of Adolph Lewisohn, the mining tycoon. One year no one felt like going home, so Arthur and Iphigene invited everyone back to their house for scrambled eggs. The breakfast became a tradition. Every New Year's Eve family members, friends, and journalists would arrive at 5 East Eightieth Street at 2:00 A.M.; be let in by Alfred, the superintendent; descend to the Sulzbergers' gleaming copper-and-enamel basement kitchen; and scramble eggs, fry bacon, and drink champagne until dawn. "Every year there were three men we had to throw out bodily at seven A.M.," recalled Iphigene.

Growing up amid this whirl of activity, the four Sulzberger children cherished whatever attention their parents and grandparents could give them. When they were small, Adolph made it his practice to drop by every afternoon about five with a present for each grandchild. By the time Arthur arrived home several hours later, tired and empty-handed, he got a comparatively tepid reception. When his protests to Iphigene had no effect, he began to show up with miniature books, ceramic animals, and other presents of his own. "That was a glorious period of time in our lives," said Ruth, who recalled it as a kind of perpetual Christmas. Arthur had cleverly made his point. Iphigene ordered her father to stop, and the daily duel of presents came to an abrupt halt.

Fatherhood brought out Arthur's whimsical, artistic side. In the many cartoons he drew for his children, he was always a bewhiskered Barney Google in a bowler marching off to the office to "make pennies." He wrote poems, illustrated a book about an elephant and an alligator named Elie and Alie, and made up a long-running tale about Isaac and Jacob, two magical kittens who worked as spies and had the power to speak any language. Every Fourth of July morning, Arthur summoned the children to his bedroom and read the Declaration of Independence aloud to a wriggling and inattentive audience. Punch later joked that it wasn't until he was twenty-one that he discovered "goddammit-sit-still" was not part of the great document.

Exactly one year after Punch was born, four-year-old Judy nearly died — and would certainly have done so if it hadn't been for Arthur. Afflicted with chicken pox and scarlet fever simultaneously, she had a temperature of nearly 105 degrees. The pediatrician gave her a special serum that set off an allergic reaction and anaphylactic shock, and her heart literally stopped beating. Terrified, Arthur raced to a nearby drugstore for Adrenalin. When he returned, the doctor administered it directly to her heart while Arthur frantically massaged his daughter's arms and legs to get the blood circulating. "She's gone!" said the doctor. Oblivious, Arthur kept at his labors until eventually Judy was restored to life.

Arthur had a natural ease with his daughters, but his feelings for his son were ambivalent. Just six days before Punch was born, Arthur's older brother Leo had died suddenly of pneumonia. It had been Arthur's grisly task to take the body to the crematorium on Long Island and see it placed in the incinerator. His grief had clouded the happiness he felt at his son's arrival, and later, as Punch grew, their relationship was characterized by masculine competition and fatherly disappointment. "I am afraid that my son and heir has not the heart of a lion," Arthur told his parents when Punch was not yet three. "He prefers to pat the dog's tail rather than its head, and walks away whenever the dog looks at him."

The Sulzbergers forbade Punch to play with toy soldiers or guns, in part because of Arthur's own unhappy experience in the military and in part because Iphigene's cousin Van Dyke Ochs had accidentally killed a child with a hunting rifle when he was ten. Encouraged by his sisters' example, Punch played with dolls. Although Arthur himself was hardly a man's man — he loved flowers, poetry, decorating, and fine clothing and had no particular interest in sports — a son's playing with dolls was a different matter. He tolerated it for a while but made it clear when Punch was five that the dolls would have to go. One day when Iphigene was gathering toys for charity, she looked up and saw Punch with his two favorites, Sunshine and Marian, in his arms, bathed and in their best ironed clothes. "What are you doing?" she inquired. "Boys don't play with dolls," he replied solemnly as he placed them in the box.

Punch sensed his father's disapproval and was poignantly determined to get close to him. One weekend when he was four, he came into the dining room of the Westchester house the Sulzbergers had rented for the summer and found that, instead of being assigned to his usual spot next to Arthur, he had been placed next to his mother. He asked the servant to move him back. When she did, he detected that Iphigene was a little hurt. With unusual sensitivity, he tried to offer an explanation that would spare her feelings. "I can see you better from that seat," he said, glancing up at his father for affirmation.

§

During his early years at *The New York Times*, Arthur worked seven days a week, including holidays, and made sure everyone from the composing room to the newsroom knew it. His aim was to "register the fact that I wasn't playing polo with the Boss's money" and, not incidentally, to convince himself that he wasn't a fraud. Julius could barely conceal his antagonism toward his rival and cousin-in-law, and the two had "some tough times together at the start." With his methodical, precise mind, Julius soon drifted toward the production and business side of the paper, areas in which Adolph himself felt most comfortable.

Arthur, however, was still in search of a purpose, a minister without portfolio. Luckily his superior, George McAneny, was indifferent to his main responsibility — acquiring the thin, grayish paper on which newspapers are printed — and Arthur rushed in to fill the void. Soon he was spending half of each day at Bush Terminal, an industrial park on the Brooklyn waterfront, where the Tidewater Mill turned pulp into paper for *The New York Times*. He traveled to Finland, Norway, and Canada to purchase supplemental shipments and investigate new suppliers. By the time McAneny retired in 1921, Arthur had become a newsprint expert. "I suddenly found myself knowing more about something than did my associates," he said. "It felt good."

Arthur could not have picked a better specialty. Newsprint remained scarce after the war, and newspaper owners were frantically casting about for reliable sources. The *Chicago Tribune* had dealt with the problem by acquiring its own mill and reforesting the adjacent land. Arthur was "distinctly nervous as to the future" unless the *Times* did something similar. In a memo to Adolph, he argued that investing in a mill would ensure a steady supply of paper at insider prices and effectively put the *Times* in the position of paying its newsprint bill — the highest single expense besides labor — to itself. Adolph was skeptical but intrigued. When Arthur heard that Kimberly-Clark was looking for a partner to build a paper plant in northern Ontario, he took a two-hundred-mile canoe trip into the Canadian wilderness with James Kimberly, the company's vice president, to investigate the feasibility of building the necessary dam, in the process cementing an important friendship. By the spring of 1926, a deal had been struck: *The New York Times* became a 42 percent owner of the Spruce Falls Power and Paper Company at Kapuskasing.

Spruce Falls was Arthur's first big solo performance, and its strategic and financial importance to *The New York Times* would soon become apparent. But until it actually started producing paper and contributing to the *Times'* bottom line, it had no discernible effect on Adolph's attitude. He continued to haze Mr. Sulzberger, as he called his son-in-law at the office, as if he were trying to run him off. He liked Arthur in many ways but found him presumptuous; after assigning him the task of screening his mail, Adolph became convinced that Arthur was diverting much of it so he could take on more responsibility. Arthur's restless desire to lead reminded Adolph of his age, which he didn't appreciate. "I'm not dead yet!" he once snapped when Arthur pressed him. To his editors, he issued a new rule: People over sixty (like himself) were no longer to be referred to as "old" in *The New York Times*.

Initially, Arthur treated his father-in-law with a deference that bordered on sycophancy. Adolph's gift of a bound set of *Current History* — a present unlikely to make Arthur swoon — elicited a profuse note alluding to how grateful he was to have his position at *The New York Times*. "It is my sincere hope that I may prove worthy of the responsibilities that you have placed on me," he wrote. But Adolph's constant harping eventually wore him down; soon he couldn't help expressing anger and defensiveness. When Brooks Atkinson, the *Times'* theater critic, commissioned a review from Adolph's friend Dr. Joseph Collins that proved unprintable, Arthur worried that Adolph would hold the contractual "kill fee" against him as "another instance of my extravagance." Then, lest his father-in-law miss the point that Collins had been asked to do the review only as a favor to the publisher, he gratuitously added, "It isn't my fault that you have such neurotic acquaintances."

To the outside world, it appeared that Julius still came first with his uncle. Following Charles R. Miller's death in 1923, Adolph appointed Miller's son, Hoyt, to the board of directors. At the same time, he removed Iphigene, replaced her with Arthur, and added Julius. The result was that while Julius and Arthur were coequals on the board, in their day-to-day work at the *Times* they were not: a list of top executives published that same year placed Julius Ochs Adler, vice president and treasurer, above Arthur Hays Sulzberger, vice president and *assistant* treasurer. When Arthur's brother David expressed a desire to work at the *Times* after his graduation from Princeton, Julius's partisans within the family succeeded in nixing the idea; they didn't want Arthur to find strength in numbers.

In 1927, after nearly a decade of working at the *Times,* Arthur finally had a chance to prove himself in a way that resonated with Adolph's love of hype, adventure, and red, white, and blue Americanism: he engineered the contract giving *The New York Times* exclusive rights to Charles Lindbergh's personal account of his historic flight across the Atlantic. Lindbergh, an airmail pilot, was a comparative unknown and Arthur didn't have much faith in his plans, but he knew that Adolph had heard good things about him from the publisher of the St. Louis *Globe-Democrat.* During a phone conversation with Harry Knight, a Lindbergh backer and president of the St. Louis Flying Club, he extemporaneously dictated a cautious contract that gave Lindbergh $1,000 down (with an additional $4,000 if he reached within fifty miles of Paris) and retained world syndication rights for the *Times.*

Lindbergh took off on May 20, and Edwin L. James, the *Times'* Paris bureau chief, was under strict instructions to "isolate" the pilot the minute he landed. But when Lindbergh's gray-white *Spirit of St. Louis* slipped out of the darkness and touched down at Le Bourget airfield at 10:24 P.M. on Saturday, May 21, fifty thousand screaming Frenchmen made that plan impossible. They burst through police barricades in a "mad rush as irresistible as the tides of the ocean" and ran onto the field. It wasn't until about three o'clock the following morning that a *Times* reporter finally managed to "isolate" Lindbergh at the American embassy, where he was sitting on a bed, drinking a glass of milk.

The New York Times ran five pages in its May 22 edition under the exuberant headline LINDBERGH DOES IT! The news was such a sensation that scalpers sold the *Times* for a dollar; one ingenious entrepreneur actually rented the paper out for five cents per half hour. Quick to grasp the promotional potential of the story, Arthur spent $11,000 advertising it. Adolph, following the news from the Hotel du Palais in Biarritz, could barely contain his excitement. "Three cheers and a tiger!" he wrote the family. "What a feat. What a glory. The world applauds and every American swells with pride. . . . It will not be long now before there is an airline to Europe from New York. . . . We are in a 'Living Age.'" Back at the *Times,* money began to pile up from the sale of rights around the world.

Arthur's handling of the Lindbergh story forced Adolph to reassess his son-in-law, and relations began to improve. "I have the feeling that some of the little rough spots between us have been smoothed out," Arthur wrote Adolph that Christmas. "I assure you that it has been my desire to remove them." In 1928 Adolph dispatched him to South America, a continent largely neglected by the *Times,* to establish a news channel and scout for correspondents. The following summer Arthur went to the Soviet Union, where in 1917 the *Times* had at first over-looked, then underestimated, the impact of Lenin. The purpose of such trips was to educate Arthur about the world and the *Times'* news operations. In both cases, Iphigene accompanied him.

By the late twenties Arthur had demonstrated a natural instinct for the news business while Julius proved far less nimble. In an effort to impress his uncle, Julius had come up with a proposal to reduce the size and scope of the Sunday *New York Times,* reasoning that people spent that day outdoors or at church and didn't have time to read. As an alternative he suggested a daily sixteen-page rotogravure section: financial on Monday; a "technical and scientific review" on Tuesday; and sports, women, and pictures on other days. His idea was both shortsighted and brilliant. Sunday was then, and is now, the best day of the week to produce a big paper: people have the leisure time to read, and advertising and profits swell accordingly. On the other hand, Julius anticipated by nearly half a century the daily thematic sections that would later be standard at the *Times* — Business Day, Science Times, Living, Home, and Weekend. His memo was put in a folder and quickly forgotten.

Despite his reappraisal of Arthur, Adolph remained as uncommitted about his successor as the decade wound down as he had been at the beginning. Julius interpreted his uncle's lack of clarity to mean that he was still a strong contender; after all, if Adolph had had no misgivings about Arthur, he would have already anointed him. Arthur had his own

doubts about whether he could ever hope to prevail without being rein-
carnated as an Ochs. In a verse composed for Adolph and Effie's forty-
sixth anniversary, he wrote in a tone of weary whimsy:

> I sometimes wonder how I fit
> Into this scheme and plan,
> And how my coat of arms appears
> Among the Wise-Ochs clan.
> It seemed a shame to introduce
> Blood that is not so blue
> And to dilute in any way
> Your virtues, and its hue.

11

A Good Name

I F ANY YEAR COULD BE DESCRIBED AS NEAR perfect in Adolph's life, it would be 1928. Buoyed by the economic boom, *The New York Times* posted $3.9 million in profit and daily circulation shot up to a record high of 442,000. Babs Adler gave birth to fraternal twins; one died, but the infant girl, Barbara, nicknamed Bobbie, was healthy and doing fine. As for the Sulzberger children, Adolph bragged that they were "all aces, four of a kind that cannot be beat."

Adolph and Effie began the year with a trip to Cuba and Panama, returning to the States through Los Angeles, where they stayed a few days to sample the Hollywood high life. Harry Chandler, owner of the *Los Angeles Times,* guided them through the Paramount, Fox, and MGM studios, where Adolph met Louis B. Mayer, had his photograph taken with the actress Pola Negri, and made an appreciative appraisal of Janet Gaynor ("a nice little trick"). Charlie Chaplin, star of the new movie *The Circus,* threw a dinner party in Adolph's honor with illegal claret and champagne and, for after-dinner entertainment, showed a Fox newsreel of Adolph working at his desk at *The New York Times.*

After years of avoiding Jewish issues, Adolph felt confident enough to tell Cecil B. DeMille that he wished his film *King of Kings* had never been made. The movie, released the previous year, had portrayed Jews as barbaric murderers of Christ and was criticized by Stephen Wise, Felix Warburg, Louis Marshall, and other Jewish leaders as anti-Semitic. DeMille, who, like Ochs, was both southern and Jewish, maintained that his intention was not to inflame, but Adolph was not convinced. "I held myself in considerable restraint in expressing my opinions," he wrote Iphigene. "I can see nothing but harm in [the film] for the Jews."

Adolph celebrated his seventieth birthday in New Orleans, where he got "flowers galore" and a surprise visit from Iphigene and his brother-in-law Harry Adler. "Three score and ten? Nonsense!" he wrote Dear

Ones All. "I felt like a two-year[-]old in the field with the shoes off, young and frisky, with the sap of Spring tickling my veins." A few weeks later he was in Chattanooga to dedicate the recently completed Julius and Bertha Ochs Memorial Temple, which he had erected in honor of his parents. Despite what he had told DeMille in Los Angeles, his speech gently chided Jews for overemphasizing bias. "We are supersensitive and conjuring up ghosts of prejudice," he said. "What wonderful strides we have made!"

Early that summer Adolph and Effie closed up the West Seventy-fifth Street house and removed to Abenia, the Victorian mansion on Lake George in upper New York State that for more than a decade had served as a luxurious summer camp for the ever expanding Ochs tribe. Abenia, which means "house of rest" in an unspecified Indian language, had originally been the summer home of Colonel Walter W. Price, a New York brewery tycoon, who built it in the 1870s. By the time Adolph acquired it, half furnished, from the subsequent owner, George Foster Peabody, the original turrets and towers that had given the house the look of a wedding cake were long gone. What remained was a rather boxy, misshapen mass that Iphigene described as "perfectly hideous but very comfortable."

By the late 1920s Abenia included a ten-car garage, a stone boathouse, a sunken croquet field, a freestanding laundry, quarters for the estate's twelve servants, chicken houses, and a cutting garden bursting with peonies — Effie's favorite flower. The main mansion was a jumble of mismatched furniture, from heavy four-posters with carved pineapple spindles to open-jawed bearskin rugs and a grand piano that was never used. Abenia's few grace notes included a stained-glass window and a fireplace in the entrance hall with a mosaic that spelled out in Hebrew "Except the Lord build a house, they labor in vain that build it."

However hot it might be outside, the air indoors was always cool, a function of the wind blowing in off the lake and the green-and-white-striped awnings that shaded the windows. Every morning the young Sulzbergers screamed in mock horror as the houseman methodically unfurled each one, freeing the bats that curled up there overnight. The children spent their days swimming, rowing, playing tennis, caddying for Adolph at the Lake George country club, and accompanying him to the Saratoga racetrack, where he always guaranteed a winner by placing five-dollar bets for each of his guests on every horse in every race. At the nearby casino he favored roulette, playing his lucky numbers — Effie's birthday, their wedding anniversary, and Iphigene's birthday — again and again.

After lunch the children went for drives with their grandmother, often ending up at the five-and-dime in nearby Glens Falls, where Effie bought two of anything that appealed to her and rarely left without her favorite delicacy, pickled pigs' feet. Electrical storms were a common occurrence in the mountains, and when they erupted at night, Effie would rouse all the children, give them candles and flashlights, and in the flickering darkness lead them in a raid of the gray, triple-doored icebox. Her idiosyncratic personal routine remained firmly intact at Abenia: sleeping till noon and staying up past midnight rearranging the furniture and leaving crumbs in the fireplace for the mice. "My grandfather tolerated her strange habits, and she was very tolerant of his," said Ruth.

There were rarely fewer than twenty around the Ochses' oak table for dinner, which was signaled by a gong struck by Frederick, the ill-tempered butler, a man whom Jules, Adolph's valet, openly accused of being "a bum, a grafter [sic] and never sober." Coat and tie were standard attire, and after everyone had assembled in the Gothic dining room, Adolph said grace in a voice that bordered on shouting.

The fare was simple — just good, fresh American cooking and plenty of it. Famous guests were commonplace. Franklin Roosevelt, Prince Machibelli, Samuel Gompers, Buffalo Bill Cody, and John Philip Sousa all enjoyed Adolph's country table. Effie was as indifferent a hostess at Abenia as she was in New York. One lunchtime, when several guests showed up uninvited, rendering the supply of lamb chops insufficient, she greedily heaped her plate and left the rest of the family, and her guests, to make do with cold cuts. "I didn't like these people anyway," she explained to a niece afterward, "and I was looking forward to lamb chops." She was also unusually fond of corn and consumed a disgraceful number of ears at each sitting, dipping her napkin in her water glass and delicately blotting the butter that dripped onto her generous front.

Evenings were usually spent in the book-lined living room, reading and talking beneath a banjo clock, painted religious scenes, and a host of dancing cupids. Sometimes Marcella Sembrich, the celebrated diva, brought pupils from Bayview, her nearby studio, to give concerts on the lawn. After the requisite operatic selections, Adolph invariably persuaded the young ladies to sing tunes more in keeping with his taste, such as "Alexander's Ragtime Band" and "Won't You Come Home, Bill Bailey?"

Late that June Adolph interrupted his summer routine to journey to Chattanooga for a three-day celebration of the fiftieth anniversary of his purchase of *The Chattanooga Times*. The honor, in which the whole city participated, meant more to him than all the accolades he had received thus far. Despite the thirty-two years he had lived in New York, Chattanooga remained his spiritual home. Editors at *The New York Times* were under a standing directive to publish Tennessee news. Whenever anyone asked him where he was from, Adolph always said Chattanooga. However rude and humble it might be, Chattanooga had given him the respect he yearned for at a critical moment in his life and had allowed him the chance to establish the reputation that made everything else possible.

Effie declined to attend the festivities, saying, "The hero should have the ground to himself," but Adolph was well looked after nonetheless. He arrived in Chattanooga on a special train that carried Arthur, Iphigene, and other family members as well as seventy guests. At the station he was met by an American Legion band, one hundred of the town's leading citizens, and his nephew Captain Van Dyke Ochs of the Sixth Cavalry, who served as his uncle's military aide for the weekend.

The next two days were an endless outpouring of affection and testimonials. *The Chattanooga Times* put out a 168-page Jubilee Edition with pictures of Adolph as a young man, the original Times Building, the Dome building, and the New York Times Tower. As Adolph approached City Hall to pick up a gold key and the designation "citizen emeritus," a thousand cheering people clustered around the entrance while factory whistles all over town let out a loud blast. Adolph played his part by slyly describing the event as a barbecue "at which an Ochs is roasted."

The climactic event was a testimonial banquet for six hundred at the Lookout Mountain Hotel, which was festooned with flags and twinkling lights for the occasion. Iphigene, dressed in a simple black evening gown with a shoulder spray of orchids, looked positively chic. Guests feasted on roast pigeon and fillet of sole and furtively sipped moonshine provided by several thoughtful Chattanoogans.

Mayor E. D. Bass read a sampling of the many telegrams, including one from Thomas Edison. Following the keynote address, a small army of shouting newsboys ran through the hall distributing souvenir newspapers designated as "Oxtras." When it came Adolph's turn to say a few words, he thanked everyone for the tributes. "I shall treasure them as my richest possession," he said, "and hope to present them to the keeper of the Pearly Gates as evidence that, if my life on earth did not deserve such praise, at least I had the ability to magnify a commonplace performance and make it appear important." Dr. Joseph Collins, a close family friend, later confided to Effie that Adolph had not just been feted; he had been "sanctified."

§

In the late 1920s many businessmen and brokers were testily annoyed at Alexander Dana Noyes, the *Times'* financial editor. In the shrill tones of a Cassandra, he had been warning that, if left unchecked, the wild stock speculation on Wall Street would result in a cataclysmic panic. On October 29, 1929, his prediction came true: the stock market crashed, U.S. securities lost $26 billion, and hysteria swept the country. "His has been a voice crying in the wilderness," said Thomas Lamont, a partner in J. P. Morgan and onetime owner of the New York *Evening Post.*

Adolph remained calm in the crisis even though advertising took a precipitous nosedive. Responsible Wall Street sources assured him that the downturn was temporary, and besides, he had amassed a $12 million surplus during the fat years of the twenties for just such a contingency. Enthusiasm and investment had always been his salvation in the past, and he again applied liberal doses of both. When Harry Adler panicked because fifteen national advertisers had canceled their contracts with *The Chattanooga Times* in a single week, Adolph encouraged him to increase spending and develop new business. "We must . . . set an example of optimism," he said. "Please urge every department to go ahead . . . as if we thought the best year in the world is ahead of us." *The New York Times* studiously minimized the crash: in December it chose Admiral Richard E. Byrd's exploration of Antarctica — an expedition the paper had sponsored — as the most important news story of 1929.

Adolph made a show of buying more land near Abenia and, in the spring of 1930, set out as usual for Europe, where he took "the cure" in Carlsbad and visited the Ochs home in Fürth. Personally, he was hardly touched by the Depression — the word President Herbert Hoover preferred to *panic* or *crisis* because he thought it sounded less frightening.

Ever since his losses speculating in Chattanooga real estate, Adolph had avoided investing in anything except *The New York Times*. He made a generous pledge to the Emergency Unemployment Relief Committee, and soon people he barely knew were beseeching him for money. "You have no idea the number of appeals that come to me every day," he wrote Milton Rodenburg, a distant relation to whom he gave $100 a month.

Laying off workers was anathema to Adolph, who took pride in the family atmosphere he had nurtured at the *Times*. He resisted making adjustments as long as he could, but when the Depression whittled the *Times'* profits to a fifth of what they had been prior to the crash, he announced a 10 percent across-the-board pay reduction, slashed executive bonuses in half, and cut the size of the paper. As an economy measure, potatoes and apples grown in Abenia's vegetable gardens were shipped to the *Times'* cafeteria. Louis Wiley pleaded with him to fire unproductive men in the business office, but Adolph preached compassion. "Where the person is entirely dependent upon his salary I would not like to see him dismissed without good cause as it would be almost impossible for him to get another position just at this time," he said.

Because of the cuts, Arthur and Iphigene had little money to give to charity after paying their living expenses, but they certainly did not suffer. They kept a full complement of servants and even added as a waitress a woman who had lost her job as a bank teller. For their fifteenth wedding anniversary, they took a six-week trip to Italy. On Sundays the Sulzberger children walked through the Hooverville in Central Park, distributing canned goods and saltines to men in ramshackle shanties made out of cardboard, tar paper, and egg crates. Even so, said Punch, "The Depression was all quite remote to me. I lived in another world."

As the economic trough deepened, Adolph's confidence began to flag. "Business is rotten," he confessed to a Chattanooga relative. An after-dinner conversation with Hoover at the White House deeply discouraged him about the future. The president told him there were at least five thousand financial institutions in the country that, if forced to liquidate at present values, would be insolvent. Hoover had no desire to be reelected, he admitted, but wanted only to get out of the "hell" in which he was living. "Of all the pessimistic views that have been presented to me, his was the most depressing I have heard," Adolph recorded in his notes on the meeting. "He . . . says we are on the brink of the most disastrous condition and that it would be nothing short of miraculous if we escape what he fears may be the worst panic that has ever occurred in our history."

Adding to Adolph's gloom was the chaotic state of *The Chattanooga Times,* which under Harry Adler had been undistinguished both journalistically and financially. To preserve an unbroken record of Chattanooga Times Printing Company preferred stock dividends, Adolph had had to dig into his own pockets and donate a surplus. For the past decade he had found himself refereeing petty squabbles over which family member should manage *The Chattanooga Times,* and as the Depression persisted, the impasse reached crisis proportions.

For several years, Harry Adler and Adolph's brother Milton had worked uneasily in harness as general manager and managing editor, respectively, of the paper. Harry, a high-strung, insecure man, was hardly an ideal match for the easygoing, undisciplined Milton, who dressed like a dandy and liked his cocktails. "Millie was a delightful guy, in some ways like Aunt Effie," said John Oakes, using the family's nickname for his uncle. "But he was never serious about what he was doing." The bickering had become so severe that Adolph had removed his brother in 1922, cushioning the blow by giving him a fancy title with few responsibilities, and put Harry squarely in charge. "I earnestly hope that you both will now maintain towards each other a pleasant brotherly affection," he told Harry.

At the same time, Adolph had saddled Harry with Milton's son Adolph Shelby Ochs, known as "A," whom he instructed Harry to groom as managing editor and, eventually, as general manager. Harry got along no better with "A" than he had with Milton. Soon the two stopped speaking altogether, choosing instead to communicate through acerbic notes.

If for no other reason than his name, "A," a restless, mercurial man, had an obvious appeal to Adolph, who even urged him at one point to call himself Adolph S. Ochs Jr., arguing that "Junior does not necessarily mean a son but the younger man." Adolph had also grown steadily impatient with Harry's plodding management; if only "A" were in charge, he reasoned, the paper might once again regain its distinction as the *New York Times* of small newspapers. In the spring of 1931, in an effort to give "A" wider authority, he sent Harry to Europe for six months to "rest his nerves." In his absence, an advertisement for *The Chattanooga Times* appeared in *The New York Times* with no reference to its having a general manager. Harry and Ada went completely to pieces. "I never saw two people so crushed or heartbroken," George told his brother.

By summertime the dilemma of how to save face for Harry and simultaneously promote "A" so threatened family harmony that George suggested that Adolph sell *The Chattanooga Times* to him and his two sons. "I don't imagine . . . that Iphigene wants to inherit your present troubles, which will multiply when you are no longer here," he argued. Adolph declined. Instead, Harry, who had always looked up to Adolph as his "father in one sense and older brother in another," provided a deus ex machina by gracefully accepting the inevitable. In order that "there may be no schism in the family," he volunteered to retire. As a balm to his ego, Adolph made Harry chairman of the board and created a trust fund so that he and Ada could continue to live in comfort. "It is all in your hands [now]," Adolph wrote "A" when the transfer of power was complete.

§

The resolution of the Chattanooga fracas came amid a series of deaths that deeply distressed Adolph. In early September 1931 Jules, his valet, suddenly dropped dead of an embolism while shaving Adolph in the special folding barber's chair he kept in Abenia's second-floor bathroom. Adolph arranged for an obituary in *The New York Times* and read from Psalms and said Kaddish at the Holy Sepulchre Cemetery where Jules, a Catholic, was buried in a plot not far from Miss MacDonnell, Iphigene's beloved governess. His letters began to take on a philosophical tone. "Why struggle and fuss over things that are only temporary, and in time have to be dropped anyhow?" he asked a relative.

At the time of Jules's death, George was touring France, Germany, and Switzerland with Nannie, Mattie, and his two sons. Though sixty-nine, George was remarkably vigorous. Every Sunday he played thirty-six holes of golf; for the past nine years he had been quietly pursuing a Ph.D. in history at Columbia. In Europe he insisted on walking everywhere and danced till the wee hours, but by the time he reached London, he complained of trouble "in my pelvic region." When he got back, his doctor recommended the removal of his prostate, an operation Adolph had undergone nearly ten years earlier. "[George's] general health and condition justify the belief that it will be nothing more than having a tooth pulled," Adolph assured Harry and Ada.

His recovery was steady but slow, with alarming episodes of leg pain, fever, and labored breathing. Four weeks after the operation, on October 26, the eve of his seventieth birthday, George was informed he could leave the hospital the following day. That afternoon he joked with friends and expressed eagerness to get back to work. Then suddenly, without warning, he collapsed; a blood clot had lodged in his heart. Within minutes George Washington Ochs-Oakes was dead.

Though visibly shaken, Adolph orchestrated every detail of the funeral. A police escort accompanied the casket from the service at Temple Emanu-El to Pennsylvania Station, where two private railway cars carried the mourners to Philadelphia. Officers accompanied the entourage to Mount Sinai Cemetery, where George was buried next to his wife, Bertie, who had died eighteen years earlier and of whom he could never speak without weeping.

George's death dealt Adolph a wounding blow, for while George had squirmed in Adolph's shadow and occasionally snickered at his sense of self-importance, he had been loyal and genuinely admiring, a Greek chorus that observed his brother and offered sometimes tart insights borne of a lifetime of understanding. He had been the one person Adolph could not fool or dazzle, the educated Ochs who always retained a faint air of superiority despite his brother's many triumphs. Now, with George's death, Adolph began to see tragedy and danger everywhere. "I am paying the penalty of living beyond the scriptural age," he told an in-law.

In the spring of 1932 Adolph's cousin Ben Franck, who had been his associate in various Chattanooga ventures and had served *The New York Times* as corporate secretary for many years, collapsed on the floor of his apartment of a heart attack and died several days later. In the face of these multiple disasters, Milton sent his brother a sympathetic telegram: I AM THINKING OF THE SHADOWS THAT HAVE GATHERED AROUND YOU WITHIN THE YEAR BUT I KNOW YOUR STOUT HEART WILL ACCEPT GOD'S DECREES WITH CALMNESS.

That summer a suspicious X ray led to the excision of Adolph's right kidney, an operation that forced him to recuperate many weeks in bed. "You have had a long siege of it, and I do hope that you are very much better," Franklin Roosevelt, the Democratic presidential nominee, told him in early September. Not long afterward John Oakes, a Princeton sophomore, passed through New York on his way to a model League of

Nations conference and stopped to call on his uncle. He was alarmed by what he found. Adolph lay in the darkened upstairs bedroom of the West Seventy-fifth Street town house, dressed in a bed jacket and propped up on pillows. "He was in an extremely gloomy mood, very agitated and kind of mumbling," said John. "He cautioned me to drive carefully and put his hand on my head as if I'd never see him again."

Adolph's spirits lifted momentarily when he and Effie moved into a sprawling fifty-seven-acre estate in White Plains in Westchester County later that fall. With the acquisition of Hillandale, as it was called by its original owner, he shed city living for good and pared back his schedule at the *Times*. He told people that he actually looked forward to the forty-five-minute commute, which he predicted would be "a relaxation for me." Effie, who at first opposed the move, became so attached to country living that she refused to stay in town with Nannie after the opera and insisted on being driven back to White Plains.

Hillandale was Adolph's great extravagance, his only truly palatial home. With its thousand-square-foot ballroom, marble floors, greenhouses, private lake, boathouse, tennis courts, six-car garage, and white-columned portico, the three-story, thirty-two-room Colonial-style Hillandale looked like a cross between Tara and a suburban country club. Westchester County had been "Our Crowd" territory since the 1860s, and by the time Adolph arrived, the Warburgs, Lehmans, Lewisohns, and Bronfmans shared the neighborhood with Protestant aristocrats such as Ogden and Whitelaw Reid, owners of the *Herald Tribune*. The Century Country Club, a bastion of the Jewish elite, was nearby. Best of all, from Adolph's point of view, he had been able to purchase the property for a mere $300,000 because of the Depression.

Soon Hillandale was bursting every weekend with a jumble of relatives, friends, and cousins to the ninth generation. Arthur, Iphigene, and the children were not just welcome, they were expected and could hardly argue that there wasn't room for them. The thousand-square-foot library was as spacious as many New York apartments. The powder room was the size of a bedroom. Despite its imposing scale, the estate was run in a way calculated to give pleasure to children. Often Effie wandered the Hillandale grounds, a canary on her shoulder, dispensing jujubes to the multitude of small relations who trailed behind her. She once held a birthday party for the neighborhood dogs in the ballroom, which the Ochses converted into a playroom with jigsaw puzzles, a piano, and a Ping-Pong table. "I helped her," said Judy, who was ten at the time. "We went around and handed out hot dogs and dog biscuits to the dogs."

§

Nineteen thirty-two was Adolph's last year as an active newspaperman. Hillandale had revived him temporarily, but the accumulating burdens of family strife, depleted profits, death, tragedy, illness, and the misery of America's homeless and unemployed had taken their toll, plunging him into the same dark melancholia that had gripped him fifteen years earlier. This time the precipitating event was the rise of Adolf Hitler, whom Adolph correctly perceived as a threat not only to peace but to his existence as a Jew. "This will lead to a second world war," he told Iphigene in January 1933, when Hitler became German chancellor.

The New York Times struck a more cautious note, assuring readers that Hitler's new post was "no warrant for immediate alarm." But within weeks Hitler had gained control of the Reichstag, and Dachau, the first concentration camp, appeared. Laws were passed stripping Jews of their jobs and rights of citizenship. Frederick Birchall, the *Times* correspondent in Berlin, revealed in a front-page lead story that the April 1 boycott of Jewish businesses was official, not spontaneous, as the Nazis had asserted.

Adolph, who was distantly related to the German poet Heinrich Heine, had a sentimental attachment to the land of his forebears. In his usual innocent way, he had refused to believe that Germans could ever be seduced by Hitler's corrupting charisma. "The German people are becoming informed about Hitler," he had told *The Jewish Journal* in 1931. "Gradually, those who have supported him are realizing the kind of man he is." Two years later, when Hitler swiftly consolidated power, Adolph had to admit that the period since World War I had been one of armistice, not peace, and that "an unprecedented reign of terror was in the making."

With considerable anguish, he made an unusual decision: he banned all letters to the editor concerning Hitler. Ever since 1896 *The New York Times* had been an open forum for readers' opinions on all sides of every issue, whether the views were personally repugnant to Adolph or not. If he were to continue that policy, he would be honor-bound to publish letters in support of Hitler, however anti-Semitic — and that he could not bear. The *Times* lamely explained to those who inquired that it had received so many letters on "the German situation" that it would be unfair to publish some and not others. Letters continued to pour in nonetheless, many from Jews furious at being denied an outlet for their condemnation of the Third Reich.

By the summer of 1933 Adolph's agitation about Hitler had ripened into a full-blown depression. "I, personally, feel helpless and almost hopeless," he wrote a man who had sent him a survey of conditions in Germany. In late September he left Abenia and arrived unannounced at Hillandale, complaining to Iphigene and Arthur of not feeling well. Dr. Tilney checked him into the Neurological Institute, where, as part of a series of tests, he was given a high-colonic irrigation. The strain of the procedure prompted a heart attack; he barely survived the night. Physically Adolph made a remarkable comeback, but emotionally he emerged from the hospital in an even deeper state of depression. "I realize I am an old man," he told Lapsley Walker, a former editor of *The Chattanooga Times.*

For the balance of 1933 Adolph spent long days in his paneled study at Hillandale and rarely appeared in public. When *The New York Times* was delivered each day, he fingered it but no longer read it. For years Louis Wiley had called Adolph every morning at 7:30; now Adolph refused to speak with him. Occasionally he walked with a nurse around the grounds, played a round of golf, or traveled to the cemetery where his mausoleum was under construction. More often he simply sat in a silence so profound, he could not be roused. When Fanny, Milton's wife, tried to cheer him up by talking about his grandchildren, he turned to her with sad eyes. "It was my grandchildren I was thinking about," he said. "What does the world hold for them? What will their fate be?" Fanny assured him that what was happening in Germany could never occur in America. He brushed her off. "Thirty years ago I was sure it couldn't take place in Germany," he said.

Adolph's incapacitation gave new urgency to the question of succession at *The New York Times.* Two years earlier he had been profoundly shaken when Herbert Pulitzer, the youngest son of his old rival, Joseph Pulitzer, had put the New York *World* up for sale in violation of his father's dying wish to keep it in the family. That a publisher's work of a lifetime could evaporate in the hands of his heirs was a point not lost on Adolph and was reinforced by the tenuous generational transition he had recently engineered at *The Chattanooga Times.*

Plagued by such concerns, and worried that announcing a successor would make him a lame duck and divide the family, Adolph did nothing. But world conditions soon made action unavoidable. When he had been depressed in the early 1920s, the nation had been prosperous and at peace, making it relatively easy for trusted lieutenants to operate in his absence. Now, Hitler's ruthless adventurism and the national economic malaise made the prospect of a rudderless *New York Times* unthinkable.

With Iphigene's encouragement, Arthur filled the vacuum, overseeing the paper's editors and correspondents and, in a departure from the measured tone Adolph preferred, sharpening its editorial voice. Shortly before the onset of his depression, Adolph had vetoed Arthur's request to endorse the National Industrial Recovery Act, insisting that the *Times*' policy was to be "conservative and cautious and not involve itself in all public clamor for a change." Now, with his father-in-law sequestered at Hillandale, Arthur "took positions and . . . took them as hard as we could. . . . I was not at all sure we weren't ruining the *Times* by doing so but . . . these were days in which the cost could not be counted."

What emboldened him, in part, was that several of his judgments about the paper's needs had turned out to be wisely prescient. *The New York Times*' financial health during the Depression was thanks in no small measure to Spruce Falls Power and Paper, which since 1929 had supplied all the *Times*' newsprint as well as the profits with which the *Times* paid its dividends. Arthur's constant efforts to change the overly generous Ochs pension plan had been rebuffed, but his analysis of the plan as a long-range financial burden had, alas, been all too accurate. Pension payments had more than doubled since 1928, yet Adolph would not hear of asking *Times* employees to make contributions or set up outside annuities.

While Arthur ran the news side of the *Times,* Julius oversaw the business and mechanical side, seemingly confident that his kinship to Adolph, his obvious dedication, and his lifetime of service would ultimately be rewarded by his selection as publisher. The rest of the Ochs family, with the exception of Iphigene, felt the same way. "Julius was a much more responsible person, much more intelligent than Arthur," said Julius's sister-in-law, Jean Steinhardt. "Arthur was very surface."

Arthur and Julius both suffered from the strain of the succession battle, as well as from the same pressures of current events that plagued Adolph. In 1932, at forty-one, Arthur suffered a coronary occlusion, caused, his doctors theorized, by worry, fatigue, and stress. The episode left him with a left hand permanently incapable of bearing any weight. A year later Julius had a nervous breakdown that was officially attributed to long hours and overwork. He entered the Austen Riggs Center in Stockbridge, Massachusetts, where he remained for six weeks.

Julius's tension had been exacerbated in recent months by the ever accelerating decline of *The Chattanooga Times*. The paper had not met its operating expenses since 1931 and "A" had had to ask Adolph for a loan in order to make ends meet. In May 1933, just before Julius entered Riggs, *The Chattanooga Times* found itself competing not just with the afternoon *Chattanooga News*, its historical rival, but with a new weekly throwaway called *The Chattanooga Free Press*, started by a disgruntled former *Chattanooga Times* ad manager whom "A" had fired, and backed by a local grocery-chain owner named Roy McDonald.

"A" had proved to be a timid manager, cowed by the depth of his paper's distress. To help him, Julius suggested that young George Oakes, whom he looked upon as more of a nephew than a cousin, go to work on *The Chattanooga Times*, with an eye toward splitting the editorial and business functions as he and Arthur were doing at the New York paper. Soon George and "A" clashed as dramatically as "A" had with Harry Adler. To "A," George was "fixed in his opinions"; to George, "A" was conservative and "afraid to move."

Julius solved the problem by bringing George to New York and offering him a job on the business side of the *Times*. Several months earlier *Forbes* magazine had run a short item declaring that Arthur had been de facto publisher for some time and it was "taken for granted" he would be Adolph's successor. Julius had been hurt by the article but paid it little mind. When George reported for work, Julius gave him the impression that if all went well — meaning, if Julius were named publisher — George would in time occupy "a position of considerable importance in the organization." Julius was building his team, waiting for the inevitable day when he would be appointed to lead *The New York Times*, the job he had been preparing for all his life.

§

In February 1934 Adolph visited *The New York Times* for the first time in more than four months but, finding it difficult to meet people after so long an isolation, dropped in just once or twice weekly throughout the spring. That summer he did not go to Abenia. At a family dinner in June, Julius and Babs served tomato juice cocktails on the advice of Adolph's doctors, who told them alcohol might further depress him. His disappointment was so keen, though, that they took pity on him and mixed up martinis.

The kidnapping of the Lindbergh baby two years earlier had caused Adolph to become terrified that something similar could happen to his grandchildren. To give her father some peace of mind, Iphigene agreed to take the Sulzberger children to Europe for an extended stay. Arthur's plan was to join them, but as the summer wore on and Adolph became more and more anxious, he was forced to abandon the idea. Arthur closed up 5 East Eightieth Street and moved into a suite at the Pierre Hotel, adding his own homey touches — a juicer, a small cabinet for his liquor, and several photos. He walked to and from the *Times* almost every day and spent as much time as he could bear at Hillandale.

In late July, while Julius was away at military camp, Arthur dined with his father-in-law in White Plains. He found Adolph consumed with the succession question, seemingly certain that Arthur was the man to run *The New York Times,* yet nearly hysterical at the thought that death would rob him of his ability to dictate what would happen. As soon as they had finished eating, he grabbed Arthur by the arm. "What is your plan of action after I die?" he demanded. Arthur replied that he didn't want to discuss it. "There are certain things that are out of your control," he explained, "and that is one of them." But Adolph begged Arthur for an answer, adding pathetically, "It's all I think about."

Adolph quizzed Arthur about how Julius would fit in. "From what you have told me, the cards are in my hands," Arthur said. "You mean that you would hold a position superior to Julius?" asked Adolph. "Yes, there can be only one head to a business," Arthur replied. Adolph then revealed that he had provided financially for Julius in his will so that "if he isn't happy he can quit." He suggested that Iphigene take the title of president, an option she had already considered and rejected. For the next hour Adolph rambled on, assuring Arthur again and again that he had confidence in him, as though he were trying to convince himself as well as his son-in-law. Two weeks later Adolph again cornered Arthur and demanded that they discuss succession. "It is beginning to have a pretty bad effect on me," Arthur told Iphigene in a letter. "It is making the hair stand up on the back of my neck."

By Christmastime Adolph assured John Oakes his "ups" were gaining on his "downs," but to Julius he still appeared "highly nervous." Three months later, on March 6, 1935, Louis Wiley, the *Times'* business manager, died following an operation; ever the social agent, the last thing he did was to dictate a congratulatory letter to a friend who had just had a baby. For Adolph, the death severed the last link to his early days of building *The New York Times*. Charles R. Miller was gone; Van Anda was in retirement.

The family worried that Wiley's passing would push Adolph further into the shadows, but curiously, it appeared to rouse him. He expressed a yearning to see the spring one final time in Chattanooga, and on Saturday, April 6, set out by train with a nurse and his granddaughter Marian. On Sunday he spent the night with Harry and Ada at the Fifth and Cedar homestead and slept well. The next morning, April 8, he ate his usual breakfast, went to *The Chattanooga Times*, and called Effie. "I've never felt more cheerful and happy in my life," he said.

For the balance of the morning, he closeted himself with "A," whose conspicuous opposition to the Tennessee Valley Authority had been troubling him. About 1:00 P.M., they joined Milton and the nurse and set out for lunch at the Coffee Shoppe, one block from *The Chattanooga Times'* gold dome. As they departed, Adolph wobbled unsteadily and nearly fell against his companions. At the restaurant the trio silently scanned the familiar menu. "What do you think you'll have, Adolph?" Milton asked. He got no answer. Looking up, he saw his brother slumped in his chair, unconscious.

The nurse hurriedly gave Adolph an injection, and at Newell Sanatorium, four doctors worked feverishly to save him. But at 4:10 P.M. Adolph S. Ochs was pronounced dead. The cause was a cerebral hemorrhage, complicated by severe benign hypertension. As his life slipped away, Ada had held his head in her arms and covered his face with kisses. "[He] made us what we are, a devoted family circle," she wrote in a distraught omnibus letter.

The next morning's *New York Times* had a black border, a gesture the paper had made only six times in its history, beginning with the death of Daniel Webster in 1852. In the middle of the front page was Adolph's picture, followed by a sixteen-column obituary, a pictorial review of his life and career, and dozens of tributes from other newspapers and national and international leaders. Several readers suggested that only Jews would produce such ostentatious coverage. When Arthur heard about the comments, he was sufficiently annoyed to ask how the *Herald Tribune,* the standard of WASP propriety, had treated the deaths of its various owners. By comparison, Arthur concluded, the *Times* had shown restraint.

As Adolph had originally hoped, he had two funerals, the first at the Julius and Bertha Ochs Memorial Temple in Chattanooga. In his honor, the city's banks closed, streetcars stopped, public buildings went dark, and stores were locked and empty. Next to the casket stood a spray of pink roses and snapdragons from Franklin and Eleanor Roosevelt; in memory of Adolph's mother, the Daughters of the Confederacy sent a pillow in the form of a Confederate flag. As the Chattanooga service began, work halted in the composing room of *The New York Times,* and the printers — Adolph's favorites, always — stood quietly in tribute.

Two special Southern Railway cars carried Adolph's body and entourage to New York City, where his simple Chattanooga casket was exchanged for a more elaborate one. On a cold, drizzling Friday morning, three thousand mourners gathered in the immense sanctuary of Temple Emanu-El to witness the last rites. Mayor Fiorello La Guardia proclaimed a day of public mourning and flew the city's flags at half-staff. The Associated Press and United Press suspended their Teletype machines for a moment throughout the world. At *The New York Times,* work halted for five minutes. Even the elevators ceased to operate, and the telephones were silent.

The service began with Mendelssohn's "Funeral March," followed by the Twenty-fourth and Ninetieth Psalms. Rabbi Jonah Wise read a prayer that began with a line that captured the philosophy that had shaped Adolph's every action: "A good name is better than precious oil." Seventy cars, eight of them filled with flowers, set out for Temple Israel Cemetery in Westchester County, preceded by sixteen policemen on motorcycles. As the mourners huddled in the rain, Rabbi

Wise stood at the top of the three steps leading into Adolph's regal mausoleum and read the committal service, first in English, then in Hebrew. Finally, Adolph was laid to rest in the marble tomb he had so lovingly prepared.

Outside, the rain and the trampling feet of mourners made a mud field of the sloping ground. In the days that followed, the family hired a nursery to plant three hundred crocus and two hundred narcissus on the site. Every year thereafter, on March 12, Iphigene faithfully placed flowers on her father's grave. She preferred to honor the day he was born, she explained, not the day he died.

PART TWO

The Stewards

12

The Man Who Would Not Be King

A S FAR AS ARTHUR WAS CONCERNED, ADOLPH had all but told him he would be the next publisher, but Julius was not prepared to accept the issue as settled, and the great man's will, which charged his heirs to maintain *The New York Times* "free of ulterior influence, and unselfishly devoted to the public welfare," did little to clarify matters. With 50.1 percent of the *Times'* common stock — a bare majority — the will established the Ochs Trust, making the trust, not a single individual, the controlling owner of *The New York Times.* Ultimately, the stock was to be divided evenly among his four grandchildren after Iphigene's death. Arthur, Iphigene, and Julius were designated trustees of the trust, which paid an income to Adolph's widow and then, upon Effie's death, to Iphigene. With 502 shares of common stock, Adolph honored his pledge to provide generously for his nephew; the sum made Julius the third-largest shareholder, after the son of the late Charles Miller and the trust itself. To Arthur, he gave two thousand shares of nonvoting preferred stock.

Babs was furious that Adolph had not explicitly named Julius his successor, but the rest of the clan took it as a sign of the patriarch's wishes that Julius had been so richly rewarded. They viewed him as the leader of the family and the obvious choice to be publisher, while Arthur, in contrast, was "sneered at." "They were all rooting for Julius," said John Oakes. "I don't think they realized it was a lost cause."

What the family failed to grasp was that Adolph had effectively given Iphigene the power to determine who would run the *Times.* Under the terms of the will, the three Ochs trustees were responsible for choosing the next publisher. The *Times'* five-member board of directors, on which they all sat, would merely ratify their decision. It was inconceivable that Iphigene would ally herself with Julius and vote against her husband. "It would have ended our marriage . . . which I had no inclination to do," she said. Yet, like a horse with blinders on, Julius tenaciously clung to the notion that he would prevail in the end.

Before the crucial vote, Iphigene invited Julius to lunch. She admired her cousin's integrity and honorable nature, but even if Arthur had not been a factor, she considered him the wrong man to lead the *Times*. "He was too righteous . . . and very conservative," she explained. "He wanted everything by the rules." Iphigene spared him this analysis during their lunch, out of consideration for his feelings, but she was blunt about how she intended to vote. Julius stiffened. "Frankly, it's a disappointment to me," he said with cool understatement. The news, expected though it should have been, made him physically ill. Arthur chaired the May 7 meeting of *The New York Times'* board, at which the decision made by the Ochs trustees was swiftly ratified. In its article about the succession, *Time* magazine called Arthur "the ideal crown prince."

The announcement of the first new publisher and president of *The New York Times* since 1896 was a story worthy of page one. But in deference to Julius, the news appeared discreetly on page seventeen of the May 8, 1935, issue of the paper. The article carefully noted that although Arthur Hays Sulzberger had won the top positions, Julius Ochs Adler had been appointed to the newly created post of *New York Times* general manager and elected publisher of *The Chattanooga Times* and president of The Chattanooga Times Printing Company. Arthur's statement of policies, printed on the editorial page, inauspiciously misquoted Adolph's famous "without fear or favor" salutatory, but he expressed the hope that, as publisher, he would "never depart from the principles of honest and impersonal journalism which [Adolph Ochs], with such force and courage, impressed upon our land." Julius struck a similar note in *The Chattanooga Times,* vowing to uphold the "cherished ideals" of his late uncle.

Among the older Ochses, there was thinly concealed dismay that Arthur had ascended the throne intended for Julius. Their congratulatory letters to Arthur mentioned both men, referring to them in the plural as Adolph's successors. "A prayer lurks in the depths of my heart that you and my precious boy may always feel strongly [sic] contentment and happiness in your association," Ada wrote in her usual florid style. Under the circumstances, "contentment and happiness" were highly unlikely. But, ever the good soldier, Julius gamely put the best face on his dashed ambitions. He vowed to be a loyal second-in-command, and over the next twenty years he was as good as his word.

In private, Julius's feelings were considerably more ambivalent. On one hand, he respected Arthur's intelligence and envied his sophistication and easy charm. "Arthur was outgoing and informal with people," said Julie Jr. "My father was strictly military." On the other, he worried about the effect on the paper of Arthur's more liberal thinking. Most of all, he was indignant that the control of the family's crown jewel — *The New York Times* — had gone not to a blood relative but to a son-in-law.

To salve his wounded ego, Julius quickly set about constructing a grand office with a big oak door at the eastern end of the fourteenth floor. When it was completed, it extended across the entire width of the building and featured a separate enclosure for multiple secretaries. Family members had always believed that, left to his own devices, Julius would have chosen the life of a soldier rather than that of a newspaperman, and his office decor buttressed the view. World War I helmets and rifles were perched atop the fireplace; to one side of his enormous desk stood the flag of the United States, and on the other the regimental flag of the fighting Seventy-seventh. Above the mantel were Julius's citations for bravery, and scattered around his vast domain were Napoleonic statuettes. He hired a number of ex-military men to serve on his staff, showing particular fondness for veterans of his former division, and inspected the uniforms of the *Times* guards for spit and polish. "He ran his part of the newspaper pretty much as his own personal army," said Punch.

The new publisher himself wisely declined to move into Adolph's immense chamber, electing instead to work out of a sizable but more modest warren of rooms next door, at the opposite end of the hall from Julius. "He didn't want people to think that he was just dropping into the slot vacated by Mr. Ochs," said Punch. Adolph's former headquarters was used for conferences and board meetings.

For all his fretting about succession, Adolph left his heirs with a messy transition. Although Arthur had virtually run the *Times* during Adolph's final illness, he had never been properly trained to be publisher. His apprenticeship had been haphazard and incomplete, a situation he later admitted made him feel frightened and alone when he finally assumed the reins. By installing Julius as a trustee of the Ochs Trust, Adolph also ensured that his nephew would be a permanent and immovable object in Arthur's organizational chart. Theoretically, Julius could be fired, but in reality he was a major stockholder with an independent power base within the family, and he had every right to expect favored treatment. "If there was any loyalty in the family, they had to take good care of him," said Ted Wagner, a lawyer and adviser for the clan decades later.

The result was that Arthur had little room to maneuver during his first days as publisher. He treated Julius with courtesy and continued to cede day-to-day oversight of the business and mechanical operations with no apparent qualms. These areas didn't interest him much in any case, and he gave Julius broad latitude, even when they disagreed. But in subtle ways he made certain that his general manager understood who had the ultimate authority. Each day Julius came to Arthur's office to report on business. In the two decades that they worked together, Arthur never made the trip down the long fourteenth-floor corridor to Julius's office — not once. Instead, said Julius's daughter Bobbie, "Arthur summoned him, like a copy boy."

The division of Adolph's job into two parts gradually created two warring camps — business and editorial — and nurtured a backbiting, courtier culture among the staff that was worthy of Louis XIV. "It was like children whose parents don't agree," said Amory Bradford, who would join the *Times* in 1947 and eventually replace Julius as general manager.

For Arthur, negotiating the delicate relationship with Julius was simple compared to bearing up under the oppressive weight of the Ochs mantle. At the time of Adolph's death, *The New York Times* was considered the best newspaper in the country, if not the world. Arthur's mission was not simply to maintain that distinction but to burnish it, fortify it, and make the paper even greater before passing it on to the next generation. The family, whose identity and values were inextricably entwined with those of the newspaper, expected and demanded no less.

Under the circumstances, Arthur felt it would be presumptuous of him to assume the role of patriarch. Instead, he adopted the role of steward, with a duty to preserve rather than create. The result was that he never had the innate self-confidence of an owner. "He didn't feel it was his," said Punch. "He felt it was a trust that had been handed to him, and he had a responsibility to it and to the family." When his managing editor, Edwin L. James, complained — as he often did — that he was just "a hired man," Arthur nodded sympathetically and told him, "I'm a hired man, too."

The inhibiting ghost of Adolph made him wary of sudden change. During the last years of the Ochs era, Arthur had participated in several planned innovations, including a merger of the rotogravure section with the Sunday magazine and a news digest feature, inspired by the success of *Time* magazine, called "The News of the Week in Review." But on his first day in the office after Adolph's burial, Arthur summoned the *Times'* picture editor and told him to put all format changes on hold for a year. "He didn't want the readers or the staff to feel a jolt," said Iphigene.

Financially, *The New York Times* was at a precarious point. Circulation had held up stoutly under the buffeting winds of the Depression, but advertising had plunged from 32 million lines in 1929 to a little over 19 million in 1935. Net income, which stood at an all-time high of $5.6 million the year of the crash, fell to $894,000 in 1936. To cut expenses, Sulzberger quickly sold off *Current History, Mid-Week Pictorial, American Year Book,* and *The Annalist,* editorial by-products that he rightly viewed as "millstones around our necks."

The entrenched, inefficient, and costly paternalism of the Ochs regime proved more difficult to eliminate. Under Adolph, *The New York Times* had been a family, with the publisher as its kindly, beneficent head. He knew the compositors by name; the lowliest employees received wedding gifts and, on hot summer days, free slices of ice cream. Bonuses were awarded arbitrarily, often after a personal plea to the publisher. Although Arthur himself had benefited handsomely — and with considerable embarrassment — from his father-in-law's generous Christmas checks, he gradually put a stop to the practice, instituting a system of salary increases based on merit. He valued the loyalty that Adolph's approach had fostered, but a bonus was a gift, he argued, something akin to charity. A raise was something employees earned for themselves.

Far more worrisome than paternalism or underperforming properties was the complicated matter of settling Adolph's $12.2 million estate. Samuel Untermyer, a friend and an attorney, had urged Adolph to transfer some of his holdings to Effie or Iphigene, but he refused, and even Abenia and Hillandale had remained in his name. As a self-made man, Adolph could not bring himself to relinquish control over any aspect of his empire, leaving an urgent problem for his heirs: how to pay federal and state death duties without jeopardizing control of *The New York Times* or, God forbid, being forced to sell the paper to raise funds.

Borrowing money from banks or wealthy individuals was an unacceptable solution; it would mean putting up *New York Times* stock as collateral and potentially giving outsiders power over the paper's decisions. On this point Arthur stood firm, ignorant of the fact that Adolph had done precisely that several times — first with Equitable and later with Marcellus Hartley Dodge.

Instead, Arthur came up with an ingenious plan under which The New York Times Company offered to purchase its outstanding 8 percent nonvoting preferred stock and then retire it. Most of these securities were held by the Ochs Trust and Ochs relatives, who had received them as generous gifts from Adolph throughout the booming 1920s. The sale generated enough money for the Ochs Trust to cover the nearly $6 million inheritance-tax bill, but it meant that the trust — the main source of funds for Iphigene — forfeited an income of $480,000 a year in preferred-dividend payments. Iphigene downplayed the sacrifice, for what was at stake was *The New York Times,* and that was far more important than money. The timing was particularly fortuitous: because of the Depression, the *Times* was valued at an artificially low level when Adolph died.

One person who was deeply unhappy about the *Times'* tax settlement was President Franklin D. Roosevelt, who had hoped that the paper's independence would be compromised by being beholden to banks or other outside interests to pay the bill. The president had long had an uneasy relationship with the *Times,* especially with its Washington bureau chief, Arthur Krock, a conservative, curmudgeonly Kentuckian who turned against the New Deal in 1936.

Roosevelt had seemed sanguine about the family's inheritance-tax strategy when Arthur first revealed it to him during a lunch at the White House on March 3, 1936, the same day the Corporate Surplus Bill was introduced in Congress. The legislation required companies to distribute earnings, something Arthur considered "un-American [and) destructive," a view he shared frankly with the president. Without the ability to accumulate earnings, Arthur told Roosevelt, the *Times* would never have had the surplus available to buy back its 8 percent preferred stock. Roosevelt listened and made no criticism.

The *Times* endorsed Roosevelt for reelection in 1936, but a year later lashed out at the administration for its plan to pack the Supreme Court, printing fifty editorials on the subject. Nevertheless, another lunch with the president, this time at Hyde Park, was cordial. But word soon filtered back to Sulzberger by way of Mississippi senator Pat Harrison that Roosevelt was furious with the *Times*. The president knew that the trust did not have the millions needed to pay the inheritance tax. He assumed that the family would have to borrow heavily or that a big block of its common stock would have to be sold, thus reducing the Sulzbergers' stake to less than a majority — a prospect that pleased him. Instead, the trust got a massive cash infusion from the company, through the company's purchase of the trust's preferred stock. Effectively, Arthur had found a legal way to use the corporation's money to pay the family's tax bill. And not a single share of voting stock was lost. "It's a dirty Jewish trick," Roosevelt had reportedly thundered to Harrison, referring to Arthur's plan to pay Adolph's death taxes and still maintain control of the paper. "When Iphigene dies, we will get [*The New York Times*]."

Within days, three more men — J. P. Morgan banker Thomas W. Lamont, presidential adviser Bernard Baruch, and Assistant Secretary of Commerce Richard Patterson — quietly came to Arthur and reported similar conversations. One quoted Roosevelt as saying that Adolph had violated the law, and that Arthur had confused his corporate and trust responsibilities. In a subsequent speech, Roosevelt lambasted the *Times* as a "fat cat" newspaper. Walter Winchell, a Roosevelt partisan whose column thrived on planted gossip, soon reported rumors that *The New York Times* was planning to sell its controlling stock. The *Times'* lawyers hurriedly assured the IRS that there was no truth to the matter.

The inheritance tax on Adolph's estate was fully paid in 1939. By then Arthur was embittered by the president's anti-Semitic remarks and his duplicitous behavior, telling his mother that he "wouldn't trust him from here to the door." To Iphigene, the feud between the president and the publisher was "ridiculous," but never one to confront her husband — or any man — directly, she quietly asked her father's old friend Henry Morgenthau Sr. to help her launch a behind-the-scenes peace initiative.

Morgenthau, whose son, Henry Jr., was then Roosevelt's secretary of the treasury, subsequently brokered a lunch between Arthur and the president at Hyde Park in late December 1939. The occasion got off to a shaky start when Sara Delano Roosevelt, the president's eighty-four-year-old mother, turned to Arthur and asked brightly, "Now, let me see, you're on the *Herald Tribune*, aren't you?" The subject of the Ochs estate came up only toward the end of the meal, when Roosevelt obliquely alluded to "personal statements" he had made about Adolph and Arthur. It was as close to an apology as Arthur ever got, and he accepted it. "I never told Arthur, to his dying day [that I had arranged this meeting]," Iphigene later confessed, adding, with the shrewd goodwill she had learned from her father, that Arthur "thought it was nice of the president to make this gesture . . . and the president was glad to hear . . . that he was willing to bury the hatchet and be friends."

§

On New Year's Eve 1935, as his first seven months at the helm of the *Times* came to a close, Arthur boasted to Frederick Birchall, the *Times'* Berlin correspondent, that advertising and circulation were gaining, "the paper is being favorably talked about . . . we have made no serious blunders and fortune has smiled." But the situation was hardly as upbeat as he portrayed it. Arthur had taken control of *The New York Times* at a critical moment in its history, a period during which it was challenged from within by the American Newspaper Guild and from without by isolationists who felt that the paper's editorial page was sounding a dangerous summons to another world war.

The American Newspaper Guild was founded as a union for newsmen in 1933, when many reporters were being thrown out of work or scraping by on severely reduced salaries. The concept quickly expanded to include ad salesmen, clerks, and cafeteria workers — any newspaper employee not covered by other unions. Adolph had had good relations with the so-called craft unions that represented the workers who manufactured and distributed the *Times*, as had Arthur. But in the late 1930s and early 1940s, when the Guild made clear its ambitions to unionize the paper's news staff, Arthur fought back fiercely.

He was not reflexively in opposition to labor. As a young man, Arthur had read *The Daily Worker* and *The New Masses*, two publications that, he hastened to say later, "were not then Moscow mouthpieces." Soon after becoming publisher, he modified the *Times'* work week to five days and forty hours and, much to Julius's consternation, did not protest the

Guild's organization of the paper's commercial departments in 1941. But like many of his fellow publishers, he strongly opposed unionizing journalists, fearing it would endanger objectivity and lead to a uniformly pro-labor viewpoint that would color news columns. "Could democracy be maintained if only Republicans reported and edited the news of the day?" he wrote in one of his many broadsides on the subject. When the Guild demanded a union shop — an arrangement under which *Times* reporters, photographers, and lower-level editors would be required to join the union — he flatly rejected the idea. "If we were ever obliged to [sign such a contract] . . . *The New York Times* would be for sale," he told a trial examiner for the National Labor Relations Board.

In 1942 the *Times* finally signed a Guild contract permitting unionization of its news and editorial departments, but at Arthur's insistence the document did not make union membership compulsory — a position he maintained throughout all subsequent negotiations. By then the leadership of the New York branch of the Guild was dominated by Communists, a development that only deepened Arthur's suspicions. Although an anticommunist faction within the Guild won control in 1948 and conducted a purge, Arthur was never convinced that the Guild did not represent a fifth column within the paper, and his antipathy toward the union that, he said, had "a pretty good record for making me sick to my stomach" only increased with the years.

As the memory of Adolph receded, Arthur gradually began to put his individual stamp on the paper, placing more photographs on page one, enlarging headlines, expanding the culture beats and number of domestic bureaus, and in 1942 introducing the now famous crossword puzzle. But it was on the editorial page that his impact was felt most acutely. Less than a year into his publishership, he named Anne O'Hare McCormick the first woman on the *Times'* editorial board, signaling an end to Adolph's extreme aversion to female journalists. Within months she was writing a signed column on foreign affairs.

Intrepid and levelheaded, McCormick possessed what Iphigene admiringly called "a real little mick face." She started at the paper in 1921 as a freelancer and became a regular contributor the following year, but although Adolph was pleased with her groundbreaking interviews with Mussolini and Stalin, he never permitted her to be hired on staff. Arthur and Iphigene agreed that putting McCormick on salary was long overdue, and their judgment was quickly vindicated: in 1937 she became the first woman to win a Pulitzer Prize in journalism. That same year Arthur struck another blow for women by hiring Ruby Hart Phillips as a correspondent in Havana.

An editorial page that reflected Arthur's strongly held views took a bit more time. Under Adolph, editorials had almost always been expository rather than evangelistic. In keeping with his philosophy, he had chosen scholarly men, classically trained, as his editorial chiefs. When Charles Miller died in 1922, Ochs replaced him with Rollo Ogden, sixty-four, a onetime minister at the Case Avenue Presbyterian Church in Cleveland who came to the *Times* from the New York *Evening Post*. Decked out in a frock coat, striped trousers, and wing collar, Ogden was Victorian in manner and nearly blind in his last years; he had to have the news read to him before writing his editorials.

This was the man Arthur unhappily inherited as the *Times'* editorial voice. On three separate occasions he walked into Ogden's office to ask him to retire; all three times his courage failed him. "I could no more talk to him than fly on my own," he said. Ogden's death soon solved the problem, but Arthur still felt inhibited about naming his own man. The paper's associate editor, Dr. John Huston Finley, a respected academic of the Ochsian mold who had been president of City College before joining the *Times,* dearly wanted the job vacated by Ogden. Arthur agreed, but only on the condition that Finley, seventy-three, would retire with the title of editor emeritus when he turned seventy-five.

Fate again intervened. Within a year Finley became too ill to continue, and Charles Merz, Arthur's friend and personal recruit, effectively ran the page. In November 1938, a month after Finley officially retired, Arthur appointed Merz "editor of the editorial page," permanently shelving the title "editor of *The New York Times*" under which his predecessors had worked.

By the time Merz took charge, he had forged an unusually close friendship with Arthur and Iphigene that included his wife, Evelyn, and their children. "We used to go on vacations together," recalled Iphigene. "They visited us all the time, always came for Christmas. There was never a family celebration without them. The children called them aunt and uncle." Tall and hefty, with steel-rimmed glasses, Merz, forty-five, had the appearance of a professor. His posture was so erect — the result of a painful back ailment — that reporters joked that he "bent over backwards" to be fair. Underneath this rather severe facade was a gentle, even-tempered man who shared Arthur's affinity for cocktails, puns, and parlor games. On weekends at Hillandale, the two composed Double-Crostics and huddled over jigsaw puzzles while Even, as Merz's wife was nicknamed, played Chopin on the piano. "We thought alike, we drank alike, and we played games alike," Arthur said of the person Iphigene came to count among her husband's "most true friends."

Educated at Yale and, like Arthur, a second lieutenant in World War I, Merz had practiced journalism at *Harper's Weekly, Collier's,* and *The New Republic* before joining the editorial board of Pulitzer's New York *World,* where he worked under Walter Lippmann. In 1931, a day before *The World* folded, he was hired at *The New York Times* on a "semi-temporary" basis, ostensibly to update Elmer Davis's 1921 *History of The New York Times* in time for Adolph's thirty-fifth anniversary as publisher. The book never appeared; the assignment, concocted by Arthur, was simply a way to persuade Adolph to hire Merz, whose work Arthur had long admired.

By the time Arthur finally had a free hand to select Merz as his editorial-page editor, the two men had coalesced as a team. Close in age, temperament, and political outlook, they shared the conviction that the *Times* must assume more leadership in national and international affairs than it had in the past. Arthur and Merz saw eye to eye on almost every issue. Their trust was so complete that in time Arthur stopped his practice of reviewing galleys of the next day's editorials.

But Merz had an additional and unacknowledged qualification for the job: he was not Jewish. Like Adolph, Arthur was skittish about showcasing Jews in *The New York Times.* Jewish reporters were convinced they got out-of-town assignments less frequently than Gentiles because such stories were more likely to merit bylines. And bylines that were granted to Jews played down their ethnicity. Abraham H. Raskin was "A. H. Raskin" to readers of the *Times;* Abraham Weiler was "A. H. Weiler." "I don't know that it was a hard-and-fast policy," said Doris Faber, who started out reporting for the *Times* under her maiden name, Greenberg. "That's just the way it happened to be."

One candidate who lobbied hard to head the editorial page was Washington bureau chief Arthur Krock. When he was passed over in favor of Merz, he was convinced it was because of backhanded anti-Semitism. The truth was that Krock's conservative views were simply not in tune with Arthur's, especially in regard to race. Krock did not consider himself Jewish, and technically he was correct; one's status as a

Jew derives from one's mother, and although Krock's father was Jewish, his mother was not. As an adult Krock became an Episcopalian, but most of the world did not recognize such distinctions.

Soon after Merz's appointment, Krock complained bitterly to his ally and patron, Joseph P. Kennedy, then ambassador to the Court of St. James's. At his first opportunity, Kennedy took up the issue with Sulzberger, telling him he was "terribly disappointed" that Krock had not been made editorial-page editor. Arthur assured Kennedy that he considered Krock "a most able newspaperman" but felt "he would be criticized if he appointed a Jew as Editor, since the ownership was in the hands of Jews." Thereafter, Krock took pains to maintain genial relations with Arthur, but he was openly hostile toward Merz. For most of the twenty-three years he ran the editorial page, Merz never submitted a *Times* editorial for a Pulitzer Prize. Krock had made it clear that any such efforts would be fruitless as long as he had influence with the Pulitzer board, on which he sat from 1940 to 1954.

Having come of age during a period of world war and repeated threats against democracy, Arthur matured into a fierce internationalist eager to thump the tub for America. He had pronounced opinions and, as he became comfortable in his role as publisher, was not timid about expressing them. "I do not believe that we should crusade in the generally accepted newspaper sense of taking up one subject and keeping continually at it," he wrote in a 1937 letter to Dr. Finley outlining the changes he hoped to make in editorial policy. "We should, however, have the crusading spirit which puts us first where wrong exists."

That spirit quickly focused on the troubled countries of Europe. In 1935 the *Times* urged sanctions against Italy for its invasion of Ethiopia, and shortly thereafter, when the first of the Neutrality Acts had been passed and an embargo placed on arms shipments to both belligerents, the paper criticized the restriction as "another ignoble chapter in American foreign policy." It led the charge to unshackle President Roosevelt from the Neutrality Act while at the same time pleading with Americans to support the principles of the League of Nations and "shoulder our responsibilities as a world power." The paper took a battering from isolationists, including many of Arthur and Iphigene's friends, who argued that it was leading the country to war, but the *Times* did not shrink from its stand. In 1936 it endorsed Roosevelt largely on the basis of its distaste for the "narrow nationalism" of the Republicans.

The world situation grew steadily more grave. In 1937 Japan invaded China, conquering most of the coastal area, while in Europe Hitler's imperialistic intentions became chillingly clear with the March 1938 annexation of Austria. Two months later Arthur traveled to Europe to hear the assessments of his foreign bureau chiefs and in London spent an hour and a half with British prime minister Neville Chamberlain. Their discussion left "no doubt in my mind that Germany represents a source of constant danger . . . [and] that Hitler is not to be trusted," he wrote in notes composed that night on Claridge's stationery. By the time Arthur returned home, he was convinced that a European war was imminent and that it might become an American war. He was just as certain that Americans, encased in their hard shell of isolationism, had to be persuaded that the rumblings of a distant conflict threatened their own interests.

Merz and the *Times'* editorial board agreed. The result was a full-throated editorial entitled "A Way of Life," written by Merz, which took up almost the entire editorial page on June 15, 1938. The *Times* predicted the advent of war and said that the United States would — and should — be prepared to defend "a way of life which is our way of life and the only way of life which Americans believe to be worth living." It was a piece Adolph Ochs would never have permitted, and it marked the beginning of a new era at *The New York Times*.

For Arthur, the editorial was a personal watershed. He joked that people often told him he had natural talent to be a decorator, a poet, or a landscape gardener; no one ever suggested that he had talent to be a publisher. Arthur would prove to have more aptitude for the job than he realized. "He is not at all what he modestly claims himself to be — a sort of pilot on a riverboat with the course already charted," said his daughter Ruth.

§

Adolph's death rearranged the landscape of the Ochs family with the force of an earthquake. Bound to their paterfamilias by love, emotional need, respect, and money, they careened without his reassuring presence. When Effie, clad in black, visited the Sulzberger home shortly after the funeral, Judy rushed up to greet her, but Effie did not answer. "She was very down," Judy recalled. "It was the first time I'd seen her like that." Ada, normally energetic, became so languid and unresponsive that she was confined to her room with a nurse. Mattie, complaining of "nerves," spent the summer of 1935 at a spa in Vichy.

Julius was soon thrust into his uncle's old role as Ochs family mediator. As publisher of *The Chattanooga Times,* his first move was to recruit Julian LaRose Harris, son of Joel Chandler Harris of Uncle Remus fame, from *The Atlanta Constitution* to serve as the paper's executive editor. Technically, Harris, fifty-seven, was subordinate to "A," Adolph's nephew and *The Chattanooga Times'* general manager, but Julius hoped that, because of the older man's experience and dynamic personality, "it will be [Harris] who will be the real General Manager."

Iphigene felt her father's loss more keenly than anyone, but there was little outward indication. Barely two weeks after the interment, she gave Milton several expensive suits Adolph had ordered shortly before he died. The gesture seemed coldly practical, but it was in keeping with Iphigene's habit of tamping down her feelings, particularly unpleasant ones. "It's her training: you just proceed, you don't let things trouble and bother you," said her granddaughter Jackie Dryfoos. "This is the way a good family operates." Her distaste for emotional exploration made her unwilling even to watch sad films or dramas. "Who wants to go to the theater or the movies to see things that are too close to the tragedies of real life?" she said.

So it was unsurprising that Iphigene's grief took the form of building monuments to her father, thereby enhancing the mystique of his memory and that of *The New York Times.* Over the next three decades, with Arthur's help, she promoted everything from an Adolph S. Ochs postage stamp to a spot for her father in the Hall of Fame for Great Americans at New York University. But in the years immediately following Adolph's death, it was the publication of a commissioned biography that dominated the Sulzbergers' efforts to honor him.

Earlier, Simon and Schuster had approached Adolph about writing a memoir, but he had politely refused, saying he might reconsider when "there are not better things to do." With the contact already made, Iphigene and Arthur selected Simon and Schuster for their project and in 1938 picked Claude Bowers, a former *New York Times* editorial writer who had become U.S. ambassador to Spain, to be the author.

It was not a happy arrangement. Bowers infuriated the Sulzbergers by missing deadlines, addressing correspondence to Arthur as "Dear Strasberger," and repeatedly misspelling Adolph's name. Arthur and Iphigene were not ideal patrons, either, for what they really wanted from Bowers was not a conventional biography but a high-minded panegyric to a free press, with Adolph as its exemplar. "My father's life was part and parcel of *The New York Times,* so it seems to me that his biography must be a history of that institution," Iphigene told Bowers. She thought it "unwise" to discuss Adolph's multiple depressions and saw no reason to mention his many travels, which, she said, were "no more important than, say, golf, in an average man's life."

After five years and a complete rewrite, Bowers abandoned the project, despairing of ever producing an acceptable book; he was paid $5,000. "I wanted to draw a portrait of a real human being," he said later. "But apparently the family wanted a steel engraving." In 1945 Arthur and Iphigene hired a second author, Gerald W. Johnson, a former Baltimore *Sun* editorial writer who had published biographies of Andrew Jackson, Woodrow Wilson, and others. When his work, *An Honorable Titan: A Biographical Study of Adolph S. Ochs,* came out the following year, it was reviewed on the front page of *The New York Times Book Review* on Sunday, August 18, the fiftieth anniversary of Adolph's assumption of ownership. In the end, Arthur thought the book "quite inadequate"; Iphigene disliked the portrayal of her father as a "stuffed shirt." Twelve years later, on the hundredth anniversary of Adolph's birth, the Sulzbergers considered commissioning a second biography but decided instead to run a long retrospective in the Sunday magazine. By then Adolph had hardened into precisely what Bowers had hoped to avoid: a steel engraving, an icon of American journalism, fixed in just the kind of exalted mythology the late *New York Times* publisher would have most appreciated.

§

After her father passed away, Iphigene had two new roles: wife of the publisher of *The New York Times* and — as one of three trustees of the Ochs Trust — key decision maker in the paper's future. Although careful never to upstage Arthur, settling instead for what she termed "pillow diplomacy," she nevertheless pointedly signed her name "Iphigene *Ochs* Sulzberger" and in private was not shy about making her views known. "She didn't want to do any damage to her husband's ego," said Abby Catledge, wife of *Times* editor Turner Catledge, "but deep down, she knew it was her paper." During the Spanish civil war, she sided with the republicans while Arthur remained skeptical of the cause. *Times* editorials, perhaps as a result, were blandly neutral. In conversations, letters, and memoranda, she goaded Arthur to pursue stories about education, welfare reform, and other issues that pricked her highly developed social conscience. "She was considerably more of a radical than my father," said Ruth.

Iphigene had no qualms about contacting top editors with her views, and for the most part, her interests never interfered with the objectivity of the *Times*. The one exception was parks, her enduring passion. She had joined the Park Association, a volunteer group, in 1928, and by 1935 was its president. "For a generation the parks were the *Times'* great and only crusade," a *Time* correspondent filed in a dispatch to his editor. The coverage was never sufficient, however, to satisfy Robert Moses, the city's tyrannical parks commissioner, who once called Iphigene a "jackass" in public.

Arthur's status as publisher of *The New York Times* instantly catapulted him to a new level of journalistic and civic involvement. He assumed Adolph's seat on the American Committee on Religious Rights and Minorities, one of the few outside activities in which the deceased publisher had participated. At Iphigene's urging, he reluctantly allowed himself to be put up for membership in the Century Association and, because of his position and highly placed gentile sponsors, had no problem being admitted. In 1938 he was elected a trustee of the Rockefeller Foundation, an honor that "marked the first time that I was selected for a post and did not reach it solely by inheritance," Arthur told John D. Rockefeller III many years later. "I was naturally most proud."

Their new responsibilities kept Arthur and Iphigene running at a furious pace during the late 1930s and early 1940s. Iphigene was often away attending meetings of her various groups. Arthur routinely came home late from the office and, if there was nothing on the social calendar, buried himself under a mound of paper. Ruth was instructed not to practice the piano on these evenings so as not to disturb him. Even the Sulzbergers' renowned New Year's Eve kitchen parties, which in earlier years had been filled with a cozy mixture of *New York Times* people, family, and old friends, became more star-studded and calculatedly business-oriented after Adolph's death. Figures like New York City mayor Fiorello La Guardia scrambled eggs alongside *Time* magazine founder Henry Luce and New York governor Thomas E. Dewey.

Iphigene and Arthur were in great demand on the social circuit and spent several evenings a week at dinner parties or official functions. At

5 East Eightieth Street, the Sulzbergers' elaborate preparations for a night on the town were an object of fascination. "We would watch them dress, and nothing in my life has ever impressed me as much as those two beautiful people decked out for an evening," said Ruth. When Arthur and Iphigene were ready to depart, Arthur would line up his children on the curved staircase in the front hall and kiss each one good night. On special occasions he allowed them to blow on his collapsed opera hat to pop it open.

Of the two, Arthur was by far the more glamorous figure, although both he and Iphigene placed a high premium on looks. Arthur teased Ruth about her "snoot," as he called her rather pronounced nose, and openly speculated about which Sulzberger female had the best legs, hair, or eyes. Iphigene valued her attractive face and beautiful skin, but she had little interest in fashion and favored simple classics over eye-catching couture. Arthur tried to update her profile by buying her clothes and personally selecting her dressmaker. His own tastes ran to the traditionally British. When in London, he patronized the tailors of Anderson & Sheppard on Savile Row and the shoemakers at Peal & Co. on Oxford Street. At home he insisted on sartorial order: inside his dresser drawers, his socks were neatly rolled and, like his boxer shorts, lined up according to color.

For a full year after Adolph's death, Iphigene and Arthur stayed close to home. But soon they were roaming the globe as often as their busy schedules allowed, using the power and privilege of their new positions to gather information for the benefit of the newspaper. When they went out West to look for a school for Marian, they prevailed on Arthur Krock to ask the head of the National Park Service and the acting director of the Bureau of Reclamation to arrange special tours of the Grand Canyon and Boulder Dam. The soil erosion they saw motivated Arthur to make conservation a regular assignment in the *Times'* Washington bureau.

A two-month trip to Europe and the Middle East early in 1937 introduced them to Palestine, where they witnessed firsthand the bitter hatreds then roiling Arabs, Jews, and the British as a result of the influx of European Jews fleeing Nazism. Arthur was so affected by the experience that he sat down in his hotel room one night and wrote a seven-page rumination on the immigration issue, some of which turned up several months later in a *New York Times* editorial headlined PARTITION OF PALESTINE.

Arthur and Iphigene were loving parents, as present and attentive as their frantic lives allowed, but there was also a certain coolness in the household, born of their frequent absences and the peculiarities of their personalities. Iphigene took an active interest in her children, listening to their problems, telling them stories, and overseeing their schoolwork. But having had an emotionally remote mother herself, she lacked conventional maternal warmth. Her aversion to being touched kept her from hugging her children or being physically demonstrative with her husband, and both she and Arthur were skittish about overt displays of emotion. In the Sulzberger household, it was embarrassing if anyone said "I love you" out loud.

Though Arthur overflowed with charm, his wit could turn acidic when his offspring displeased him. "It was a lot easier for him to relate to us when we were little," said one. "As we got minds of our own, he would get angry." Late one night Judy, whose fourth-floor bedroom was directly above his, became annoyed with a cat wailing in the yard next door. She got up, went to the window, and loudly yelled, "Shut up!" awakening Arthur from a deep sleep. The next afternoon when she came home from school, she noticed a stack of paper on the front hall table with a sign that read TAKE ONE. On the sheet was a poem, written by her father, entitled "Lines Written After Two Hours Sleep," in which he declared:

> It's my good fortune though, as I have said,
> That not to Judy will I e'er be wed.
> But, I assure you, it's not quite ideal
> To lie beneath her stormy iron heel
> And suddenly to have the ceiling quake
> And jolt from gentle sleep to wide-awake.
> To hear her heavy tread and angry shout,
> As vixen-like she leans herself without
> And bids the neighborhood a fierce 'shut up'
> In voice becoming as a female pup.
> And when some quiet does again prevail
> How I would like to boot her in the tail!

The Sulzbergers viewed their parental roles largely as that of teachers. When Arthur received a letter from thirteen-year-old Ruth, then visiting France with her mother and siblings, he was exasperated with her

"shockingly bad" handwriting. "You should make her take time and separate her letters — she runs them all together now in a ridiculous manner," he complained to Iphigene, adding rather grumpily that "after an
8-day trip [Ruth] might have written more than one page." Iphigene,
too, tended toward the sermonic with her children. One weekend when
Arthur and Iphigene were out of town, Marian invited her White Plains
neighbor, June Bingham Birge, to stay overnight at Hillandale. Both girls
received letters from their mothers at the same time. "I was sitting up in
bed chuckling and giggling [over my letter]," said June, "and Marian was
glowering because her mother had told her to work harder and get better marks. Marian didn't want to hear that."

Like many children of prominent families, Marian, Judy, Ruth, and
Punch spent much of their time in the company of governesses, cooks,
butlers, and chauffeurs. At night when their parents were gone, they
would lie in bed and hear the servants talking and laughing in their
spare quarters on the top floor. "We were all alone in that huge house
with these voices from upstairs," said Ellen Sulzberger Straus, who often
stayed overnight with her cousins. "It was a lonely existence." Punch was
particularly close to the family retainers and regularly sought out the
safety of the kitchen when his parents entertained.

Primary among the caretakers was Jeanne Lajus, the French governess, who took up residence in the Sulzberger home with Boo-Boo,
her toothless Pekingese, in the early 1930s. Tall, thin, with a great mass of
frizzy hair, Mme. Lajus had been hired as a replacement for Punch and
Judy's kindly Irish nurse, Nana, because Iphigene wanted the children to
learn French. She accomplished her goal: Mme. Lajus spoke French constantly with the young Sulzbergers, and they became fluent. But in the
process, the "dragon lady," as one visitor called her, managed her charges
with a military rigor that was both comical and cruel. Compulsively
neat and orderly, Mme. Lajus was a firm believer in schedules. Clothes
for the next day were laid out the night before. If a child did not produce
a bowel movement promptly after breakfast, Mme. Lajus would threat-
eningly appear with a glass of orange juice laced with castor oil. Her
methods bordered on the sadistic. When Punch and Judy discovered a
tiny field mouse in their bathtub at Hillandale, Mme. Lajus turned on
the water and forced the children to watch as the poor creature swam
frantically around the tub until it finally gave up in exhaustion and
drowned.

When they were younger, Punch and Judy had formed a warm sibling bond, often talking at night across the expanse between their beds. Upon Mme. Lajus's arrival, however, Judy moved in with her, and Punch inhabited a room by himself. Soon, said Judy, "we got so we fought all the time. She pitted us against each other." Sensitive, rebellious, and iconoclastic, Judy was dubbed "the duchess" by her father and "the spoiled brat" by her cousin, Cy Sulzberger. To Mme. Lajus, she was a made-to-order headache. At Hillandale the two once got into such a row that Mme. Lajus slapped Judy in the face. To her amazement, the girl slapped back, and then fled over the manicured lawn with the wiry governess in pursuit until she came upon the soft sanctuary of Effie, who halted the chase by enfolding her granddaughter in her arms, fixing a fierce gaze on Mme. Lajus and exclaiming, "You leave her alone!"

Marian and Ruth were old enough to escape the worst of Mme. Lajus's excesses, and with Judy as lightning rod, Punch was relatively safe as well. As a small boy, he had a short fuse; he once struck his Chattanooga cousin Billy Ochs on the head with a croquet mallet because he was mad about losing. But as he matured, Punch developed a deceptively even-tempered way of dealing with disagreeable requests. Whereas Judy would scream and yell when asked to do something she didn't want to do, and then do it, Punch would simply nod sweetly and say, "Yes, yes, I'll do it," then proceed to do nothing of the kind.

Thrown together by their parents' frequent absences, and united against a common foe — Mme. Lajus — the four Sulzberger children gradually became a closed corporation. "We weren't competing so much for our parents' attention except when they were around," said Judy. "And when they weren't around, it made us close." Like Iphigene, who had been raised among extended relatives and few outsiders, the young Sulzbergers were warm rather than intimate, and keenly aware of the fifth child in their midst: *The New York Times*. "They were brought up as royalty," observed a Hillandale neighbor and contemporary. "They had their responsibilities, and the *Times* was the kingdom."

The task of inculcating the Sulzberger children with the significance of *The New York Times* fell to Eddie Greenbaum, the family's attorney and valued friend. Once a year or so, beginning when Punch was eleven, Greenbaum gathered the young Sulzbergers in his office at Greenbaum, Wolff & Ernst for free-ranging discussions about the newspaper, the structure of Adolph's will, and the hazy, distant future when, as a group, they would inherit and control *The New York Times.* "He kept drumming into our little heads, 'This is yours; you'd better learn it,' " said Marian.

Under Greenbaum's tutelage, the Sulzbergers mastered what subsequent generations of the family came to call "the rules of the road." At the philosophical center of the list was the exalted importance of *The New York Times* — "the holy *New York Times*," as Judy ruefully called it — and the relative insignificance of the family. "We were never ever allowed to think that we were special," said Ruth. "The idea was, through the service of the family, to keep the newspaper together." Conflict was to be avoided, and it was considered bad manners to discuss money. *Times* profits were to be plowed back into the paper to make it better, not to enrich their lives. Even after he grew up and went to work at the *Times* himself, Punch never knew how much his father made. Years later a New York Times Company director would marvel that the four Sulzbergers viewed the newspaper more as a public institution than a private possession, saying, "It's as if they were overseeing the National Gallery of Art."

As they grew older and more capable of understanding the intricacies of the business, Greenbaum debated with his charges whether family members should hold certain jobs or cede them to trained professionals. The message he conveyed was always a little mixed: yes, family members should be involved at the highest levels of the paper, but they must rise on merit and be treated like everyone else. "The feeling was: you're not entitled to anything," said Marian's daughter Susan Dryfoos, who, along with the rest of her generation, eventually inherited the "rules of the road." "You're entitled to serve, but not to have power or a certain position."

The tone of Greenbaum's seminars was relaxed and jocular, a form of indirect communication with which the Sulzberger siblings felt comfortable. The truth was that while the Sulzberger children fully embraced the lessons of family unity, they were often bored with talk of stock transactions and trusts. Judy regularly nodded off in Greenbaum's law office and eventually came to resent the newspaper, which she considered a rival for her parents' attention. "Around the dinner table we'd always be talking about what happened at *The New York Times,* not what I did in school," she said. "I thought, 'Damn the paper!' I just felt I was competing with this faceless Gray Lady."

13

Married to *The New York Times*

L
IKE MANY FAMILIES, THE SULZBERGERS PIGEON-
holed their children. Marian was the Pretty One, Ruth was the
Scholar, Judy was the Rebel, and Punch was the Hapless One. So
fixed were these notions that when Effie died in 1937 and the Sulzbergers
inherited Hillandale, Iphigene automatically assigned Marian the bedroom with a dressing table and Ruth the bedroom with bookcases. "I
thought to myself, 'How does she know *I* don't want a dressing table?' "
said Ruth.

In part, the stereotypes reflected each child's performance in school.
Because of her own unhappy experiences with traditional education at
Dr. Sachs's and Benjamin-Deane, Iphigene enrolled her oldest children,
Marian and Ruth, in the Lincoln School, an experimental adjunct to
Teachers College at Columbia. The teaching methods were so unstruc-
tured that by the seventh grade Marian could barely read or write and
Ruth hadn't the slightest notion of geography or the multiplication
tables.

By the time Arthur and Iphigene realized their mistake, the girls were
so far behind that they had to be privately tutored before they could be
accepted at other institutions. Ruth spent a semester studying for the
entrance exams to Brearley, a private school on the Upper East Side, but
flunked every one and had to be tutored five days a week for an entire
summer before she finally managed to get in. Even then, the school
made her repeat a grade. Once accepted, she soon caught up and
excelled, becoming a prefect and playing class basketball.

A year of tutoring likewise enabled Marian to get into Rosemary Hall,
a boarding school near White Plains where she played tennis and
jumped horses, but the school quickly decided that she was not up to its
standards. After a summer touring Europe in the company of a female
tutor and chaperone, Marian entered Manhattan's Lenox School, the

college preparatory school for the now defunct Finch College. She barely managed to graduate.

By her own admission, Marian was lazy and didn't apply herself. At one point Arthur became so discouraged with his daughter that he suggested she quit school and go to work. "Nonsense," Iphigene told him. "Marian does need to learn something." A large part of Marian's difficulty was due to dyslexia, the same learning disorder that had plagued her mother. A Philadelphia psychologist correctly diagnosed the condition, and the Sulzbergers found special teachers. By then, however, Marian was more interested in boys than in Balzac. "She was the world's worst student," said Iphigene.

Judy benefited from her sisters' academic misfortune, sidestepping the Lincoln School in favor of the Froebel League, a laboratory school for kindergarten teachers, then handily entering Brearley a year before Ruth. She did well, singing in the chorale and participating in dramatics. Each morning as the Sulzbergers' chauffeur drove Judy and Ruth to school in the family's limousine, Judy lay on the floor, embarrassed at being seen in such an ostentatious car. Getting her to school at all was a major undertaking. "She'd kick and scream that she was dying, she had a stomachache and couldn't go," recalled Punch.

On the whole, the Sulzbergers' was a secular household. Despite Arthur's being a trustee and member of Temple Emanu-El and a member of the Central Synagogue, where Iphigene's uncle was a rabbi, the family attended temple only on high holy days, and even then not faithfully. Iphigene and Arthur never hosted a Passover seder, normally spending the holiday at the home of Roger Straus, a founder of the publishing company of Farrar, Straus & Giroux. On Rosh Hashanah and Yom Kippur, the children were kept out of school, but according to Judy, they didn't know why. Even lox and bagels were unknown in the Sulzberger house.

Arthur and Iphigene did, however, make a conscious attempt to familiarize their children with Judaism. For several years the three girls, their cousin Ellen, and Eddie Greenbaum's son, David, met in the basement of 5 East Eightieth Street for Bible classes. The family's Jewish identity was of little consequence when the children were small. The Lincoln School was heavily populated by Jews, including Henry Morgenthau Jr.'s son, Bob, and Rube Goldberg's two boys. But at Rosemary Hall Marian was one of only four Jews, and at Brearley Ruth was one of two. The year she entered, everyone in her class attended a certain dancing class, and Ruth told her mother she wanted to go, too. Iphigene made a few inquiries and then matter-of-factly told her, "You can get into that dancing school if I grovel, but I'm not going to grovel, so you're not going to go."

Although Marian and Ruth weren't happy about being passed over for gentile debutante parties and other social events, they took it in stride. For Judy, the embarrassment of exclusion cut deeply. She was terribly wounded when a friend at Brearley told her, "I'd love to ask you to our summer place in Southampton, but we can't invite Jews." When her cousin Ellen innocently dubbed her Ju for short, Judy insisted that she change the nickname to J.P. — her first and middle initials. "I was very anti-Semitic," said Judy. "I felt because I was Jewish, I was less attractive. I didn't have the same boyfriends that my friends had." At fourteen she announced that she didn't want to be a Jew, indeed that she didn't believe in organized religion at all. Her father advised her to "write all your feelings down and talk to me about it when you're older."

As the youngest child and the only boy, Punch sailed above the social slights that tortured his sisters. "I was raised in a very protective household," he said. "Anti-Semitism just washed over my head." Like his sisters, Punch received a dollop of Jewish education, but he learned almost nothing; when the time came for him to be bar mitzvahed, Arthur and Iphigene let the date pass without comment. "I think they knew it was hopeless," he said.

"Hopeless" was also an apt description of Punch's experience as a student. Like Marian, he suffered from a learning disability that caused him to lack concentration and reverse letters and numbers. To make matters worse, he was left-handed, a condition considered improper at St. Bernard's, the strict British school on East Ninety-eighth Street that Arthur and Iphigene chose for their son. Each time Punch wrote with his left hand, the teacher hauled him up in front of the class and whacked him over the hand with a ruler. When he tried to write compositions with his right hand, the results were so indecipherable that for a while he had to trace letters using special cardboard stencils. Punch said the brutal regimen "screwed me up in spades," but the result was that he became ambidextrous, writing with his right hand and throwing a ball with his left.

Iphigene met with the headmaster and Punch's teachers; nothing they did penetrated his resolute indifference to learning. "I just wasn't very responsive," he said. "I said, 'I'll do better, I'll do better,' but I really didn't. I didn't like it very much." Punch's lack of progress prompted his parents to move him to Browning, a private academy on the Upper East Side, but he did no better there. "Nearly every school in the vicinity of New York was graced with Punch's presence at one time or another," Ruth said later. "They were all delighted to have him but wanted something other than a spectator."

Punch was an unusually self-contained boy, fastidious in dress and appearance, polite, and seemingly pliable. Quiet and somewhat timid, he had "a" friend when others had many, and was content to pursue solitary hobbies — collecting seashells, china eggs, and hotel soap; tinkering with gadgets; and hunting for turtles in the Hillandale gardens. At his first political convention in 1936, he lingered over the news ticker, more interested in how the machine worked than what the words said.

At home Punch had few unconditional allies. His mother clearly loved him, but as she put it later, "There was no worship on either side." And Arthur, with his artistic tastes and temperament, was not naturally drawn to his son, who, though small for his age, excelled at traditional masculine pursuits such as track and soccer — activities for which Arthur had no talent and even less interest. "He just never really gave Punch the time of day," said Judy. Even those loving paternal gestures he did make contained bite. On the occasion of Punch's thirteenth birthday, he wrote:

> Of all the sons I've ever had
> You are the best one for your Dad.
> But don't forget that rating first
> May also mean you are the worst!

With few friends his own age, and a father who spent little time with him, Punch grew up in a largely female world. As he approached adolescence, Iphigene worried about the lack of masculine role models. Her solution was to hire male companions for Punch: an arts and crafts teacher from the Mount Vernon school system named Mr. Raffo, and a young British graduate student at Columbia named Brinley Rhys, who tutored Punch for six hours a day and occasionally roller-skated with him in Central Park. Rhys was soon replaced by an attractive, French-speaking Columbia law student named Thibaut de Saint Phalle, a cousin of the famous sculptor Nikki de Saint Phalle.

Tip, as the Sulzbergers called him, became a fixture in the Sulzberger home, playing the part of tutor and big brother to Punch, father confessor to Ruth and Judy, and boyfriend to Marian. During his job interview, he had asked Iphigene what she wanted him to do. "I want you to help Punch grow up," she replied, but it was a task that Thibaut pursued with less than total enthusiasm. In deference to his Columbia commitments, he spent only weekends and summers with the family, drilling Ruth for her college entrance exams as she lounged by the Hillandale pool and courting Marian while Judy and Punch giggled from behind the protective shield of a hedgerow. With Punch, he did little schoolwork, preferring instead to accompany him to the movies, share a game of tennis, or toss a football.

As time went on, Thibaut became particularly close to Arthur, driving out to Hillandale with him on Friday afternoons and back into the city on Monday mornings. "He was like a father to me," he said. "I really loved that man." So filial was the relationship that Arthur broadly hinted there might be a job waiting for Tip at the paper when he finished law school. "I think he would've liked very much if I'd married Marian and gone to work for the *Times* and eventually taken his [place]," said Thibaut. But the romance eventually cooled, and he went on to become a successful lawyer and investment banker, later ending up as director of the Export-Import Bank.

After the Ochses' death, Arthur and Iphigene, horrified by the combined cost of maintaining Hillandale and Abenia, put both properties on the market. With the aid of an auction house, they located a buyer for Abenia — a friend of Adolph's from Lake George who got the Victorian mansion and three hundred acres for just $35,000. But at the height of the Depression, it proved impossible to sell Hillandale, and soon the Sulzbergers gave up trying.

The children were just as glad. For them, Hillandale was part playground, part amusement park, part resort, and part family homestead, a tie to their late grandparents and the scene of many of their fondest memories. On rainy days they loved to shoot billiards in the estate's cavernous ballroom or play bounce in the spacious library on the third floor directly across from Punch's bedroom. Fair weather found them splashing in the pool or playing baseball in the Hillandale field. The house saw such a constant stream of relatives, dignitaries, *Times* editors, and accomplished neighbors that Arthur joked that Iphigene "runs a hotel." "There were crowds of people around, between the butlers and the nurses and the nannies and the four children," said Ellen Sulzberger Straus, a frequent guest. "You can't conceive of what the meals were like. Aunt Iphigene was like an administrator."

With its grand ballroom, 1,200-square-foot living room, large dining room, and broad lawns, Hillandale was ideal for entertaining. Beginning in 1938, when Arthur was elected to the board of directors of the Associated Press, the Sulzbergers regularly hosted a Sunday luncheon to kick off the annual board meeting the next day. The dazzling guest list included presidential candidates and government officials as well as editors and managers of the *Times* and other New York newspapers.

Though they rarely read the paper, the young Sulzbergers knew more about current events than most people their age simply from listening to household conversations. At one AP lunch Mayor William O'Dwyer, "Bill-O," then under a cloud for alleged complicity with organized crime, approached Judy's nearly full table as if he might join them. She turned to the group and said with knowing sophistication, "Don't let Mayor O'Dwyer have the extra chair. It would be too degrading."

One year Colonel Robert McCormick, publisher of the *Chicago Tribune,* made a dramatic and ungracious entrance by arriving in a bright red helicopter emblazoned with gold lettering that read THE CHICAGO TRIBUNE, AMERICA'S GREATEST NEWSPAPER. Arthur had carefully instructed McCormick to land in a nearby field, but he descended instead in the middle of the Sulzbergers' lawn just as their guests were having drinks. The wind and commotion sent people flying in all directions. "He was an extraordinarily self-centered character," said Iphigene.

§

Several months after the first AP party, Hillandale had a more controversial guest: Madeleine Carroll. Arthur first met the stunning twenty-nine-year-old British actress on board the SS *Normandie* in May 1938, three years after her success in *The 39 Steps* and the year after David O. Selznick's *The Prisoner of Zenda.* Madeleine was on a mission to Europe to promote *Blockade,* her provocative new film about the Spanish civil war. Seated together at the captain's table, Arthur, Madeleine, and several members of minor European royalty stayed up until well past 4:00 A.M. three nights in a row drinking and dancing. The group reunited in Paris, and by the time Arthur returned to New York in June, he was thoroughly smitten with "la belle Madeleine."

Whether Arthur began his affair with Madeleine Carroll when he met her or later on is unknown. But among family members and close friends, it was widely assumed that the relationship was a full-blown romance. In addition to her beauty, glamour, and celebrity, Carroll possessed vivacity, strength, intelligence — unlike most actresses, she was college-educated — and a British primness that no doubt appealed to Arthur's Anglophilia. Perhaps the attraction simply came down to what Madeleine once jokingly referred to as her worst vice: "my passion for making conquests." In the letters they exchanged over the next twenty-five years, Arthur called her Marie (her real name was Marie-Madeleine); she called him Wings.

Madeleine first visited Hillandale in the summer of 1938, prompting Arthur's teenage niece Jean Sulzberger to write a mocking poem for her uncle that began "On one thing he will always dote / 'Tis meeting Carroll on a boat." It then slyly went on to observe how "strange" it was that on the day she stayed at the Sulzbergers', "All his family were away." From then until her marriage to Andrew Heiskell in 1950, Madeleine was an intermittent weekend guest at Hillandale, whenever her work and travel schedule permitted.

Arthur did not hide his lover from Iphigene, who was almost always present during such visits and reigned with grace and imperturbability over the clamorous Hillandale dinner table. "I think she preferred not to have it behind her back," said Thibaut, who, as a fellow Roman Catholic, attended Sunday mass with Carroll whenever she was in residence. The Sulzberger children were largely oblivious to the modern marital arrangement in their midst. Only later did they come to understand that Madeleine was their father's mistress and that he had had affairs before and after her. Marian was sixteen when she first heard the whispers. "Suddenly it dawned on me that he wasn't perfect, that he had his girlfriends, that he went his way and Mother held the place together," she said.

Even before Adolph died, there had been speculation that Arthur had his eye on Mabel Rossbach, the thin, chic wife of his Hillandale neighbor

Max Rossbach and the mother of Marian's close friend June. As teenagers, the two girls openly wondered whether their parents were sexually involved. Years later in a poem, Marian wrote, "June's Mom / My Pop / We think they liked each other an awful lot." Whether Arthur actually consummated that particular infatuation is open to question, but it is indisputable that he had a number of extramarital liaisons during his long life. "He had lady friends," said Punch. "I don't know whether he necessarily slept with all of them."

The Sulzbergers' marriage had begun to cool during the 1920s and 1930s. Arthur still made homemade valentines and wrote Iphigene sentimental birthday poems, but by the time Punch was born in 1926, the couple, then in their thirties, slept in separate bedrooms. Years later Iphigene confided to Marian that she "didn't care much for sex." She had no talent for flirting or being coy, and though she appreciated Arthur's puns and lighthearted humor, she was by nature rather serious. "Iphigene really had a wall," said Thibaut. "I don't think anybody ever got through that wall. Arthur respected her enormously as a person, but she was not the kind of person you could throw your arms around. [It must have been] very difficult for a man like Arthur to be married to a woman like Iphigene."

As important an explanation for Arthur's seeking relationships with other women was his nagging sense that he was not his own man. "When you work for your wife's father, there's an enormous desire to assert yourself in some way," said Charley Bartlett, a family friend and former Washington correspondent for *The Chattanooga Times*. In all his years as publisher, Arthur literally never made a speech without mentioning that he had gotten his job by "marrying the boss's daughter," as if by acknowledging it first, the taint would somehow be removed. When *Times* editor Turner Catledge informed him that one reason the paper had never had a female education editor was that she would have to "superintend the work of males," Arthur cheerily said, "That's done in my home!" Bedding beautiful women boosted his self-confidence, gave him something indisputably his own, and kept Iphigene off balance, thereby maintaining his masculine prerogatives of power and potency. "I just bet that [Iphigene] understood that," said Elly Elliott, a family friend who thought Arthur might have made a pass at her mother after she was widowed in 1940. "She [Iphigene] didn't take it so much as being against her as having to do with his ego."

On the surface Iphigene was remarkably tolerant of Arthur's infidelities. "She never raised a finger about it," said Sally Reston, who spent several weekends at Hillandale with her husband when Arthur's girlfriends were in attendance. "She would always sit and talk to [these women] alone in the most intelligent and polite way." In later years she even competed for their attention. Once she invited *Times* editor Clifton Daniel and his wife, the former Margaret Truman, to dinner to meet a handsome, middle-aged French woman she knew. During the course of the meal, Iphigene proudly told the Daniels, "You know, this lovely woman started out as Arthur's friend, but now she's mine."

"I am all for good old Victorian and French hypocrisy," Iphigene once said, adding that she agreed with the adage "If you have not virtue, at least assume its mantle." Raised by a father who himself had an eye for the ladies, Iphigene firmly believed, as she told Martin Ochs, that "men have sexual needs that don't have anything to do with love. . . . Women are the only ones who can control their emotions." Besides, she loved Arthur and wanted him to remain publisher. "The rest of us can get divorced," said June Bingham Birge. "But when your husband's career is also in your power, you think twice and turn the other way if you don't want to destroy the guy." Paramount in Iphigene's mind was her duty to preserve the dynasty her father had built. "I think she endured [the dalliances] because her family was the most important thing," said her friend Audrey Topping. "If she had to put up with her husband's [affairs] to keep the family together, she did it. She was married to *The New York Times.*"

Still, that her husband sought the intimate companionship of women more attractive than her wounded Iphigene deeply. Madeleine Carroll was a particular threat. Iphigene once confided to her friend Lady Susan Pulbrook, the wife of the chairman of Lloyd's of London, that she had been "terribly hurt" when "this beautiful creature crept into [our lives]." But for the most part, she buried her pain. "She concealed [the affairs] from herself," said *Times* correspondent Harrison Salisbury. "It was a conscious strategy."

As a result of this intricate dynamic, Iphigene grew to be unusually lacking in self-assurance around Arthur, and he took advantage of this insecurity by denigrating her in front of others. "She was very tentative when she talked in front of Arthur," said John Oakes's wife, Margary.

"Very often he would cut her down with this withering wit of his. I think her consummate goal in life was to please Arthur and just make him love her." Once during a birthday celebration, Arthur got up from his place at the table, walked over to where she was sitting, ceremoniously pulled a small jewelry box out of his pocket, and handed it to Iphigene. Inside was a pig made out of seashells with the message "Happy Birthday to My Shellfish Pig."

Members of the family gossiped about how he mistreated her, but she seemed not to notice what others viewed as her husband's insulting behavior. At least she never admitted it, preferring instead to apply a rosy gloss to even the most traumatic and tender memories. "I don't think she really ever saw her relationship with Daddy as clearly as anybody else saw it," said Judy. "[Even after he died] she said he never did anything that humiliated or hurt her. Ever."

§

Arthur and Iphigene did not host their annual New Year's Eve kitchen party in 1940. Instead, guests received a typed message headed NOT AN INVITATION announcing that the Sulzbergers had decided to "fold the family wings around ourselves, retire to a quiet spot in the country and drink our toast to the New Year with a touch of solemnity." A week later they headed south for a monthlong vacation at the Jupiter Island Club in Hobe Sound.

Elsewhere the country was in a state of suspension, sharply aware of the problems abroad but tentatively optimistic at the first flush of prosperity in more than a decade. Unemployment was down by nearly 2 million from the previous year, workers were putting in double shifts, and car manufacturers were having their best year since the crash. But for Arthur, the war in Europe had inflamed a heightened sense of urgency. Shortly after Hitler's invasion of Poland in September 1939, Britain and France declared war against Germany; within months France was near collapse. As Arthur watched the unprepared nations of Europe crumble before Hitler's armies, the *Times* continued its crusade for American readiness.

Gradually he came to the conclusion that battling isolationism was not sufficient. In early June 1940 he gathered his editorial board together. "I cannot live with myself much longer, and I doubt that this country can live with itself much longer," he said. "We have got to do something." During the discussions that followed, it was decided that the *Times* should advocate universal military training, a stand Julius had urged for months without success. The first of a series of editorials appeared June 7; a week later the Germans entered Paris. President Roosevelt quickly endorsed the position of *The New York Times,* the only major paper at the time to support a peacetime draft. By the end of the month, Congress took up a selective service bill, and Julius was asked to testify.

As a result of the *Times*' bold stand, Arthur and Julius received hundreds of threatening letters and phone calls from people accusing them of turning young men into cannon fodder. *The New Masses* suggested that Roosevelt himself had planted the draft editorials. By the fall of 1940 the strain of events had begun to show on Arthur. He had trouble sleeping and would often get up in the middle of the night and paint. One self-portrait shows a man in an unbuttoned blue shirt set against a blue background, his blue eyes staring back at the viewer with haunting directness. "These are sad and weary days," Arthur wrote an advertising manager in the *Times*' London bureau. "I only hope that we will not all be too old before we can again lie under the trees and watch the clouds sail overhead with no other thought."

Despite his bitter experience with the army, Arthur had hoped to sign up for the service as soon as the draft became effective, but the military would not take him because of the coronary attack he had suffered eight years earlier. Julius, who had advanced in rank as a reservist since World War I, departed in October with a year's leave of absence from the *Times,* a move that halved his salary, and enlisted for active duty. He was assigned to train men at Fort Dix in New Jersey, and in less than a year, Roosevelt nominated him to be a brigadier general.

Arthur's resolve regarding the war was matched by his politics. Disturbed by Roosevelt's fiscal policies, court packing, and bid for a third term, the *Times* in 1940 took the unusual step of endorsing Wendell Willkie, a Republican and Sulzberger family friend, for president. Under Adolph, the *Times* had described itself as "independent Democratic," although in fact it had backed two Republicans during his long tenure. The Willkie endorsement, coming as it did during a period of heightened tensions abroad and at home, was widely viewed as Arthur's attempt to drop *Democratic* from the phrase. The paper lost circulation as a result, but Arthur held firm because he thought "that Willkie had a correct international point of view."

§

In the summer of 1940 Judy visited her relatives in Chattanooga while Ruth traveled by car from Los Angeles to Seattle with her cousin Jean Sulzberger. A tall, striking girl of nineteen, Ruth had just completed her freshman year at Smith College, where she had earned the unfortunate nickname of Slutz because her *New York Times* subscription had arrived the first week mistakenly addressed to "Ruth Slutzberger." Consumed with patriotic fervor, Arthur had urged his second daughter to do war work in a factory instead of going to college, but Iphigene had overruled him, arguing that the country needed educated people more than it did factory workers.

Punch spent the summer playing at Hillandale and taking occasional lessons with Thibaut. He was still small for his age and lagged academically. Iphigene and Arthur considered sending him to Culver Military Academy in Indiana, the same school in which Julius's son, Julie Jr., had enrolled two years earlier, but Punch recoiled at the prospect of such rigid structure and instead, in the fall of 1940, began at Loomis, an all-male boarding school in Windsor, Connecticut. "In comparison to Culver, I would have taken anything," he said.

At twenty-two, Marian was in the last year of a three-year teacher-training program at the Froebel League, where Judy had gone to nursery school. Given her dyslexia and aversion to studies, teaching was an unnatural vocational choice, one made more to mark time between the end of high school and the beginning of marriage than to pursue a career. As a teenager, Marian had been unusually attractive, with long black braids and dark eyebrows; by her early twenties, she had matured into a young woman with unbounded confidence in her looks and charm, and none in her intelligence.

Young Jewish women of Marian's age and station regularly attended dances organized by families of similar backgrounds. It was at one such party, hosted by her parents, that Marian met Orvil Dryfoos. As with many important moments in her life, Marian could only vaguely remember their first encounter. "He claims someone told him to cut in on me and no one came and cut out," she said. "Doesn't sound altogether true, but anyway . . . we met at a dance." Orvil was so short that he wore lifts, but he was a terrific dancer, with twinkling brown eyes, a flirtatious smile, and a cheerful disposition. He and Marian shared a love of sports and had many mutual friends; soon they were seeing a lot of each other.

Like Marian, Orvil accepted life as it was and did what was expected of him. "I can't think of an unconventional or daring thing Orv has ever said or done," said a close relative. He possessed a sweetness rare in men, and a physical warmth and informality that was a welcome counterpoint to the chill of the Sulzberger home. When Orvil visited Marian at her East Eightieth Street house, he did not hesitate to hug her siblings or ask them occasionally to scratch his back. With Iphigene and Arthur out at dinners and official functions, and Ruth and Punch away at school, he often had Marian and Judy to himself in the evenings. Sensing Judy's loneliness, he would climb the stairs to her room and in a brotherly fashion kiss her good night. "I had a crush on him," Judy said. "I thought he was wonderful."

Arthur and Iphigene were unaware of how serious Marian and Orvil had become until one morning early in 1941, soon after they had returned from their winter vacation in Hobe Sound, Marian approached her father as he was eating breakfast and said, "Daddy, guess what? I got engaged last night, and I'm going to marry Orvil!" Arthur looked up at his daughter blankly and said, "That's wonderful. Orvil who?" That evening when Orvil paid a call on his future in-laws, Judy rushed up, threw her arms around him, and offered her congratulations. Arthur and Iphigene awkwardly extended their hands.

Superficially at least, Orvil was an agreeable match for Marian. His grandfather, Otto E. Dryfoos, had emigrated to New York from Germany in 1865, founded a hosiery manufacturing firm, and amassed a fortune sufficient for him to buy a town house on the same block of East Eightieth Street that the Sulzbergers would later inhabit. When Otto died in 1928, he left an estate of nearly a quarter of a million dollars. Orvil's father, Jacob (he legally changed his name to the less Jewish-sounding Jack in 1923), was a textile wholesaler, and Orvil and his two brothers grew up in relative comfort. Like Arthur, Orvil had gone to Horace Mann, where he played soccer and tennis and wrote a sports column humorously entitled "The Dug Out" for the school paper. At Dartmouth College, which he entered in 1930, fraternities refused to pledge Jews. His response was to revive the Bema, a nonfraternity club that was open to all.

Orvil was an indifferent student, earning mostly Bs and Cs and finishing in the lower half of his class, but he was not lacking in ambition. After graduating in 1934, in the middle of the Depression, he started work as a runner on Wall Street. Four years later he borrowed the $104,000 necessary to buy a seat on the New York Stock Exchange and began a career as a two-dollar broker — a trader who earned a small commission on stock transactions — affiliated with the firm of Sydney Lewisohn & Co.

Orvil could have continued making a respectable living on Wall Street, but his abiding fascination was *The New York Times*. The first time Marian visited him at his mother's East Thirty-ninth Street apartment, where he maintained a room, Orvil made a point of showing her a closet piled high with old editions of the newspaper. "He just liked to save them," she explained. Few who knew the couple doubted that Orvil loved Marian, but, said one friend, "I don't think that was the only reason he married her."

The wedding took place on Tuesday, July 8, 1941, on the west lawn of Hillandale before several hundred guests. The day before, in anticipation of the first marriage in their generation, the Sulzberger children had signed a "buyback" agreement promising to give one another a right of first refusal on their shares of common stock in the company once they came into their inheritance. The document was the first of many intended to ensure that *The New York Times* would never stray from family hands.

That afternoon Arthur took Marian out for a walk. "I think I had better tell you the facts of life," he said solemnly. Marian stifled a laugh. Not only had she been initiated into the joys of sex long since, but three weeks earlier Orvil's mother had taken it upon herself to accompany her prospective daughter-in-law to a doctor to be fitted for a diaphragm. Iphigene was incapable of such breathtakingly modern motherhood. When Judy had begun dating, she had asked her mother what she should talk about with boys. "Well," ventured Iphigene, "you might discuss the charms on your charm bracelet."

After the vows, guests chatted over a buffet catered by Louis Sherry in the Hillandale ballroom and remarked on the sign Arthur had affixed to his back: IF YOU LIKED THE SETTING AND THE CEREMONY, REMEMBER I HAVE TWO MORE. Later in the day the room was cleared, and couples twirled to three of Marian's favorite songs: "This Is New," "Girl of the Moment," and "September Song." When the time came for toasts,

Punch, fresh from tutoring camp, delivered his speech while standing on a chair, for he was too short to be seen otherwise.

Following a honeymoon in California, the newlyweds settled into an apartment on East Seventy-second Street and Orvil returned to Wall Street — but not for long. Iphigene was determined that *The New York Times* be owned and run by her children, who would eventually inherit and share her controlling interest, and she worried about what might happen if she or Arthur were to die suddenly. At the moment, there was no one of maturity or training in the family to take over the business or hold the Sulzbergers together. With Marian's marriage to Orvil, a solution became apparent, as clear to Iphigene as had been her own husband's ascendancy to the office of the publisher six years earlier.

In the fall of 1941 Iphigene and Arthur suggested to Orvil that he quit the stock exchange and join *The New York Times*. After some deliberation, he agreed. "I told him it [was] almost essential . . . in view of the manner in which the Estate is left," Arthur explained to Julius in a letter in late November, after Orvil had made his decision. "He may be called upon to act as a sort of cohesive force to hold the varied interests together in what I hope is going to be the distant future." The job offer came with no commitment about Orvil's career path and no guarantee of advancement. Perhaps to hedge his bets, Orvil did not relinquish his seat on the stock exchange until 1949. In such a critical moment for the family and the paper, it was once again Iphigene who had been the pivotal figure. "I don't know that she did it," said Orvil's friend Ardie Deutsch, referring to her role in persuading Orvil to change the course of his life. "I just know that she was a very dynastically minded woman."

14

Arthur's Crucible

ORVIL JOINED *THE NEW YORK TIMES* ON JANU-
ary 2, 1942, less than a month after the Japanese bombed Pearl
Harbor and barely three weeks before the first American
troops of World War II landed in Ireland. He was eager to enlist and had
already applied for a commission in the navy, but a physical exam in the
Times' medical department soon revealed inactive rheumatic heart disease. Orvil's heart was so enlarged that the doctor ordered him to give
up playing squash, singles tennis, and the other strenuous sports he
loved. "He was as surprised [by his heart ailment] as we all were, and terribly hurt and upset," said Marian. "It's pretty awful when all your
friends have gone to war and you're not allowed."

Arthur had detested the haphazard apprenticeship Adolph had
inflicted on him, and with Orvil, he tried to be more systematic. For a
year Orvil worked as a city-room reporter, covering the police beat, city
hall, the courts, and — in an unbroken string of seventeen night assignments — windy after-dinner speakers. He quickly impressed the *Times'*
hard-boiled newsmen as "genial and willing . . . but no ball of fire." His
biggest story was an explosion in an arms plant in Bridgeport, Connecticut, an event that introduced him to the distasteful task of counting
bodies and interviewing survivors. As a "legman" — someone who
helps out more experienced reporters — he never earned a byline.

It hardly mattered; Orvil's future was not in the newsroom. A little
more than a year later, Arthur brought him to the fourteenth floor as
assistant to the publisher. Orvil's sudden rise to management was due in
part to his new status as a father. With the birth of Jacqueline Hays Dryfoos, called Jackie, in the spring of 1943, Arthur and Iphigene thought it
best for their son-in-law to trade in the 8:00 P.M. to 4:00 A.M. reporting
shift he had often been assigned for a less punishing schedule. The
new job came with an office, a secretary, a $5,000 raise, and unspecified

duties. Arthur soon assigned him responsibility for *Overseas Weekly,* an abbreviated tabloid edition of *The New York Times* for American servicemen, and for preparing the paper's Pulitzer Prize nominations. He sent letters to his New York banking contacts, asking them to meet Orvil and then "introduce him to some of your associates."

The war changed all the Sulzbergers' lives in dramatic ways. As crises erupted around the world, Arthur spent longer and longer hours at the *Times,* often sleeping in the small bedroom he had added to his office. Iphigene acted as senior hostess at the weekly officers' party at Delmonico's, where during college vacations Ruth and Judy were pressed into service as dance partners for the men. With Marian married and the other children away at school, she often invited visiting foreign servicemen to stay in the empty bedrooms at 5 East Eightieth Street, which gradually assumed the chaotic hotel atmosphere of Hillandale.

Frustrated by his inability to enlist, Arthur pushed Ruth to go overseas with the American Red Cross soon after her graduation from Smith. At twenty-two, she was three years younger than the minimum age requirement for women, but Arthur was on the Red Cross's central committee and, despite the potential danger to his daughter, got the rule set aside. "I'm sure he knew what war was all about," Ruth said. "But I was his surrogate."

Ruth and her father had developed a close bond, nourished by a similar sense of humor and long, late-night talks about *The New York Times.* She called him Poppy; he called her Ruthie. "I had a tremendous crush on my father," she said. "We had a very special relationship." Arthur introduced her to bourbon and taught her how to cure its headthrobbing consequences with ample doses of Alka-Seltzer. His teasing about the size of her nose took the form of letters addressed to "Dear Aardvark." When she was at Smith, he sent her elaborate food boxes and a gigantic stuffed bear named Angel, which she loved so much that she reserved a separate seat for him on the train when she went home for visits. While Ruth was overseas, Iphigene gave the bear to a children's hospital. "My mother never forgave her for that," said Ruth's youngest son years later.

Of all the Sulzberger children, Ruth was the only one who decided at an early age that she wanted to work for *The New York Times.* In college she pedaled her bicycle to Northampton's Western Union office to file a story about the WAVES, then headquartered on the Smith campus, and a Sunday magazine piece, "That Crumbling Ivory Tower," about the changing atmosphere of women's colleges in wartime. During the summers and Christmas holidays, she worked at the *Times* under the gimlet eye of managing editor Edwin L. James. "I hope that I will prove more than a burden to an Editor," she told him in an application letter. "If I find myself unable to cover a wedding without forgetting the bride's name, I will retire quietly."

Ruth performed ably as a reporter, ever mindful that the publisher was monitoring her behavior. "My father would walk through the newsroom from time to time and if he ever saw me not typing, I would get fussed at when I got home," she said. Her most memorable assignment was a story based on her experiences as a New York city cabdriver. With so many men away at war, male hacks had become scarce and the taxi companies started to hire women. During her two-day stint one man climbed into the backseat, muttered his destination, looked up, saw the gender of his driver, and promptly got out.

Ruth joined the Red Cross as an unpaid volunteer in September 1943 and, after a brief training period in Washington, D.C., was assigned to an unfinished air base called Boreham, near Chelmsford, England, about thirty miles outside of London. As an assistant in the base's Aeroclub, she made snacks for enlisted men and organized occasional dances, pool games, and other recreation. The metal Quonset hut she shared with another woman was heated by a coal stove that fought a losing battle with the damp British winter, and the ongoing construction site outside was treacherously muddy. The women had to throw a wooden plank across a puddle to enter their quarters. Running water was scarce, forcing Ruth to catch rainwater in her helmet to wash her hair. By December she was so homesick that she wrote a heart-tugging letter to her family in which she reminisced about all the lovely Sulzbergerian Christmas traditions she would miss because of the war. Arthur published it in *The New York Times* as a letter to the editor, with a short introduction informing readers that she, and he, "must remain anonymous." He signed the submission, "The Girl's Daddy."

When the air base was completed, the 394th Army Air Force Bombardment Group moved in, and Ruth stayed with it throughout the war, eventually following it to the Continent. She and her Red Cross colleagues greeted combat crews returning from bombing missions, dispensing doughnuts, hot coffee, good cheer, and comfort at all hours of the day and night. It was hardly a safe assignment. During the Blitzkrieg German planes routinely dumped excess explosives left over from pounding the British capital. "Whatever they hadn't dropped on London, they dropped on us," said Ruth. She huddled under a desk for protection; there were no bunkers.

It was in Britain that Ruth first confronted what it meant to be a Sulzberger. She was talking with a coworker when he stopped her in mid-sentence to ask whether hers was the family that ran *The New York Times*. Ruth was stunned. "How did you know that?" she replied, genuinely perplexed. He looked at her as though she had insulted his intelligence. "I was aware that everybody knew there were Hearsts, Pulitzers, and Reids," she said later. "But since Poppy always stood so consistently behind and not in front of his job, I had never realized that 'Sulzberger' was also a name."

§

Steeped in a strong family tradition of military service, every able-bodied male Ochs rushed to enlist. Julius, who had already been on active duty for months by the time the United States entered the war, went overseas as assistant commander of the Sixth Infantry Division, followed soon by Julie Jr., who served as an Army Air Force bombardier with the 325th Squadron. The Oakes brothers joined the army, both ending up in intelligence work. True to his father's maverick nature, John Oakes deliberately signed up as a private on the principle that men of his privileged background and education ought to go through the process of being drafted. By the war's end, he had risen to the rank of major and earned the Bronze Star and the Croix de Guerre.

For "A," general manager of *The Chattanooga Times* since 1931, the family pressure for military achievement gave him a chance to escape his personal and professional problems. In recent years the *Chattanooga Free Press*, launched in 1933 by Roy McDonald to advertise his Home Stores grocery chain, had relentlessly hammered away at *The Chattanooga Times*. The *Free Press* had subsequently swallowed up *The Chattanooga News*, a fifty-year-old liberal paper, and had gone from a weekly to a daily. Calculatedly local and shamelessly boosterish, the *Free Press* reflected the reactionary politics of Mr. Roy, as McDonald was known, a man so steeped in the nineteenth century that he once proudly proclaimed he was "against progress in all its forms."

By the time Pearl Harbor was attacked, *The Chattanooga Times* and the *News–Free Press* were in a bitter circulation and advertising battle that was costing *The Chattanooga Times* $1,000 a day. The *News–Free Press* had launched a Sunday edition to compete with the morning *Times;* in retaliation, the *Times* had started a poorly conceived afternoon daily. Over a two-year period the Ochs Trust poured $280,000 into the new edition in a vain attempt to shore it up, in the process absorbing a considerable proportion of the limited funds that remained after the payment of Adolph's inheritance taxes.

By the spring of 1942, the tension had become too much for "A." Several months earlier Arthur had come up with a plan to end the destructive competition by merging the business operations of the *Times* with those of the rival *News–Free Press*. The "joint operating agreement" was one of the first of its kind and called for combining all departments except news and editorial while shutting down the afternoon *Times* in exchange for a shutdown of the Sunday *News–Free Press*. "A" considered the idea an indication of his failure. When he showed up two hours late for the first merger negotiation with McDonald, nervous and highly excited, Arthur strongly suspected the cause was "A"'s by now well-known drinking problem.

When the partnership was finally signed in May 1942, Julius became apoplectic. He had continued to hold the titles of publisher of *The Chattanooga Times* and president of The Chattanooga Times Printing Company during his absence in the army and was indignant that the story announcing the merger made no mention of him. In a letter to Arthur, he said he was "deeply hurt" that, without being consulted, he suddenly found himself subordinate to "A," who had been appointed chairman of the new joint entity, called The Chattanooga Publishing Company, as well as to the "unspeakably unpalatable" McDonald, who had been made president. Arthur tried without success to mollify Julius, who wrote a curt letter to "A," huffily demanding that he discontinue Julius's salary as publisher and president. He had considered shedding the titles as well, Julius told "A," but in the end decided against it in order "to prevent people from assuming family strife."

As part of the merger, the *Times* agreed to move its operations from the gold-domed building Adolph had erected in 1891 to McDonald's plant. On June 9, 1942, the first issue of *The Chattanooga Times* edited and published in its new headquarters rolled off the presses, a development that sent Julius to new heights of distress. "I must appear to the public to have been swallowed up," he complained. However disturbing the merger was to Julius, it proved a boon to *The Chattanooga Times*, which immediately experienced a rise in advertising and circulation and was soon operating at a profit.

For "A," by nature a sensitive and fragile man, the discord was too much. Less than a month after the merger, he requested a leave of absence from *The Chattanooga Times* to seek a commission in the army. "My job is done," he wrote Arthur. "I feel that I am now entitled to be relieved of responsibilities which have become extremely painful." With the paper at such a delicate juncture, Arthur tried to talk him out of his plans, but "A" would have none of it. By late July 1942 he was in New York, commissioned as a major and preparing to go to England to be business manager of *Yank*, a new weekly for servicemen.

But the military proved no safe haven for "A." En route to England, the inchoate anxiety that had gripped him in Chattanooga expanded into full-blown mental illness. By late August he was in an Oxford hospital, diagnosed as a psychotic with paranoiac tendencies. Thin, unshaven, and occasionally violent, he refused medication, certain that the medics were Nazis. Arthur, in England on business at the time, saw "A" several days after he had been admitted, and the two men had a reasonable conversation. Later he discovered that "A" did not believe it was Arthur who had visited him; it had been someone else, "A" asserted, disguised as Arthur. "He's suffering severe nervous depression, suspicion, and [is] frankly quite nuts," Arthur informed Iphigene in a telegram.

In January 1943 "A" was transferred to Walter Reed Hospital outside Washington, D.C., and by May was deemed well enough to retire from the service and return to Tennessee. There, at Arthur's insistence, he resumed his title of general manager of *The Chattanooga Times*, though it was understood that Charles Puckette, the *New York Times* vice president whom Arthur had dispatched to Chattanooga to act as the top executive during "A"'s absence, would continue to run the paper. From then on, "A" rarely went in to the office, preferring to spend his time at home or, in the summer, on Signal Mountain in the house he called the Ochs Box, playing chess and taking walks with his cocker spaniel. Arthur generously made him *The Chattanooga Times'* correspondent in Washington, but even "A" admitted that his output there was "poor and meager," and he soon abandoned the job. The manic depression that earlier had engulfed his uncle Adolph would exact a higher price from "A," whose melancholic apathy plagued him for the rest of his life.

§

One of the enduring myths about *The New York Times* is that it nobly sacrificed profits from revenue-generating ads during World War II in order to print more news. Arthur was immensely proud of the policy, which had been his decision, and decades later Iphigene was annoyed that it wasn't mentioned more prominently in her husband's obituary. But the truth is somewhat more complicated.

The war forced paper mills across the country to redirect their efforts toward the production of cardboard and waterproof paper for packaging materials, which resulted in a national shortage of newsprint. Arthur served on the Publishers Newsprint Committee, which came up with a rationing plan, known as Order L-240, that kept all newspapers supplied equitably without giving unfair advantage to papers that owned mills, as the *Times* did.

The limitation presented newspapers with a quandary: how large should they be in size and circulation, and how should they balance money-making ads and news? In 1943, when Order L-240 went into effect, the economy was humming with wartime spending. Most papers, the *Times* included, had more ads than they had paper on which to print them. Faced with a surfeit of both ads and world news, Arthur made the critical choice not to accept all the ads the *Times* was offered, instead filling up the rest of the paper with breaking stories. The decision did not, however, result in a "profit squeeze" or a "financial sacrifice," as several books about the *Times* later contended.

The *Times* did print a copious amount of war news: in the first eight months of 1944, it published 1.9 million more lines of reporting than any other New York paper, forfeiting several million lines of advertising that were there for the taking. But the paper slashed its "news hole" — the amount of space devoted to news — far more severely than it cut the space devoted to ads. In 1939 nearly 60 percent of the paper had been taken up by news; in 1944 the figure had fallen to below 50 percent. That, coupled with an advertising rate hike made possible by the surge in advertiser demand, sent the *Times'* ad revenue soaring to its highest level since 1931.

Arthur, who did not realize the *Times'* actual situation, was stunned, and none too pleased, when the paper's acerbic managing editor, Edwin L. James, sent him a memorandum in January 1945 calculated to prick the publisher's balloon of self-sacrifice. James wrote:

> I was cogitating today on the effect of a possible further 5% newsprint cut on news coverage and I thought of the following two figures: Reduction in news lineage since 1941 — 29.8%; Reduction in advertising lineage since 1941 — 2.6%.

Arthur immediately asked The New York Times Company secretary, Godfrey Nelson, to give him the figures on how much the *Times'* ad revenue had decreased since 1941 and how much its news-gathering expenses had risen. Alas, Nelson had to disappoint him. Ad revenue, he told Arthur, had actually increased during the period, from $13 million to $15 million, while the amount of money spent on news had slumped slightly from $3.9 million to $3.7 million. Moreover, the number of news and editorial employees in 1945 stood roughly where it had been in 1937.

Arthur's decision may not have been quite the high-minded privation he believed it was, but it was a shrewd policy nonetheless. Instead of stuffing the *Times* with all the ads it could hold and thereby reaping a windfall — an approach taken by the greedier *Herald Tribune* — he satisfied readers' hunger for news, using the *Times'* newsprint allotment to print more, rather than larger, papers. The result was that by the spring of 1945, daily circulation was up by more than 100,000. When newsprint restrictions were lifted after the war, readers stuck with the *Times* — they had come to rely on it — and many advertisers defected from the *Herald Tribune,* which soon began its slow descent into oblivion.

Despite the limits on newsprint, the *Times* during World War II still managed to deluge its readers with official war communiqués and speeches, most published in full. Every day on page one a map showed the latest battlefront and troop maneuvers; beneath it was a summary of war news. At the height of the conflict, the *Times* had fifty-five correspondents overseas, more than any other American newspaper. Many, like drama critic Brooks Atkinson, who was deployed to Burma, India, and China, were far afield from their regular beats. To assuage Arthur's concern that his war reporters lacked nourishment, the paper supplied them with monthly vitamin and food packages prepared by B. Altman's department store. A disproportionate number of the *Times'* correspondents were British, which troubled Arthur, who came to feel that, despite their loyalty and talent, "an American newspaper should be served primarily by Americans." Lurking beneath his words was the assumption that the *Times'* foreign staff — the paper's elite ambassadors — should also be "well-educated, attractive Protestants," not Jews.

The notable exception was Arthur's nephew, Cy Sulzberger, who joined the *Times* in September 1939, three days after Hitler invaded Poland. Tall, craggy, brilliant, with a booming voice and clothing so threadbare that a magazine once described him as looking "like a hick," Cy was a dogged reporter with a flair for the dramatic. As a student at Harvard, he had once written a poem using his own blood for ink. While working at the *Pittsburgh Post-Gazette*, he slept, ate, and panhandled with homeless men, producing a gripping six-part series called "Hobo for a Week." A stint with the United Press ended abruptly when he published *Sit Down with John L. Lewis*, a book about the controversial labor leader that the wire service considered too sympathetic.

By the spring of 1939, Cy was in Athens stringing for several London papers when he received an urgent telegram from his uncle asking to meet him in London. There, over dinner, Arthur and Berlin correspondent Frederick Birchall — one of the paper's Englishmen — tried to persuade him to join *The New York Times*. Cy declined, saying he "had no desire to join a family enterprise." But by the end of the evening, Arthur and Birchall had exacted from him a promise to reconsider if war arrived. The day Hitler marched into Poland, Birchall phoned Cy, who was then in Bucharest and immediately became the *Times'* Balkan bureau manager, covering Hungary, Romania, Yugoslavia, Albania, Bulgaria, Greece, and Turkey.

Cy quickly earned a swashbuckling reputation by driving a Mercedes purchased from a Polish count and offering daily infusions of vermouth and soda to Felix, the wirehaired terrier who served as his constant companion. In Greece Felix saw combat when a small metal bomb sailed through a hotel window and landed on Cy's bed, where the dog was sleeping; it failed to explode, but the impact broke his hind legs.

Arthur had balked at hiring Cy while Adolph was alive, fearful that the addition of another Sulzberger would endanger his succession to the publishership. Now that he was in charge, however, Arthur was glad to welcome the son of his late brother, with whom he had developed an affectionate surrogate-father relationship. Cy was coarser and less refined than Arthur, but they shared a manly taste for martinis, gin rummy, and beautiful women.

When Cy was classified 1-A soon after Pearl Harbor, Arthur confronted a difficult dilemma. He had pushed Ruth into the Red Cross and supported Orvil in his efforts to serve in the military, thinking, quite rightly, that his bad heart would prevent him from seeing combat. But when he was faced with losing Cy, whom he considered not only a close relative but a crack war correspondent, he did everything in his power to keep him out of harm's way. Arthur argued to the draft board that Cy was indispensable to the *Times*. When that failed, he appealed the board's decision — again unsuccessfully. In desperation, Arthur implored a sympathetic official at draft headquarters in Washington to intercede directly with the president. Whether the man did so or not is unclear, but by mid-September a new regulation was promulgated designating newspapers a "vital industry" and providing that no journalist could enlist or be commissioned without his employer's express approval. Although Arthur assured his nephew that his resulting deferment had nothing to do with the prominent last name they both shared, Cy remained doubtful — and deeply embarrassed.

Nevertheless, Cy was soon back overseas, based in Cairo and traveling widely to cover the war. In the fall of 1944 Arthur named him chief foreign correspondent, a portfolio that made Cy the overseer of an offshore operation of foreign reporters and gave him carte blanche to circumnavigate the globe. *Time* did a story about the promotion, illustrating the piece with a photo of Cy lounging leather-jacketed in a boat during his escape to Turkey from Greece in 1941. Not long afterward the Manchester *Guardian* dubbed Cy *The New York Times'* "Crown Prince," suggesting an eventual succession to power within the Ochs and Sulzberger dynasty — an implication Cy did little to discourage.

§

With the onset of war, Iphigene took it upon herself to organize public-service lectures in the Times Building on everything from food canning and victory gardening to map reading and evacuation procedures. When the paper's foreign correspondents returned from abroad, she persuaded them to speak about their experiences in Times Hall, a former working theater on West Forty-fourth Street. By 1944 she officially had a position on the staff of the promotion department, with her own office and stationery.

Before America's entry in the war, Iphigene had worked to attract female readers through ladies' teas at the paper and public-affairs programs at women's clubs. As part of that effort, she had insisted, against Edwin L. James's wishes, that the paper publish a food column. Her promotion of "women's news" resulted in the hiring of Natalie Wales Latham, founder and president of Bundles for Britain, who arrived at the *Times* shortly before Pearl Harbor to create the first rough cut of a women's page. Mrs. Latham lasted only until 1943; she was inclined to give public speeches that embarrassed the *Times,* and within the paper she was widely rumored to have had a flirtation, or worse, with Arthur. But the idea of a women's page remained, gradually evolving into what would come to be known at the *Times* as the "four F's" — food, fashion, furnishing, and family.

Women's news was just one area where Iphigene's influence was felt during the war. She took care to couch her "interest" in stories in a polite and deferential way, but there was no escaping that a word from the daughter of Adolph Ochs and the wife of the publisher carried outsize weight with editors. Once, when she protested to Edwin L. James that the strength of her influence was exaggerated, he fixed his eyes on her and said in his Tidewater accent, "Little lady, you don't realize the power of your own voice."

Iphigene's voice rang out loudly, for once, in a *Times* series on Americans' ignorance of their own history. She had a particular fondness for history and was appalled that American students, her own children included, understood so little about their own Constitution, the Civil War, and other key events and concepts. The *Times* articles, written by education editor Benjamin Fine, were based on thousands of questionnaires and a specially devised American history test, administered to seven thousand freshmen in thirty-six colleges and universities. The poor test results caused surprise and alarm, and in response, a number of states adopted laws requiring courses in American history in both high school and college.

The series won the Pulitzer Prize for public service in 1944, a fact that deeply gratified Iphigene and disgruntled Cy, whose dispatches on Tito's Partisan movement had also been nominated. In his memoir, published more than twenty-five years later, Cy said that Arthur had asked him to withdraw from the Pulitzer competition in order to ensure that the history series would receive the award. Arthur "was sure I would understand," he said, because the subject was so vital to Iphigene. Technically, the *Times* could never "ensure" a Pulitzer, of course, but at the time it was understood by *The New York Times* and the Pulitzer board that the paper would get no more than one each year.

Just as presidents often appear larger and more statesmanlike on the world stage than at home, the historical accident of a foreign war gave Arthur an opportunity to step smartly into the spotlight. It marked the beginning of a personal campaign for recognition and legitimacy that would continue for the rest of his publishership. Nearly every week he traveled to Washington in connection with his duties as a member of the American Red Cross central committee. His speeches on subjects such as national sovereignty and the status of the draft after the war were covered as news on the pages of his own newspaper. Columbia University and the Metropolitan Museum of Art put him on their boards.

In 1945, a year after the *Times* acquired WQXR, a classical music radio station, Arthur wrote and recorded the first of what came to be annual New Year's greetings from the publisher. Moralistic in tone and delivered in a patrician Yankee voice and cadence that sounded startlingly like FDR's, Arthur's addresses aired at the stroke of midnight each New Year's Eve. "A year of sacrifice for victory is past," began one such message. "[The New Year] also must be a year of sacrifice and toil and effort if we are to gain our goal."

Arthur's radio pronouncements struck some at the paper as unsuitably self-promotional — more appropriate to a world leader than a man pledged to preserve the anonymous and "impersonal journalism" of Adolph Ochs. To Arthur, they were a natural outgrowth of his changing role. He once told Ruth that his main objective in life was to "fight to keep democracy alive in this country," a goal that could be accomplished, he thought, only if America preserved "peace in the world." To that end, he commiserated with presidents, prime ministers, and military leaders so often and so confidentially that he began to think they were all working for the same cause. In short, he began to think of himself as one of "them."

Arthur's position with the American Red Cross made it possible for him to travel more freely than other publishers, but it also meant that he had to juggle a number of conflicting roles: reporter, war worker, unofficial envoy, curious citizen, news source, PR man, and even employment agent. After a bomb killed her sister during the London Blitz, Madeleine Carroll left moviemaking, vowing to "fight Hitler with everything I have." With Arthur's assistance, she secured a job with the Red Cross, working in French and Italian hospitals and, later, in rehabilitation centers for victims of concentration camps. The Red Cross trips Arthur took permitted him to confer privately with many of the top Allied leaders. As a condition of these government-sanctioned journeys, he agreed never to write stories about what he learned, but he did manage to get a firsthand look at how *New York Times* reporters performed their jobs under life-threatening conditions. By venturing overseas, he hoped at least to "subject myself to some of the same difficulties" as his correspondents.

During a visit to Britain in 1942, ostensibly to examine Red Cross facilities, he awakened one night in London's Savoy Hotel to the thunder of a bombing raid. Hurrying to the workroom the *Times* maintained in the hotel, Arthur watched in respectful fascination as his men cranked out news dispatches till dawn. The scare was an exception in what was, on this particular trip, a rarefied itinerary that included lunch with Lord Mountbatten, dinner with the American ambassador, and conferences with General Dwight D. Eisenhower, who arranged for Arthur to tour British military installations in return for hearing the publisher's candid observations afterward.

During the same stay, Arthur lunched at Chequers with Prime Minister Winston Churchill, who claimed kinship to *The New York Times* through his maternal grandfather, Leonard W. Jerome, a director of the paper during the pre-Ochs era. Arthur was impressed with Churchill's heroic consumption of alcohol (eight glasses of wine, two glasses of port) and carefully recorded in his "Strictly Confidential Note for the File" that the prime minister's eyes looked "watery" and his lips "appeared to drool a bit." Despite its eccentric aspects — Churchill greeted Arthur in his trademark jumpsuit overalls — the meeting marked the start of what would become a long and warm association.

Arthur's circumspection about what he had seen and heard in Britain made it possible for him to visit Russia the following year, again under the passport of the Red Cross. He first had to make a self-aggrandizing argument for the trip to President Roosevelt, who had a policy prohibiting newspaper publishers from visiting war zones. His mere presence in the Soviet Union, Arthur argued, would demonstrate that "at least one great newspaper in this country thinks the Russians are in its world. Not only does it send its correspondents there but the Publisher himself goes over to see the country and its people."

Arthur left for Russia in June 1943, purportedly on a mission to monitor the delivery of Red Cross medical supplies to the Red Army. Accompanying him was Scotty Reston, who came along to keep a record of the journey. Scotty, a native-born Scotsman and former AP sportswriter, had joined the London bureau of the *Times* in 1939 but did not come to Arthur's attention until the publisher's trip to Britain three years later. At the time, Scotty was on leave of absence from the paper, helping set up the Office of War Information at the American embassy. During discussions with John Winant, the American ambassador, Arthur inquired how British newspapers were handling German propaganda. Winant summoned Scotty to respond. Arthur was dazzled by his quick, incisive answer and invited him to come to New York when his leave was up to work as his personal assistant, helping out with speeches and making a study of the postwar problems of the *Times*.

In Moscow Arthur and Scotty stayed three weeks at Spaso House, the American ambassador's residence, and enjoyed the services of a Chinese valet, while Cy Sulzberger, who served as his uncle's unofficial guide, camped out with the other foreign correspondents at the Metropol Hotel. The visit included a meeting with Foreign Minister Vyacheslav Molotov; an elaborate lunch with Maxim Litvinov, the Soviet ambassador in Washington, who happened to be in Moscow; and a surreal Fourth of July concert of American music that included a Russian rendition of "Ol' Man River." Scotty complained that the endless vodka toasts scorched his throat, but Arthur downed glass after glass while also sampling the excellent Russian caviar, which he "ate like jam." For years afterward Scotty referred to Arthur as Mr. Gus — from *gospodin*, the Russian word for *mister* — and Arthur called Scotty "Pectoh," *Reston* as it appeared in Cyrillic.

At a small farewell party held at a well-appointed Moscow apartment, the Russians thoughtfully provided three beautiful women to pay special attention to Arthur. Scotty had heard the office gossip about the publisher's extramarital affairs and kept a close eye on his boss. "I had to recognize that this was not silly, that he was really fiddling with these girls," he said. When the Russians brought out cameras to record the hilarity, Scotty took Arthur's arm, telling him, "I think we've got to get out of here." Arthur understood, and as soon as it was graciously possible, they left.

Arthur and Scotty came home predicting — correctly, as it turned out — that the Soviet Union would increase its military might but remain weak economically during the postwar era. In the interest of peace, Arthur concluded, the United States should try to cooperate with the Russians "even if it hurts." In general, he felt that his so-called Mission to Moscow had been an unqualified success. Cy, who saw in Scotty a potent rival for his aspirations at the *Times* as well as for his uncle's admiration, took a more jaundiced view, remembering only that Arthur was "entertained lavishly, although he accomplished little."

§

In addition to the predictable burdens that came with a world war, Arthur had the responsibility of running *The New York Times* during the reign of Hitler and the horror of the Holocaust. These events would have challenged any publisher, but for Arthur, they also had a deeply personal effect, crystallizing his own conflicted feelings about being Jewish. He resisted singling out Jews for special treatment on the pages of the *Times* and battled such Jewish groups as Zionists, whom he considered wrongheaded and extreme. Like his late father-in-law, he did not want the *Times* to be viewed as a "Jewish paper." But in his single-minded effort to achieve that end, he missed an opportunity to use the considerable power of the paper to focus a spotlight on one of the greatest crimes the world has ever known.

Because Arthur rejected the idea that Jews were members of a "race," he was vehemently against collective phrases such as *the Jewish people* and launched a campaign to roust them from the *Times*. He instructed editors to substitute expressions like *people of the Jewish faith* or simply *Jews*, which he felt subtly conveyed the notion that being Jewish was something one could freely choose, like being a Methodist or a Presbyterian. "Deep down, my father probably would just as soon not have been Jewish," said Judy.

Arthur had encountered little anti-Semitism himself until he entered Columbia University, where he was shunned by fraternities, a rejection that embittered him. "I'm not kept out because I'm not American," he wrote a friend at the time. "I'm not kept out because of my looks, or my manners or what ever else you may say. No — I'm a Jew, and that's all, and that's enough!" Several Jewish students invited him to join them in founding a Columbia chapter of Zeta Beta Tau, the Jewish fraternity, an overture he resisted, "despite my childish feeling of loneliness." To him, Judaism was "a religion, and a religion only, and . . . should not be a common denominator of social intercourse or political activity." He opposed any kind of "ghetto living or thinking or acting."

The fraternity incident was mild compared to what Arthur euphemistically described as the "jolt" he later experienced at a Cape Cod resort during a summer motor trip he and Iphigene took with their Hillandale neighbors, the Rossbachs. The two families had stopped at the inn in the early evening; Marian and the Rossbachs' daughter, June, then about thirteen, slumped sleepily in the backseat. Arthur and Max Rossbach went into the front office to register, only to emerge moments later in a towering rage. No one said a word, but it was clear they had been turned away because they were Jewish. "I have never seen grown men in that kind of frustration and anger," recalled June. "It was so humiliating to have this happen [at all], but worse to have it happen in front of wives and children."

Experiences like these left their mark on Arthur, who later struck an uncomfortable compromise that made him party to the anti-Semitism he despised. At his direction, the *Times* printed ads for businesses that included words like *restricted* and *selected clientele*, shorthand for *No Jews Allowed.* His rationale was that Jews should be forewarned of bias, so they could avoid the sort of embarrassment he had suffered. He didn't halt the practice until 1943, and he did so then only because Frank S. Hogan, the district attorney for New York County, informed him that it was illegal.

Like Adolph, Arthur also feared that Jews, if placed in prominent positions in large numbers, would sow the seeds of suspicion and resentment that could ultimately lead to a backlash. In 1933, when his friends Morris Ernst and Nathan Straus Jr. were both thinking of running for mayor of New York City, he had urged them to reconsider. Herbert H. Lehman was then governor of New York, and Arthur felt it would be "a distinct mistake for a city to consider a Jewish mayor at the time the state had a Jewish governor." Several years later he counseled President Franklin Roosevelt not to name Felix Frankfurter to succeed U.S. Supreme Court Justice Benjamin N. Cardozo, a Jew and a distant relative on his mother's side, who had just died. He had no objection to Frankfurter himself, he just thought it "unwise" for Roosevelt to create a de facto Jewish seat, making it "look as though there was always to be a Jew, whether or not he was qualified." At the end of their conversation, the ever duplicitous Roosevelt told Arthur, "I agree with you completely," and then promptly proceeded to nominate Frankfurter, who served on the Court until 1962.

Arthur's determination to avoid the perception of the *Times* as a "Jewish" newspaper intensified in the 1930s and early 1940s, a period when anti-Semitism found fertile soil in America as well as overseas. One reason was economic. As educated Jewish professionals fled Hitler's oppression, many Americans, still reeling from the Depression, worried that the newcomers would claim the best jobs. Such fears, coupled with allegations that American Jews weren't doing their full share in the military, nurtured a bigotry that abated only with the end of the war. In five polls taken between March 1938 and April 1940, some 60 percent of Americans thought Jews had "objectionable" qualities. Another survey taken in 1938 found that the same percentage believed the persecution of the Jews in Europe was either entirely or partly their own fault.

In such a highly charged atmosphere, Arthur felt that the *Times* had to "lean over backwards" to be objective and balanced in its stories about Jews. Even before the anti-Semitic press made much of the fact that *Times* spelled backwards was *Semit(e)*, he was vigilant about correcting any suggestion that he or the paper might represent Jewish interests. When *Time* referred to the paper as the "Jewish-owned *New York Times*," Arthur complained to the proprietor, Henry Luce, alleging that the phrase implied the *Times* was biased.

These personal and professional strains converged with increasing power during the Holocaust, making Arthur more cautious about its coverage than he might have been otherwise. The *Times'* reporting of Jewish persecution was remarkably thorough, and the paper often raised its voice forcefully in editorials, but crucial news stories were frequently buried inside the paper rather than highlighted on page one. A July 2, 1944, dispatch citing "authoritative information" that 400,000 Hungarian Jews had already been deported to their deaths and an additional 350,000 were to be killed in the next three weeks received only four column inches on page twelve, while that same day a story about Fourth of July holiday crowds ran on the front page.

To be sure, Arthur did not consider "story placement" part of a publisher's job. "He had the idea that if it was in the *Times,* it was just as good on page thirty-nine as on page one," said assistant managing editor Turner Catledge. Moreover, during the 1930s the newsroom was structured so that the so-called bullpen, a group of night editors made up largely of Roman Catholics, decided what went into the paper and where it was placed, long after managing editor Edwin L. James had left the office for the evening. In those days it was a running joke that the *Times* was a paper "owned by Jews and edited by Catholics for Protestants."

The *Times* was hardly alone in downplaying news of the Final Solution. In the late 1930s and early 1940s, other major dailies, including the *New York Herald Tribune,* the *Chicago Tribune, The Washington Post,* and the *Los Angeles Times,* like the public at large, disbelieved reports of Jewish genocide in Europe or suspected that they were exaggerated in order to attract relief funds. But the *Times'* was unique in one respect: as the preeminent newspaper in the country, with superior foreign reporting capabilities, it had much power to set the agenda for other journals, many of which took their cue from the *Times'* front page. Had the *Times* highlighted Nazi atrocities against Jews, or simply not buried certain stories, the nation might have awakened to the horror far sooner than it did.

On its opinion page, the *Times* focused consistent attention on all victims of Nazi aggression, with only occasional references to Jews as a group. Editorials concerning the Warsaw resistance and the subsequent ghetto uprising, for instance, referred obliquely to "the Poles" and "Warsaw patriots." An internal survey of *Times* editorials on "minorities" from 1931 to 1943, commissioned by Arthur himself, showed that of the 345 editorials examined, "Jews in Germany & German-occupied Countries" were the minority most often written about, with the exception of American blacks. But just eleven editorials about persecution of Jews appeared in 1938 — the year that Hitler's Aryanization campaign was fully realized — and three editorials appeared in each of the years 1941, 1942, and 1943 — a period in which Hitler's extermination plan was increasingly apparent.

As the situation of European Jews became more and more desperate, Arthur found himself monitored by a range of Jewish groups, most of whom disagreed violently with the *Times* coverage. He got used to headlines such as the one that appeared in the September 2, 1943, edition of *PM:* JEWS SAY SULZBERGER MISUSES "THE TIMES." With pressure mounting to find refuge for Hitler's victims, Zionists in America and elsewhere called for the establishment of a Jewish homeland in Palestine and immediate withdrawal of Britain's 1939 white paper restricting Jewish immigration there. Arthur rejected Palestine as a haven, except as one of several places to which Jews could escape, and instead supported utopian schemes for settlements in Australia and southwestern Africa. "If I, as a Jew, can help to impress the world that what Jews want far more than a home of their own is the right to call any place home," he declared, "then I believe I shall have been faithful to the tradition of justice which is my heritage as an American of Jewish faith."

The rhetoric on both sides became overheated early in 1942 when American Zionists, meeting at the Extraordinary Zionist Conference at New York's Biltmore Hotel, called for a Jewish military force under the Star of David and, for the first time, demanded that Palestine be established as a Jewish commonwealth. A *Times* editorial solemnly declared the idea to be "unwise," and in early November Arthur injected himself personally into the debate with a speech before the Brotherhood of the Madison Avenue Temple in Baltimore, Maryland. In his remarks, which were summarized in a wire service story published in *The New York Times,* he called upon Jews to drop their efforts for a Jewish army and a Jewish national state and urged non-Jews to be cautious before endorsing Zionist aims. As an alternative to a Jewish Palestine, he suggested the postwar creation of a "great state," carved out of several nations in the Holy Land, which would "welcome all who wish to come," Jews and non-Jews alike. *The Jewish Record* responded by calling Arthur a "Jewish Bourbon" and a "self-hating Jew." Rabbi Abba Hillel Silver, chairman of the American Zionist Emergency Council, charged him with using the newspaper as a "transmission belt for anti-Zionist propaganda."

The moment was a turning point for Arthur. In a sharply worded reply to Rabbi Silver, he said the "Zionist barrage of misrepresentation" following his Baltimore address had converted him from a "non-Zionist" to an "anti-Zionist." Entrusting statehood to a group that "willfully perverts and distorts facts" and "seeks to destroy the character of individuals who differ with it" would be "fundamentally bad judgment." He then concluded with a reference to Hitler's minister of propaganda, a comparison calculated to inflame Silver and his followers: "I am opposed to Goebbels' tactics whether or not they are confined to Nazi Germany."

Behind his defiant words, Arthur was badly shaken by the exchange. "I don't want to make myself the spearhead of the attack on the Zionists," Arthur told Rabbi Morris Lazaron, head of the Baltimore Hebrew congregation, a week after the speech, "and that isn't because I don't like a scrap but rather because I cannot disassociate myself from *The New York Times*. If I were to become too much involved people would think the *Times* was prejudiced in its reporting." To keep him "straight" on Zionism and Jewish issues, he hired Bernard Richards, the head of the Jewish Information Bureau, as an adviser.

Arthur had met Richards, a Lithuania-born author and journalist, years earlier through his father, Cyrus Sulzburger. Richards was an active Zionist, but Arthur considered him accurate and fair. For $100 a month, he summarized what the Jewish press was saying about the *Times* and answered Arthur's queries about the paper's Jewish coverage. From time to time he also provided a spirited defense. When *The Jewish Times* reviewed *The Disappearing Daily,* a book by Oswald Garrison Villard that attacked Arthur for having failed to "voice indignation against Nazi assaults on and butcheries of the Jews," Richards responded by writing a letter to the editor praising *The New York Times* for its coverage of Jewish persecution and its "large number of editorials condemning the indignities." Missing from Richards's correspondence, however, was any indication that he had a working arrangement with the *Times.*

If Arthur's public role concerning the plight of the Jews was well known, his private actions to help Jewish relatives escape Hitler were not. He and Iphigene never discussed the Holocaust, or their own efforts to save people, with their four children. As far as their offspring were concerned, the only visible evidence of the Sulzbergers' beneficence was the presence of the Raicks, a family of Belgian Catholics — father, mother, and three young daughters — who emigrated to America under the sponsorship of the Sulzbergers and lived at Hillandale in the early years of the war. Arthur had met the mother, Marie-Claire, in Brussels in 1912, when she was a girl and he had boarded with her family during a college vacation. When the Low Countries were invaded in May 1940, he sent an urgent cable instructing her to take her family to Paris, where a *Times* correspondent would help them reach America. Once the Raicks were safely in the United States, Arthur and Iphigene gave them funds as well as a temporary home and helped the father, Julien, find a job in the steel industry.

During the 1930s and early 1940s, Arthur and Iphigene also quietly sponsored the emigration of at least twenty-five Ochs and Sulzberger relatives and rescued a handful of other individuals who either worked for *The New York Times* in Europe or touched the Sulzbergers' hearts with their stories. Some claimed kinship simply because they shared the same last name. "Judging by the number of refugees that have been arriving, I have rather come to the opinion that the name 'Sulzberger' has become as common as 'Smith,' " Arthur wrote an uncle in 1939. One recipient, Fred (né Fritz) Sulzberger, was a physician who eventually settled in Southbridge, Massachusetts. Another, Clark Abt, an Ochs relative who began his life in Cologne as Claus Pessiak, rose to prominence as founder and president of Abt Associates, a social-policy consulting firm in Cambridge, Massachusetts.

Years later, when she had become more open about the issue, Iphigene always maintained that she and Arthur had managed to get all their relatives out of Germany. But at least one family member, Louis Zinn, a distant cousin on the Ochs side, found himself in a situation so tangled that he was beyond help. Zinn was born in San Francisco of German parents who returned to their homeland for health reasons when he was a small boy. World War I forced Zinn to choose between the country of his birth and the only real home he had ever known. He made the painful decision to relinquish his American citizenship and officially became German, although he never served in the army. After the war he ran the family's toy factory, delighting his niece and nephew with elaborate steam engines and bathtub ducks magnetized so that the ducklings bobbed in a row behind the mother. Artistic and a natural bon vivant, he played host to visiting Americans in his elegant Nuremberg home, which was filled with valuable etchings and woodcuts — some, it was said, by Albrecht Dürer.

Zinn's life changed dramatically in the summer of 1936, when he was arrested and denied a passport. Hitler's campaign against "undesirables" included homosexuals as well as Jews, and Zinn was a lifelong "bachelor." Within the family, the real reason for his alarming disappearance was covered up. When Arthur was apprised of the situation, he counseled Frederick Birchall, the *Times*' Berlin bureau chief, to "do nothing." Arthur had been persuaded by Zinn's brother-in-law not to antagonize the Nazis. As a result, neither Birchall nor the Sulzbergers made any effort on Zinn's behalf.

In February 1937 Zinn was released from prison, shamed and despondent. Within months he lost a sister to ill health. By Christmas he was in such a state that he cried openly at another sister's dinner table in Fürth. By then she was making plans to leave Germany with her husband and small daughter. As a German citizen, a Jew, and a purported homosexual with an arrest record, Zinn had no such option. Several weeks later, in January 1938, he hanged himself in his own home. "He was a broken man," said a relative.

Despite the many people she and Arthur managed to save during the Holocaust, Iphigene would forever feel remorse about the people she did not. "I didn't do all I should have during these Nazi atrocities," she said. She was not a woman given to emotion, observed one of her grandchildren years later, "but that subject brought her to tears."

15

Wartime Footing

RTHUR WAS SLEEPING COMFORTABLY ONE NIGHT in early November 1944 when the phone rang. Groggy and disgruntled, he picked up the receiver and growled, "What is it?" The man on the other end of the line didn't miss a beat. "It's a boy!" cried Orvil, referring to his second child, Bobby, who had just been born. With his usual backhanded humor, Arthur declared the new arrival "homely" and dubbed him Ichabod after the awkward, beaknosed schoolmaster immortalized by Washington Irving.

While Iphigene gracefully accepted her status as a grandparent, Arthur was ambivalent. When Marian had presented him with Jackie, his first grandchild, a year and a half earlier, he had declared that he did *not* want to be called Grandpa or Gramps, insisting on Grumpy instead. But Jackie could not pronounce the word. One day she pointed her finger at him and blurted out, "Bumpy," and the moniker stuck. Iphigene settled for the more conventional Granny.

With the arrival of grandchildren, the senior Sulzbergers took on roles patterned after Adolph and Effie, with Marian and Orvil in the positions Arthur and Iphigene had once occupied as young marrieds. Within the family, Orvil called Arthur "Father"; at the office he observed hierarchical decorum and greeted him as "Mr. Sulzberger." Every summer during the war, the Dryfooses lived with Arthur and Iphigene at Hillandale, moving into the empty bedrooms, eating vegetables grown in the Sulzbergers' version of a victory garden, and watching the children play on the wide lawns. "We lived with them, summer after summer," said Marian. "I think it was hard on Orv."

Gas rationing was strictly enforced during the war, and even the publisher of *The New York Times* was not exempt. Luckily, a bus ran by Hillandale and proceeded on to the railway station, making it possible for

Arthur and Orvil to commute between White Plains and West Forty-third Street. In a bow to wartime exigencies, the Sulzbergers raised chickens, pigs, and even two steers on their vast acreage, slaughtering them for food. The experience didn't sit well with Iphigene, who found it difficult to become friendly with animals she knew would end up as entrées.

Judy was largely absent from the Hillandale ménage except during vacations from Smith College, where she had enrolled in the fall of 1942. Despite their persistent friction, Arthur admired his youngest daughter's intelligence; she was, he said, the brightest of his four children and possessed "a challenging and quick mind." She had also been accepted to Vassar and Bryn Mawr but had decided on Smith because Ruth, then in her senior year, was still there and could ease her entry. "I was afraid of leaving home," she admitted. It did not take long for Judy's exhibitionist nature to manifest itself: in the junior play she read the prologue standing on her head.

Within the family, Judy was considered rather ditzy and emotionally volatile, in part because of her un-Sulzbergerian tendency to blurt out what she really felt, but she was also a serious student, determined to become a doctor. So solid was her academic performance that she left Smith after three years under a plan that made it possible for her to take her final year as an entering medical student at the College of Physicians and Surgeons, part of Columbia University, and still receive her Smith diploma. Judy's interest in medicine had begun with her own near fatal illness as a child and was later reinforced by success in ninth-grade biology and what she described as chronic hypochondria. In the end, though, her primary motivation was that medicine was far afield from *The New York Times*. "Judy wanted to separate herself from the Sulzbergers, the Ochses, and make a name for herself," said Dick Cohen, her second husband.

Punch, meanwhile, was enjoying the experience of being "out from under the [tyranny] of women" at all-male Loomis. He didn't mind waiting on tables or cleaning classrooms, chores required of all students regardless of wealth or social pedigree. But academically he was no more successful in the regimented routine of boarding school than he had been in the elite private academies of Manhattan. He frittered away his time "having fun and daydreaming." A math teacher once became so exasperated that he paddled Punch on the rear end with a math book, an act that had an instantly edifying effect on the boy's grades. "I guess it was all in there somewhere," he said later. "I just didn't like [studying], and nobody pushed me terribly hard." His performance was so poor, he had to repeat his freshman year.

Punch's real education took place outside the classroom. As one of only a handful of Jewish students, he was singled out for hazing, his clothes thrown out dormitory windows. He never complained to his parents or Loomis's headmaster, Nathaniel Batchelder, a Unitarian minister. "We had to learn how to deal with this kind of atmosphere," Punch's classmate Alan Rabinowitz said. "It was one of the burdens in life."

Later Punch would joke that Pearl Harbor "saved me from perpetual servitude as a sophomore." In January 1943, at the age of sixteen, Punch impulsively decided to change his life and, like the Illinois farmboy who escaped his plow to pursue glory in *The Red Badge of Courage,* left Loomis, never to return. His intention was to enlist in the marines, a plan that required his parents' permission since he was underage. Iphigene and Arthur were reluctant but were finally persuaded by Punch's argument that in a little over a year's time he would be eighteen years old and eligible for the draft anyway. At least this way, he told them, he would be able to choose the branch of the armed services he wanted.

While waiting to be called, Punch spent his mornings on the seventh floor of the Times Building, making transmitters and receivers for Times Facsimile, a subsidiary that manufactured portable facsimile machines for the Signal Corps. Arthur knew his son had an aptitude for electronics and thought the work would help him prepare for a position as a military radio operator. In the afternoons Punch attended Morningside School, a small academy on the Upper West Side that specialized in one-on-one instruction for young actors and other students with unorthodox schedules. It was there that Punch found his first real girlfriend. The combination of work, study, and a semblance of a social life had a transformative effect. "Punch is beginning to develop into a thinking human being," Arthur marveled in a letter to a relative.

In December 1943, two months before Punch was eligible to be drafted, a family friend and captain in the Marine Corps intervened and saw to it that his application was acted upon. Punch was aware that his life up to that point had been a series of failures and disappointments. Instinctively, he had sought out the Marine Corps — the toughest branch of the military — not because he was certain he could succeed there but because he longed to be tested in a purely masculine milieu, free from the burdens and protections that came with being a member of the family that owned *The New York Times*. "It let me prove to [myself] that I could carry my own weight equally or better than anybody else," he later said of his service in the corps. "It just grew me up completely."

Punch reported to Parris Island, a desolate patch of South Carolina lowland, on January 22, 1944, for a brutal three-month training period. In this unforgiving atmosphere he experienced the first real success of his life. He was still short for his age, but his speed and athletic prowess, honed by school sports, helped him stand out. He was also a crack shot and a key contributor to the Thirty-eighth Platoon's near perfect rifle score of 98.7. Within weeks of his arrival, he was named a corporal of his squad — the same leadership position his father had held in 1916 at the first Plattsburgh camp. Simply finding something he was good at and gaining recognition for it boosted his battered self-confidence. He even tried, ultimately without success, to reinvent his image by shedding his childhood nickname and using the more adult name of Art.

§

By the spring of 1944, it was well known that the Allies were planning an invasion of France, but the actual date and circumstances were a deeply guarded secret. Just thinking about the momentous event put Arthur in a wistful mood, and one Sunday in late May he climbed up to the flat roof of 5 East Eightieth Street, stripped to his shorts, and lay down on a faded blue mattress he had taken from the playroom. While baking in the sun and writing a speech, he heard bands rehearsing martial music in Central Park. His mind drifted to Ruth and Punch, "who wear the uniform I used to wear." Filled with unabashed patriotism, fear for his children, and a sense of his own advancing age, he wrote a verse about what it meant to be an American and sent it to Ruth in England.

When D-Day dawned, Arthur was in Tennessee. He had accepted an honorary degree the night before from the University of Chattanooga and was asleep in the president's house when a phone call from New York informed him of the first reports of the invasion. On the plane home he wrote an emotional letter to Ruth full of envy and yearning for his own lost chance at heroism: "I'd give my eye teeth to be in it and if I were would probably give the skull that holds them, but still I'd like to be there. You are a lucky girl, you know. Life hasn't passed you by."

Arthur arrived back at West Forty-third Street to find that the *Times* had printed three editions of the paper overnight, the first two based on early dispatches and the last with confirmation of the invasion, which had come into the newsroom at 3:32 A.M. The electronic "news zipper" girding the Times Tower, inaugurated by Adolph in 1928 and now long dark because of blackout regulations, snapped on and worked eighteen hours straight with news of the troop landing. "We have come to the hour for which we were born," said the *Times* editorial the next day. "We go forth to meet the supreme test of our arms and our souls, the test of the maturity of our faith in ourselves and in mankind."

Ruth spent D-Day at the Boreham air base in England. When the success of the invasion was assured, she traveled with her Red Cross colleagues and the 394th Army Air Force Bombardment Group to the southern coast to await transfer to France. The high drama of the situation only deepened the romantic drama that had been apparent for several months between Ruth and Ben Golden, a field officer with the 394th. The couple had met shortly after Ruth arrived at Boreham, and on the surface at least, they made an unlikely match.

A native of the Kentucky mountains and the son of an automobile dealer, Ben had the husky build of the high school football star he had once been. His full lips, dark eyes, ruddy complexion, and slightly curly hair, combined with Golden as a last name, made people mistake him for a Jew. In fact, his family attended the First Christian Church and his forebears hailed from County Tyrone, Northern Ireland, in the mid-eighteenth century. At the University of Kentucky, he had joined Pi Kappa Alpha, a fraternity known more for its embrace of the Confederate mystique than for its polish. "I can just see him down there in the South, going hunting with the boys," said Luellen Bowles Hewitt, who served in the Red Cross with Ruth and knew Ben at Boreham. When Ben had volunteered for the Army Air Force, he was western manager for the Tennessee Valley Authority in Knoxville, a position of which he was inordinately proud.

Ben loved beautiful cars, swing music — he was an excellent dancer — and good bourbon and scotch. Many women found him sexy. Ruth, a comparative innocent who lacked confidence in her looks and had never dated until just before college, was mesmerized. Despite Ben's lack of refinement, she was drawn by his traditional masculinity and the sudden intimacy fostered by the war. "Relationships over here cannot be weighed successfully because circumstances, need for companionship and a new life play too much part," she later wrote her parents, long after she and Ben had become involved. "Even those who feel they've found something cannot know for sure. . . . No one, no matter how stable, should be away from everything they know and want for a year. For they forget what they know and doubt what they want and regard things totally without perspective."

The disparity between Ben's and Ruth's backgrounds would have been sufficient cause for Arthur and Iphigene to worry, but they were troubled by another, more disturbing factor: Ben was married. Later, as if marshaling justification for her liaison with a married man, Ruth would tell her children that the fact that Ben and his wife had had no offspring after ten years of marriage was a sign that the union was in trouble. "The idea was that the marriage was not working came first, and then she came on the scene second," said her son Michael.

When Arthur learned of the situation, he took action to stop it. At his request, the Red Cross director at Boreham sat down with Ben and Ruth and tried to persuade them to disentangle themselves. Ruth soon told her family that the relationship was over, but within weeks it was apparent to Arthur's younger brother, David, who was in England in connection with his work for the National Refugee Service, that such was not the case. "Don't be impressed with the fact that she has written you that all is off between them," he wrote Arthur, adding that "[Ben] is all right, I guess, but from some things I hear he hasn't got much class."

In France Ben and Ruth were stationed first in Normandy, then in Orléans, where the military men and Red Cross workers worked side by side in a bombed-out airfield and slept in tents pitched in a nearby apple orchard. With her command of French, Ruth was soon able to get an apartment, which was not only more commodious but afforded her a discreet way to see Ben.

While Ruth watched the approaching light of victory in Europe, Punch, his basic training over, waited to be shipped out to the Pacific. By the fall of 1944, he was stationed at Camp Pendleton, several miles from San Diego, awaiting transfer. In mid-December his orders came through, assigning him to the island of Leyte in the Philippines. Punch is "off to the Pacific taking his chances with a lot of others," Arthur wrote a relative in Chicago.

The statement was disingenuous, and Arthur knew it. Punch was not "taking his chances" with everyone else; instead, at General Douglas MacArthur's request and with Arthur's grateful acquiescence, Punch had been released from his marine unit and was soon to be attached to the headquarters of the supreme commander of Allied forces in the Southwest Pacific Area at Tacloban, which was staffed by an all-services unit. He worked in the basement under MacArthur's house, a square stucco structure that had been an officers' club during the Japanese occupation, first as a radio operator in naval interception and then, when it was determined he wasn't fast enough in Japanese code, as a "Jeep driver, a gofer, a jack-of-all-trades." The work was not particularly interesting, but it had one key virtue: it was relatively safe.

Punch's special berth had been arranged several weeks prior to his shipping out, during a Red Cross junket Arthur had taken to the Pacific war zone with assistant managing editor Turner Catledge. Arthur had not gone to the Pacific with the intention of "fixing" a spot for Punch, but MacArthur had his own reasons for wanting to be of service to the publisher of *The New York Times* and made the offer.

A man of unbridled ego and ambition, MacArthur had been mentioned only months earlier in connection with the Republican nomination for president, giving him ample reason, as he looked ahead, to want to court Arthur. On the day Arthur and Turner arrived at headquarters, MacArthur arranged a lunch for them in his mess, with Arthur carefully positioned on MacArthur's right. Afterward the two fell into conversation. MacArthur asked whether Arthur had any relatives in the service, and Arthur replied that he had a son in the marines. "I hate the marines," said MacArthur. "They sacrifice their men. They have no sense of the value of life. Why don't you let me request him for my headquarters?" Arthur explained that Punch had chosen the marines himself. "I can't interfere with him," he told the general. "All right, but I think you're making a big mistake," said MacArthur.

For the next two days, Arthur brooded about whether he had made the right decision. He had never gotten over his own lack of combat service during World War I. Indeed, when prior to seeing MacArthur he and Turner had unexpectedly found themselves in the midst of Japanese sniper fire on the tiny island of Peleliu, the situation had privately given Arthur great pleasure. He understood Punch's desire to prove himself on the battlefield, as generations of men had done before him.

However, Arthur also very much wanted him to survive the war; Punch was not only his son but, as the sole male in the Sulzberger line, the putative heir to head *The New York Times* some day. As a marine private, Punch was more likely than most to be sent to the front lines; as a radio operator armed with an aerial antenna, he would be a particularly visible target. Finally, after much soul-searching, Arthur went to MacArthur and said obliquely, "I cannot say yes or no. I have to leave it to you." That was sufficient for MacArthur, and the deed was done. Later Arthur told the general that he was "eternally grateful."

Punch was never informed that he had been singled out for special treatment, but when he was ordered to report to MacArthur's headquarters, he was suspicious. "It became quite obvious when I discovered where I was that some sort of miracle had happened," he said. Soon after his arrival at Tacloban, he asked his commanding officer for a transfer to a marine combat unit. The request went nowhere. He wrote to Orvil, bitterly complaining about his situation, and sent his father a letter expressing outrage at what he assumed had been done.

Arthur did not reply. Even after the war he did not tell Punch the circumstances that had prompted his decision, and Punch, as was customary in the mannered culture of the Sulzberger clan, did not ask. For years Punch nursed a simmering anger at his father for taking away the one thing he had accomplished on his own: the right to fight as a marine. "For the first time, Punch was one of the guys, he belonged to a group," explained a close friend. "For the first time, he'd really *done* it. And this action singled him out totally as the son of the publisher of *The New York Times.* His father didn't understand how lonely that boy was, how isolated he'd been." Ten years would pass before Punch would finally summon the courage to confront Arthur. One day, after Punch had downed several drinks during a party on the sunporch at Hillandale, he exploded with full force at his father, as other guests looked on in horror and amazement. "Punch, I didn't want you to get killed!" Arthur protested. The storm subsided as quickly as it had arisen, but the bitterness remained for a long time. "I never really forgave him," said Punch. "But I understood what he had done, and we moved on in our relationship."

§

Germany surrendered on May 7, 1945, the tenth anniversary of the day Arthur had become publisher of *The New York Times.* Although confirmation did not come until the following day, the unofficial news brought thousands of jubilant people swarming into Times Square, where, despite the continued policy of paper conservation, the streets were soon littered with excelsior. As the festivities echoed below him, Arthur sat in his office pondering the anniversary note Charles Merz had sent him, congratulating him on his performance as publisher "during the ten most critical years in modern history." Later that day he penned a short message of thanks to his foreign and domestic correspondents.

By June Arthur was in Paris with managing editor Edwin L. James celebrating the reclamation of the *Times* bureau, which had been taken over by the Germans during the occupation and rented out to French companies. He also used the visit to map out the postwar assignments of the paper's foreign staff, strategically placing his nephew Cy, the *Times'* chief foreign correspondent, in the plum location of Paris. By then Ruth had moved with her Red Cross unit to the German-Dutch border, where she was billeted with a "very anti-Semitic" German family. To surprise her, Arthur asked the bureau secretary in Paris to call Ruth and tell her that Cy and Drew Middleton, another *Times* reporter, would soon be coming to see her. Everyone but Ruth knew that Arthur was part of the group.

On the morning of the appointed day, Ruth's roommate, Joan Hughes, told her she should wash her hair and press her uniform. "Hell, I'm not going to all that [trouble] just for Cy!" she replied. At lunch the colonel in charge of the 394th Bombardment Group informed her that her guests had just flown in. "Take my car," he said nonchalantly. "Your car?" she gulped, still suspecting nothing. With Ben at the wheel, she arrived at the airfield. Looking out the window, she saw two familiar figures approaching. As she got out, she noticed a third. Shrieking, she rushed toward her father and burst into tears. Arthur, too, was overcome. "The [other] fellows who were with us drew discreetly to one side and let us cry in peace," he later wrote to Iphigene.

With Arthur's help, Ruth got a pass and accompanied him back to Paris, where they took rooms at the Ritz and had long, soulful talks. "It always comes out the same," said Arthur. "Neither one of us can believe it's real." Tanks rumbled down the Champs-Elysées and men in uniform sipped coffee at battered outdoor cafés. Compared with its prewar insouciance, Arthur found the City of Light "rather depressing." Still, he was delighted to be included in the official dinner for General Dwight D.

Eisenhower, who only days earlier had been decorated by French president Charles de Gaulle at the foot of the Arc de Triomphe.

By late July 1945 Arthur was back in New York, overseeing the coverage of the war in the Pacific and tending to business as usual. The routine was deceptive, for weeks earlier he had become privy to a secret known to almost no one in private life and to only a handful within the government: he had learned about the government's effort to test an atomic bomb.

In the spring of 1945 General Leslie Groves, head of the Manhattan Project, had quietly approached Edwin L. James and asked to borrow science reporter William L. Laurence for a top-secret war assignment. James agreed, without knowing the precise nature of Laurence's job. For the next several months Laurence worked anonymously out of an office in Oak Ridge, Tennessee, one of the bomb-production sites, absorbing information about the weapon's development so that he could write press releases and stories about it when it was put to use. He labored twelve hours a day, seven days a week, under conditions so secure that the contents of his bright red wastebasket were burned every day and he felt "afraid even to talk to myself." He visited the secret labs and the three main production plants and witnessed the first test in New Mexico.

On August 2, 1945, an army captain dressed in mufti came to New York to see Turner Catledge, who was acting as the paper's managing editor while James was away on vacation. He instructed Turner to report to Washington the next day to learn more about "the Laurence matter." Turner knew that Laurence was on loan to the government but, like James, did not know the details. After alerting Arthur, Turner traveled by overnight train to Washington and the next day found himself seated at a conference table with six or eight men, some in uniform, some not. At the urging of General Groves, who chaired the meeting, the men briefed Turner on the background of the bomb. Groves told him that a decision had been made to drop one or more of the weapons on Japan; at that very moment crews were poised for takeoff. The *Times* was the only paper informed in advance about the bomb's imminent deployment, in part as a gesture of gratitude for the use of Laurence.

Turner returned to New York that night, and the next day, Friday, went up to Hillandale to report to Arthur. He found the publisher standing on the lawn entertaining some of Iphigene's friends who had come for lunch. The two men walked solemnly to the swimming pool, where Turner gave him the news. That weekend Arthur was so nervous and distracted that Iphigene asked him what was wrong. "It's nothing, nothing personal," he assured her. "I'm not worried about anything." The following Monday, August 6, a B-29 named *Enola Gay* dropped the world's first atomic bomb on Hiroshima. The *Times'* front-page story, unbylined, featured an across-the-page headline three lines deep: FIRST ATOMIC BOMB DROPPED ON JAPAN; MISSILE IS EQUAL TO 20,000 TONS OF TNT; TRUMAN WARNS FOE OF 'RAIN OF RUIN.' Three days later a plutonium-based bomb ravaged Nagasaki. Laurence was aboard the instrument plane that accompanied the bomber, and for his eyewitness account he won the Pulitzer Prize.

When Japan surrendered on August 14, Times Square again erupted into a spontaneous frenzy of kissing, hugging, and dancing. Half a world away in the Pacific, Punch, recently recovered from a bout of jaundice, accompanied MacArthur to Japan three days before the official treaty-signing ceremonies. From Yokohama, where he bedded down in an old silk factory, he could see Tokyo, blackened by the fire bombings.

Julius was aboard the USS *Missouri* to report the formal moment of Japanese surrender for *The New York Times*. To his everlasting disappointment, he had been sidelined from military service the previous year by a gallstone attack in New Guinea. After an operation at Walter Reed Hospital and several months of recovery, he had resumed his prewar duties at the paper. When Secretary of the Navy James Forrestal and Secretary of War Henry Stimson had invited Arthur and several other top newspaper executives on a seven-week tour to observe the Pacific military operations firsthand, he had declined, designating Julius instead. The group had been on Okinawa when Japan's offer of surrender came through, and Julius quickly arranged press credentials to cover the ceremonies. Despite his lack of training as a reporter, he filed a vivid series of dispatches and followed up with several stories about the first days of the American occupation.

Punch's period with MacArthur during his first triumphal weeks in Japan should have been the highlight of his wartime service, but he spent most of that time in a hospital bed, first with a siege of amoebic dysentery and then with a series of skin eruptions made worse by the Asian climate. Because of his condition, he was sent back to the States in early October and had a fifteen-day furlough in New York before reporting to Camp Lejeune. Soon after Punch's arrival, Arthur wrote a letter to

MacArthur thanking him for watching out for his son. "I fear that he couldn't have been of very much use around headquarters and that his tour of duty in hospitals was rather excessive," he said. "But the kid certainly had a bad break in that respect and, of course, it wasn't his fault."

Her Red Cross duty done, Ruth soon followed her brother home, sailing from Le Havre on board the SS *Mariposa,* a former U.S. cruise ship that been converted to a troop transport. With forty other women, she slept in a large room that had once been the ship's dispensary, clambering onto the top of a double-decker bunk each night and playing endless rounds of bridge to wile away the time. Attached to her bed by a leash was a live bit of contraband — Ruben, a longhaired dachshund on which she had taken pity in Le Havre and had smuggled aboard in a duffel bag. The presence of an animal was completely against the rules; Ruth did not dare take him for walks on deck for fear of detection. As the days wore on, rivulets of dog urine trickled toward the luggage, and the stench, heightened by the smell of unwashed linen and unwashed bodies, became overpowering. "This trip is like a long drawn-out illness," Ruth's bunkmate, Betty John, wrote in her account of the journey. "Tempers are short. Everyone is smelly."

The *Mariposa* anchored in Boston Harbor on October 24. Ruth had been away from home for almost two years and, despite her parents' concern for Punch's safety, had been in far greater danger than her brother. Like so many other weary Americans, she was restless to get back to her former life, but she and the other women aboard the *Mariposa* had to wait on deck while the thousands of troops were let off first. While standing there leaning on the rail, she spied a small government tug approaching the ship. "I know this is going to sound silly," she told the soldier next to her, "but that looks like my father standing on the deck of that boat." "Yeah, sure," the man replied, rolling his eyes. As the small launch came closer, a banner unfurled bearing the greeting HI RUTHIE! With that, the entire ship erupted in a chorus of "Hi-i-i-i, Ruthie!" Ruth broke out in a broad grin. Using his connections in the military, Arthur had managed to meet his daughter in a boat that carried the harbormaster, a senior armed forces official, and Punch. "It's my daddy!" cried Ruth, jumping up and down. "It's my daddy!"

16

Fantasy and Reality

L IKE THE UNITED STATES, ARTHUR EMERGED FROM the war with new confidence in his capabilities and powers. He had run *The New York Times* with relative independence during the most threatening conflict of the century and had become thoroughly intoxicated with the heady world of Roosevelt, Eisenhower, MacArthur, and Churchill. The strain of events had taken a toll on his heart, however, necessitating hospitalization and two months away from work in 1943. In addition, he was afflicted with Dupuytren's contracture, a condition that gradually curled his fingers into claws and required three painful operations. But he took solace in the fact that his internationalist views had been vindicated; more than ever he believed that America — and by extension, the *Times* — had a unique responsibility to serve as the guardian of freedom. "The eyes of the world are on [us]," he told *Times* reporters in a message from the publisher in December 1945. "We have to make our democratic system work for their benefit as well as for our own."

The visible manifestation of Arthur's new status was an ambitious enlargement and renovation of the New York Times Building on West Forty-third Street. Fearful of a postwar recession, Julius had argued against spending money on new construction, but Arthur had boldly moved ahead. When the modern eleven-story expansion opened in 1948, reporters in the previously cramped newsroom suddenly had space to breathe. The addition meant that some reporters in the third-floor city room were nearly one hundred yards from the editors, a distance so vast that the staff presented assistant managing editor Turner Catledge with opera glasses. Arthur installed fifteen new presses and ordered bedrooms built on the fourteenth floor so that top executives could stay overnight during emergencies. "What we are headed for I don't know," he told an inquiring reader, "but at least we . . . are not going to die of dry rot or suffocation."

He also commissioned an overhaul of the lobby, for the first time putting his personal imprint on one of Adolph's architectural creations. Visitors now entered a high-ceilinged space of white marble with indirect lighting. Straight ahead was a bust of Adolph and the "without fear or favor" motto, incorrectly quoted as usual. To the left was a new addition, a half globe of the world, bolted to the wall and accompanied by two lines from an 1889 poem by Sarah Chauncey Woolsey: "Every day is a fresh beginning / Every morn is the world made new." The sentiment was archaically romantic, but to Arthur it captured the joy he felt at the daily miracle of a newspaper and served as a satisfying counterpoint to "All the News That's Fit to Print," which remained on the lobby wall in a less prominent location.

Arthur's strategy of printing more, rather than larger, papers during the wartime newsprint shortage paid off handsomely in increased readership. In May 1946 the circulation of the Sunday *New York Times* shot past the 1 million mark for the first time in its history. The paper's advertising lead over the *Herald Tribune,* which had narrowed to a sliver during the war, rebounded dramatically.

Despite a postwar boom and the United States' expanded international role, Arthur stayed with a narrowly focused mission for *The New York Times.* He opened new bureaus in San Francisco, Los Angeles, and Hollywood and began to ship papers by air to Washington, Detroit, and Cleveland in time for breakfast delivery, yet made it clear that the *Times* had no intention of becoming a national newspaper. Instead, he said, it aspired to be a "New York newspaper with a national circulation." While the New York *Daily News,* the *Los Angeles Times,* and the Louisville *Courier-Journal* bought television stations, Arthur judged the medium inappropriate for newspaper owners. "The question is not whether television is a good business, but whether it is our business," he told the New York State Publishers Association.

Although Arthur's views on Zionism and other Jewish issues had, if anything, hardened during the war, Iphigene's had been transformed. For her, the systematic murder of 6 million Jews made a separate state of Israel "comprehensible — and necessary." "I am afraid the world regards the Jews just as the pioneers did the American Indian: The only good one is a dead one," she wrote Scotty Reston. She contributed to the cause and, incidentally, stopped going to temple, no longer able to bear listening to prayers about a God of Israel who freed captives and loved the Jews. "Has God ever heard of Auschwitz?" she asked the rabbi indignantly.

Julius continued to resist the establishment of a Jewish homeland, yet when he inspected Dachau and Buchenwald in the spring of 1945, just before Germany's surrender, he couldn't help but be moved. In a barracks at Buchenwald, living skeletons — "husks of men," as he described them — let out a feeble cheer when they saw the eighteen-member press delegation assembled by General Eisenhower; Julius left the building in tears. "I know you all want to know about it and I'll tell you," he informed the family when he returned. "But I don't ever want to talk about it again. I want to try and forget." Despite the powerful effect of such experiences on the owners of *The New York Times,* readers detected no change in the coverage of Nazi barbarism. The front-page story on the liberation of Dachau never mentioned the word *Jew.* A week later Cy Sulzberger's story about Russian estimates of the death toll at Auschwitz appeared on page twelve, with no indication that most of the victims were Jews.

In 1946 Arthur himself visited Dachau and sat in on the Nuremberg trials. The grisly tour included ovens, torture chambers, open graves, and even several unburned and unburied bodies, yet it failed to touch him as it had Julius. While in Germany, he picked up a piece of marble and a shard of glass from the ruins of Hitler's desk and for years displayed them in a small box as souvenirs. Despite the misery he had witnessed, he returned home unshaken in his opposition to Israel as a separate state, opposition he freely admitted was fueled by the "character assassination" that had been visited upon him by Zionists during the war.

When the United Nations recommended the partition of Palestine into Jewish and Arab states in August 1947, *The New York Times* supported the plan, not because it supported Jewish sovereignty, Arthur was quick to explain, but because it wanted to lend a voice of confidence to the still-fragile United Nations. The following spring the *Times* did not endorse Israel's declaration of independence; it merely accepted the act as a fait accompli. "My attitude toward Israel is the same as my attitude toward Indonesia," Arthur told the Newark *Jewish News.* "I wish it well, but am completely without nationalistic fervor toward it."

Eventually, the *Times* established a bureau in Jerusalem, although no Jewish reporter was ever based there during Arthur's publishership and Israel was forbidden to be referred to as "the Jewish State" on the editorial page. But he was pragmatic enough to recognize that New York City's Jews were a formidable force, so he assigned Irving "Pat" Spiegel, a *Times* reporter, to cover "Jewish news," a beat unlike any the paper had ever had. For the next two decades, Spiegel kept up with the important rabbis in town and got tickets to high holy day services for Arthur to pass out to his friends. "He was the house fixer for the Jewish community, that was his job," said Bill Kovach, a *Times* reporter and bureau chief who knew Spiegel toward the end of his tenure.

The enmity of Zionists and other critics notwithstanding, Arthur was unquestionably in full command of *The New York Times* after the war in a way he had not been earlier. In the late 1940s, at an awards ceremony at the University of Missouri School of Journalism, the dean introduced the evening's other honoree in exhaustive detail but his words were tellingly succinct when it came Arthur's turn. "Arthur Hays Sulzberger is the biggest man on the best newspaper in the world." Marshall Loeb, a future Time Inc. editor, was a student in the audience that night and recalled the reaction. "Everyone accepted it without question," he said. "It was a given."

§

Armed with a new military title — major general in the Officers Reserve Corps — Julius reestablished his beachhead at *The New York Times* with more bluster than ever after the war. General Adler, as he preferred to be called, expected the male receptionist on the fourteenth floor to stand at attention whenever he came into view. His personal assistant, John Sheehan, an Irish Catholic whom Julius affectionately addressed as Boy, accompanied him every summer to Camp Drummond in Plattsburgh, New York, where more than a dozen *New York Times* business executives — former officers hired by Julius — gathered for two weeks of drill and military exercises. "It was the damndest sight," said Mike Ryan, a *Times* office boy at the time. "The head of circulation had a helmet on, and important people in advertising. [The business side of the *Times*] came to a halt." One of Julius's odder recruits was Commander Cortland J. Strang, a 1921 Annapolis graduate who served as the *Times'* mechanical superintendent and could often be found sitting at his desk, assembling a ship in a bottle. "He was famous for polishing the leaves of his plants with an oilcloth," said Tom Campion, Strang's eventual successor.

Julius commanded respect from his subordinates, but he also engendered fear. After a sweat-inducing session with the General, people "would go out to Sardi's and have a couple of belts just to recover from the experience," said a former assistant business manager. But his gruff demeanor was largely a facade, and Julius was widely admired for his decisiveness, fairness, and decency. He was gratified when someone spoke up to him, and possessed idiosyncratic quirks that made him lovable. Chief among them was his apparent failure to grasp telephone technology. When speaking long-distance, he faced in the direction of the call and modulated his voice according to the mileage. Connecticut merited a conversational tone, California a full-throated blast.

But he was miscast as a modern manager. Obsessed with control, Julius made himself the hub of the wheel on the business side of the paper: production, circulation, advertising, and promotion radiated outward from him. Because no major decision could be made without his participation, departments battled one another for Julius's favor, creating a poisonous atmosphere of subterfuge and backbiting.

The *Times* had never seen fit to institute budgets, so Julius had only a vague idea of whether individual departments were efficiently managed. The result was that he would arbitrarily issue orders to cut back on new personnel, new equipment, and other expenditures, infuriating Arthur, who felt that Julius was trying to block his creation of a great newspaper. "Adler thought Sulzberger was a liberal spender and liberal thinker," said Amory Bradford, who came to the *Times* after the war. "Sulzberger thought Adler was a tightfisted reactionary."

At home, Julius ranted about Arthur's "gallivanting" trips to Europe and expressed disdain for the manner in which Punch's postings had been "greased" for him during the war. His wife, Babs, was only too happy to echo his fury and add a few complaints of her own. She was especially disparaging of Iphigene, who as the wife of the publisher enjoyed an exalted position of power and privilege Babs felt should have been hers. She thought Iphigene's clothes dowdy, her treatment of servants "familiar," and her dinner parties tastelessly informal. "Babs was a tragic malcontent," said her former daughter-in-law, Anne Freeman

Turpin. "She looked at her life and figured the only way to deal with it was to criticize everybody."

The Adler marriage had long before become a marriage in name only. In 1939 Julius, Babs, and the three "kidlets," as he called Julie Jr., Bobbie, and Nancy, had moved into a twenty-two-room apartment at 630 Park Avenue, where the couple, who had previously shared a bedroom, occupied separate quarters. While Julius was overseas, Babs took two lovers: Alan Rinehart, the son of mystery writer Mary Roberts Rinehart, and Joseph V. McKee, a noted Roman Catholic layman and lawyer — his nickname among the Adlers was Holy Joe — who had served as acting mayor of New York in 1932 after the resignation of James J. "Jimmy" Walker. Whether Julius knew about his wife's infidelities is unclear, but Iphigene certainly did, and she was surprisingly sympathetic. "I feel so sorry for Babs," she said years later when Holy Joe died. "He meant so much to her."

Arthur noticed the reserve in the Adler marriage and urged Julius to find a mistress, advice that he was emotionally unequipped to take. Unlike Arthur, who flaunted his extramarital conquests and often had long-term relationships, Julius quietly fulfilled his needs by frequenting Madeleine's, an East Side nightclub where the downstairs was a saloon with a black jazz trio and the upstairs was a high-class bordello. For a man of Julius's Victorian sensibilities, divorce was out of the question. "One doesn't wash one's dirty linen in public," he told his daughter Bobbie when she asked why he had never ended the marriage. "Besides," he added in a rush, "I've always loved your mother." Bobbie considered his expression of devotion purely a formality. "I don't think he ever knew anything about loving; I don't think anyone in my family did," she said.

With her voracious appetite for money, possessions, glamour, and prestige, Babs was a brittle and unforgiving harridan, impatient with Julius's austere ways. For several years she accepted his birthday and anniversary gifts, then began to return them. "I would prefer a check," she told him coldly. In defense, Julius kept his finances secret. He asked Babs to sign blank income-tax forms and never revealed what he made as general manager of *The New York Times*. "She would rag him about money," said Bobbie. "She was always saying that he and Arthur didn't pay themselves enough."

Nine live-in servants catered to the Adlers in their enormous apartment, decorated with reproduction Louis XV furniture. Babs, called

Muh-MAH by her offspring in the manner of the British upper class, took her morning meal in bed and declined to see her children off to school. Julie Jr., Bobbie, and Nancy ate hot cereal and honey with their father, who silently read his *New York Times*, the paper raised before his face. When he was done, he snapped it closed. "Well, gotta go and make you kidlets a new pair of shoes!" he announced before descending to the lobby, where Sam Baker, the chauffeur, waited to ferry him to the office. "For the longest time, I thought my father was a cobbler," said Bobbie.

On Sundays Julius observed an unchangeable routine that began with horseback riding in Central Park, Julius astride Miracle, the horse he rode in military parades, and the younger Adlers on rented steeds. He then visited Nannie, who since George's death in 1931 had lived alone in the San Remo, an elegant building on Central Park West. Sunday lunch followed at the Adler apartment; it, too, was always the same: old-fashioneds, soup, and rare roast beef, carved in the kitchen and passed by servants. Anne O'Hare McCormick and her husband, or Edwin L. James and his French wife, Simone, and other guests from *The New York Times* rounded out the table. "It was their version of having people to Hillandale," said Julie Jr. Discussion revolved around the day's news. "Now, I'm interested in what you young people have to say about Scotty Reston's column," Julius would begin, lighting up an unfiltered Chesterfield and turning to his terrified offspring.

Julius's long absences in the army and at the office, coupled with Babs's harshness and indifference, damaged each of the Adler children in one way or another. In Julie Jr. the result was a kind of destructive self-delusion. Tall and athletic, Julie Jr. had wanted to pursue a professional baseball career, but as Julius Ochs Adler's namesake, he was expected to march in lockstep with his father. As a young boy he had joined the Knickerbocker Greys, a drill team, and attended Culver Military Institute and Lawrenceville, the boarding school where his father had graduated as the valedictorian. After the war Julius insisted that his son enroll at Princeton, his own alma mater. Julie Jr. obeyed but did no work, flunking out after one semester.

He got a job in sales at Westinghouse Electric Supply Company and lived at home, where he antagonized Babs with his smelly cigars, boorish manners, and candidly expressed carnal desires. He was on the verge of being thrown out of the house when he met Anne Freeman, the refined, Vassar-educated daughter of Douglas Southall Freeman, the retired editor of the *Richmond* (Va.) *News-Leader* and biographer of Robert E. Lee. *Editor & Publisher* ran an item about their marriage in the summer of 1950, describing it as the union of "two distinguished newspaper families." The suggestion of dynastic royalty pleased Babs, although she failed to understand what Anne saw in her son. "I'm worried about this marriage, because she's such an intelligent girl," she told a friend.

On the first day back from his honeymoon, Julie Jr. entered a five-year training program at *The New York Times*. His assumption, never explicitly stated, was that he would one day inherit his father's place as general manager. In the meantime, he behaved like a prince who did not have to pay his dues. "He was lazy," said Tom Campion, who oversaw Julie Jr. in the mechanical department. "He was arrogant and haughty, always puffing and blowing about how great he was, probably because he was so unsure of his position." Julius did not help matters by summoning various department heads to his office to give their frank and bruising appraisals of his son and by demanding that Julie Jr. report to him every day at 5:00 P.M. If Julie Jr. found his father's treatment demeaning, he kept silent about it and fixed his gaze on a gauzy future as a top executive at *The New York Times*, if not *the* top executive of the company. From the first, however, Julius had made it clear that such a notion was folly. "It's just not in the cards," he cautioned his son. Julie Jr. took no notice. "It was wishful thinking," Bobbie said of her brother's ambitions. "There's a lot of fantasizing going on in this family."

§

The end of the war brought a spate of marriages in the Sulzberger clan, all of them, it would turn out, ill-fated. The first to wed was Ruth, who despite her parents' misgivings, married her wartime beau, Ben Golden, in June 1946. "I've always felt that if I had been there at their wedding, I could have saved them a lot of grief by telling them, 'Don't do this; this is a mistake,' " said their daughter, Lynn, many years later.

Arthur and Iphigene's earlier objections to the romance on the grounds that Ben was married had quickly given way to a more personal and generalized antipathy. They found Ben bewilderingly brash, abrasive, and unsophisticated. Iphigene, who rarely voiced displeasure with anyone, was appalled at his demand for sliced white bread at every meal, even during visits to Hillandale. She did not consider *Ben* a proper name and insisted on introducing him to her friends as Benjamin Hale Golden, until Ruth demanded that she stop. The Sulzbergers watched in mystified horror as their sensible, Smith-educated daughter melted in the presence of this autocratic, hard-drinking man with few discernible intellectual interests. Arthur's vision of his daughter as unattractive and Iphigene's distaste for sex blinded them to the sincere and cracklingly electric passion Ruth and Ben shared. Her parents never saw Ruth the way a *Time* correspondent did: "a tall, willowy, dark-haired, dark-eyed, pretty, intense young woman."

When their criticisms failed to dissuade her, Arthur raised the question of finances. If Ben kept his job at the Tennessee Valley Authority in Knoxville, their combined income, including the $2,500 Ruth received annually from the Ochs Trust, would amount to just $5,300 a year. How would they live? Ablaze with romantic idealism, Ruth replied that "Beng" could transfer to the TVA operation in Chattanooga, and she could work for *The Chattanooga Times.* "I'm going nuts, and Beng is too," she told her father in a letter pleading for marriage "as soon as possible." "I don't mean to be difficult. I'm just in love."

Reluctantly, Arthur and Iphigene gave in. Ben's mother came to the wedding, which took place at Hillandale; his father and brother sent regrets, saying they "couldn't make it." Although the senior Sulzbergers questioned Ben's suitability on many grounds, his being gentile wasn't one of them — unlike others in the clan. During the engagement, Ruth had gone to Philadelphia to tell Aunt Mattie the happy news. "Is he *Unser?*" Mattie had inquired, meaning "Is he one of us?" Ruth hadn't understood at the time, but when she returned to New York, she realized with sudden fury that what Mattie had wanted to know was whether Ben was Jewish. "What difference does it make?" she demanded of her parents.

After a brief wedding trip, Ruth and Ben began their married life in Knoxville — "which I hated," said Ruth — where the new Mrs. Golden, who had become pregnant on her honeymoon, spent the balance of the summer fighting off morning sickness. In the fall of 1946 the couple relocated to Chattanooga so that Ben could begin a new career on *The Chattanooga Times.* The added costs of a child and Arthur's fear that his favorite daughter was in danger of drifting into Ben's world had, in the end, proved persuasive. Arthur could have trained Ben in New

York, but Ruth felt that, with her husband's lack of newspaper experience, he would fare better on the family's less demanding farm team,
which had the added advantage of being located in the South, his home
territory.

Ruth and Ben arrived in Chattanooga during a postwar renaissance
fueled by low labor costs and the cheap power of the TVA. Under the
skeptical eye of Charles Puckette, who had functioned as the paper's top
executive since "A"'s mental breakdown, Ben went through a rapid
indoctrination at *The Chattanooga Times*, starting out in news and
sports, moving on to the copy desk, then to advertising, circulation, and
promotion — every department except the composing room and the
presses. Tongues soon wagged that Ben was being groomed to take over
from Mr. Puckette, as the erect, bow-tied "Southern gentleman in the
classic mold" was universally known, when he retired. But as of 1950
Ben's status remained unclear. A *Time* reporter found him "pleasant but
ill at ease. . . . He obviously feels the pressure to which he is being subjected as the boss's son-in-law and as a result gives the impression of
being always tautly at attention."

The truth was that Ben's relationship with the Sulzbergers was a Faus-
tian bargain: he felt he had sold his soul, and the more comfortable the
family made his life professionally and materially, the more he lashed
out at Ruth. When Stephen Arthur Ochs Golden was born nine months
and ten days after the wedding, Ben was attentive and seemingly content. But a sharp-edged resentment soon manifested itself in an explosive temper and put-downs reminiscent of the worst of Arthur's
behavior toward Iphigene. "He'd been a boxer at one time," said their
second son, Michael, born in 1949. "You don't do that because you love
animals." Ben's anti-Semitic remarks became the talk of Chattanooga.
"My name may be Ben Golden, but I want you to know I'm not Jewish,"
he told a local matron he had just met. "Ruth is Jewish," he went on,
pointing to his wife. "*She's* Jewish. *I'm* not Jewish."

Arthur and Iphigene were largely ignorant of the growing tension in
the Golden household. They bought Ruth and Ben a car, arranged an
advance from the Ochs Trust so that the couple could purchase a house on
prestigious Lookout Mountain, and provided a housewarming present
of a new terrace and furniture. To Ruth, family bounty was business as
usual. "I think we are the luckiest people in the world," she told her father.
To Ben, the gifts were emasculating reminders of who in the marriage

had power and who did not. He was painfully aware that while good things were always there for the asking, asking was required. In his mind he was a perpetual supplicant. "It was this two-hundred-pound rhinoceros sitting in their house all the time," their daughter, Lynn, said of the central presence of the family and *The New York Times* in their lives. "They never sorted it out, and it was there from the beginning."

§

Ruth was not the only Sulzberger daughter forging her way through the early stages of marriage with a husband of whom her family did not approve. In December 1946, six months after the Golden wedding, Judy married Matthew Rosenschein Jr., whom she had met in medical school. She found Mattie, as he was known, delightfully funny, but the rest of the Sulzbergers thought him rough-hewn, a sloppy dresser, and "not very polished" — code words that telegraphed their distaste for his Eastern European Jewish background. To Judy, the family rebel, such negative assessments only made Mattie more attractive. At one point she had broken off the engagement, prompting an outpouring of relief. "He's the worst," her cousin Ellen Sulzberger Straus had told her. "He's not for you." The criticism had propelled Judy straight back to Mattie, who soon learned all the terrible things the Sulzbergers had said about him.

On the surface, Mattie had superior credentials. He was bright and on the verge of graduating from medical school with a residency at Columbia University's Psychiatric Institute. But there was something biting and sarcastic about his manner, as though he were constantly on the lookout for slights or spoiling for a fight. Despite his education and professional training, he was from a different social class and, though no one had the bad taste to say it, was what was known in the Sulzbergers' world as a "real Jew." "I don't think my parents liked that last name and I didn't, either," said Judy, who had defiantly declared as a child that she didn't want to be Jewish. "It was as Jewish as Jewish could be."

In a role he had by now grown accustomed to, Arthur again played host to an opulent wedding at Hillandale. In honor of the season, artificial icicles dangled from evergreen trees, and ropes of greens were coiled around the mansion's many pillars. Like her mother and two sisters before her, Judy wore Effie's tulle veil bordered by rose-point lace, and the groom, his parents both dead, relied on his maternal grandmother to represent his side of the family. In a reprise of Marian's nuptials,

Arthur amused his guests at the reception by sporting a sign that read, ALL SOLD OUT. GOING OUT OF BUSINESS. When it came time for toasts, Jean Sulzberger, a cousin, stood up and raised her glass. "Judith Peixotto Sulzberger Rosenschein," she said solemnly. "I'm glad it's your name and not mine."

After a honeymoon in Guatemala, Mattie completed his coursework and spent one year at the Psychiatric Institute before deciding to switch specialties to the general practice of medicine. Judy, who graduated medical school in 1949, began a pathology residency at Grasslands Hospital in Westchester County. Arthur was enormously proud of his daughter's status as a doctor. "It's been tough, hard sledding . . . but you have gone at it like a real soldier," he told Judy in a letter informing her that he and Iphigene were giving her a Chevrolet coupe as a graduation present. Still, he thought pathology, with its ghoulish autopsies, was an odd occupation. Once, when Judy was at Hillandale for the weekend, he introduced her to his other guests by saying, "This is my daughter, the doctor. She cuts up dead bodies."

Mattie's and Judy's careers put them well outside the orbit of *The New York Times* and *The Chattanooga Times,* but soon the same pressures that had affected Ben began to bother Mattie. The Sulzbergers and the Ochs Trust advanced the Rosenscheins money for a house, for psychoanalysis connected with Mattie's residency, for office equipment, and for the reestablishment of his private practice after two years in the navy. By 1952 Mattie's anger and resentment had became so apparent that he felt impelled to write a tortured explanation to his in-laws. "It is not that I have not felt gratitude," he said. "It is just that I am so proud[,] I could not accept help graciously. . . . I can't tell you how particularly exasperating this has been to me. . . . I am not unaware that my position in the family circle has been adversely affected . . . by my irritability."

§

Thanks to the Marine Corps, Punch's bearing was straighter, he was more mature, and he came back to the States after the war having consciously decided to make something of his life. While lying in a military hospital in the summer of 1945, with nothing to do but think, he had surveyed the other patients in the ward and realized that, compared with most of them, he was more intelligent and more capable. Certainly he was not the fumbling loser his father imagined him to be. In a moment of epiphany, the future had become clear. He felt prepared to assume the mantle of expectation at *The New York Times* that he had, in his own genial way, resisted for so long. "He knew he had the stuff, and it was high time to show it," said Alan Rabinowitz, Punch's Loomis classmate. "It was time to step up to the plate."

Punch's first act was to redeem his sorry academic record. While serving out the final months of his tour at Camp Lejeune in North Carolina, he took the high school equivalency exam through the Armed Forces Institute. His scores were significantly higher than those of other GIs, even in spelling and math, and the results emboldened him to set his sights on Columbia, where his father was a trustee. "He's a good kid and an able one even though he has been slow in maturing," Arthur wrote a university administrator a week after Punch had been discharged as a marine corporal. Columbia judged Punch too unprepared, but the dean agreed that if he enrolled in the School of General Studies extension program and maintained a B average, he could enter the university as a regular student starting in January 1947.

He handily won admission and as a Columbia freshman found himself thrown together with a postwar assortment of eighteen-year-olds and battle-savvy veterans, who amused themselves by tormenting the professor in Columbia's mandatory sex-education course. When Punch made the dean's list his first semester, his parents were astounded. That summer he accompanied Arthur to Europe as his secretary, charged with the responsibility of keeping an account of the trip, but taking notes during important interviews under the critical eye of his father proved to be more than Punch could bear. By the time they arrived in Berlin, he complained of stomach pains and a persistent headache. In London he developed a festering boil on his jaw and diarrhea reminiscent of his wartime tangle with dysentery. He spent a week in the Hospital for Tropical Diseases, prompting Arthur to cavil that his schedule had been reduced to tatters because he was obliged to "visit the brat morning and afternoon."

Back in the States, months passed with no trip report from Punch. After weeks of prodding, he finally turned in a halfhearted attempt that sent Arthur into fresh paroxysms of disapproval. Punch had waited so long to record an interview with Winston Churchill that he had "missed the flavor of it," Arthur complained, and the conclusions he expressed were not his own but "conclusions you heard me express." Despite everything, Arthur added as an afterthought, "I still love you." It had never occurred to Arthur, or to Iphigene, that Punch's learning disabilities might have made efficient note taking and report writing difficult.

Punch's first semester at Columbia proved to be the zenith of his academic career, and his grades never again reached a noteworthy level. He took history courses, some science, and a smattering of other subjects, settling for effortless gentleman's Cs. He had more important things on his mind: he was in love with a young woman he had met shortly after he had entered the marines in 1944.

Barbara Grant exuded the fresh, blond sexiness of a high school cheerleader, which she had, in fact, once been. People were entranced by her sparkle. "She had a face that lit up," said a woman who knew her then. Orvil had first noticed the animated sixteen-year-old stamping envelopes and hanging newspapers in racks on the fourteenth floor of the New York Times Building — a summer job that Lillian Lang, Arthur's secretary and an acquaintance of the Grants', had helped arrange. Orvil invited Barbara to dinner as a blind date for Punch, who was about to come home on leave before shipping out. The evening was a great success, and within weeks Barbara, who lived a mile from Hillandale, found herself immersed in the Sulzbergers' world.

Barbara was impressed with Punch's sweetness and handsome good looks, though she noticed that he didn't talk much and had few friends his own age. His life was firmly rooted in his family, a family much closer than her own. She had been fascinated by the swirl of important people at Hillandale, the wealth, the stimulating conversation. Though she was younger than Punch, she was harder and more cynical, largely because her mother, Helen, an abusive, explosive "witch of a woman," had instilled in her a catlike wariness. "I learned to look into people's eyes," she said. "I zeroed into my mother's eyes every time I walked into that house."

Helen MacDonald Grant, a descendant of Scots who had immigrated to Prince Edward Island and become high-class servants, ran her home with an arbitrary willfulness that bordered on madness. She once locked her son in a closet for several hours; when guests came for dinner, she dressed Barbara in a maid's uniform and ordered her to serve at table. To gain approval, Barbara became proficient in ballet and won a full scholarship to the American Ballet School. Not long afterward she came home to find her mother in front of the fireplace, burning all her costumes and toe shoes. Helen had been so determined to destroy Barbara's ambitions that she had dragged a massive trunk of ballet equipment down the stairs. When she looked up and saw her daughter, she swore at her. With no support from her passive father, Barbara gave up ballet forever.

Compared with Helen, Iphigene was a refuge of maternal warmth and understanding. She conscripted Barbara to be Punch's friend, social secretary, and potential girlfriend, just as she had once hired male companions for him. "She desperately cared for Punch and wanted him to have a group of friends — and I had a lot of friends," Barbara said. Though they were not a couple, she and Punch exchanged letters while he was in the marines, a correspondence strongly encouraged by Iphigene, who sent Barbara a steady stream of gifts. When Punch returned from the war, Barbara saw him in a different light. The quiet restraint was still there, but he was more outgoing and gregarious, and possessed an alluring "physical, manly strength." As for Punch, the months of separation from Barbara had only heightened her attraction. Almost every weekend he drove to Goucher College, just outside of Baltimore, where she had enrolled in the fall of 1946.

Punch had an unwelcome ally in his courtship: Helen. Intent on marrying off her daughter to a future mogul, she permitted no other dates in the house and chipped away at Barbara's self-esteem by telling her she was "stupid," "nasty," and a "mental case." Goucher should have been a sanctuary; instead, Barbara became depressed, tentative, and dependent. "I was worried about what was going to happen to me," she said. During school vacations Punch ingratiated himself with the Grants by cutting their grass, trimming their trees, and generally spending so much time away from the Sulzbergers that Arthur penned a sarcastic poem suggesting that Punch also served as Barbara's father's personal barber.

The engagement was announced shortly before Christmas 1947. Babs made her usual withering appraisal of the prospective bride — "A drum majorette from a public high school? What could be more déclassé?" — but Arthur and Iphigene were pleased. They might have been expected to be perturbed by Barbara's religious background, if only because Punch was the only son, but, said Alan Rabinowitz, "they were much too sophisticated to say you couldn't marry her because she isn't Jewish." The larger concern was that Punch and Barbara were "barely out of nursery school" and too immature to get married. "They both were so excited and thrilled to find each other, but so ill-prepared for anything in life," said Jackie Dryfoos.

Punch and Barbara were wed in a civil ceremony in the garden of her parents' home, Clochemerle, on July 2, 1948. After a honeymoon in Scandinavia, the couple set up housekeeping at 21 Claremont Avenue, one block from Columbia and Barnard, where Iphigene, a Barnard trustee, had helped Barbara transfer for the balance of her college years. While their classmates attended parties and football games, Punch and Barbara's greatest delight was taking care of five-year-old Jackie Dryfoos when Marian and Orvil were out of town. Punch assumed the role of playmate, rolling on the floor and frolicking as an equal. Barbara — "absolutely gorgeous, magnificently beautiful" — made dinner for Jackie, took her to the theater, and in a poignant and unspoken way made her own neediness apparent. "She adored the fact that I adored her," Jackie remarked.

Punch and Barbara's idyll ended abruptly on June 25, 1950, when North Korea launched a surprise attack on South Korea across the thirty-eighth parallel. Four years earlier, to absolve himself of the shame of his privileged posting in World War II, Punch had signed up for the Marine Reserve. "I wanted to show myself and the others that I wasn't dodging," he told Iphigene at the time. The news of North Korea's attack came while Punch was touring South Africa with Barbara, and he soon got word that his Marine Reserve unit had been called up. With a student deferment, he finished out his final semester at Columbia, and in February 1951 applied for an officer's commission. While awaiting orders, he worked on *The New York Times'* city desk, where he wrote his first story. "Chinese Youngster Rescued from Apartment Blaze" appeared on page thirty-three.

17

Freedom and Disillusionment

J UNE 7, 1951, WAS AN OCCASION THAT ARTHUR considered "quite a Sulzberger day." He watched from his seat among Columbia's trustees as Punch and Barbara received their bachelor's degrees from Columbia and Barnard, and Iphigene was awarded an honorary doctor of laws degree from Columbia in recognition of her place as "a distinguished daughter of a distinguished father [and] an active worker in the new generation which is carrying forward with a sure hand the century-old but never more vigorous *New York Times.*"

Iphigene's distinction was just one of many that came to the family and to the *Times* during the paper's centennial year. Arthur had declined to publish a hundredth-anniversary edition, arguing that he didn't want to "hold up people for advertising," but he did hang a centennial flag from the building, install a neon TIMES sign on top of the tower, and commission an updated history of the paper. *The Story of The New York Times 1851–1951,* written by Meyer "Mike" Berger, a revered *Times* reporter, was rife with omissions. Originally, Berger had included an account of the tension between Arthur and Julius over succession; Arthur had excised it, along with other critical details of his publishership. "Mike was ashamed of that book," said Ruth Adler, his close friend and a former editor of *Times Talk,* the paper's in-house newsletter. "He felt it was honest, it just left out a lot."

On September 17, the one hundredth anniversary of the day that Henry J. Raymond and George Jones had first put to bed what was then known as *The New-York Daily Times,* Arthur appeared in the composing room at 10:15 P.M. to watch the front page of the next day's issue roll off the presses, with the headline A CENTURY OF THE TIMES on its front page. "I have a young grandchild trying to get born tonight," he confided to Turner Catledge, who stood at his elbow.

Punch's first child, Arthur Ochs Sulzberger Jr., was indeed due to arrive that day but did not make an appearance until September 22. Judy was with Barbara at Mount Kisco Hospital during her labor and administered the chloroform. As he had at the birth of all his grandchildren, Arthur sat down soon afterward and wrote a commemorative ode. This one instructed his new grandson — another Arthur — to be a good and worthy king of the family's version of Camelot. "Here is to Arthur — long may he reign!" it began. "Let him have grief, spare not his pain."

Punch himself was not present at his son's birth. Two months earlier he had reported as a second lieutenant to Quantico, Virginia, for twenty weeks of training. Arthur was proud of Punch's reentry into the marines, which he viewed as a reflection of the patriotism with which he had been imbued at home, while Barbara regarded it as "an interruption in his life as it had been planned." But with her new baby she dutifully joined her husband in off-base housing and tried to make the best of it.

They returned to New York in December so that Punch could commute to Fort Slocum in New Rochelle for an eight-week course at the Armed Services Information School. By mid-April 1952, as a newly minted public-information officer, he was stationed with the First Marine Division just south of Panmunjom, where the Korean peace talks were taking place. Enlisted combat correspondents considered him a "mouse-quiet Reserve shavetail" and called him Little Artie. "We wondered covertly what a rich kid like him was doing here," said one.

By August Punch was back in the States, living with Barbara at Hillandale and awaiting the birth of their second child. As his terminal duty assignment, he was sent to Washington, D.C., to work for General James D. Hittle, legislative assistant to the commandant of the Marine Corps. In a second-floor office in the Navy Annex, across from Arlington National Cemetery, Punch reviewed cases, answered mail, and made suggestions on legislative matters. Hittle was so impressed with his performance that he asked Punch to write an analysis of Marine Corps policy and national security. When *Concept for Catastrophe* was published, a New York congressman eager to ingratiate himself with *The New York Times* called it "one of the most important writings of contemporary military literature" and had excerpts printed in the *Congressional Record*.

But there was no denying Punch had done a good job. As a sign of his approval, Hittle asked an overjoyed Punch to work on a second report — a history of the unification struggle in Korea, something no one up to that point had attempted. "He loved Hittle," said Charley Bartlett, then Washington correspondent for *The Chattanooga Times.* "He loved the uniform. He would have been a very happy career marine."

Barbara, on the other hand, felt stranded in the couple's tiny house in Alexandria, Virginia. She spent her days ironing Punch's shirts, tending to Arthur Jr., and washing diapers for their new daughter, Karen Alden Sulzberger, born that November. With no car or social contacts, she felt desperately alone. She and Punch had dinner a few times with "a couple of those colonel types," but she found them mind-numbingly boring. When she complained about her isolation, Punch completely missed the point. "Don't worry, Barbara. I'll give you a gun," he said. "My God!" she responded. "What am I going to do with *that?*"

§

The *Times'* centennial also coincided with a major shift in the senior Sulzbergers' circumstances. They sold their town house on East Eightieth Street and moved thirteen blocks north to 1115 Fifth Avenue. With eleven rooms, including three servants' rooms and a specially made walk-in bar for Arthur, the new apartment was regally spacious, with a panoramic view of Central Park. "This completes our adjustment to reality," Arthur remarked to Herbert Bayard Swope, the former executive editor of the New York *World.*

The "reality" was that the Sulzbergers' children had all grown up and moved out of the house. That had motivated their parents to reduce the scale not only of their city lives but of their country lives as well. For years Arthur and Iphigene had longed to dispose of Adolph's sprawling White Plains estate, which cost $60,000 annually to maintain. Its frayed carpets and massive sideboards decorated with winged lions and urns of carved fruit made Hillandale a dated relic. In 1949 the Sulzbergers had gratefully accepted an offer of $150,000 for the property, even though the price had represented a loss.

Arthur was now finally free to create his own rural palazzo, and he found the ideal raw material in Wind Ridge, a white Colonial-style home with hand-hewn shingles and flagstone trim seven miles from downtown Stamford, Connecticut. The sixteen-room house, situated on eleven acres, had been built in 1938 by George Washington Hill, the head of the American Tobacco Company. Mature trees shaded its front lawn; in back a stone patio overlooked a generous yard, woodlands, and a small lake. The overall effect was of an extra-large, comfortable, middle-class American home, not the colossal mansion of Adolph's era. "We are in love!" Arthur exclaimed to their friend Lady Susan Pulbrook, shortly after the Ochs Trust acquired Wind Ridge for $125,000.

Arthur liked everything about the estate except its name, so by fiat he decided that the new Ochs-Sulzberger compound would henceforth carry the same name as the old: Hillandale. With the pent-up creativity of a frustrated designer and landscape architect, he built a swimming pool and a pool house, a six-car garage, new roads, a footpath, and a second terrace. In the library, with its elegant bay window, he selected dark green paint; for the living room he chose a shade "a little darker than oyster white" and installed a pull-down screen in the ceiling above the fireplace so that he could entertain visitors with first-run movies. He also enforced a new rule: No more than four people could gather in the library at any one time. "I want the living room to be lived in," he declared.

Orvil and Marian could have taken the Sulzbergers' removal to Stamford as an opportunity to strike out on their own, but that was not the family tradition. "You're pulled in, you're sucked in, and there's not much room for you," said Jackie Dryfoos. "It's this rubber fence boundary, so that there seems to be room at times, but there really isn't." For two summers the Dryfi, as Arthur called the Dryfoos family, rented a house partway up the hill leading to the new Hillandale. In 1951, on land purchased from the senior Sulzbergers, they built Rock Hill, a modest contemporary dwelling made out of cypress and glass that was a three-minute walk from Hillandale — so close that Susan Dryfoos, born in 1946 and known within the family as Susie, got in the habit of visiting her grandparents every morning as they ate their breakfast. Arthur usually joined Iphigene in her bedroom, sitting on the couch or the chaise longue while she took her tray in bed. Sometimes as a treat he would place a sugar cube on a demitasse spoon, pour a small amount of coffee on it, and hand it to Susie, who delighted in the taste as well as the color change.

The Sulzbergers' urge to transform their living quarters was mirrored by similar changes at the paper. A year earlier *Time* had described *The New York Times* as a sleepy, overstaffed, dust-covered place that specialized in long, dull, turgid stories. The Washington correspondent for the Louisville *Courier-Journal* had been quoted as saying, "There are mornings when I grab hold of a copy of the *Times* and say to it: 'Damn you, I'm going to read you if it kills me!' " Unfortunately, the newsweekly's assessment was all too accurate: the *Times'* newsroom had indeed become an anachronism. As a practical matter, however, it had been impossible to modernize while Edwin L. James was alive.

Dressy James, as Heywood Broun dubbed him, had reigned as managing editor since 1932, treating Arthur with ill-concealed contempt even as he cultivated Iphigene with a prickly charm accentuated by his trademark cane, Tampa cigar, and bright yellow vest. Surprisingly indifferent when it came to news, James had a policy of either printing foreign correspondents' copy exactly as it was filed or throwing it away. ("We don't rewrite it," he explained.) He disliked colorful prose, fearful that it would tart up the paper, and considered analysis a violation of the Ochsian orthodoxy of objectivity. During his tenure the bullpen — the group of night editors who decided what went on the front page after he left the office — became increasingly powerful, making news decisions that by rights should have been his. The result was, as Henry Luce once quipped, "the best unedited paper in the world."

Arthur could have taken the situation in hand, but it was not in his nature to do so. While he felt comfortable hobnobbing with the paper's urbane overseas correspondents, he was rather timid in the *Times'* home office, rarely making appearances off the fourteenth floor. He mingled uneasily with the staff, many of whom did not recognize him when he walked by, and hated to make decisions on the phone, preferring to communicate by the dreaded "blue note," so called because of its colored paper. If the recipient didn't agree with his criticisms or suggestions, however, the matter often ended there.

In December 1951 James died, clearing the way for the revolution that Arthur — urged on by Orvil — had long wanted. To be James's successor, Arthur chose Turner Catledge, the bluff, courtly forty-nine-year-old southerner who had been his boon companion on several overseas trips during the war. Turner's first order of business was to make the *Times* more readable, with shorter, tighter stories that allowed for interpretation as well as presentation of the facts. Banished were the rambling sentences that had flourished since the days of "space rate" — a system of paying correspondents by the volume of their reports. "I wanted the paper not only to be needed," Turner said later, "I wanted it to be wanted."

With Catledge's backing, assistant managing editor Ted Bernstein launched what amounted to a one-man in-house course to improve *Times* prose. *Winners & Sinners,* Bernstein's two-page internal bulletin, "goaded, goosed and jollied" the paper's six hundred reporters and copy desk editors to unsnarl awkward syntax and reach for literary high notes. At the same time, Bernstein, like his predecessor during the James era, stubbornly blocked Turner's efforts to curb the power of the bullpen. It was Bernstein who ran the 4:00 P.M. news conference that determined what would appear on the next day's front page; Turner usually listened in silence. "Every now and again he might put in a word, but he didn't really say much," said Tom Wicker, who started at the *Times* in 1960.

Turner made little headway toward another of his goals: changing the prevailing culture so that reporters thought of themselves as members of *The New York Times,* not as subjects loyal to one of three distinct city-states — the foreign staff, the Washington staff, and the local staff. The main obstacle in his path was Cy Sulzberger, who since his appointment in 1945 as the *Times'* Paris-based chief foreign correspondent had run the paper's international staff as his own personal offshore corporation. When Arthur had invited Turner to be managing editor, the first question Turner asked was, "Am I going to be managing editor of all of *The New York Times*?" Arthur had answered with knowing weariness: "You're talking about Cy."

There was no doubt that Cy brought luster to the *Times* with his tireless reporting and high-level contacts, but he was also touchy, officious, egomaniacal, and not above waving his blood tie to the publisher in front of editors like a spiked club. He wrote in a style only the State Department could love, droning on at lengths guaranteed to put readers to sleep, yet he exploded if so much as a word was changed in his copy or a story was not prominently displayed.

James had long ago given up trying to discipline Cy, who made costly trips without asking permission and never bothered to tell New York in advance what he was going to write about. A significant portion of his expense account went to Lucas Carton, the Right Bank Paris restaurant where he often lunched with sources, his beagle companion at his feet feasting on steak and carrots Vichy. Certain that his colleagues were out to steal his stories, he sent his copy to New York by Western Union rather than using the bureau's in-house telegraph desk. To Arthur, he spoke of "the cabal against me in the office."

Cy's dark-haired Greek wife, Marina, whom he had met and married during the war, was a cheerful counterpoint to her husband's scowling fits of temper. Though not conventionally beautiful, she had a radiance and charm that pulled people toward her as irresistibly as Cy's high-handed ways pushed them away. Aware of the favorable impression Marina made on people — she spoke three languages fluently and three imperfectly — Cy took her with him on many of his long reporting trips, but he did not always treat her well. His nickname for her — Dopey — seemed to belittle her intelligence, and he did nothing to hide his extramarital escapades. Once, finding himself with an hour and a half to kill before a dinner engagement, he picked up a twenty-five-year-old prostitute who proceeded to tell him that Salvador Dalí, a longtime client, had become so enamored of her naked derriere that she posed in various positions for him in his Paris studio whenever he came to town. "Now where but Paris would you run into this gaudy [sic] tale?" Cy had written in his diary the day after the encounter.

As early as 1949 Cy had informed Arthur of his desire to assume Anne O'Hare McCormick's foreign affairs column when she retired, but Arthur had made no promises. Three years later Cy was vacationing on Cyprus when he got the news that Mrs. McCormick had passed away. After admitting he sounded "like a ghoul pushing my way over the memory of Anne," he begged Arthur not to make a decision about her replacement until he could come to the States and make his case.

Arthur was reluctant to give the column to Cy. Not only had he hoped to hire another woman, but he had grown impatient with his nephew's ten-dollar words and serpentine sentences. He was also well aware of Turner's exasperation with Cy. Months earlier, in a confidential memo, Turner had confessed that "[I am] coming to my wit's end. . . . I cannot do the job I would like to do . . . under [Cy's] harassments and lack of cooperation."

In the end, Arthur cannily used McCormick's column as a bargaining chip to bring the supervision of the foreign staff back to New York. He offered Cy the thrice-weekly column, but only on the condition that he give up control of the *Times'* overseas reporters. Cy agreed, and on October 27, 1954, Cy's forty-second birthday, "Foreign Affairs" made its debut. "Today I ceased being a reporter and became a journalist," he wrote proudly in his diary. To gather material for his maiden effort, Cy came to the States and called on "my old friendship with Eisenhower." Arthur chided his nephew for using *I* and *me* too much but three weeks later gave him a raise when Cy demanded one. As for Turner, he thought Arthur's compromise an "excellent arrangement. . . . I am very happy for [Cy] and for all of us."

§

Although Arthur called himself a Democrat, he was, at heart, uncomfortable with many of the party's policies and candidates. During his long tenure as publisher, he had seven opportunities to endorse a president; four times the paper supported Republicans, and three times Democrats. In 1948 it had backed Republican Thomas E. Dewey over Harry S Truman, whose veto of the Taft-Hartley Act, which outlawed the closed shop, and inability to rein in inflation so disturbed Arthur that by 1951 he was sickened by the prospect of the *Times'* having to give him its approval if the GOP failed to put up an acceptable opponent in 1952.

Feeding his anxiety was a groundswell among the Republican Old Guard for the nomination of Ohio senator Robert A. Taft, a conservative isolationist who had the muscle to beat Truman and who, Arthur feared, was determined to march the country off the world stage and back into its cocoon. These concerns, coupled with his postwar self-image as a member of the elites running the country, led Arthur for the first time to involve himself directly in partisan politics, taking on a kingmaker role that Adolph never would have assumed and certainly never sanctioned.

The man he chose to help crown was the nation's favorite hero, General Dwight D. Eisenhower. Arthur had been starstruck by Eisenhower during their wartime encounters, impressed by his internationalist outlook and "great moral courage." Along with Thomas J. Watson Jr., president of IBM, and other Columbia trustees, Arthur had persuaded Eisenhower to accept the job of university president, a post critics considered a bald attempt to "civilianize" the former head of the Allied forces so that he could pursue a political career.

By the fall of 1951 Eisenhower was stationed in Paris, on leave from Columbia to negotiate European military commitments to NATO, and dedicated to fostering "an aura of mystery" about his political plans. On a brief visit to Washington in early November, he lunched with Truman at Blair House. The president had recently decided not to run again — though only his closest aides knew it — and a Taft victory in 1952 was as repugnant to him as it was to Arthur. The liberal wing of the Republican Party had recently begun an effort to draft Eisenhower, and Truman wanted to sound out the general about his intentions, since he had never made his party affiliation publicly known. If he ran as a Democrat, Truman told Eisenhower, he could "guarantee" him the nomination and give him his full support. "What reason do you have to think I have ever been a Democrat?" Eisenhower asked Truman. "You know I have been a Republican all my life and that my family have always been Republicans." Besides, he disagreed with the Democrats on too many issues — labor legislation in particular — to ever consider accepting such an offer.

Three days later, on November 8, Arthur Krock, using a highly placed source, broke the details of the Truman lunch on the front page of *The New York Times*. Truman and Eisenhower both denied the account. That same day an agitated Eisenhower wrote Arthur asking about an earlier conversation they had had concerning how the general might reveal his Republican sentiments. "The pounding I have been taking recently has somewhat addled my memory," he said.

Arthur's response, hand-delivered through Cy for security reasons, made it clear that he felt no qualms about using *The New York Times* to help Eisenhower "bridge the gap between your present post to that of a candidate." Because Ike needed to "identify himself in some way" with Republicans, Arthur suggested that Eisenhower instruct his brother, Milton, to leak to *The New York Times* that he had voted for Dewey in 1948. Eisenhower professed reluctance, arguing that seeking the presidency from his European post would violate "my prime duty" to his overseas assignment. However, Milton Eisenhower, authorized by his brother, soon made a public statement that his family had always been Republicans.

Still eager to be of assistance, Arthur asked Arthur Krock and Scotty Reston to give him their assessments of Eisenhower's potential, which he then passed along to the general without their knowledge. In his memo, Krock said the draft-Ike movement would never get off the ground without "more jet propulsion by the General." If he waited beyond January to declare his plans, Krock believed he would be "imperilling the whole project and injuring his supporters." Scotty, in contrast, admired Eisenhower's refusal to jeopardize his NATO work by declaring his candidacy. If he waited until May, when the NATO job was due to end, he would only fortify his appeal as a draft choice, Reston felt. "His great strength is the public belief that he is putting the national interest before anything else."

On January 6, 1952, a few days after Eisenhower had written Truman a letter saying the chances of his ever being drawn into politics were "so remote as to be negligible," Senator Henry Cabot Lodge announced that he was entering the general's name on the Republican ballot in the New Hampshire primary and would be forming an Eisenhower for President campaign. Eisenhower was livid. Lodge had made the move independently to force Eisenhower to a decision — and the ploy worked. On January 7, in Paris, Eisenhower announced that he was prepared to accept the Republican nomination if it was offered. The same day, *The New York Times* came out with a remarkable editorial, headlined simply EISENHOWER, in which it promised to support Eisenhower "enthusiastically" if the Republicans made him their nominee. Never before in its history had the *Times* declared its presidential preference seven months before the convention and before even knowing who the Democratic candidate would be.

Over the next several months Arthur unsuccessfully urged Eisenhower to come home and campaign, insisting, "The crisis is now, not in June." In late April, a month after Truman let it be known he would not seek another term, Arthur sent Charles Merz to France so that he could "get a little of (the) candidate's charm at first hand." After his return Merz and John Oakes, who had joined *The New York Times* Sunday department in 1946 and moved to the editorial page in 1949, penned a series of columns called "Taft Can't Win," calculated to soften Taft support and pave the way for Eisenhower's coronation.

In July Eisenhower won the nomination in what the *Times* hailed as "a people's victory." Two weeks later, when the Democrats chose Illinois governor Adlai Stevenson as their standard-bearer, the paper reaffirmed its devotion to Eisenhower, but its enthusiasm began to dim as the presidential campaign got under way. For Arthur, the pivotal factor was Senator Joseph McCarthy, who for the past two years had exploited the public's fear of communism with his savage accusations of treason in high places. Fearful of damaging his chances with pro-McCarthy voters,

Eisenhower proved unwilling to speak out against the deceit and demagoguery. In fact, the Wisconsin Republican deserved credit, Ike told Arthur, "for having awakened the country to some of its security problems."

Arthur and other Eisenhower backers clung blindly to the belief that their candidate would eventually repudiate McCarthy, but in late September, when Arthur discovered that the candidate planned to speak in Milwaukee on the same platform as McCarthy, who was running for reelection, he confessed to Sherman Adams, the general's personal campaign aide, that he was "in despair." To mollify him, Eisenhower invited Arthur to the president's residence on the Columbia campus and explained his dilemma: Wisconsin was an important state, he said; he was under enormous pressure to appear with McCarthy. Arthur replied that if he really must go, he should use the occasion to pay tribute to George Marshall, the brilliant general who had been Eisenhower's friend and military mentor, Truman's secretary of state, and later his secretary of defense. The previous year, in a three-hour harangue from the Senate floor, McCarthy had accused Marshall of taking part in a Communist conspiracy; since then he continued to vilify Marshall, who had resigned from the Cabinet in September 1951.

Eisenhower agreed to include praise for Marshall in the speech he planned to give in Milwaukee, and using an advance copy of the talk, Arthur ordered up a *Times* editorial to run the morning after the appearance, quoting from the text. But when the moment came, Eisenhower buckled to pressure from McCarthy and deleted the references to Marshall. "Do I need to tell you I am sick at heart?" Arthur wired Sherman Adams, adding that he was "close to physically ill."

Like Arthur, John Oakes had been naturally drawn to Eisenhower, but after the Stevenson nomination and the general's spineless performance in Milwaukee, he had a change of heart. He renounced Eisenhower and tried to persuade Arthur and Charles Merz that, despite the *Times'* earlier commitment, Stevenson was the superior man. His arguments went nowhere, and for the duration of the general election campaign, he wrote no political editorials, in keeping with Adolph's long-standing policy that no one should write an editorial with which he disagreed.

When it came time to draft the *Times'* formal endorsement of Eisenhower, however, Merz decided to include some kind words about the opposition, and at his request, Oakes contributed a few paragraphs. The editorial, which appeared October 23, took Eisenhower to task for his endorsement of McCarthy, his failure to provide details on foreign affairs issues, and the slush fund that his running mate, Richard Nixon, had allegedly kept. It praised Stevenson while also scoring him for his inattention to inflation and China policy. Then, point by point, it laid out the reasons why voters should support Eisenhower.

In the newsroom of the *Times* — a hotbed of Stevenson support — reporters correctly assumed that the publisher's wife disagreed with her husband and her own paper. Iphigene had been lukewarm about the Republican nominee to begin with, but the Milwaukee incident had damaged him irreparably in her eyes. "[Eisenhower] was a good general, a nice man," she said later, "but he's not one of my heroes." In late October, after McCarthy made a televised speech linking Stevenson to Communist sympathizers, hundreds of angry *New York Times* readers deluged 229 West Forty-third Street with phone calls and telegrams, demanding that the paper switch its allegiance to Stevenson.

Four days before the election, rumors flew that the *Times* was about to reverse itself and come out for Stevenson. Fed by that hope, some fifteen thousand people wrote letters urging the paper to reconsider its stand. On October 31 alone, the *Times* received 2,200 phone calls and telegrams, of which all but 155 were pro-Stevenson. The pressure was so great that the paper felt compelled to publish a story headlined THE TIMES IS NOT CONSIDERING TO SHIFT FROM IKE TO ADLAI.

On election day Iphigene went to the polls and reluctantly pulled the lever for Eisenhower. "I voted for him . . . only out of solidarity with the family and the paper," she confessed. Years later Arthur maintained that if he had it to do over again, he would "unhesitatingly repeat" the choices he had made in order to help Eisenhower enter the race and win, but privately he admitted that he had lost a lot of his political naïveté. Writing to an overseas friend at the height of the 1952 campaign, he expressed a degree of disillusionment he had kept hidden from almost everyone: "You get so interested in a man and then with the limelight on him and the guns directed at him, you find certain weaknesses showing up. I find it all a bit nauseating."

18

Redemption

I F THE EISENHOWER CAMPAIGN LED ARTHUR TO stray perilously far from his central identity as a publisher, the *Times'* battle against McCarthy and his disciples eventually pulled him back to his roots. Arthur's own view of communism had evolved over the years from one of sympathy to virulent opposition. As a young man, he had been violently anti-czar, believing that only through bolshevism could Russia's oppressed masses bestir themselves and claim their patrimony. Yet in 1929, when he saw the country firsthand, he had become so depressed by its drab hopelessness that he had cut his trip short. His distaste increased in the 1930s when the New York Newspaper Guild, which he considered awash with Communists and fellow travelers, tried to organize members of the newsroom. By the first flush of the Cold War in the late 1940s, Arthur had evolved into a staunch anticommunist who declared he would not knowingly employ any "Communists or other totalitarians or subversive characters" in the news operation of the paper.

The recklessness of McCarthy's witch-hunt wreaked havoc with this neat philosophy. "I wish my mind were clear as to what is right," he wrote a friend at the time. While Arthur supported the goal of rooting out Communists, he detested the demagogic manner in which McCarthy made accusations and destroyed lives. As a result, the paper's early editorials did not rail against McCarthy as an invidious evil; instead, they emphasized the need for the orderly administration of loyalty oaths and other procedures.

On the news pages, reporters were hampered by Adolph's dogma about objective journalism. "We tell the public which way the cat is jumping," Arthur once told *Time.* "The public will take care of the cat." Yet as the McCarthy period progressed, it became glaringly apparent that this approach — reporting what a news source said without telling the reader whether it was true — was no longer sufficient. When McCarthy first appeared on the national scene, Turner Catledge's campaign to intro-duce analysis into stories had not yet been implemented, so few *Times* articles in the early 1950s went beyond repeating McCarthy's charges and the denials of his targets.

When it came to advertising that touched on the issue of commu-nism, Arthur vacillated wildly. He refused to run an ad advocating the commutation of the death sentence for Julius and Ethel Rosenberg, who had been convicted of giving atomic secrets to the Russians, on the grounds that public opinion had the power to sway judicial decisions and the *Times* did not accept ads aimed at doing that. Yet he permitted an ad for the book *Spartacus,* self-published by Howard Fast, a former writer for *The Daily Worker* who had refused to tell the House Un-American Activities Committee whether he was a Communist.

McCarthy and his henchmen systematically made their way through nearly every sector of American life, including the State Department, academia, Hollywood, and the army, in each case charging Communist infiltration, espionage, and conspiracy. By 1953 it was clear that the news media, and specifically *The New York Times,* would soon be their next target. In January Walter Winchell reported in his syndicated column that a government undercover man named Harvey M. Matusow had testified before the Senate Internal Security Subcommittee that there were approximately five hundred dues-paying Communists working in newspapers; of those, "well over 100" were at *The New York Times.* Arthur sent the column to Eddie Greenbaum, with a note: "Walter Winchell apparently knows who the Communists in *The NYT* are," it read. "I should think God would be very envious of Walter Winchell."

Still, he was sufficiently concerned by Winchell's report to dispatch Eddie and Julius to Washington to meet with J. Edgar Hoover, head of the FBI. The relationship between Arthur and Hoover had always been one of mutual aid tinged by a respectful wariness. In 1946 Hoover had invited Arthur to make the graduation speech at the FBI National Acad-emy, and in the ensuing years the *Times* had discreetly asked the FBI to share whatever it could about employees suspected of being Commu-nists. Arthur assumed that Hoover knew a great deal about Matusow; he also assumed that Hoover was the primary source for much of the mate-rial that found its way to Winchell and the other Red-baiting colum-nists. During his meeting with Eddie and Julius, however, Hoover characterized Matusow as an "opportunist" and expressed concern about the Winchell allegations. Two months later, when Winchell repeated Matusow's charges about Communists at the *Times,* Julius again asked Hoover whether the claim had any basis in fact. This time, Hoover brusquely told him that whatever information Matusow furnished to the FBI was "confidential." Eddie tried to take up the question directly with Matusow, sending a registered letter to him, but it came back "addressee unknown."

Then, in late September 1953, Matusow called Frank Adams, the *Times'* city editor, from Reno, Nevada, and said he wanted to change his story. Adams paid for Matusow to fly to Los Angeles, where the local *Times* correspondent Gladwin Hill met the plane. What followed was one of the more bizarre episodes of the McCarthy era.

The elusive Matusow turned out to be a heavyset man in a blue suit and bow tie, ingratiating and chatty one moment and nervous and suspicious the next. Over the next two days, in a room at the Hollywood Roosevelt Hotel, Matusow bragged to Hill that it was he who had first denounced the folksinging group The Weavers, and he cheerfully conceded that while he had repeated the charge of one hundred dues-paying Communists at *The New York Times* at least one hundred times, he actually knew of only six. He was delighted that such nonsense had rattled the mighty *Times* and equally unrepentant about his false claims against CBS, the YMCA, the Boy Scouts, the Voice of America, the USO, and the state of Montana, which Matusow had alleged to have "more Communists per capita than any other state." Senator McCarthy was well aware that he had made up most of his allegations, Matusow said, but had encouraged him, even paid him, to carry on. At the end of Hill's exhaustive debriefing, Matusow signed an affidavit attesting to his revelations and declared himself ready to go public with the truth.

Although the Matusow affidavit had the power to damage McCarthy, Arthur decided not to publish the story. Instead, in a maneuver calculated to disseminate the information without being tied directly to it, he sent the document to J. Edgar Hoover with a note explicitly urging him to share it with Walter Winchell. Hoover was outraged. "I could never, under any circumstances, attempt to influence any columnist or writer," he replied indignantly.

Later, *Times* executives close to the decision would say that, at the time, they feared a story exposing Matusow would only serve to further publicize his allegations, which had never appeared in the *Times*. Arthur was also concerned that the paper would be left vulnerable to a potentially devastating counterattack from the McCarthy forces.

The televised Army-McCarthy hearings in the spring of 1954 served as a national showcase for McCarthy's true aims. By the end of the year, he was censured by the Senate and, with the Democrats again in control of Congress after the 1954 elections, his days of Red-baiting were numbered. But that did not mean newspapermen could breathe easy, for Senator James O. Eastland of Mississippi, head of the Internal Security Subcommittee, soon picked up where McCarthy had left off.

Eastland, a detractor of *The New York Times*, was especially incensed by recent editorials demanding that Mississippi obey *Brown* v. *Board of Education*, the May 1954 Supreme Court ruling declaring an end to separate but equal schooling, and a 1955 decision requiring that desegregation proceed "with all deliberate speed." Julien G. Sourwine, the deceptively soft-spoken forty-seven-year-old former newspaperman and chief counsel for the subcommittee, was an even more ferocious enemy.

The assault on the *Times* began in earnest shortly before the 1954 congressional elections when Walter Winchell revealed in a TV broadcast that a former editor of *The Daily Worker* had identified a *New York Times* reporter who, though an alleged Communist, was covering McCarthy. Unfortunately, this time Winchell was right. Two days later Clayton Knowles, a reporter in the Washington bureau on the security beat covering McCarthy, confessed to Arthur that in 1937, while at the *Long Island Daily Press*, he had joined the Communist Party, but he had dropped out six years later when he began at the *Times*. He had considered alerting Arthur to his past, he said, but decided against it because his "misguided idealism . . . was so many years behind me, so tentative and so insignificant that it would serve no useful purpose." Knowles agreed to go before the subcommittee and tell everything he knew, including the names of others who had been in his cell.

Three months earlier, in a speech at John Carroll University in Cleveland, Arthur had advocated an amnesty program for former Communists. Many people had come under the spell of Communist rhetoric when they were young, he argued — perhaps thinking of himself — but later had realized their mistake and abandoned the party. Persecuting them was cruel and unreasonable. However, anyone who was still in the party or a front organization after the 1948 Berlin Airlift was probably irredeemable and should be considered a threat. Applying this standard, Arthur did not fire Knowles. Instead, at the insistence of Scotty Reston, who had recently succeeded Arthur Krock as head of the Washington staff, Knowles was banished from the Washington bureau and spent the rest of his career as a leprous figure in low-profile jobs in New York, alternately pitied for the purgatory in which he labored and scorned for naming names.

In the wake of the Knowles exposé, Arthur designated Louis Loeb of Lord, Day & Lord, the *Times'* general counsel, to investigate which other employees of the paper might have a Communist past. Despite the policy he had enunciated at John Carroll, it was hardly clear in Arthur's mind which workers deserved to lose their jobs and which did not. He struggled to find a way to be compassionate without appearing to be a Communist dupe; the result was an ad hoc system of justice in which the principles kept changing.

Particularly troubling was the Fifth Amendment — the right of a citizen not to incriminate himself. When Melvin Barnet, a *Times* copyeditor, took the Fifth before the Eastland subcommittee, admitting only that he had not been a Communist since 1942, Arthur discharged him, saying his lack of cooperation had caused the paper to "lose confidence" in him. The decision prompted criticism that Arthur was advocating amnesty on one hand and firing Barnet on the other. After all, Barnet had left the Communist Party long before the cutoff date of the Berlin Airlift. "You, Mr. Sulzberger, have violated your trust," said one furious reader.

To Arthur, the matter came down to his belief that Barnet, who had been nervous and evasive during his discussions with Louis Loeb and had refused to name others, was essentially untrustworthy and unpatriotic. Several months later, in an attempt to draft a policy statement on the question, Arthur wrote that while all Americans have a Fifth Amendment right to be protected against self-incrimination, "in our judgment no one working in the news or editorial departments of this newspaper should invoke it."

In early December Sourwine held four days of closed-door hearings in New York City to probe Communist influence in the newspaper industry. Of the thirty-eight witnesses subpoenaed, thirty were current or former *New York Times* employees. Publicly, Arthur's position was that he welcomed an inquiry into Communist infiltration of the press.

Privately, however, he regarded the Eastland hearings as a calculated effort to discredit *The New York Times*. In Washington the word was that Sourwine's strategy was first to undermine confidence in the nation's preeminent newspaper and then to go after the Associated Press, the *Herald Tribune*, *Time*, CBS, and other media critics of McCarthyism.

As 1955 came to a close, Eastland announced that he had scheduled more hearings for the first week of the New Year, this time in Washington and open to the public. Four days later *Times*men began to receive subpoenas. As the date neared, a new air of defiance made itself apparent at the paper. Instead of soft-pedaling racial strife in Mississippi out of deference to Eastland, Catledge fired a broadside, publishing a story on Christmas Eve in which the bishop of the New York Episcopal diocese denounced Mississippi's treatment of blacks as a "reign of terror." Senator Eastland's battle cry calling on states to defy the Supreme Court decision outlawing segregation, the bishop said, was "subversion just as real, and, because it comes from a United States Senator, far more dangerous than any perpetrated by the Communist Party."

Tension in the newspaper industry was palpable; everyone knew what was at stake. "The slightest sign of retreat by the most important newspaper in the country would not only do great damage to the freedom of the press, but would have a very bad effect on the fight for civil liberties," a *Times* reporter who had worked under Adolph told Arthur. If the Eastland subcommittee tried to intimidate *The New York Times*, Arthur was determined to fight back.

But what, practically, would that involve? After a Publisher's Luncheon shortly before the commencement of the hearings, Arthur and his top advisers worried aloud about what the *Times* could do to sound a cannon roar if it was required. "I think I've got a solution in my desk drawer," said Charles Merz. The group trooped down to the tenth floor and crowded into Merz's small office. Merz then read aloud an editorial he had been working on. "The Voice of a Free Press" summed up the role of the *Times* with such force and poetry that several listeners had tears in their eyes. If it was needed, Arthur had his cannon.

On January 4, 1956, the first day of the hearings, the packed meeting room was flooded with TV lights. The lead witness was a former *Times* employee who had left the paper to join *The Daily Worker*. Then came a former *Times*man who screened Russian films at a New York theater, followed by Clayton Knowles. Then came Sam Weissman, who worked

Adolph Ochs standing between his parents, Julius and Bertha, during the family's short-lived period of prosperity in Knoxville in the late 1860s. *(NYTCA)*

Below left: Effie Miriam Wise, age twenty. A daughter of the celebrated rabbi Isaac Mayer Wise, she escaped her irascible stepmother by marrying Adolph, only to come under Bertha Ochs's control. *(NYTCA)*

While negotiating to purchase *The Chattanooga Times,* Adolph, age twenty, grew a mustache in order to appear older. *(NYTCA)*

When Ochs bought *The Chattanooga Times* in 1878, the equipment was dilapidated and money tight. Ever mindful of image, he invested in a finely tooled leather checkbook to create the illusion of solvency. *(NYTCA)*

In 1892 Ochs erected a dramatic gold-domed building to house his paper, in part to quiet rumors about his precarious finances.
(The Chattanooga Times)

In 1898, two years after acquiring *The New York Times*, Ochs (in the hat, with managing editor Henry Loewenthal), slashed the price of the paper to a penny to boost circulation and prevent an anti-Semitic former employee from exposing inflated readership figures. (NYTCA)

At midnight on New Year's Eve 1906, Ochs dropped a large illuminated globe from the top of his newly constructed Times Tower in Times Square. The event has since become a national ritual. (New York Times *photo*)

Background: In the August 9, 1896, *Times*, the first under Adolph's leadership, he vowed "to give the news impartially, without fear or favor, regardless of party, sect or interests involved." Ever since, the paper and members of the Ochs-Sulzberger family have repeatedly misquoted the famous credo.

Adolph's only child, Iphigene, and Julius Ochs Adler were dressed as a miniature bride and groom for a relative's wedding. Many in the Ochs clan hoped the first cousins would in fact wed one day, ensuring undiluted family control of the *Times*. *(NYTCA)*

Ochs adored the child he called "my ownest daughter and onliest son" and led her to believe she might succeed him as publisher. But when she came of age, he refused to permit her even to work for the paper because of her gender. *(NYTCA)*

At Barnard, Iphigene struggled to gain independence from her dominating father. She gave money to the suffragist cause and embraced the egalitarian political movements then roiling Russia. "I never quite lost my leftist leanings," she later said. *(NYTCA)*

Rachel Hays Sulzberger was proud of her Sephardic ancestry and insisted that her children join the Sons of the American Revolution to demonstrate that Jews had been patriots during the War of Independence. With her sons (from left) Leo, David, and Arthur, in their World War I uniforms. *(NYTCA)*

Adolph had tried to prevent Iphigene's marriage to Arthur Hays Sulzberger in 1917, and their wedding portrait was unusually grim. Best man Julius Ochs Adler (with mustache) stands behind Arthur. *(NYTCA)*

Decorated for bravery in combat during World War I, Julius Ochs Adler was hospitalized after being gassed. Fears for his nephew's safety contributed to Adolph's debilitating depression. *(NYTCA)*

When she married Julius, Babs Stettheimer believed that her new husband was in line to succeed Adolph at the *Times.* Her greed and thwarted ambition made the Adlers' family life miserable. From left: Julie Jr., Babs, Nancy, and Bobbie.

As publisher of the *Times,*
Adolph (left) regularly associ-
ated with "great men." In 1928
he lunched with George
Eastman, Thomas Edison,
General John J. Pershing, and
Sir James Irvine, a distin-
guished British chemist.
(NYTCA)

After the stock market crash,
Ochs adopted a stance of
aggressive optimism, refusing
to lay off workers and supporting scores of destitute relatives.
But a private dinner with
President Herbert Hoover in
1931 gave him pause. "Of all
the pessimistic views that have
been presented to me, his was
the most depressing I have
heard," he recorded in his
notes. *(NYTCA)*

Adolph's brothers and sisters and their spouses gathered for his seventieth birthday. Seated from left: Fannie, Mattie Talimer, Effie, Nannie, Ada Adler. Standing: Bernard Talimer, Milton, Adolph, George, Harry Adler. *(NYTCA)*

Ochs built the Times Annex in 1913 and added several floors in the 1920s, patterning the building after the castle of Chambord in France. (New York Times *photo*)

After three daughters, Iphigene and Arthur finally produced the male heir Adolph had yearned for. From left: Marian, Iphigene holding Arthur Ochs "Punch" Sulzberger, Judy, and Ruth. (NYTCA)

In 1925 Adolph presented Iphigene and Arthur with a sprawling $180,000 town house on East Eightieth Street in Manhattan, half a block from the Metropolitan Museum of Art, and pointedly put it in his daughter's name. (Louis H. Dreyer)

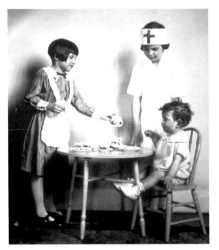

Ruth (left) and Marian (in nurse's uniform) serve Punch, then barely a year old. (NYTCA)

The Sulzberger children pose in a formation they would repeat in photographs throughout their lives, with Judy, the self-described maverick, refusing to put her arms around her brother's waist. From left: Punch, Judy, Ruth, and Marian. (NYTCA)

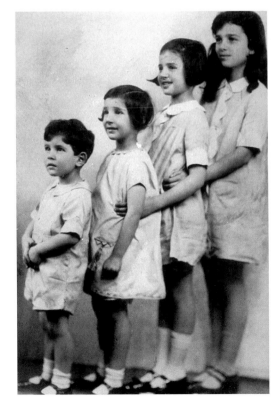

Adolph and Punch at the beach. With his grandchildren, Ochs experienced the childhood he never had, buying toys, holding squealing contests, and performing coin tricks. *(American Jewish Archives)*

Adolph's purchase of Hillandale, a fifty-seven-acre estate in White Plains, New York, was his only real extravagance. The Sulzbergers were expected every weekend. *(NYTCA)*

Adolph and Effie's official fiftieth-wedding-anniversary portrait in 1933. Soon thereafter, Ochs fell into a profound depression that lasted almost until his death. *(NYTCA)*

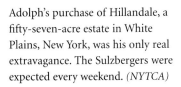

Arthur's affair with actress Madeleine Carroll was common knowledge within the family. As a rule, Iphigene studiously ignored her husband's dalliances, but later admitted that she had been "terribly hurt" when "this beautiful creature" entered their lives. *(Photofest)*

While they had misgivings about the match, Arthur and Iphigene were in high spirits at Ruth's wedding to Ben Golden at Hillandale in 1946.

Arthur (with pipe), outside Hitler's bunker. On a visit to Germany in 1946, he toured Dachau and sat in on the Nuremberg trials. Despite the misery he witnessed, he returned home unshaken in his opposition to Israel as a separate state. *(AP/Wide World)*

Arthur (center) helped Eisenhower's 1952 campaign by publishing a *Times* endorsement an unprecedented seven months before the nominating convention. Julius (left) was an equally enthusiastic supporter; Iphigene favored Stevenson but, out of loyalty to her husband, pulled the lever for Ike. *(NYTCA)*

Arthur in 1956, the year Senator Eastland's Internal Security Subcommittee singled out the *Times* during its investigation into Communist infiltration of newspapers. Arthur's response, a defiant editorial titled "The Voice of a Free Press," inspired journalists everywhere. *(NYTCA)*

Though Arthur and Iphigene thought them little more than children, Punch and Barbara Grant were determined to marry. Their 1948 wedding at Hillandale included a Sulzberger favorite, the explorer Rear Admiral Richard E. Byrd.

In the early years of Ben and Ruth's marriage, their happiness was evident. Over time, however, Ben came to resent his financial dependence on his in-laws and focused his gathering rage on his wife.

A series of postwar weddings was followed rapidly by grandchildren. From left: Punch and Barbara; Ben and Ruth; Orvil and Marian; Mattie and Judy. And in their laps, the four oldest in the fourth generation: Bobby Dryfoos, Stephen Golden, and Susan and Jackie Dryfoos. *(NYTCA)*

When Arthur (here with Orvil) marked his twentieth anniversary as publisher with a male-only party at "21," Iphigene, stung by her husband's latest romantic escapade, scandalized the family by saying in a recorded message that was played after dinner, "If I had been the boss's son instead of his daughter, this party might have been for me instead of you." *(NYTCA)*

Managing editor Edwin L. James, known as Dressy James because of his sartorial flair, needled Arthur by complaining that he was just a "hired man" on a family farm. Arthur, ever sensitive about having married the boss's daughter, would respond sympathetically: "I'm a hired man, too." *(NYTCA)*

Charles Merz, the *Times'* editorial-page editor from 1938 to 1961, shared Arthur's taste for cocktails, puns, and parlor games. Arthur Krock had wanted the job, but Arthur feared criticism if he gave it to a Jew. *(NYTCA)*

Scotty Reston (seated) was the "adopted Sulzberger" whom Arthur and Iphigene sought out for advice. A shrewd office politician, Reston succeeded the prickly Arthur Krock (standing) as head of the Washington bureau. *(NYTCA)*

In 1961 the *Times* downplayed what it knew about the Bay of Pigs operation, yet after the calamitous invasion President Kennedy publicly denounced the paper as irresponsible. Privately he told managing editor Turner Catledge that more candid coverage might have saved his administration from "a colossal mistake." *(AP/Wide World)*

In 1959 Orvil (right) was two years away from being named publisher, and his family (from left: Bobby, Marian, Jackie, and Susan) seemed supremely blessed. *(NYTCA)*

A picket line outside the *Times'* West Forty-third Street head-quarters during the 1962–63 strike. The 114-day conflict, prompted primarily by a struggle for dominance among the news-paper unions, led to the closing of four of New York's seven dailies. *(NYTCA)*

Orvil handwrote a memorandum welcoming striking staffers back to work and, in an act of journalistic courage, published a shockingly frank account of the strike. Within two months he was dead of heart failure. *(NYTCA)*

in the editorial index at the *Times*. As the afternoon wore on, it became clear that the *Times* had been singled out, and Arthur gave the green light to run Merz's editorial.

The piece was long and discursive, with a detailed recounting of the *Times'* opposition to communism and a history of the Eastland inquiry. Painstakingly, the editorial made its case and slowly gathered speed and power, like a preacher warming to his sermon. By the end it became a clarion call, and in the final sentences Merz soared. It was these last paragraphs that prompted *Times* reporters to weep and their rivals in the newsroom of the *Herald Tribune* to break out in spontaneous cheers as they read the words in the early edition. The editorial concluded that

> if further evidence reveals that the real purpose of the present inquiry is to demonstrate that a free newspaper's policies can be swayed by Congressional pressure, then we say to Mr. Eastland and his counsel that they are wasting their time. This newspaper will continue to determine its own policies. It will continue to condemn discrimination, whether in the South or in the North.
>
> It will continue to defend civil liberties. It will continue to challenge the unbridled power of governmental authority. It will continue to enlist goodwill against prejudice and confidence against fear.
>
> We cannot speak unequivocally for the long future. But we can have faith.
>
> And our faith is strong that long after Senator Eastland and his present subcommittee are forgotten, long after segregation has lost its final battle in the South, long after all that was known as McCarthyism is a dim, unwelcome memory, long after the last Congressional committee has learned that it cannot tamper successfully with a free press, *The New York Times* will still be speaking for the men who make it, and only for the men who make it, and speaking, without fear or favor, the truth as it sees it.

Reaction to the editorial was overwhelming. Hundreds of letters poured in. "Thank heavens for courage," wrote Eleanor Roosevelt. Jacob Potofsky, president of the Amalgamated Clothing Workers of America —

not a *Times* admirer — lauded the "concluding, ringing words." Theodore White declared the editorial "noble," adding, "I do not know whether you realize how much the *Times* means to all of us other newspapermen. . . . If the *Times* should cringe, then the courage and pride of all of us would be diminished." One letter simply said, "Bravo, Bravo, Bravo, Bravo, Bravo, Bravo, Bravo."

At the paper, reporters and editors overflowed with pride for their institution. Lee Kanner, a copyeditor, was emboldened to tell Arthur that the editorial was "magnificent . . . a milestone in journalism." A particularly satisfying salute came from Arthur Krock, who in the summer of 1953 had praised the Senate Internal Security Subcommittee as "an example of Congressional investigation at the very highest level." The editorial, he told Arthur, "is another and profound demonstration of how wisely Mr. Ochs chose his successor." *The Washington Post,* the Louisville *Courier-Journal, The Minneapolis Tribune,* and many other papers reprinted it, and the *St. Louis Post-Dispatch* urged its readers to devour the editorial "to its last syllable." On Sunday the *Times* ran it a second time, along with dozens of letters.

The day the editorial appeared, Sourwine sarcastically said that he was "flattered" by the attention, and the hearings ground on for two more days, with more testimony from *Times* employees. Although the *Chicago Tribune* bruited the subcommittee's suggestion that the *Times* was infested with Communists, most newspapers focused on its bold editorial. Senator Eastland issued a statement that the testimony had disclosed "a significant effort on the part of Communists to penetrate leading American newspapers," and he promised that there would be more hearings, with more newspapermen called. But there were no more hearings, and two weeks later Sourwine resigned as the subcommittee counsel.

In the afterglow of the editorial, Arthur was magnanimous toward employees who took the Fifth Amendment, and none except Barnet was fired. Three were cited for contempt; eventually all three successfully fought the charge. Despite his stand against the encroachment of the Eastland subcommittee, Arthur never lost his suspicion of Communists. One of those who took the Fifth was Matilda Landsman, a Linotype operator who "looked like a commissar" and before Eastland's committee had refused even to say when she had started setting type for a living. A few days after the hearings ended, Arthur told Turner that he wanted her watched for fear that she might be making errors on purpose to change the content of a story.

§

Arthur had wrestled with Eastland and Sourwine largely without the help of Julius, who might have been of particular value because of his connections in the military and intelligence communities. Julius had died on October 3, 1955, three months before "The Voice of a Free Press" was published. He went out like a soldier, with a demonstration of courage that won the respect of everyone who witnessed his dignified, lonely battle with pancreatic cancer.

Only a year earlier he and Arthur had walked the five blocks to Leone's restaurant for a surprise party in honor of Louis Loeb. When Julius had entered the darkened cellar used for such occasions, the lights flashed on and the jammed room burst into "For He's a Jolly Good Fellow." The party, arranged by Nat Goldstein, the *Times'* bespectacled circulation manager, was in fact a commemoration of Julius's fortieth anniversary at the *Times.* Late in the evening a photographer captured a radiant Julius wearing a printer's hat made of folded newspaper, leading the well-lubricated assembly in old army songs.

Even then, Julius had not been feeling himself. Shortly after Christmas 1954 he underwent exploratory surgery at the same hospital where his oldest daughter, Bobbie, awaited the delivery of her first child. The doctors found that he had inoperable cancer. Babs decreed that Julius was to be kept in the dark about his condition, and she swore her children and a few key people to secrecy. Arthur was among those she told, and he joined in the conspiracy of silence even as he prepared to find a replacement as general manager.

For public consumption, the story was that Julius had jaundice, and by spring he told friends he was making slow progress. "My strength is reluctant to come back in a hurry," he said, adding that soon, no doubt, "I shall be again hitting on all cylinders." On the fourteenth floor of the Times Building, Julius's affliction was an open secret. In March, he came to work for a couple of hours each day, but his vitality never fully returned. When Milton Ochs died in late April at the age of ninety-one, Julius sent an anguished telegram to Aunt Fan: "Am heartbroken that my doctors will not permit me to come." In an ironic echo of the deception going on around him, Julius decided not to tell his mother, Ada, that her brother had died. She suffered from Parkinson's disease, and he feared she was too fragile. He sent his loyal aide, John Sheehan, to Philadelphia to break the news to Aunt Mattie, with orders that the blow should come at the end of a nice, long lunch.

By late spring Julius had visibly faded and his pain had grown worse, but he continued to make appearances at the *Times*. Executives sometimes saw Julius making his way to his office, leaning against the wall for support, barely able to stand. He was determined to attend his Princeton reunion in June and march with his class in the boisterous annual procession known as the P-rade. He went as usual, but for the first time he roomed alone and did not march.

It is unclear precisely when Julius realized his true situation, but in midsummer he rewrote his will. Since learning of his condition, Babs had thought of little else. She did not know the specific details of his finances, but she was well aware that Julius had inherited stock from Adolph, and she was determined to make sure that she, not her children, got it. What is more, she had made it clear she would challenge any will not to her liking.

Julius and Eddie Greenbaum conferred about how to deal with the matter. Adolph had left Julius two kinds of stock: preferred shares, which were nonvoting but paid an annual income, and common shares, which had not paid a dividend for twenty years but represented a percentage of The New York Times Company, one of the biggest blocks outside the Ochs Trust. With Eddie's help, a will was drawn that left Babs the preferred stock with its cash income, the Adler apartment, and most of Julius's other property. The three children — Julius Jr., Bobbie, and Nancy — were named inheritors of the common stock.

In late July Julius signed his will and shortly afterward summoned Julie Jr. and Bobbie to his office at the *Times*. He was about to reenter the hospital, where he knew he would be under Babs's surveillance, and he had something to explain to his children. "I want you to understand why I've written my will the way I have," he told them. "I never want your mummy to have any voting rights in the paper, and I never want her to challenge the will. So I've left her everything except the *Times* voting stock." And, he added, "I've left your stock in trust because I'm afraid your little sister Nancy might leave her share to a dog-and-cat hospital."

When Julius returned to the hospital, Babs made it difficult for even close friends to see him. To the very end, she wheedled and cajoled, trying to persuade him to alter his will again, to cancel the trust and leave her everything. Just days before he died, Babs forbade her sister to visit him because a meeting with the lawyers had been scheduled in the hospital, and she did not want to drain any of his remaining strength. Her obsession with money was so overwhelming that when she learned that Julius had left instructions ordering her to share any leftover cash with their children, she stripped the money from their joint account just three days before his death.

Julius knew that he had not had a good marriage and that, after he was gone, the prospects of the Adlers remaining intact as a family were dim. In his last days his mind wandered back to happier times when his children were young. On one of the few visits that Babs allowed, Bobbie brought him a ball of trinkets and toys wrapped in crepe paper, a traditional favor at birthday parties in years past. Inside the ball was a set of jacks. As Julius unwrapped it, he asked Bobbie and Nancy to sit on the floor beside his bed and play jacks as they had done years before. "I just want to remember you as little girls," he said. His dying words were to his oldest daughter: "Bobbie, try and hold this little family together." He then lapsed into a coma, and on October 3 he died.

After years of being overshadowed by Arthur and Iphigene, Babs was determined to take center stage in an extravagant funeral. As a major general in the Army Reserve, Julius was entitled to full military honors. His body lay in state at the Seventh Regiment Armory, accompanied by an honor guard; survivors of the company he had commanded in World War I came to pay tribute. The funeral was slated for Temple Emanu-El, the most elite synagogue in New York and a place rarely visited by the Adlers. Bobbie was assigned to arrange the service, prompting an exchange that spoke eloquently about the Adlers' ignorance of Judaism.

When Bobbie told her mother what musical pieces she had selected, Babs remarked, "What about Daddy's favorite hymn, 'Onward, Christian Soldiers?' " As everyone in the family was well aware, whenever Julius was in high spirits, he would march up and down the hall outside his bedroom belting out, "Onward, Christian soldiers, marching as to war, with the cross of Jesus going on before." Babs could not fathom why Temple Emanu-El would mind if Julius's favorite hymn happened to be a Christian summons to battle. "I don't care — call them up," she ordered Bobbie. The answer, to her consternation, was no.

After the service the family and special friends boarded a private railroad car for the trip to Washington, where they were met by a convoy of black limousines that transported them to Arlington National Cemetery. At the gravesite, located near the Tomb of the Unknown Soldier, a rabbi said Kaddish, something Babs had strongly resisted, relenting only under pressure from Iphigene. On Julius's headstone were the words JOURNALIST-SOLDIER-LEADER.

As events would prove, the bugler's sounding of "Taps" at Arlington also marked the end of the Adlers as a family. "When the General died, the glue disappeared," said Douglas Adler, Julius's grandson. The three Adler offspring knew of their mother's efforts to disinherit them, and to add further insult, Babs had attended the funeral with Holy Joe, her wartime lover. When the train returned to New York, Julie Jr. said good night to his mother and didn't speak to her again for three years. "His death gave me the fortitude to effect that break, which I never would've done if he had been alive," he said. Bobbie and Nancy did not cut Babs off so dramatically, but relations were frosty and bitter.

Until her own death in 1971, Babs continually changed her will, depending on which of her offspring she wanted to punish. "My mother wrote more codicils than the Pope has bishops," said Bobbie. "We used to laugh about who was number one on her shit list." Relations among the Adler siblings fared no better; as trustees of one another's trusts containing the *Times* common stock, the three squabbled over their inheritance, with accusations of deceit and shady maneuverings. Eventually they simply stopped speaking altogether.

Julius's death also effectively spelled the end of his son's career at *The New York Times*. Julie Jr. stayed in the advertising department for four more years, but his desultory work habits and misplaced sense of entitlement made it easy for Arthur to suggest he look elsewhere for employment. "He was a sad case," said Amory Bradford. "There was nothing we could do with him." In 1959 he left the *Times* to invest in a bowling alley on Staten Island, where he lost almost half his inheritance. Seven years later he and his wife, Anne, divorced. "He just downright did not like family life, that was not the focus," she said. "The focus was this very infantile idea of being a powerful person."

§

Julius's death in 1955 came twenty years after Adolph's. For Arthur, being untethered from his wife's conservative cousin meant that for the first time in his life, *The New York Times* and its associated enterprises were fully, wholly his in a way they had never been before. The first step he took was to push for changes at *The Chattanooga Times* in an area that had long troubled him: race. Julius's racial attitudes had been influential at the Tennessee paper, where he had served as publisher and president of The Chattanooga Times Printing Company since 1935. Like the town, the paper was racially segregated. The death notices of Chattanooga's blacks ran under the title "Colored" on the obituary page; in news stories the courtesy of honorifics was reserved exclusively for whites.

In December 1955 Arthur exerted his new authority by demanding that *The Chattanooga Times* do away with segregated obituaries. "I don't think God is standing next to Saint Peter to check the color of the spirits as they come through the gates," he told Ruth, Ben, and Mr. Puckette, the paper's general manager. Arthur was preaching to the converted. All three were in sympathy with his idea, but they feared the effect it might have on the paper's standing and fortunes.

Locally, *The Chattanooga Times* had taken a drubbing for its support of *Brown* v. *Board of Education,* and it continued to labor under the perception that it was a puppet of what its reactionary rival, the *Chattanooga News–Free Press,* called "Communist-infested New York." Detractors dubbed the paper "Pinky Puckette's Pravda"; Ruth and her family were sneeringly referred to as "those Yankee Democrat Jews." "I would prefer not to give race haters and rabble rousers any further ammunition," Ben wrote Arthur, while Ruth accused her father of using the issue of race as a way to vent his frustrations with *The Chattanooga Times* in general and with the city of Chattanooga in particular — a place he considered deeply anti-Semitic. "You are in part solving your own personal disturbance in this fashion," she told Arthur. "I don't think it will help the paper."

For a few weeks Arthur did not address the obituary issue, exacting instead an agreement that *The Chattanooga Times* would henceforth adopt a standard *The New York Times* had followed on its news pages since 1946: to keep racial identification out of the news altogether, especially in crime stories, unless it was "germane." In January 1956 Arthur renewed his campaign for integrated obituaries, and this time Ruth, Ben, and Mr. Puckette reluctantly accepted his decree — with predictable results. Enraged whites threatened to boycott the paper's advertisers, and *The Chattanooga Times* lost three thousand subscribers. But the new policy stuck. As the decade wore on, *The Chattanooga Times* emphasized "gradualism" in the dismantling of segregation while Arthur prodded the paper to echo the harder line of *The New York Times*. However principled his stand, events would later prove that he was unwittingly contributing to an erosion of *The Chattanooga Times'* fragile foundation.

The morally superior tone Arthur assumed when pressing for changes regarding race at *The Chattanooga Times* was, in fact, slightly disingenuous. At *The New York Times* and in private life, he had often been equivocal, displaying the guilt of a well-meaning white liberal while harboring many of the prejudices and stereotypes he ostensibly scorned. As a member of the Red Cross central committee during the war, he had tried to reverse the army's policy of segregating white and black blood, arguing that many black women wet-nursed white children, and milk and blood were both bodily fluids. Yet while on a Red Cross tour of England, he was horrified by the sight of black American soldiers "fraternizing" with white women. "Rape by Negroes is just one degree worse than by whites, and black illegitimate children just one degree more unfortunate than white ones," he told General Eisenhower at the time. Later he admitted, with some shame, that even *he* "would not want his granddaughter to go to school with Negro boys."

At the *Times* Arthur's record on race was typical of most major newspaper publishers until well after World War II. A Newspaper Guild survey taken in the 1950s found a mere thirty-eight blacks among the nation's seventy-five thousand newsroom employees. To his credit, Arthur was enlightened enough to have had the desire earlier than most to try to rectify the situation. In 1945 he had agitated to hire a black reporter, a move he characterized as an experiment.

George Streator, a Fisk graduate with a master's degree from Western Reserve University, arrived at *The New York Times* after working on several black weeklies, including a stint as managing editor of *The Crisis*, the organ of the NAACP. "I am a product of American middle-class education," Streator had told a *Times* editor in his letter of application. "I like concerts, the theater, all angles, and it is not all Marian Anderson."

Arthur found the letter "very moving" and ordered that Streator be hired at $100 a week, $25 more than he had asked for.

The experiment proved to be a disappointment. Having worked only at activist publications, Streator had no training in the *Times*' tradition of objectivity. Turner discovered that sometimes Streator made up quotes in order to present blacks in a more positive light: "Once he admitted to me he'd invented some quotes for A. Philip Randolph, because he was sure he knew what Randolph meant to say, whether or not he said it." Corrections and critical memoranda piled up in Streator's file. The final straw was the omission of an important fact from a story about a black university in Texas, necessitating yet another "humiliating" correction in the *Times*. Shortly thereafter, Catledge fired him.

The *Times*' experience with Streator did not discourage the hiring of blacks in the newsroom and other white-collar jobs, but it very likely slowed the process. In 1961, when the *Times* began converting to automatic elevators and the elevator operators lost their jobs, Arthur ordered a report on the paper's record of employing blacks. The result was a confidential memo revealing that several departments had no blacks at all. Only eight of the forty-one displaced black elevator operators had been able to get better jobs elsewhere at the paper. The news department had one black copyeditor; there were two black reporters.

Black advocacy groups considered the *Times*' editorial and employment record maddening. By the standards of the South, *The Chattanooga Times* was racially progressive, but compared with other mainstream papers in New York, *The New York Times*, according to the NAACP, was barely ahead of the Hearst papers on the index of racial fairness. Indeed, until about 1950 the NAACP considered the *Times* "anti-Negro" — an especially troubling notion because the paper "has such immense prestige."

In the paper's actual reportage, changes came in tentative increments. The *Times* criticized the Daughters of the American Revolution's refusal to allow Negro performers to use Constitution Hall and supported the desegregation of organized baseball, but until the 1950s, said John Oakes, "the paper could never have been called a front-runner, other than to denounce a lynching." Although photographs of blacks occasionally appeared, they were carefully chosen to avoid any suggestion of social integration, especially anything hinting at interracial sex. Sometimes black wedding announcements ran without photographs and with no indication of race, but it wasn't until 1954, a scant year before Julius died, that the *Times* was emboldened to publish its first picture of a black couple on the society pages. The bride was a former head of the student government at Radcliffe, the groom was a surgeon, and the marriage had taken place in the chancery of St. Thomas' Church, an Episcopal venue favored by Manhattan's upper crust. Julius, who had protested the integration of the military and scrupulously hired only white help at home, registered no complaint with Arthur. The couple was light-skinned and no readers even took note of it.

§

Unlike Julie Jr., who lumbered through *The New York Times* with all the subtlety of an errant bull, Punch began his career at the paper with a soft-spoken, self-deprecating, and unpretentious demeanor. As the only Sulzberger male, he knew he would probably occupy a decent position at the *Times*, but exactly what that spot might be and when he would get it were unclear. "The handwriting was on the wall: Orvil forever," said a friend from that era. "He had no illusions that he was ever going to be in an important job." While Punch was in Washington writing reports for General Hittle, Arthur had come up with what he called a "typical Stalin five-year plan" that called for Punch to work for one year on *The Milwaukee Journal*, a year each on the business and news sides of *The New York Times*, and two years in a foreign bureau. In the end, the only part of Punch's training program that came to pass as outlined was his year in Milwaukee.

Arthur felt strongly that Punch should start out on a paper other than *The New York Times*, where, as the son of the publisher, he was bound to receive favored treatment. Of the several places he could have chosen for his son's apprenticeship, *The Milwaukee Journal* had particular appeal. To Arthur, it was important for Punch to understand the sensibility of the Midwest, the locus of the isolationist sentiment he loathed. The *Journal's* employee stock-ownership plan, in operation since 1937, was also a model that the four Sulzberger children might follow when they inherited the controlling stock of *The New York Times* at Iphigene's death. Arthur Krock knew the *Journal's* editor, J. D. "Doc" Ferguson, and asked him whether there might be a place for Punch. In the fall of 1952, after a flurry of letters between Milwaukee and New York, the deal was made.

Punch, Barbara, and the children arrived in Milwaukee in February 1953, two months after Punch had been discharged from active duty as a Marine Reserve officer. Their modest rental apartment on East Jarvis Street in Shorewood, a middle-class suburb north of the city, contained just one obvious extravagance: a large, all-in-one Magnavox entertainment center with a TV, record player, and radio. Punch reported for duty at the *Journal*'s city desk and was immediately put to work writing obituaries, a job that he jokingly complained prevented him from ever meeting his subjects. In yet another effort to finally escape his childhood nickname and remake himself in a place where no one knew him, he introduced himself as Art, to no avail.

Punch's record as an obit writer was less than dazzling. In one case he got the day of the funeral wrong. In another he wrote that the deceased "died suddenly," prompting the *Journal*'s legendary city editor, Harvey Schwander, to scribble, "Ask Harvey, pls." — his trademark — in the upper-right-hand corner of his copy. When Punch showed up at his desk to see what was wrong, Schwander informed him the phrase was redundant. "Everyone dies suddenly," he said. "One minute you're here, the next you're dead." Years later, when queried about his time at the *Journal,* Punch said the main lesson he took away was that "in Milwaukee, you died unexpectedly."

Punch spent ten months on the city desk and two on the state desk, receiving dull assignments and rating few bylines. Occasionally, chief political editor Ed Bayley let him tag along to ward meetings and rallies, events that had a profound effect on Punch's political thinking. The *Journal* was opposed to McCarthy, a stand unpopular with many Wisconsinites, who chanted, "Give it to the *Journal,* Joe" at the senator's speeches. With no firm beliefs of his own, Punch had followed his father's lead in 1952 and voted for Eisenhower. Now he was face-to-face with the dark, reactionary side of Republicanism. "He began to see a different kind of Republican — not these Eastern gentlemen," said Bayley. "I think he became more open to a nonpartisan position."

If Punch gave the impression of an unassuming, somewhat bumbling novice, Barbara came across as a sophisticated and even slightly dangerous flirt. "She was electrifying looking, with flashing blue-gray eyes, and so well turned out," said Ed Bayley's wife, Monica. "She had a boldness that set her apart." Several months after their arrival in Milwaukee, Barbara suffered a potentially threatening miscarriage that, in retrospect, marked the beginning of a downward spiral in the marriage. The day began normally enough, with Monica and Ed Bayley in the Sulzberger apartment helping to prepare Wisconsin wild duck for a dinner party. Before the meal was on the table, Barbara complained of sharp cramps. She went to the bedroom to lie down, leaving Punch to play host. During a lull in the meal, Monica peeked in on her and was alarmed by what she saw. "All right, now tell me: do you need a gynecologist?" she demanded. Barbara had mentioned nothing about being pregnant. "Maybe I do," she replied weakly.

As it happened, finding a gynecologist was particularly difficult that weekend because they were all attending a convention in downtown Milwaukee, and it ultimately took the help of the *Journal*'s medical reporter to locate one. After an examination, the doctor checked Barbara into Columbia Hospital, where she had a miscarriage so severe that she felt it had brought her to the brink of death. The next morning Punch called Monica to tell her what had happened. "We went through a grim thing there," she said. "He didn't want to talk about that much to anybody."

For Barbara, Punch's behavior during the emergency undermined a fundamental trust. Whether her anger was already present, waiting for a spark to set it off, or whether Punch had genuinely let her down, is uncertain. What was clear, however, was her disillusionment with Punch for what she considered his lack of decisiveness and attention in her moment of need. "He just never took hold of the situation," she later complained to a friend. "He acted like a boy instead of a man."

In the wake of the miscarriage, Barbara's coquettishness took on a darker cast. At parties she brought her own records, telling every man she danced with, "This is *our* song." After lots of drinking at one gathering, she pressed Ed Bayley — whose "song" was "Too Marvelous for Words" — to run away with her. At the end of another long evening, Punch had trouble persuading her to leave the dance floor and go home. When he insisted and took her arm, she just went on dancing.

Later Punch claimed he had no indication that his marriage had begun to unravel in Milwaukee, explaining, "I had my eyes closed to it." Yet at the time, he admitted to his father in a letter that he and Barbara were "having some difficulty." Like Iphigene, Punch had the ability to shutter his emotions, to settle for a surface serenity. "He always finds a way of showing a good face, even when he is unhappy or under stress," said a friend. "He can communicate a sense of being relaxed even when the house is falling in around him."

As Punch's year in Milwaukee neared its end, Iphigene, sensing her son's distress, stepped in to change Arthur's neatly mapped-out plan for his future. Instead of spending two years in New York followed by two years overseas, Punch was to come to New York only for several months and then go directly to the Paris bureau. Punch was delighted. He was certain his troubled marriage would fare better away from what he called "the social rat-race" of New York. "I am dying to go to France," he told his father. What he could not have known then was that his yearning to leave New York would prove to be a cataclysmic mistake, one that would result in his hating Paris forever.

19

The Sorcerer's Apprentices

B Y THE TIME ARTHUR TURNED SIXTY-FIVE, HIS body, already afflicted by a host of chronic conditions, started to give out. His blood pressure shot up to precarious levels, prompting the enforcement of a strict diet devoid of salt, butter, cream soups, and gravy. For years Arthur had had eggs every day for breakfast; now he chastely limited himself to one a day and carefully trimmed the fat from his steaks and chops. Drinking had always been a source of relaxation; Arthur maintained a well-stocked bar in both the city and the country, and he was particular about how his Jack Daniel's was served (in an old-fashioned glass with cracked ice and a twist of lemon peel). "He was a moody man," said Judy. "He was always better after a cocktail." Now gout and a duodenal ulcer, diagnosed two years earlier, forced him to restrict even this simple pleasure. His doctor limited him to one small jigger of bourbon a day, taken in a glass of milk, and ordered him to cut out the cigarettes and cigars he occasionally enjoyed.

His maladies were certainly real, but they were undoubtedly aggravated by the inner anxiety he concealed from almost everyone. "I've never seen you when you didn't give the outward appearance, at least, of placidity," his friend C. T. Lanham wrote Arthur soon after the ulcer was diagnosed. "I suppose that this very thing — the bottling up inside of your emotions — lies at the very root of the trouble."

In cold weather his hands, still weak and deformed despite the surgery for Dupuytren's contracture, often became so uncomfortable that he had to cancel engagements, take a pain medication, and go to bed. He complained to his doctor about periods of despondence and began to show signs of forgetfulness. He sent an angry note to Elliott Sanger, president of WQXR, objecting to the airing of short news bulletins from the newspaper in between pieces of classical music early in the morning. "Are we trying to insure that no one reads the paper?" he thundered. "When did we start doing this? Was I asked? I don't like it." In patient tones, Sanger informed Arthur that not only had he been asked, he had formally approved the practice a full year earlier. Embarrassed and upset, Arthur tried to save face the next day in a memo to Orvil. "I'm not certain that I didn't make a mistake [in approving the news bulletins]," he wrote grumpily.

Despite his multiplying health problems, Arthur's eye for beautiful women remained sharp. In 1955, just before his twentieth anniversary as publisher, he had fallen for a recently divorced blond actress named Irene Manning, who hoped to catch the approving attention of New York critics by performing in summer stock. Arthur poured out his feelings to her in verse: "This isn't the season / I haven't a reason / And yet I admit I'm in love," it began. He nudged Turner Catledge to give some "legitimate" coverage to "a friend of mine" who was performing in *Pal Joey* in Wallingford, Connecticut; soon afterward Irene Manning's picture appeared in the Sunday theater section.

Iphigene had no doubt been aware of the liaison because, about two weeks after Arthur composed his love poem, she had aimed an unusually tart barb at her husband. In the weeks leading up to Arthur's May 7 anniversary, elaborate arrangements had been made for a dinner in his honor. Even though Iphigene had played the decisive role in his selection as publisher two decades earlier, Arthur excluded her from the event by insisting on a stag black-tie party at "21."

The dinner, held on a Friday night one day before the actual anniversary, included all the paper's top executives as well as male family members and friends. The group presented Arthur with a bound volume of tributes, along with a large linden tree for Hillandale. Iphigene's gift was truly spectacular: a coastal scene entitled *Near Venice* painted by Winston Churchill. To obtain it, she had had to use all of her persuasive powers; the former British prime minister was notorious for not selling his works.

The most dramatic moment of the evening came after the dinner had been devoured, when, over brandy, the crowded room was silenced so that Arthur could hear a series of recorded greetings from President Eisenhower, Adlai Stevenson, Churchill, and other dignitaries. After these paeans were over, it was time for Iphigene's tribute, a toast she had recorded at WQXR less than a week after Arthur had penned his gushing verse to Irene Manning. "Dear Arthur," said the disembodied voice floating through the cigar smoke. "Once more you must admit I am right. If this were not a man's world, as I've always insisted it is, I would not be left out in the cold tonight."

Then Iphigene made a comment she had never uttered before: "If I'd been the boss's son instead of his daughter, this party might have been for me instead of you." She hastened to add in her usual deferential way that had she been male, the party might have been "a wake instead of a celebration" because she would have made an inferior publisher. Then she ended on a wistful note: "All I want is to be your wife, even when I'm left at home."

A garbled version of what Iphigene had said raced through the Ochs family thanks to Aunt Mattie, who had written in astonishment to Aunt Fan, Milton's widow, that the "whole dinner" had heard Iphigene say to Arthur: "What would have become of you if I had been a boy?" In her addled way, Mattie had zeroed in on the brutal truth. Even after thirty-seven years at *The New York Times,* twenty of them as publisher, even after his many successes, honors, and accolades, and the near complete power he now wielded in the wake of Julius's death, that was the question still haunting Arthur.

§

At the *Times,* Arthur kept a grip on the publisher's office even as he groomed Orvil to be his successor. Following the war, Arthur had consciously tried to broaden Orvil's duties — inviting him to attend editorial-board meetings, asking him to answer official correspondence in the publisher's absence. Still, Orvil remained assistant to the publisher, with no promotion or change in title, for twelve years. It was not until 1954, when New York Times Company secretary and vice president Godfrey Nelson died, that Orvil inherited the vice-presidential part of Nelson's title as well as his seat on the board of directors. With the death of Julius Adler the following year, Orvil assumed some of the General's business and advertising responsibilities and moved into his capacious office suite, although with characteristic modesty he chose to inhabit only a fraction of what had been Julius's vast territory.

Despite Arthur's intention to avoid repeating the unpleasant aspects of his own apprenticeship under Adolph, relations with his heir apparent were remote and equivocal. "It was the son-in-law of a son-in-law relationship — and uneasy," said John Oakes. "Orvil knew the succession was certain, but I'm not sure that he eagerly looked forward to it.... He was worried about whether or not he was up to the job." Superficially, the two men had little in common besides Marian and *The New York Times.* They both enjoyed the company of women and regularly made winking asides to each other about the "very attractive dish" or the "pretty number" they had spotted at a party, but Arthur was far more urbane, sophisticated, and artistic than Orvil, who liked nothing better than to spend his leisure hours watching football or playing golf. While Arthur and Charles Merz exchanged original doggerel during weekends at Hillandale, Orvil, Marian, and their friends played sardines, an adult version of hide-and-seek.

His Ivy League education notwithstanding, Orvil was surprisingly awkward with language and prone to making embarrassing — and often hilarious — malapropisms. In his office diary he once noted that he and Marian had a date in Washington to dine with Senator John F. Kennedy, but that Jackie Kennedy, then pregnant, would not join them because "she is incarcerated." (He meant *incapacitated.*) "I think you should be more careful about your English and your use of words," Arthur admonished Orvil in a "personal and confidential" memo reacting to several inserts Orvil had written for the annual report. "You say at one point . . . that the advertising of the International Air Edition helps to 'allay' the cost. Of course, you mean it helps 'defray' the cost." Orvil gratefully thanked Arthur for his candor and invited him to "correct any error any time."

He was equally compliant about Arthur's quirky demand that he change the style of his signature. Penmanship was something of a fetish with Arthur, whose aesthetic sensibility was offended by sloppy, ill-formed letters and undignified peculiarities. When Orvil first joined the *Times,* he had a flamboyant signature; for years Arthur hectored him to produce a more sober version. "I feel certain that if you work on this a bit, you will come up with something very good indeed," Arthur told Orvil just before he became vice president. Within a few years Orvil had transformed the dramatic swirls into a stately signature — O. E. Dryfoos — that resembled printing more than cursive.

Arthur himself disliked making public speeches, but he knew that they came with the job of publisher, and as part of Orvil's training, he launched a campaign to coax him onto the dais. "Sooner or later you are going to have to make a speech," he told Orvil, who resisted as long as he could, no doubt out of fear that the deficits in his language would be exposed or that he would be compared unfavorably with his witty, self-possessed father-in-law. "I would prefer to consider myself on sabbatical while I learn certain aspects of the *Times* business that I know very little about," he told Arthur after assuming some of Julius's duties. Arthur would have none of it, however, and kept up the pressure until Orvil eventually succumbed, agreeing to give a talk at Dartmouth.

Like Adolph, Arthur thought a potential publisher should be well traveled and to that end orchestrated several global trips for Orvil and Marian, who familiarized themselves with the foreign bureaus en route and dined with politicians, royalty, and the Sulzbergers' many friends. In New York their schedule overflowed with dinner parties and official functions. "He was the heir apparent, and we were always invited to different things because of that," Marian said. "He loved it, and I loved it."

If Arthur was dutiful and distant with his son-in-law, Iphigene was surprisingly intimate. Despite her lack of physical maternal affection with her own children, she found it easy to express love with Orvil, gradually becoming his counselor, sounding board, and surrogate mother. "My father had this wonderful ability to put all kinds of people at ease," said Orvil's youngest daughter, Susan. "It was an opportunity for [Iphigene] to feel safe with someone. I can't imagine that she had that kind of openness with many people." Almost every weekend they walked in the woods surrounding Hillandale and talked about politics, business, the newspaper, and whatever drama was brewing among the Ochses and the Sulzbergers at the moment. "He said [Iphigene] was someone apart," remembered Orvil's friend Ardie Deutsch. "He just said she was so great, he couldn't believe that he had this relationship with her. He idolized her and he idealized her." Orvil's own mother was an eccentric original — what Marian described as "a real Auntie Mame type." While Orvil addressed her by her first name, Florence, he took to calling Iphigene "Mother."

With Iphigene's support and his own effortless amiability, Orvil carved out a unique place for himself in the complex Ochs-Sulzberger universe. "Orv had a way of assuming that he was completely part of that family," said Alan Rabinowitz, "a full member, not an in-law." He made an effort to know everyone in the family, especially those connected with the newspaper. During the summers in the early 1950s, when he and Marian lived at Rock Hill and John Oakes and his wife,

Margary, rented a house nearby, he would drive over each weekday morning in his old rattletrap station wagon, pick up John, and give him a lift to the Stamford station so that the two men could commute into the city together. "Orvil genuinely liked me, and I certainly liked Orvil," said John. "That was the beginning of a warm kind of feeling." Even crusty Cy Sulzberger, whom many in the family considered hopelessly irascible, had a soft spot for Orvil. In the summer of 1954 the two couples — Cy and his wife, Marina, and Orvil and Marian — spent several weeks together touring Cy's old haunts in Greece and Yugoslavia.

Orvil's congeniality was not limited to members of the family. While Turner Catledge was in Europe on a tour of overseas bureaus, his first wife, Mildred, suddenly required the care of a psychiatrist and was briefly hospitalized. Orvil kept in touch with her and her doctors, arranging for her to take sculpture lessons and sending almost daily telegrams of encouragement to Turner. "I can't begin to tell you . . . of my gratitude for what you did," Turner told Orvil. "I hope I never have to do the same for you."

Well before he was named managing editor, Turner had made the assumption that Orvil would one day be publisher of *The New York Times*. With the cunning of the Mississippi politicians about whom he had once reported, he took pains to cultivate the relationship and contribute to Orvil's training. During Orvil's early years, the two often took sandwiches to a pond in Central Park — a place they called "the sanctuary" — and spent their lunch hour discussing the changes they felt needed to be made at the paper. Turner schooled Orvil in his personal definition of news — "anything you didn't know before, had forgotten, overlooked or didn't understand" — and squired him around the annual Gridiron Dinner, an off-the-record banquet and skit sponsored by Washington-based reporters at which the president, cabinet secretaries, and key members of Congress, who were usually in attendance, were mercilessly lampooned.

Orvil considered Turner a great friend and adviser, but he never felt the strong personal rapport with him that he did with Scotty Reston, who was closer to his own age and personified the bedrock values and soaring ambitions of *The New York Times*. Scotty had emigrated from Scotland at the age of eleven with his poor and pious parents, and like many immigrants, he had a romantic faith in the American experiment that at times bordered on the naive. Despite rapid success, his foreign

birth and gritty beginnings made him ever conscious of being an outsider, a feeling shared by Orvil, who in his own way had immigrated to a
comparably foreign land when he married into the Sulzberger family.
The New Yorker once mockingly suggested that *The New York Times'*
tone of voice was that of God — "not the God of the Bible or the Koran
but the God of a philosopher — Spinoza, perhaps." If any one writer
could be said to embody that tone, it was Scotty, a strict Calvinist whose
personality was redeemed from stuffiness by subtle humor.

After the war Arthur had brought Scotty to New York to serve as his
assistant, with the assignment of helping map out a postwar news strategy for the paper and figuring out "what to do with the next generation."
At Arthur's urging, Scotty took Orvil under his wing, and even after
Reston moved back to Washington, the two remained close.

No doubt it also mattered to Orvil that his key patron, Iphigene,
favored Scotty over Turner, whom she thought "very jolly [and] full of
life . . . [and] a great raconteur" but whose perpetually bent elbow and
late-night antics made her uneasy. She resonated more with Scotty's rectitude, old-fashioned values, and persistent optimism — qualities that
reminded her of her father. Like the preacher his Presbyterian mother
had hoped he would one day become, Scotty kept the Sulzbergers' sights
set on the majesty of their mission and the nobility of the enterprise that
had been bequeathed them. "You see the present misery of your life; I
see the glory," Scotty once told Arthur when he was feeling discouraged.
"Who in our profession has been more faithful in redeeming the obligations of a lifetime? Who has carried the baton over rougher ground?"
Little wonder that for Iphigene, and for Arthur, too, Scotty became an
"imaginary son-in-law" and the "adopted Sulzberger."

Guided by his mentors, Orvil gained confidence and gradually took
some of the day-to-day responsibilities off Arthur's shoulders. But if
anyone wondered whether Arthur still exerted dominion over the paper,
those doubts were extinguished during the presidential election of 1956,
when he again kept an authoritative grip on the *Times'* politics in the
face of near total opposition. In many respects, Arthur was dissatisfied
with the president's performance; he was critical of the secretary of
state, John Foster Dulles, and Eisenhower's recent heart attack and
recurrent ileitis also gave him pause. The president was only one year
older than Arthur; if he were to die, the country would be saddled with

his vice president, Richard Nixon, who had the strong backing of the reactionary wing of the Republican Party.

In spite of his long and close personal relationship with Eisenhower, these factors were sufficiently serious to prompt Arthur to wrestle with his conscience about whether the paper should endorse the president for a second term. "I don't think I was ever faced with a more difficult decision," he told John Oakes at the time. Iphigene had no such qualms. Ever since Nixon's smear campaign against Helen Gahagan Douglas, she had considered him "an evil man," and she had little use for Eisenhower after his feeble response to McCarthy. She made it clear that she intended to vote for Adlai Stevenson, who had been nominated again by the Democrats, and hoped that the *Times* would agree with her.

Most of the paper's top editors did. Scotty wrote columns suggesting that Eisenhower's ailments made him a "wounded soldier" whose time had passed. In an effort to persuade Arthur to abandon Ike, John Oakes composed a ten-page memo titled "The Case Against Richard Nixon," detailing the vice president's voting record, his political techniques, and his questionable associations. "He invites distrust," John wrote. "His eye is on the main chance, irrespective of principle." Turner tactfully kept his counsel in Arthur's presence but in private made no secret of his preference for the Democrats. Orvil and Marian remained in the Eisenhower column even as most members of the Sulzberger family, including Punch and Judy, were outspokenly pro-Adlai.

Confronted with this majority sentiment, Arthur hesitated, but in the end he decided that as publisher, he had the right to make a unilateral judgment. A presidential endorsement, he said, "should not be subject to a poll among [the paper's] editorial writers." His reasons for backing Eisenhower were weak, confused, and deeply conservative. "I find that I am inclined to vote for or against the party in power, rather than be swayed too much by the promises made by the outsider," he told John Oakes in a memo explaining his position. "While we have criticized the Eisenhower Administration quite frequently, we have nonetheless given it a passing grade."

The endorsement, written by Charles Merz and blandly titled "The Choice of a Candidate," dutifully enumerated Stevenson's outstanding attributes as well as the points on which the *Times* disagreed with him, notably his desire to eliminate the draft and his support of a guaranteed minimum wage. Eisenhower was treated similarly. So balanced were the two sides that at the end, a reader could easily have assumed that the *Times* might come out for either candidate. Indeed, Estes Kefauver, Stevenson's running mate, described the endorsement as being one that "gives all the arguments on our side and then comes to the wrong conclusion."

The next day at the Publisher's Luncheon, Iphigene made a rare appearance and for once made no effort to contain herself. "She doesn't like [the endorsement] and makes no bones about it," Turner reported to Punch, who was out of town. Turner was deeply disturbed by the *Times'* editorial, which he felt lacked vision and conviction. "What we have come out for is the 'status quo,' " he said "[and] that is not enough for a paper of our standing." One reader was so upset with the *Times'* equivocal position that he sent Arthur a check for two cents, declaring that was what he thought it was worth.

When election night arrived, Arthur, as was his custom, invited a small group of dignitaries and special friends to have cocktails and sandwiches in his office at the *Times* so that they could closely follow the returns. In an attempt to inject humor into the situation, he set up two small tables bordered with black crepe paper. On top of each was a box of Kleenex, in front a sign. One said FOR EISENHOWER MOURNERS; the other said FOR STEVENSON MOURNERS.

§

Punch left Milwaukee in late January 1954, with high hopes that the pain of Barbara's miscarriage and their subsequent marital difficulties were now in the past. After a brief tour at marine headquarters in Washington, he reported for a three-month stint on the *Times* foreign news desk while Barbara settled the children temporarily into 1115 Fifth Avenue, which was empty because of Arthur and Iphigene's absence in California. When the senior Sulzbergers returned in mid-March, Punch's brood adjourned to Hillandale and prepared for the imminent move to Paris.

The foreign desk interregnum was Punch's idea. Although Arthur had originally wanted his son to work in the *Times'* promotion department so that he could be exposed to advertising and circulation problems, Punch had argued that, since he was going overseas, it would make sense to spend some time learning how editors handled copy coming in from the paper's foreign bureaus. Soon Turner was able to report that Punch was a "member of the team right down to his pencil box, his big cigar, his diligence and his lovely nature." Punch's most challenging task was to decipher the Seventh Avenue "mumbo jumbo" that came across his desk nearly every night from the paper's verbose fashion editor in Paris. He took it upon himself to chop the prose into digestible bits — with questionable results. "If, during the Fifties, women's skirts went up and down in a random fashion, you have no one to blame but me," Punch later joked to a *Times* editor.

Barbara was as opposed to the Paris assignment as Punch was enthusiastic. The miscarriage and the constant care of two small children had left her exhausted, and after her nightmarish childhood and the multiple moves of the past several years, she was desperately in need of stability. "She represented the syndrome of the motherless child who was looking for the security upon which to build her life," said a former Ochs in-law who knew her well. "And [Punch] was no more equipped to be her father than she was equipped to be his mother." When her entreaties to Punch went unheeded, she appealed to Arthur and Iphigene, explaining that she wasn't ready physically or mentally to handle another big change. The Sulzbergers, discomfited by such an overt expression of distress, assured her that everything would be fine, and she meekly acquiesced. "I was young and I didn't stand up for myself," she said.

By the summer Punch, Barbara, and the children were in Paris living in Cy Sulzberger's spacious apartment on avenue de Ségur, which they rented while he was in the States on his triennial three-month leave. At first, the marriage seemed to regain its ground, but within a few weeks Barbara became so nervous and agitated that the *Times* doctor checked her into what she ruefully came to call her "favorite pension," the American Hospital. "I was very, very depressed," she said.

By early fall her condition was sufficiently worrisome that Iphigene decided to make a hasty trip to Paris to "see whether or not it's wise to leave her there or bring her home." What she found was that Barbara had serious problems, having been hospitalized for both depression and amoebic dysentery. At the suggestion of Dr. Howard Rusk, a family friend who also wrote a medical column for the *Times*, Iphigene arranged for Barbara to see Dr. Jean Delay, professor of psychiatry at the University of Paris. The consultation produced no definite diagnosis. By mid-October Barbara began to calm down on her own — "I have routed my perfectionist spirit forever," she triumphantly told Arthur — and Iphigene felt comfortable enough to return home.

Barbara's illness had been hard on Punch, personally and professionally. When he had first reported to the *Times'* office at 37 rue Caumartin, he was given the so-called fourth-man slot, a position that the bureau chief, Harold Callendar, regarded as "patronage or baby-sitting, or a combination of both." After the war it had been filled first by the son of then managing editor Edwin L. James, then by Martin Ochs, Punch's cousin. The post permitted Punch to fill in for correspondents on vacation but gave him no regular assignment, leaving him feeling superfluous and at loose ends. He wanted a more substantial job, but his father refused to make the personnel changes necessary until Barbara stabilized.

With Barbara's crisis apparently over, Punch finally secured a beat, but as in Milwaukee, his performance was uninspired. When his first story with a Paris dateline appeared, Arthur quietly contacted assistant managing editor Robert Garst and asked him to compare Punch's original dispatch with what had actually been published in the paper. He wanted to find out, he said, "how much Punch learned while he was on the [foreign] desk." Garst gave him a forgiving answer that nonetheless conveyed the truth: "[Punch] did polish the top [of the story] a lot."

Punch did not impress the other Paris reporters as having keen news instincts. While attending an automobile race at Le Mans on his day off, he witnessed a terrible disaster. One of the drivers lost control of his car, which jumped the road, sailed through the air, and plowed into a group of spectators, killing eighty-three people. Punch was horrified at the sight, but it never occurred to him to rush to a phone and call in the story.

No one took more pleasure in Punch's blunders than Cy. Before Punch's arrival, Cy had declared that he was "absolutely delighted" his cousin and Barbara were coming to Paris, telling them, "It will be lots of fun getting to know you folks after all these years." But once Punch was on the scene, Cy studiously avoided him, setting a dismissive tone that permeated the bureau. Cy's wife, Marina, however, went out of her way to be kind, organizing picnics with the children and donning a black leotard to join Barbara in the dance exercises she loved. After Punch and Barbara moved into their own apartment at 86 rue de Grenelle, they invited Cy and Marina for dinner; Cy seemed to make sure the date was on a night when Punch was assigned to cover a story.

Arthur hoped Punch would make high-level contacts during his stay in Paris and arranged a generous entertainment allowance for that purpose. Cy, who prided himself on his access to political and social grandees, could have easily facilitated such connections by inviting Punch to his celebrity-studded dinner parties. One wall of his office was covered floor to ceiling with autographed photographs of presidents, kings, emperors, and heads of state. But Cy had no interest in helping an ineffectual younger cousin whom he considered a competitor, albeit a sorry one, for Arthur's affection, esteem, and support. "Punch was very badly hurt by that," said Ellen Sulzberger Straus.

In March 1955 Arthur and Iphigene came to Paris to mark the tenth anniversary of the reopening of the bureau after World War II. Barbara appeared to them to be completely cured of the depression that had incapacitated her the previous fall. The truth was that her anxieties had simply gone underground, and by May they surfaced in a new and more potent form. By her own description, she "started to act out" and began an affair with Don Cook, a reporter for the *Herald Tribune* in Paris. "He and his wife, Cherry, had the most mixed-up goddamn sex life I've ever heard of," said Clifton Daniel, who as a *New York Times* foreign correspondent had known the couple socially. "Cherry was just as indiscreet as her husband was. They lived in the same household; they never separated. She must have known about Barbara."

Punch was oblivious to the infidelity until one day when he came home from an assignment earlier than expected and found Barbara and Cook together. "At that point, we talked [about our problems] for the first time," said Barbara. Punch was initially devastated, then humiliated by the affair. "It was a very public, embarrassing spectacle," recalled Flora Lewis, a *Times* columnist based in Paris. Barbara's romance with Cook proved to be volatile and brief, and she soon professed her desire to rebuild a life with Punch "for the sake of the children." At the same time, she made it clear that she was still in love with Cook. "Punch is easygoing and all that, but he wasn't going to sit still for that," said Joan Dryfoos, Orvil's sister-in-law. Soon thereafter, the marriage quickly spun out of control.

Having had a taste of psychotherapy with Dr. Delay, Barbara now pleaded with Punch to join her in marital counseling, but he would have none of it. He was uncomfortable with psychologists and totally lacking in curiosity about the whys of human behavior. "Why should I try to remember what I've spent a lifetime trying to forget?" he would later say to a close family member. Barbara compared his impenetrability to a "locked box." Even his sisters noted that he had a "wall" around him, that he was incapable of sustaining a conversation of any length or depth if it spilled over into the realm of emotions. Like Iphigene, Punch was now face-to-face with the fact of an unfaithful spouse, and just like her, he preferred to keep things smooth, to ignore unpleasant realities rather than probe them.

For Barbara, psychotherapy became a nonnegotiable demand, and if Punch would not take part in it with her, she felt he should at least allow *her* to seek out its comforts. "There is no question but that I need some therapy," she told him. "For the good of this family and for these two children, I have got to do it." But Punch stood firmly against it, afraid that Barbara's examining her demons would only push them farther apart. "If you do therapy, it will break up the family," he said. "If you pursue it, that's the end of the marriage." Faced with such a stark choice, Barbara opted for therapy — and a divorce. "It was my call," she said. "I think the marriage would have lasted if I had gone along [with what he wanted]."

Barbara left Paris almost immediately, taking Arthur Jr. and Karen to Menton, a small town on the French Riviera. Punch, too, had no desire to stay in a city abuzz with gossip about him. He wrote to his father, telling him in general terms what had occurred and requesting a change of assignment. By August he was in the Rome bureau of *The New York Times*, living on Via San Crecenziano, learning Italian, and, in a half-hearted fashion, getting acquainted with news sources. Scotty Reston, who was in Europe that summer, saw Punch and reported to Orvil that he looked "rather woebegone."

Punch, Barbara, and the children returned to New York within a day of one another in late October, living together uneasily at Hillandale while Barbara looked for a home of her own. Julius Adler had died only three weeks earlier, and his responsibilities were beginning to be parceled out to members of the younger generation. Orvil, naturally, was destined to get the lion's share, but Arthur, sensing his son's grief, wanted to "keep Punch closer to me." He offered him a position as assistant to the publisher, beginning after the New Year. Punch, happy to finally be included in the executive ranks, even at a low level, agreed.

The pain of his Paris experience never quite left him. It was the city where his cousin Cy had snubbed him and others in the bureau had treated him "like he was the publisher's son who would never amount to anything, who was just kind of dumb." It was also the place where his marriage fell apart in a manner that left him powerless and publicly disgraced. Forever after he hated Paris. "For the longest time, when he went to Paris he would get violently ill," said a close associate. "He would throw up."

§

Barbara soon settled the children into temporary quarters in Port Chester, New York, not far from Hillandale. For Arthur Jr. and Karen, moving from the sun and tropical greenery of the French Riviera to the dun-colored landscape of a suburban New York winter was a melancholy change that suited their new status as children of an impending divorce. "To me, it was a continual winter," said Karen.

When Punch took up his duties as assistant to the publisher in late January 1956, he treated his responsibilities lightly. There was plenty of time for socializing, and although he was not "that loose on the town," as he put it, he was certainly open to meeting new women. In February Orvil's younger brother, Hugh, and his wife, Joan, invited Punch to a small dinner party at their Upper East Side apartment. Among the dozen other guests was an attractive divorcée named Carol Fox Fuhrman. The Dryfooses had become acquainted with Carol the previous summer at their beach club on Long Island and thought she might make a good dinner partner for Punch. During the cocktail hour Carol startled everyone by scooping up a dollop of caviar that had fallen from a cracker and popping it into her mouth. "You can't waste that!" she said cheerily. Punch was impressed. "I thought, 'That's for me — a nice, frugal girl,'" he joked years later with considerable sarcasm.

When the dinner was over, Punch asked if he could drive her home, and Carol assented. Once they had settled into the car, he invited her to join him for a nightcap at "21." Carol had earlier taken note of his wedding ring and politely demurred, telling him, "I'm sure your wife and children are waiting for you." Punch quickly explained that he and Barbara were separated and in the process of getting a divorce. "Well, in that case, fine," she said.

What Carol found in Punch that night was a "good-looking, bright, attractive [but] unhappy character" whose painful marital history roughly paralleled her own. His sense of wounded abandonment aroused her empathy as well as her protective instincts. With her Audrey Hepburn–like silhouette, long, glossy hair, and shy demeanor, Carol radiated a subdued vulnerability that was far less threatening to Punch than had been Barbara's recent bouts of vampish charm. "Carol was a very insecure woman," said one Sulzberger family member. "She would never be the life of the party or run off with the *Herald Tribune* guy. She wouldn't attract that kind of attention."

Carol was also unlike Barbara in her Jewish heritage and privileged upbringing. Her father, David Fox, had made millions in the garment industry well before she was born. Although he continued to dabble in the trade, he effectively retired in his forties, shuttling his family between apartments at the Sherry Netherland Hotel in New York and the Hôtel Royal Monceau in Paris during the worst years of the Depression. In the summers the Foxes repaired to the Hôtel Miramar in Cannes; in the winters to the Palace Hotel in St.-Moritz. Carol's father was a warm, outgoing man who loved gambling, boxing, good food, and fine wines; her mother was a domineering social snob with meticulous taste. "She cared about clothes and tables being set a certain way and curtains being closed a certain way," said Carol. "I don't think I ever had a meal in my house without a finger bowl. It was a very rarefied kind of life. My sister and I were little American princesses."

Carol had no professional ambitions, but like many women of her era and class, she expected to go on beyond high school, and chose Goddard, a small, progressive junior college in Vermont. In the summer between her freshman and sophomore years, she took a vacation to California and, while on a blind date, met Cy Fuhrman, a dark, handsome ex-marine and graduate of the University of Southern California. Cy's parents were Eastern European immigrants with a successful fur business in Beverly Hills, and quite unlike the cosmopolitan, well-traveled Foxes. Cy was an accomplished dancer with a wide circle of friends who were constantly on call for card games and swimming parties. "It was like those beach movies," said Carol. "What I loved was that you were never really alone."

By August Carol and Cy were engaged; by October they were married. Cy went into his family's fur business, but soon, under pressure from Carol's parents, the young couple moved to New York, where Cy accepted his father-in-law's offer of a job as a coat buyer with Jay Thorpe, an upscale women's retail store in which Mr. Fox had an investment. Life in a Park Avenue apartment with their small daughter, Cathy, born in 1949, was lonely compared with what they were accustomed to in California. Cy's hours in the retail trade were long and unpredictable, and he and Carol did not have a ready-made set of friends. Within a year Cy had had enough. He went back to California; Carol and Cathy moved in with her parents on Central Park West.

By the time Carol met Punch, she had been divorced for three years and was working as a publicist for Jonathan Logan, a line of women's clothing. Their first real date was at the Copacabana, where Punch showed up "with pants too short and reservations too early." The celebrated nightclub rarely swung into action before 10:00; Punch had asked Carol to meet him at the outré hour of 7:30. He made up for his misstep by securing opening-night tickets to *My Fair Lady* and treating Cathy with fatherly sweetness. "I loved him right away," Cathy recalled. "He used to come over [to our apartment] and tickle my stomach and guess what I had for dinner. I thought that was a miracle — that he could feel my stomach and figure it out." By the time Punch invited Andy Fisher, assistant to the *Times'* business manager, and his wife, Connie, to meet Carol several months later at a small Manhattan restaurant, they were "madly in love with each other," as Connie remembered.

Punch gave Carol a gold friendship ring and the two made plans to marry as soon as he was divorced. But before they wed, Punch had to confess something to his prospective bride that over the ensuing decades would become an open though rarely discussed secret within the Sulzberger family. Soon after Punch took up his duties as assistant to the publisher, he had had a brief liaison with a widowed *Times* reporter named Lillian Bellison Alexanderson. "I slept with a woman, she got pregnant, she was sleeping with other people in the news department," Punch said years later. Lillian claimed he was the father and refused Punch's entreaties to get an abortion. Her pregnancy was in progress even as he courted Carol. "The timing was exquisitely awful," he recalled, adding that when he finally informed Carol of his predicament, she was remarkably sympathetic.

Indeed, Carol was far more understanding of Punch's dilemma than she was of the affection in which the Sulzberger family continued to hold Barbara, despite her infidelity. Iphigene had given Barbara $100 and a paisley purse the previous Christmas. That summer Judy vacationed with her on Martha's Vineyard. When Punch and Carol made it clear that they intended to marry, they had dinner with Orvil and Marian. "Well, you know we like Barbara," Marian blurted out at one point.

Carol kept her counsel, and the next morning phoned Marian. "I'm glad you like Barbara," she said crisply, "but that has nothing to do with me." Marian apologized.

Before Punch could get divorced, he and Barbara had to agree on a property settlement, which took several months. "She was really divorcing *The New York Times,* not this thirty-year-old kid," said Carol. "And, of course, the family didn't want to read about it in the gossip columns." Because of the structure of the Ochs Trust, Punch was wealthy in theory but not in fact; he would not come into any serious money until Iphigene died. In the interim he lived on his salary, as well as gifts and loans made to him by his mother. Whether Barbara and her attorney fully understood his situation is unclear. "I did not want their money," said Barbara. "That is not why I married Punch. That money, I did not earn." What she did want — and eventually got — was an apartment in New York, funds for furniture and the children's education, and psychiatric counseling for herself.

The property settlement was signed September 28, and the next day Punch flew to Nevada to begin the six-week residency that was required before he could obtain a divorce. He stayed in a two-room cabin at Washoe Pines, a dude ranch several miles north of Carson City on the road to Reno, where he found the food "even better than Sardi's" and the nearby casinos diverting, if not remunerative. During the days, he composed funny skits to amuse his fellow guests and took up horseback riding. "The hard thing to find out is what to do with your balls at full gallop," he wrote Turner Catledge. Ten days into his stay, Iphigene came out to keep him company, followed quickly by Judy.

Judy's visit was not entirely sisterly. After nearly ten years of marriage and the birth of two sons, Daniel and James, she was also in Nevada to get a divorce. "I just didn't want to have sex with Mattie anymore," she explained. "I don't know [what happened]. He began to turn me off." The real reasons were far more complex. Heavy expenses for their medical educations and an unforeseen need to support Mattie's grandmother had forced the couple to turn repeatedly to Iphigene for money, a hat-in-hand situation that rankled Mattie. After completing her residency in pathology at Grasslands Hospital, Judy had become pregnant with Daniel and for all intents and purposes never practiced medicine during the course of their marriage. "[Mattie] was distinctly jealous and did everything he could to discourage her," said Iphigene. The couple tried counseling, but eventually they became resigned to the inevitable. "I should never have gotten married when I did," commented Judy. "I was just so immature."

Two days after Iphigene departed for Nevada, Lillian Bellison Alexanderson successfully delivered a boy. She gave the baby her late husband's name — George Alexanderson — although he had died more than two years earlier and could not possibly have been the father. A few months later she filed a paternity suit against Punch. He denied being the father, but when a blood test failed to rule him out, he agreed to a settlement that required him to pay child support and medical costs for the next sixteen years. "I couldn't prove that it wasn't mine, so . . . I did the honorable thing," he said later. There was no way to conceal the embarrassing development from his parents: he had to borrow money from them to make the deal. But, he said, "I got no lectures from anybody."

In the years that followed, Punch would make no attempt to contact the child. "I've never seen him," he said. "It's a piece of history, it's over, it's done." The twin experiences of a failed marriage and then a traumatic affair conspired to make him an "emotionally deprived character," as Sydney Gruson would later put it, a man whose most intense wish was to forget these painful episodes — something he accomplished without apparent regret. "I don't think it's Punch's most shining hour," Gruson remarked.*

In an era before no-fault divorce, Punch needed grounds to dissolve his marriage to Barbara; he alleged "extreme cruelty, entirely of a mental nature." On November 16, after a brief hearing, a Nevada district court judge granted the decree, and Punch immediately took the red-eye back

---

*Both Arthur Jr. and Karen would grow up with no knowledge of George Alexanderson's existence. "Carol is the one who told me about it," said Karen. George, on the other hand, was certainly aware of his "other family." As a child, he would occasionally visit the *Times* newsroom, where his mother continued to work. Once, when Punch walked by the boy unawares, a reporter overheard George murmur to his companion, "That's my father."

In 1972 Lillian filed a second paternity suit to extend child support, which Punch fought and won. Ten years later George himself filed a suit seeking a share in the eventual distribution of the Ochs Trust. In exchange for dropping any claim of inheritance, Punch agreed to create a trust for Alexanderson. Lillian died in 1982. George has broken his ties to the remaining Alexandersons and moved away from New York. The authors' repeated efforts to contact him were unsuccessful.

to New York. At Idlewild Airport, Carol was waiting to greet him when his plane arrived the next morning. The path was now clear for Punch and Carol to marry, but with his divorce and the birth of George Alexanderson so recent, Iphigene tried to persuade her son to wait. "You shouldn't rush," she told him. "It's unseemly. Everyone will think that Carol is pregnant and you have to marry her." When her pleas were rejected, she asked Turner to take Punch and Carol out to dinner and deliver the same message. His sermon, too, fell on deaf ears.

The wedding took place on five days' notice; no engagement announcement appeared in *The New York Times*. The date was fixed with such haste that Arthur had to reschedule a WQXR board of directors meeting and cancel opera tickets. Punch was so flustered that he mistakenly transposed the initials of his name on the marriage license so that they came out like his grandfather Ochs's — A.S.O. "[Carol] is very charming and attractive and has already won our hearts," Arthur wrote his Belgian friend Marie-Claire Raick on the day of the nuptials. "As to how we feel about the whole thing, I don't really know." Punch's great-uncle, Rabbi Jonah Wise, presided at the afternoon ceremony on December 18 in the chapel of Temple Sholom in Greenwich, Connecticut. The senior Sulzbergers and Carol's parents were the couple's only attendants. Afterward the group adjourned to the Foxes' Manhattan apartment, where friends had gathered for a party. "Nobody knew it was [to celebrate] a wedding until they got there," said Carol.

That evening Punch and Carol had a wedding-night dinner at Sardi's with three other couples, including the pair who had first introduced them, Hugh and Joan Dryfoos. Slightly tipsy from champagne, Hugh stood up to make the first toast. "Here's to Punch and Barbara," he said. The table convulsed in laughter as Hugh, realizing his gaffe, turned red and sat down in humiliation. The next day, as Carol was perusing the small announcement of the wedding that appeared on the *Times'* social page, a peace offering arrived from Hugh. It was a hundred-word Western Union telegram that read I KNOW IT'S CAROL, CAROL, CAROL, CAROL, CAROL, CAROL. . . .

20

An Owl and an Omen

A RTHUR BEGAN 1957 IN A SPIRIT OF RELIEF AND
renewed hope. In a letter to the actress Irene Rich, one of his
rumored conquests, he recounted the problems that had burdened him during the preceding twelve months: his unpredictable
health, the personnel changes at the paper following Julius's death, three
strike threats, and Punch's and Judy's divorces. "In other words, as someone once said, 'Brother, you can't go anywhere but up,'" he wrote. "I'm
glad to start a new year."

Uppermost on Arthur's agenda as he surveyed the coming months
was continuing the process of turning over direction of the business to
members of the next generation. By his own admission, he had run *The
New York Times* as Adolph had — "like a czar" — with all authority
concentrated in the publisher, who also held the titles of chief executive
officer and president of the company. Like Adolph, Arthur had no intention of retiring, nor did he believe that his successors were yet ready to
run the New York and Chattanooga properties without his guiding
hand. Still, after his own unhappy experience following Adolph's death,
he knew it was important to plan for a smooth transition. To resolve this
quandary, attorney Eddie Greenbaum came up with the idea of revising
the bylaws of both *The New York Times* and *The Chattanooga Times* to
create a new position — chairman of the board — that permitted Arthur
to retain ultimate power while gradually transferring various degrees of
responsibility to younger men in the family.

With this change in place, Arthur orchestrated two promotions of
Sulzberger sons-in-law during the early months of 1957. The first was
on Valentine's Day, when Ben Golden became president and publisher
of *The Chattanooga Times,* succeeding Arthur, who had held the titles
since Julius's death. Following Arthur's exhortation to "wear your new

honors with modesty and distinction," Ben published a short statement in the next day's paper pledging a "continuance of the Ochs tradition of a free and responsible press."

Ben's ascension was made possible by the absence of Charles Puckette, *The Chattanooga Times'* general manager, who had died unexpectedly of cancer the previous month. Mr. Puckette had had little respect for Ben and for more than ten years had effectively refused to train or advance him despite Arthur's repeated orders to do so "whether we like it or not." "Ben was from a limited country background," explained John Popham, who, as *The New York Times'* southern regional correspondent, operated out of Chattanooga. "He basked in the wealth and position [of the Sulzbergers] but he resented them, too. Mr. Puckette saw this insecurity." Ben did not help his cause by playing pinball at a cigar store across from the paper during office hours and disappearing on alcoholic binges. "Mr. Puckette would come to my office, and Ben would be sitting there just drunk as a fool during the day," said Bob Sudderth, a former *Chattanooga Times* hand.

Arthur and Iphigene had nonetheless insisted on Ben's steady advancement from general trainee to assistant general manager to assistant publisher and, finally, to the top position. "Why did my parents make Ben publisher of *The Chattanooga Times?*" wondered Judy. "It kept it in the family, but it made no sense, when you think about it." Arthur, a son-in-law himself, had his own doubts about Ben, but he never considered Ruth a potential candidate. He did not believe a woman could manage a newspaper; indeed, he was fond of saying that the Sulzberger women had "had the good sense to marry men to run their business." Still, in recognition of her future stake as an owner and her work as a cultural reporter and director of special events at the paper after her four children were born, Ruth was named vice president the same day Ben was promoted.

If by making Ben publisher and president Arthur signaled his willingness to step back dramatically from the active management of *The Chattanooga Times*, he was still not ready to make so sweeping a statement at *The New York Times.* Instead, in April, by a vote of the board of directors, he surrendered just one of his multiple titles, appointing Orvil president. The move enabled him to keep editorial control of the paper while handing off to Orvil the day-to-day oversight of the business — thus reinstating, temporarily at least, the division of labor that had existed when Julius was alive. Amory Bradford, who was promoted from company secretary to vice president and business manager at the same time, urged Orvil to fight Arthur for the title of chief executive officer, which had traditionally gone in tandem with that of president. Orvil, typically, opted for strength through diplomacy. "I'm going to be able to handle this within the family," he assured Amory. "I don't want to make a fuss about it."

To Arthur, Orvil showed nothing but gratitude for his latest demonstration of trust and confidence. In a handwritten note composed on the day of his promotion, he told his father-in-law how much he respected the "way you have encouraged many of us to 'take hold.' Relinquishing the title of president after these many years can-not [sic] be easy. . . . I tip my hat to you, sir. And I hope and pray that you will never give up the [three] titles you now hold." In return, Arthur penned a comic poem commemorating the occasion, titled "An Ode to OED," using the three initials with which Orvil signed all internal notes and memos.

After reorganizing the management, Arthur turned his attention to planning a three-month trip around the world. "Iphigene and I are running away from a fortieth anniversary celebration," he explained in a letter to President Eisenhower, referring to the four-decade mark coming up in November. That was hardly the only reason, of course: Arthur, who had traveled widely in Europe, wanted to see Japan, India, Thailand, and other points in the Far East before age and infirmity made it impossible. He also thought it wise to absent himself for a while in order to let Ben and Orvil try their wings.

Arthur and Iphigene departed New York in late September, linking up with their good friend Louie Woods, wife of First Boston Corporation chairman George Woods, in Hawaii. Cy and Marina joined the group in Tokyo. At each stop on the Sulzbergers' itinerary they were treated like visiting royalty, with cocktail parties, banquets, and special tours arranged in their honor. The whirlwind schedule was exhausting, and Arthur bowed out of several of the more strenuous engagements. "I feel fine although I look like hell," he wrote Orvil from Bangkok. "If only India were behind us!"

Arthur had appeared drawn and tired before he left the States. He had had an occlusion removed from his left eye, and his heart — his "pump," as he called it — had been bothering him. From the minute he landed in Asia, he found the heat oppressive. In Singapore he was delighted to find his large Victorian suite at Raffles Hotel air-conditioned. "If we can keep up this standard [of accommodation], why maybe I will get back alive," he wrote in his diary.

On Sunday, November 3, the Sulzberger party arrived in Rangoon, Burma, and settled into the Strand Hotel, where Arthur downed two scotches without ice before retiring at the unusually early hour of 10:00 P.M. The next night they dined with Ambassador Walter McConaughy and his wife at the U.S. embassy. As they filed into the sitting room for after-dinner coffee, Cy noticed Arthur dab his right eye with a handkerchief, wincing in pain. On the way back to the hotel, Arthur complained that he had suffered a sinus attack. He took a painkiller, climbed into bed, and promptly fell asleep.

Several hours later Iphigene awoke to see Arthur staggering toward the bathroom as though he were drunk, his voice thick and his speech slurred. It was nothing, he assured her; the medication had simply upset his stomach and he would sleep it off. The following morning he insisted on taking his breakfast in their suite and forbade Iphigene to summon a doctor. At 9:15 A.M. Iphigene went down to the hotel lobby, where Cy and Marina were waiting in anticipation of the day's sched-uled outing to a Buddhist shrine, and asked Cy to take a look at Arthur.

When Cy arrived in the room, he found his uncle still in his pajamas, sitting in an armchair, his left arm hanging limply at his side, talking gibberish. Certain that Arthur had had a stroke, he phoned Ambassador McConaughy, and soon Dr. Suvi, an Indian general practitioner trained in Edinburgh, showed up to confirm his suspicion. For three days Arthur sweltered in his tiny room at the Prome Road Nursing Home, an English facility next to the American embassy, as his condition wors-ened. During the first terrifying day he sent Iphigene out to fetch a cold drink. When she departed, he motioned Cy to come closer. "I hope I don't make it," he whispered. "Don't tell anyone."

But by November 9 he had shown clear improvement and felt well enough to see humor in his situation. He wrote "On Arsending the Throne of Burma," a poem about being carried to the toilet, each arm around the neck of a nurse, while his hospital gown flapped open in the back. When he cabled New York demanding the previous month's circu-lation and earnings figures, his children and their spouses knew he was going to live.

President Eisenhower ordered the State Department to do everything it could to make Arthur comfortable; within days two air conditioners magically appeared in Arthur's room. The Sulzbergers spent November 17, their wedding anniversary, in the Prome Road Nursing Home making preparations for the long journey back to the States. "The great day was not all it should have been, but things are looking brighter," Iphigene wrote Arthur's secretary. A week later the weary Sulzbergers finally returned to New York. Arthur, unable to walk, was taken off the plane by forklift and returned by ambulance to his Fifth Avenue apartment, which had been outfitted with an electronically controlled hospital bed in his absence.

Soon the elegant Sulzberger home looked like a gymnasium, with parallel bars installed in the hallway and a wheelchair, a crutch, and several canes becoming elements of the decor. Arthur's progress was slow. He popped twenty pills a day to stimulate his heart, help him sleep, and control the constant ache in his left arm and leg, which he likened to "a bad tooth." Unable to concentrate and plagued by a damaged left eye, he found it difficult to read. Instead, he watched television and did home-made crossword puzzles created for him by the wife of the Broadway composer Richard Rodgers. He became introspective, lethargic, and "boring as hell." "I am . . . too willing to lie around like an oyster," he told Dr. Suvi, who corresponded frequently with his prominent patient.

In late December Arthur decided that he would be unable to sustain a visit to the recording studio for his annual New Year's message on WQXR radio. Even when station president Elliott Sanger suggested tap-ing the segment in the Sulzbergers' apartment, Arthur declined. Instead, with Arthur's agreement, Sanger reran a publisher's message from the early 1950s. Arthur's rousing words, which appealed to Americans to be "ever strong . . . physically and morally," seemed calculated to serve as a kind of pep talk to himself in his newly straitened circumstances.

Arthur's condition cast something of a pall over Judy's marriage to Dick Cohen, which took place at the Sulzbergers' apartment two months after their return from Asia. Unlike Mattie, who had shown barely disguised ambivalence toward the Sulzbergers, Dick, a Yale-educated insurance broker, actively sought their approval. His life had been subtly intertwined with theirs for years. His father, a clothing merchandiser, had grown up across the street from the house where Arthur spent his adolescence. He had known Judy long before she met Mattie and, after their marriage, had dined at the Rosenschein home. At the wedding of Judy's cousin Ellen Sulzberger, Dick had served as an usher for the groom, his Yale classmate Peter Straus.

These connections, together with Dick's gruffly ingratiating personality and business experience, made Arthur eager to bring him to the *Times*, but Judy would not hear of it. As compensation, Arthur threw several of the company's insurance accounts his way and put him on the *Times*' board of directors as Judy's representative — making Dick the first in-law to become a director without also holding a position at the newspaper.

The doctors had warned the Sulzbergers that Arthur's convalescence would take at least six months, and their prediction was right. Although his blood pressure remained high, his left eye still bothered him, and he had a pronounced limp, by the summer of 1958 he was able to walk well enough to accept an invitation to a White House dinner in honor of the West German president. He dined with friends at "21" and wrote pun-filled letters to the editor, signed "A. Aitchess," a nom de plume that played on the sound of his initials (A.H.S.). "We cannot trust Nasser," said one letter published in the *Times* ten months after his stroke. "Remember how Egypt us over Suez?"

The surface cheer was deceptive, for Arthur worried that his condition had undermined his ability to serve as publisher of *The New York Times*. Like an aging monarch, he strutted and roared in an exaggerated effort to demonstrate his power. "He was a different person [than before the stroke]," said Harrison Salisbury, then a *Times* reporter based in New York. "He was much more aggressive and interfering." He vetoed Orvil's request to invite Soviet leader Nikita Khrushchev to a Publisher's Luncheon on the grounds that "he would not understand a free press." When an editorial on Eisenhower's State of the Union Address didn't include "a single one of the reactions" he had expressed to Charles Merz the night before, he sent his old friend one of his fabled blue notes, observing that "[the editorial] sounded as though it was written by a sour Stevenson rooter." To Turner Catledge, he complained that he was bypassed too much; he saw items in the paper, he said, that he should have been told about in advance. One former *Times* reporter had the temerity to note that, by ceding the presidency to his son-in-law, Arthur had generously "given up the driver's seat" at the paper. "I still call the tune," Arthur replied coldly. That was all too apparent to Orvil, who often bore the brunt of Arthur's displeasure. "I was flabbergasted today for I received a beautifully printed copy of *The New York Times* on excellent newsprint," Arthur told him in one of his more sarcastic blue notes. "How did this happen to get out?"

Arthur's recovery was brief. In October 1959, while in Abano Terme, a health resort in northern Italy known for its mud baths and arthritic cures, he suffered a second stroke. It seemed so minor at first — Arthur simply woke up one morning with a slight loss of balance — that he didn't mention it to Iphigene. But after a day of sightseeing in Venice with George and Louie Woods, he came back to the Royal Orologio Hotel, began to undress, and fell on the floor.

The next day the Sulzbergers left for London to get medical attention. By the time they had settled into their usual suite at Claridge's, Ruth had shown up to escort them back home on the ocean liner *Mauretania 2*. "You would hardly know he'd had an attack, except for his gait," Ruth wrote reassuringly to her siblings. "He's cute and funny and just his old self." Her analysis proved to be sadly premature. Arthur's second stroke appeared slight at the time but marked the beginning of an irreversible decline that, over the next ten years, would make his life, and Iphigene's, a debilitating trial.

For years Arthur had recorded his thoughts in a kind of disjointed journal — first-person musings on everything from religion to politics to members of his family. Now his attention turned to an appreciation of his privileged life and the death he professed not to fear. "I saw a guy dragging himself along the street the other day and that sure wiped out a lot of self-pity," he said in an entry written one month after the Abano Terme incident. "When I come home, I return to beauty, charm and cleanliness. What a difference! One can look forward to dying like a gentleman." At Thanksgiving two weeks later, he found himself "crying for no reason at all," reduced to weeping by a musical comedy and the mere thought of parting from Iphigene, "wife, companion, irritant but always lovely, good beyond compare."

Arthur's mercurial temperament was due in part to the drugs on which he had come to rely since his first stroke. Troubled by pain and insomnia, he found it nearly impossible to sleep without barbiturates. For the three-week trip to Abano Terme alone, he had packed 1,900 pills. By January 1960 the years of dependence began to catch up with him. Blood thinners caused him to hemorrhage internally, and following an emergency transfusion, he had a violent allergic reaction to the dozens of drugs he had been taking. After five weeks in the hospital, his physician, George Carden Jr., ordered Arthur to detox for two months in a warm climate.

In March, accompanied by their Hillandale housekeepers and dogs, the Sulzbergers rented a two-bedroom house in Tucson, and Arthur set about the task of weaning himself from the chemicals that had taken over his body. "I still clench my teeth and shake and behave generally like a broken-down drug addict who can't get his poison," he reported in a letter to his family. "Maybe time will do the trick." At the end of his self-supervised treatment, Arthur felt much better, although he had to drink fifteen glasses of water a day to continue flushing the drugs from his system, and he was under strict orders not to ingest alcohol — a major deprivation. By August he was back in the office two days a week, riding a water bicycle around the lake at Hillandale to strengthen his legs and taking Librium to regulate his moods and relieve fullness in his head. "I don't approach the evening with fear as I used to," he told Dr. Carden. "On the other hand, I wouldn't say that my spirits are elated in any way."

In the months following his second stroke, Arthur became a more sentimental grandfather. He named the pond at Hillandale Lake Susan, after Orvil and Marian's youngest, and the small islands and inlets after his eleven other grandchildren. He asked Marian, Ruth, Judy, and Punch to send him accounts of "the funniest thing each [grandchild] has done or said" so that he could assemble a loose-leaf scrapbook, and he proudly wore a tie imprinted with his grandchildren's names. Still, like Iphigene, he felt uncomfortable with overt displays of affection. When Orvil's son, Bobby, reached up to kiss him during an office visit, he recoiled. "Don't kiss me!" he commanded. "What's the matter with you? Don't you know men shake hands?"

Arthur's reduced capacities and battle with drugs placed new burdens on Iphigene. "Goddamn it, Iphigene!" he would bark, livid about irritations ranging from her late arrival at dinner to food he didn't like to singing commercials on television. Yet she reacted to her husband's abuse with the same serenity with which she had dealt with his affairs. "I never saw her mad or angry," said Sally Reston. "No tears. Just control, absolute control." Her sense of duty and ability to look life "straight in the eye," as one friend put it, served her well. She coped without complaint, confiding in no one, keeping the peace. In public and private alike she protected Arthur's image, boosted his ego, and showed the face of a loyal, loving wife. "She liked things to be pleasant on the surface," said Doris Faber, a *New York Times* reporter hired by Iphigene several years later to help with her memoirs. "She liked everything nice and neat, everything pretty, the way it should be in a happy memory."

To Dr. Carden, who was also Iphigene's physician, she spoke more freely about her frustrations. He was well aware of the damage that stress had done to her body. For years she had suffered from chronic intestinal disorders that produced periodic incontinence, and diverticular bleeding so severe that on two or three occasions she had required transfusions. "In a lesser character, this malady could almost paralyze you," Carden said. "But she never lost a stride in her lifestyle because of the illness. She dealt with it absolutely without emotional involvement."

If there was any sign that Arthur's irascibility was extracting a price from Iphigene, it was subtle. Her grandchildren noticed that when she told stories about him, they were always tales of joint travel and the exciting people they had met. She never mentioned their early romance and courtship or gave any hint that she had ever had intimate feelings for him. Dick Cohen, the family's newest addition, assumed from the first that his in-laws lived in a marriage of convenience. Dr. Carden admired Iphigene's loyalty and her desire to bolster Arthur "for the sake of the paper," but he did not think that she loved him by then. Her friend Audrey Topping also felt that Iphigene was ambivalent about Arthur. "I got the sense that she had to put up with a lot," she said. "She talked about all the wonderful things [she and Arthur] did, but I could tell by her attitude that there was an anger underneath."

§

On January 1, 1960, Americans awoke to greet a new decade, a decade of upheaval that would permanently shift the tectonic plates beneath themselves and their government. The launch of the Soviet satellite *Sputnik* three years earlier had already stunned the country out of its postwar complacency and into a space race. Nikita Khrushchev, who had replaced Soviet premier Nikolai Bulganin in 1958, was lowering the already frigid temperature of the Cold War. And in a few short months, Francis Gary Powers would be shot down in a U-2 spy plane over Russia, exposing the United States in an embarrassing lie — the first wedge in what would come to be an ever widening credibility gap between Washington and its citizens. In every sphere — political, social, economic — the comfortable verities that had governed the placid and prosperous years following World War II were rapidly giving way, questioned and reshaped by a younger generation poised to lead.

No one personified this new era more than John Fitzgerald Kennedy, a politician whose youthful hope and telegenic charisma dazzled the nation; yet Arthur, still enamored of Eisenhower, a man of his own vintage and the president whom he had personally known, found it difficult to embrace Kennedy over his challenger, Vice President Richard Nixon. He considered Kennedy's Boston Irish background slightly smarmy and was particularly suspicious of his father, Joe, whose questionable business maneuverings had made him a millionaire. Like many Americans, he doubted that a Catholic could separate his religion from his politics, which was particularly ironic given Arthur's struggle against a similar prejudice against Jews. He also worried that any Democratic president would pander to the detestable labor unions. However, these factors paled in comparison to the effect Iphigene's support of the Democrats had on him, support he considered so "blind and biased" that he feared it "will drive me in the other direction to keep on an even keel."

Although Arthur had serious concerns about Nixon, he found him "very personable and engaging in private" and liked him more with each exposure. Iphigene's disdain, on the other hand, was apparent. Even after getting to know him better at a Publisher's Luncheon, her judgment did not change. Turner Catledge felt the same; he considered Nixon icy and eccentric. During a recent post–Gridiron Dinner party, the vice president had played the piano while the Times' managing editor had sung. Once the conviviality was over, Nixon had abruptly left without a word to Turner, and at their next meeting failed to recognize him.

What ultimately turned Arthur around was southern conservatives' fervency for the Republican nominee. "I guess that means I've got to vote for Kennedy, little as I like doing so," he said. In keeping with his reluctance, the Times' endorsement of Kennedy was unusually tepid. Afterward Arthur made a special point of telling Scotty Reston that he did not approve of the "blatant" pro-Kennedy tilt he detected in Reston's column and the column of his own nephew, Cy Sulzberger. "I like to think of you as reporters, not as pundits," he said, ignoring the fact that columnists, by definition, are meant to express opinions.

The 1960 election, which Kennedy won in a squeaker, was to be Arthur's last as publisher. Just as the torch had been passed to a younger man in Washington, so a generational shift was about to take place at *The New York Times*. Arthur knew the time had come. Physically he was so frail that he took "steps the size of an infant" from the elevator to his office. One day while eating waffles at Hillandale, he discovered that he could not pour the maple syrup; his left hand was too weak to grip the pitcher. Despite a valiant effort, he had again become dependent on drugs, particularly Nembutal, a powerful sleep aid. At Dr. Carden's recommendation, he entered Harkness Pavilion at Columbia-Presbyterian Medical Center in an effort to kick the habit once and for all.

Early in 1961 Arthur confidentially shared his decision to step down as publisher with close family members and intimates. His intention, he said, was to make Orvil publisher in late April and to retire Charles Merz, Arthur's great friend and the *Times'* editorial-page editor for the past twenty-three years, at the same time. Merz was sixty-eight, after all, and Arthur well remembered his frustration with Adolph's aging holdovers. He considered it important for Orvil to have a contemporary as his editorial chief. With Merz's concurrence, Orvil choose John Oakes, Iphigene's cousin, who had penned distinguished editorials for the past twelve years.

Shortly before the *Times* announced the changes at the top, Orvil, though not yet officially publisher, was asked to make one of the paper's toughest judgment calls. The precipitating incident was the Bay of Pigs invasion, an ill-conceived attempt by U.S.-trained Cuban exiles to overthrow the government of Fidel Castro. At the time, the paper was in a sensitive position because of its coverage of Castro, who had come to power by deposing the dictator General Fulgencio Batista on New Year's Day 1959. Herbert Matthews, the brilliant *Times* correspondent primarily responsible for covering Castro, had become so emotionally involved with his subject that by 1961 Arthur, Orvil, Turner, and other editors questioned whether he could report the story objectively. Hanging in the balance was the *Times'* reputation for clear-eyed journalism.

By 1960 it had become apparent that Castro's government was in the thrall of the Soviets; the regime was hardly "free, honest and democratic," as Matthews insisted. A congressional committee publicly attacked the *Times* reporter and hate mail poured into the paper, much of it accusing Matthews — and by extension, the paper — of being Communist.

Posters of Castro appeared emblazoned with the statement I GOT MY JOB THROUGH THE NEW YORK TIMES — a play on the wording of a *New York Times* promotional campaign. Still, the *Times* observed its tradition of not interfering with its reporters; Matthews was eventually moved off the news beat to the editorial page, where he continued to write about Cuba. "I agree we can't muzzle him," Orvil told John Oakes confidentially. "However, I wish he would pipe down."

It was in this atmosphere of heightened sensitivity that Orvil grappled with the question of what to publish about the coming Bay of Pigs invasion, an operation that was, by the time it occurred in mid-April 1961, effectively an open secret. Early on, the Cuban leader had infiltrated the exile volunteers with his own agents, who gave him regular, reliable reports. "The only information Castro didn't have by then was the exact time and place [of the invasion]," Pierre Salinger, President Kennedy's press secretary, wrote later.

As early as November 19, 1960, *The Nation* had published a report that the CIA was training Cuban exiles for an invasion of Cuba at a base in Guatemala. When the *Times'* Central America reporter, Paul Kennedy, who happened to be in Guatemala on assignment, asked President Miguel Ydígoras about the training site, Ydígoras denied its existence, and Kennedy's story, published in the following day's *New York Times,* made no mention of the base or the CIA. Over the next seven weeks the *Los Angeles Times* and *Time* magazine both confirmed *The Nation's* account. Determined to prove Ydígoras a liar, Kennedy returned to Guatemala; the result was a page-one article on January 10, 1961, expanding on *The Nation's* report with a map pinpointing the training base but making no mention of the CIA.

In the early spring *Times* correspondent Tad Szulc stumbled across the invasion story while visiting friends in Miami. Worried that other reporters would get wind of his information if he discussed it over the phone, he flew to New York and reported to Turner and Orvil what he knew: that American-backed Cuban exiles were massing in Florida and elsewhere for an attack on Cuba. Turner sent Szulc back down to Florida with three other reporters to flesh out the details. From that point on, stories about the Cuban exiles appeared almost every day in the *Times.*

On Thursday, April 6, Szulc filed a report that was a red flag to the *Times'* bullpen editors — who read all stories likely to appear on the front page. Szulc declared that the CIA was the sponsor of the coming invasion and pinpointed the day it would happen: April 18. To protect the paper, the editors softened Szulc's prediction, describing the invasion as merely "imminent." After all, they reasoned, Szulc could be wrong, or if he was right, his story could cause the government to alter its plans, thus embarrassing the *Times.*

It was late in the afternoon when Turner first saw the edited version of Szulc's story, and it set off alarm bells. He immediately brought it to the attention of Orvil, whose concerns were threefold: he worried that the piece would endanger the lives of the men landing on the beaches, interfere with national policy, and effectively aid Castro, thus lending support to those who thought the *Times* — and Herbert Matthews in particular — had helped bring the dictator to power.

Orvil and Turner gathered in Turner's office to confer by speakerphone with Scotty, who said he would make some inquiries and report back. He then called Allen Dulles, director of the CIA, whom he had often used as a background source. Dulles advised Scotty that, for national security reasons, it would be best not to publish the story. However, if the *Times* decided it absolutely must publish, it should keep the CIA out of it. When Scotty called back Orvil and Turner, he did not reveal with whom he had spoken but told them, "I wouldn't publish that story at all."

Orvil knew the *Times* had a long history of protecting the government. Arthur's vigilant anticommunism and his close association with Eisenhower had made him particularly disposed to comply with Washington's wishes, sometimes inappropriately. In 1954, at the height of the McCarthy era, he had temporarily pulled *Times* correspondent Sydney Gruson out of Guatemala because Allen Dulles had told Julius, Dulles's friend and Princeton classmate, that the CIA believed Gruson was too "liberal" to report objectively on the impending revolution there. Several years after the ouster of the leftist Guatemalan leader Colonel Jacabo Arbenz Guzmán, the truth emerged: the CIA had feared Gruson was dangerously close to exposing the agency's role in the coup, which at one point included a "disposal list" of assassination targets. In the midst of the anti-Gruson hysteria, Eisenhower himself, in a meeting with Dulles, had characterized *The New York Times* — a paper he admitted he rarely read — as "the most untrustworthy newspaper in the United States."

In response to Scotty's counsel, Turner removed the word *imminent* and all references to the CIA from the invasion story. He didn't doubt that government intelligence of some sort was involved, but he was not convinced that Szulc had proved that the CIA was responsible. To protect the *Times*, he substituted more general terms like *United States experts* and *officials*.

Early that evening assistant managing editor Ted Bernstein and news editor Lew Jordan laid out a dummy of the invasion story, signaling its importance by making it the lead story on the front page under a four-column headline. Turner disagreed. Without a prediction of an "imminent" invasion, he thought the story merited a lower profile and ordered the headline changed from four columns to one.

Bernstein and Jordan had been used to making up the paper each night without the supervision of the managing editor. Turner's interference, for what they assumed were political reasons, enraged them. They marched into Turner's office to make an appeal; when he proved implacable, they demanded to hear from Orvil himself why the change had been made. "Flaming mad," Turner swiveled around in his chair, picked up the telephone, and asked Orvil to come down to the third-floor newsroom. For the next ten minutes the publisher-to-be explained his reasons for downplaying the story: national security, national interest, and the safety of the Cuban exiles. What he didn't say, of course, was that by emphasizing the news of the coming invasion in a four-column headline, the *Times* would run the risk of again being criticized as sympathetic to Castro, something he wished to avoid.

On April 7 the one-column Szulc story, headlined ANTI-CASTRO UNITS TRAINED TO FIGHT AT FLORIDA BASES, appeared on the front page of *The New York Times*, above the fold, with a Miami dateline. Strangely enough, although Orvil and his editors had fiercely debated whether to report even a hint of a timetable for the invasion, there was a "shirttail" — a separate but connected piece from another source — at the end of the Szulc story quoting a CBS News report that said the landing was in its "final stages."*

The calamitous Bay of Pigs invasion occurred on April 17 — a day earlier than Szulc's prediction — resulting in 1,000 captives, 114 dead, and international embarrassment for the Kennedy administration. Two

---

*Tad Szulc told a friend at CBS Radio in Miami what he knew, and CBS ran with it. By printing a shirttail, the *Times* allowed CBS to say what it had not been willing to report on its own responsibility.

days later Allen Dulles told newsmen at a State Department briefing that the debacle proved there should be an "official secrets act." President Kennedy took up the cry, lashing out at the press for its "indiscriminate and premature reporting about the preparations for the invasion." Publishers should "re-examine their own professional responsibilities," he said in a speech to the Newspaper Advertising Bureau; they should ask about every story not just "Is it news?" but "Is it in the interest of national security?"

Aroused to action, Turner organized a delegation of editors and publishers to meet with Kennedy at the White House. Pressed to give examples of irresponsible reporting, Kennedy repeatedly singled out *The New York Times,* and specifically the Paul Kennedy story that had appeared on January 10. Turner countered that the same essential news story had appeared months earlier in *The Nation.* "But it was not news until it appeared in the *Times,*" the president replied. As the conference was breaking up, in an aside uttered too quietly for anyone else to hear, Kennedy told Turner, "Maybe if you had printed more about the operation, you would have saved us from a colossal mistake."

§

As planned, on April 25, eight days after the Bay of Pigs, the board of directors appointed Orvil publisher of *The New York Times,* replacing Arthur, who remained as chairman. That morning on his breakfast tray Arthur found a handwritten letter from Orvil acknowledging the "emotional overtones that must be present today" and thanking him for "training this team" and "asking us to take the field." Arthur, too, had ordered a message to be hand-delivered to his son-in-law. "Good luck to you on your big new venture," it read. "I'll be rooting for you and hope I can be of help without getting in your hair." A secretary had typed the letter, but Arthur, his fingers crippled and his coordination impaired, had insisted on signing his barely legible initials.

Later in the day the stockholders of *The New York Times* gathered in the paper's fourteenth-floor boardroom to hear Arthur deliver the farewell statement over which he had long labored. "Whereas I, of necessity, grow older, the *Times,* of necessity, *must not,*" he began. "The Publisher of this newspaper should have a spark that I no longer possess." With consummate grace, he acknowledged every group at 229 West Forty-third Street, including the "telephone girls," the reporters, and even the compositors and pressmen whose strike threats threw the paper into biennial chaos. Employing a metaphor that was perhaps too apt given his private peccadillos, Arthur admitted his heart was "sad at breaking any bonds . . . with this too-demanding mistress." Finally, as he had done so many times throughout his life, he gave one last thanks to "Mr. Ochs."

Later that day Arthur sat in his office surrounded by affectionate messages and letters, including one from President Kennedy, who jokingly welcomed him to the "rocking chair club" — an allusion to the rocking chair the young president used to ease his bad back. From his hospital bed, Eddie Greenbaum expressed the hope that his old friend would now "begin to enjoy life again" and no longer experience that "guilty AWOL feeling" when he left the building. Several *Times* executives and members of his family chipped in to buy a golf cart in the hope that he could now putter around the Stamford compound on his own; the Washington bureau gave him a cherry tree, which he promised to plant in front of the main house at Hillandale.

As Arthur basked in these gestures, he contemplated the legacy he had left his successor. Certainly there were quantifiable achievements: during his twenty-six-year reign as publisher, daily circulation had risen by more than 200,000 and Sunday circulation by more than 600,000; advertising volume had increased more than threefold to a high in 1960 of almost 62 million lines; and the newspaper's staff had more than doubled. *The New York Times* was relatively modern in appearance, with more photos, larger headlines, a stronger editorial voice, and signed columns. As important, Arthur had steered the paper through a remarkable period of American history, a period that encompassed the Depression, World War II, the McCarthy hysteria, postwar prosperity, and the Cold War. Throughout the era, Arthur had kept *The New York Times* true to its Ochsian roots. "What a glorious family story this is," Scotty Reston wrote him. "It was the sense of family continuity and responsibility that struck Sally and me more than anything else."

Arthur had a great deal to be proud of, not the least of which was the maturity and self-control he had demonstrated in handing the reins to a younger man — something Adolph had never been able to do. But he could not help feeling sorrow and loss. "Misery likes company," he wrote Charles Merz, who took the title "editor emeritus" the same day Arthur gave up the publishership. "I know that you and I are pursuing the right course [but] I also know there's a lot of heartache associated with it. As someone told me the other day, 'This is the first milestone you have ever passed that hasn't pointed up.' " When his brother David called to see how he was doing, Arthur became so tearful that he made a mumbled apology and abruptly hung up the phone.

At the opposite end of the fourteenth floor, letters of congratulations piled up in Orvil's office. He had worked steadily toward this moment for almost twenty years. Now that it had actually arrived, he was a little breathless. "It was like he'd been hit by a ton of coal," said his old friend Ardie Deutsch. Phil Graham, the publisher of *The Washington Post,* who had also gotten his job through marriage, sent Orvil a message that unintentionally played to his insecurities. "You've now become the occupant of the most important chair in the American newspaper business," he said, "and [you] have my every good wish, and sympathy as often as needed, in holding it down."

To mark the occasion, Ruth, Judy, and Punch jointly purchased a gift for Orvil: a clear glass owl, six inches high, made by Steuben. It sat serenely on an onyx base mounted with a plaque inscribed with the date and a quotation from the Roman playwright Plautus that read, "Not by years but by disposition is wisdom acquired." Wisdom was, in fact, required within the first few hours of Orvil's publishership. That night, a wildcat strike broke out in the composing room, and instead of enjoying a congratulatory dinner as he had planned, Orvil stayed at the office until 2:30 A.M. to help settle the dispute. If the altercation had gone on much longer, the edition of *The New York Times* announcing his promotion would not have been published. When the paper finally did hit the streets, a profile of the new publisher, written by foreign editor Emanuel Freedman, was nowhere to be found. The story had described Orvil, among other things, as a man who "holds no passionate convictions on public questions, nor does he cultivate intellectual interests." Arthur thought the piece unflattering and had ordered it pulled from the lineup. Orvil's statement, in which he promised to "maintain vigilantly the high standards set by our predecessors," misquoted Adolph's famous "without fear or favor" language, just as Arthur had done decades earlier.

When Orvil arrived at his office on Wednesday, April 26, exhausted from the previous night's drama, he found the Steuben owl lying on his desk, mysteriously split in two, as if someone had sliced it cleanly in half. It may have been faulty workmanship by Steuben craftsmen; it may have been the result of a careless cleaning woman. But "things like that don't happen," said Ruth, adding that her grandfather Adolph, with his superstitious nature, no doubt would have read dark portents into the accident and its timing. Steuben quickly sent over a replacement. The incident only added to Orvil's worries about whether he was up to his new responsibilities. "I hope it's not a bad omen," he told his secretary.

21

The Coach

O RVIL'S THREE-ROOM EXECUTIVE SUITE WAS subtly symbolic of what many reporters and editors hoped would be an era of innovation and informality at *The New York Times,* an era as youthful and energetic as the New Frontier taking shape in Washington. Whereas Arthur's office featured an American eagle statuette and a sofa upholstered in a deer-and-hound pattern — totems of conventional masculinity — Orvil's was strikingly modern. He sat in one corner behind a sleek, kidney-shaped desk with fresh flowers to one side and an English silver tray with writing utensils directly in front of him. In the opposite corner was a lush jungle of green plants and a conference table. Although he never wore a wristwatch, he kept an elegant two-faced Tiffany clock on his desk so that he, and his visitors, always knew the time. His three secretaries, who inhabited an adjacent room, called him Mr. D. — a level of familiarity unknown in the Arthur Hays Sulzberger years. A small sitting room completed the ensemble.

The symbolism was deceptive, however, for despite his years of preparation, Orvil began his reign as publisher with no overarching plan for the future. "He wasn't a very deep or philosophic thinker," said John Oakes. "He really was quite insecure." Like Arthur, Orvil commenced his publishership in the shadow of Adolph. Through the accident of marriage, Orvil was now the steward of the greatest newspaper in the country, if not the world, a paper made preeminent by a man he had never met but whose principles were as inviolate as if they had been handed down on stone tablets. What right did he — a former two-dollar broker — have to tamper with them? When *Newsweek* inquired what Orvil hoped to accomplish in his new post, he safely replied that he planned no changes: "I see the *Times* going along just about as it is."

On the business side, a steady-rudder policy was not necessarily what the *Times* needed. The paper itself was barely breaking even; in 1960 it had made just $348,000, compared with $1.86 million the year before. The picture brightened when the *Times'* 42 percent stake in Spruce Falls Power and Paper was taken into account. In recent years Spruce Falls, which supplied two-thirds of the *Times'* newsprint, had accounted for roughly 53 percent of The New York Times Company's total profit. Even so, corporate net income in 1960 stood at a disappointing $1.65 million, about half what the company had made in 1959.

There were several reasons for the *Times'* sinking finances. The international edition of the paper, started in 1949, had been a big drain. For years the paper had been published from whole pages produced in New York and then flown to Paris for printing, a time-consuming technique that made the international edition out-of-date the moment it hit European newsstands. During his last months as publisher, Arthur had tried to remedy the situation by sending the paper to Paris by Teletypesetter, a device using telephone wires and radio transmission. There, it was printed the same day, and copies were flown all over Europe, six days a week. But the cost of establishing the perfected international edition had been overwhelming, and the revenue remained slight.

Another reason for the *Times'* slump was the family's commitment to quality and its remarkable lack of concern for personal enrichment. In the twenty years between 1937 and 1957, the company's profit after taxes had averaged a meager 4.5 percent, and without the annual infusion from Spruce Falls the margin would have been far smaller. Most of the profit remained in the business, either invested in presses and other improvements or retained to see the paper through economic downturns. Relatively little was paid out in preferred stock dividends. In 1958, when John Hay "Jock" Whitney had been on the verge of buying the *Herald Tribune* from the Reid family, he had probed Orvil about the pluses and minuses of the newspaper business. When he discovered that the *Times* had made just 1.7 percent net profit after taxes in 1957 and that WQXR had barely cleared $50,000, he asked in bewilderment, "But you *could* make money, couldn't you?" Orvil replied that of course it was possible, but "that would spoil the quality."

In many ways, the *Times* operated more like a foundation or an educational institution than a commercial enterprise. Like many disciples of inspirational leaders, Arthur and Iphigene — and, under their tutelage, Orvil — were Ochsian fundamentalists, convinced not only that reinvesting money in the *Times* was good but that being financially shrewd, even in the interest of the paper, was potentially corrupting. Arthur had deliberately remained ignorant of where the *Times* put its surplus cash, fearful that he might make an editorial decision, however unintentionally, that favored the investment. He kept his personal money exclusively in U.S. Treasury bills, insisting that the Ochs Trust do the same, and refused even to put the trust's funds in short-term government paper, despite the pleas of First Boston chairman George Woods, his friend and adviser, who argued that "money is worth its hire." When Arthur was considering donating his personal papers to a library, Eddie Greenbaum suggested he take a tax deduction for it. Arthur declined; such schemes were cheap and unpatriotic, he said. As for Iphigene, she considered it bad form for family members to speak about wealth. "Money is without any question one of those taboo subjects," said a grandson. "You don't talk about money. You don't even think about it."

The insistence on quality, coupled with the family's aversion to discussing finance, produced a business culture similar to that of a mom-and-pop store. From 1935 through the mid-1950s, the company's financial statement was so closely guarded that only Arthur; Godfrey Nelson, the *Times'* secretary; and Julius had any working familiarity with it. At the annual meeting, stockholders saw furtively circulated carbon copies, which Nelson carefully collected before anyone left the room. The *Times'* guardedness, shared by other family-owned newspapers, was partly defensive; Arthur did not want the *Herald Tribune* or other rivals to know how much the *Times* was spending on promotion, news gathering, and so forth. But a good deal of the feeling sprang from a desire to shield the reporters — Adolph's acolytes — from the crass verities of the collection plate. Their job was to build the cathedral and to embody its spirit, not to pay for it.

By the time Orvil assumed the publishership, the *Times'* financial insularity had begun to break down. In 1958 the company for the first time released a public financial statement. Arthur claimed the reason was that *Times* stockholders, which now included a few educational and charitable institutions, had a "legitimate interest in seeing our reports." That was partly true; without such documentation, the company left itself open to stockholder suits. But the real motivation was far more complex, and had to do with the family's desire to retain control of *The New York Times* in the next generation.

From 1934 through 1957 the common stock of *The New York Times* paid no dividends, the reason being that, under the intricate provisions of the Ochs Trust, common dividends were effectively a charge against the trust. Only the 8 percent preferred stock, held by Arthur, Iphigene, the Sulzberger children, and various *Times* associates and their heirs, generated cash. It was from these holdings that the family's income was largely derived, in addition to salaries and coupons from U.S. Treasury bills. Needs over and above that amount were usually met by the Ochs Trust, which owned several of the Sulzbergers' houses and even the cars they drove.

This unwieldy arrangement worked for many years and the family had little concern about inheritance problems: when Iphigene died, the Ochs Trust would dissolve and the children would inherit the stock without further tax. But no provision had been made for payment of taxes upon the deaths of Punch and his sisters, nor was there a financial structure to ensure that the family could retain control of The New York Times Company into another generation. Under a recapitalization scheme conceived of by board member George Woods and approved by shareholders in May 1957, two classes of common stock were created, Class A nonvoting and Class B voting. The Ochs Trust and the Sulzbergers got the majority of the Class B stock, and for the first time in over twenty years, the common stock began to pay dividends. When the Sulzberger children died, their heirs would retain control through the Class B voting stock while selling as much of the Class A common stock as necessary to pay death duties. There was just one hitch in the plan: without public financial statements, there would be no market for the common stock. Hence the seemingly abrupt willingness of *The New York Times* to announce its profits and losses to the world. "This will permit the children to have a marketable security when they inherit the property from the Ochs estate," Arthur explained to a friend who inquired why the *Times* had submitted its finances to public scrutiny. "That's the reason for this sudden appearance."

The changes came none too soon, for there were signs that the newspaper business in general could not continue as it had for much longer. Although seven daily newspapers scrapped and fought in New York City in 1961, behind that impressive front lay a set of disturbing facts. Daily newspaper readership had risen nationwide by 6 million over the previous decade, yet in New York it had fallen by 358,000; Sunday circulation was even worse. Only the *Times* had scored any gains, picking up 220,000 readers, for a total daily circulation of 744,763. Hurt by the growing popularity of television news, an exodus of readers to the suburbs, and strong labor unions that made it difficult to take advantage of cost-saving technology, two of the four morning papers and all three of the evening papers were hanging by a thread. For the first time, articles appeared posing the question, Can New York support seven daily newspapers? Orvil's answer was a definite no. Without naming names, he told *Time* magazine three months after becoming publisher that several of the threatened newspapers were clearly doomed. "Within ten years," he predicted, "there's bound to be a different line-up."

§

By making Orvil president and publisher of *The New York Times,* Arthur had reunited the business and news sides of the newspaper under one head for the first time since Adolph's death in 1935. Although Arthur himself had had the same two titles, and had unquestionably been the ultimate authority in both areas, the day-to-day reality was that, out of deference to Julius's partisans within the family and his own preference for editorial involvement, Arthur had spent most of his time focused on the *Times'* news reportage, editorials, and presidential endorsements, while Julius attended to advertising, circulation, and union contracts. Now Orvil, who had started out in the newsroom but had spent most of his training years on the executive floor, was expected to hold sway over both arenas with equal expertise.

It was an impossible task, of course; as a former stockbroker, he was naturally inclined toward business and remained somewhat in awe of the editors who, as he tellingly put it, "really run the paper." Whereas Arthur had plunged freely into editorial matters, Orvil almost never did. He "drives with the loosest rein of all," said the profile of the new publisher that Arthur had refused to print in late April 1961. "Rarely, if ever, does he order anything into or out of the paper. He may send a mild memo, 'FYI only,' to a top editor and takes no cheerfully as yes."

Orvil seemed reluctant to use the power with which he had been invested. "The word 'management' annoys me," he told Arthur Krock.

"Shouldn't we all consider ourselves part of the editorial team?" Having come of age professionally during the 1950s — the era of William H. Whyte's *Organization Man* — he was bureaucratic and unchallenging. "I view my job as the coach," he once told two executives who asked him to intervene in a business matter at the paper. "I stand on the sidelines and coach the team." Not everyone considered his style to be appropriate. "It's a goofy way to view your job," said Tom Campion, a former production manager and director of operations. "Orvil did not see himself as a leader."

Appropriate or not, Orvil's hands-off philosophy meant that the top men on his "team" had unusually broad latitude to shape *The New York Times*. On the news side the key player was Orvil's friend and mentor Scotty Reston, even though, as Washington bureau chief, he resided a couple of hundred miles away and Turner Catledge, by virtue of his title as managing editor, should have had that power. The rivalry between the two men was "wary, knowing and often witty." Scotty subtly encouraged a perception, in the Washington bureau at least, that Turner was a lazy, do-nothing southerner who made speeches, attended meetings of the American Society of Newspaper Editors, and did very little as an editor. "Turner was technically Scotty's boss," said *Times* columnist Russell Baker, "but Scotty's relationship with Orvil made that irrelevant. He could call New York and get whatever he wanted."

On the editorial page, Orvil's man was John Oakes, the *Times'* first Jewish editorial-page editor, who was determined to inject new life into what had become a "dull, heavy, mournful" pastiche of opinion. One of his first acts was to ban the use of Charles Merz's trademark phrase *on the other hand,* an indication that the paper would henceforth speak with a more assertive voice. "For years I thought the editorials were very flabby," he said. "[They were] so damn low-key that no one read them."

John had firm beliefs, clearly enunciated — so clearly enunciated, in fact, that in the late 1950s Arthur had expressed doubts about the wisdom of John's ever becoming a foreign correspondent, fearing that such an opinionated personality would make a poor ambassador for the paper. "[John] could broadcast but he had no receiver," said Ivan Veit, the *Times'* promotion director. Still, many readers liked the new voice of the *Times'* editorial page. "It has all at once come alive — and alive to such an extent that one almost feels the vitality," Archibald MacLeish wrote to John several weeks after he had taken charge.

Politically, Orvil and John were an odd couple. John was an iconoclast like his father, George Washington Ochs-Oakes, whose heavy oak desk he took as his own and moved into his tenth-floor office. But unlike his father, he was a liberal. "I was a little more what Joe McCarthy used to call a 'knee-jerk liberal' than the *Times* was," he said. "I was very much more ready to go after corporations or Wall Street." Orvil often feinted right when John feinted left, but was mainly nonideological, with no strong views either way. His colleagues at the paper hadn't a clue whether he voted Democrat or Republican.

Because of Orvil's lack of firmly held beliefs, he and John had few disagreements, and the ones they had never escalated to the level of Orvil's having to assert his authority with the final word. Beyond requesting that he see photocopies of *Times* editorials before they were sent to the composing room, Orvil was seemingly content to let John operate the page as he saw fit. "I don't remember him pushing hard on anything," John said. But for Arthur, the *Times'* sharp veer to the left was a jarring change.

In the summer of 1961 Orvil returned from a vacation in Europe to find his father-in-law and John at swords' points over the issue of admitting Communist China to the United Nations. For years the *Times* had given its unswerving support to Chiang Kai-shek's government on Taiwan, a position John considered rigid and unrealistic. He produced an editorial backing the admission of Beijing and showed the draft to Arthur, who promptly rewrote it to reflect his own view, which was that "for us to unilaterally break a wartime treaty which we made with Nationalist China was just as offensive as would be the Russian unilateral rupture of a treaty covering Berlin." Confident that his new publisher would agree with him, Arthur advised Orvil to "have it out with Johnny now, right at the beginning. It will make things easier in the future." The result was an editorial supporting American willingness not to put up roadblocks to UN debate on the issue of Chinese representation — a sure sign that John had won. Clearly smarting, Arthur told Charles Merz: "The more I stay around here, the more difficult I find it to adjust myself to the fact that I am not the Publisher anymore."

If the editorial page was undergoing an overhaul, the *Times'* business methods were still in desperate need of one. The personnel department was a quill-pen operation; salaries and promotions were haphazardly dispensed and inscribed by hand in a little black book. There were no budgets, no long-range plans, no analysis, and little cooperation. Each of the major departments — advertising, promotion, news, and production — was a separate kingdom with a ruling monarch and a retinue of scheming nobles. "We started from zero, as far as any kind of orderly business procedure is concerned," said John Mortimer, who joined the paper in 1962 as industrial-relations manager.

Amory Bradford, the *Times'* general manager, and Andy Fisher, the assistant general manager, were Orvil's personally picked dream team on the business side, top executives with Ivy League credentials who, he hoped, would impose discipline, make tough choices, and create up-to-date systems that would help the *Times* face a complex and increasingly competitive future. The two men joined the paper within weeks of each other in the summer of 1947, Amory from the white-shoe New York law firm of Davis, Polk, Wardwell, Sunderland & Kiendl, and Andy directly from Harvard Business School — a radical departure for the *Times*, which until then had never hired anyone with a Harvard MBA. Both men were demanding and decisive, full of fire and ambition, ego and intensity.

Amory, tall and regally handsome, was the oldest son of a Congregational minister and a descendant of William Bradford, the second governor of Plymouth Colony. He exuded the haughty, self-assured air of a New England patrician, and his degrees from Andover, Yale, and Yale Law School bolstered the image. In fact, he did not come from a privileged background but was a lonely, angry bootstrapper, advancing in life through self-reliance, gut determination, and carefully cultivated connections. Profoundly alienated from his family, especially his father, who had struggled financially and suffered from depression, Amory became self-supporting at fourteen. A scholarship student at Phillips Academy in Andover, Massachusetts, he waited on tables, ran the school laundry, and graduated first in his class. At Yale he was tapped for the elite secret society Skull and Bones. Out of law school he joined Davis, Polk, and after a wartime stint doing intelligence work at the Pentagon and State Department, he returned to the firm, only to become quickly bored with his assignment: AT&T debentures. It was in this state of restiveness that Orvil, then assistant to the publisher, had first asked Amory about his plans for the future.

They had met through Amory's wife, Carol Rothschild, a granddaughter of the philanthropist Felix Warburg and a former girlfriend of

Orvil's. In the early years of the Dryfooses' marriage, the two couples shared occasional outings. In the spring of 1947 Orvil invited Amory to a meeting of the Overseas Press Club and mentioned that the *Times* was looking for a bright young lawyer to understudy the company secretary, Godfrey Nelson, who was sixty-nine and in poor health. The idea of an executive job appealed to Amory, and after a perfunctory talk with Arthur, he came to the *Times* — but not for the job he had originally been hired to do. In the interim, Nelson had balked at having an assistant. Amory was informed that, instead, he could do "whatever [he] wanted to learn about the business," and at Arthur's suggestion, he chose to work as an aide to the publisher.

The unyielding, combative style that would characterize Bradford's tenure at the *Times* was glaringly apparent from the first. He consciously modeled himself after Dean Acheson, Truman's secretary of state, who was a family acquaintance and for whom he later worked while on a year's leave of absence from the *Times*. Amory respected Acheson's preemptory manner and his reputation for verbally decapitating those he thought foolish or inferior. "I liked his style, which was justifiably arrogant," he said. "He had the talent to be arrogant, to be pleased with himself about it." He especially admired that Acheson had resigned as undersecretary of the treasury during the Roosevelt administration over a policy dispute with the president. For Amory, threatening to resign would become standard operating procedure, a way to achieve results and husband power. "I was ready to leave," he said. "This was true at any time over any issue."

With these attributes, Bradford advanced quickly, becoming company secretary when Godfrey Nelson died, business manager and vice president in 1957 at the time Orvil was made president, and general manager three years later. Many at the paper joked that he was the Sulzbergers' "front office-Gentile," a moniker Arthur unwittingly encouraged by garbling Amory's high-WASP name with that of Harding Bancroft, the aloof Yankee who succeeded Amory as company secretary. Arthur regularly referred to Harding Bradford or Amory Bancroft.

Orvil played good cop to Amory's bad cop, an arrangement that suited his personality. "I used to remind Orvil that we weren't there to make friends, we were there to run *The New York Times*," Amory said. "And he would smile and go ahead and stay on a friendly basis with everybody." In turn, Orvil tacitly agreed to protect Amory from "family problems," meaning the concerns of Arthur, Iphigene, and their children and spouses, thus freeing Bradford to concentrate entirely on the business. To Orvil, of course, "family" and "business" were one and the same; to Amory, who had pointedly refused to join his wife's family company, Federated Department Stores, they were separate and distinct. "My sense of myself was not that I was working for a family," he said. "The family wasn't important to me."

Amory was less accomplished a general manager than he believed himself to be. "He had no more talent in the field of business management than the man in the moon," said Tom Campion. Nonetheless, because of his relationship with Orvil, he had a sweeping mandate to run the newspaper operations of *The New York Times*, and he imposed his rigid ideas on many aspects of the place. No one knew his eccentricities better than Orvil's other key lieutenant, Andy Fisher.

Andy, a blue-eyed former boxer, was a ruggedly masculine man, who began his *Times* career as an administrative assistant working in labor relations. In the 1950s Orvil asked him to serve as his aide, a position he remained in as Orvil advanced from vice president to president of the company. By 1960 Andy was eager to assume line responsibilities, and Orvil agreeably named him assistant general manager, a slot that made him Amory's top subordinate. Leaving the warmth of Orvil's orbit for the chill of Amory's was a shock, but Andy prided himself on his professionalism, loyalty, self-control, and decisiveness. He quickly carved out a place for himself as the *Times'* guru of contemporary management techniques, bringing in consultants, pushing for quantifiable information, and talking excitedly about "optimum" results. "He sort of awed me because of his Harvard Business School approach to everything," Turner Catledge said in a tongue-in-cheek comment that captured the skepticism with which traditionalists at the paper viewed Fisher's ideas.

The biggest challenge facing Orvil and his new team was how to find new sources of income to protect *The New York Times* from the profit-draining shocks of newsprint hikes, strikes, and rising labor costs. Papers such as the *Dallas Times-Herald*, which received one-third of its income from its profitable TV station, had proved that electronic media could be moneymakers, and Orvil was enthusiastic about following their example. But Arthur remained firmly against television, which he considered a medium of entertainment, not news — "and news is our bailiwick," he said.

Building a newspaper chain was also out of the question. While *The Chattanooga Times* had sentimental value, especially for Iphigene, in the New York office it had become nothing but a headache. Despite a nearly twenty-year-old joint operating agreement with Roy McDonald's *News–Free Press,* the paper had required steady infusions of cash from bank loans secured by the Ochs Trust. It had never fully recovered from the loss of circulation resulting from its advocacy of school desegregation in the mid-1950s, and Arthur's insistence that *The Chattanooga Times* follow *The New York Times'* presidential endorsements and general editorial line only wounded it further. "I have no sympathy for the multiple ownership of newspaper properties," Arthur told his children. "They are not grocery stores or outlets for merchandise. . . . To make policy for one newspaper is more than enough for any one man."

Bound by these restrictions, Orvil had little room to maneuver, so he simply kept to the proven course. He expanded *The New York Times'* investment in newsprint, buying 49 percent of Gaspesia Pulp and Paper Company Ltd. in Chandler, Quebec, in a joint venture with Price Brothers Company. Newsprint was hardly an independent source of income; its fortunes, like the *Times',* were tied to strikes and other vagaries of the newspaper business. Still, between 1952 and 1961 Spruce Falls Power and Paper accounted for the major portion of the company's profits in four years out of nine. Less than a year into Orvil's publishership, the *Times* itself was very close to falling into the red, with operating profits of only $59,802. Orvil's desperate hope was that the Gaspesia purchase would, like Spruce Falls, do its part to prop up the "real" business of the company, *The New York Times.*

A western edition of the paper, announced in the fall of 1961 and inaugurated a year later, was, like the international edition, an attempt by the *Times* to expand its readership and advertising base. But while the Paris-based edition had thus far been a financial disappointment, Orvil was determined to make the Los Angeles–based version of the paper a success and, eventually, to publish a *New York Times* that would be available across the country. *The Wall Street Journal,* already a national newspaper, albeit one aimed at a business audience, had been producing a Pacific Coast edition for more than thirty years. *The Christian Science Monitor* also had a long-established western edition.

The western strategy, two years in the making under the code name Westward Ho, called for the *Times* to supplement, not supplant, papers such as the *Los Angeles Times*. The paper contained no local news, except for weather and theater listings, and no local ads. Instead, the *Times* sought out national advertisers, a situation that put it in direct competition with *Time*, *Newsweek*, and the well-heeled *Wall Street Journal*. West Coast residents clearly wanted *The New York Times*; the western edition's initial circulation figure was 100,000. But because its readers were scattered over thirteen states, including Alaska and Hawaii, the paper was demographically unappealing to advertisers. Adding to the pressure was Arthur's insistence that the paper pay its own way.

It also faced mechanical problems. Editorial control remained in New York, as it did for the international edition, with news and pictures transmitted by Teletypesetter to Los Angeles; *Times* readers got their papers six days a week by mail, home delivery, or through newsstand sales. However, the punched tape coming out of New York was riddled with errors, requiring time-consuming corrections at the *Times*' Watts printing plant, and the Teletypesetter technology frequently broke down. Andy Fisher, who had led the Westward Ho planning group and was in charge of the western edition, bought a house in Los Angeles and shuttled frantically between California and New York City trying to iron out the kinks. Within a year of its start-up, "we had the most beautiful newspaper ever produced," said production chief Walter Mattson, who, like Andy, moved himself and his family to the West Coast. The western edition had yet to prove it could make money but was well on its way to becoming Orvil's breakout showpiece, a paper where, freed from the straitjacket of the New York City labor union agreements, the company could theoretically experiment with new cost-efficient printing techniques. "It was a bold new venture, a high-profile opportunity for the best kind of diversification," said Andy proudly. "This is where Orvil showed some real independence." Such optimism would prove short-lived.

22

A Separate World

EVERY MORNING, EXCEPT IN THE WORST WEATHER, Orvil rendezvoused with four or five *Times* executives near his Upper East Side apartment and walked with them to the paper more than two miles away, arriving at his office shortly after 10:00 A.M. In the winter his heavy fur-collared coat, thick-soled boots, and bushy fur hat gave him the appearance of an unusually genial Russian commissar. He delighted in regaling his walking companions with details about the White House dinner he had recently attended or what the women were wearing at a party the night before, but he was equally observant about new buds and falling leaves or changes in the buildings that they passed. En route he stopped several times at a pay phone to ask his secretary, "Anything doing?"

Orvil used the walks not only as a form of exercise and a way to keep abreast of office gossip, but as a way to work off anxiety. Turner Catledge often joked that he never had to waste his time worrying, because Orvil loved to worry and was good at it. "He did his fanciest worrying over small things," he said. "On the larger ones he seldom seemed ruffled."

Orvil's inner tension was largely imperceptible. In extremis, he became quiet and slightly pensive, but most of the time he simply hid his troubles. To colleagues, he was unfailingly courteous and upbeat, a good listener and an affable companion who, said John Popham, "lifted the spirit of anyone in his presence." Even Amory Bradford, who ruled by fear, emerged glowing from office visits with Orvil. "He would always look up when I came in the door, and a big smile would come over his face as if he were really glad to see me," he said. "I don't know whether he really was or not, but there was this wonderful welcoming sense."

By the time Orvil became publisher, Marian had successfully re-created an updated version of her mother's life — at home, at the *Times,* and in the larger world. Although Iphigene was more intellectual and better educated than Marian, mother and daughter were remarkably alike in their lack of pomposity and their highly developed social conscience. Just as Iphigene had started to work at the *Times* during the war, Marian joined the paper when Orvil became publisher. She shared her mother's office in the promotion department and set about learning the job of special-activities director in anticipation of the day, not far off, when Iphigene would retire and cede the title to her. Arthur, who was vigilant about family featherbedding, impressed upon Marian that in her new role, expenses "must bear the examination of an unbiased outsider," an allusion to the Internal Revenue Service, which in recent years had questioned everything from the personal use of the Sulzbergers' company cars to the cost of Marian's travel when she accompanied Orvil on business trips.

Iphigene had used her brains and her persistence to achieve her positions as a Barnard trustee, chairman of the Barnard Development Committee, and president and chairman of the Park Association, but Marian, who had never felt confident about her intelligence, relied on her charm. When she wrested $10,000 out of a foundation for the Community Services Board, a New York City–based charity, she discovered, "much to my horror," that she was good at raising money. Thereafter, she was in constant demand as a fund-raiser, and she became wildly successful at it. Like her father, Marian admired order; she employed a cleaning woman so fanatically thorough that the Dryfoos children referred to her as the "white tornado." In public, her neatness found an outlet in the "Keep New York City Clean" campaign launched by Mayor Robert Wagner in the 1950s; soon even Orvil was spearing scraps of trash on his morning walks and declaring, "This one's for Marian."

Her chairmanship of the city's Council on the Environment, another mayoral group, led to an appointment to fill the unexpired term of a recently deceased member of the Kennedy administration's Outdoor Recreation Resources Review Commission. Marian knew little about the conservation issues with which the panel dealt, but she was a quick study and basked in the prestige of a volunteer job at the national level. The experience, as she later put it, was "the beginning of my life. . . . Everything evolved from that."

Less than a year later, Secretary of the Interior Stewart Udall appointed her to his department's Advisory Board on National Parks, Historic Sites, Buildings and Monuments, a seat previously occupied by her cousin John Oakes, who had just completed a six-year term and had a long association with environmental causes. That one member of the Ochs-Sulzberger family had succeeded another was prima facie evidence that Udall valued a connection to *The New York Times,* but Marian seemed oblivious to the realpolitik of her situation. The board was made up of archaeologists, naturalists, architects, and historians; Marian was the only layperson and the only woman. Yet when asked why she was chosen, she said with genuine lack of guile: "I think [Udall] liked me." Regardless of the reasons for her appointment, Marian considered the national parks board a personal triumph. "[My mother] was so jealous of my being on the National Parks Board while she'd only been on the city park board," she remarked. Arthur, too, was satisfyingly shocked that his daughter — "the pretty one" — had been tapped for such a serious responsibility.

In the Dryfooses' second-floor apartment at 1010 Fifth Avenue, eleven blocks from the senior Sulzbergers, Marian maintained a household complete with finger bowls and maids she summoned to the table by a small bell. A succession of nurses and nannies cared for the three children, and a chauffeur carried them to and from school. The responsibility of being members of the family that owned and ran *The New York Times* was carefully impressed upon each of them. Even as a young child, Bobby was expected to wear a jacket and tie when he went outside, "because that's the way we present ourselves to the public," he said.

Compared with Orvil, Marian was an emotionally absent parent. "She just wasn't that interested in us," said Jackie. "She and Daddy went out five nights a week and then we went to the country, and often there were friends [there]. Everybody sort of drifted." Like Iphigene, Marian had a tendency to be opaque and remote. Years later Marian would tell Jackie that, as the oldest of the Sulzberger children, she had taken care of her three younger siblings and that "I was tired of being a mother by the time I had children."

Orvil, in contrast, was an enthusiastic and exuberant father. On a trip to the Far East, he made a point of doing one thing individually with each child: with Bobby he went to a "den of iniquity where girls in tights and strapless tops . . . look cute while a jukebox blares"; with Jackie he danced at a Japanese nightclub; and with Susie he visited a Tokyo teahouse. In New York he regularly took the children to Broadway shows and the ballet, with dinner beforehand at Sardi's. Like Arthur, he was more comfortable with his daughters than with his son. "He was very companionable with his kids," said his secretary, Alice Kernan Berlinghoff. "But Bobby was a loner. He just kept it all to himself."

Jackie was eighteen when her father became publisher, an awkward adolescent — bright, dark-haired, and slightly overweight. Marian urged her to "work on that diet," and Arthur insensitively informed her that while he was sending his other grandchildren Halloween candy, she was not on the list, explaining, "I don't want to put temptation in your way." Orvil was well aware that Jackie suffered by comparison with her beautiful mother, and he went out of his way to make her feel special. One evening she came home to find her parents hosting a party for Nelson Rockefeller. From the chattering masses Orvil rushed up and threw his arms around her, exclaiming, "Ah, my favorite person!"

Susie struggled with dyslexia and was a slow learner like her mother but, being the baby of the family, was the adored apple of her father's eye. Orvil scratched her back before she went to bed just as he had Judy's when he was courting Marian, and he pulled Susie onto his lap during dinner parties, no matter how distinguished the company. For her Sweet Sixteen party, he hung sugar cubes from ribbons and dangled them from the dining-room chandelier. "In my circle of friends he was the favorite father," she recalled. "I just wanted more of him than I could have."

Bobby, the darkly handsome middle child, was the odd man out in the Dryfoos ménage. "Every opportunity they had, Jackie and Marian would put him down," said Jackie's former husband, Stuart Greenspon. "They gave him no respect, no emotional support." Orvil's ease with girls, coupled with Marian's cool brand of motherhood and the pressure of being the only male offspring of the *New York Times* publisher, conspired to produce a solitary, angry, and alarmingly self-sufficient spirit. Among his siblings and cousins, Bobby was known as the "lone wolf." He often sat through meals without saying a word. "My brother is not cocktail party–fluent," said Jackie. "He does not schmooze; he's never known how to schmooze."

At the Hill School in Pottstown, Pennsylvania, which he entered in 1958, Bobby scored a perfect 800 on his math SATs but made only average grades. He constantly ran afoul of boarding-school regulations, most of which he considered foolish and arbitrary. "My teenage rebellion was not directed at my parents," he said. "My wars were [about] rules with no reasons. If you can't convince me there's a good reason for doing something, then we're not going to get along too well." Sensing her grandson's isolation, Iphigene invited him to Shakespearean plays in Stratford, Connecticut, and to a viewing of a lunar eclipse in Canada. Orvil tried to engage him in debates about issues at the paper. But Bobby remained elusive, and even Jim Weiskopf, his Hill School roommate and best friend, had no idea what was going on in his head. The quotation under Bobby's yearbook picture summed it up. "Every bird loves to hear himself sing."

Despite his spotty record, Bobby managed to get into Dartmouth, aided no doubt by his father's prestigious title and status as an alumnus and trustee. But Orvil thought his son too immature for college and insisted that he defer entry for a year and work instead. Bobby clerked briefly on Wall Street and then did research for IBM, a job Orvil and Marian had arranged through IBM president Thomas J. Watson Jr., a family friend.

That summer, as usual, Orvil and Marian closed up their city apartment and made the seasonal exodus to Rock Hill. The forested estates of suburban Connecticut held no allure for an adolescent boy, especially one in a state of active revolt. At the Dryfooses' request, Orvil's younger brother, Hugh, a round teddy bear of a man who manufactured Christmas ornaments, took Bobby into the Park Avenue apartment he shared with his wife, Joan, and their two young boys. For Bobby, living with them was like slipping into a soothing bath. "They were very, very warm," he said. "They treated me like their eldest son."

That kind of closeness was clearly lacking in the Dryfoos marriage. As early as the mid-1950s, Orvil would stop off at his brother's apartment on his way home from the *Times* and talk to Joan while she fed the children. He liked the cozy informality of the cluttered kitchen and Joan's hands-on mothering, both of which contrasted sharply with the nannies, starched napkins, and uniformed servants of his own household. He envied the easy laughter and love that was apparent between his brother and sister-in-law. "Hugh and I were mad about each other, and it showed," said Joan. "I think in many ways Orvil was an unhappy man."

By the time he became publisher, whatever passion had existed at one time between Orvil and Marian was clearly spent, although they both maintained appearances and were perfectly cordial with each other. How Orvil coped with the void in his emotional life is unclear. He once made a pass at Bobbie Adler, Marian's cousin, after a Century Country

Club dance, and politely backed off when she informed him it was not welcome. As for Marian, she followed her father's example and sought comfort outside her marriage. Later, when her daughters were having their own marital troubles, she would advise them not to divorce. "Just get a lover and keep your marriage going," she said. "It's European."

§

Despite his many infirmities and his vow to pull back, Arthur continued to loom as a powerful and demanding figure in his positions as chairman and undisputed family patriarch. "I don't just talk to hear myself!" he ranted to Orvil in one of his infamous blue notes soon after giving up the publishership.

At every turn, Arthur encountered reminders that his influence at *The New York Times* was on the wane. One day he called from Hillandale and asked for Mr. Sulzberger's office; he was connected to Punch. He then asked for the chairman's office, and was connected to the chairman of the local branch of the printers union in the composing room. His eyesight was so poor that Iphigene had to read books and editorials to him, and some days he didn't even bother her to do that. "I have grown mentally lazy and, quite frankly, somewhat indifferent," Arthur confessed to Charles Merz. By his seventieth birthday he was visibly depressed. "He was down; he had lost his joie de vivre," said Judy.

Hillandale was his only tonic. Using the golf cart he had received as a retirement present, he navigated the grounds, ordering bushes moved to widen paths or a stone wall torn down to enlarge a gate. Occasionally he let Judy's two sons ride with him. On one such trip they dubbed the estate Bumpy's Acres, a name that implied ownership, which pleased Arthur enormously because he well knew that the Ochs Trust held the deed.

Because of his position at the *Times*, Arthur had never been free to invest in the stock market; the danger of a conflict of interest was too great. So, after the move to the "new" Hillandale in the early 1950s, acquiring property became his one extravagance. Soon he owned small, scattered tracts of land adjacent to the estate. His goal was to buy up enough property so that, upon his death, some of it could be sold off, and the profit used to develop the remainder into a park that would be donated to Connecticut or New York State. By 1965 of the more than 277 acres that made up the compound, 100 acres were in Arthur's name.

Finally, after ten years of underwriting Arthur's personal version of Monopoly, Iphigene had had enough. When he announced that he intended to buy yet another fifteen acres, she refused. Arthur was stunned at being defied, and he and Iphigene had what he later described as the "first serious argument" of their forty-five-year marriage. He explained his side of the dispute in a letter to his children and, in a sarcastic aside, asked if it would be all right for him to spend $1.25 for a new pair of boxer shorts, explaining, "I need some." Like her siblings, Marian knew how it felt to be on the receiving end of her father's wrath, and she took this opportunity to dress him down. "Mother has given of herself extraordinarily," she told him in a scolding tone. "I have rarely, if ever, heard her complain or disagree with you. . . . Now she is standing her ground. I admire her for that."

It was Hillandale, in part, that motivated Iphigene to "stand her ground." Though she had never been domestically inclined, the woods and gardens awakened in her a surprising proprietariness. Arthur gave her an apron with a smiling face on it and instructed her to wear it backwards; if all he was going to see of her was her rear end when she was weeding, he said, at least he wanted to view a pleasant expression. Iphigene knew the names of all her flowers and made it clear to Gino Rossi, the Italian-born gardener, that she had a decided preference for blue delphiniums and only white or pink geraniums, never red. "She never raised her voice but she told me what she thought," said Rossi. "She didn't hit the donkey; she hit the saddle so the donkey understand [sic] it."

The struggle over Hillandale's landscaping soon became a metaphor for the unacknowledged undercurrents of power and resentment in the Sulzbergers' relationship. Once Arthur told Gino to cut down a tree that was blocking his view of the lake. The next time Iphigene passed by the spot, she was appalled to see the ragged stump. "What happened to my favorite tree?" she demanded. Rossi meekly replied that he had simply followed Arthur's instructions. "I still own this land," Iphigene told him in an uncharacteristically hard voice, drawing out every word. It was a phrase she came to use often with regard to arrangements at Hillandale, and her meaning was unmistakable.

Arthur's retaliation took its traditional forms: yelling and — despite his failing health — assignations with young women. Many afternoons Arthur would retreat with one of his nurses to a small building near the Hillandale tennis courts outfitted with a daybed and a few other amenities. In his better days, Iphigene had nonchalantly told visitors the cottage was "the place where Arthur takes his girlfriends." Now she cautioned the grandchildren never to interrupt their grandfather when he was there because he was "having his rest." "She put up with it because my father was sick," said Judy. "She thought, 'Well, if that makes him happy...'"

After Iphigene discovered that Arthur was paying one of the nurses to have sexual relations with him, the nurse, in turn, assumed such a mocking, impertinent air with Iphigene that the Sulzberger matriarch could no longer tolerate having her in the house. Iphigene would never be so crude as to confront the woman directly; instead, she spoke with Arthur's physician, Dr. George Carden Jr., who was fully aware of his patient's extracurricular activities. "I don't think much of this nurse," said Iphigene pointedly. "I don't, either," agreed Carden, instantly intuiting her real meaning. With that, Carden dismissed the nurse on medical grounds; as a parting gesture, Iphigene gave her a generous check. "She handled this with so much sophistication," said Carden. "I changed nurses on several occasions because of something she said."

The domestic unpleasantness was largely hidden from the Sulzberger children, grandchildren, and guests, who considered Hillandale their own personal paradise. With its neatly mowed lawns, lush gardens, accommodating servants, and predictable routines, it was an idyllic and self-referential community, a touchstone for the Sulzbergers just as Hyannis Port was for the Kennedys, and a place where every generation renewed the bonds of blood, affection, and shared history that held them together. Yet by unspoken consensus the embrace was never too tight, never too intimate. "This may be one of the reasons we get along as well as we do," said Judy. "Because we don't have this very deep kind of emotional relationship with each other."

For Marian, Judy, and Punch's children, who lived in New York City or its suburbs, the estate's protocols were a more exalted version of their normal lives. But for the "long-distance cousins" in Chattanooga — the children of Ruth and Ben Golden — Hillandale was a place of near mythical proportions, a place that, long after they became adults, they continued to describe as "magical," a "fantasy," a "wonderland." "The smell of it, the whole feel of it was so evocative," said Ruth's daughter, Lynn. "It was just this separate world."

Every summer, usually before the Fourth of July, the four young Goldens arrived at Hillandale without their parents, making the trip from Chattanooga by train in the early years and later by plane. In New York they were met by Joseph, the Sulzbergers' personable chauffeur, who took their luggage and ushered them into the family limousine. Often Arthur was in the backseat, his legs covered by Adolph Ochs's lap robe, which still bore the initials ASO. When the car passed a certain red barn near the Sulzberger compound, the children let out a loud squeal, knowing that in a few moments they would climb up Rock Rimmon Road to a secluded, special haven.

Meals were the axis around which Hillandale life revolved, and they were as regular and ritualized as a religious ceremony. For the Goldens, who lived during the year in what Arthur described as the "sweetest, sloppiest Southern home I've [ever] seen," the formality was daunting. "God forbid your roast beef should fling off your plate," said Lynn. Everyone was expected to dress for dinner, which meant skirts or dresses for the girls and for the boys long pants, a clean shirt, and, on certain occasions, a tie. At the appointed hour the group gathered in the sunroom for cocktails and hors d'oeuvres of shrimp, nuts, olives, and crudités. The dining-room table was set with elegant china, sterling silver, and stemware, and at each place was a finger bowl, a plate with a small hand-rolled ball of butter, and an individual service of salt and pepper. Once seated, the family and their guests solemnly awaited the sacrament of the corn, for a sacrament it was.

Every summer the Hillandale garden yielded thousands of ears of corn, carefully planted in sequence so that several bushels were always available at the peak of freshness. Iphigene was especially fond of young corn — so young that the individual kernels did not touch one another — and issued strict instructions that the corn was not to be picked until the cooking water was boiling. Corn was the first course at every meal except breakfast as long as the season lasted, and no one ever complained of monotony. "We *like* corn," Arthur told one of the estate's several gardeners in a letter instructing him to plant extra rows. "As far as I'm concerned you can throw the rest of the garden out!"

When the corn was barely boiled, a servant in a starched uniform burst from the kitchen carrying a silver platter with her precious cargo wrapped in a white linen napkin. As she went around the table, each person took an ear, holding it by the small handles embedded at each end, and placed it in the glass corn dish at his or her place. After buttering and seasoning the corn, the diners attacked with gusto, some eating circumferentially, some eating typewriter-fashion, some gnawing away in arbitrary bites, all of which was observed in clinical detail and thoroughly discussed. Arthur was particularly critical of diners who ate circumferentially instead of in rows, a technique that inexplicably violated his sense of order. When the first round was done, the maid collected the shorn cobs and brought around a steaming platter with seconds. A dinner of lamb, chicken, or beef usually followed, summoned by Iphigene, who pressed a floor buzzer with her foot to signal to the help that the next course was to be served. Afterward the family retired to the library for coffee, nonpareils, and candied ginger.

Lunch was only slightly less formal. In good weather Iphigene would order a table set up in the yard complete with white tablecloth, silverware, and china. Iced tea mixed with orange juice — an Iphigene signature — appeared in tall glasses. If it was a Saturday, Punch could be counted on to cook hamburgers on a portable barbecue set up near the front door, a male servant standing at attention by his side holding a silver tray stacked with raw patties. The Sunday meal was yet another distinct ritual, mainly because Judy, her sons, Daniel and James — known as Dan and Jace — and her husband, Dick Cohen, were always present.

In spring the fare ran to shad roe, in summer to steamed artichokes, which Iphigene persuaded the children to eat by letting them make designs with the discarded leaves. Manners were paramount. "A knife and fork are like Bumpy and Granny: inseparable," Iphigene intoned. "They go together at the top of the plate when you're eating and when you're finished, they go together in the middle of the plate."

After a nap Arthur would emerge from his bedroom, gather whatever grandchildren were available, and take them on a tour of the grounds in his Hillman Minx convertible, a milky white English sedan that bore his initials on the left-hand door and Iphigene's on the right. Several of the children thought Arthur "scary" and "distant." At meals he was often silent. "Every once in a while a fire would light and he would charge into the conversation," said Stephen Golden. "It would continue sometimes, for just a few minutes, and then he would fade back into quietness." Even in his diminished state, he was capable of humor. When one of Michael Golden's baby teeth disappeared down the bathroom sink and he worried that he had nothing to offer the tooth fairy, Arthur gave him the walrus tusk Admiral Richard Byrd had brought back as a gift from one of his expeditions.

For Dan and Jace, the Hillandale Sundays provided an oasis of order in their emotionally perplexing lives. Their father, Mattie Rosenschein, had failed to make child-support payments after his divorce from Judy and saw his sons infrequently. In 1960, under pressure from Judy, he agreed to give them up, and Dick Cohen officially adopted them and gave them his last name. After the adoption, Dan and Jace were instructed to call Dick "Daddy" while Mattie disappeared almost completely from their lives, even though he lived just a few miles from them in Pound Ridge, New York. One day Jace was standing at a major intersection in Pound Ridge and recognized his father, who was preparing to park his Volkswagen and go into his medical office. Jace waved excitedly, but when Mattie saw him, he just turned his head and continued on his way. "He remarried and had four sons with his new wife, and I guess he just decided it was better for all of us to start our families afresh," said Dan.

23

Hapless Punch

LTHOUGH PUNCH HAD BEEN AT *THE NEW YORK*
Times for more than ten years by the time Orvil was made publisher, he had not advanced very far. Shortly before the transfer
of power, a *Time* reporter had asked Arthur about his son's role in the
company and Arthur had vaguely replied that Punch was "studying
the business and pitching in." The fact was that Punch had become the
Times' version of the Prince of Wales: hapless, not taken seriously, and
without a job of substance. "He was undersold [by his family] and
underemployed," a senior executive later told *The New Yorker*. "He was
kept away from the hub."

Arthur bore much of the blame for the situation. After carefully
orchestrating Punch's moves to Milwaukee, Paris, and Rome, he did not
seem to know what to do with him in New York. His dutiful hope was
that Punch would one day succeed Orvil as publisher, assuming that he
had "demonstrated his capacity to take on the big job." But Punch's poor
academic record, failed first marriage, and seeming lack of ambition did
not inspire confidence. Orvil was firmly in place for at least the next fifteen years; there was little for Punch to do but wait.

Like Arthur and Orvil before him, Punch spent several years as assistant to the publisher, doing "whatever I was asked to do." Because so
little was expected of him, he took a rather casual attitude toward his
training and quickly got a reputation as a rich, pampered playboy, a
characterization his father did nothing to discourage. One of Arthur's
own secretaries referred to Punch as a "glorified office boy" behind his
back without fear of reprisal. He attended news conferences and Publisher's Luncheons but often seemed distracted, more interested in
examining the air-conditioning ducts in the ceiling than in the business
at hand.

When Arthur named Orvil president of *The New York Times* in 1957, he made Punch assistant treasurer, a change motivated largely by his desire to give Punch the opportunity, as an officer of the company, to sit in on board meetings. The financial responsibilities of the job were minimal, which was fortuitous since Punch, by his own admission, could barely balance his own checkbook. His chief duty was to hand-sign payroll checks, a chore so tedious that he bought the company's first check-signing machine. Even this minor achievement was undercut when he put the checks in upside down and all the signatures came out on the upper-left-hand corner. Punch attended the board meetings faithfully — it was the only time other executives saw father and son together — but rarely contributed to the discussion.

From his seventh-floor office, Punch also oversaw his father's pet project: the construction of a new *Times* plant on the West Side. Arthur had never known the satisfaction of erecting a statement-making building, and he yearned for it. On a three-block-long tract on West End Avenue, not far from what is now Lincoln Center, he envisioned a future home for *The New York Times*, a gleaming structure of steel and glass with a twelve-to-twenty-story tower rising from its center. The site's most appealing feature was its proximity to West Side rail lines, which, it was hoped, would eliminate the need to truck papers and newsprint through the snarled traffic of midtown Manhattan.

The building's design, in which Arthur took an active role, was totally impractical. The first stage, an auxiliary printing and distribution facility, was, said Walter Mattson, then the *Times'* production manager, the "worst of Forty-third Street moved up to West End Avenue." Tractor-trailers could not turn around in the narrow driveways; there was no room to stack the giant rolls of newsprint efficiently. The press conveyors were the longest in the business and broke down constantly. "From a technological point of view, the building was a disaster," said Mike Ryan, who oversaw the facility as assistant general manager. On its inaugural night — July 28, 1959 — the plant managed to produce only 1,250 papers.

For Punch, who loved all things mechanical, the West Side plant was a perfect assignment. He chaired the *Times* committee that thrashed out architectural and technical decisions, dictating detailed minutes that sometimes ran fifteen to twenty pages. After anguished debate, he persuaded his father to sell Adolph Ochs's Times Tower, arguing that the coming West Side plant made it an extravagant heirloom. The *Times* retained only a small fourth-floor office to run the zipper, the electronic news bulletin that encircled the tower, which hadn't housed any operating units of the paper for forty-seven years.

Like a pharaoh inspecting his monument, Arthur took great pleasure in visiting the West Side plant as it went up, dashing off blue notes to Punch about matters as minuscule as dirt in the unused mailroom and a disorderly box of fire hoses. At his behest, a ten-foot-high aluminum eagle with an eight-foot-wide wingspan was hoisted over the entrance, a replica of an eighteenth-century carved pine eagle Arthur had purchased in a London antiques shop in 1958. Soon Arthur insisted that the eagle become the *Times'* emblem, a likeness of which appeared in the upper-left-hand corner of the editorial page and on the paper's corporate seal. The original wooden bird, whose folded wings suggested to Arthur both peace and strength, stood in the West Side plant lobby.*

At the *Times,* Punch called himself a jack-of-all-trades, and his father certainly treated him like one. When Punch became responsible for the paper's cafeteria, Arthur passed along Iphigene's complaints about the quality of the coffee, which she considered "the dregs of the dregs." He asked Punch to water the trees outside the West Side plant and to locate a slide for the Hillandale pool. "You would see Punch wandering around the newsroom," said Joe Lelyveld, who started at the paper as a copyboy in 1962. "He was the ne'er-do-well son, supposedly, and he was said to be largely concerned with the disastrous reconstruction of the men's room on the third floor." So demeaning were Punch's duties that several executives quietly took it upon themselves to discuss the matter with Orvil. "Punch is getting no training at all," Ivan Veit told him. "Someday you'll want to give him more responsibility, and he won't be ready." Orvil, who frequently voiced doubts about whether Punch even read the newspaper, reacted with uncharacteristic impatience, replying, "Well, this is all he wants."

Orvil, who carefully monitored Arthur for cues, was ambivalent about Punch. As an in-law he was friendly, but at the office he was often dismissive. "He considered Punch as a little brother," said Orvil's secre-

---

*The West Side plant, considered an impractical albatross by many at the *Times,* was never fully completed and closed in 1976.

tary, Alice Kernan Berlinghoff. "Not incompetent, just immature." Along with Amory Bradford, Orvil had come to believe that despite the senior Sulzbergers' hopes, Punch might not be the appropriate choice to succeed him in the distant future. When, at Iphigene's urging, Arthur suggested making Punch a vice president, Orvil and Amory opposed it on the grounds that it would send a signal to Punch and to others that the publishership would inevitably be his one day. "Orvil and I both agreed that it would be a disaster to have [Punch] take over the paper," said Bradford. "We needed to look for some other family solution."

Without committing himself as to Punch's long-term future, Arthur acceded to Orvil and Amory's wishes. In a letter from the Virgin Islands in the winter of 1961, he said he would not make Punch a vice president now as long as it was understood that if he, Arthur, were to die soon, Punch's name and title would be included on the masthead. At the end of the letter, under Arthur's wobbly signature, was a handwritten message from the person who no doubt had instigated the protective condition: "I agree with this. IOS."

Believing that Punch might benefit from more discipline and focus, Orvil gave him a new title: assistant to the general manager. The change put him under Amory's wing and brought him back up to the fourteenth floor, where he occupied a little office next to Bradford's that had originally been intended as an executive bedroom. To Amory, who prided himself on hard work, Punch was a protected, spoiled rich kid. "I [sat] down with him the way I would have with a young lawyer at Davis, Polk and explained the problem and gave him something to do," he said. "And I never got anything back that was worth anything."

Privately Punch considered Amory "a very strange duck"; publicly he was always polite and friendly. "I don't think I ever had a dispute with [Punch]," said Amory. But Punch's affability was misleading. He had long seethed about the humiliation Amory had inflicted on him in the mid-1950s, shortly after Punch had returned from Paris. As assistant to the publisher, Punch had inhabited a small office on the fourteenth floor not far from Orvil. When Bradford became a vice president in 1957, he, too, had arrived on the executive floor and immediately laid claim to a suite of rooms, including Punch's tiny cubbyhole. "You don't mind moving downstairs, do you?" he had inquired. Punch *did* mind, but he was damned if he was going to give Amory the satisfaction of knowing it. Carol and many of Punch's friends were vocal in their outrage; his father, who disdained special treatment for family members, did nothing. Punch, though inwardly furious, kept his counsel.

Technically, Punch had no right to complain about the move; he had just been made assistant treasurer, and it was appropriate for him to be on the same floor as the company treasurer, Frank Cox. But Punch was not just another *Times* employee; he was the Sulzbergers' only son, the putative heir apparent, and he had been treated in a manner he considered high-handed and disrespectful. Moreover, he had lost face in front of his new bride. "Punch has a long memory for slights," said a *Times* executive and close friend. Amory's subsequent campaign to prevent Punch from becoming a vice president only deepened the animosity.

Those early years were lonely and disheartening for Punch, who was less desperate about his situation than frustrated. "I think Punch had given up on the *Times*," said Harrison Salisbury. "He didn't think he was going anywhere on the paper. He was a wandering spirit." In this vast desert, there was a single oasis: Turner Catledge. The *Times*' avuncular managing editor attached himself to Punch and gave him what he needed most — comfort, guidance, a sympathetic shoulder, and a sense of belonging. "My feelings went way beyond liking [Turner]; I really loved the guy," said Punch, who rarely made such baldly emotional statements. "He was the biggest influence in my professional life." As if to underscore the point, Punch dubbed Turner "the Professor."

It was Turner's nature to adopt strays and orphans, and he took special care with displaced members of the Ochs and Sulzberger family. He had befriended Julie Jr. during his troubled tenure at the *Times* and attended his annual New Year's Eve party. Later he looked after Julie's never married sister, Nancy, when she became a reporter. In Punch's case, Turner had watched Arthur's and Orvil's behavior with increasing annoyance. It was degrading, he thought, to assign a future owner housekeeping chores. "He felt I was being totally wasted in what I was doing," said Punch.

Turner and Punch had divorced and remarried at about the same time, which made for a certain bond, and their new wives soon became friends. Catledge was also keenly aware that because Scotty Reston and Amory Bradford had Orvil's ear, his own influence in the Dryfoos regime was greatly diminished from what it had been under Arthur's. His remaining seat of power was what was known as the Club, the informal cocktail party he held in his office every afternoon after the news

conference. At Turner's invitation, Punch became a Club regular, dropping by for a glass of bourbon and good fellowship with men such as
advertising manager Monroe Green, promotion manager Irvin Taubkin,
circulation manager Nat Goldstein, and Ivan Veit.

Frequently the talk would turn to newspapers. "It was like a little seminar that anybody could participate in," said Clifton Daniel, an assistant
managing editor and occasional Club visitor. "Punch got his education
in running a newspaper from this group." Turner didn't lecture; he was
never didactic. He let Punch listen to the debate and ask questions. From
these discussions, Punch took away a nugget that became, for him, an
enduring aphorism: You make a newspaper for one person only — the
reader. "Turner gave me that wonderful advice, and it helps clarify
things," he said later.

§

Throughout the late 1950s and early 1960s, Punch was continually
strapped for money. Arthur and Iphigene were generous, making him
personal advances, smoothing the way for bank loans, and ordering the
bylaw changes necessary to elect him a director of *The Chattanooga
Times*, a job that paid $3,000 a year in directors' fees and alarmed Carol,
who feared it presaged a transfer to what she considered a "scruffy railroad town." Even so, Punch felt the need to borrow on his life insurance
and ask his sisters to advance him funds against his residuary interest in
the Ochs Trust. By their tenth anniversary, Punch and Carol jointly owed
Arthur and Iphigene $132,500 and smaller amounts to various banks.

One reason for the spiraling debt was child support and the divorce
settlement with Barbara, but Carol's taste for fine things was also a factor. She had a discerning eye for expensive antiques and loved to decorate;
every few years she would completely overhaul their living quarters. "She
has shopped every day since the day she married him," said Punch's secretary, Nancy Finn. "It's her avocation." As the keeper of Punch's personal checkbook, Nancy paid the household bills; when the balance was
perilously low, she would warn Punch. Usually he was too embarrassed
to ask his mother directly for funds, so Nancy would take it upon herself
to call Eddie Greenbaum. He would quietly approach Iphigene, who
with a quick payment would extricate Punch from what his father delicately called his "financial jam."

Punch and his siblings were forced to turn to Iphigene for money mostly because of the way the Ochs Trust was structured, but the arrangement eventually came to suit her, giving her a measure of power and control over her children, as well as over Arthur. "I think she liked to feel that they had to come to her," said Lady Susan Pulbrook. Most onlookers assumed that since Punch, Judy, Ruth, and Marian would one day inherit *The New York Times,* they must be rich. For each of the four families, however, the day-to-day reality was quite different. While they certainly had money at their disposal, much of it was not actually theirs.

That, coupled with the family ethic against ostentation, produced an unusual dynamic: despite being raised in great comfort, several of the Sulzberger grandchildren considered themselves practically destitute. Jackie Dryfoos fretted that she was in financial jeopardy every time she spied her father in the library poring over his large black ledger. When she entered Smith College in the fall of 1961, she applied for a job in the school cafeteria, explaining, "I was always worried that there wasn't enough money." For those of Punch's generation, years of going hat-in-hand to Iphigene had the effect of ossifying them in childhood. Regardless of their actual age, they were forever "the children." In letters they often addressed their parents as Mommy and Daddy. "There is an infantile streak in all of them," said Marit Gruson, a family friend. "They talk a little like children. Even Punch has a childlike voice."

Unlike Orvil and Dick, Judy's husband, Carol was determined to resist the centripetal pull of the Sulzbergers, especially Iphigene, whom she considered cold and opinionated, a dowager queen who wielded a power over Punch that Carol felt should be hers. To Carol, Iphigene was a baffling bluestocking who cared so little about her appearance that she chose to wear what Carol sneeringly referred to as "little old lady" clothes.

When Carol married Punch, the Sulzbergers had tried to make her feel welcome. During her first Christmas at Hillandale, she received an exquisitely wrapped wicker basket full of scarves, sweaters, and handbags — the gift Arthur always gave each of his daughters and daughters-in-law. "I was so impressed because I was immediately treated, at least as far as I could see, like all the other girls," said Carol.

But the open arms pulled in quickly, on both sides. Carol was at first hurt, then angered, by the family's devotion to Barbara, who at Iphigene's instigation continued to be invited to the clan's major gatherings.

"Her theory was, 'This person is the mother of my grandchildren, and I'm not going to just chuck that away; it's too important to the children,'" said Punch. For years after the divorce, Arthur kept Barbara's photograph on his bedroom bureau, a reminder to Punch of his humiliation in Paris and a calculated annoyance to Carol. Judy and Ellen Sulzberger Straus thought the picture so insulting to Carol that one day they slipped into Arthur's bedroom and stole the portrait from its frame, much to Arthur's fury. He was sufficiently embarrassed, however, to write Carol soon thereafter and ask for *her* picture. But as his secretary noted in a handwritten aside on the office copy of Arthur's letter: "Somehow I don't think he really wants one."

Carol didn't help matters by calling Punch by his given name — Arthur — and launching a concerted and ultimately unsuccessful campaign to make the rest of the family follow suit. "She feels that *Punch* is a child's name," explained her daughter, Cathy. "When they were married, he was the baby, [but] she never saw him in that way."

Carol's relations with Marian, Ruth, and Judy were equally cool and correct. "They didn't think Carol was good enough," said Nancy Finn. "[They considered] her Seventh Avenue," shorthand for New York's teeming garment business. As far as the sisters were concerned, Carol was whiny, unhappy, and superficial, a woman who refused to fulfill her duties as a member of the family that owned *The New York Times.* She often declined to accompany Punch to business functions that wives attended. Even at social events hosted by old friends, Punch often showed up alone. "For years she wouldn't play ball," said Elly Elliott, who had known the Sulzbergers since childhood. "Carol just didn't want to be involved." Few recognized that Carol was simply too shy and lacking in self-confidence to plunge into a crowd of people she didn't know. "Carol is really quite narrow," said Iphigene's friend Audrey Topping. "It's an innate thing: she feels very uncomfortable with anyone who isn't in her circle."

These fissures in the Sulzbergerian commonweal closed temporarily in May 1959, when Punch adopted Cathy. Her biological father, Cy Fuhrman, had continued to live in California, and although he clearly cared for his daughter, he rarely saw her. Carol urged Punch to do what was best for Cathy — to make her feel like a full member of the Sulzberger family "rather than the one who stuck out," as Punch put it — and he agreed.

The rhythms of the younger Sulzberger household were largely dictated by the obligations of Punch's divorce. Every other weekend he took charge of Arthur Jr. and Karen. In the winter they stayed in the city; in the summer they gathered at Hillandale. The urban weekends were a bit cramped because, although Punch and Carol had rented a seven-room apartment at 1010 Fifth Avenue, twelve floors above Orvil and Marian, there was no separate bedroom for visitors, so Arthur Jr. and Karen had to make do with a pullout couch. Like most divorced dads, Punch filled his visits with nonstop activity: *Cinderella* and *Mary Poppins* one visit, the rodeo the next, the Empire State Building and the Statue of Liberty the next, each event followed by a Chinese dinner of spareribs and egg rolls washed down by Coca-Cola.

The divorce was hard on the children, and on Barbara, who had found in the Sulzberger family the security and acceptance so lacking in her own. By the time Punch remarried, she and the children had settled on the Upper East Side of Manhattan in the same building as Julie Jr.; his wife, Anne; and their young son, Doug. In these new surroundings, Barbara tried to be a better mother than she had been in Paris, but Arthur Jr. and Karen needed some convincing. When their French nurse, Georgette, returned to France and Barbara didn't hire a replacement, Karen asked in bewilderment, "Who's going to take care of us now?" "Well, I will," said Barbara. Karen stared at her mother in disbelief. "I remember thinking, 'Well, she is this very nice, pretty lady, but she doesn't know what toys I like in my bath or how I like my food cut up or any of that kind of thing.'"

Arthur Jr. had grown into a quiet, handsome boy, small for his age, slightly wan, and naturally sweet toward his mother. Soon after the divorce he suggested to Barbara that they have a tea party, "just the two of us." Barbara went to the kitchen to fix a tray. When she reappeared in the dining room, she could hardly believe her eyes. The windows had been shuttered, and the room was bathed in candlelight. A vase of flowers, taken from the living room, adorned the table. Arthur Jr., wriggling with delight, sat on the couch while his favorite song, "Old MacDonald Had a Farm," played on the record player. Mother and son sipped tea and ate cookies for a few moments, until Arthur Jr. broke the silence. "Oh, Mother, isn't this fun?" he exclaimed. "It's so cozy!"

Having been virtually ignored by his own father, Punch had little idea how to be a warm, understanding parent, especially to a son. "He didn't touch his children a lot," said Barbara. "He adored them; it just didn't show." In the absence of hugs and roughhousing, Punch connected with his kids in the one way with which he was most familiar: working with his hands. In his Manhattan apartment he converted a small maid's room into a workshop and kiln. During their weekends together, he and Arthur Jr. and Karen worked on endless enamel and tile projects and fashioned bowls out of clay. "I remember making a thousand ashtrays," said Karen.

Punch's absence was particularly difficult for Arthur Jr. "He wanted a male in his life," said Barbara. "Anybody I would date, he would ask me whether I was going to marry." In David Christy, a New York business-man and divorced father of three, Barbara believed she had found what was missing in Punch: a man who was physically affectionate and won-derful with small children. "He was a big, fun, charged, energized father figure who played with us on the floor," said Arthur Jr. "He was the kind [of man] who would throw the ball and walk you to school." Barbara and David married in 1958 and soon had two children of their own, a boy and a girl. Arthur and Iphigene sent baby presents on both occa-sions. Punch found out about the first one by accident when one of his father's secretaries made an idle remark about it, and the news sent him into a frenzy of profanity. "If my father wants to be generous, he should pick somebody else's ex-wife!" he yelled.

§

For Orvil, the autumn of 1962 was a period of both triumph and strain. On October 1 he was in California to oversee the successful launch of the western edition. Then, three weeks later, he was forced again to face the grave question of whether the *Times,* in the interest of national security, should print an important story. This time the issue was the Cuban mis-sile crisis.

On Sunday morning, October 21, in a conversation with Kennedy national security adviser McGeorge Bundy, Scotty Reston confirmed that the Russians had placed missiles in Cuba, just ninety miles off the Florida coast. When Bundy told the president that Scotty was aware of the top-secret information, Kennedy called Reston directly. He was planning to go on television the following evening to tell the American people about the missiles, he explained, and needed twenty-four hours to complete his plan for retaliation — a naval blockade of Cuba. If the

Times published the news about the missiles before the blockade was in place, Soviet premier Nikita Khrushchev could give Kennedy an ultimatum before he went on the air or, even worse, threaten to activate the missiles and force an attack. "I'll report what you have said to my office in New York," Scotty replied. "If my advice is asked, I will recommend that we not publish, but it is not my duty to decide."

Kennedy then phoned Orvil, who — true to his vision of himself as "coach" — tossed the question of whether to withhold publication back to Scotty and the Washington bureau. The paper's recent decision regarding the Bay of Pigs weighed heavily on their minds. In that case, the *Times* had edited out a crucial word and de-emphasized the story; still, a piece of some sort had appeared. In the case of the missiles in Cuba, however, the paper was being asked to say nothing about a potentially explosive situation. Max Frankel, the State Department correspondent in charge of writing the missile story, had by prearrangement listened in on Scotty's phone conversation with the president and now challenged his inclination to capitulate to the government's wishes. "How do we know there's going to be a blockade, and if there is, that there won't be a landing to seize the missiles?" he asked. "Kennedy doesn't have the right to take the country to war while asking us to be silent. If we withhold the story, we should get assurances that no blood will be spilled." Scotty called the White House back and asked whether, in exchange for holding the story for a day, the *Times* could be certain that Kennedy would not use military force. The president gave his word of honor.

Scotty relayed this information back to Orvil in New York. Coincidentally, five weeks earlier, on September 13, the *Times* publisher had met privately with Kennedy at the White House to discuss national security and the press. During their forty-minute conversation, Kennedy had cursed "a great deal" and pushed for press controls, even suggesting that the CIA report all conversations between newspapers and the Pentagon. Normally mild-mannered, Orvil had surprised the president and even himself by taking the offensive. He had urged Kennedy not to make rules for the press about what was and was not in the national interest, but simply to permit editors to continue making judgments on a case-by-case basis. He reminded the president that the *Times* had altered and downplayed the Bay of Pigs story, and Kennedy repeated what he had told Turner Catledge two weeks after the botched invasion: "I wish you had run it — I wish you had run everything on

Cuba." Uppermost in Orvil's mind were words in the briefing memo Turner had prepared for him in anticipation of his White House meeting: "National security should not be confused with political security."

Now, barely a month later, with the perceived threat of nuclear war, Orvil made up his mind to hold the story for twenty-four hours. What appeared in the *Times* the following day was a carefully worded piece, written by Max Frankel but unbylined, saying that there was "an air of crisis in the capital tonight" prompted by speculation that there was "a new development on Cuba." That evening Kennedy appeared on television to announce the presence of Russian missiles and the U.S. naval blockade. Three days later, after Khrushchev had backed down, he sent Orvil a letter thanking him for his "cooperation."

Whether the *Times'* self-censorship contributed to a peaceful resolution of the crisis is difficult to assess. Frankel, for one, came to feel that although the paper made the best decision it could at the time, nothing cataclysmic would have happened if the paper had printed everything it knew. "Kennedy wanted total surprise and a united world on his side," he said later. "It was a matter of convenience and propaganda skill that Kennedy was buying, not safety. And that's not a powerful enough reason [to withhold a story]."

Arthur was barely aware of the critical decisions with which his son-in-law had been faced. He had had his own personal trauma to deal with: the death of his younger brother, David, at the age of sixty-four. For years David had battled a bad heart made worse by heavy drinking. Toward the end, he had required an oxygen tent. "His last years were so wasted," Cy wrote Arthur. "[I recall] your trips abroad when you acted as a kind of nursemaid and private-personal vomitorium. . . . All of this must, I fear, make you feel very old and somewhat lonely." Marian, who understood the affectionate yet competitive relationship her father and uncle had had, admired the "courage and fortitude" Arthur showed in the wake of his brother's passing. "It certainly has been an inspiration to me," she told him in a condolence note. "I only hope we have inherited a small part of this." At the time, she could not know how very soon she would be forced to find out.

24

A Quiet Leader

SINCE ITS BIRTH IN 1851, *THE NEW YORK TIMES* had managed without fail to print a newspaper every day of its existence, with the exception of a nine-day period in 1953, when a strike by photoengravers shut down the *Times* and every other major newspaper in New York City. Strikes by the drivers who hauled papers to newsstands and other distribution points had occasionally prevented the newspaper from reaching readers, but the *Times* itself had always been printed. Its near perfect record was due largely to Arthur's publicly stated position that he would never allow a strike to occur because of a disagreement over money. He had long ago drawn the line at permitting the Newspaper Guild to impose a union shop on the newsroom, but if higher wages or shorter hours were the issue, he preferred to accommodate union demands rather than suspend production of the newspaper.

To many, Arthur's strategy was incomprehensible, as it gave the Guild and the nine printing-craft unions at the paper carte blanche to push for whatever financial concessions they wished, confident that the *Times* was likely to grant them and that the Sulzbergers would be satisfied as long as the company made a modest profit. Other New York papers disapproved of the higher costs that resulted from the *Times*' contracts, which, because the craft unions generally negotiated the same deal with all newspapers, they were pressured to match. But at least they had subsidies from chain ownership or family fortunes in nonjournalistic enterprises to cushion the blow. *The New York Times* had neither. Still, Arthur believed it was his democratic duty to "keep the newspaper alive," as he put it, in order to provide the community with "its chief defense weapon: the right to be fully informed." He also reasoned that permitting a strike only encouraged readers and advertisers to defect to rival papers. Besides, if the *Times'* plush contracts forced added costs on his competitors, wasn't that ultimately to the *Times'* advantage?

Arthur's philosophy was still intact in December 1962, when the printers, represented by the International Typographical Union (ITU), led a strike against *The New York Times,* the *Daily News,* the *Journal-American,* and the *World Telegram & Sun* that lasted a record-breaking 114 days. The siege sounded the death knell for much of New York journalism. Within several years of the strike's conclusion, the number of papers in the city dwindled from seven to three — the *Times* and two tabloids, the *New York Post* and the *Daily News.*

On its face, the disagreement appeared to be about money, working conditions, and job security, but what the *Times* and its sister publications did not realize was that the president of the ITU, a canny, forty-one-year-old Irishman named Bert Powers, had a hidden agenda that had almost nothing to do with the stated issues. Powers calculated that a long, drawn-out strike would crack the hegemony of the Newspaper Guild, which had long called the shots in the world of New York newspaper labor agreements by virtue of the fact that its contract expired October 31, five weeks earlier than those of the craft unions. Since the early 1950s it had been an article of faith among publishers that whatever terms the Guild agreed to during its biennial negotiations would be accepted by the craft unions. Powers wanted to wrest this standard-setting power away from the Guild by requiring that all union contracts share a common expiration date. In the process, he hoped to catapult himself and the ITU into a more powerful position within the New York labor hierarchy.

Powers had been spoiling for a strike well before his election as president of ITU Local No. 6 in May 1961. In the fall of 1960 his predecessor, Francis Barrett, had negotiated a contract so unpopular with the membership that by early 1961 it still had not been ratified. Further hampering its acceptance was the *Times'* dismissal of a printer for swearing at his foreman. Arbitration upheld the firing, but eager to forestall a strike, the *Times* reinstated the man shortly before the ITU election. The conciliatory gesture helped Powers win, and he in turn helped get the contract ratified by a slim margin.

The episode lulled the *Times'* point man in labor negotiations, Amory Bradford, into believing he could handle Powers, even manipulate him, but Powers knew he was just biding his time until the ITU contract came up for renewal in 1962. That was when he planned to take his union out on strike, thereby forcing a reluctant Guild and the other craft unions to go out in sympathy.

When the 1962 contract talks began in late July, Amory was confident that he and Powers could find common ground. Impressed by Bradford's gritty independence, the Publishers Association had chosen him to be spokesman and chief negotiator for all the city's papers; Orvil sat on the association's owners' committee as the *Times'* representative. In four months of talks, the publishers gave in on twenty contract changes proposed by the ITU while Powers, knowing that his real goal was a strike, not settlement, made only minor concessions. Amory was flummoxed. "It was the appearance of negotiation but no give," he said. "No give at all."

At 6:00 P.M. on December 7, eight hours before the ITU contract was set to expire, Amory assured the publishers that there would be no walkout. When the 2:00 A.M. deadline arrived, the printers calmly put down their rulers, vacated the *New York Times* composing room, and began their strike. On the eleventh floor of the New Yorker Hotel, where the negotiations had been taking place, Bradford looked across the table at Powers and in steely tones accused him of "a real double-cross."

Picket lines instantly appeared in front of the *Times,* the *Daily News,* the *Journal-American,* and the *World-Telegram & Sun,* while the *Mirror,* the *Post,* the *Herald Tribune,* the *Long Island Star-Journal,* and the *Long Island Press,* which had not been struck, stopped their presses and locked their doors in a show of ownership solidarity. At the *Times* Orvil personally took charge of the nine hundred employees who remained on the job out of his former workforce of five thousand. Soon advertising salesmen were running elevators, and three-quarters of the paper's city room was kept dark in an effort to save electricity.

For New Yorkers, the strike amounted to a news blackout. Some turned to television and newsmagazines; others picked up newsstand copies of *The Christian Science Monitor* or *The Wall Street Journal.* The *Times'* radio station, WQXR, more than doubled its broadcast time, adding live reports from nonstriking *New York Times* correspondents, most of whom had little concept of the impact of the spoken word. When Turner Catledge suggested reading a Scotty Reston column about southern blacks in Negro dialect, the idea went unremarked by other editors, and it was not until WQXR president Elliott Sanger diplomatically suggested that the notion might be "inadvisable" that Turner abandoned it.

Readers addicted to *The New York Times* had to content themselves with the scarce copies of the western edition that were air-shipped back to New York. As the impasse wore on, NBC-TV and NBC Radio launched "The New York Times of the Air," a Sunday program featuring the paper's editors and columnists. Everywhere, readers bemoaned the absence of the newspaper they had come to regard as their daily history book. At Wake Forest University in North Carolina, an editorial headlined WE MISS THE TIMES noted that Americans had lost "one of the mainstays of our civilization."

Amory, on edge before the strike, became increasingly tense as the weeks wore on. He possessed an alarming capacity for what his fourth wife vividly described as "righteous anger," and he was not shy about expressing it. "I could blow at any time," he said. Years before, during a labor dispute with the Newspaper Guild, he had bitten his pipe stem in two when a representative of the Hearst papers inadvertently bungled the negotiation. Now the days and nights of fruitless talks that frequently dragged on till dawn brought him to the snapping point. One evening he emerged from the negotiating room and, plunging into a crowd of waiting reporters, purposely kicked over several television cameras.

He soon resorted to brinkmanship to get his way. In mid-January 1963, in an effort to resolve the crisis, New York mayor Robert Wagner invited all sides to meet at City Hall. Amory fought the action furiously. The publishers were dead set against Wagner's becoming involved; they believed he would be pro-union for political reasons. But knowing it would look bad to snub the mayor's invitation, they unanimously overruled Amory, who, livid at being defied, put on his hat and coat and stalked out, declaring that he would not join them. The next morning he was back, persuaded by a frantic Orvil to change his mind.

During the seventeen days of talks that followed, Amory was so arrogant and offensive to the mayor's handpicked chief mediator, Theodore Kheel — a skilled negotiator who as a member of a presidential panel had just helped settle a longshoremen's strike — that he drove him to quit. Kheel had come up with a fresh solution to one of the thorniest issues in the dispute, but as he began explaining it to the publishers, Amory interrupted him. He told Mayor Wagner that he was "sick and tired of the whole proceeding" and thought the publishers were wasting their time at City Hall. At that, Kheel turned on Bradford. "If that's the way you feel, why don't you leave, because if you don't, I will," he said. After the publishers had adjourned, Kheel notified Wagner that he was pulling out. "Amory was trying to dominate the negotiations, and I felt strongly that a mediator should dominate," he explained later.

The next day Orvil visited Kheel at his law office at 30 Broad Street. "Bert Powers is out to kill us," he pleaded. "You are our only salvation. Please don't quit." Kheel agreed, and from that moment on, he said, "Amory was out of the picture." Kheel kept his job as city mediator and saw Amory at the negotiations, but his direct dealings with him were infrequent. Instead, he developed a relationship with the two most forceful newspapermen at the talks — Jack Flynn, publisher of the *Daily News*, and Walter Thayer, president of the *Herald Tribune*, who became the de facto spokesmen for the Publishers Association. Almost every evening the three men met secretly at "21" to review the bidding.

Back at the *Times*, Orvil set up a strike-defense office on the fourteenth floor, where he and his top news and business executives gathered, usually late at night after the end of that day's talks, to hear a progress report from Amory and to plot their next move. "We would be sitting around having martinis, and Amory would come in like Zeus: 'Here's the oracle, we can listen to the oracle now,'" said former production manager Tom Campion.

Amory treated his colleagues at the *Times* with the same hauteur he displayed at the bargaining table, and he was only slightly more respectful of Orvil. His attitude toward his boss was one of polite disdain, and he seemed determined to keep Orvil out of the loop regarding the talks. "I don't know why Amory won't tell me anything, why he doesn't call me," Orvil complained confidentially to assistant general manager Mike Ryan.

Amory's peremptory manner only added to Orvil's burden. Although he didn't have a New York paper to publish, the *Times* still generated 80,000 words a day for the western edition and 36,000 for the international edition. Every day he spent four or five hours walking through the building, trying to boost morale. Every night he sat in the strike-defense office, commiserating with his executives about strategy and trying to pry information out of Amory. His once-full social calendar was reduced to the essentials; on weekends he took short naps in his Fifth Avenue apartment. As the negotiations persisted into the night, he slept at the paper. The strike "has been the most exasperating and tiring experience I ever expect to have," he confided to John Oakes during the fourteenth week of the walkout. "It has been a night-and-day performance. . . . Just between us, the tension and nerve strain have not been a great help."

Orvil's tendency to worry took the form of a misplaced sense of responsibility for the crisis. Deep down, he felt that the debacle proved he was incapable of being publisher. "He took the strike so personally," said Punch. "It was as though it was his fault that all of these things were happening. It just ate at him in a most destructive way." By the end of January 1963, *The New York Times* was operating at a monthly deficit of $1.5 million and, with so many other papers out on strike, Spruce Falls, historically the *Times*' safety net, was suffering a 50 percent dip in demand for newsprint. When it was decided that only a draconian pay cut for *Times* employees would allow the paper to stay afloat, Orvil agonized like a man lashed to the rack.

At first he agreed to a 50 percent across-the-board reduction, but two days before the scheduled announcement he changed his mind. "I couldn't sleep last night worrying about it," he told Helen Durall, one of his secretaries. "I can't ask people to take a cut like that. How would they manage?" He hastily called a Sunday-night meeting at his apartment and revised the figures so that only the highest-paid employees — officers and senior executives — would experience the full 50 percent. Even so, when the memorandum explaining the cuts went out over his signature, it was "one of the hardest days in his life," said Mike Ryan. "He went around and told each person individually."

The anxiety took a toll on Orvil's health. After contracting gout on a 1958 trip to Russia, he had reduced the fat in his diet and given up his pipe. Like Arthur, he got regular massages to help him relax. But his cholesterol remained high, and as the strike wore on, the exhaustion of back-to-back eighteen-hour days began to show in his face. Colleagues remarked to one another that the *Times*' publisher was aging before their eyes. When Orvil slept at the office, his breathing was so labored that it could be heard in the hall. Judy noticed he was in trouble during a phone call when "he was panting all the time."

The cause of his distress was the enlarged heart that had kept him out of the service during World War II. The pressure and late nights caused fibrillation and discomfort, and his doctor put him on digitalis to regulate his heart, but it was no more than a stopgap measure. As long as the stress of the strike persisted, his heart would continue to be perilously strained.

Amory had no inkling that Orvil had a cardiac condition. It was not until the first week of February, when he sat next to Orvil's physician, George Carden Jr., in the Century Association dining room, that he learned of it. Unless Orvil got complete rest, Carden told Amory, he would almost certainly die. "Well, what about having him go down to the Caribbean and relax?" Amory inquired. Knowing Orvil's personality, Carden said, he would worry even more being out of touch. "Then what is the answer?" Amory asked. Carden's reply was blunt. "To have the strike over soon. Isn't there anything you can do?" "No," said Amory, visibly hardening. He bid Carden good day and walked out of the club. "I'm still surprised that I didn't stop and think that it would be worth almost any amount of money to save Orvil's life," Amory said many years later. "It didn't enter my consciousness at all."

§

As the strike approached its third month, the Newspaper Guild and the other craft unions pressured Powers to settle. Their strike benefits were nearly depleted, and several of Powers's demands were not important to them. When Powers gave no sign of budging, Elmer Brown, president of the ITU national in Colorado Springs, felt that it was time to rein him in, and quietly phoned Kheel. "This strike's gone on long enough," Brown said. "I'm prepared to help develop a settlement." From that point on, the only meaningful deliberations were conducted behind Powers's back.

For several weeks Kheel, Brown, Flynn, and Thayer met clandestinely at Kheel's office and hammered out a settlement while, at the official negotiations in the Commodore Hotel, Kheel kept up a charade of mediating between the publishers and Powers. When the time came to unveil the rogue plan, Kheel suggested that it would have a better chance if Mayor Wagner were perceived as its author. The so-called Wagner proposal, distributed to both sides on March 7, contained virtually everything Powers had pressed for, including a common contract-expiration date. Still, Powers continued to resist, even after Brown threatened to cut off ITU strike benefits if the contract was not approved. The publishers announced their acceptance at 1:45 A.M., but it took several more hours of hard bargaining before the unions finally agreed to recommend the package to their members.

More than three weeks later, on Sunday, March 31, after a series of tense ratification votes by the Guild and the nine craft unions, the 114-day newspaper strike finally came to an end. The episode proved to be a disaster for *The New York Times*. The final agreement added more than $3.5 million a year in costs at a time when the company was already suffering from losses on the western and international editions. Many readers, forced by the walkout to find news elsewhere, had changed their reading habits permanently and never returned to the *Times*. By the end of 1963 revenues would be down $16 million, daily circulation would drop by 80,000, and the company would slash its charitable giving in half. For the first time since 1946, the price of the paper went up, doubling from a nickel to ten cents.

Orvil hand-wrote a memorandum welcoming striking staff members back to the *Times* and promised salary advances if they needed them. On the day work resumed, he was everywhere in the building, shaking hands, swapping stories, inquiring how people were faring. While *Times* employees appreciated the publisher's gallant effort, they couldn't help noticing the dark circles under his eyes and his sunken appearance. What they did not know was that in the days leading up to the final agreement, Orvil had overseen not only the resolution of the strike but the preparation of a pull-no-punches, play-by-play account of the debacle that candidly skewered publisher and unionist alike for hubris, stubbornness, and miscalculation. Chief among those criticized was Amory Bradford, his own vice president. The story, written by Abe Raskin, a crack labor correspondent who had recently left the *Times* newsroom to work on the editorial page, was set to appear April 1, the day the paper published its first post-strike edition.

"This is a history of failure," the article began, quoting a ranking official of the Publishers Association. The story went on to describe Bert Powers as "cold, ambitious and utterly incapable of setting any realistic priorities for himself" and Amory as a man of "icy disdain" with a "short fuse." Raskin never uncovered the secret pact arranged without Powers's knowledge that had led to the final settlement, but he had virtually every other detail nailed down tight.

Orvil refused to read the story before it appeared in the *Times*, relenting only when Turner convinced him that, because he was a character in the drama, he ought to look at it. The afternoon before publication, Orvil sat down with the piece in Central Park. "It's unbelievable, the accuracy of that story," he told Turner when he returned, suggesting just one small change: a point of fact in the section concerning his role in persuading Kheel to stay on as mediator. He then gave Turner a green light to send it to the composing room to be set into type.

When Amory saw the galleys, he urged Orvil to kill the story, ostensibly on the grounds that the *Times* would be perceived as unethical to report on itself. The real reason, of course, was that Raskin's reporting reflected harshly on Amory's character and judgment. As he had in so many other cases — the Bay of Pigs, the Cuban missile crisis — Orvil deferred to his editors. He told Amory to pursue his criticisms with Turner, insisting that it was up to the managing editor whether to publish. "I won't talk to him," Bradford replied curtly. Seeing that his action had had no effect, Amory resorted to a familiar threat. "You can go ahead and publish it," he told Orvil. "Just take my name off the masthead." "If that's what you want, OK," Orvil replied. With that, the two men parted and Amory went to the Century Association for dinner.

Orvil had in fact grown disillusioned with Amory and his imperious behavior during the strike. Although he had no desire to protect or placate Bradford, he was sufficiently unsettled to ask the *Times'* corporate secretary, Harding Bancroft, who was familiar with Amory's strike reports, to take a look at the Raskin story. He reached Bancroft at 8:00 P.M. on a Sunday night at his country home in Millbrook, New York, and told him to drive back to the city, meet Turner at his apartment, and go over the story one last time. Bancroft arrived at 2:00 A.M. "What a piece of reporting!" he exclaimed after he was done. "There is no question but [that] this story has to be printed." In the meantime Amory had had a few drinks — and a change of heart. "I realized I didn't want to deal with my friend in that way," he said later. "I called Orvil, said I'd had time to think it over, and was ready to accept whatever he decided."

The next morning *The New York Times* featured the fifteen-thousand-word Raskin story on its front page. Publishers across the country were astonished that the *Times* would cover itself, and other newspaper owners, with such frankness. Press critic A. J. Liebling, a miser when it came to complimenting publishers, found it "almost unbelievable" that Orvil did nothing to stop the Raskin story and wrote in *The New Yorker*, "I doff my bowler." *New York Post* columnist James Weschler hailed the performance as "one of journalism's finest hours."

The decision to publish the Raskin piece was certainly *Orvil's* finest hour. Arthur, with his reverence for precedent and animus for unions, would have been unlikely to do the same. Some considered the article proof that Orvil had become more confident in his role as publisher. Others believed it showed just the opposite: the Raskin story, they felt, was Orvil's tortured mea culpa for the straits in which the *Times* now found itself. "Orvil never really felt secure," said John Oakes. "I think he felt [the Raskin story] was an atonement for some major mistakes."

§

The day after the strike account appeared, Orvil and Marian left for a vacation in Puerto Rico. "[The strike] has been a terrific strain, I know," Arthur wrote Orvil, "and I want you to take all the time you need to recuperate." Orvil needed no encouragement; he was ready for a rest. Still, he could not leave work behind entirely. Each day he spent several hours in his room at the Dorado Beach Hotel talking with the office and making his way through a thick packet of what he called "unfinished business" — memos, reports, and letters that had accumulated during the walkout.

By two or three days into their vacation, though, Orvil found he could barely walk the golf course and had to rest at regular intervals in the cooling shade of a tree to catch his breath. On April 8 — the twenty-eighth anniversary of Adolph's death — Marian awoke to find her husband sitting in front of the air conditioner, gasping. Frightened, she located a doctor who examined Orvil, administered oxygen, and pronounced his affliction to be heart failure. After a week in Saint Jorge Hospital near San Juan, Orvil told Marian that he wanted to go home. On April 15 Punch met the Dryfooses at the airport and drove them directly to Harkness Pavilion at Columbia-Presbyterian Medical Center, where Orvil was given daily doses of oxygen and subjected to cardiograms and X rays of his heart. Two days later a one-paragraph article in *The New York Times* reported that Orvil had been admitted to the hospital for treatment of "heart strain."

The Sulzbergers had known since his war deferment that Orvil had a heart defect, and the physical cost the strike had exacted from him was apparent. But a conspiracy of silence had kept them ignorant about the severity of his condition. Orvil had said nothing about it, not even to Marian; neither had Orvil's physician. Ironically, the only person whom Dr. Carden had confided about Orvil's health was Amory Bradford. "When I heard that Orvil was coming back [to New York] for oxygen and medication, I didn't expect he would make it, because that is what Carden had told me months earlier [at the Century Association]," said Amory.

Orvil himself assumed that his hospital stay was temporary. He made plans to join friends at the theater in late April — a date he had to cancel — and joked good-naturedly with Marian during her daily visits. "He was wonderfully jolly," she recalled. Judy, working at nearby Francis Delafield Hospital, dropped by with containers of salt-free food she had cooked herself, in keeping with his dietary restrictions. Orvil read newspapers and books and answered some mail, but Dr. Carden limited personal visits to one or two a day.

Nevertheless, against all reason, Orvil kept up with work, and neither Arthur nor Amory nor anyone in the Sulzberger family made a move to stop him. He pursued "Canada," the code name for a proposed merger of operations between *The New York Times* and the *Herald Tribune*, with singular determination. The two papers had first discussed joint operation in 1959, and the idea had taken on new urgency during the revenue-draining strike, sparking a series of confidential conversations between Orvil and the *Herald Tribune*'s Walter Thayer that later expanded to include Arthur, Iphigene, and top executives at the *Times*.

By late April Orvil was strong enough to sit up in a chair. "His doctor is reassured that with the rest Orv is now getting, he ought to be fine, and we are betting on that," Arthur cheerfully told a well-wisher. But to Amory, who went to the hospital twice a week to brief Orvil on the *Herald Tribune* deal and other business, "it was obvious every time I went up there he looked weaker and weaker."

Back at West Forty-third Street, Orvil's duties were parceled out. Punch took over the paper's annual party honoring the Associated Press board of directors, and Amory conducted the company's annual meeting. The more disturbing question was what the paper was going to do if Orvil's illness became prolonged, a prospect that seemed increasingly likely. Dr. Carden had made it clear that Orvil could never again climb stairs, and Punch had already spoken to builders about installing an elevator at Rock Hill. "I thought Orv was going to come back in some capacity," said Punch, "but not as publisher."

Punch himself had matured greatly during the strike, taking command of letters to the staff and showing himself to be a valued member of the team. Yet Arthur never considered him a candidate to take Orvil's place as publisher, even temporarily, nor did he think Punch a suitable replacement for Orvil on the Ochs Trust. Instead, he sounded out his old friend, George Woods, then president of the World Bank, about the possibility of becoming an Ochs trustee. Woods, who was almost a second father to Punch, wisely counseled Arthur that his own son was the more appropriate choice. Punch was certainly qualified, he argued, and not naming him would do great damage to his self-esteem. Arthur took Woods's suggestion under advisement but did nothing.

On May 13 Arthur visited Orvil at Harkness Pavilion and, alarmed at what he saw, dictated a memo suggesting that he himself resume his former duties as publisher. "[Orv] will . . . be absent from his post here for some further weeks," began the memo, which was addressed to the paper's top executives. "During this period, I propose to come back to work, something which, I am glad to say, the condition of my eyes will now permit." Arthur never discussed his idea with Punch and, in the end, never sent the memo. If he had, the most shocked recipient would have undoubtedly been Amory, who was biding his time, waiting for the call to assume temporary leadership of the company in Orvil's stead.

After he had been in the hospital nearly six weeks, Orvil grew depressed as he began to realize that he wasn't going to get better. When Judy dropped by his room for her usual visit, a nurse stopped her from going in, telling her, "He doesn't even want to see *you*." On Friday, May 24, Carol found her brother-in-law in a black humor. "I don't mind it when the mayor calls," he said, "but when the cardinal calls, I know I'm in trouble." Assured by Dr. Carden that Orvil was stable, Marian went to Tarrytown, New York, to spend the weekend with her old friend Joe Cullman, head of Philip Morris, and his wife, Sue, at their country home.

Orvil died several hours later, on Saturday, May 25, shortly after 3:00 A.M. Punch was the first to get the call. "I was dumbfounded," he said. "It didn't dawn on me that he wasn't going to make it." He pulled on his clothes, picked up Dr. Carden, and headed out to Tarrytown to perform the grim duty of informing Marian.

Bobby was in the Dryfoos apartment when his mother and uncle returned. Carol had succeeded in stopping him just before he left for his job at IBM. She hadn't felt it was her place to tell him about Orvil; she left that up to Punch and Marian. Though clearly upset, Bobby registered little outward emotion but left the apartment and spent several hours that day in a darkened movie theater watching *War and Peace*. Punch found Susie at the home of a classmate from Nightingale-Bamford, the private school she attended on the Upper East Side; the two girls had spent the night together and were studying for final exams. When Susie reached home, she raced past the crowd that had already started to gather, rushed into her bedroom, shut the door, and turned the radio dial to the *Times'* station. "I didn't believe it until I heard it on WQXR," she said. "I was devastated."

Because the *Times'* secretary, Harding Bancroft, had a weekend home not far from Smith College, Punch had asked him to drive to Northampton to notify Jackie. Harding pulled up in front of her dormitory in his Volkswagen Beetle about 10:30 A.M., confident that Punch's instructions to Jackie's housemother had been carried out. Punch had roused the housemother in the middle of the night, alerted her to Orvil's death, and implored her not to tell Jackie, who had an 8:00 A.M. exam that day. But the woman had ignored Punch's request, and Jackie's screams of grief echoed throughout the dorm. Many at the *Times* viewed Harding as austere and chilly, but in that critical moment he was "terribly sweet," recalled Jackie, comforting her on the long ride back to New York with warm, funny stories about her father.

Arthur was sitting in his wheelchair in the Dryfoos apartment when Jackie returned, and he burst into tears at the sight of her. By then the living room was filled with family, friends, and dignitaries, who continued to arrive in a steady stream until a week after the funeral. Ruth and Judy took charge of Marian, who moved through her duties in a numb state of shock. Bobby occupied himself by tending bar. "All I remember of those few days is sitting behind the bar serving drinks," he said. "People came in and out and in and out by the hundreds."

Orvil's secretary, Alice Kernan Berlinghoff, was at her weekend house when she first heard the news on the radio. She rushed to the city, changed into work clothes, and was in Orvil's office by early afternoon. When she walked in, she found Amory, who had already been there for several hours. He told her that he "had the situation under control" and suggested that she return home. Amory and other top executives had been retrieving Orvil's papers concerning the proposed merger with the *Herald Tribune,* and Arthur had already phoned Walter Thayer to assure him that, Orvil's death notwithstanding, the *Times* was eager to proceed. The paper's financial situation was far too precarious to slow the pace of negotiations, even in the face of tragedy. Indeed, Orvil's obituary in the next day's *New York Times* candidly noted that under his leadership, the paper had "operated at a profit margin so modest as to startle some businessmen . . . even while it was breaking advertising lineage [records]."

Tributes poured in from Emperor Haile Selassie of Ethiopia; Golda Meir, foreign minister of Israel; New York governor Nelson Rockefeller; and Secretary of State Dean Rusk. President Kennedy wrote Marian a letter commending Orvil's restraint during the Bay of Pigs and Cuban missile crisis, while the New York *Journal-American* berated "those who dragged the strike out for 114 days," essentially accusing the unions of killing Orvil. Bert Powers, in a well-intentioned but clumsy act, sent Marian a plant.

But it was J. P. Morgan financier Thomas S. Lamont who best captured what it meant for the country to lose a publisher of *The New York Times.* "Beyond the family loss is the loss of *The New York Times,*" he wrote Arthur and Iphigene. "For I have come to feel that what is good or bad for the *Times* is good or bad for every American — for all of us. . . . Three generations of your family have contributed to the creation of a public institution which . . . has done as much as any other single institution to make our American democracy work by . . . giving our people an informed and tolerant view of their problems at home and throughout the world."

On Sunday, May 26, Orvil's mahogany casket lay in an upstairs room at the Frank Campbell Funeral Home on the Upper East Side. Marian had agreed to an autopsy, which showed the cause of death to be an enlarged heart, but she had balked at cremation. Irrationally, she feared that Orvil would be burned alive. "That was my concern at the time — that they might make a mistake," she said. "I was slightly hysterical in those days."

At 10:00 A.M. the following morning, two thousand people gathered beneath the soaring ceiling of Temple Emanu-El for Orvil's funeral. William Randolph Hearst Jr., Samuel I. Newhouse, and other titans of the newspaper industry sat in respectful silence alongside John Dickey, president of Dartmouth; New York City mayor Robert Wagner; and Brigadier General Chester V. Clifton, who had come from Washington as President Kennedy's personal representative.

At Marian's request, Scotty Reston delivered the eulogy, which transformed Orvil's modest life of decency and gentle humor into something celestially grand. "The death of Orvil Dryfoos was blamed on heart failure," he began, "but that obviously could not have been the reason. Orv Dryfoos's heart never failed him or anybody else. . . . It was steady as the stars." When he praised Orvil for the "courteous questions and wise judgment" that had resulted in the toned-down Bay of Pigs story, several *Times* editors shifted in their seats. During those tense hours in April 1961, they had wanted to publish everything the paper knew, and it had been Scotty's influence on Orvil that had led to their being overruled.

In the front pews the Sulzbergers were stoic and dry-eyed; not even seventeen-year-old Susie violated the family ethic of keeping a stiff upper lip. "You don't indulge in things that might unravel you or those around you," she explained. "Not falling apart was very important." Later Arthur commended his grandchildren for not crying, and told a family friend how "wonderful" Marian had been for "taking everything like a soldier and keeping her feelings to herself." The next day he addressed Bobby as "the man of the house" and reminded him to "keep your chin up [and] be brave."

After the funeral Nathan A. Perilman, the rabbi at Temple Emanu-El, said the Jewish prayer for the dead over Orvil's casket in the Ochs plot at Temple Israel Cemetery before a small group of family and friends. Like most of the men who had married into the Ochs and Sulzberger family, Orvil was laid to rest among his in-laws. Carved on the stone that marked his burial site were the words A QUIET LEADER, the headline that had appeared the day before on *The New York Times* editorial about his death. The spot was just steps from the grand marble mausoleum that was the final resting place of Adolph, Effie, and two of Adolph's sisters — Nannie, who had died in 1947, and Mattie, who in an eerie coincidence had died the same day as Orvil. The Dryfoos children were not present for the interment; Marian feared it would be too upsetting. Orvil's mother, Florence, was also absent from the cemetery service. She did not believe in attending funerals or burials, a policy she did not alter even for her own son.

In the years that followed, Marian never went back to visit Orvil's grave, explaining that she didn't feel the need and it only dredged up bad memories. "I have a great tendency to block out anything that's sad," she said. "I can remember the date of Orvil's birthday; I just can't remember the day he died." The same was true for the Dryfoos children. Without being instructed explicitly, they understood that, for a Sulzberger, grieving was inappropriate. One should get on with life and avoid what a friend of Iphigene's called "useless despair." "We didn't talk about my father," said Susan Dryfoos. "He was gone, he was gone."

PART THREE

The Inheritor

25

The Divine Right of Kings

THE DAY BEFORE ORVIL'S FUNERAL, SCOTTY AND
Sally Reston arrived at Amory's East Ninety-fourth Street town
house and were welcomed in for an elegant lunch. The five-story
Bradford home, located just one block from Arthur and Iphigene's Fifth
Avenue apartment and around the corner from John Oakes's, featured
its own elevator, halls illuminated by skylights, and a dramatic curved
staircase leading to the second-floor living room. As they settled into
their seats around the impeccably set table, the mood was solemn and,
for the Restons, a little stiff.

Ostensibly, Amory had invited the Restons to join him and his wife,
Carol, for a quiet meal so that they could share their grief and ruminate
on the future of *The New York Times*. But the true purpose was more calculated. Orvil's death meant that the publishership and presidency were
vacant, and Amory, now fifty and aware that he had little chance of
securing both, hungered for the president's mantle, which would give
him power over every aspect of the company except the newsroom. His
hope was that Scotty could be persuaded to become his partner in what
would amount to a package deal: Scotty as publisher and himself as
president, an arrangement he was confident Scotty could sell to the family if he wished. "Amory was clearly trying to get his position solidified,"
said Sally. "It was a very uncomfortable lunch."

When Amory made his pitch, Scotty, with Delphic vagueness, admitted that what the *Times* needed was a "tough son of a bitch" but stopped
short of committing himself to an alliance. Privately, he considered
Bradford a disastrous manager. He had bungled the strike, and his hostility and arrogance made him temperamentally unsuited to a place as
paternal as the *Times*. Still, given the uncertainty of the situation, he
didn't want to alienate a potential confederate or reduce his own
maneuvering room. After all, Amory might actually succeed in his quest.

With the utmost tact, Reston explained that he did not feel it was his place to volunteer his views on succession to the Sulzbergers; as the top nonfamily executive at the paper, Amory was the appropriate party to present Arthur with the idea of making Scotty publisher. Amory agreed to do so at the first opportunity and left the lunch giddy in his belief that Scotty had embraced his campaign.

A few days later Amory was sitting behind his long, boat-shaped desk when he heard the familiar sound of Arthur's wheelchair coming down the hall, pushed by a nurse. Arthur stopped at Amory's open door and asked him to come to his office; he had something he wanted to discuss. When they had settled in, Arthur paused briefly, looking away, his fingertips touching. Except for me, he said to Amory, you are the senior executive at the company, and "I think it's appropriate that I talk to you about the problem of succession. . . . I know that you and Orv have felt that Punch was not up to the job. While Mrs. Sulzberger and I have not agreed with that, I'm wondering whether, in order to gain time for consideration, I should not resume the title of publisher for the time being."

Bradford was dumbstruck; having been charged up to present the scheme he had outlined to Reston, he had now been thrown a curveball, and he scrambled to play it to his advantage. "That is a possibility," Amory answered diplomatically, "but the question of whether you are in a condition to take on this added strain is one for your doctor and your wife to decide. I can't advise you on that, but I do have some thoughts on the general question of succession, which I would like to share with you if I may."

After Arthur nodded his assent, Amory laid out his strategy in detail, arguing that the *Times* needed a commanding hand "now more than ever before." He was "fond" of Punch, he said, using a word that in the Bradford lexicon dripped with derision, but thought Arthur's son lacked the experience and judgment the top job required. He counseled Arthur to consider going outside the family for a successor, for the good of the paper. "I am reluctant to urge this, being one of the obvious candidates," he added disingenuously, going on to say that of the two men besides himself whom he deemed qualified — Scotty Reston and company secretary Harding Bancroft — he thought Scotty the better choice.

By then, it was clear to Amory that Arthur had begun to lose his concentration. "We're both exhausted from the strike and the shock of

Orvil's death," Amory said, rising to leave. "Let's defer this question for at least a month. That will give you a chance to talk with your family, and me a chance to rest and recover." After they shook hands, Bradford returned to his office, packed up some papers, and departed for a monthlong vacation at his country home in Vermont, confident that his future as the next president of *The New York Times* was secure.

Under the terms of Adolph's will, it was the three trustees of the Ochs Trust who were charged with deciding who would be the next publisher of *The New York Times*. Since Julius's death in 1955, Orvil had served as the third trustee. Now that he, too, was dead, the remaining trustees — Iphigene and Arthur — shared the task of filling the post. In the newsroom, many feared that the senior Sulzbergers would choose someone from the business side rather than from the news end, and their worries were well founded. In the ensuing days, as they agonized over succession, Arthur suggested to Iphigene that perhaps Amory should run the paper while Punch completed his apprenticeship — a proposal to which she was unalterably opposed. Amory had never spoken to her about the Reston-Bradford plan he had floated by Arthur, and she was justifiably offended. More important, she believed he was the wrong man for the job. "He had made himself thoroughly unpopular," she argued. "We would have had a revolt [if he had been made publisher]."

By blood, Punch remained the obvious choice, although outside observers speculated that John Oakes, Cy Sulzberger, or even Ruth might be dark-horse candidates. The stumbling block was Arthur. "My father lacked confidence in Punch," said Ruth. "He thought he was awfully young and immature." Punch himself was seemingly a dispassionate observer, content to obey the family's unspoken rule against self-promotion. He certainly wanted the job, but it would never have occurred to him to lobby for it with his parents, their advisers, or his sisters. In the trusting manner of a child, he sat back and waited for the adults to come to a decision.

Carol Sulzberger, however, was ferocious in her ambitions for her husband. "She was rabid on the subject," said Celia Ochs, wife of Punch's Chattanooga cousin Martin, who visited Punch and Carol in the days following Orvil's death. "She just felt that he got walked on all over the place." Her combativeness stiffened his resolve to fight for his birthright, if it came to that. "Carol was good for Punch," said Ruth Adler, a former *Times* staffer. "She made him grow up."

As she had at other critical moments in the history of the *Times,* Iphigene stepped forward to play an outsize role in the selection of the next publisher. She believed that Punch had the courage and instincts for the job, even if he lacked the experience. Unlike Arthur, she was willing to take a gamble on their son. "Iphigene felt [Punch] had been mistreated by his father," said the *Times'* Sunday editor, Lester Markel. "This had a lot to do with her decision that, by God, Punch ought to have a crack at this."

Iphigene's arguments ultimately proved persuasive, and after conferring with Marian, Ruth, Judy, and Eddie Greenbaum, the senior Sulzbergers privately agreed that Punch would become publisher. The only remaining question was whether he should also be president. In the newsroom, gossip swirled that the Sulzbergers would end up devising a power-sharing arrangement that paired Punch with a mature *Times* veteran. Unbeknownst to them, George Woods, a *Times* board member and close family friend, had already confidentially written to Arthur, suggesting that Punch be teamed with Scotty. "A lot of people thought there would be a kind of regency," said Max Frankel, then in the Washington bureau. "There was much clucking about how ill-prepared Punch was for the job."

The first weekend in June, Arthur and Iphigene invited the Restons to Hillandale, where the discussion inevitably turned to succession. For Arthur, the question was complex. He did not want to put the *Times* at risk by burdening his son with more responsibility than he was capable of shouldering. At the same time, he hoped to maintain peaceful relations with his wife, avoid wounding Punch, and not lose Amory, who he was convinced provided a strength and continuity that the company needed, especially in the absence of Orvil.

He turned to Scotty and asked him point-blank: What did he think of Punch sharing his responsibilities with Amory? It was the moment Amory had known would come, when Scotty would be invited to share his views on succession. But Reston declined to help Bradford's cause. "It's a bum arrangement," he told Arthur, reminding him how unhappy he himself had been sharing sovereignty over *The New York Times* with Julius Adler. Arthur protested that he wasn't sure he could trust Punch to run the company. "If you don't trust Punch now," Scotty replied, "you'll never trust him, and you'll cripple him."

Scotty's blunt words finally convinced Arthur. The next day the senior Sulzbergers informed Punch, in the manner of issuing summary judgment, that he was to be the next publisher of *The New York Times.* Although they didn't spell out precisely what that meant, Punch assumed he had been tapped to take over Orvil's job in its entirety, with both of his late brother-in-law's titles. He was awash with pleasure. "I have something very confidential to tell you," he told his secretary, Nancy Finn, with obvious excitement. "I'm going to be named publisher — and I'm taking you with me." Over the next several days, Nancy held her tongue as other executive secretaries tried to prepare her for the letdown they felt sure was to come when Scotty or Amory was named to lead the company.

Amory was working in his garden in Vermont shortly before 11:00 A.M. on June 6 when Arthur called from his office at the *Times.* "Amory, I know you do not agree with this, but I have decided to make my son, Punch, the next publisher of *The New York Times.*" Amory was stunned. "I'm surprised you've acted so soon," he replied, believing that he and Arthur had agreed on a monthlong hiatus before any decisions would be made. "Do all the children agree?" Arthur replied that they did. "Are you making any other changes?" Amory asked, an oblique reference to the possibility that Arthur might divide up Orvil's job and name him president. "No," said Arthur. "It would be unfair to Punch to do that." "Well," Amory answered stiffly, "I'm not sure that I want to go along with it." Aware that Bradford's words amounted to a threat to resign, Arthur stalled for time. "Why don't you think it over, and perhaps you'll come to a different conclusion," he suggested. Amory promised to call back that afternoon with his response.

Arthur's apparent calm was deceptive; Amory's displeasure had spooked him. He knew that his general manager had a reputation for brinkmanship, but losing Amory and Orvil in a single month was something the family and *The New York Times* could ill afford. He hastily summoned Eddie Greenbaum and Louis Loeb, the *Times'* outside counsel, and soon the trio had cooked up a compromise: making Punch publisher but holding the presidency in abeyance. That would still leave Punch in the top job, and with time, as he and Amory worked together, Punch might welcome naming him president. Meanwhile, Amory would have operational control of the company; what he would lack, at least for the time being, was the presidential title.

At noon Louis Loeb picked up Arthur's private phone and called Amory to make the new proposal. Amory was indignant. "This makes things even fuzzier than I thought they were," he complained. If Punch was to be publisher, then the president should be selected at the same time so that there would be a "clear and immediate understanding" as to who had what responsibility. Loeb urged Bradford not to judge the plan too hastily. "I assure you that I have given this a lot more thought than you have," he told Loeb coldly before hanging up. Amory's reaction sent Arthur reeling. He told Iphigene that he had no choice but to make Amory president now, or risk losing him. Punch could still be the publisher in the traditional sense, concerning himself exclusively with editorial policy, but the company needed Amory to run the business.

Punch was sitting in his office talking with Turner Catledge when his mother came in to explain the latest turn of events. "I'm sorry," she told her son, "but that's the way your father wants it." Punch turned pale. Once again, his father had humiliated him, this time in favor of an old nemesis who had shown him nothing but disdain. Punch knew he could never share power with Amory. He had observed how Amory had manipulated Orvil with his tantrums and threats, and how he had commandeered the business side as his own, leaving Orvil uninformed and dangling, and he was determined not to repeat the experience.

He got up and strode into his father's office, fully aware that what he was about to do would almost certainly prompt Amory to quit, something Punch frankly preferred. It was a turning point in his life, not unlike the moment when he had decided to enlist in the marines or when, lying in a military hospital, he had had an epiphany and realized he wasn't the hapless man many assumed him to be. He stood before his father and announced that he would take the publisher's job without conditions, or he wouldn't take it at all. "It just won't work," he said of Arthur's plan.

As quickly as Arthur had embraced the idea of making Amory president, he abandoned it. Iphigene had made her preference for Punch clear, and he, too, had grown weary of Amory's unyielding rigidity. "I don't blame you," he told Punch with a sigh. "The more I think about it, I can't get along with the son of a bitch, either." At 4:30 that afternoon, Amory, unaware of what had transpired on West Forty-third Street, dictated a letter of resignation over the phone.

Scotty was largely ignorant of what had happened during the critical days since his weekend visit to Hillandale, so when Arthur showed him the letter Amory had dictated from Vermont, Reston sat down and wrote Bradford a note. "Your resignation . . . depresses . . . [and] frightens me," he said, "for if there was ever a time in the long history of this paper when it needed to cling to strength, this was it." Scotty went on to profess astonishment at the process by which the Sulzbergers had arrived at their decision, claiming, "I do not know how it all happened. . . . Nobody on the paper outside the family was asked for an opinion. This at least was true in my case."

On June 11 Arthur formally accepted Amory's resignation. All that remained was for the *Times'* board of directors to ratify Punch as the next publisher and president at its June 20 meeting and to orchestrate the public announcement. Having vanquished the specter of Amory Bradford, Punch brimmed with self-confidence. "I know I'm young," he told Hugh and Joan Dryfoos over dinner at a Manhattan restaurant. "But I can do it." When Susan Dryfoos heard the news that her uncle would soon fill her late father's job, she burst into tears and fled the room.

Amory cut short his vacation and drove to New York to pack up his office and complete the formalities of leaving the company where he had worked for sixteen years. The initial draft of his public letter of resignation had indicated that he was quitting because he disagreed with the choice of publisher, but after Louis Loeb and Harding Bancroft persuaded him that a direct slam at Punch would injure the paper, he modified it to read that he was not in agreement with "the proposed plan of organization." After the final statement had been agreed upon, Bancroft congratulated Amory on the gentlemanly way he had handled the situation. Amory did not respond. "I was pissed off," he said later.*

The board of directors met at 10:00 A.M. on Thursday, June 20, and after a moment of silence in honor of Orvil, ratified Punch as publisher

---

*Bradford soon took an executive position with Scripps-Howard Newspapers and in 1970 headed a Nixon administration study group that designed and recommended the new federal Environmental Protection Agency. He divorced his wife and by 1972 was a jobless alcoholic on the verge of suicide, having lost most of his money in a fruitless lawsuit against the *Times* over his retirement benefits. He quit drinking, began psychiatric treatment, and studied massage and Gestalt therapy at the Esalen Institute in Big Sur, California. In 1978, at the age of sixty-five, he sold his house in Vermont, burned all his personal papers, and set out in a Volkswagen van for what would become four years of living on the road.

and president. As his first act, he designated Bancroft to replace Bradford as vice president; Amory's other title — general manager — was
retired. That night Arthur took Punch, Carol, and Carol's parents out
for a celebratory dinner. "To say that I am relieved is to put it very mildly
indeed," Arthur wrote Eddie Greenbaum, who had departed several
days earlier for Europe. "Just getting the whole thing over with and
being able to lie down and not think about it will be . . . a tremendous
relief."

The next day's front-page story, headlined ARTHUR OCHS SULZBERGER
NAMED TIMES PUBLISHER, noted that, at thirty-seven, Punch was the
youngest chief executive the paper had ever had, including his grandfather Adolph Ochs, who was one year older when he took possession of
The New York Times. European bureau chiefs "beamed when they heard
that you and the family were still going to steer the ship," Eddie Greenbaum wrote Arthur from the Ritz Hotel in Madrid. "There had been a
vague fear that the new publisher was to be a 'business man' without
that intangible something which the words 'tradition' and 'principle'
best describe."

Punch was flooded with letters from more than 750 well-wishers,
including President Kennedy, New York governor Nelson Rockefeller,
and media titan Walter Annenberg. After years of being viewed as what
Clifton Daniel aptly described as "the pet dog of the family," Punch
savored his overnight rise in power and status, even as he felt its daunting weight, but his humor remained intact. The day the story of his promotion appeared in the *Times*, Judy called her brother to congratulate

---

It was during this period that he met a female psychic named Phoenix and, over
lunch in a Toronto diner, told her about his relationship with Orvil. As they were
talking, she suddenly shifted her eyes to a spot just above Amory's shoulder. "What
did Orvil look like?" Phoenix asked. "Did he have a high forehead, a prominent
nose, a warm mouth?" Bradford stammered that yes, he did. "Well, I'm seeing him
right now and he has a message for you: he says that he needs to move on and so do
you. He says you can talk to him while you drive west, and that will be a way of saying good-bye."

So Amory did talk to Orvil as he drove west, which he said helped him resolve his
guilt over the part he felt he had played in his death. Bradford eventually settled on
Edisto Island, South Carolina, where he practiced Siddha Yoga meditation and, with
his fourth wife, Laurene, taught massage. In 1998 he died at the age of eighty-five.

him. "I have just made my first top-level decision," he told her in the deadpan voice he reserved for jokes. "I have decided not to throw up."

§

As he gingerly settled into his new duties as publisher, Punch cut a singularly unprepossessing figure. He had inherited neither Adolph's taste for tailored suits nor his father's matinee-idol physique. If left to his own devices, he tended to look more Kiwanian than cosmopolitan. His sole sartorial flourish was his Marine Corps tie clasp, which he wore every day just at the tip of his breastbone.

When *The Gallagher Report,* a newsletter for advertising, media, and marketing executives, wrote that Punch "must learn in 15 months what he was intended to learn in 15 years," it voiced the fears of many observers that the Sulzberger scion was hopelessly in over his head. At the *Times,* no one knew whether his aim was to actually run the paper or to serve as a kind of symbolic leader. Executive holdovers from Arthur's and Orvil's regimes were smugly certain they could manipulate him for their own purposes. "They felt he wasn't going to do anything," said *Times* general counsel James Goodale. "They were just going to do it themselves and spin him around in circles."

What these men had failed to take into account, however, was droit du seigneur — the divine right of kings. Because Punch was the first publisher since Adolph Ochs to come to his post as a blood relative rather than as a son-in-law, he would never suffer his father's self-doubts about being "the man who married the boss's daughter," nor would he consider himself a "coach" rather than a leader, as Orvil had. Punch had grown up with *The New York Times* as a fifth child. His place had been automatic, assured by the simple fact of his name and his blood tie to *The New York Times.* Not since Adolph Ochs had a publisher possessed such an effortless sense of ownership and prerogative. "It gave him a power that Orv probably felt he didn't have," said Stuart Greenspon, Jackie Dryfoos's former husband. "Punch was free to do what he wanted to do."

He was free only within the constraints of his situation, of course, which were considerable. Punch came to his position with no circle of trusted contemporaries to advise him; his subordinates were almost all men who were older than he was and were somewhat intimidating to him. Outside of Turner Catledge's "Club," few at the *Times* knew him well, and fewer still had bothered to cultivate him. "He leaned on three or four people a lot at first," said Ivan Veit, who, as vice president for circulation and promotion, befriended Punch and was soon included in his inner circle.

Punch was also limited by the condition of *The New York Times* as he had inherited it from Orvil, a paper bled dry by the strike and poor management, bereft of morale in the wake of Orvil's death, and thin on experience at the top. "The whole thing was really shattered," said Punch. "My first job was to try to pick up the pieces." With little fanfare, Punch moved into Orvil's fourteenth-floor suite, turning what had been the conference room into his office and equipping it with a special reading chair and a portable bar. Marian appropriated Orvil's curved, modernistic desk and moved it to the twelfth-floor office she occupied as director of special activities. With characteristic sensitivity, Punch hung Orvil's framed photograph next to those of his father and Adolph Ochs in the executive wing at West Forty-third Street and ordered that it be displayed in all the foreign bureaus — something Orvil had forbidden, for fear of appearing immodest.

Publicly, Punch signaled his intention to chart a cautious course at the paper. "There is a new management team and it will consider change," he told *Time*. "But it has never been in the nature of the *Times* to go for drastic change." Hampered by Adolph Ochs's legacy, Arthur and Orvil had voiced similar sentiments when they became publisher and had moved with painstaking circumspection. Punch had fewer inhibitions. The strike had taught him that the paper *had* to change in fundamental ways if it was to survive. It had to extricate itself from indentured servitude to the unions, and it had to be more aggressive about making money. But he also knew he could not effect such a metamorphosis immediately. He needed time to learn, to assess the paper's problems, to eliminate ventures that weren't working before creating new ones.

If his father's Achilles' heel had been his marriage to the boss's daughter, Punch's was his lifelong belief that he wasn't bright; and like Arthur, he rushed to broadcast his deficiency before others did. At meetings, he cheerily admitted he couldn't read a balance sheet; in "View From the 14th Floor," a signed column he initiated for the in-house newsletter, he confessed that the younger people at the paper today "are a lot smarter than I sure was." Even when he made a skillful presentation or offered an astute comment, he downplayed his contribution. "You know me — I screwed up again," he would tell aides, smiling and rolling his eyes. During the first few years of Punch's tenure, his self-deprecation, combined with his genuine lack of knowledge about the business, prompted *Times* executives to continue to brood about the lack of leadership at the top. "The perception was that Punch was so ineffectual as to be essentially absent," said James Goodale. "He made few, if any, decisions."

That perception was largely unjustified, for although Punch had none of the intellectualism, strong opinions, or overpowering charisma usually associated with publishers, he possessed common sense and a healthy irreverence for doing things the way they had always been done. "He had the impatience of a man who is underrated and wants to prove himself," explained Turner Catledge. Less than two months after taking over as publisher, he put a halt to "Canada," the proposed merger between *The New York Times* and the *Herald Tribune,* despite the fact that his father still favored it, because the proposal just "didn't make any long-term sense to me." In January 1964 he closed the western edition, which had no hope of being profitable by the end of a five-year projection. The regional edition's paid circulation had slumped to just seventy thousand. "It was a question of dropping that or the European edition," said circulation manager Ivan Veit. "We had a commitment to do the European; we didn't for the West Coast."

When Andy Fisher, who had headed up the western edition since its inception, moved back to New York after almost two years in Los Angeles, he had no idea what might be in store for him. His main responsibility had been judged a failure, and without his patrons, Orvil and Amory, he was glumly certain he would be made the scapegoat. Instead, he emerged as one of Punch's key aides. At forty-two, Fisher was the executive closest in age to the new publisher, and although they had known each other only glancingly during Orvil's regime, he and Punch quickly discovered that they had much in common: a love of order and analysis, and a proselytizing faith in technology.

As publisher, Punch hoped to bring a modicum of rationality to the paper's inefficient management structure, which he described as "hopeless" and "truly horrendous." He was exasperated with the chain of command that Amory had created, with himself at the pinnacle, a pyramid requiring that nearly every major decision be made at the highest level. At one point, the *Times'* executive floor had fifteen separate departments reporting to it, a situation Punch likened to a tall stand of reeds with roots in the same soil and nothing to join them at the top. "It was obvious to me we couldn't continue to exist that way," he said.

In February 1964 the *Times'* top business and news executives boarded a bus and rode through a snowstorm to Atlantic City, where they met for several days to thrash out how they might work together for the first time as a team. Eight months later Punch reconvened the group at the Greenbrier, a resort in West Virginia, to discuss goals, financial planning, and the first budgets the company had ever instituted. The result was a complete overhaul of the business structure, one that made Harding Bancroft executive vice president with three vice presidents arrayed beneath him. One was Andy Fisher, who was put in charge of production. The reorganization, a textbook application of modern management theory, was meant to bind together Punch's unruly "reeds" into "a single strand — strong, sharp and effective."

Punch revamped the news side in similar fashion by appointing Turner Catledge to the newly created post of executive editor. Long before Orvil's death, Turner had discussed the need to unite the Sunday and daily news departments under a single editor, an idea Orvil had eagerly embraced because it suited his notion of the *Times* as one paper rather than a collection of autonomous and warring fiefdoms. Arthur, however, had never acted on it. During his publishership, he had served as his own executive editor and had actually grown to like the separation of the Sunday and the daily papers, since it gave him the power to resolve disputes in the area he cared about most — news.

But the more compelling argument for continuing the status quo had been Lester Markel, the irascible head of the Sunday department, whom Adolph had hired in 1923. Markel ruled his kingdom with ruthless brilliance. Over his forty-one-year-long reign, he had built the Sunday *New York Times* into a veritable behemoth of information and advertising. At the end of the 114-day strike, the Sunday paper had set a new record for weight — six pounds, fourteen ounces, the size of a newborn baby — and surpassed 1.3 million in circulation.

The price for this success was the toleration of a despotic and highly temperamental one-man show: no word went into the Sunday magazine without Markel's personal approval. "I looked on him as a psychiatric case," said Dan Schwarz, Markel's longtime assistant, who lived through several of his boss's incapacitating breakdowns and frequent tirades. With his aversion to confrontation, Arthur had never had the stomach to remove Markel, despite the fact that the man was seventy years old and, under *Times* rules, a candidate for retirement. Nor had Orvil been willing to tackle Markel. But Punch wanted to shake things up, and he knew he couldn't do that if his Sunday editor remained in his post. After a few stiff drinks, he marched down to Markel's eighth-floor office and told him that he planned to centralize the news flow under Turner as executive editor. He cushioned the blow by offering Markel the title of associate editor and gave him an office on the fourteenth floor, where he was put to work in the newly established department of public affairs. Punch was not thrilled about having Markel practically next door to him, but, he said, "nobody else would take him."

Turner's promotion to the position of executive editor also signaled a reversal of fortune for Scotty Reston, whose friendship with Orvil had given him great clout. Now it was Turner who enjoyed a favored relationship with the publisher, a relationship that for the first time made the Washington bureau accountable to New York in fact, rather than merely on paper, as it had been during the Orvil years. The power shift resulted in Scotty's resignation as bureau chief. "When Punch became publisher, that gave Turner the upper hand, and Scotty did not want to be in a position of answering to Turner," explained Russell Baker, then a Washington-based reporter.

For a while Scotty mulled over an offer from *The Washington Post*, first made in 1953 and revived soon after Punch was named publisher, but decided in the end to stick with the *Times*, the institution he loved with an almost religious fervor. He, like Markel, accepted the title of associate editor, and although he no longer reigned as Washington bureau chief, he continued to work out of the capital, concentrating on his column.

For Punch, clarifying the company's organizational chart and kicking Markel upstairs proved to be easy compared with trying to exert control over John Oakes, his cousin and editor of the *Times'* editorial page. Under Orvil, John had become accustomed to running the page with little interference; as such, it had become a mirror of his liberal convictions.

Like his predecessors, Punch saw copies of editorials before they went into the paper, but he didn't necessarily read them. His learning disabilities made reading a chore, and political and policy debates put him off. Whereas Arthur had treated the editorial page as his own personal megaphone, Punch felt it should reflect the institutional voice of *The New York Times;* his private opinions, though seldom strongly expressed, were generally conservative and in sympathy with business, but he believed they were largely beside the point. "He is such an unusual sort of publisher he does not even call his newspaper 'my newspaper,' " wrote Dick Schaap, the television sportscaster, nine years into Punch's publishership. "He calls it 'the *Times.*' "

Still, when John published an editorial in early 1964 attacking proposed U.S. subsidies to build a supersonic transport, Punch felt impelled to take a stand. John objected to the plane because he thought it would damage the ozone layer, generate too much noise, and inappropriately involve Washington in what he felt should be an exclusively private enterprise. Punch, however, who was enraptured by all things scientific, was intrigued by supersonic technology and did not want the *Times* to stand in the way. In a letter that "astounded" John because of its "peremptory tone," Punch declared that the *Times* should reverse its condemnation of the plane, and asked John to produce an editorial to do just that.

Whether John fully understood the request is unclear, but the result certainly did not satisfy Punch, who rejected the proposed editorial John sent him for inspection. "[This] is not exactly what I asked for," he wrote John in a note attached to the editorial. "In fact, it is just the opposite." He had no intention of forcing any *Times* editorial writer to write something he didn't believe, though, and told his cousin, "If no one on your floor feels the way I do, I shall be glad to write the editorial myself, or get someone to write it for me."

Suddenly, for John, the issue escalated from a discrete disagreement over supersonic aviation to a matter of principle. From the first day he had taken over the editorial page in 1961, he had consistently maintained the publisher's right to have "the last word" on whatever views were expressed in the paper while at the same time believing that, as editorial-page editor, he had to "stand by" every syllable that appeared on the page. "If I couldn't persuade [the publisher] to take a different view or at least a compromise that I could live with . . . then the only honorable course would be for me to resign," he said. "I was my own man; I wasn't going to be anybody's mouthpiece."

For Punch, the question was much the same: who, ultimately, was going to prevail when a controversy arose over *The New York Times'* editorial policy — the editorial-page editor or the publisher? Already he had been put in the embarrassing position of absorbing angry blasts at dinner parties for *Times* opinions with which he didn't agree. Neither Punch nor John wanted to force a resignation, especially so early in Punch's publishership. As a conciliatory gesture, John offered to come up with a compromise editorial that would satisfy everyone, subject to Punch's review.

The revised editorial, which appeared April 14, 1964, under the headline JOINT VENTURE FOR SUPERSONIC, was ultimately a victory for John. The only concession he had made was to withdraw his attack on federal subsidies for the American entry into the race for supersonic aircraft. No reversal of the *Times'* earlier opinion was apparent, and on the other issues — ozone damage and noise pollution — the editorial was silent. Shortly afterward, at Punch's request, John produced an internal document outlining his guiding principles for *Times* editorials: "modern and moderate liberalism, with strong emphasis on civil liberties, civil rights, the Federal Government's responsibility to assure them and also to further peaceful relationships with all countries of the world."

Following the supersonic incident, Punch basically left John alone, a tacit admission that he was no match for his editorial-page editor's obstinancy. Quietly, he deputized Harding Bancroft, who had a good relationship with John, to read every editorial and pursue any differences of opinion. Unless he had a specific interest in a topic, Punch rarely read the *Times'* opinions before his readers did. "You take your chances," Punch said of his approach to the editorial page. "Once in a while things come out that you don't particularly agree with."

§

Punch may have been reluctant to beard John Oakes, but he quickly demonstrated that he had the backbone to stand up to a president. The White House had initiated the meeting, billing it as a private getting-to-know-you session between John F. Kennedy and the new *Times* publisher, then only five months into his tenure. Punch was noticeably nervous as he walked with Scotty Reston from the paper's Washington bureau to Pennsylvania Avenue. "What do I say to him?" he asked. "What does he say to me?" "It will just be small talk," Scotty assured him. In fact, the encounter turned out to be nothing less than a blatant attempt by Kennedy to remove a *Times* reporter from his assignment.

Relations between Kennedy and *The New York Times* had long been tense. Before becoming editorial chief, John Oakes had roused Kennedy's ire by pursuing persistent rumors that his speechwriter, Ted Sorensen, had ghostwritten Kennedy's Pulitzer Prize–winning book, *Profiles in Courage.* During an interview in his senatorial office, Kennedy had pulled out his notebooks and gone over them line by line to demonstrate that he had, in fact, authored the book. To John, the documents proved little except that Kennedy had done work of some sort on the manuscript. "I sure wasn't convinced by this," he said. "Undoubtedly Ted or someone else wrote it."*

The *Times* had been supportive of the Kennedy administration in its early days, but under John's leadership, editorials had become increasingly critical. Privately, he disapproved of Kennedy's marital infidelities and what he viewed as the White House's showcasing of the arts for political purposes, a phenomenon he sneeringly referred to as KKK — Kennedy's Kultural Kick. "Jack thought Johnny Oakes was off the wall," said Charley Bartlett, Washington correspondent for *The Chattanooga Times* and a close personal friend of Kennedy's since the 1940s. " 'If I tried to run the country the way Oakes writes those editorials,' he would say, 'we'd all be in a ditch.' " Robert Kennedy likewise sniped about the Sulzbergers after the *Times* charged nepotism in his appointment as attorney general. To Anthony Lewis, a *Times* reporter covering the Justice Department, he sarcastically remarked that, of course, Punch had been "made [publisher] on the merits, struggling up from the bottom."

It was against this background of mutual antipathy that Punch and Scotty entered the White House in late October 1963. Paramount on Kennedy's agenda was the *Times'* reporting on Vietnam. Since his inauguration, Kennedy had increased the number of American military advisers attached to the South Vietnamese army from 685 to nearly 16,000 and had approved National Security Action Memorandum 52, which declared that the objective of the United States was to "prevent Communist domination of South Vietnam." Since then, dissatisfaction with the ineffective and corrupt Diem government had grown; indeed, a

---

*Ironically, *New York Times* columnist and former Washington bureau chief Arthur Krock had "advised" Kennedy on the rewriting of an earlier book, *Why England Slept.*

little more than a week after Punch's meeting with Kennedy, a military coup, in which the United States was tacitly complicit, would topple the regime, leaving Diem and his brother, Ngo Dinh Nhu, dead.

David Halberstam, the *Times'* reporter in Saigon, was one of the few full-time American correspondents in the South Vietnamese capital. In the fifteen months since his arrival, he had developed excellent sources and — unlike reporters during World War II or Korea, who had considered themselves part of the American "team" — believed his job was to report the news, whether it reflected well on the United States or not. Kennedy was furious about the tone of American reporting out of Saigon, and he was especially irate about Halberstam. He told Punch that Halberstam had lost his objectivity — he was "too close to the story, too involved" — and suggested that it might be better if he were assigned elsewhere. For Punch, the issue was not whether American involvement in Vietnam was right or wrong, or even whether Halberstam was objective or not. It was, rather, whether a president of the United States had the right to tell *The New York Times* what to do with its reporters. Not hesitating a moment, he replied that as far as he was concerned, Halberstam was *not* too involved and would remain where he was. Punch emerged from the meeting clearly shaken and immediately instructed Halberstam to cancel his scheduled vacation so that it would not appear that the *Times* had capitulated to White House demands.

When Scotty returned to the bureau late that afternoon, he was beside himself with pleasure, crowing to his colleagues, "Punch was very tough," and repeated the story for years afterward. "He retold that tale with respect and real pride [as an example of] exactly the way a newspaper publisher should behave," said Hedrick Smith, a young reporter in the Washington bureau at the time. In 1954, when faced with similar pressure from CIA chief Allen Dulles, Arthur had removed *Times* reporter Sydney Gruson from Guatemala shortly before a U.S.-backed coup overthrew the leftist government of Colonel Jacobo Arbenz Guzmán. When Kennedy had complained previously about Vietnam coverage, Orvil had suggested that the president call Turner Catledge. Punch, however, had taken direct responsibility and seemed to know instinctively where to draw the line. "Where [*The New York Times*] is concerned, he's got a central core of principles that are untouchable and unchangeable," said Gruson.

Exactly one month after Punch's triumphant meeting with Kennedy, the president was assassinated in Dallas. Punch got the news while presiding over a Publisher's Luncheon on the eleventh floor of the Times Building. Because Turner was in Miami at a press meeting, assistant managing editor Clifton Daniel was the paper's highest-ranking editor. Toward the end of the meal, a waitress called him to the phone. The national news editor, speaking from the third-floor newsroom, told Daniel what had happened. The luncheon speaker was still holding forth when the ashen Daniel returned to the publisher's private dining room and broke into the discussion. "President Kennedy has been shot in Dallas . . . and he may be dying," he said. "Anybody who has work to do had better go downstairs."

At 2:30 P.M. *Times* reporter Tom Wicker, in Dallas covering the presidential trip, called in the news that Kennedy had died. Two and a half hours later he sat down at a writing desk on the mezzanine of a terminal at Love Field and started to type what would turn out to be a long, four-thousand-word story. Turner raced back from Miami, arriving at the office at 8:00 P.M. In a gesture of mourning, the *Times'* radio station, WQXR, canceled its regular programs and commercials and played religious music all afternoon.

The next day the *Times* ran a black border around Kennedy's portrait, though not around the news articles, as it had following Lincoln's assassination in 1865. Throughout that momentous and horrifying weekend, the *Times* produced such accurate, analytical, exhaustive reporting that ABC anchorman Harry Reasoner was moved to write a paean to Abe Raskin, the paper's assistant editor of the editorial page. "I don't recall in my lifetime ever seeing the profession of journalism carried on at a higher level," he said. "All the facets . . . were so shining and splendid that you would think the *Times* had been planning its coverage for years. In a way, of course, I suppose it had." The only mishap was the front-page headline after Jack Ruby gunned down Lee Harvey Oswald, which said PRESIDENT'S ASSASSIN SHOT TO DEATH. Turner later admitted *assassin* was inappropriate because Oswald had never been tried and convicted.

In Chattanooga, where Kennedy had been demonized as a liberal Yankee and a "nigger-lover," Ruth and the Golden family were in a distinct minority of mourners. Eleven-year-old Lynn, who heard the news of the president's death while sitting in her sixth-grade classroom at

Lookout Mountain Elementary School, recalled that "everybody started cheering." Jackie Dryfoos, Marian's oldest, saw in the Kennedy assassination a replay of her father's death six months earlier. All the grieving she had kept inside since the funeral suddenly surged forth. "I was totally, totally hysterical," she said. "The news reports kept showing these children and a father. I could not stop crying and I could not stop watching the television and I could not go to school."

The day after the assassination, while attending a Manhattan dinner party, John Oakes was summoned to the phone to take a call from White House special assistant Walter Jenkins. "Mr. Oakes, the president of the United States," he said, and John gulped as Lyndon Johnson came on the line. John was stunned; why was the president contacting him at this busy and emotional moment? As it happened, Johnson simply wanted to express his thanks for the editorial that had run that morning in the *Times*. At first, John thought Johnson meant the editorial about the slain president, which Oakes had personally written the day Kennedy was shot. "This shows how innocent I was," he said later. "Then I realized he was interested in [the editorial about] himself." John was so addled that he started to assure the new president that he could count on the paper's support, but stopped himself just in time, saying instead, "Mr. President, you know you're going to have our *sympathy.*" Later John learned that Johnson had made hundreds of similar calls in the first few days after the assassination in a strategic effort to build backing.

The Kennedy assassination demonstrated to the nation, if indeed it needed to be demonstrated, that *The New York Times* was still the preeminent source of news in America. Two months later, in its diennial survey, *Time* magazine declared the *Times* to be the best paper in the country. Financially, though, the assassination proved to be a burden. Fearful of appearing ghoulishly mercantile, stores canceled their pre-Christmas ads, costing the *Times* hundreds of thousands of dollars. That, coupled with the revenue forfeited during the 1962–63 strike and the $8 million the paper had lost on its international and western editions over the past four years, led to the *Times'* ending 1963 in the red — hardly an auspicious start to Punch's publishership.

The effects of the 114-day strike had convinced Punch that the *Times'* long-term economic health depended on liberating itself from the tyranny of the unions. The paper's labor relations were "sick," he said, and "the greatest single hazard to our future." In 1965, when the Newspaper Guild and craft union contracts came up for renewal, he was determined not to repeat the paper's sorry history of appeasement. But he was still a very raw publisher, untested in the area of labor negotiations, and he found it harder than he had imagined.

For the International Typographical Union, the big issue in 1965 was automation. Some fifty newspapers across the country had already installed computers to set type, and the threat to printers' jobs was clear. Bert Powers, president of the ITU, had emerged from the 114-day strike as the pacesetter for the craft unions, and he triumphed again, in large part because the *Times* still refused to take a strike, once more forcing the other publishers to follow its lead. After only a brief work stoppage in the *Times'* composing room, the ITU gained a wage increase to $12 an hour — the second-most expensive agreement the paper had ever made — and a veto over how and when the *Times* and other New York papers would install automation equipment.

Six months after the ITU face-off, the Newspaper Guild succeeded in shutting down the *Times* for twenty-five days. Relations among the publishers were so fractious and the economic stakes so dire that the *Herald Tribune* broke ranks with the Publishers Association and resumed publication before a settlement had been reached. In the end, the *Times* again caved in to labor demands, this time conceding a principle on which Arthur had vowed never to yield: a union shop for the newsroom, an agreement that meant that, henceforth, all employees in Guild jobs would be required to pay dues. "No possibility was offered of continuing the individual choice you have enjoyed for several years," Punch wrote in a letter to "affected employees." "I am sorry."

The truth was that the *Times* simply had no alternative; its finances were too precarious to remain closed for long. It had little reserve cash and no ancillary businesses, except its newsprint mills, on which to rely for outside income. As Orvil had predicted in 1961, New York newspapers gradually began to be killed off by costly union contracts, the rise of television, and mismanagement. In 1966, barely a year after the Guild strike, the *Herald Tribune* expired. Its owner, Jock Whitney, merged the remnants of his operation with those of two other struggling papers — one a Hearst property, one Scripps-Howard — into an impossible hybrid, the *World Journal Tribune,* whose initials, WJT, prompted wags to dub it the *Widget.* Less than eight months later, it failed, too. Of the fifteen newspapers that had thrived in New York in 1900, only three remained: *The New York Times,* the *New York Post,* and the New York *Daily News.*

The collapse of the *WJT* made an orphan of the Paris edition of the *Herald Tribune,* a situation that *The New York Times* quickly turned to its advantage. Rather than abandon the *Times'* money-losing international edition, also based in Paris, Punch merged it with *The Washington Post* and Whitney Communications, the owner of the Paris *Herald.* The new, jointly owned newspaper, the *International Herald Tribune,* rolled off the presses in the spring of 1967. Some critics considered the disappearance of the international edition to be the *Times'* second major failure in recent years, the first being the shutdown of the western edition. Such talk did not bother Punch; as far as he was concerned, the *Times* was in a battle for survival, and he was prepared to take whatever steps were necessary to win. "He didn't care about face," said Stuart Greenspon. "He wanted to save money."

26

The Center Will Not Hold

IN THE MONTHS FOLLOWING ORVIL'S DEATH, Marian and her three children struggled without success to comfort one another. The force that had bound them together was Orvil, with his sweet, affectionate accessibility and his position at *The New York Times*, which had given them all a sense of mission and place. With those elements suddenly ripped from their lives, they careened, and eventually found solace elsewhere. The result was a series of weddings that, with the exception of Susan, who was in high school and therefore too young, left every member of the family married or remarried less than two years after Orvil's passing. "Everyone needed a home," explained Jackie.

Marian's reaction was to seek a life as close to the one she had had with Orvil as she possibly could. In the process, she effectively separated herself from the offspring she described to her parents as "pretty nice . . . (though at times pains in the neck)," just as she had detached herself from Orvil, whose grave she never visited. In the weeks following the funeral, she coped by keeping busy — salmon fishing in Canada, traveling to the Grand Canyon with the Advisory Board on National Parks, returning to New York, repacking her bags, and heading out the next day to Mexico. Left alone much of the time, Susan stayed with Punch and Carol or with John and Margary Oakes, whose daughter, Andra, was her close friend. "It would be far too much to say Susie grew up at our house," said John. "But she spent a lot of time with us . . . and probably felt more at home in our home [than her own]." On parents' day at Nightingale-Bamford, Susan's school, Jackie did the honors, as Marian was out of town. "I was lost," said Susan. "I was completely lost."

Though prematurely gray at forty-four, Marian retained enough of her earlier beauty to make her a captivating commodity on the dating circuit. Within two or three months she was seeing a variety of men, including journalist Clayton Fritchey, manufacturing executive and former congressman Fred Richmond, and Adlai Stevenson, who, after failing to win the Democratic nomination in 1960, had been appointed U.S. ambassador to the United Nations. The younger Dryfooses were unimpressed with Fritchey, whom they referred to as "the Old Shoe," and Richmond made them anxious.

Stevenson, on the other hand, proved to be an agreeable suitor. Late one night he coaxed Susan out of her bedroom in her bathrobe and regaled her and Marian with enchanting stories of life among the Pygmies in Africa. "I was smitten," said Susan. "I had hoped that my mother would marry him." But except for a few perfunctory passes and an embarrassing moment when he appeared at the door of his Waldorf Towers apartment in his underwear when she came to pick him up, Stevenson never got very far with Marian.

The man who did capture her interest, however, was Andrew Heiskell, chairman of Time Inc. In April 1963, shortly before Orvil died, he had turned up at the cocktail party the *Times* threw each year in honor of the Associated Press board of directors, where Marian, in a break from her vigil at the hospital, was serving as the paper's official hostess. Andrew had long been a fixture at the paper's annual soiree, in part because of his position and in part because of his marriage to Arthur's former mistress, Madeleine Carroll, from whom he had been separated for several years. Fed up with the "utterly frustrating and humiliating business of being a *Time* and *Life* wife" — an existence she compared to "purdah" — Madeleine, who had become a naturalized American citizen during the war, had moved back to Europe in 1961.

At the end of the reception, after Marian had shaken "four thousand hands coming in, and four thousand hands going out," she noticed Andrew sitting on the couch behind her. Much later he confessed that he had lingered for a reason. "You looked so sad," he told her. "I thought someone should take you home." When he deposited Marian at her apartment, he offered to serve as her escort to *Time*'s upcoming fortieth-anniversary party at the Waldorf, saying gallantly, "I know you've been invited and your husband is sick." On the appointed evening, Marian answered the door to see Andrew looking "handsome as could be" in a top hat with his "real" date, the actress Joan Fontaine, in the car. From his hospital bed, Orvil had joked that "the minute I'm down-and-out, that damn Heiskell moves in."

Andrew respectfully waited several months after Orvil's death before asking Marian out, and the romance was instantaneous. Born in Italy of American parents and educated at the Sorbonne and Harvard Business School, Andrew had been associate editor and then publisher of *Life* magazine before becoming chairman of Time Inc. Temperamentally, he was as dominant, sophisticated, and self-assured as Orvil had been cautious and unobtrusive. "Andrew walks into a room and he owns the room," observed Marian. "Orv walked into a room and had to go around and introduce himself." One element in Andrew's favor was his height: at six foot five inches, he towered over every gathering and certainly over the petite Marian.

When, several months later, the couple decided to marry, Marian knew that she could look forward to a life that in status and security was roughly comparable to the one she had lost. Her job would essentially remain the same: to serve as a helpmeet to a powerful and publicly visible man, a role that suited both her ambitions and her nature. "She's a great career facilitator," said June Bingham Birge. "In that sense, she's an old-fashioned wife."

Jackie liked Andrew, but somehow whenever he dined at the apartment, she and Marian got into screaming fights. "Marian was always putting Jackie down," said a former in-law who was present at the skirmishes. "The way she looked, the way she conducted herself. Marian was a tough mother." Bobby, troubled before his father's death, was in a state of bitter rebellion by the time Andrew arrived on the scene. He made his unhappiness plain by speaking to Marian with such disrespect that Andrew finally felt compelled to intervene. Several hours later, Bobby came to his mother and calmly declared, "I don't care what you do, if you marry him or you don't, but that man will never be my father and I will always call him 'Mr. Heiskell.' "

As disruptive as the Dryfoos children could occasionally be, they were outclassed by Madeleine Carroll, who was furious at Andrew for ending their fourteen-year-long marriage in order to wed Marian. Arthur had burst into laughter when he heard that his daughter intended to marry the husband of his former lover; Iphigene simply declined to discuss the matter in terms that acknowledged Arthur's prior relationship. Marian thought the tangled history "great fun" and had no feeling one way or the other about Madeleine, whom she had come to know during the actress's many visits to Hillandale. Madeleine had always been kind to her, and to Orvil; during the Dryfooses' honeymoon in California in 1941, she had invited the young couple to visit her on the set of *My Favorite Blonde.*

On January 22, 1965, Andrew and Madeleine were officially granted a divorce. Eight days later, in the senior Sulzbergers' Fifth Avenue apartment, Marian, dressed in a sea-foam-green cocktail dress, wed Andrew before several dozen family members and close friends, including Adlai Stevenson. Despite the fact that Andrew was a Gentile and she herself was not religious, Marian had insisted that a Jewish judge perform the ceremony, an idea Arthur considered "cockeyed." After a honeymoon in the Virgin Islands, the newlyweds returned to New York and took up residence in the twelve-room apartment Marian had shared with Orvil at 1010 Fifth Avenue.

Andrew changed Marian and her household in ways large and small. Having been raised in Europe, he drank wine with meals and made it his business to select the best vintages for the Sulzbergers' birthday and anniversary celebrations. Iphigene, who had treated Orvil with a certain maternal authority, adopted a more respectful tone with Andrew. At the end of a letter suggesting that *Life* run a story on a cooperative educational program for gardeners, she signed off: "Hopefully and humbly submitted . . . your Mother-in-Law." Susan, the only Dryfoos child living at home, was openly antagonistic toward the man who had supplanted her father. In a letter addressed to Sir Andrew — her nickname for him because he was so tall — she wrote: "I hope you understand why I hate you. . . . I want my father back and you're not him."

As for Marian, she blossomed under Andrew's care. He finagled an appointment for her as the *Times*' representative on the board of the Inter American Press Association, a group he had once chaired, and challenged her to discuss her views on public issues. In keeping with her new loyalties, Marian vacated Rock Hill and spent her weekends instead at High'n Dry, the rambling clapboard house in Darien, Connecticut, that Andrew had shared with Madeleine Carroll. Andrew had put the house on the market soon after his marriage to Marian, but his asking price was so high that it was clear he didn't really want to sell. With its oversize armchairs custom-built to accommodate his large frame, its cozy library, and the dazzling view of Long Island Sound, High'n Dry was a perfect retreat for Andrew, all the more so because, though just a half-hour drive from Hillandale, it was at an agreeable remove from the

Sulzbergers' sometimes-suffocating brand of gemütlichkeit. As a successful forty-nine-year-old executive, Andrew considered himself the
equal of any Sulzberger; he was not about to spend every weekend at
Hillandale playing the role of supplicant.

Less than a year later, the Heiskells left Marian's Fifth Avenue apartment and moved into the United Nations Plaza residential complex near
the East River, which, though only recently completed, was well on its
way to becoming a glamorous address. With their change of location in
the city, the last vestiges of Marian's former life were swept away, and her
transformation from *New York Times* widow to wife of the chairman of
Time Inc., civic leader, board member, and Manhattan socialite was
complete.

Jackie and Bobby preceded their mother in marriage, cementing
matches within eight weeks of each other in the summer of 1964. "I married my father," Jackie said of her husband, Stuart Greenspon, the sweet,
stable son of a German Jewish doctor from Newport News, Virginia,
whom she had been seeing at the time of Orvil's death. The couple had
met on a blind date in January 1962, when Jackie was home from her
freshman year at Smith College and Stuart was studying at Columbia
Business School. That summer, the relationship began in earnest.

Jackie was refreshingly open and direct compared with the compliant
girls Stuart had met in the South; Stuart, in turn, was résumé-perfect for
the oldest daughter of the publisher of *The New York Times*. "He met the
criteria," said Jackie. "My family liked him. He was thoughtful, he was
polite, he looked good." One of the last things Orvil had said to Jackie
was "Stuart is a nice man, he'll take good care of you." As she squabbled
with Marian and looked ahead, Jackie saw only one choice. "It was very
clear that I couldn't go home and live with [my mother]," she said. "We'd
kill each other. Therefore, I had to get married."

Jackie and Stuart chose July 2, 1964, as their wedding date, the same
day Punch and Barbara Grant had married sixteen years earlier. In the
absence of Orvil, Bobby escorted his sister down a makeshift aisle on the
lawn at Hillandale, and when they reached the rabbi standing under a
yellow-and-white *huppa*, Arthur, too frail to make the walk, joined his
grandson in giving away Jackie. But the joy of the moment was miti-
gated by memories of the recent tragedy. "I missed Daddy dreadfully
and was upset the whole day," she said.

At the time of his wedding, Stuart was working for the investment-research department of Chase Manhattan Bank, uncertain what direction his career might take. In December 1966 Punch and Carol invited Jackie and Stuart to their home for dinner. Following dessert, Punch motioned Stuart to join him in his study for a private conversation and, after a brief speech about the importance of keeping *The New York Times* in the family, invited him to join the paper. Punch had taken pains to befriend Stuart long before his marriage to Jackie. While he was still at Columbia, living in a student walk-up on the East Side, Punch had regularly swung by on weekends, picked up Stuart, and taken him to the Century Country Club for a round of golf. He was impressed with Stuart's seriousness of purpose, his diligence, and his facility with numbers. "We don't have many business people at the *Times*," he told him. "You're the kind of guy we need. Not only to help us now; we would look upon you as the leader of the next generation."

It was that last phrase that seduced Stuart, and indeed, even at this early stage in his publishership, Punch was looking ahead. His own son, Arthur Jr., was only fifteen; it would be ten years or more before he could even begin an apprenticeship at the paper, assuming he wanted to. Stuart, on the other hand, was twenty-seven, a graduate of a prestigious business school, and married to the oldest grandchild in the family, not to mention the daughter of a former *Times* publisher. "There will be other people from that generation who may join the *Times*," Punch went on. "But if things work out, I would assume you would be my successor."

Stuart left Punch and Carol's home in a daze, and in the cab on the way back to their apartment at 880 Fifth Avenue, he told Jackie, six months pregnant with their first child, about his talk with Punch. "I was afraid of that," she said, smiling. "It's your decision." Over the next several months, Stuart consulted Andrew Heiskell, Andy Fisher, and others, trying to figure out what to do. His biggest stumbling block was nepotism; he wanted to earn his place at the company, he said, not advance merely because of a fortuitous marriage. Jackie, however, was thrilled. "I was on my career path," she said. "My husband was going to become publisher. . . . If Adolph Ochs's daughter's husband becomes publisher, then the first-born [grand] daughter's husband becomes publisher. Somewhere along the way, I assumed that I would be married to the publisher. That was the pattern."

In May 1967, two months after the birth of their daughter, Carolyn, Stuart began what would turn out to be a long and complicated grooming at *The New York Times*. Punch and several senior executives mapped out a multiyear training program for him. He spent six weeks on the news side as an observer before moving on to library services and eventually acquisitions, production, the Sunday department, advertising, and consumer marketing. But despite Punch's professed interest in succession, he was an inscrutable mentor. When Stuart tried to talk to him about his career, Punch was as remote with him as he was with his own children. "There was a vagueness that reminded me of my mother," said Jackie. "It wasn't that either [my mother or Punch] pushed you away, but you couldn't quite get what you needed."

Bobby, meanwhile, had left his job at IBM and entered Dartmouth in the fall of 1963, three months after Orvil's death. He shared a large suite in Streeter Hall with Jim Weiskopf, his former roommate at the Hill School, who had enrolled in Dartmouth the previous year, and gravitated quickly to the campus computer center, where he worked with BASIC, an operating program invented by two Dartmouth professors that within a few years would help bring about the personal-computer revolution. At a freshman mixer during the first week of school, he met Katie Thomas, a student at nearby Colby Junior College. Katie was a descendant of Seth Thomas, the famous clockmaker, but by the time she was born, the company had long been out of family hands. With her fresh-faced good looks, appealing naïveté, and middle-class background, Katie personified a kind of all-American ideal. And she was just as emotionally needy as Bobby. "I was terribly homesick and terribly lonely," she recalled. "I really needed a friend. Bobby came along and — *boom!* — he was my best friend."

Bobby called her every evening; she spent every weekend at Dartmouth, eating dinner with Bobby and Jim before retiring to Bobby's room. Katie was alternately flattered and alarmed by the attention. "I had never had anybody that crazy about me in my life," she said. "It was kind of frightening." Bobby did not allow her to date anyone else; if one of his friends spotted her at a fraternity party, he would erupt in anger. Malleable and eager to please, Katie meekly complied with his wishes. Bobby found her passivity attractive, as well as her selfless desire to take care of him. "I felt that he needed mothering, and I'm a mothering type," said Katie. "I guess that's why we hit it off." As Thanksgiving neared, Bobby announced to Katie outside Hopkins Center, Dartmouth's performing-arts building, that he had decided they were going to marry. "I remember standing there and thinking, 'I don't even know if I love this person,' " Katie recalled.

While she was impressed with Bobby's apparent self-confidence, wide-ranging knowledge, and worldly sophistication, she didn't know at the time that he was related to the family that owned *The New York Times;* he never mentioned it. Indeed, she thought he was not only fatherless but poor. "I felt so sorry for him," she said. "He always wore these old clothes. I used to bring sandwiches and dinners to him because I didn't think he could afford to take us out." It wasn't until Bobby invited her to spend a weekend in New York that she discovered the truth of his circumstances. Marian, Jackie, and Susan were so exquisitely turned out that Katie suddenly felt embarrassed by her own skirts and sweaters. When she returned to college, a friend dragged her to the library and pointed out Orvil's entry in *Who's Who.* "It didn't mean anything, because I didn't know what a family like that was all about," she said. "I'd never met one before."

At the end of the academic year, shortly after Jackie's wedding, Katie discovered she was pregnant. When the couple announced they were getting married, Bobby's family couldn't mask its disapproval. "They had been trying to split them up," recalled Stuart Greenspon. "Whenever you mentioned Bobby's name, there was trouble." The nuptials were so sudden that Katie's parents had to interrupt their vacation on Martha's Vineyard in order to attend.

On August 31, 1964, a judge in Yonkers, New York, performed what Punch described as a "shotgun wedding." Only thirty people attended the reception, which consisted of finger sandwiches laid out on Marian's dining-room table. "We all want the best for you, Bob," she said by way of a halfhearted toast. "It was not a happy occasion," said Jim Weiskopf, who served as Bobby's best man. "The family was livid. This was just after Jackie's wedding with Stuart, who was everything the family ever wanted."

The newlyweds returned to Dartmouth, where Bobby worked on the college yearbook, shot pool, and barely cracked a book while Katie awaited the birth of their baby. Although others in the family did little to hide their disapproval, Iphigene tried to make Katie feel accepted by welcoming her warmly to Hillandale at Christmastime and giving her a copy of *The Joy of Cooking* as a gift. "Granny handled it like a champ," said Bobby.

Bobby dropped out of Dartmouth soon after James Dryfoos was born on March 2, 1965. That summer he and Katie lived in an apartment over the garage at High'n Dry and took their meals with Marian and Andrew in the main house. Many evenings, after everyone else had adjourned to the living room, Andrew and Katie would remain at the table for hours, talking. "Andrew just kept pouring the Beaujolais," said Katie. "He used to ask me a lot of questions. . . . I liked his European flair. I liked his manners; he was such a gentleman." It was Katie who came up with the name her son eventually called his stepgrandfather: Grandrew.

Education was a sacrament to Iphigene, who insisted on paying the tuition bills for all her grandchildren as they progressed through private high school and college. She was outspokenly disapproving when Bobby decided not to return to Dartmouth after the birth of his child, but her admonitions had no effect. In September Bobby, Katie, and the baby moved to an apartment in White Plains, New York, where Bobby resumed work at the local office of IBM. Marian asked her friend IBM president Thomas J. Watson Jr. to tell her honestly whether he had rehired Bobby as a personal favor to her. "That boy has gotten his job because he's good at it!" Watson told her, clearly annoyed. "Never think that I would hire anybody as a favor."

In the two years following Orvil's death, Susan watched helplessly as the members of her family formed new lives with new partners, leaving her isolated and effectively on her own. Compounding her difficulties was a learning impairment that made reading a trial and writing in script so onerous that she printed homework assignments. Marian had had similar problems, but oddly, no one in the family had ever told Susan; it was years before she would be correctly diagnosed as suffering from dyslexia. When the time came for her to decide on a college, it was Iphigene, not Marian, who took her on campus visits. Susan's academic record was so poor that she wound up attending Lake Erie College in Ohio, a school that she admitted was then "very mediocre at best."

One bright spot in Susan's confusingly rearranged life was Anne Madeleine Heiskell, Andrew's daughter by Madeleine Carroll. A.M., as Susan came to call her stepsister, lived with her mother in Paris, and it was there in the summer of 1965, during a dinner with Madeleine, Marian, and Andrew, that the two first met — a prelude to a family vacation through Eastern Europe and Scandinavia. At eighteen, Susan was four years Anne Madeleine's senior, but A.M. was so elegant and statuesque that, remembered Susan, "she looked about seven years older." During their month of travel, the two girls stayed up late sorting out all the complicated couplings that had brought their families together; by the end of the trip, they had become fast friends.

Anne Madeleine hated the strict convent boarding school in which her mother had placed her; when she graduated, she came to the States to live with her father. The arrangement lasted barely a year. "I guess I kicked her out," admitted Marian. "She was involved with a lot of very unattractive people. I didn't know who the hell they were. It was more than I could take." Anne Madeleine refused to return to her mother in Europe, choosing instead to move into a tiny apartment on East Twenty-eighth Street.

Over the ensuing decade, Anne Madeleine became involved in drugs and alcohol. She ran with a rough crowd and turned every disagreement with her father into a screaming fight. "I remember slapping her once," Andrew wrote in his memoir, *Outsider/Insider.* Stays at rehab centers in White Plains and New Canaan had no lasting effect. When she contracted liver poisoning, her four-week hospital stay resulted in a staggering bill: $146,000. Ravaged by anorexia and a string of beatings from various boyfriends, the onetime beauty began to look "more and more coarse."

Marian was in Detroit on the day Anne Madeleine was found dead in her apartment of an apparent drug overdose. Susan was notified and immediately set out for the grisly scene. When she arrived, Andrew was in his daughter's kitchen, dazedly answering questions from the police as Anne Madeleine's body lay in the next room. "He talked and cried," said Susan. "It was a horrible but touching time. He's not a man who unburdens himself."

At the funeral in Manhattan, Andrew sat with Marian on one side and Madeleine Carroll on the other. Susan, who had been too young to participate in her father's service at Temple Emanu-El, bravely delivered the eulogy. She spoke of how she and Anne Madeleine had confessed their "dreams" and "hopes for our future" to each other. "Somewhere, these dreams fell short," she said. "Somewhere her life got tangled in a demanding adult world. . . . And we, her parents and friends, couldn't help her. I can't make sense out of why that had to happen to her." For

Susan, that last sentence was particularly resonant, for even decades after the fact, her father's death also remained a bewildering mystery.

§

Ruth loved to cook and disliked television, yet most evenings at the Golden home on Chattanooga's Lookout Mountain found her in the sunroom with Ben, a tray in front of each of them, eating a dinner prepared by the family's black maid and watching television. She had adopted the routine long ago out of deference to Ben, who didn't like dining at the early hour required by their four children but insisted on his wife's company, even though Rufus, as he called her, invariably sulked on the sofa and ignored the blaring set. Whether they were nursing an old argument or battling afresh, the evening would usually play itself out in an established pattern. Ruth would retreat to the bedroom, and Ben would summon Michael, who had eaten supper hours before in the breakfast room with the maid and his brothers and sister. In a brittle voice, Ben would command his son to "go upstairs and get my pillow and my pills" — a signal that he had decided to sleep in the downstairs den.

The tension apparent in the early days of the Golden marriage had grown steadily over the years, fed in large part by Ben's increasing resentment of the central place the Sulzberger family played in their lives. While he felt a grudging gratitude to Arthur and Iphigene for his job, his house, even his car and overseas vacations, he was all too conscious of his in-laws' disapproval and knew that they had named him publisher of *The Chattanooga Times* more out of familial duty and concern for Ruth than confidence in his abilities. By the early 1960s his rage engulfed the household. "I'm so goddamned angry, I can't see straight!" he would exclaim at least once a day.

It was Ruth who bore the brunt of Ben's wrath; Ruth, with her superior education, artistic and intellectual interests, depth, self-discipline, and blood tie to *The New York Times*, came to epitomize all the qualities Ben lacked. He asserted himself by subjecting her to snide remarks, crude language, and devastating put-downs, often in public. "It was nothing but insecurity, knowing who she was," said Martin Ochs, Ruth's cousin. "He wanted to show her, 'I've got you, I can be rough with you.'" Friends became accustomed to the embarrassing sight of Ben bullying Ruth at parties and Ruth "fussing" back — the genteel word Chattanoogans preferred to *fighting*. "Ben wanted me to change — to become nicer, more docile, I don't know," said Ruth. "But you don't marry people to change them."

Ruth and Ben tried to shield their children from the worst of their battles. On weekends they would give them money; put them in the car, with Stephen at the wheel; and send them off for a few hours to a local bowling alley. But the ongoing feud between their parents was hardly a secret among the younger Goldens, especially Stephen, who drew down his father's fury like a lightning rod. Bookish and sensitive like his mother, with an interest in poetry, music, philosophy, and acting, Stephen was the antithesis of Ben, and Ruth's closeness to him was an added annoyance. "Ben took out on Stephen all the things he didn't like about me, which were numerous," said Ruth. Michael, on the other hand, was his father's favorite. "Dad could watch me play football and baseball," he said. "Stephen wasn't interested in that."

Lynn, consumed with hamsters and trolls, was the only girl in the family and, as such, was effectively out of the line of fire, as was the Goldens' youngest, Arthur, who had been born in 1956 with clubfeet. Until he was a toddler, Ruth drove Arthur to Atlanta every couple of weeks so that a specialist could change the casts on his tiny limbs and gradually bring his feet into alignment. His life was so peripatetic that when a woman in the doctor's waiting room asked him where he lived, he said, "The car." For nearly eight years, Arthur wore braces on his legs at night.

Despite the obvious strain between Ben and Ruth, it was not misery every moment at the Golden household. "We had very happy times, and we had very bad times," recalled Ruth. Unlike Marian, Ruth had pointedly rejected her parents' grand standard of housekeeping. "My children are not going to be raised by nannies," she had told a cousin. "They're going to be raised by *me*." While other Lookout Mountain hostesses hired uniformed staff for their dinner parties, Ruth served meals herself and pressed her guests into helping out in the kitchen.

The Goldens loved to entertain, and although he had few close friends of his own, in a social setting Ben could be charming and gregarious, with an easy laugh that occupied his whole body. If there was any doubt about his Irish ancestry, he dispelled it with his talent for storytelling. "We'd laugh till we cried, he was that funny," said Martha Bartlett, wife of Charley Bartlett, *The Chattanooga Times'* Washington correspondent. Thanksgiving was a special occasion, with a guest list that included many "Oxen," as Iphigene called the numerous Chattanooga relations, as well as people from the paper. Despite his love of football, Ben didn't take his children to the big game held every Thanksgiving at the University of Chattanooga. Instead, John Popham, who had left *The New York Times* to become managing editor of *The Chattanooga Times* in 1958, piled them into his car along with his own brood. "I couldn't care less about the University of Chattanooga," Popham said. "But . . . I know what a ball game means to kids. Ben just wasn't made for fatherhood."

On Christmas Eve the Goldens usually dined at the Read House, a hotel in downtown Chattanooga, then drove back up Lookout Mountain, delivered presents to family and friends, and, once home, opened a single gift apiece under the brightly lit tree as an hors d'oeuvre before the main event Christmas morning. At Eastertime the family played "char-eggs," a game they invented based on charades. Each person was given an egg, along with sequins, ribbons, buttons, and colored paper with which to decorate it. The sport was to guess who — or what — each egg was supposed to represent.

Like her parents, Ruth was a nonpracticing Jew who enjoyed celebrating the major Christian holidays, but in ultraconservative Chattanooga, her Jewish "blood" mattered. That, coupled with her northern roots and her ties to *The New York Times,* made for a highly suspect combination. When the local Junior League invited Ruth to become a member, she made a point of joining the Julius and Bertha Ochs Memorial Temple at the same time, despite the fact that she rarely attended services. "I didn't want anyone to think I wasn't Jewish," she explained. As it turned out, Ruth was the first Jewish member the Junior League had ever had, and for the next twenty-five years, she remained its *only* Jewish member. Being a pioneer didn't faze her. "She had a missionary sense of, This is good for you, to have me, as a Jew, beside you; you're going to learn something from this," said Lynn. The city's more observant Jews, meanwhile, didn't know what to make of the Goldens. Ben belonged to the Mountain City Club, a businessman's club that had admitted several Ochs relations but generally spurned Jews. Lookout Mountain, where the family lived, was a bastion of wealthy white Protestantism.

With little that was explicitly "Jewish" in their lives, the Golden children were hazy about religion. When his classmates at Baylor, a local military high school, taunted Michael for being Jewish, he was bewildered. "That I was a Jew was news to me," he said. Ben refused to allow his offspring to be brought up Jewish, making their religious education yet another combat zone between Ruth and himself. One Sunday Ben would dress up the children and truck them off to the Episcopal church. The next Sunday, in what she considered a compromise between Judaism and Christianity, Ruth would take them to the Unitarian church. "I was sitting there hoping this [tug-of-war] ends soon," said Michael. To make matters worse, some Chattanoogans made it their personal mission to convert the young Goldens to Christianity. "When I was in high school, saving a Jew was a big deal," said Lynn.

The tactics were benign enough: one of the Golden children would be invited to sleep over at a friend's house on a Saturday night and told to bring nice clothes. The next morning the parents would take everyone to church, where the young Golden was encouraged to join in the service. One Sunday afternoon seven-year-old Arthur came home from such an outing, clearly befuddled. "Mom," he asked Ruth. "How come everybody in this family is Jewish but me, and I'm Presbyterian?" At least "there was enough of a sense of Judaism around the house that Arthur had this view," said Stephen.

If their Jewishness made the Goldens controversial on a personal basis, *The Chattanooga Times'* support of civil rights and the perception that it was a mouthpiece of *The New York Times* made them pariahs in their public life. At Baylor, Michael was called "nigger lips" and "nigger lover." Roy McDonald, the reactionary owner of the rival *Chattanooga News–Free Press,* declared that he was "almost ashamed" to occupy the same building as *The Chattanooga Times* after the paper supported the admission of the first black to the University of Mississippi. When they were very young, the Golden children were oblivious to Chattanooga's segregationist policies. But as they got older, they came to think of their family, along with the people at the paper and a small band of like-minded friends, as a wagon train rolling through hostile Indian territory. "I grew up with a strong sense that we were right and they were wrong, that we had better values," said Lynn.

The Goldens' sense of embattled isolation only added to the tensions between Ben and Ruth, tensions exacerbated by Ben's lackluster performance at the paper. Mr. Puckette's reluctance to train Ben, and Ben's failure to apply himself, meant that by the time he became publisher of *The Chattanooga Times* in 1957, he was woefully unprepared. "Ben would have made a good automobile dealer," John Popham frequently told colleagues, "but not a publisher." Arthur and Iphigene knew their son-in-law was ill-suited to the job when they appointed him, but eager to please Ruth and maintain family leadership in Chattanooga, they pressed ahead anyway, hopeful that, with strong supervision and the assistance of the paper's senior management, Ben would grow into his responsibilities.

Whether it was latent rebellion against the Sulzbergers, anger at Ruth, or personal insecurities that deepened with the weight of increased expectations, Ben became even less engaged and dependable after he was named publisher. "I think he knew he was in over his head," said Norman Bradley, the paper's associate editor. "He would sit in his office and watch TV." Instead of asking for help or delegating some of his duties to subordinates, he lashed out like an ill-informed autocrat, and in letters to New York complained bitterly about his top staff.

Weak leadership might have been tolerable in a period of success, but *The Chattanooga Times* was in a fight for its life. Not only had the paper's principled stand on *Brown* v. *Board of Education* and other racial issues eroded circulation, but Roy McDonald had kept *The Chattanooga Times* in a state of perpetual insecurity concerning their joint operating agreement. Over the years, McDonald had renewed the mutually beneficial pact whenever it was due to expire, but never without complaining about *The Chattanooga Times'* "extravagant" expenses in the name of quality and threatening to either separate the papers' joint operations or sell the *Free Press* to an outsider.

Despite these differences, and McDonald's barely concealed dislike of Ben, relations were cordial enough until the 1950s, when McDonald began diverting earnings from the *Free Press* to shore up his ailing Home Stores grocery chain. His precarious finances caused him to default on an agreement with *The Chattanooga Times* to split the costs of constructing a new building, as well as on repayment of hundreds of thousands of dollars in advances and loans the paper had made to help him out. As a consequence, McDonald eventually lost his position as an equal partner in the joint operating agreement and was reduced to paying rent to his rival for office space. "That was more than he could stand," said Ruth. The bad feelings were reciprocal, fed by *The Chattanooga Times'* well-founded suspicion that the advertising manager for the joint operation, whose job was to sell ads in both papers, had long been pushing advertisers to favor the *Free Press*.

By the time Ben was made publisher, the strain at the newspaper and the strain in the Golden marriage had begun to feed off each other. Ben's extramarital affairs, which had been going on for some time, became more blatant and widely known. "Once he started running around with girls, he's in trouble here," said John Popham. "It's a small town that way." Formerly a social drinker, Ben also began consuming bourbon far past his limit.

At the same time, his abuse of Ruth took on a frightening physical dimension. One night in a drunken rage, he slashed a Sulzberger family portrait with a knife. During another fracas, Judy said, "he threatened Ruth with a gun." Arthur and Iphigene were aware that the Golden marriage had its problems, but Ruth never confided the embarrassing details to them. Punch and Orvil, however, knew how fragile the relationship had become. On more than one occasion, Orvil had phoned Martin Ochs's wife, Celia, and asked her to drive over to the Goldens' to make sure Ruth was all right. "Ben was knocking her around a bit," Celia said; by the time she would arrive, Ben would be somewhere else cooling off, and Ruth would be alone in the house. "Every time this happens, I love Ben just a little bit less," Ruth would tell Celia in a resigned tone. "It cuts away and cuts away and cuts away."

Meanwhile, in May 1962 matters with Roy McDonald reached a new crisis point. As usual, he had heightened everyone's anxiety by warning yet again that he wanted out of the joint operating agreement. His financial troubles and his ongoing disgruntlement about paying rent to *The Chattanooga Times* had frayed relations, and this time it sounded as though his saber rattling might be serious. If ever *The Chattanooga Times* needed a strong hand, it was now.

It was at this precise moment that Ben decided to make a trip to Poland. His plan was to rendezvous with Charley Bartlett, who was in Warsaw on a press junket, and proceed with him by train to Moscow, where Bartlett was to file stories for *The Chattanooga Times*. In New York an agitated Arthur dictated a tough letter to "Ruthie," informing her that while he didn't want to "injure the relationship between the two of you . . . it isn't only you and your happiness that is involved here." As vice president of *The Chattanooga Times,* he said, she must now provide leadership in Ben's absence. "The fact that Ben is ill is apparent. No one who is healthy could have gone away at just this juncture," he insisted. Arthur signed the letter to his daughter but never sent it. Instead, Punch, in his role as a *Chattanooga Times* director, covered the essential points with her when he went to Tennessee with *Times* treasurer Frank Cox to help negotiate a deal with McDonald.

In Chattanooga Punch and Cox talked candidly with *The Chattanooga Times'* top staff, who told them of their "deep frustration at the lack of any driving force" at the paper. In early June Ben returned from his Russian adventure to a fiercely protective Ruth, who remained his ally in the face of the Sulzbergers' disapproval. A month later Ben agreed to a six-week stay at Silver Hill Hospital in New Canaan, Connecticut, which specializes in alcohol and drug dependency and has counted among its patients such celebrities as Rita Hayworth, Joan Kennedy, and Truman Capote.

When the Silver Hill treatment was completed, Punch gave him a Dutch uncle talk, ordering him in no uncertain terms to create "clearcut lines of authority and responsibility." To that end, Ben had to meet every day with his managing editor, editorial-page editor, and circulation director — an innovation that did not go down well with any of the participants. "I tell you, one afternoon I came out of there and I thought somebody had me by the throat," said former editorial-page editor Martin Ochs, who had had what he diplomatically called a "clash of personalities" with Ben. "New York had all the evidence in the world that Ben wasn't going to make it, but they insisted on one more try."

Despite the warnings, Ben objected to any interference from his staff and failed to report effectively to New York. "Ben's deficiencies in understanding himself, his associates and . . . the deeply ingrained personality habits which he has do not offer much hope for ever expecting that he will be able to maintain control as the manager and publisher of the paper," Frank Cox wrote in a "personal and confidential" draft memorandum for the file. "At the same time, Ruth is devoted to his defense and is apparently unable to see the other side of the picture." Indeed, with Iphigene as her model, Ruth remained steadfastly loyal to her husband. "My technique is to feed [Ben] ideas that will look as his own, just like Mommy has done all these years to Daddy," she informed Cox in a telephone conversation.

In October 1963, four months after Punch had become publisher of *The New York Times*, Ben was given an ultimatum: he had one year to shape up; if he didn't get his house in order by then, he would have to resign as publisher and president of *The Chattanooga Times*. No sooner had the threat been delivered than McDonald announced that he wanted to terminate the joint operating agreement. The *Free Press* was required to give five years' notice; that meant the two papers would actually separate in 1969. In New York the news sent Arthur into a panic. McDonald's move made it "critically urgent that we . . . be in control of our own destiny," he told Ben in a letter informing him that he could expect an "outline" from Punch of what had to be done "immediately and in the near future."

By the fall of 1964, near the end of Ben's probationary year, there had been little improvement in his management and the Golden marriage was in a state of collapse. In early October Ruth called Punch to tell him that she had finally concluded that "for the good of her family [and] the paper," Ben should leave *The Chattanooga Times*. "I told her I thought this is a real step forward in her thinking," Punch reported to his parents in London, "and [I] would help her get on to the second part, in other words, her personal life."

Together, Ben and Ruth consulted a psychiatrist in Atlanta in a last-ditch effort to save their marriage, but by then the love Ruth had once felt for her husband was spent. She was numb, eager only for their mutual misery to be over. "[The divorce] was something that she just thought had to happen," said Stephen. "When she gets to that point about some-thing, she's single-minded about it." In November Ruth announced she would not accompany Ben to Boca Raton, Florida, for the annual meet-ing of the Southern Newspaper Publishers Association (SNPA). She knew that Ben was in line to be elected SNPA president, and in light of their impending divorce and his upcoming departure from *The Chat-tanooga Times*, she had urged him to decline the post. Fearful of losing face, Ben had insisted that they maintain the fiction of normalcy.

With his wife conspicuously absent, however, Ben had little choice but to tell the SNPA nominating committee of his dilemma. They advised him to accept the presidency anyway, which he did, but the honor did little to cheer him. Once back in Chattanooga, he was "pathetic," said Eddie Greenbaum, the senior Sulzbergers' old friend and attorney. In accordance with an agreement Eddie had brokered, Ben lived only in the downstairs portion of the Golden house and was not allowed to participate in any business discussions about the paper, at home or at the office. Every other day he saw the psychiatrist in Atlanta.

In mid-December Ben resigned as president and publisher of *The Chattanooga Times* but remained on the board of directors — a compassionate concession that permitted him to serve out his term as president of the SNPA. In a stiffly worded letter to Arthur, he described his time in Chattanooga as a "most wonderful experience" and "the high point of my business career." In return, Arthur sent Ben an equally formal letter outlining the payments he could expect over the next three years "in recognition of your long and valuable service."

As soon as Ben was served with divorce papers, he departed for Jacksonville, Florida, where his mother had an apartment. On his way out of town, he stopped at a local liquor store, loaded up his trunk with Jack Daniel's, and charged it to Ruth. Three months later Ruth, "delighted and happy," left the Chattanooga courthouse with her divorce decree in hand and spent that evening having a "good and gay time" with Martin and Celia Ochs and Punch, who had traveled to Chattanooga to testify on her behalf.

The decision of who would replace Ben as publisher and president of *The Chattanooga Times* was up to her parents and Punch — the trustees of the Ochs Trust — and while the choice may have been obvious to everyone else, it was not to Ruth. "Guess who the new publisher is going to be?" Punch had gleefully asked his sister over the phone shortly after she informed her family that she was filing for divorce. "You!" Ruth was genuinely surprised. She hadn't asked for the job, her parents hadn't inquired whether she wanted it, and her father had always been against a woman's running a newspaper. Like Punch, Ruth had been taught from birth not to campaign for herself. If the Ochs trustees thought she was the best person for the position, she reasoned, they would inform her. In the meantime, she had sat back and waited to see what would happen. "There is a strong streak in Mother that the world doesn't owe you a living," said Stephen. "The worst thing that you can do is to assume that there are things that are yours by right."

In the photograph that accompanied the article announcing her promotion, Ruth looked serious and determined. "I was born into the Sulzberger-Ochs family," she stated by way of declaring her principles, "and am deeply committed to the quality of journalism that these two names have come to exemplify." After moving into the large office that had once been Ben's, she invited the paper's top executives to her house for dinner and asked for their support. "So far we seem to be surviving here," she wrote Turner Catledge in New York. "I haven't yet put a slip-cover on the copydesk or painted the news room pink."

For years Ruth had stayed in the background out of consideration for Ben, but once she became publisher, she showed an unexpected decisiveness and stepped out boldly. To improve the editorial page, which she felt "took itself too seriously" and was "either too righteous or too oblique" in tone, she dispatched Martin Ochs to an American Press Institute seminar for editorial-page editors. To stress that *The Chattanooga Times* was not simply an echo of its liberal New York cousin, she told the local Rotary Club, "You would not want a *New York Times* published in Chattanooga, and this is not the kind of newspaper we aspire to provide you." When Roy McDonald patronized her by saying that he was sorry he had to bother a lady with numbers, Ruth briskly informed him that she had had to learn all about "figures."

At home, Ruth made it a point of honor never to bad-mouth Ben to her children and, in a noticeable change of routine, began to cook dinner and eat with them every evening. She was shocked by what she found: after years of dining with no parental supervision, the younger Goldens had the table manners of animals. One night Ruth was summoned to the phone and struggled to hear her caller over the din in the breakfast room. She shouted out several times for quiet, to no avail. Suddenly she appeared in the doorway, crimson-faced. "I am *not* going to put up with this!" she told her family, pounding her hand down forcefully on the table. "You *cannot* behave this way." Quiet descended over the quarreling foursome, who looked up at their mother expectantly. "And you're probably going to think *this* is funny, too," she said, gingerly lifting her hand from the table. "She had embedded her hand into a fork," laughed Lynn. "There were four little holes in her hand."

In June 1965, three months after Ruth's divorce decree and six months after becoming publisher of *The Chattanooga Times*, her oldest child, Stephen, graduated from high school. His troubled relations with his father were apparent in his academic record; Stephen had left Baylor in the ninth grade; had an unsuccessful summer at Loomis, Punch's alma mater; and finally enrolled in Chattanooga High School, making him the first member of his extended family to be publicly educated. Grow-ing up, he always knew that Chattanooga was "not my place," and desperately wanted to leave. But to help his mother during her period of turmoil, he had decided to stay and attend the university there, beginning the following fall. After listening to Ralph McGill, the leg-endary editor of *The Atlanta Constitution,* give a stirring commence-ment address, Stephen filed out of the auditorium with the other graduates. As he approached the exit, he could not believe his eyes. There, in what could only be interpreted as a gesture of conciliation, stood Ben. "At the last minute, Ben decided to show up," Ruth wrote her parents. "I think Steve was very glad to have him there."

Ben's life gradually disintegrated after he and Ruth split up. He lived in a series of apartments in Jacksonville, smoking, drinking, playing golf, and going through a number of girlfriends. He took little responsi-bility for the breakup, and during his children's visits would often recite a long list of grievances. "He'd go into some damn near tirade about what had happened and why," said Michael. "There was a lot of anger roaring around." Other times he would become sentimental. "Your mother's a wonderful 'woe-man,' " he would tell one child or another in his Kentucky accent, "and I love her." Ruth encouraged the children to see Ben, and they usually spent spring vacations with him, riding bikes to the ocean and playing endless hands of gin rummy. "He really didn't do anything," said Lynn. "He was depressed."

Years later, after she had happily remarried, Ruth agreed to allow a Golden family in-law to interview her on camera, along with her mother and daughter. The interviewer asked each of the women what event had been the most significant of her life. Iphigene answered, "World War One," explaining that "it was the first time my whole world had changed." Lynn, a college student at the time, said, "Vietnam." When it came Ruth's turn, she bowed her head and fingered her pearls, then straightened up and looked directly into the camera with a face etched with regret. "The most significant thing in my life," she said, "was my divorce."

27

A Parallel Existence

P UNCH'S UNSENTIMENTAL APPROACH TOWARD *Times* tradition was hard on his father, whose health and spirits declined noticeably in the months following Orvil's death. In his era, Arthur had relished the daily Publisher's Luncheon, where he had played host to the best minds of the *Times* and the world's most important decision makers. It had given him a distinct seat of power while preserving the formal distance between him and his subordinates that he found agreeable. For Punch, the role held more terror than appeal, and he was less strict about forcing his editors and executives to attend — a development that Arthur took as a personal affront. "You have to keep plugging, otherwise the luncheon and all that it has come to mean over the years will fall apart," he told Punch in a worried memo. "It's up to you."

Punch also broke with Arthur's custom of broadcasting a New Year's Eve message over WQXR. When his father reminded him in early December 1963 that the date was coming up — his first as publisher — Punch firmly demurred. "I doubt if anybody is really interested to hear my greetings of goodwill," he replied in a memo. "Unless you have any reservations, I would be happy to forgo it." Across the bottom of the memo, Arthur scribbled his defensive reaction: "I don't care."

There was another, more personal reason that Punch resisted such functions: he hated public speaking. Several years earlier he had substituted for his father at a charity event supported by *The New York Times*. Though terrified, Punch dutifully went through the motions, but when he got home and took off his suit, he discovered he was covered with hives — only under his clothes, where it wouldn't show. "Now, that's control," laughed his daughter Karen.

New social duties came with the job of publisher, and in that realm, too, Punch veered from the historical course. While his parents had traveled easily in the company of scholars, business moguls, and the cultural doyens of New York, Punch was a natural homebody who shied away from intellectual conversation and looked to his family and a limited circle of colleagues at the paper for friendship. What he desired most was order and predictability, and *The New York Times* was a place he knew well; in personal relations, he rarely strayed from its enfolding arms.

Carol, too, was ill at ease with new people, preferring to rely on a small coterie of old friends. "God, what a group!" said Judy. "They were the typical Jewish country-club set." Moments before her first appearance as publisher's wife and hostess of the *Times'* cocktail party honoring the AP board of directors, Carol was literally trembling. "I don't know how I'm going to get through this," she told the wife of a *Times* senior executive. "I don't know a soul." As publisher, Punch had new opportunities to travel to newspaper conventions and other gatherings where spouses were expected, but except on rare occasions, Carol declined. Her fear of flying made it difficult for her to board a plane without several drinks, a pack of cigarettes, and a fistful of tranquilizers.

Although Iphigene resigned from the boards of the Urban League and the Girl Scouts to make way for her daughter-in-law, Carol showed little interest. "Most of it is so boring," she complained. "With my mother-in-law around, don't you think one was enough?" To Marian, who had loved the social and political clout of the publisher's office, Carol's hermitlike attitude was unfathomable. One night, as she mulled over her own lost status, her frustration boiled over and she burst into tears. "You're a damn fool!" she told Carol. "You're the wife of the publisher! You've got the world open to you! Go ahead and do something with it!"

To Iphigene, Carol's recalcitrance was nothing less than a willful shirking of duty. When Punch informed his mother that he had recently bumped into Nelson Rockefeller at the home of Arthur Gelb, the *Times'* metropolitan editor, Iphigene pointedly inquired why he had had to go to an editor's apartment for such encounters. "Again may I suggest that you and Carol do more entertaining," she wrote her son. "You are an attractive couple and have a charming home. You can invite anyone you wish, you don't have to be buddies." That night Punch sat down with Carol and discussed potential guest lists, but the Sulzbergers' at-home social schedule did not pick up appreciably.

Such pressure only hardened Carol's resentment of Iphigene, who continued to keep in touch with Barbara Grant — she even paid some of her medical bills — and chastised Carol for smoking. To Carol, Iphigene was not "Mother" or even "Iphigene," but that far more distant creature — "my mother-in-law." Despite the Sulzbergers' polite silence on the subject of her education and her social standing as a daughter of a man in the "rag trade," Carol was fully aware that they considered both second-rate. Out of self-protection as much as desire, she became the consummate outsider, going her own way, repudiating the family that had failed to clasp her to its bosom. "She was absolutely rude to Iphigene," said Dick Cohen, Judy's husband. Never one to make an enemy, especially of an in-law, Iphigene studiously ignored the animosity. "She did not confront, she just stepped back," said Ellen Sulzberger Straus. "She was very wise in family relationships."

Caught in the middle of these warring factions, Punch tried to balance the demands of his parents and siblings with those of his wife. But having grown up as the only boy in an undemonstrative family, he was singularly ill-equipped to grapple with raw emotion or ponder what motivated people. His visceral response, honed since childhood, was to retreat to that familiar, private place inside himself where no one could reach him.

His remoteness had cost Punch his first marriage, yet it remained the defining element of his personality. At home with Carol and Cathy, he was affable and good-natured, rarely sharing problems from the office. Occasionally he would lose his temper over something unrelated, but for the most part, he lived a parallel existence to those around him, a man who appeared pacific on the outside, unreachable and unknowable.

For Carol, as for Barbara, the loneliness of being mated to such a man would eventually become intolerable. Barbara had used infidelity to provoke a reaction from Punch; Carol's technique was to needle him, hurling taunts and statements she knew to be outrageous until he had no choice but to explode. Their friends became familiar with the warning signs of when Punch was about to blow: first his feet would shuffle, then he would rub the tops of his thighs and move his mouth as if chewing his tongue. Finally, in a sudden and explosive burst of frustration, he would erupt, pounding the table. "You don't know what the fuck you're talking about!" he would shout at her. "Carol thinks it's good for him," explained former actress and film producer Marit Gruson, a family friend. "She reminds him that he has feelings, that he can react. She's so afraid that he will become stone-hearted."

By the time Punch became publisher, his marriage to Carol had settled into a complex blend of need, distance, and sincere but wary affection. The starry-eyed romance of their early days had given way to a tightly scripted two-person drama. Carol's part was to push Punch; his part was to resist and usually — but not always — give in.

These elements came together in the fall of 1963, several months after Punch had become publisher, when Carol announced that she was pregnant. Whether the pregnancy was a premeditated attempt to produce a rival to Arthur Jr. as a future publisher or simply an accident, one thing was clear: Punch was not happy. He had been so certain when he married Carol that they would never have children that he had tried to eliminate the maternity benefit from his health-insurance coverage, convinced, erroneously, that it would lower his premium. "I'm too old for this stuff," he moaned to his secretary, Nancy Finn, when he told her the news.

When Cynthia Fox Sulzberger was born on June 3, 1964, however, Punch was instantly besotted. With her lush, dark hair and sunny disposition, Cynthia was easy to love. She came along at a time when Punch was older and more mature. He could relax and enjoy fatherhood in a way that had been unthinkable in Arthur Jr.'s and Karen's early years. With Cynthia as their focus, Punch and Carol found a satisfying way to reconfigure their marriage. "I think that Cynthia was the savior of their life together," said Nancy Finn. "That was what they had in common. I can't imagine they would be together [otherwise]."

Carol was a doting parent, uncomplainingly shuttling Cynthia back and forth to specialists when it was discovered that she, like so many Sulzbergers, was afflicted with learning disabilities. "She was a terrific mother, and Cynthia took up her whole life," said Audrey Topping, a sometime sculptor who, at Carol's request, produced a bust of Cynthia. "But she also used it as an excuse not to do anything [as wife of the publisher]. I don't know how many times I've heard her say, 'I can't leave Cynthia.' " When Cynthia was old enough, the *Times'* chauffeur drove her to school, with Punch in the front seat and Cynthia in the back. En route, Punch would flip open his briefcase, extract three hand puppets, turn around, and put on an impromptu show for his little girl, complete with made-up voices. Later he invented a character called the Throxy

Bird, whose adventures he chronicled with Cynthia nestled in his lap. To him, she was "sweetie" and "baby," terms of endearment he used with no one else.

Before Orvil's death, Punch and Carol and various combinations of their collective offspring had spent nearly every weekend with the senior Sulzbergers in the main house at Hillandale. When Marian left Rock Hill to move in with Andrew at High'n Dry, Punch took over the house and grounds and delighted in making them his own — installing a sprinkler system, adding a playroom, landscaping the yard, hanging an old rifle over the bar, and erecting a movie screen similar to the one his father had put in the main house. The furnishings were undistinguished — what Ruth tactfully called "Bloomingdale pleasant" — but Punch didn't care. To him, Rock Hill was an oasis whose every twig and bush he loved, a place where he found the uncomplicated leisure he so craved after his week at the *Times*.

Most Saturday mornings Punch was up early, decked out in the Churchillian jumpsuit he preferred for gardening. In Punch's early years as publisher, he and Carol often invited Bill Jacoby, a designer who had done some redecoration work at the *Times,* and his wife, Rhoda, for the weekend. With Bill silently weeding with Punch, and Rhoda puttering around after Carol, the Jacobys provided a quiet, undemanding kind of companionship that fulfilled Punch and Carol's desire for peace and privacy. In the old-fashioned sense of the term, the two couples "kept company." In private, some family members cattily referred to them as the Jaco-bores. "It was a little like having a pet dog around," said one. "The Jacobys never made waves, and everything was very pleasant."

On Saturday nights Punch often entertained his children and guests with a rented 16 mm film. His taste ran toward traditional Westerns or spy movies — anything with a simple story line and a clear moral. If he read a book, it was almost certain to be a mystery or a spy novel. Before going on vacation to Europe or the Caribbean, he routinely dropped by the office of *The New York Times Book Review* and asked for copies of "the kinds of books I can toss overboard." On Sundays Punch loved nothing better than to eat a plain grilled hamburger topped with a fried egg, served on a tray, and watch *Wild Kingdom* and the Walt Disney show with Cynthia. At some point during the weekend, he walked up to the main house to visit his parents, paying special attention to Iphigene. In time, the two were able to discuss ongoing business problems at the

Times with the same intimacy Orvil had once enjoyed. "He was enormously caring of his mother's feelings and her position," said Sydney Gruson. "He was a very good son."

It was precisely these qualities that fed Carol's frustration over what she viewed as her forced encampment at Rock Hill. While Punch loved weekending on his parents' estate, she was more urban than rural in her tastes. Moreover, Rock Hill was not only not her house, it was a mere stone's throw from her mother-in-law, who, as far as Carol was concerned, summoned Punch for their weekend tête-à-têtes with the commanding air of a dowager queen. Carol would have preferred a place in the Hamptons, the Long Island retreat of wealthy and well-connected New Yorkers, but Punch would not hear of it.

For Arthur Jr. and Karen, the contrast between weekends with Punch and life with Barbara and her second husband, David Christy, was glaring. "It was not a happy household at the Christys," said Karen. No one was quite certain what David did for a living; at various times he was reputedly a coal and mineral broker, a financial consultant, an investment banker, and out of work. His main redemptive virtue was that he was big and fun-loving and had a magical way with small children. Under David's tutelage, Arthur Jr. learned how to ride a bike and roll down a hill. When Arthur Jr. expressed his desire for a dog — "someone to keep me company at night" — David brought home Booth, a boxer that drooled continuously and slept in Arthur Jr.'s bed. "I became very close to [David]," Arthur Jr. said. "He was very much a father figure in my life." At their mother's request, Arthur Jr. and Karen called him Dad.

But as the children began to acquire minds of their own, David's charm faded. "It's when you start to try and have a conversation when you get older that everything breaks apart," said Karen. With Punch's help, Arthur Jr. and Karen went to private schools in Manhattan, and to Lake George and New Hampshire for summer camp, but by every other measure their life was starkly middle-class and unstable compared with their father's. Though they never wanted for anything, the prevailing mood in the Christy household was one of anxiety over money. As products of the Depression, both David and Barbara were practiced penny-pinchers. During rare family dinners at a neighborhood restaurant, they insisted that Arthur Jr. and Karen split an entrée long after they were old enough to warrant their own. Punch and Carol, meanwhile, lived in a world in which money was of no consequence. "It was wonderful," Karen said of the vacations she and Arthur Jr. took with Punch and Carol. "You could go to the hotel dining room and order off the menu."

David was active in St. James Episcopal Church, and having grown up with virtually no religious training herself, Barbara decided to join him. She called Punch to tell him that she was becoming an Episcopalian and added that she thought Arthur Jr. and Karen should have some kind of religious life, too. "If you want them reared as Jews, that's fine with me," she said. "But you'll have to do it; I don't understand it." Like his father, Punch considered himself an American of Jewish faith. He had been comfortable with the idea of his children being raised "neutral," as he put it, but the prospect of their being raised Christian touched something visceral. For the first time in his life, he sought the advice of a rabbi. "It was my last consultation," he said. "He was for the birds. . . . It didn't help me one single iota." The children attended St. James and eventually were confirmed as Episcopalians.

Arthur Jr. was small and slight for his age, afflicted by allergies, subdued and lacking in confidence. "I don't like to think of myself as [having been] a serious child," he said later. "I think of myself as [having been] fun-loving. . . . But I confess [that for] most of my childhood I was in a fog." He was always the last chosen in pickup games of baseball; running bases, he was inevitably tagged out. The experience left him with a lifelong distaste for team sports — any "games with rules," as he put it.

But despite his physical shortcomings, he showed admirable perseverance in other areas. Every day he doggedly practiced the trumpet, blaring out the apartment window or holed up in a closet while Julie Adler Jr. and his family, who lived two floors above the Christys at 168 East Seventy-fourth Street, served as an involuntary and unappreciative audience. "I thought there was never going to be a day in this world that I would live long enough to hear 'My Country! 'Tis of Thee' from beginning to end," said Anne Freeman Turpin, Julie Jr.'s former wife.

§

After several years as publisher, Punch showed signs of developing into a capable manager, but his lack of experience still made itself apparent from time to time in glaring and sometimes costly misjudgments. One of the most public examples occurred in early 1968 in a blowup he came ruefully to call "*The New York Times*' Bay of Pigs."

The ostensible problem was what to do about Tom Wicker, the paper's Washington bureau chief, whose performance had disappointed Punch, Turner, and other top news executives in New York. The deeper and more intractable dispute involved a decades-long tug-of-war between the Washington bureau and New York. Under Arthur Krock, Scotty Reston, and now Wicker, the Washington bureau had gone about its business with enviable independence, brooking little interference from New York. As executive editor, Catledge was determined to bring Washington into line; the historic rivalry between Turner and Scotty only heightened the stakes.

In 1964 Scotty had personally selected Wicker, a garrulous North Carolinian who was roughly Punch's age, to succeed him as head of the Washington office. Punch had approved of the appointment; he admired Wicker's work, and at Scotty's urging, he and Carol had also become friends with Wicker and his wife during several European excursions. As important, he did not want to cross Scotty and possibly lose him to another paper. However, he had not taken into consideration the dispiriting effect his decision would have on Clifton Daniel, his new managing editor, who felt that he should have been consulted, and on Turner and the other New York editors, who longed to address the cronyism and lack of imagination they felt flawed the paper's Washington reportage.

The chief complaint about Wicker was that he did not produce enough front-page exclusives, a charge that contained a good deal of truth but was not entirely Wicker's fault. Keenly aware of television's power, politicians and policymakers had started to give newsbreaks that had once gone to the *Times* to the networks instead. At the same time, the formerly ineffective *Washington Post* had shown drive under its new editor, Ben Bradlee. Hardly a day went by that the *Post* didn't scoop *The New York Times* on some story or angle, a matter of deep embarrassment to Turner and the New York cadre.

Turner's solution had been to propose offering Wicker a column, giving him Arthur Krock's space when Krock retired in September 1966, and turning over administration of the bureau to a new man. Wicker had been surprisingly antagonistic to the idea, and when Catledge had gone to Washington to canvass the situation, he found a bureau demoralized by what it considered to be nit-picking by the bullpen in New York. Bureau reporters had also been decidedly unenthusiastic about the list of candidates to replace Wicker. In the face of such resistance, Turner advised Punch that, for the time being, it was probably best to stick with the status quo. Relieved not to have to confront Wicker, Punch agreed. The ironic result was that Wicker had actually come out ahead: not only did he continue to run the Washington bureau, he got Krock's thrice-weekly column as well.

By early 1968 news coverage out of Washington had not improved, and the *Times* was facing a presidential-election year. Since Wicker was certain to be away from the capital more than usual, gathering material for his column, the moment seemed ripe to name his replacement. This time New York didn't take a broad survey of Washington's opinion. Instead, Punch, in consultation with his top editors, tapped James Greenfield, a former executive with Continental Airlines and assistant secretary of state in the Johnson administration who had come to the *Times* seven months earlier as an assistant under metropolitan editor Arthur Gelb. Greenfield's chief attributes were that he was loyal to the paper's New York commanders, yet knew his way around the capital, and that with no desire to write, he could devote himself full-time to running the bureau. He was also something of a Trojan horse, a way for the ambitious Rosenthal, who was frequently mentioned as a possible future managing editor, to plant his own man in the all-important Washington bureau and at the same time eliminate Wicker as a rival for managing editor. That particular element of the political arithmetic seems never to have occurred to Punch, who endorsed Greenfield and set the wheels in motion for his appointment.

In the first week of February, Punch flew to Washington to personally inform Wicker. Over dinner at the Metropolitan Club, he told him in almost apologetic tones of the decision to replace him. Wicker was shocked: he knew that New York was dissatisfied with him, but it was the first he had heard that his removal was imminent. "Turner told Punch everything had been worked out," said Stuart Greenspon. "Then he went down there and [found out] . . . Turner had done zilch [to prepare the ground]."

The next morning Punch returned to New York, shaken but unbowed in his determination to carry out the Greenfield appointment. Wicker in the meantime had spent a sleepless night, furious at being bullied by New York and getting trumped by his rival Rosenthal. When he arrived at the bureau, he typed up his resignation and tacked it to the bulletin board. As the news raced through the office, correspondents heatedly vowed to resign in protest. "The idea that New York was going to impose some New York guy on the bureau was a red flag," said Wicker.

When Turner learned what had happened, he placed a frantic phone call to Wicker and talked him out of resigning. To protect the *Times*, Wicker agreed, and that afternoon he flew to Claremont, New Hampshire, to report on the New Hampshire primary while his wife, Neva, on her own recognizance made two indignant phone calls to complain about how her husband had been treated — one to Scotty Reston, and the other to Carol Sulzberger, who rose up with protective fury. "[Neva and I] were just not going to let this go by," said Carol. "Tom is a friend, and if you're a friend of mine, you've got me forever."

A few days later Scotty injected himself into the situation. Just three weeks earlier he had warned Punch that "a smooth transition to Greenfield is out of the question, and a stormy transition may be more costly than it is worth." Now that his prediction had come true, he made a point of going to New York, using the excuse of a Council on Foreign Relations meeting. Hearing that Scotty was in town, Punch popped by to see him. Reston's displeasure was apparent before a word had been uttered. "Boy, you're *really* upset by the Greenfield thing, aren't you?" Punch said with a tone of forced joviality.

In reply, Scotty conveyed the impression that he might resign if the Greenfield appointment went through. Punch was not entirely sure what Scotty's true intentions were, but he felt distinctly uneasy. If he stuck with Greenfield, he risked losing Reston and perhaps other valued *Times* reporters in what had the potential to become a mass mutiny. If he reneged, he would appear weak, his word would mean nothing, and his top New York editors would feel betrayed. In short, he felt that he was in a no-win situation, a position he particularly loathed.

The next day Wicker arrived in New York from New Hampshire, prepared to demand an audience with Punch and Turner. Finding most of the newsroom out for lunch, he adjourned to the Century Association, where by coincidence he bumped into Scotty. The two fell into an intense conversation, and that afternoon Scotty met again with Punch, telling him in no uncertain terms that installing Greenfield was the worst idea since Eisenhower had chosen Nixon as his vice president. "If you do this, you're going to have a nasty scandal," he said. Rather than face that, or possibly Scotty's resignation, Punch relented. He summoned Wicker, who was elsewhere in the building at the time, and told him that he had decided to retain him as bureau chief.

At 4:30 P.M. Punch called Turner out of the afternoon news conference and informed him that he couldn't go through with the Greenfield appointment. When he returned to the meeting, Turner couldn't hide his extreme frustration and annoyance. As the conference was breaking up, he asked Clifton Daniel and Abe Rosenthal to remain behind. "Gentlemen," he said. "I have bad news for you. The publisher has reversed his decision on the Washington bureau." Neither Catledge nor Daniel nor Rosenthal — Greenfield's three principal supporters — had been consulted in advance. "I was madder than hell," said Daniel. "I was absolutely livid with fury."

After Rosenthal had unsuccessfully tried to place an angry call to Punch, he strode into the newsroom and, in a windowless cubicle, told Greenfield what had happened. Greenfield was stunned. He had never campaigned to be Washington bureau chief and, indeed, had been surprised that the *Times* wanted to put a neophyte in such an important slot. *Times* colleagues had already begun congratulating him on his new job; *Newsweek* had scheduled an interview with him for the next day. Now the publisher had rescinded the promotion and had not even had the courtesy to deliver the news himself. Under the circumstances, he decided there was no way he could remain at the *Times*. Greenfield submitted his resignation on the spot and minutes later stormed out of the building without his sweater.

That night the news of Greenfield's resignation made the NBC radio and TV news. Two days later *The Washington Post* gleefully published a story about the contretemps, including the cheers that had erupted in the *Times'* Washington bureau when it became known that Punch had reversed himself. "We've won," one staffer had crowed. Indeed, the vanquished forces in New York were left to stagger home and bind their wounds as best they could. Far from unifying the paper, the incident further balkanized it. "I'm sorry all this has happened, but I hope we'll be able to work things out in the future," Wicker told Catledge hours after the incident. Turner stared back, stone-faced. "Well," he said, glowering, "we'll see about that!"

In the ensuing days, Punch scurried around trying to mollify the New York staff. Turner pointedly ignored him, finally succumbing to Punch's argument that their years of friendship should not be held hostage to a single event, but Clifton Daniel was not so quick to call a truce. For almost two weeks he refused to meet with the publisher, fearful, he told Punch, that "one of us might say something we would live to regret." When he finally agreed to a conversation, his angry denunciation of Punch for the Washington bungle was so shrill and so loud that Turner and the other editors could hear his voice through the closed door. "He lectured Punch like he was a schoolboy and Clifton was the headmaster," said Sydney Gruson. Punch never forgot the dressing-down; it was an error that would eventually cost Daniel the executive editorship.

Over the next several months, the wounded parties tried to recover their dignity and reestablish their authority, but newsroom morale was severely shaken. No one knew who really ran the news side of the paper. Though he declined to take much blame for the debacle, Punch admitted that "the Washington thing was sloppily handled from top to bottom." Iphigene, too, was worried that the *Times* had lost not only face but its inner compass. "Where are we going?" she demanded of Punch not long afterward.

In a series of private memos he sent his mother starting in the winter of 1968, Punch tried to come up with an answer. As he contemplated where the *Times* stood and how it should change in the future, one thing became clear: it was time for Turner to depart. The Greenfield episode had undermined Punch's confidence in his top editor, and at sixty-seven, Turner was not as sharp as he used to be. He nodded off in meetings and occasionally drank more than he should have. As executive editor, he had largely failed in his main mission: to unify the daily news department and the Sunday department. On the personal side of the equation, Turner had never quite made the leap from Punch's avuncular mentor to respectful subordinate.

Before he could remove Turner, however, Punch had to decide on a replacement. Clifton Daniel, the managing editor, would have been the obvious choice, but he had burned his bridges permanently with Punch. Iphigene weighed in on the side of Scotty. If anyone could restore the paper's stature, serve as a symbol of its values, and salve its internal injuries, she argued, Scotty Reston could. Furthermore, bringing Scotty to New York would remove him as the effective potentate of the Washington bureau, giving the *Times* a chance — finally — to centralize authority at West Forty-third Street. Scotty was reluctant to take the job because he liked Washington and didn't want to leave. But in the interests of the paper, he agreed; his only condition was that he could continue to write his column.

Now all that remained was the painful task of telling Turner. "It was hard because he was as close as anybody in my family," said Punch. "But it was the right thing to do." Unfortunately, Punch handled the announcement of the impending change as ineptly as he had the Washington episode, confiding the news first to Sydney Gruson, one of the paper's great gossips, in the certain knowledge that it would trickle down to Catledge in a matter of hours. The strategy was meant to prepare Turner and spare Punch pain, but the next day, when Punch informed "the Professor" that he planned to install Scotty as executive editor, Turner was shocked. Remarkably, in a newsroom full of secret-tellers, no one had informed him. "I was . . . somewhat hurt," Turner said later. "Quite a few people here knew about it before I did. . . . I thought at least [Punch] should have discussed it with me."

As it turned out, Punch had not discussed the matter with another person who had felt slighted by the omission: his father. Several days after Punch and Turner's discussion, Arthur asked Catledge to come to his fourteenth-floor office. When Turner arrived, he spied Punch, clearly embarrassed, furtively hovering in the corridor outside the chairman's door; upon entering, he saw Iphigene, who hugged him and greeted him warmly as a new *Times* director — the compensatory plum Turner had been given when he was fired. Arthur sat in a wheelchair behind his desk and offered Turner a glass of sherry, and for a fleeting moment the two recaptured their old camaraderie. Then Arthur looked down, gathered himself, and in a voice thick with emotion said, "I just want you to know this is not the way I wanted it."

28

Searching for Lost Fathers

ONE SUNDAY AFTERNOON IN THE WINTER OF 1966, Arthur Jr. sat in his room at Loomis, the Connecticut boarding school his father had attended, hoisted his feet up on the radiator for warmth, and gazed disconsolately out the window at the bare quadrangle below. The previous year he had phoned his father with prideful delight to tell him that he had been accepted at his alma mater. Despite Punch's own abysmal experience at the school more than twenty years earlier, the news had pleased him. Now, after just one semester, Arthur Jr. knew that he and Loomis were not a good match. He missed the vitality of New York and found the highly structured Loomis atmosphere stifling. "It was all those old rigid rules at a time when society was clearly breaking away," he said. "I was not cut out for that." His unhappiness had become so overwhelming that he had recently started seeing a child psychiatrist.

In March Arthur Jr. left Loomis, never to return. Withdrawing before the end of the school year, with all the failure that implied, was hard enough. Then, compounding the drama, he made an even harder decision, one of the most difficult and important of his life: he decided to move in with his father. Arthur Jr. had long yearned to escape the disorder of his mother's household. Over the past six years, Barbara had had two children by David Christy, and their apartment had grown noisy and crowded, its rhythms determined by the routine of diaper changing and bottle-feeding. Moreover, the Christy marriage was beginning to show cracks and strain. Barbara, needy and flailing, had begun to focus her considerable emotional wattage on fourteen-year-old Arthur Jr., a situation that made him uncomfortable and only added to the confusion of his emerging manhood.

The more compelling motivation for Arthur Jr.'s decision, however, was his desire to become better acquainted with his father and to claim his rightful place in the extended Sulzberger clan, in which he had begun to feel like an outsider. He entered the magical world of Hillandale and Fifth Avenue only on major holidays and every other weekend, while his stepsister, half sister, and cousins lived there every day of the year. They inhabited their heritage in a way he did not. Stirred by an inchoate fear of dispossession, Arthur Jr. determined to act.

Arthur Jr. did not ask his mother's permission to live with Punch, but rather informed her; and though she was devastated, she assured him that she understood. "I knew that [Punch's family] would pull a lot more than I could," Barbara explained. "I have nothing to offer the children. Except me." But when Karen, observing her older brother's bold action with a mixture of envy and annoyance, declared that she, too, wanted to live with Punch, Barbara put her foot down. "I can't let you go; it would kill me," she told Karen. "I've got to have you here." Karen was accustomed to caring for her mother: at the age of eight she had consoled Barbara after the death of the family cat rather than the other way around. Karen gave up without a fight the idea of moving in with her father, although she found a way to make her displeasure clear. "Karen has completely fallen apart," Punch told Arthur and Iphigene soon thereafter in a letter detailing his daughter's poor report card.

At 1010 Fifth Avenue, Cathy's room was split into two to make a bedroom for Arthur Jr., an accommodation Cathy made with magnanimity, as she would be leaving for college in a year. Making room for Arthur Jr. in the established order of the Sulzberger household was another matter. Punch said he was "just absolutely delighted" with his son's decision, but neither he nor Carol had any experience bringing up a boy, especially a boy on the verge of adolescence. "I was fourteen when I came to his house, so he had me for a year and a half before I became an asshole," Arthur Jr. remarked.

Although Arthur Jr. now had his father at close range, forging a bond would prove to be no easier than before. During the week Punch was often out at business functions and absent for dinner. Weekends were better, a time when everyone escaped to Rock Hill and Punch gardened and barbecued and slipped into his familiar role of family man. But his predilection for tinkering, weeding, and other solitary activities effectively erected a shield around him that was hard for a teenage boy to penetrate. When Arthur Jr. shot baskets with his cousins Dan and Jace Cohen in the Rock Hill driveway, Punch made no effort to join in.

Arthur Jr.'s desire to connect with his father was poignantly obvious. That summer when he departed for camp, he took with him the same olive green trunk and name-tagged underwear as all the other boys, but among his gear was also something unique: his father's battered typewriter case, identified in clear lettering as being the property of A. O. SULZBERGER, THE NEW YORK TIMES. "If I had to name one moment when the bells went off," said Carol, "that would have been it." From the earliest age, Arthur Jr. had declared his intention to be in the newspaper business, but after Punch was named publisher, his ambition became more specific: to succeed his father. "He wanted to be publisher of *The New York Times,* [for] as long as I can remember," said Dan Cohen. Growing up without Punch had made him eager to please his father and hungry to know him, and what better way to corner him than to follow him into *The New York Times*?

Arthur Jr.'s lack of athletic ability only reinforced his interest in newspapering. "I think that made him feel a little bit an outcast and pushed him in other directions," said Dan. "He narrowed his focus, not necessarily by choice." At the Browning School on East Sixty-second Street, where he repeated the ninth grade upon his return from Loomis, Arthur Jr. was so short, blond, and fresh-faced that in his class photograph he looks startlingly out of place, like a child prodigy. "I was four feet two inches forever," he recalled. At an age when boys measure their worth by their skill on the playing field, Arthur Jr. dabbled in soccer and softball, excelling at neither.

Public speaking was one area in which he distinguished himself. As a member of the Browning Debating Club, he discovered that a well-placed witty remark could turn a situation to his advantage. He developed a tongue that, when necessary, he wielded like a rapier; in time, he earned a reputation as a smart aleck. "That's where the defense [mechanism] came from," said his mother. "He developed a fabulous sense of humor because of his height."

In tenth grade Arthur Jr. joined the *Grytte,* Browning's student newspaper; eventually he would rise to the position of associate editor. Even at that young age, he was determined to demonstrate that he was his father's son, the heir to *The New York Times.* Despite his own childhood difficulties, Punch had always assumed the job was his birthright. He had been raised in an insular world of wealth and connections, a world so unself-conscious in its sense of entitlement that he and his grammar-school contemporaries had staged races among their chauffeurs. In the social churn of the sixties, that world was rapidly disappearing. As a child of divorce growing up in the Christy household, Arthur Jr. had experienced none of that peculiar brand of security, an absence that left him with all the daredevil courage and all the fear of one who feels he must succeed on his own capacities. "Punch is totally comfortable in his own skin," said Carol Sulzberger. "Arthur Jr. is not. He has to prove himself to so many people."

Outward Bound, a wilderness-survival program in which Arthur Jr. participated the summer between his junior and senior years in high school, gave him a chance to test his abilities. The tenets of Outward Bound — collective decision making, confronting and overcoming fear, uncovering the power within — were made to order for a boy who had spent his life as an outsider. Griswold Smith, Arthur Jr.'s godfather and a director of Outward Bound in North Carolina, first proposed the idea over dinner in New York, believing that his godson needed a physical challenge and adult male attention. Arthur Jr. was skeptical. "I didn't embrace this," he recalled. "I had to be convinced it wasn't the Marine Corps."

The twenty-eight-day course was grueling. From a base camp in the Carolina mountains, Arthur Jr. and the ten other boys in his group slept in canvas bunks, cooked their meals over an open fire, and tramped into the woods for five- to seven-day expeditions. Rock climbing, rappeling from cliffs, and crawling and walking across ropes and logs strung between trees some thirty feet off the ground rounded out the activities. The program, similar to basic training in the military, molded a disparate group of teenagers into a team. "They try to build that platoon-like sense of working together and caring about each other under conditions of stress," said Arthur Jr. "You're exhausted, you're wet, you're cold, but you're with people who are just like you."

The worst moment for Arthur Jr. came during the three-day "solo." Each boy was dropped off alone in the wilderness for three days with only half a day's dry rations and some paper and a pencil. The exercise was designed to allow the boys to decompress, reflect on the lessons of the past weeks, and experience the self-reliance that comes with fending for oneself. In an article Arthur Jr. later wrote for the *Grytte,* he described the feeling as one of having been "abandoned." After he arrived at his assigned spot, he put up his little tarp, unrolled his sleeping bag, and started to cry.

Arthur Jr. had taken one book with him to North Carolina: *The Fountainhead,* by Ayn Rand. The novel is a monument to individualism and vividly illustrates one of the fundamentals of Outward Bound — that each person has the capacity to do more than he ever thought possible. Arthur Jr. would later describe the experience as "a defining moment," a time when he realized that "I could take control of my life." "He faced something he wasn't sure he could do, and he didn't just do it, he kicked its ass," said his half brother, David Christy Jr. "It gave him a lot of confidence." Yet it was the emphasis on teamwork — the opposite of individualism — that would stay with him as he matured. "The more important theme [of Outward Bound] is that there are some things you cannot do alone," he said. "You're going to have to find a way of making the group work for the betterment of everyone." When Arthur Jr. got home, he was so grateful to Griswold Smith that he spray-painted his mountain boots silver and mailed them to his godfather as a gift.

No sooner had Arthur Jr. returned from this intense experience than he was off on another: a six-week trip to Israel with Ellen and Peter Straus, relatives on his father's side of the family, and several of their children. For a year after he had moved in with Punch, Arthur Jr. continued to attend St. James Episcopal Church with his mother and stepfather, a habit that had gradually tapered off. By the time he arrived in Israel, he considered himself an Episcopalian, even though he hadn't practiced religion of any kind for several years.

The group spent half the time at a kibbutz near the Lebanese border and the remainder touring Israel. In Jerusalem Peter Straus used his contacts to arrange a dinner with several senior government officials, and during the evening one remarked that no matter what happened in the world, everyone around the table would always have a homeland in Israel. Arthur Jr. was deeply offended. "Excuse me, but I'm an Episcopalian," he said loudly. "Is this still *my* country?" As Peter and Ellen went white with embarrassment, the Israeli official diplomatically retreated. "It was racist," Arthur Jr. later said of the man's comments. "The minute he discovered I wasn't who he thought I was, the statement was no longer valid."

Arthur Jr.'s outburst was deceptive, for his visit to Israel had a profound and lasting effect. "I never felt Jewish before then," he said. "I went in there as an Episcopalian and emerged with some sense that there was a side of me worth pursuing, some threads that needed to be pulled." That fall, when he returned to Browning to start his senior year, he wrote a long article for the school paper headlined GRYTTE STAFFER HAS INTERVIEWS WITH ISRAELI OFFICIALS. "Israel will survive," it concluded. "Arabs may finally overrun the country, but she will survive. It is impossible to work with the people, talk with them, and live with them and to think otherwise. Israel will survive simply because she has everything to gain, and everything to lose."

§

After years of living with Dick Cohen, his adoptive father, Dan Cohen had become an expert at annoying him. As he boasted, "I could set off his fuse anytime I wanted." A favorite technique was to catch Dick in an inconsistency or to pretend not to understand what had just been said. If that didn't work, Dan would insult Dick with a sharp remark, a move guaranteed to provoke the older man into an explosion of brute force. "Dick was really harsh," said Judy. "He used to bat [the kids] around."

As Dan matured, he began to tire of the cat-and-mouse game. Once, after Dick had cuffed him on the side of the head to get his attention, he looked his father straight in the eye and said, "Listen, I'm really sick of this. I don't know what you think you're accomplishing. Hitting me isn't going to serve any purpose." They had a talk, and as an incentive to curb his temper, Dick agreed to pay Dan a quarter every time he hit him. Several days later Dan couldn't resist another taunt. "I went so far under his skin, he lost it," he recalled. Unable to contain himself, Dick inflicted several glancing blows on Dan's head. At the end of the drubbing, Dan looked up and said, "That will be $2.75." Dick began to quake. He stormed upstairs, brought back a five-dollar bill and slapped Dan three more times. "Here," he said, handing his son the money. "Keep the change."

Judy had married Dick Cohen in 1958 largely because she felt that her children needed a father after her divorce from Mattie Rosenschein, but Dick was unprepared to care for two troubled boys. His presence was not helpful; if anything, it was negative. "If I had to have a father like [Dick], I didn't want a father in the house," said Dan. But in fairness, the Cohen boys were hardly model children. Angry at Mattie for giving them up, and furious about the attention Judy showered on her new husband, they lashed out in whatever way they could.

There had been sexual sparks between Dick and Judy when they had first met, but for Dick, the Sulzbergers' wealth, warmth, and connections were of equal appeal. Whereas Mattie had resented the family's double-edged generosity, Dick was only too happy to accept loans and cash gifts, and stay in expensive hotels such as the Hassler in Rome on family vacations. He consciously courted Iphigene, and she in turn doted on him. "I was basically her favorite," Dick said. While he eagerly reaped the rewards that came with being married to a Sulzberger, he didn't know how to give back in kind. Never having had children of his own — Judy had a miscarriage soon after their marriage — he had no inkling how to be a father.

Dan and Jace received only marginal assistance from Judy, who, true to the Sulzberger tradition, was an undemonstrative mother. She built model airplanes and cars with her sons, meticulously painting each tiny part, and felt completely at home on the floor with an Erector set. But as she herself acknowledged, "I was very close to my children, I really loved them, but as far as hugging and kissing, no." When, several years after they were married, Dick and Judy began to experience difficulties, the tension found its way back to Dan and Jace. "A lot of that was taken out on us as kids," said Dan. "We didn't know what was going on, but it wasn't a house filled with a lot of love." With so little warmth to go around, Dan and Jace competed for it rather than clinging to each other.

Each morning a chauffeur drove the young Cohens from their home in Stamford, Connecticut, not far from Hillandale, to New Canaan Country Day School and picked them up in the afternoon. New Canaan went up to only the tenth grade, and for the balance of high school, most parents sent their offspring away. When Dan reached that point, Judy and Dick chose Westminster, a small, all-male, heavily Protestant boarding school near Hartford, Connecticut. "The relationship [with Dick] was so bad, they wanted me out of the house," Dan said.

When he arrived on the Westminster campus in the fall of 1966, Dan was a volatile compound of anger and insecurity. Because he was a late arrival — nearly everyone else had started in the ninth grade, a year earlier — he was assigned a single room. "I never felt so abandoned in my whole life," he recalled. On his first day he went to mandatory chapel wearing the black tie that identified him as a new boy. As the minister said, "Let us pray," the students bowed their heads, but Dan, one of a handful of Jews, did not. Within moments he felt a blow from behind that threw him into a more reverent position. "Pray, Jew," growled his unseen assailant. "That was my first exposure to anti-Semitism," said Dan. "I had never been called a Jew in my life. I didn't know what it all meant."

Dan quickly learned that disparaging his Jewishness before anyone else did could have a disarming effect. Although he had gone to temple only four times in his life — and two of those occasions were funerals — he began to refer to himself as "the Yid Kid." He even imprinted a Westminster coffee mug with the words and made anti-Semitic remarks at his own expense. "I felt I had no value," he said. "I was nothing." For a boy of his sensitivities, the environment at Westminster was *Lord of the Flies* incarnate. Afflicted with what would later be called attention deficit disorder, he had trouble concentrating; writing was torture. The school's rigid requirements — compulsory breakfast, room inspection at 7:55 A.M. — made him seethe. "I hated authority, I fought authority," he said. "[If] someone had arbitrary rules, I'd go nuts."

For nearly a year Dan pleaded with his parents to let him come home. "You'll work this out," they assured him. "You'll get through this." Finally, Dan gave up begging and resigned himself to fitting in with his predatory Westminster classmates. Like Arthur Jr., Dan was small for his age — so small that his nickname was Leprechaun. And, like Arthur Jr., he discovered the defensive potential of a sharp tongue. So armed, he held his own, but his awareness of his power to wound others only made him feel worse. "I was a despicable kid at that point," he said. "I wasn't proud of any of it. I *hated* myself."

Summers and school vacations provided a reprieve, and during these interludes he spent as much time as he could with Arthur Jr., the Sulzberger cousin closest to him in age, circumstance, and sensibility. Even as young children, they had fallen into set roles. During the war games they had played in the woods behind the Cohen home, Arthur Jr. was always the strategizing general; Dan, the sergeant, barking out orders; Jace, the bullet-riddled private; and Karen, the nurse. No one, not even Dan, questioned Arthur Jr.'s right to be the commander, for as Karen said, "That was his part. He wanted to be on top."

By the time they were teenagers, Dan and Arthur Jr. had become so seamlessly connected that they were like brothers — closer than brothers, in fact. "We spoke in code," said Arthur Jr. "It must have been horrible for everybody else." Cynthia agreed with that assessment, complaining,

"It was awful to be around them. They were so obnoxious." That became dramatically apparent one summer weekend at Hillandale when Dan and Arthur Jr. decided to light matches near the pool house while everyone else was eating lunch. The small patch of grass where they were playing was brittle and dry, and soon a flame escaped, shot out, and raced down the hill.

Panic-stricken, Arthur Jr. and Dan galloped to the main house to get help. On the way, they breathlessly agreed that they would lie, saying that they had seen two boys start the blaze, and had given chase but failed to capture them. When they arrived in the Hillandale living room and announced the crisis, Punch and Dick and the other able-bodied men took off immediately for the pool house, leaving Arthur sitting in his wheelchair in a state of hysteria. "I don't feel so good," he groaned, clutching his heart, terrified that his beloved Hillandale was about to go up in flames.

After the fire had been subdued, Punch took Arthur Jr. into one room, and Dick took Dan into another, and the two fathers interrogated their sons about the real cause of the near catastrophe. "Arthur Jr. knew that the minute my father got me by myself, I was going to cave, because [he would] beat the shit out of me," said Dan. "I was going to die if I didn't confess instantly."

Dan's sense of fatherlessness deepened when, during a summertime bicycle trip through England and Scotland, he received word that Mattie Rosenschein had died at the age of forty-five. Mattie had had an allergic reaction to a chemical — possibly an insecticide — and although he was able to make it back to his office, where his nurse was waiting, he didn't get the lifesaving dose of epinephrine in time. He died of anaphylactic shock; Judy went to the funeral.

Over a decade later, Jace would seek out Mattie's second family and gradually become close to his four half brothers, but Dan would have nothing to do with them. For him, all that remained of Mattie was a single photograph, a picture he did not display but could not bear to part with. Among Mattie's effects was a letter, written to him by a medical colleague — a psychiatrist — during the period in which he had wrestled with the decision of whether to give Dan and Jace up for adoption. It would be in the best interests of the boys, the doctor had advised Mattie, if they were allowed to grow up in a "whole family" rather than shuttling back and forth between two households. Mattie's oldest son by his second wife had found the letter and had given it to Jace. For Jace, the knowledge that Mattie hadn't been cavalier or unfeeling, that he had agonized, sought counsel, and tried to do the right thing, made it possible, finally, to accept his father, even to love him, long after he was dead. He gave the letter to Dan in the hope that it might produce a similar response in his brother. Dan cried when he read it, but his heart remained closed. "I've never really forgiven him [for abandoning us]," he said.

29

The Age of Discontent

I N RETROSPECT, MAY 1968 WAS A TENSE MOMENT of breath-catching between two national catastrophes — one month after the assassination of the Reverend Martin Luther King Jr. and one month before the assassination of Robert F. Kennedy. His credibility destroyed by the failure of his Vietnam policy, President Lyndon Johnson had recently declared his intention not to seek a second term. Hippies were a common sight, even at *The New York Times,* where copyboys and -girls adopted such relaxed standards of dress and cleanliness that Punch circulated a cranky memo complaining that he had had his "stomach full" of their "strange-looking" attire. Sexual liberation had arrived at the paper two months earlier in the form of a story about premarital sex at Barnard, a piece Iphigene had denounced as "outrageous" and a virtual endorsement of "loose living" among college students. "What are those girls on the Women's Page trying to do to the reputation of the *Times* and Barnard College?" she had demanded of Punch in an angry letter. "Premarital affairs are nothing new, but they are not desirable as a way of life. . . . If we have a family page, let's stick to the subject."

One afternoon during this period, four-year-old Cynthia Sulzberger looked out the window of her parents' eighth-floor apartment at 1010 Fifth Avenue and saw a large group of protesters with placards. They were shouting what, to her ears, was a thrilling chant. "Sulzberger, Sulzberger, tell the truth! *New York Times,* tell the truth!" Cynthia ran to find Carol. "Mommy, Mommy!," she cried. "They're having a parade and they're talking about *us!*"

Several days earlier, in the biggest campus demonstration since the free speech movement at the University of California at Berkeley, Mark Rudd, chairman of the Columbia University chapter of Students for a

Democratic Society, had led students in a takeover of five Columbia buildings and held several administrators hostage. The ostensible issues were Columbia's ties to the Institute of Defense Analysis, a consortium conducting research for the Defense Department, and the proposed construction of a university gym in a section of a park used by local blacks.

But that mattered less than the prevailing mood of confrontation on campus. Horrified by the King assassination and disenchanted with an undeclared and costly war, students were restive, itching to register their indignation in the streets. Punch had recently taken his father's seat on the Columbia board of trustees, and when the uproar on campus reached crisis proportions, he joined with his fellow trustees in directing Grayson Kirk, Columbia's president, to "maintain the ultimate disciplinary power over the conduct of the students."

On April 29 Arthur Gelb, the *Times'* metropolitan editor, sat next to a senior New York City administrator at an official dinner. After a few drinks, the man confided that there was about to be a bust at Columbia: a thousand helmeted policemen were readying themselves to move in, recover the buildings, and roust the students. "In two or three hours, we're going to clean out the dorms that have been taken over," he said sotto voce. "I'm giving this tip to you alone." Gelb thanked him profusely, raced back to the *Times* and, at 10:00 P.M. dispatched to Columbia every reporter he could lay his hands on. When he tracked down Abe Rosenthal, who had become the paper's assistant managing editor, at a Broadway theater, where he was watching *Hair,* Rosenthal said he wanted to see the action for himself. With Nat Goldstein, the *Times'* circulation director, he hitched a ride with the police up to Columbia, a decision he later admitted was "not the most brilliant . . . in the world."

As he stood amid the swarm of cops and students on the darkened campus, Rosenthal was aghast. "I'd never seen anything like it in America," he recalled. Some students shouted obscenities; others sobbed. One young man stopped near Rosenthal and two other newspapermen and yelled with unrestrained fury, "I hope you old fucks die!" When the police rushed up the stairs of Low Library and into the occupied office of President Kirk, Rosenthal followed. The protesters had turned the place into a garbage heap. Half-eaten sandwiches and dirty blankets littered the room; the furniture had been smashed; the green rug was spattered. For Rosenthal, forty-six, who, like many first- and second-generation Jewish immigrants, had proudly enrolled at New York's City College in the 1940s, the disrespect for academic authority was incomprehensible.

The presses were stopped at 4:00 A.M. to insert the story, which was put on page one. Absent from the piece, however, was anything more than the most cursory details of the police rampage that had occurred after most copies of the *Times* had been printed. In the predawn melee, dozens of students had been badly kicked and beaten and hundreds arrested, yet the *Times* story indicated that the only serious contact with the police had occurred when a faculty member who had blocked the entrance to Low Memorial Library had been hit on the head with a nightstick. Nowhere had the *Times* qualified its account by saying that its reporting had been "as of 4:00 A.M." To readers — especially to the rioting students — the story appeared to be the *Times'* final word on the conflict, a whitewashed version of reality that was silent on the subject of police brutality and portrayed Kirk, who was later characterized by William Manchester as "aloof, frosty and a poor administrator," as a sympathetic figure.

In an unusual move for a top editor, Rosenthal had written a passionate eyewitness account headlined COMBAT AND COMPASSION AT COLUMBIA. He spoke of President Kirk's pain, of the ambivalence many students felt about the demonstrators, and of the "harsh force" of the police, many of whom nonetheless seemed "almost fond, in a professional way, of the students." Within New York journalism circles, there was talk that he had purposely assigned himself the Columbia story because Punch was a university trustee. Rosenthal denied having any political agenda, and when Jack Newfield attacked him in *The Village Voice* for one-sided coverage, he angrily responded that Newfield was trying to "damage the major asset of *The New York Times* — its reputation for integrity." Officially *The New York Times* never admitted any error, but privately the paper was embarrassed.

It was in the immediate aftermath of these events that placard-wielding students showed up outside Punch's apartment. In a mimeographed letter handed out to passersby, the protesters questioned Punch's role as a trustee in the decision to bring in the police and suggested that *Times* editorials on the sit-in reflected his bias as a partisan of the Columbia administration. In his response, published the next day, Punch wrote that he saw no conflict between working for a newspaper and serving on boards of philanthropic organizations, and defended the *Times'* coverage as "full, accurate and dispassionate." The students remained unconvinced, and two weeks later refused to admit a *New York Times* reporter to one of their press conferences.

If Punch was perceived as a mouthpiece of the Establishment during the Columbia shutdown, to President Johnson he was the publisher of a newspaper whose coverage of Vietnam bordered on treason. Although a loyal ex-marine, Punch was also a pragmatist who bristled at the idea that a small band of generals in the Pentagon might be wasting soldiers' lives, almost as much as he bristled at the hippies and peace protesters who burned the American flag and sneered at the military. He felt no particular moral outrage about U.S. involvement in Vietnam, but early on he questioned whether America could succeed in a country where the regime was corrupt, unstable, and unable to articulate a clear goal behind which the country's people could unite. "I am not sure that what we offer the Vietnamese peasant or what their own leaders offer them is any better than what the Communists offer," he wrote John Oakes candidly in the spring of 1964.

During the 1950s and well into the 1960s, the *Times,* like most major papers, had subscribed to the domino theory and treated the defense of Vietnam against the Communists as vital to "the free world." When John Oakes became editorial-page editor in 1961 — the same year the United States began sending support troops to South Vietnam — the paper's position became more ambivalent. Though still eager to contain communism, it warned against being drawn into the commitment of a full-blown war. In August 1964 the *Times* loyally supported the Tonkin Gulf resolution, drafted by the Johnson administration, which provided a mandate for military action in Vietnam and declared the country critical to U.S. security interests. That fall, based largely on the president's confident leadership and positive assurances that he would not seek a wider war, the *Times* endorsed Johnson.

But by February 1965, it had become clear that Johnson's portrayal of himself as the peace candidate had been an expediency to get elected. In an operation called Rolling Thunder, the United States launched bombing raids on North Vietnam and Communist-controlled areas in the south; by the following year, 190,000 U.S. troops were stationed in Vietnam, with more on the way. Johnson's strategy was to pummel North Vietnam into peace talks, a plan John Oakes felt sure would have the opposite effect of stiffening Hanoi's resolve.

John, like Punch, was an intensely patriotic man — a decorated World War II veteran and a former member of the OSS. But once he became convinced that a land war was unwinnable, the *Times'* editorial page became ardently dovish, warning of the "catastrophe" that could befall the United States if it continued to pursue "the present process." "Nothing is more important for Americans today than to face these hard truths before it is too late," warned an editorial in the spring of 1965. The *Times* did not advocate a pullout; rather it favored a settlement, which John described by coining a new term, *de-escalation,* a word he used with increasing frequency in strongly worded editorials.

Johnson was furious at the *Times'* criticism and told his assistant Bill Moyers that he was certain the paper wanted him to lose the war. At an off-the-record meeting with Washington bureau chief Tom Wicker in late April 1965, the president spoke "harshly and caustically of critics, particularly ... *The New York Times,"* frequently mentioning John Oakes by name. In a separate session with John Pomfret, an executive at the paper and an old friend of Punch's from his *Milwaukee Journal* days, Johnson complained, "I can't fight this war without the support of *The New York Times."*

Among those in the extended Sulzberger family who were directly responsible for the paper's stance, Johnson did, in fact, face a virtual united front. The most liberal members, John Oakes and Iphigene, had simultaneously come to the same conclusion about the war. Initially, Iphigene had thought there "was something to this domino theory," but she gradually became disillusioned with the American rationale. "Frankly, I think we [at *The New York Times*] were a little slow [on Vietnam]," she said years later. "We were going along with the government, it's the natural thing to do." By 1966, after the *Times* had been squarely against Johnson's policies for some time, she told Punch that the paper's Vietnam editorials were "wonderful."

While not as liberal as his mother and cousin, Punch was in accord with the paper's position on Vietnam, his only concern being that the *Times* sometimes expressed its opinions too stridently. When Punch read Herbert Matthews's emotional editorial on the Christmas truce of December 1966 in the early edition of the *Times,* he called John at home and ordered him to kill it. John felt that Punch's demand was a "rather unusual interference on the part of the publisher," but he agreed to tone down the piece in order to save it. Readers of later editions never saw Matthews's original opening line — "Kill and maim as many as you can up to 6 o'clock in the morning of December 24 and start killing again on the morning of December 26." Instead, they read a version that began with Matthews's more sedate second paragraph: "By all means, let there be peace in Vietnam for a few hours or a few days over Christmas and the New Year. It is not much, but it is that much better than uninterrupted war."

Characteristically, Arthur was far to the right of his relatives at the *Times.* "I hope we will not — repeat not — have anything in the paper tomorrow opposing the President's resumption of bombing North Vietnam," he fumed to Punch in late January 1966. "I feel very strongly about this and I know that Johnny feels just the opposite." As Arthur feared, the editorial in question denounced the bombing, predicting that it would hurt the peace process and only lead to "more wounded, more dead."

The division within the Sulzberger family was mirrored by a similar but very public schism on the news staff of the paper. In both 1965 and 1966 *Time* magazine — itself a notorious hawk — ran articles about the "less than unanimous" opinion of the *Times'* senior reporters and editors on Vietnam. Hanson W. Baldwin, the paper's military specialist since 1937, led the crusade for aggressive American involvement. In the lead article in the *Times'* Sunday magazine of February 21, 1965, soon after Johnson had commenced his undeclared policy of expanding the war, Baldwin suggested sending in a million troops, if necessary, to secure a victory — a position that, John Oakes told Punch, "absolutely appalls me." Cy Sulzberger, while not as hawkish as Baldwin, stood virtually alone among the *Times'* columnists as an opponent of "flabbiness in Vietnam." Living in Paris, where he was surrounded by reminders of America's triumph during World War II, and by nature easily impressed by official authority, Cy had little idea what was really going on back home. Vietnam doomsayers, he wrote, were guilty of a "deep-seated doubt about ourselves and deep-seated ignorance of the world we inhabit," as well as a "smarmy dislike for President Johnson."

The Tet offensive came as a vindication of the *Times'* stance on Vietnam. Launched on January 31, 1968, the first day of Vietnam's biggest holiday, the Vietcong's surprise attack on more than half the supposedly impregnable provincial capitals of South Vietnam stunned Washington. In the process of recapturing the occupied cities, U.S. and South Vietnamese troops ended up ravaging much of what they had ostensibly sought to save. "What is the end that justifies this slaughter?" Scotty Reston asked in his column. "How will we save Vietnam if we destroy it in battle?" President Johnson assured the country that "the enemy will fall and fall again" because "we Americans will never yield," but the *Times* charged that such optimism was unfounded. After Tet the mood of the country shifted. When CBS anchorman Walter Cronkite returned from a visit to Vietnam in late February, he shed his trademark neutrality. The United States, he said, must promptly negotiate its way out.

By mid-June American military deaths in Vietnam totaled nearly 34,000, and the dissatisfaction with Washington's policies took a more active form. Riots broke out at the Republican convention in Miami, which nominated Richard Nixon, and were soon followed by far worse violence in Chicago, where the Democrats selected Vice President Hubert Humphrey. The Chicago police, under shoot-to-kill orders from Mayor Richard Daley in cases of extreme unrest, clubbed young peace demonstrators and smashed reporters' cameras in the streets while inside the convention hall, disorder reigned. When J. Anthony Lukas, a *Times* reporter in Chicago, described the police's behavior as "brutality," Abe Rosenthal back in New York changed the word to *overreaction.* Harrison Salisbury, who was directing the paper's convention reporters, angrily called to complain. "You're taking the guts out of the story!" No, Rosenthal replied, he was taking out the "goddamn editorializing."

That fall, after Punch and other prominent news officials had signed a telegram to Mayor Daley protesting harassment of the press in Chicago, the *Times* enthusiastically endorsed Humphrey. Once the election was over and Nixon had won by a mere half a million votes, Punch composed a letter to each candidate — a custom of his father's that Punch continued. Normally, such letters were deliberately polite and noncommittal, lest either politician assume he had a special relationship with *The New York Times.* But after everything he had witnessed in 1968 — a year of tragedy, calamity, assassination, and upheaval — Punch's letter to Humphrey was transparent in its expression of fear for the future. "I can't really begin to tell you," he wrote, "how deeply sorry my family, my associates and I are at the outcome of the election."

§

Confined to his wheelchair, Arthur had grown so forgetful that when a Columbia University oral-history interviewer questioned him about the events of 1952, he had no recollection of the *Times'* unprecedented pre-convention endorsement of Eisenhower. His short attention span and weak eyesight made reading impossible. Most evenings he mindlessly watched *Perry Mason* or *Maverick* with Gigi and Zita, his two papillons, on his lap. "He was bad-tempered and had no interests," said Ruth. "He had been such a handsome, glamorous kind of person and what happened to him, he never could accept."

On his seventy-fifth birthday, Arthur was wheeled onto the front lawn of Hillandale, where a large blanket was ceremoniously spread out at his feet. As speakers blared "The March of the Siamese Children" from *The King and I,* Arthur's four children, thirteen grandchildren, and two secretaries marched up to him single file and solemnly bowed, as if paying court. Each one read a short, funny statement about each year of Arthur's life, starting with his birth, and then deposited a bottle of Jack Daniel's at his feet. By the end, seventeen full-size bottles and fifty-eight small, airline-size bottles were lying on the blanket.

Two weeks later Arthur and Iphigene traveled to London, where they stayed at the Savoy in a two-room suite with a nurse. Claridge's, their traditional hotel of choice, had become too noisy for Arthur. But even the Savoy's charming rooms overlooking the Thames provided no diversion from his afflictions. He spent the days in London suffering from "nerves," unable to rest or sleep, too sick even to venture out and see his old friend Lady Susan Pulbrook.

In the autumn of 1968 Arthur felt well enough to attend a meeting of The New York Times Foundation, but soon his health became so precarious that, privately, family members feared his time was near. During one visit, Judy could see that her father was in great discomfort. "I wish I were dead," Arthur moaned, words that had a chilling meaning for Judy. From her years of practice as a doctor, she was used to hearing requests for physician-assisted suicide from terminally ill patients and their loved ones. Now she wondered whether her father was trying to signal his desire for a similar end. "Do you want to talk about it?" she asked him gently. "No," Arthur replied. "Just get me the nurse."

Later that fall, at Hillandale, Arthur had an attack severe enough to put him in Stamford Hospital. Iphigene asked Dr. George Carden Jr., the family physician, to arrange for Arthur's transfer to Columbia-Presbyterian Medical Center in the city, but Carden counseled against it. "I think we've gone far enough," he told her. "We ought to bring him back home and make him as comfortable as possible." Iphigene agreed, and later told a friend, "I felt that was exactly what Arthur wanted."

At 2:25 P.M. on December 11, Arthur Hays Sulzberger died peacefully in his sleep at 1115 Fifth Avenue. Iphigene, ever loyal, ever vigilant, was at his bedside. About the same time, Marian, who was walking on a nearby street, suddenly said to herself, *I haven't seen Mother and Father in a while, I think I'll go visit them.* She arrived at her parents' apartment just moments after her father had passed away. "It was vibes, I guess," she said. "Instinctively, I knew something was wrong." Judy was driving up Madison Avenue, doing Christmas shopping, when she heard the news on the radio. She pulled her car over and, with the motor still running, sat there for a few minutes, stunned. Punch was in mid flight, en route from Chattanooga to New York.

The next day, Arthur's picture and obituary ran on the front page of *The New York Times,* while inside, on the editorial page, was a commemorative editorial that John Oakes had drafted the previous summer. It noted that Arthur's death had come almost fifty years to the day since he had joined *The New York Times.* For twenty-six of those fifty years, he had been publisher, a man "who preferred to lead and direct rather than exercise the mailed fist," who "liked to play as well as work," a man "of deep conscience, steady purpose and fair play."

During his reign, daily circulation had risen 40 percent and Sunday circulation had nearly doubled. The paper came to include more coverage of specialized subjects such as science, and more analytical and interpretative reporting than it had when he took over in 1935, yet Arthur's *New York Times* had remained true, always, to its Ochsian roots. He had viewed his role as a steward rather than an owner, and while that path had sometimes been confining, he had hewn to it with grace, strength, and good humor. Now, as old assumptions in every sector of society were coming under assault, Arthur's version of "Mr. Ochs's" ideal had begun to seem outdated and a little quaint.

Over the years, Arthur had drafted and redrafted instructions to his executors about the disposal of his body. He wanted to be placed in a plain pine box in the clothes he was wearing at the time of death, and cremated. "Please do not dress me up," Arthur had written in 1932. "I generally sleep in my pajamas." His survivors were free to select any music they wished for his memorial service, as long as it was not Mozart, whose compositions he detested. His ashes, he said, should be placed "without ceremony" in the underground vault at Temple Israel Cemetery, in front of the Ochs mausoleum. Over his plot, on the stone bench that shaded the spot, he asked that the name SULZBERGER be inscribed. "My father had said he had lived all his life under the name of Ochs, and he was damned if he was going to be buried under it," said Ruth.

Arthur's wishes were carried out to the letter. On a bitterly cold Sunday afternoon four days after he died, more than one thousand people made their way through the season's first snowfall to Temple Emanu-El on New York's Upper East Side. Once again, Scotty Reston provided a healing benediction for the Sulzberger family while at the same time honoring Arthur's personal request that his eulogy avoid the morbid. Standing at a pulpit donated to the temple by Adolph and Effie, he described Arthur as "an incorrigible poet, cartoonist, storyteller, amateur painter, interior decorator, drink mixer and furniture-mover," a man who had neither self-confidence nor the confidence of his associates when he took over, "but [who] by any standards of excellence or commerce or ethics . . . was a remarkable success."

During the half-hour service, the family sat up front near the brightly lit altar, dry-eyed as was their custom. "We were told, 'Granny's not going to cry, and none of you should cry,' " said Karen Sulzberger. "It was 'We're here as a family, we should be dignified and keep the upset private, don't make it public.' " One who found it impossible to heed the admonition was Susan Dryfoos, for whom the scene brought back such vivid memories of her father's funeral that she broke down. Conspicuously absent from the family pews was Cy Sulzberger, who through an oversight had not been notified of the service for his uncle. Later, from Paris, Cy would write a wounded note, and Punch would send a pacifying response. The ceremony had been hastily scheduled out of consideration for Iphigene, who was exhausted, with a bad case of the flu, Punch told Cy. "Dr. Carden and Marian convinced me the sooner we had the service, the better, as Mother would not rest until it was accomplished."

President-elect Richard Nixon arrived at the temple ten minutes before the first strains of Schubert's "The Lord Is My Shepherd," causing many a craned neck and raised eyebrow. He owned a Fifth Avenue apartment not far from Temple Emanu-El and, despite *The New York Times'* antipathy toward him as a politician, had chosen to come out on what Iphigene said was "the world's worst day in December" to pay his respects. As he exited, Nixon made a point of speaking to Iphigene, who graciously assured him that Arthur had always liked him, even though the *Times* had never supported him.

There were no family members at the interment of Arthur's ashes at Temple Israel, and the burial was swift, just as Arthur had ordered. "I want no undertaker pawing over me," he had instructed his executors in 1963, three days after the Kennedy assassination, in yet another version of his final wishes. Among his personal effects was a letter to Iphigene asking her to send $1,000 checks to Arthur Krock, Nat Goldstein, Ivan Veit, and other *Times* friends, with a note attached that read, "Thanks. It was fun!"

On the marker above his grave, Arthur had asked that his epitaph consist of the words inscribed on a silver martini shaker he had received from his friends and family in 1948, on the occasion of his thirtieth anniversary at *The New York Times*. It was a recipe for an "Arthur Hays Sulzberger cocktail": "One part wisdom, one part wit, one part humanity."

30

The Phoenix Rises

I MMEDIATELY FOLLOWING ARTHUR'S FUNERAL, Marian, Andrew, and the Restons took Iphigene to Caneel Bay, a resort in the Virgin Islands. During the boat ride to the hotel, Iphigene stretched out on one of the wooden benches and fell into a deep sleep; she was completely enervated. The last ten years of caring for Arthur had drained her, physically and spiritually. When he was healthy, she had willingly played the role of supportive wife, consciously staying in the background to avoid challenging her husband's ego. He, in turn, had thoroughly dominated her, exacerbating her insecurities. As his afflictions multiplied, she had organized her life completely around his moods, his whims, his schedule, what he could do, what he couldn't. She had enjoyed almost no existence of her own.

With his death, Iphigene was emancipated, not just from the tyranny of Arthur's illness but from Arthur himself. Far from fading and declining without his commanding presence, as some in the family had feared, she flourished. "There was an extraordinary change in Iphigene's whole attitude, which had nothing to do with whether she loved Arthur or not, [because] she did," said John Oakes. "After his death, Iphigene blossomed. She became much less repressed, much warmer." Friends noticed a new accessibility; she was outgoing, happy, released from the reins that had restrained her during her fifty-one-year marriage. She began to host parties as she had in earlier years, carefully observing the starched niceties of a bygone era: finger bowls, doilies, and the after-dinner convention of brandy and cigars for the men in the library and coffee for the women in a separate room.

Iphigene was delighted to be the center of attention among her friends and the repository of moral authority within her family. "She didn't have to be the wife, she could be the matriarch," said Elly Elliott, her friend and fellow trustee at Barnard. "She became *the* person of that generation, because her husband was gone, General Adler was gone, Charlie Merz was gone. She was the survivor." With Arthur no longer around to chip away at her self-confidence, Iphigene's tentativeness gradually vanished, to be replaced by a slightly cranky assertiveness. Punch's secretary, Nancy Finn, could hardly believe her ears when Iphigene ordered that flowers be repositioned in Nancy's office so that Punch could see them. She then turned her attention to a row of clocks sitting on a shelf. "That's my clock!" she declared, pointing to a timepiece given to her father decades earlier, which she promptly seized for Hillandale. An overweight houseguest was astonished when Iphigene reached out and patted his protruding belly. "Suck in your gut!" she commanded.

At home her routine was vigorous and regimented. She read the *Times* from front to back over breakfast in bed, then worked on her voluminous correspondence and her many civic and political interests until late morning. On their frequent visits to Hillandale, Sally and Scotty Reston were expected to join in her religiously observed preluncheon walk. After the midday meal came rest and, in summer, brisk laps in the pool. "She swam the breaststroke in a very dignified way," said Sally, who spent hours sitting with Iphigene around the water's edge discussing politics, books, current affairs, and history.

With John Oakes, Iphigene had long shared the distinction of being the family's most committed liberal, but in public she had always kept her opinions to herself for fear of appearing to contradict Arthur. Now she was finally free to speak her mind on a host of hitherto forbidden subjects. During a trip to Israel with her granddaughters Karen and Cathy, she told *The Jerusalem Post* that *The New York Times* was "definitely for the survival of Israel" — a sentiment Arthur would never have expressed — and added that she was sure her son, Punch, "would very much like to visit here."

From time to time during Arthur's illness, Iphigene had escaped overseas with friends and relatives. On visa applications, she had always modestly listed her occupation as "housewife." But by the time Iphigene trekked to China in 1973, five years after Arthur's death and a year after Nixon had made his historic mission to open the mysterious country to the West, she no longer thought of herself that way — or acted it.

She muscled her way onto the trip, which was arranged by Chester Ronning, a seventy-eight-year-old retired Canadian ambassador who had been born in China and was once stationed there. The original party included Ronning's daughter, Audrey Topping, who was the wife of *Times* assistant managing editor Seymour Topping, and Ronning's young granddaughter. When Iphigene declared that she wanted to join them, Audrey cringed. "I didn't want to take her," she said. "I thought, *I can't handle two old people in China on a very rugged trip.*" But Iphigene wouldn't rest until Audrey put the question to Ronning himself. When he, too, refused, she invited him to Hillandale for dinner and in her own firm but polite way worked on him till he agreed.

By the time they departed, the group had expanded to include Iphigene, her granddaughter Susan Dryfoos, and, as a hedge against medical disasters, the Toppings' old friend Dr. Herman Tarnower, author of *The Scarsdale Diet* and later the victim in the notorious love-triangle case involving Jean Harris. Iphigene considered the trip the grandest of her life. Everyone, including Mao Tse-tung himself, seemed to know Ronning, and at each stop the group was treated like visiting heads of state. At the countless banquets and ceremonial receptions in their honor, Iphigene took pains to find out the names of every person responsible. The next day she would compose handwritten thank-you notes, a custom utterly bewildering to the Chinese. She danced with Ronning atop the Great Wall and celebrated her eighty-first birthday at the Summer Palace.

The climactic moment of the trip was a banquet in Beijing's Great Hall of the People hosted by Premier Chou En-lai. Iphigene was seated on the premier's left, the place of honor. Drawing on a lifetime of experience conversing with powerful men, from Andrew Carnegie to Winston Churchill, she charmed and cajoled the aging Chou so thoroughly that by the end of the meal he told her that he would be glad to welcome Punch to China the following year. The invitation was no small feat, for although several *New York Times* correspondents had visited China, the paper had had no success in opening a bureau there. A personal visit by Punch, it was thought, might pave the way.* Moreover, relations between the *Times* and China had been at a low ebb since the previous May, when the paper had printed an advertisement from the Nationalist regime on Taiwan referring to Taiwan as the "Republic of China." When Beijing lodged an official protest with the *Times,* the paper reported the government's displeasure in a news story, further aggravating the situation.

---

*Punch didn't go to China until 1976; the *Times* opened its Beijing bureau in 1979.

Iphigene helped smooth over these differences by telling the premier she believed in recognizing governments that hold effective power in their countries. "When Chiang Kai-shek left, the United States should have recognized your regime immediately," she said, expressing her personal view while also echoing editorials John Oakes and his staff had written. She then boldly asked Chou En-lai why the visa of her nephew Cy Sulzberger had been revoked. "We don't like his point of view," he replied. Iphigene said she didn't always agree with him, either, but wasn't it helpful to have a variety of opinions? Whether it was her argument that led the Chinese to reconsider is an open question, but two days later Cy's visa was reinstated.

§

The day after Arthur died, Punch went into his father's office with a garbage bin and began the process of taking over. As Arthur's secretaries watched from their desks just outside the room, he methodically threw away his father's stationery and other emblems of his chairmanship. Like Iphigene, Punch found himself liberated by Arthur's death. He knew that his father loved him, but he never felt he had his full respect. Now that Arthur was gone, two of Adolph's direct descendants — Punch and Iphigene — were firmly in charge of *The New York Times*, without encumbrance, for the first time since the patriarch's passing in 1935.

Iphigene's own relationship with Punch had never been a completely comfortable one. With her academic interests and love of debate, she was in many ways more compatible with Cy Sulzberger and John Oakes. Cy was worldly and could gossip endlessly about the great men he had known, as she could; John shared Iphigene's liberal politics and conservationist causes. Punch's strengths were his unpretentious personality and his sound instincts, qualities that Iphigene appreciated but, with her literal, rationalist bent, was at a loss to know how to value. When a *Time* reporter asked her to describe her relationship with Punch, she was both affectionate and clinical. "We have never had a serious falling out," she said. "Friendly disagreements, always. But, then, I believe in telling my children and grandchildren what I think. They can disregard my advice, but I always give it."

In Punch's case, Iphigene offered advice in a manner that some considered tantamount to lecturing but that others found merely direct. "After Arthur died, she became much more open in her willingness to say things to Punch," observed Sydney Gruson. "She never interfered directly at the paper, but she was never hesitant about saying to Punch what she liked or did not like, and what was good for *The New York Times* or not good for *The New York Times.*" Punch himself seemed not to mind, for he considered his mother the *Times'* institutional gyroscope, the one person he could always trust to tell him whether the paper was on course or losing its way.

As a result, his weekend visits with Iphigene took on added importance. Their private audiences at Hillandale were a ritual no one was permitted to interrupt, as Dan Cohen learned one afternoon when a servant told him that he couldn't see his grandmother because "Punch is finishing his visit." No one knew what they talked about, but it was clear that the time was important to both of them. "Punch wouldn't really do anything of any major consequence without talking to his mother about it," said Mike Ryan, a *Times* corporate attorney.

Barely six months after his father's death, Punch had something quite significant to discuss with Iphigene: he was appointing forty-seven-year-old Abe Rosenthal managing editor, replacing Clifton Daniel, the man who had dressed him down so thoroughly over his handling of the Washington bureau fracas. Punch was also sending Scotty Reston back to Washington with instructions to concentrate on his column, leaving the post of executive editor vacant. The Rosenthal appointment was a bold repudiation of one of his grandfather's and father's key shibboleths: that a Jew could never be top editor of *The New York Times.*

The personnel changes signified the final transition from Arthur Hays Sulzberger's generation to Punch's on the news side of the paper, changes that proved Punch was far tougher and shrewder than many believed. By relieving Scotty of his duties as executive editor and installing a strong leader like Rosenthal, Punch not only effectively put an end to the influence of the "adopted Sulzberger," the man who had been Arthur's wartime traveling companion, Iphigene's trusted confidant, Orvil's mentor, and the family's counselor, but also concentrated power, finally and completely, in the New York office.

Despite his fondness for Scotty, Punch was not sorry to see him go. Reston had performed the job of executive editor halfheartedly, commuting up from Washington every week and living in a rented apartment. Even his primary focus, his column, had lost much of its bite because, as the paper's top editor, he feared his opinions would be read as those of the *Times* rather than as his own. "You gave me the greatest prize in your possession — to be executive editor of the *Times* — and I let you down," Scotty wrote Punch with sincere contrition years later.

There was also ample evidence that Scotty had outlived his era, an era in which great men in the press protected great men in government. When Mary Jo Kopechne died in the waters off the bridge at Chappaquiddick in July 1969, Scotty was the logical man to write the story. He was vacationing on Martha's Vineyard, where he had just bought the local *Vineyard Gazette,* and he knew Ted Kennedy. But when Scotty's copy arrived in the newsroom, Abe Rosenthal, then associate managing editor, read the first sentence with incredulity: "Tragedy has once again struck the Kennedy family." He called Scotty and, as tactfully as he could, told him the emphasis was misplaced. "The story is this girl, it's not a Kennedy family tragedy," he insisted. A grumbling Scotty rewrote the piece, but to make certain the *Times* wouldn't be embarrassed by Reston's follow-up coverage, Rosenthal dispatched a young reporter named Joe Lelyveld to Martha's Vineyard to "help out." "Why do that?" Scotty asked Rosenthal, perplexed. "The girl's dead. It's a one-day story."

In background, style, temperament, and vision, Rosenthal was as different from the *Times*' preceding managing editors as any man could be. His Russian-born father, Harry Shipiatsky, had adopted the name Rosenthal when he emigrated to Canada on the eve of World War I. Eventually, the family, including Abe and his five sisters, moved to the Bronx, where Harry worked as a housepainter. When Rosenthal was nine, his father fell off a scaffold and spent three years languishing in agony before he died.

Rosenthal's grief over his father's death was compounded by a mysterious ailment that, by his early teens, sent pain shooting through his legs. By sheer will, he continued to walk, using a cane; he was eventually diagnosed as having osteomyelitis, an acute bone infection, and began years of botched treatment. After an operation left him encased in a cast from his feet to his neck, one of his sisters persuaded a charity to pay for a railroad ticket to the Mayo Clinic in Minnesota. Rosenthal took the trip alone and, following an eighteen-hour operation, spent months recuperating without a single visitor from home. After returning to New York, he entered City College, where he joined the student paper and suddenly discovered his calling. By 1944 he was a twelve-dollar-a-week campus stringer for *The New York Times.* When wartime manpower shortages provided an opening for a regular job, he quit college to work at the paper full-time.

After covering the fledgling United Nations, Rosenthal had been posted to India, Poland, and Japan, earning a Pulitzer Prize and a reputation as the paper's preeminent foreign correspondent. Years after it appeared, his lyrical and poignant essay about a visit to Auschwitz still resonated in the memories of many *Times* readers. In 1963, shortly after Punch had become publisher, Rosenthal had returned to New York to run the *Times'* metropolitan desk, where, along with his indefatigable, idea-spouting deputy, Arthur Gelb, he had covered New York as though it were a foreign capital that needed to be explained to readers in all its quirks and peculiarities.

As a new editor, he was appalled by the stiff, shoddy writing that crossed his desk. "I almost fainted the first time I saw raw copy," he recalled. "My God, I almost threw up." He encouraged reporters to inject imagination, humor, and literary panache into their work and assigned what for the time were atypical *Times* stories — on interracial marriage, the Mafia, and the increasing visibility of the city's gay community. "I think he was deliberately testing the limits," said Joe Lelyveld, whom Rosenthal had spotted and promoted as an up-and-coming young stylist.

Rosenthal had quickly advanced to assistant managing editor and then in 1968 to associate managing editor, a position that, because of Clifton Daniel's fatal misstep during the Washington bureau flap, effectively gave Rosenthal dominion over the entire paper. From that perch he had vanquished Theodore Bernstein, the thin, bespectacled man who for decades had run the *Times'* bullpen with a dictatorial hand, making up the front page that signaled to the world what the paper judged to be the most important news each day. The power shift — which was a crushing blow to Bernstein, who had been Rosenthal's mentor — for the first time put the decision of what went on page one, and where, in the hands of the *Times'* editor. Punch admired Rosenthal's vision and his willingness to be ruthless in the interest of the paper, which counted largely in his decision to make him managing editor. What the paper needed, he said, was a "hands-on, roll-up-your-shirtsleeves editor."

Punch had personal as well as professional reasons to have chosen Rosenthal. A self-described "obsessive-compulsive" about *The New York Times,* Rosenthal loved the paper, loved it in his marrow as Punch and the family did. Like Adolph, Rosenthal was the son of poor Jewish immigrants who felt a strong idealistic attachment to America. He considered being a journalist a patriotic act. "The Ochses, Sulzbergers, Restons . . . the Rosenthals and so many, many others," Rosenthal wrote Scotty Reston years later. "Sometimes it seems to me, in my euphoric moments, that what we have done with our lives is to create something good together and give it to the country and say, 'this goes with our thanks.'"

Punch was also grateful for the fatherly attention Rosenthal had paid to Stephen Golden, who had come to *The New York Times* in 1966 to work as a general assignment reporter on the metropolitan desk. Stephen had dropped out of the University of Chattanooga after barely a semester, amassed some clips at *The Chattanooga Times*, and headed to New York to claim his connection to the family. His plan was to work at West Forty-third Street for a few months and then go to London as a member of the *Times* bureau there, but Rosenthal had gently persuaded him to learn his craft before using his name to push his way into a job he wasn't prepared for.

Stephen took the advice seriously, reading the byline files of every *New York Times* reporter who had won a Pulitzer Prize, walking the streets at night in search of stories, and carving out a niche for himself writing features about hippies. Like Rosenthal, he was one part explosive temper, one part transparent need and vulnerability. Over long drunken evenings at Sardi's, the older man and the younger man had explored such metaphysical issues as whether great reporters made the *Times* or the *Times* made great reporters.

When Stephen decided he wanted to go back to college, Rosenthal, who keenly felt his own lack of a degree, wrote a personal letter to Columbia's director of admissions. In the fall of 1967, Stephen enrolled in the university's School of General Studies, the same program Punch had pursued after the Marine Corps. Within six months he had married June Tauber, a speech and linguistics teacher at Yeshiva University with whom he had begun living soon after arriving in New York. The older Sulzbergers went to great lengths to avoid acknowledging their cohabitation. "Do you know where Stephen is? His mother would like to reach him," Punch would ask June when he called the apartment. "No," June would respond, "but if I talk to him, I'll tell him." She would then hand the phone to Stephen, who would call Ruth.

When the couple was finally wed in the Baroque Room of the Plaza Hotel, Rosenthal, who was on a long-planned trip to Tokyo, was the only "regret" on the guest list that Stephen really cared about. Ben showed up and spent much of the wedding drunk, crying about his divorce from Ruth and his troubled relations with Stephen. "Behave like a man, for God's sake!" Joan Dryfoos, Ben's dinner partner and Orvil's sister-in-law, told him. "You mustn't let them see how upset you are!" The display — "emotional bordering on maudlin," said Michael — troubled Stephen enormously. So it was all the more touching when Stephen spied Rosenthal making his way toward him in the receiving line. At the last minute, he had flown back to New York for the occasion. He stayed just one night, returning to Tokyo the next day.

The gesture had made an impression on Punch. Stephen was the first of his generation of blood-related Sulzbergers to work at the paper. Others surely would follow, including, Punch hoped, his own son. He remembered what Turner Catledge's friendship had meant to him when he was struggling to find his footing at the *Times*. By sensitively tutoring Stephen, Rosenthal had demonstrated that he understood and embraced the Sulzbergers' role as stewards of the *Times* and was prepared to do what he could to ensure that it continued. Those qualities were critical, Punch felt, in any nonfamily member who hoped to work at the top of the company, whether in news or in business. In the future, there would be those who would fail to recognize that particular truth, and as events would prove, they would do so at their peril.

§

Arthur's death had a shattering effect on Ruth, who by nature had been more compatible with her father than her siblings had been. Whether they were sharing a glass of Jack Daniel's, composing light verse, or discussing the newspaper business, theirs was a relationship based as much on friendship as on blood. In 1950 *Time* magazine had interviewed Charles Puckette, then *The Chattanooga Times*' top executive, who had stated flatly — though not for attribution — that Ruth was Arthur's favorite child. Without her beloved Poppy, Ruth was emotionally at sea.

Then, a little over a month after Arthur's death, *The Chattanooga Times*' general manager, William "Mick" McKenzie, died of cancer at the age of forty-five, leaving Ruth to deal with the paper's deteriorating finances by herself. It was the indispensable McKenzie to whom she had delegated responsibility for everything from labor relations to the acquisition of new equipment, reserving for herself the part of the publisher's job she liked most: guiding news coverage and bettering the community through civic good works.

The paper's fortunes had taken a turn for the worse in 1966 after *The Chattanooga Times* had dissolved the joint operating agreement with Roy McDonald's afternoon *Free Press* and launched an afternoon paper of its own, *The Chattanooga Post*. By selling advertising jointly for both papers at a price so low that McDonald would go broke trying to match it, *The Chattanooga Times* hoped to force the archconservative publisher out of the market. But McDonald had stubbornly refused to be broken, and within a year *The Chattanooga Times* and *The Chattanooga Post* together were losing money at an annual rate of $1.4 million. When *The Chattanooga Times*' cash reserves dwindled to nothing, the Ochs Trust, which owned the paper separately from *The New York Times*, once again had to make up the shortfall.

Ruth's third loss came in March 1970, when Ben died in Florida of emphysema. Encouraged by their mother, the four young Goldens had continued to visit him several times a year, but his vitriolic anger remained an impregnable barrier between him and his children. Even Michael, the one to whom he had been closest, had begun to experience the blunt force of his father's wrath. After a pitched battle late one night in Ben's Jacksonville apartment, Michael defiantly picked up the phone and made a reservation for the first flight back to Chattanooga. "Yeah, you ought to leave," Ben growled at him. The next day father and son drove to the airport in stony silence. "I realized for the first time the character that Stephen and Mother had known," Michael said. "I'd witnessed it, I'd seen it, but it hadn't been [aimed at] me."

Yet to the end it had been Stephen who had the most fraught relationship with his father. In the years following the divorce, Ben had gotten in the habit of calling his oldest son at three or four in the morning. "I really want you to come down," Ben would say. "I will," Stephen would reply. They would both mean it at the time; it just never happened. "I'm not sure what prompted those calls," Stephen said later. "He'd talk about what was going on in his life, and I would talk about what was going on in mine. The only times I ever really felt close to him were at those times."

So it was to Stephen's astonishment that Ben had named him executor of his estate. He arranged for his father to be cremated, and with the
rest of the family he attended the funeral, which Ruth paid for, but he
did not go to the interment in Kentucky, near where Ben was born. Ten
years later, on a journey to explore his paternal roots, he was drawn to
the cemetery in Barbourville where his tormented and elusive father
was buried. To his great relief, he felt only tenderness as he stood by the
grave. "I wasn't angry," he said.

Ruth had never dated seriously while Ben was alive, but now that he
was gone, she felt free to do so. She found a kindred spirit in William
Holmberg, a sweet, soft-spoken *New York Times* circulation executive
whom Punch had dispatched to Chattanooga shortly after McKenzie's
death to help Ruth until she found a new general manager. Shy and
balding, Bill was anything but glamorous. His soft belly protruded over
his belt, and his rumpled clothes were frequently sprinkled with ashes
from his omnipresent cigarette. But to Ruth, he was a savior.

When he first arrived in Chattanooga, Bill was also married. He had
moved his family to Tennessee for the summer and spent his time creating a budget, installing cost controls, and working unsuccessfully with a
search firm to find a new general manager. In the fall he returned to New
York and continued to help out in Chattanooga, commuting there for
two weeks every month.

His presence was certainly needed, since the situation at *The
Chattanooga Times* could hardly have been more dire. The Ochs Trust
had to borrow funds to keep advertising rates low enough to continue
the squeeze on McDonald. Losses covered by the trust ballooned to
more than $6 million, with no end in sight. In addition, McDonald had
filed a complaint with the U.S. Justice Department asserting that *The
Chattanooga Times* and *The Chattanooga Post* had violated antitrust
laws with their advertising scheme. So serious was the allegation that
Punch asked Herbert Brownell, a former U.S. attorney general under
President Eisenhower and one of *The New York Times*' longtime outside
counsel, to join Ruth's legal team. Brownell predicted an embarrassing
court fight that would inevitably taint *The New York Times*.

On February 25, 1970, the front page of *The Chattanooga Times* carried
the humiliating news that The Chattanooga Times Printing Company
had signed a consent decree with the Justice Department and was closing *The Chattanooga Post*. Investigators had concluded that the paper's

rate structure and some of its competitive practices had indeed violated antitrust laws, and although Ruth and her advisers publicly disagreed with that conclusion, they settled to avoid a protracted and expensive legal battle. "What defeated us was the 'deep pocket' philosophy," said Ruth. "Had we been making money at the rates we were charging or had we not received money from the Ochs Trust, then the case would not have held up."

Although Bill's work in Chattanooga officially ended with the consent decree, he had grown to like the town. He asked for and was given McKenzie's job as general manager; within two months he was elected president of The Chattanooga Times Printing Company and put on the board of directors. By then, local gossips were speculating about whether Bill's return was motivated by more than just his love of Chattanooga. "That was just an out-and-out thing: Ruth went after him and said, 'I'm going to get him,' " said Connie Fisher, who had come to know the Holmbergs in Los Angeles when her husband, *Times* executive Andy Fisher, worked with Bill on the western edition. It was also true that Bill's marriage had long since soured. As he had become immersed in the sophisticated environment of the newspaper business, his wife, a woman he had known since childhood, had become devoutly religious. They had less and less in common, and she pointedly disliked Chattanooga. "Look, they weren't happy together, or this wouldn't have happened," Ruth later told Michael in an effort to explain why, once again, she had gotten involved with a married man.

Ruth's children were delighted that she had at last found a gentle, supportive man to love her. And as Bill filed for divorce and began showing up at family events, they were also amused by the shy way their mother dealt with the affair. The Goldens were visiting at Rock Hill when Ruth abruptly announced that she had something important to tell them. For several minutes she stuttered and stammered and plumped pillows on the sofa. "It must be important because she's cleaning obsessively," June whispered to Stephen. At last she got around to the news that she and Bill were engaged.

They were married in May 1972, in the living room at Hillandale, surrounded by close friends and family. "That's a very happy marriage," remarked Iphigene. "Ruth's over fifty, but you'd think she was sixteen." Years later, asked about what had attracted her to Bill, Ruth said, "What did I see? I don't know. I just know I didn't make a mistake."

31

Fits and Starts

O N BOTH ITS NEWS AND BUSINESS SIDES, *THE New York Times* had become a thicket of brutal competition and backbiting. Reporters locked their desks at night out of fear that colleagues might steal their stories. Business executives referred to rival departments as "camps" and "forces" as though they were Vandals plotting raids against the Visigoths. Every large corporation in America practiced its own brand of gamesmanship, of course, but the *Times'* deep-rooted paternalism gave routine turf battles and politicking a peculiarly familial twist. Editors and executives vied for preeminence at the paper in much the same way that siblings might compete with one another for the approval of a powerful father. "They're still trying to please their parents, but there are these sharp elbows," observed one editor who came to the *Times* from another paper.

No one was more exasperated by the feuding than Punch, who was convinced that if the *Times* was to thrive in the future, news executives and business executives would have to find a way to work together. He had been disappointed by his earlier efforts at Atlantic City and the Greenbrier to foster teamwork, and by 1969 he was ready to try again. This time he latched onto a management guru named Chris Argyris, chairman of Yale's Department of Administrative Sciences. Argyris had done work for IBM, Polaroid, General Electric, and the State and Defense Departments, but never a news organization. Although initially Punch had simply wanted Argyris to help his managers communicate better, Argyris had more ambitious plans. He sold Punch on the idea of a multiyear program of "management study and executive development" — a kind of corporate psychoanalysis that would result in the publication of a book or article about the *Times*. Punch agreed, naively asking only that Argyris mask the identity of the company and its employees in whatever he produced.

Argyris was given unprecedented access to the paper, and from his base in what had once been Lester Markel's office on the fourteenth floor, he attended executive meetings, budget sessions, and story conferences, tape-recording each as he went. In the first stage of the project, he conducted individual interviews with forty top news and business executives at the paper, including Punch, who set an example by being the first to be questioned.

What emerged from these sessions was a mixed assessment of Punch's leadership. *Times* executives liked him personally but complained that he wasn't decisive and wouldn't crack heads. When Argyris asked why these men had never shared their concerns with Punch, they were bemused. He would never stand for such a conversation, they explained; he was too insecure. After all, everyone knew he had gotten his job through an accident of birth. The Punch that Argyris came to know, however, was quite different from the person his executives described. "His" Punch had few doubts about his courage or personal abilities but was also painfully aware that his senior people did not share his vision of himself. Stung by their lack of confidence, he was "committed to showing them — more than himself — that he could run this organization," said Argyris.

With the exception of general manager Andy Fisher and production chief Walter Mattson, Argyris found the Old Guard on the business side of the paper so lacking in drive that he compared them to the complacent administrative staff of a sleepy college. On the news side, he described a group of highly intelligent and strong-minded professionals who declined to examine their assumptions and biases. They bristled at authority, yet seemed to respond only to an authoritarian. In between these disparate camps sat Punch, who had neither the aggressive temperament nor the certainty of vision to be a dictator.

Argyris observed that Punch was unlike most chief executives he had met in that he didn't flex his muscles in front of subordinates or mount power plays. His goal was to feel comfortable and to make others feel comfortable, which he achieved through a disarming lack of self-importance. Argyris described Punch's habit of unassuming kindness as akin to making deposits in a "positive bank account" of good feelings and goodwill. Such "accounts" allowed him, when necessary, to reprimand, disappoint, or even fire people without causing himself too much emotional discomfort. No matter how much pain he might inflict,

Punch could tell himself that he had a long record of friendship with that particular person.

These reserves gave Punch an inner strength that his executives frequently misunderstood because they so rarely saw it in evidence. When he appeared easily malleable, they believed they were managing him; what they didn't understand was that Punch kept his long-range plans to himself and picked his battles carefully. Skirmishes that he considered unimportant passed by without his participation. But it was this very opaqueness that was the basis of Punch's greatest weakness as a manager. Although he was able to discuss any topic with seeming frankness, he rarely put all his cards on the table.

A prime example was the process by which he decided, after endless internal wrangling, to create a page of opinion opposite the editorial page, to be written by *Times* columnists and outside contributors. By the time Argyris arrived at the paper, Punch and his editors had been debating the placement and management of this new Op-Ed page for three years. As Argyris moved into the second stage of his project — so-called interventions, in which he critiqued executives' behavior and refereed searingly direct discussions among them — the Op-Ed battle turned into an ugly, head-bashing exercise between John Oakes and Abe Rosenthal, both of whom wanted control of the page. If an Op-Ed page was to go forward, Punch would ultimately have to side with one of these men, but with characteristic inscrutability, he gave no indication which way he was leaning, hoping instead that "the process" would produce an answer.

The idea of an Op-Ed page first surfaced in 1943, when Scotty Reston mentioned it to Arthur during their trip to Moscow. It went no further until 1956, when a friend of John Oakes's sent him an article on the Suez crisis that was too long for a letter to the editor and too short for the *Times'* Sunday magazine. The piece was, in fact, an essay — and there was no place to run such a thing in the *Times.* On a walk with Orvil, John had proposed publishing a page of serious commentary, a "forum for intellectual exchange" similar in format to the featurey Op-Ed page Joseph Pulitzer's defunct New York *World* once ran. Orvil dismissed the idea out of hand; he felt certain that Arthur would never agree to move the obituaries, which then ran next to the editorials, in order to make room for it.

After Orvil's death, John had raised the subject with Punch, who thought well enough of it to form a committee to work out how it might be done. The ensuing debate quickly devolved into a squabble about who would control the space — a commodity *Times* editors battled over like feudal lords. At the time, the space in question "belonged" to the news department, and if Oakes's editorial operation took it over, Rosenthal stood to forfeit a major piece of his domain. Neither man would budge.

Given that Punch had already decided that an Op-Ed page was a worthy idea, why had he not long ago cast his vote and put an end to the bickering? To many of his executives, his inaction appeared weak, but as Argyris explained, "I don't think he's afraid to make a decision as much as [worrying], 'How do I get these people to become much more responsible?'" In the end, Punch had to admit that his experiment in decentralized management was a failure. "I would have preferred that an agreed decision among you had been brought to me for approval or rejection," he wrote John and Rosenthal in an exasperated memo. "This has not proved possible, leaving me no alternative except to exercise my responsibility as Publisher." His ruling — that the editorial department would run the Op-Ed page — was a victory for John, whose pleasure was soon diluted by Punch's insistence that Harrison Salisbury, an editor on Rosenthal's staff, be the first Op-Ed editor, reporting to John but with day-to-day responsibility for putting out the page.

Finally inaugurated in the fall of 1970, the Op-Ed page carried a variety of outside opinion as well as regular columns by Russell Baker, Anthony Lewis, Scotty Reston, Cy Sulzberger, and Tom Wicker. John was gratified when his pioneering innovation received admiring attention, but to his intense annoyance, Salisbury's strong personality meant that often it was he, rather than Oakes, who was given credit in media coverage as the creator of the page. Even when Salisbury died and his *Times* obituary accurately described him as having been "in charge" of the Op-Ed page, "supervising" it until his retirement in 1973, to John's ears, the words gave the false and infuriating impression that the Op-Ed page had been Salisbury's idea and that he had functioned without Oakes's oversight.

If the sometimes harsh exchanges induced by Argyris opened up the decision-making process at the paper, they had the unfortunate effect of setting in motion the departure of Andy Fisher, the *Times'* general manager and, ironically, the paper's leading advocate of radical change and new thinking. On its face, the Argyris approach seemed an ideal way to showcase Andy's strengths, but through his own impatience and gross misreading of Punch's personality, he ended up doing himself in. Andy had been eager to assume more authority when Argyris arrived at the *Times,* and he was especially hoping to take over the company's diversification effort, which was headed by Ivan Veit, a gentlemanly, bow-tied *Times* vice president who had gotten his start at the paper in 1928 working for Louis Wiley, Adolph's general manager. Andy thought Veit too mired in the old way of doing things, but Punch was reluctant to push him out. In the early days of Punch's publishership, Veit had befriended him and served as a fatherly Turner Catledge figure on the business side of the paper.

In one-on-one talks with Punch, Andy poured out his frustration. Veit was diversifying too slowly, he argued. His only acquisitions had been a handful of penny-ante companies, when what was needed was something dramatic. Punch listened sympathetically, as he did with everyone, and said little. Even though he tended to agree with Andy, carping behind closed doors was exactly what he was trying to stop. Argyris's cure for corporate backbiting was to prod people to express their complaints openly, on the theory that frank talk would clear the air and lead to improvement. But when Sydney Gruson, assistant to the publisher and a close friend of Punch's, tore into Fisher during a three-day "learning seminar" of top managers at Seaview Country Club in Absecon, New Jersey, accusing him of working "ruthlessly" to become the company's president, many assumed that Punch had sanctioned the attack as a way to send a message to Andy. The public evisceration stunned him. "My question now," Andy told the group in a daze, "is, What the hell am I going to do when I get back?"

Seven months later Punch named Andy and Ivan Veit executive vice presidents, a move that put them on the same level as Harding Bancroft, who until then had held the title alone. The promotions didn't enlarge the scope of Fisher's responsibilities, which included production, circulation, and advertising, or those of Veit, who continued to oversee corporate development and industrial relations. But because Bancroft and Veit were both nearing retirement age, Andy, at forty-nine, stood out as the logical candidate to become president of The New York Times Company in the not-too-distant future. That knowledge should have given him some peace of mind, but in mid-January 1971, when Punch added "vice president" to Gruson's existing title and began handing off to him several departments that had previously reported to Veit, Andy was convinced that Gruson, who had no financial training, was a threat to his future, and that of *The New York Times.*

By the time of Gruson's elevation, Andy was a knot of frustration. He was executive vice president and general manager of *The New York Times,* yet he had no control over corporate development or labor relations — key elements of the job. And when it came to aggressive, creative thinking, Andy considered himself a voice crying in the wilderness. He felt that he was "treading water" and "up against a stone wall" at the *Times.* "I knew that nothing was going to happen, or it was going to happen at such a slow pace," he said. "The reality of it was that Punch had to lead us there, and that wasn't happening."

In late January, a few days before going to the Caribbean for the winter board meeting of Gaspesia Pulp and Paper Company, Andy met privately with Punch. Again he hammered hard on the twin issues he considered most important: diversifying "with a vengeance" and getting tough with the unions in order to introduce new technology in the composing room. He hinted strongly that if he wasn't given the power to make these changes, power that now rested with Ivan Veit, he might resign. "Punch, I'm really considering leaving," he said. "I'm not making any demands on you, I just don't see enough challenge [for me] ahead." As usual, Punch listened receptively, revealing little and promising nothing.

After the board meeting, Andy and his wife, Connie, stayed in the Caribbean for a vacation on the island of Guadeloupe. "We just used that week to really talk about what we wanted to get out of life, what the rest of life was going to mean to us," she said. They agreed that while the *Times* had been a fine opportunity, it had taken a toll on their marriage, health, and family. On the beach, Andy roughed out a letter of resignation to Punch on a yellow legal pad.

In February, soon after Andy returned to New York, he asked for an appointment with Punch. Once they were settled in their chairs, Fisher handed over his typed letter of resignation. "You are well aware of strong differences which exist between my business views and those of your other top advisers," it said. One of the most important differences, it explained, was Andy's conviction that the "diversified activities" and the "newspaper product" should be guided by "a single business strategy and a unified management." He closed on a more personal note. "I thank you for your patience with my impatience for change."

At first, Punch refused to take the letter seriously. As far as he was concerned, all Andy had to do was wait until Veit and Bancroft retired. Why push to be made president now? "I don't understand this," Punch said. "What's your rush? It's all going to flow into your lap anyway. I've depended on you to be with me to go forward with this." Andy was adamant. "Punch, nothing is happening, and I don't see that anything can happen the way we're set up now. Your other business advisers, I differ with them." The comment, Punch knew, was a veiled reference to Sydney Gruson.

Fisher never stated explicitly that he would withdraw his resignation if Punch accelerated Veit's retirement and gave Andy those duties, but that was certainly how Punch interpreted it. More galling was the implication that Fisher thought Punch should step aside, become a figurehead, and let Andy operate the company. "I'm quite sure [he] thought he could run the paper better than Punch," said Turner Catledge. "He wanted to be president of the paper. There's not much future in that ambition, unless you're a member of the family."

Punch hated to be painted into a corner; and when he was, he could turn in a flash from the pleasant, compliant publisher most people knew into a cold, tough son of a bitch. In Andy's case, he felt he had plenty of goodwill stored away in his "positive bank account" to allow him to do so. While he genuinely liked Andy and had yielded to many of his demands in the past, the time had come to make a large withdrawal. "Don't push me this way, because it's not going to work," Punch warned. When Andy indicated that compromise was not an option, Punch curtly accepted his resignation, wished him well, and ushered him out the door.

The next day's *Times* carried an announcement that Andy Fisher would leave the company on March 1 "to seek a new and different career." Because he had quit rather than being let go or retired, he received none of the financial benefits the *Times* normally showered on its senior executives who acceded to being let go or retired. Andy eventually found work as a management consultant in newspaper acquisition and publishing. Later he would become chairman, president, and publisher of the Wilmington (Del.) *News Journal*, but nothing would ever equal his experience on West Forty-third Street. "I loved my work at the *Times*," he said more than twenty years later. "I dream about it now."

In 1972 Argyris abandoned his experiment in corporate group therapy, convinced that the *Times* was not committed to organizational change.

The book he produced, *Behind the Front Page,* appeared in 1974 and so poorly concealed the identity of the newspaper and its executives that the journalism review *MORE* reprinted excerpts of the actual "interventions" with real names attached. Later, Punch came to feel that Argyris was "a little bit too psychological for us at the particular time. We were real amateurs [and] it was a terrible invasion of privacy." As for the effect of Andy's departure, it would be two years before Punch would name a new general manager, and when he did, it would be a man less outwardly ambitious than Andy but far more authoritarian: Walter Mattson.

§

Andy left *The New York Times* just as it was about to do the one thing he had so desperately wanted: diversify in a dramatic way. Three weeks after his official leave-taking, the company bought Cowles Communications, which owned regional newspapers, television stations, and magazines as large as *Look* and *Family Circle.* The $67 million deal, carried out with 2.6 million shares of *Times* Class A common stock, would not have been possible without Punch's decision three years earlier to take The New York Times Company public.

Although Punch had inherited his father and grandfather's single-minded mission to maintain *The New York Times* as the country's preeminent newspaper, the world in which he lived was far different from theirs. No longer could profit be considered desirable but somewhat beside the point, as it had been for Arthur, nor could the company refuse as a matter of principle to dabble in television or acquire other papers. The 1963 strike's thinning of the field of New York papers, coupled with the *Times'* capitulation to labor again in 1965, had made it clear that the power to stand up to the unions would come only through financial independence. "It became so obvious that having all our eggs in one basket was a dangerous business philosophy," said Punch. Making money suddenly took on grave importance, and diversification was essential. Punch's decision to aggressively pursue both had represented a wrenching shift in the culture of the family and of the *Times.* As Mike Ryan, then a *Times* attorney, recalled, "This was such a radical departure, to own anything else. The favorite expression was that General Adler . . . and Mr. Ochs would turn over in their graves if they ever heard the discussions that we were thinking of . . . buying another company. . . . It was that kind of atmosphere that [Punch] came into."

The company's first purchases had been modest. In 1966 the *Times* had paid $500,000 for a majority interest in Teaching Resources and Systems Corporation of Boston, a firm that produced visual aids for schools, businesses, and government. It would take six years and $2 million in investment before the new venture would turn a profit. A majority interest soon followed in Arno Press, which specialized in the reproduction of out-of-print reference works and classics. Both companies were close to the *Times'* traditional business, and both were pointedly not newspapers.

By 1968 Punch had reluctantly concluded that if The New York Times Company was ever going to make any significant acquisitions, it would have to go public. "All the business types said we were never going to survive unless we went public and did some deals for stock, because we didn't have the cash to do anything," said Mike Ryan. "In the end it was Punch's decision — another very lonely decision for him to make."

Behind the "business types'" desire to trade stock for companies had been a different and unstated motive: they hoped public accountability would impose rigor on *The New York Times'* antiquated management practices. As general counsel James Goodale said, "Unless there was some public pressure brought on us that would embarrass us with respect to our profit, we would never make a profit, and therefore we would never knock off the unions." At a meeting with executive vice president Harding Bancroft and treasurer Frank Cox, Goodale had made the case that going public would, essentially, save the Sulzbergers from themselves. *The New York Times* was a principal shaper of world opinion, he argued; for it to exist on such a marginal financial basis was downright dangerous. His colleagues agreed.

Once the decision had been made, however, the American Stock Exchange refused to list the shares because the *Times'* Class A common stock, created in 1957, had no voting rights. Voting control was vested in the Sulzberger family through their majority ownership of Class B shares. To break the impasse, a compromise was adopted that gave Class A shareholders limited voting rights — the ability to elect three *Times* directors to Class B's six.* Shortly before he died, Arthur had signed the

---

*This provision ultimately ended up with Class A shareholders electing 30 percent of the board, regardless of board size.

final documents authorizing the sale of *New York Times* stock to the public. On January 14, 1969, the issue had appeared on the American Stock Exchange, opening at $42 per share.

As soon as underwriters realized how undisciplined the *Times* was, however, the stock began to plummet. "We didn't have a planning process, we didn't have any goals, we didn't have any of the usual things public companies [have]," said Goodale. By the second quarter of 1970, the *Times'* after-tax profit margin stood at 3.4 percent, the lowest of eleven top media companies, including Dow Jones and *The Washington Post*, and the stock had sunk to $20 a share. Goodale worried that it might fall as low as $2.

More problems appeared in the form of an ad slump, a drop in circulation, and increased costs. Between 1969 and 1970, the *Times* lost 10.5 million lines of advertising as a result of rate hikes and the distant rumble of oncoming recession. Circulation fell 15 percent, fueled by a five-cent rise in the price of the paper and the continuing exodus of readers to the suburbs. Desperate to court this market, the sales department invited suburban housewives to "*Times* parties" modeled on Tupperware parties, and Punch banned the word *here* in stories referring to New York City. But delivering papers to outlying areas was expensive, and circulation there was so anemic that to compete with dominant publications such as Long Island's *Newsday*, the *Times* had to sell ads below cost.

To make matters worse, in its 1970 labor negotiations, the *Times* had again capitulated rather than take a strike. In a contract that added nearly $11 million annually in labor costs, ITU president Bert Powers had won a staggering 42 percent wage increase over three years without a single concession on automation. The deal had made Punch a laughingstock among other publishers and even among labor leaders, who privately considered him "soft."

To turn the situation around, Punch had gone on a cost-cutting binge that, he said, was "the most unpleasant task I have had to do as publisher of the paper." By late 1970 the *Times* had trimmed a total of $3 million, mostly by holding down expenses. When several advisers proposed that he make a symbolic sacrifice by selling his beloved company plane, known internally as *Punch's Pilot*, he refused, though he did agree to exchange the limousines and chauffeurs the *Times* made available to its seniormost executives for ordinary cars and drivers. Cy Sulzberger, who owned a $7,000 Camaro convertible and enjoyed the luxury of two secretaries — twice Punch's allotment — was told to pare back the budget of his Paris office. Punch even canceled the paper's annual party honoring the Associated Press board of directors, ordering that the $20,000 saved be used to paint the newsroom and spruce up the elevators.

After years of complaining that "God is our personnel manager" — meaning that people left only when they died — Punch had let the equivalent of three hundred jobs go unfilled and entertained suggestions that the paper reduce the number of reporters assigned to the political conventions, use more wire service photos, and shrink the size of the Washington bureau. The staff reductions prompted one market analyst to ask whether editorial quality had suffered as a consequence of all the belt-tightening. Scotty Reston, appearing as part of a *Times* presentation for Wall Street, replied that it hadn't, but he admitted feeling uncomfortable having to worry whether the *Times* was making money or not. "I don't know anything about maximizing profits, and I frankly don't think about your problem in this regard," he told the analysts. "I think the time we begin thinking about the news in terms of how *you* look at it, that's the day . . . we begin to go down the drain. . . . I must say to you quite candidly, since we have gone public, we on the news side find ourselves in a wholly new world."

Despite the *Times'* cost-cutting efforts, by early 1971 Wall Street still considered the company a dog, and its stock hovered at just $16 a share. Rumors flew that the company was poised for a hostile takeover, even though the family's controlling interest made that technically impossible. Then, as if on cue, a miracle happened. Ben Handelman, who worked for Ivan Veit, head of the *Times'* diversification effort, happened to read in *The Wall Street Journal* that Cowles Communications was in trouble with the government because of its subscription sales tactics. Only two days earlier, Veit had told Handelman that Punch was ripe for a dramatic "big buy" instead of the small bets the *Times* had been acquiring. Cowles (pronounced "Coles") had a rich array of properties, and a quick glance at Standard & Poor's revealed that the company's stock price was one-quarter that of the *Times'*. Handelman suggested to Veit that the *Times* make an offer, giving Cowles a half share of *Times* stock for every share of Cowles.

Veit thanked him and promised to mention the idea to Punch, who was scheduled to see Cowles's chairman, Gardner "Mike" Cowles, on another matter a few days later. Because Punch had known Mike Cowles for years — his sister was a close friend of Iphigene's and his father had been acquainted with Adolph — he had no hesitation about being frank. "We would like to grow our company and we like much of what you've got," he said. "Would you be interested in selling to us?" Cowles indicated that he would indeed.

Handelman had advocated buying Cowles Communications in its entirety and then selling off its less-viable subsidiaries, but the *Times,* historically uncomfortable with closing businesses, bought only the pieces it wanted. On the reject list were the money-losing *Look;* a newspaper in Suffolk County, New York; and several television stations whose license renewals were at risk. Punch, who loved puns, gave the Cowles negotiations the code name "Newscastle," playing off the expression "coals to Newcastle." The night before he signed the final deal that brought to the *Times* the *Family Circle* magazine, three newspapers in Florida, the *Modern Medicine* group of magazines, a CBS-affiliated television station in Memphis, and Cambridge Books, Punch took his children to Sun Luck Imperial, a restaurant in the East Sixties where he was fond of the egg rolls and spareribs. At the end of the meal, he was astounded to read the name of a Cowles magazine printed inside his fortune cookie: "You will find good fortune within the family circle." He stuffed the slip of paper into his pocket and later framed it and hung it on his office wall.

While not all of the Sulzbergers were comfortable with the Cowles acquisition — one sneeringly referred to *Family Circle* as "that supermarket magazine" — in the management ranks on West Forty-third Street, there was universal rejoicing. Overnight, the *Times* had gained credibility with Wall Street. "All of a sudden we became a diversified company," said Goodale. "We pulled the rabbit out of the hat by doing the deal with Cowles."

The allusion to magic was apt, for however fortuitous the Cowles acquisition, it had materialized by chance, not as the result of a carefully planned diversification strategy. Like newspaper deals in the earlier part of the century, its success had depended on the historical friendship between two families — the Cowleses and the Sulzbergers. "The negotiations were mostly on the level of gentlemen sitting down to trade polo ponies," said a Sulzberger acquaintance.

Whether Punch and his managers were capable of handling so major an acquisition remained to be seen. With Andy Fisher's departure, the

Times had almost no financial expertise at the top. The vice presidents who had previously reported to Andy now reported directly to Punch, and the knowledge vacuum terrified the young, forward-thinking executives who had considered themselves members of "Andy's team." "I was scared, because to leave this company in the hands of Harding Bancroft and Ivan Veit was very dangerous," said one. "The Old Guard felt *The New York Times* was 'different' from other businesses and even other news organizations, and that was their excuse to make decisions from the gut, not based on information or numbers." Some of the more seasoned hands agreed. "I don't think Punch was doing so well at that point," said John Mortimer, head of industrial relations. "He hadn't found himself yet."

§

Despite her broad exposure to the world and her innately democratic nature, Iphigene was surprisingly ignorant of the way most people lived. Her own grandchildren speculated that she didn't know that toast was made from bread. Once, when Michael Golden showed up at Hillandale with buckets of Kentucky Fried Chicken, she professed amazement that such a feast could be had on a moment's notice, without phoning ahead. "What if they run out?" Iphigene asked. "They don't run out," Michael explained. "They just make more."

Television had completely passed her by. When Carol Sulzberger excitedly informed her mother-in-law that she was having dinner with Barbara Walters, Iphigene looked at her blankly. She had so little understanding of the medium's power that years later as Ronald Reagan began his successful campaign for the presidency, she couldn't fathom his appeal: while even Reagan's enemies begrudged him his telegenic charisma, Iphigene judged him entirely on transcriptions of his speeches and articles about him in the *Times*.

Her indifference to television was rooted in a determination to control her world. The very shows her family thought she would most enjoy — news, nature, history — were the sort she wished most to avoid, for Iphigene had no desire to be confronted with violent images of the Vietnam War, animals stalking prey, or newsreel footage of goose-stepping Nazis on *The Twentieth Century*. Television was random and unpredictable; how could a person possibly filter out what might be unwelcome? With complete logic, she simply declined to turn it on.

Despite her personal guardedness, the younger Sulzbergers were often amazed at Iphigene's progressive attitudes. She allowed unwed couples in the family to share rooms at Hillandale and didn't blink when one of the grandchildren brought an interracial husband and wife to spend the weekend. "White women have been sleeping with black men for ages, it's about time they married them," she said matter-of-factly. At the same time, she was furious at Cathy for attending Woodstock, which she considered a convention of depraved, drugged-out hippies. If she found it unseemly for the *Times* to publish stories about free love among college students, she nonetheless urged her unmarried grandchildren to be responsible about birth control. In many ways, she was far more liberal than her own offspring. Still, some among the younger generation thought their grandmother a bit too self-satisfied in her views. "Within a narrow confine of subject matter, you could talk to her at great length, but she wasn't going to come out of the box," said Arthur Jr.

That limitation, however, had no effect on Iphigene's role as the vital link to the fourth generation in the Ochs-Sulzberger dynasty. She was the axis around which her thirteen grandchildren spun, and as she came more forcefully into her own in the years following Arthur's death, her influence on their lives deepened. To them, she was a patron, teacher, and refuge, the living embodiment of "the family," that communion of blood and purpose they all shared.

Grandmotherhood hadn't softened her appreciably, and in keeping with her rational approach to life, her manner was oddly masculine. Rather than comforter, she was an instructor and a prodder who treated her grandchildren like adults and expected them to be engaging companions. She had little interest in their playmates or pets or other child-ish pursuits. What she wanted to know was what they had been reading, a query that always led to a conversation. No matter the topic, Iphigene injected personal recollections of the great personages she had met with her father and windy digressions about context. "She could be terribly boring, sitting around the lunch table, going on and on about history," said Jace Cohen.

Whatever frustrations they may have had with her, the cousins' generation agreed that she made each of them feel special. Without words, without hugs, she communicated an intense interest in them and their welfare. She never said, "I love you"; her way of showing affection was to demonstrate that she enjoyed their company. If she hadn't heard from a particular grandchild for a while, she would call and ask when she could expect a visit. "She conveyed a closeness and a warmth," said Jackie Dryfoos. "You knew when she was mad at you. You knew when she was disappointed; you knew when you were loved; you knew when she felt worried for you. There's a lot of communication that goes on in this family without language."

Dan and Jace were in particularly urgent need of Iphigene's brand of grandmothering. In the spring of 1972, Judy separated from Dick Cohen in order to pursue a middle-aged married businessman named Budd Levinson, whom she had met several months earlier at a cocktail party in Stamford. After fourteen years of marriage to Dick, she had grown restless and bored. "I'd been thinking, *I've got to get something going here*," she said. Budd had asked her to dance and they had spent the rest of the evening talking. As they were putting on their coats, he said he would like to see her again. "Well, why not?" Judy replied. Soon, they were meeting in motels. "It was an unhappy marriage; I'm not blaming her," Dick said later. "Judy was swept away. She did things on impulse."

Dan felt a mixture of relief and pleasure at the news that his mother had found someone new. He often complained that she didn't really love him, but he also knew in his heart that she was his most dependable ally. After Judy formally announced her divorce to her sons, she took them out for what Dan described as a "good, cementing lunch." "Dad was now out of the picture [and] he had been a divisive force," he said. "Jace, my mother, and I felt unified."

Judy was absolutely obsessed with Budd, who, though married, was well on his way to a split by the time they met. A man of Russian Jewish lineage who had gone to Penn State and then night law school in Baltimore, he prided himself on his single-minded determination to succeed. He had quit law school to take a position in a textile firm, where he had married the owner's daughter. Eventually he left, started his own business, sold out, and retired at forty-eight. When boredom set in, he had bought his former competitor's business, sold it after a few months, and retired again. As a personality, he was rugged, self-absorbed, and more charismatic than Dick. With his own small fortune and an apartment on Fifth Avenue, he was looking for a fresh start when Judy turned up.

Once separated from their spouses, Judy and Budd behaved like characters in a New Wave film: caught up in an illicit romance, on the run, inseparable. They traveled together, were silly and adventurous and eager to do anything, with Budd always the dominant partner. As a disciple of the famous psychologist Theodor Reik, he had no qualms about applying the master's techniques to Judy and her family. He noticed, for instance, that the Sulzberger siblings, though well into their fifties, had a disturbing fondness for their childhood roles. At a surprise party for Iphigene on her eightieth birthday, the four lined up by age to pay tribute to their mother in a tableau reminiscent of a nursery-school production. Budd failed to see the charm of such moments and said so, even though his unsolicited dissection of Judy's relationship with her mother thoroughly alienated Iphigene.

The solidarity Dan and Jace felt with their mother in the first flush of her divorce evaporated quickly, for in the months between separating from Dick and marrying Budd, Judy effectively vanished. "She never spoke to us," said Dan. "We never saw her, we never heard from her. She just went off with Budd." Ironically, the separation caused Dan and Jace to draw closer to Dick, who was so distraught about Judy's abandonment of him that he reached out to them with uncharacteristic neediness.

On the day after Christmas, roughly ten months after they had first met each other, Budd and Judy were married by a judge at Rock Hill. Iphigene in particular was careful not to make condemnatory pronouncements about her daughter's second divorce and third marriage. She continued an affectionate relationship with Dick, and with his new wife when he eventually remarried. When Budd bristled at Dick's continuing relationship with the Sulzbergers and Judy complained, Iphigene would patiently say, "Well, he *is* the boys' father."

But Judy didn't only want Dick out of the family; she wanted him out of the *Times* as well. In 1960 she had been content to have Dick take her place on the company's board of directors, but as soon as their divorce became final, she deputized Budd to inform Punch that she wanted her ex-husband thrown off immediately so that she could have the seat herself. Although his term would have expired in six months, Judy didn't want to wait; after all, she reasoned, since she and Dick were no longer married, what right did he have to represent her interests? Although Punch cushioned the blow by promising to send him more *Times* insurance business, Dick was bitter about being summarily dismissed. "The irony was: no one took less interest in the operation of the paper than Judy, and she replaced me," he said. In due course, Judy was elected to the board and joined her siblings and her mother around the enormous polished table in Adolph's former office. Had her father been alive, no doubt he would have marked the occasion with a wicked poem.

Dan was hurt by his mother's distance, but he coped with her new marriage with relative grace. Jace, who was just about to graduate from high school when Judy separated from Dick, took it much harder, and spent the summer after his senior year at Hillandale, drawn by the familiar company of his cousins and by Iphigene, the rock to which he clung for security and support. He told his grandmother that he did not want to go to Syracuse University as planned, but instead to get his license as a tractor-trailer driver. With protective sensitivity, Iphigene arranged for Jace to live on the Hillandale grounds in a small house near the gardener's cottage. When he got his tractor-trailer license, Jace went to work delivering construction materials for a local lumber company.

During that year, while Judy disentangled herself from Dick and married Budd, Iphigene and Jace established a companionable routine that assuaged the loneliness they both felt. She spent two or three days each week in New York, then came to Hillandale Thursday through Sunday. Jace was often her sole dinner partner, and they made an odd pair. Iphigene, as usual, wanted to talk about history or current events, while Jace's interests ran more to cars, trucks, women, and board feet of lumber. "I could tell she really enjoyed having me around, even though I probably wasn't the greatest conversationalist," he said. When she got tired of what amounted to a monologue, Iphigene would vent her frustration. "Tell me what's going on!" she would demand. "Why don't you respond to some of the things I've said?"

Living at Hillandale enabled Jace to know his grandmother in the intimate way that only her household staff did. When Hannah Heidenreich, the estate's cook, invited Iphigene to lunch at the home she shared with her husband, Robert, the butler, in a nearby town, they asked Jace as well. He arrived alone in his own car, with Iphigene showing up moments later, driven by Richard, her black chauffeur. For the next several hours, Iphigene, Jace, Hannah, Robert, and Richard sat comfortably around the Heidenreichs' modest dining room, enjoying a meal together. Afterward Iphigene went into the kitchen and started to wash the dishes.

"She was a cool lady," said Jace. "She loved these people that looked after her."

It was Iphigene's ceaseless pressure that made Jace agree to enroll at Syracuse when his year in the Hillandale cottage came to an end. Barely six months after arriving on campus, a love affair took up most of his time and he dropped out, returning to the forgiving world of Hillandale, this time with his Syracuse girlfriend, Rebecca Haskell, who had once been his cousin Cynthia's baby-sitter. In 1977 they married, bought a horse farm in Maine, and in rapid succession had two sons.

The generosity Iphigene extended to "the family" went far beyond just the descendants of Adolph Ochs. Although the Adlers and the Milton Ochses had been for the most part demoted to the marginalized role of "peripherals," as Punch offhandedly called them, to Iphigene, they were a living, breathing part of her father's legacy, and she took as much care to bind them to her, and to one another, as she did her Sulzberger grandchildren.

The main vehicles of her largesse were highly practical. "She had two strong beliefs that she would help you with," said Punch. "One was expenses toward your education, and the other was toward buying a new coat." She paid prep school and college tuition for a far-flung host of Ochs descendants whose kinship to her was often almost too distant to determine. Sometimes there was no direct kinship at all. Barbara Grant's children by David Christy were two of Iphigene's beneficiaries, as were the six members of a Vietnamese family who lived temporarily with Billy Ochs and his wife in Washington after the fall of Saigon.

In the decade after their father's death, the Adler offspring had required constant help. When Julie Jr.'s bowling alley on Staten Island failed, Iphigene had quietly asked the assistance of Bernard Gimbel, the department store mogul and an investor in the then new baseball team the New York Mets. In short order, Julie Jr. was offered a job as the team's promotion manager. Only years later did he discover that she had played a pivotal role in his employment. "She knew I was nuts about baseball, and in her own way, she went about easing my path," he said.

Iphigene had also bailed out the Adlers' oldest daughter, Bobbie, after the printing business she and her husband had started was forced to close and Bobbie found herself in serious legal jeopardy for having written a bad check to cover unpaid withholding taxes. In desperation, Bobbie had gone to Punch, who had immediately called the *Times*' treasurer and ordered him to cover the $17,000 check, but that turned out to be only the beginning. To settle all her debts, Bobbie needed another $350,000, and the only person who could manage a sum of that magnitude was Iphigene. Bobbie made a date to have lunch with her and laid out her dilemma. "I wouldn't do this if it hadn't been for your father," Iphigene had told her coldly after agreeing to pay off the banks. It took Bobbie thirteen years to made good on her debt, but despite Iphigene's less-than-tender treatment, "I don't remember a particular rubbing of the nose in the *merde.*"

Iphigene also lavished special attention on the descendants of Milton Ochs in Chattanooga, many of whom felt resentful of the Sulzbergers' dominant position in "their" town, on "their" newspaper. Like his father, "A," and his great-uncle Adolph, Martin Ochs, *The Chattanooga Times*' editorial-page editor, suffered from manic depression, which had begun to assert itself in the late 1960s. His erratic behavior and garbled writing soon made work impossible. When Ruth suggested that Martin go on a leave of absence, then a year later refused to hire him back, he spiraled into despair. As she had with so many other relations, Iphigene raced to the rescue, this time with a $25,000 severance package, an offer to put Martin's three children through school, and comforting phone calls to Martin's wife, Celia. "[Depression] is in the family," Iphigene assured her. "I remember my father going through this."

32

Betting the Enterprise

ON A BLUSTERY FRIDAY IN LATE MARCH 1971, Neil Sheehan, a Washington correspondent for *The New York Times,* and his wife, Susan, a writer for *The New Yorker,* arrived in Cambridge, Massachusetts, and checked into the Treadway Motor House near Harvard Square, registering as Mr. and Mrs. Thompson. Hours later Sheehan called Bill Kovach, the *Times'* Boston bureau chief, from a pay phone. "I need some help," he said. After weeks of negotiation, Sheehan had persuaded Daniel Ellsberg, a researcher at MIT's Center for International Studies, to let him see a top-secret historical study of America's involvement in Vietnam. The forty-seven-volume work had been commissioned in 1967 by Secretary of Defense Robert McNamara, who had grown increasingly disenchanted with the war and had ordered a research project to trace the roots of the United States' engagement. Lyndon Johnson had known nothing about the study, and of the fifteen copies distributed at the time of its completion in 1969, only one went to an official in the Nixon administration: National Security Adviser Henry Kissinger.

Ellsberg himself had written part of the report for the Pentagon and, after gaining access to the full seven thousand pages, had come to believe that the government's decades-long record of lies, missteps, and wasted carnage should be exposed. Two years earlier he had surreptitiously copied the documents and set about looking for the appropriate way to make them public.

His quest had led him to contact Sheehan, whom he had met in Vietnam and who he knew shared his pessimistic view of the war. Ellsberg told Sheehan about the existence of the Pentagon study and what it contained and, after a series of thrust-and-parry conversations, agreed to let him see it. When Sheehan arrived in Cambridge on that Friday in late March, Ellsberg took him to an apartment where the documents were stored. To protect himself from criminal liability, he told Sheehan that he could read the classified material and take notes but did not explicitly give permission to reproduce anything. Ellsberg simply handed Sheehan the key to the apartment, told him he could come and go freely over the weekend, and left.

Sheehan interpreted these actions to mean that Ellsberg expected him — even wanted him — to copy the material, and he wasted no time in getting to work. "We've got to get some important documents from MIT copied over the weekend," Sheehan told Kovach from the pay phone. "Do you know where the hell we can do it?" As it happened, Kovach had a friend in a nearby town with a copy shop and high-speed copiers. He told his friend that Sheehan and his wife were physicists reproducing a book that had to be at the publishers on Monday, and not to worry about SECRET and TOP SECRET stamped on the pages, because the Sheehans had clearance.

Twelve weeks later Punch gave the green light to publish what came to be known as the Pentagon Papers, despite having been advised by the paper's lawyers that the *Times* might be sued and driven into financial ruin and that he himself might go to jail. The far greater worry, by his own reckoning, was that readers might judge the *Times* to be treasonous. Punch had weighed all these factors carefully, but once he finally made up his mind, he became immovable. When Louis Loeb, the paper's outside counsel, refused to defend the paper's actions in court, Punch dismissed the man who had represented the *Times,* and the Sulzberger family, since 1948, and sought legal advice elsewhere. "We are going to look back on these days as some of the most exhilarating in the history of the *Times* and . . . in the history of American journalism," Punch wrote managing editor Abe Rosenthal after the Pentagon Papers episode was over, with the *Times* more secure than ever in its greatness.

The same could be said of Punch. The publication of the Pentagon Papers was his grand, defining moment, a moment in which he took his bearings from his heritage and his own values and instincts, and steered the paper safely and surely toward the "right" decision. The *Times* had not displayed such courage since George Jones had taken on Boss Tweed and the Tammany machine exactly a century earlier. While exposing Tweed's corruption had put the paper in great peril, at the same time it had inspired a generation of American journalists, including a young Adolph Ochs.

The Pentagon Papers had much the same effect. Punch was deeply anxious about the consequences of his decision, but he had no real qualms that his choice was correct. He had not consulted his mother or his sisters, but simply informed them of his verdict shortly before publication. Likewise, the *Times'* directors had no idea ahead of time that the paper was about to put itself at risk. "The board doesn't discuss editorial matters," Punch explained. On the night before the first installment, he attended a family dinner party and was called away so many times to speak to the office that the others began to suspect something was up. "Tomorrow I'm doing something that the world is going to hate," he whispered to his cousin Ellen Straus, "but it's the right thing to do."

Punch's conviction was heavily influenced by the dramatic shift in the relationship between government and the media that had taken place during the preceding decade, in part as an outgrowth of disillusionment with Vietnam, in part because of court rulings that had expanded First Amendment protections of the press. In *The New York Times* v. *Sullivan,* the U.S. Supreme Court established that public officials could not recover damages for defamatory statements, even false ones, unless they could prove that the press had recklessly disregarded the truth. In another landmark case, *Times* reporter Earl Caldwell had refused to testify and submit his notes to a federal grand jury investigating the Black Panthers in Oakland. Never before had the press so brazenly defied the federal government. Caldwell was held in contempt, the *Times* appealed, and by March 1971 the case was an ongoing irritant to the Nixon administration.

It was in this charged atmosphere that James Goodale, the *Times'* in-house counsel, had flown down to Washington to attend the annual Gridiron Club dinner as the guest of Washington bureau chief Max Frankel. *Times* attorneys rarely received such prized invitations, and Goodale was both surprised and flattered by Frankel's attention. It soon became apparent, however, that Frankel had something other than Goodale's sterling company in mind. Sheehan had recently informed Frankel that he was trying to obtain some top-secret documents, but neither of them had any idea what the legal ramifications might be if the *Times* published such material. During the Gridiron weekend, Frankel casually asked Goodale if he saw any problem with publishing classified documents. Goodale, consumed with the Cowles acquisition at the time, said he was too busy to deal with the question, but on his return to New York he began looking into the issue of legal liability.

Within days Sheehan had made his trip to Cambridge and returned to Washington with all but four volumes of the report; Ellsberg, concerned about compromising intelligence interests, had withheld the section covering the diplomatic history of the war from 1964 to 1968, along with its footnotes. What Sheehan did get, however, was a treasure trove of material, albeit a chaotic one. The report had been copied in such haste that pages were out of order, and there was no way to tell which portions of the historical narrative were linked to which supporting documents. James Greenfield, who had been enticed to return to the paper as foreign editor, sent Gerald Gold, one of his most trusted assistants, to Washington to help Sheehan sort through the mess and assess what was there. It took a month for them to organize the papers sufficiently to make a presentation to the *Times'* top editors.

On April 20 Sheehan and Gold crowded into Scotty Reston's Washington office with Greenfield, Abe Rosenthal, Max Frankel, and columnist Tom Wicker. After vouching for the papers' authenticity, Sheehan briefed the editors on the origin and scope of the Pentagon study. The historical analysis, he said, proved that administration after administration had systematically deceived the American people regarding Vietnam; the supporting documents provided prima facie evidence of the government's duplicity. Everyone in the room agreed that the secret history was a blockbuster story and should be published.

A few days later, in a conference room off the *Times'* third-floor newsroom, Rosenthal, Scotty, and other top editors told Punch about the Pentagon report for the first time. "The more I listened, the more certain I became that the entire operation smelled of twenty years to life," Punch would recall more than two decades later. At the time, he said little. "I'm not sure we should publish this stuff," he muttered to Sydney Gruson as they went back upstairs. "The question is not whether we should publish it," Gruson replied. "The question is how we'll publish it. That's all."

A few days later Punch convened a conference of editors, senior executives, and lawyers in the *Times'* boardroom to discuss what should be done. With Adolph looking down from his portrait above the fireplace, the meeting quickly turned tense. Louis Loeb argued passionately against disclosure of secret information. By publishing classified material, the paper not only would be in violation of the Espionage Act, he warned, it would violate its own tradition of responsible journalism. Executive vice president Harding Bancroft, a former legal adviser in the

State Department, agreed: to publish would be to invite economic and political ruin.

The editors lined up unanimously on the opposing side. The *Times* had published classified documents many times in the past, they pointed out. After all, hadn't Scotty Reston won a Pulitzer Prize for his stories on the Dumbarton Oaks Conference, which were based on privileged information? Of the lawyers present, only Goodale, the *Times*' general counsel, allied himself with the editors. If the stories were presented carefully, he said, higher courts would never sustain an injunction or criminal conviction against the *Times*.

After listening to the debate, Punch told Rosenthal to continue preparing the material but that he had not yet made up his own mind about whether the *Times* should publish it. Though Punch almost never interfered in the news judgments of his editors, in this case, he said to Rosenthal, he and he alone would make the final decision. "Well, if the *Times* doesn't publish them, I'll publish them in the *Vineyard Gazette!*" Scotty exclaimed, sensing Punch's hesitation. The meeting broke up without resolution. As Goodale recalled, "Everyone was pissed off at each other."

Rosenthal moved the Pentagon Papers project to New York and installed an expanded team in suite 1107 of the New York Hilton, a nondescript convention hotel in midtown Manhattan. The task of preparing the material for publication was monumental. Editors had to painstakingly compare what government sources had said for public consumption with what the secret history revealed as the behind-the-scenes truth. As April turned into May, the seven-day-a-week effort took on an increasingly cloak-and-dagger cast. Punch had his office swept for bugs. Only one hotel maid was allowed to clean the rooms that housed Project X, as it was called; on her days off, the room remained unvacuumed and undusted. Some editors feared that Ellsberg would give the documents to a rival paper and the *Times* would be scooped, or that the government would learn what was happening and prevent it. At one point, fearing that a federal raid was imminent, two *Times* executives raced the twelve blocks to the Hilton with empty suitcases, loaded up every scrap of paper, and removed the entire operation to the tenth floor of the newspaper.

Meanwhile, the battle for the soul of Punch was in full cry. About three weeks after the acrimonious meeting in the boardroom, a delegation from Louis Loeb's law firm, Lord, Day & Lord, convened with

Punch and three of the paper's senior executives; this time no editors were invited. Accompanying Loeb was senior partner Herbert Brownell, an éminence grise of the Republican Party. As Eisenhower's attorney general, Brownell had drafted the presidential executive order establishing the system for classifying documents. In the publisher's back sitting room he solemnly predicted that if the *Times* printed the Pentagon history, Punch and others would probably go to jail and the *Times* would be damaged beyond imagining. "He scared the bejesus out of me," recalled Punch. Goodale, who was present, urged Loeb and Brownell to at least look at the documents before they made such a rigid judgment, but they refused, claiming that even to read them constituted a crime. Loeb then invoked a name certain to resonate with Punch. He was absolutely certain, he said, that Arthur Hays Sulzberger would never publish such material.

For weeks Punch had wrestled with every aspect of the dilemma, knowing full well that the decision before him was actually a series of decisions. First he had to choose whether to publish anything at all; then, how much material; and finally, in what form. Each element provoked a roiling debate. His gut told him that Goodale was right: even if the government went after the *Times,* the courts would ultimately leave the newspaper alone. "I did not believe that the risks were what Herb Brownell had told me," he said. "I didn't think they were going to come and lock me up, but I thought they could fine us one hell of a lot, and we didn't have all that much money."

One of Loeb and Brownell's strongest arguments was that by disclosing top-secret documents, the *Times* risked losing its credibility with readers. Punch, however, was equally concerned about losing credibility with his editors, who had told him that *not* publishing the account would forever bring dishonor on the *Times.* "After all, [the report] should be in the public domain because it was history, and it was not secret; it had been illegally stamped SECRET," said Punch.

An issue that had to be resolved was whether to print the entire report at once or space it out over several days. Goodale argued that bringing it out in one huge installment would make it impossible for the government to seek an injunction to halt publication. Frankel and others countered that such a ploy would appear cowardly. "We found offensive the idea that we ought to be running with one eye on the sheriff," as he put it. Some of those working on Project X believed strongly that the *Times* should ignore an injunction if one was issued, and continue publishing in defiance of a court order.

By far the most heated battle was over whether to publish verbatim the memos, letters, and cables that supported the report's historical narrative. John Oakes, whose editorials on Vietnam had angered Kennedy, Johnson, and now Nixon, was of the opinion that the documents should be paraphrased or, at most, briefly quoted. Bancroft and former Sunday editor Lester Markel, whom Punch had invited to join the debate, were also strongly against publishing actual documents because of the possibility of unintentional damage and the perception of treason.

Rosenthal argued that not publishing the documents would be "catastrophic," for not only could short quotes and summaries be taken out of context, but the *Times* would forfeit one of the strongest weapons it had. The newspaper was contemplating publishing extremely controversial material, he reminded everyone, and the government was bound to challenge the articles' veracity. By printing the actual documents, readers could decide for themselves whether the *Times*' analysis was correct.

Early on, Punch had told Rosenthal that he wanted to read what was intended for publication before making his final decision. In late May Rosenthal, with barely contained glee, wheeled a grocery cart containing the relevant documents into Punch's office. Until then, remarked Punch, "I did not know it was possible to read and sleep at the same time." He found the material so turgid that he began to wonder whether it was worth the expense of releasing it.

The tentative publication date of June 10 was fast approaching, and Punch still had not given a clear signal of his intentions. While he ruminated, he found himself returning again and again to the question Turner Catledge had posed years ago over drinks in his back-office Club, the place where Punch had gotten his real journalistic education: Who are you writing this paper for? "That cleared it up, pretty much," acknowledged Punch. "We weren't writing for the benefit of the government; we were writing for the benefit of the reader, who is entitled to know."

That still left the thorny issue of whether to publish the classified documents themselves or merely quote or paraphrase them. The day before he was to render his final judgment, Punch dispatched his stalking-horse, Sydney Gruson, to see if Rosenthal could be persuaded to alter his position about printing the documents verbatim. Gruson made his pitch in the early evening while driving Rosenthal home, and that night

Rosenthal, Frankel, and Greenfield debated the issue at Greenfield's house until 3:30 in the morning. Early the next day they told Gruson that they were united in their opinion. "No documents, no story," said Rosenthal, who felt so strongly that he had privately resolved to resign if Punch did not agree. Gruson relayed the message back to Punch.

On Friday morning, June 11, Rosenthal and Frankel gathered in Punch's office to hear his decision. Neither editor had gotten much sleep; both were in a fog after weeks of worry and hard work. With a serious, deadpan expression, Punch made his pronouncement: "I've decided you can use the documents" — at which point there was a slight pause, and then he added — "but not the story." In their glassy-eyed state, it took Rosenthal and Frankel a moment to get the joke. So there would be no question about his position, Punch had prepared a formal memo that stated: "I have reviewed once again the Vietnam story and documents that would appear on Sunday, and I am prepared to authorize their publication in substantially the form in which I saw them." The secret history was to appear as a series of articles over several days rather than in a single issue. If the federal government secured an injunction to stop publication, the *Times* would honor it.

The first installment was scheduled to appear two days later, on Sunday, June 13. On Saturday at 6:16 P.M. the presses began rolling out the next morning's front page. Above the fold on the left was a two-column photo of Tricia Nixon on the arm of her father at her White House wedding, and to the right a headline that, by order of the publisher, was calculatedly unprovocative and did not even use the word *secret*: VIETNAM ARCHIVE: PENTAGON STUDY TRACES 3 DECADES OF GROWING U.S. INVOLVEMENT. Accompanying the article was column upon column of reprinted cables, presidential orders, position papers, and other official material. "It was perhaps the most extraordinary leak of classified documents in the history of governments, and it was only a beginning," author William Manchester later wrote. "Subsequent installments, the editors promised, would reveal more."

§

On Sunday James Goodale was at his weekend home on Connecticut's Lake Waramaug, anxious about "what the hell would happen." He tuned in to the hourly news update on WINS, an all-news radio station on which the Pentagon study "just got a sentence here and there, practically nothing." At *The Washington Post*, executive editor Ben Bradlee's heart sank when he saw *The New York Times*. For nearly two weeks he had heard rumors that the *Times* was working on a knockout scoop. Now there was nothing to be done but order his reporters to rewrite the competition.

Most other news organizations, however, including the three television networks, gave the "Vietnam Archive" scant attention — as did *Times* readers, who offered no denunciations, no praise. A few of the paper's editors were so concerned about the lack of response that they surreptitiously asked friends to send congratulatory cables to Punch. After so much hand-wringing about adverse reaction from the public and the federal government, the silence was disappointingly anticlimactic. Since the Nixon administration hadn't raised any objections, Punch felt no hesitation about leaving town. On Monday morning he boarded a Quantas flight and left for a long-planned trip to London with Carol and two of his children, Ivan Veit and his wife, and another couple.

Ironically, it was Richard Nixon and Henry Kissinger who shared responsibility for finally alerting the nation to *The New York Times'* moment of journalistic courage. Even after reading the account, Nixon initially reacted with uncharacteristic calm, calculating that whatever damage the revelations might do to U.S. military and diplomatic interests, they had the political benefit of excoriating previous Democratic administrations.

A thirteen-minute phone call Sunday afternoon with Henry Kissinger, however, changed Nixon's mind. Speaking from California, Kissinger pushed Nixon to publicly oppose "this wholesale theft and unauthorized disclosure," for, he warned, doing nothing "shows you're a weakling, Mr. President." That characterization, coupled with Kissinger's more substantive claim that the leaked material could "destroy our ability to conduct foreign policy," fired Nixon's resolve to retaliate against *The New York Times*. By the time the second installment of the "Vietnam Archive" appeared on Monday morning, the president was furious at the *Times* and whoever was responsible for leaking the classified documents.

All day Monday Goodale waited in his office for a reaction from the government; when none was forthcoming, he left for home. At 7:30 P.M., two hours before the third installment of the Pentagon Papers was to go to press, Harding Bancroft, who was in charge in Punch's absence, received a call from Assistant Attorney General Robert Mardian. Mardian read him a telegram addressed to Punch from U.S. Attorney General John Mitchell, which stated that publication of "the Pentagon's Vietnam Study" was directly prohibited by the Espionage Act; further disclosures, it asserted, would cause "irreparable injury to the defense interests of the U.S." The telegram concluded by "respectfully" requesting that the *Times* "publish no further information of this character." Nowhere was legal action threatened, but to make sure the *Times* got the message, Mitchell simultaneously placed a call to Herbert Brownell, whom he had seen over the weekend at Tricia Nixon's wedding. Mitchell told Brownell that the paper had two choices: pull the Pentagon Papers, or face a Justice Department lawsuit.

Summoned from his Upper East Side apartment, Goodale returned to the *Times* to find Rosenthal and Gruson "screaming and yelling at each other," with Gruson urging that the paper consider suspension of the articles, pending resolution in the courts, and Rosenthal "in a frenzy over that suggestion, warning it would create the impression that the *Times* was buckling under to government pressure." Bancroft wasn't sure how to proceed, and the Bay of Pigs incident was very much on everyone's mind. If the *Times* complied with the Justice Department's request, it would reinforce that earlier precedent of crumbling in the face of government pressure. That could have devastating consequences not only for the *Times* but for all American journalism.

Bancroft called Loeb, who advised the *Times* to obey the attorney general, but when Bancroft seemed inclined to agree, Rosenthal demanded that Punch make the final call. At about 2:00 A.M. London time, Punch was roused from an untroubled sleep at the Savoy Hotel. In New York, his voice was broadcast over a speakerphone, and as Goodale recalled, "Punch sounded like 'I wish I weren't publisher of *The New York Times*. I wish this would go away.'" Punch asked what everyone thought, and as Goodale listened to the various opinions, he sensed that the publisher was especially influenced by the arguments of Bancroft and Loeb and that he was going to halt publication. Defiance of the attorney general would almost certainly mean a court fight starting the next day. The *Times* had done its duty and published the first two installments, and there was every incentive not to tangle with Washington over classified documents. Finally, Punch asked Goodale whether continuing to publish would increase the paper's liability. "Not by five percent," he replied.

With that, Punch indicated, albeit with great ambivalence, that the paper should continue publication. "He really never was comfortable with the whole thing," Goodale said later. "He was generally persuaded that it was a crime." When Rosenthal returned to the third-floor news-room, the one hundred and fifty people waiting to hear the publisher's verdict erupted in cheers. Punch's decision to proceed with the series was in many respects more courageous than his original one. No longer were the stakes theoretical, and the penalties were potentially grave.

Back in the *Times'* legal department, Goodale placed a call to Lord, Day & Lord to discuss the legal battle that now seemed inevitable and was shocked to learn that the firm had decided not to go to court on behalf of the *Times*. The ostensible reason involved something Mitchell had said to Brownell during his saber-rattling phone call earlier that night. Any suit the government might bring, Mitchell had told him, would be based on the classification system Brownell himself had drafted while working for Eisenhower, creating a conflict of interest. If Lord, Day & Lord chose to represent the *Times* against the government in this case, the Justice Department would move swiftly to have it dis-qualified as counsel. The spectacle would embarrass both the newspaper and the law firm.

Left without outside counsel, Goodale briefly considered arguing the case himself — a daunting proposition for a lawyer whose previous courtroom experience consisted of two uncontested divorces — but soon came up with a better solution. Because of the Caldwell case, Goodale had become familiar with every top First Amendment attorney in the country, including Yale professor Alexander Bickel. By coinci-dence, Bickel that very day had attended a program Goodale had orga-nized about the Caldwell case, where he had made a point of congratulating the *Times* for its publication of the Pentagon Papers. Goodale reached Bickel after midnight at his mother's apartment on Riverside Drive, and he agreed to help. That night Goodale also drafted Floyd Abrams, a sophisticated media lawyer and stunningly effective lit-igator with the street-tough firm of Cahill Gordon.

On Tuesday, June 15, the third installment of the Pentagon Papers appeared, along with a front-page account of Mitchell's telegram, his telephoned threat to Brownell, and the *Times'* response. "The most satisfying headline I've ever seen in the *Times* is the one that read MITCHELL SEEKS TO HALT SERIES ON VIETNAM BUT TIMES REFUSES,"

Rosenthal told *Time* magazine. Later that day, as expected, the attorney general went to federal court and persuaded a judge who had been sitting on the bench for only five days to issue a temporary restraining order to halt further publication of the Pentagon Papers.

Although Punch had made it clear that he was willing to defy the attorney general's request, he had made it equally clear that he would abide by the courts. *The New York Times* suspended publication, marking the first time in the nation's history that a newspaper was restrained in advance by a court from publishing a specific article. On the same day, the government filed a lien against the *Times* to cover the Justice Department's litigation costs and fees, an action the *Times* discovered only years later when it wanted to sell one of its buildings.

The attorney general's attempt to muzzle the *Times* accomplished what the Pentagon Papers themselves had been unable to: it provoked the outrage of the national media and focused attention on what the purportedly explosive documents actually revealed. As important, the relationship between the press and government became the subject of public debate, with the nation's most respected and Establishment-minded paper leading the charge. Punch and the *Times*' staff suddenly found themselves regarded as heroes in certain circles. Soon people at the paper were sporting protest buttons that read FREE THE TIMES XXII — a reference to the twenty-two *Times* executives and employees whom the federal government had named as defendants in its complaint. When a group of *Times*men wore the buttons to Christ Cella, a popular New York steak house, everyone in the restaurant stood up and applauded. A Bill Mauldin cartoon in the *Chicago Sun-Times* showed a man reading a newspaper headlined TRUTH ABOUT VIETNAM with a brilliant beam of light shining from behind a sky full of dark clouds. On the beam of light were the words *"The New York Times."*

Most news organizations gave vivid accounts of the *Times*' fight but were reluctant to join the struggle. When Daniel Ellsberg learned that the *Times* had stopped publication, he offered to give the three television networks copies of the Pentagon Papers if they would make them public. After all three declined, he turned to *The Washington Post*. On Friday, June 18, *Post* publisher Katharine Graham defiantly began publishing the documents; four days later *The Boston Globe* obtained portions of Ellsberg's cache and began printing them. The government moved against both papers just as it had against the *Times*.

Punch flew back to New York the day after the restraining order was issued. At an airport press conference, and in the many interviews he gave over the next few days, he eloquently argued the *Times'* case. "This was not a breach of national security," he explained. "We gave away no national secrets. We didn't jeopardize any American soldiers or marines overseas. These papers . . . are part of history." As for charges that he had published classified material, he remarked, "I think that is a wonderful way, if you've got egg on your face, to prevent anybody from knowing it; stamp it SECRET and put it away." When he was asked who had made the decision to publish the Pentagon Papers, Punch gestured to his chest with his pipe and silently mouthed, "Me."

While Punch appeared confident and calm during his press conference, he was, in fact, intensely nervous. The night he returned from London, he went to Rock Hill and barbecued chicken for dinner — one of his specialties. He was so distracted that by the time it came off the grill, "It was like it had been on a funeral pyre," said his daughter Cathy. "Internally, he was just terrified." Adding to Punch's agitation was his fury at Louis Loeb and Herb Brownell for not having given him advance warning that they would not take the case. Within a month, to Loeb's shock and distress, the *Times* transferred almost all its legal work out of the firm.

The government had argued that the Pentagon Papers represented a threat to American security interests, but on June 30, in a 6–3 ruling, the U.S. Supreme Court disagreed, finding that prior restraint was not justified and that the *Times* could resume publishing the documents. The Nixon administration could have continued its attempt to silence the media by bringing other charges under the Espionage Act but, convinced by John Mitchell that it had no chance of winning a criminal prosecution, abandoned that strategy. Instead, Nixon secured an indictment against Ellsberg for stealing classified documents and, in the course of amassing evidence against him, sent E. Howard Hunt and G. Gordon Liddy to break into Ellsberg's psychiatrist's office, a crime that came to light later during the Watergate scandal. In 1973 a mistrial was declared, the charges were dismissed, and Ellsberg went free.

When word of the Supreme Court's decision reached the *Times,* there was uproarious jubilation. Punch and Rosenthal heard the news in New York on an open telephone to the Court and spontaneously hugged each other. "Get some champagne quick, because we're drinking it like mad here," Rosenthal telegrammed Frankel in Washington. "We ran out of French and are reduced to domestic," came the giddy reply. At a press conference at the *Times*, Punch was asked whether he would ever go through such a legal high-wire act again if the paper obtained information it considered as important as the Pentagon Papers. His answer was typically wry: "Yes, but I'd time my vacation to Europe so I could avoid being there when it happened."

The Pentagon Papers represented a milestone for Punch, and not simply because their publication resulted in journalism's highest honor, the Pulitzer Prize for meritorious public service, for the first time on his watch. Punch had had to make the toughest call of his publishership mere months after his closest business adviser, Andy Fisher, had left. He had done so against some of the most sophisticated legal advice in the country, and with the knowledge that the consequences for the *Times* and the Sulzberger family could have been dire.

The Andy Fisher showdown had proved that Punch was capable of unexpected toughness; the Pentagon Papers demonstrated that he was worthy of esteem. "[It] gave him a lot of strength, respect, from others, from himself, that he never had before that," Stuart Greenspon told a *Time* correspondent. Within the family, he enjoyed a new regard, as did the institution they all embraced as a living, breathing relation. The day after the government had halted publication, Stephen Golden had written Punch an admiring letter. As a child, he said, he had grown up feeling "impressed, embarrassed, boasting, secretive and otherwise emotionally tussled" about being a member of the family that owned *The New York Times*. But the past few days had made him swell with unadulterated pride. He saluted his uncle's "tremendous courage" and the reputation for courage that the *Times* had maintained throughout the Ochs-Sulzberger ownership. "That's what I'm applauding and am proud of. It's the first time I've personalized it like this, but I'm proud of you and the other members of our family who have made and are making the *Times* one of the world's greatest [news] organizations."

33

The Summer of the Gypsy Moths

O NE WEEKEND MORNING NOT LONG AFTER THE resolution of the Pentagon Papers case, Punch awoke at Rock Hill and went down to the kitchen to fix himself breakfast. When he opened the pantry, he saw the usual boxes and cans, neatly lined up, but someone had pasted on each one identical little military hats meticulously cut out from construction paper. On the brim of each hat were Punch's initials — AOS — and on the side of each box and can was a saluting arm. Atop the shelves of groceries-at-attention was a banner that read ARTHUR OCHS SULZBERGER! YOUR ARMY OF COMESTIBLES AWAITS YOU!

Punch's compulsion for neatness, drummed into him by Mme. Lajus and later reinforced by his father and the marines, was something of a family joke. He emptied ashtrays two seconds after they had been used and straightened pictures if they were one bubble off plumb. At home, identical pairs of white underwear lay in ordered rows in his dresser drawer. Aspirin bottles and shaving implements stood in straight lines in his immaculate medicine chest. Soup cans were lined up alphabetically on the kitchen shelves. If a dinner invitation called for an 8:00 P.M. arrival, he could be counted on to ring the doorbell at precisely 7:59 P.M., and to drive his chauffeur crazy by telling him the fastest route to get there. "His idea of a good time is coming to visit and cleaning my car," said Ruth. The filth and disarray of the newsroom horrified him. He once wrote a memo threatening to send a cleanup crew to the third floor with strict orders to dispose of all "cartons under the desks, material leaning against the walls, junk on desk tops, and furnishings that are not part of the decor." The cigarette-butt-strewn lounge maintained by the Newspaper Guild reminded him of a "restroom [in] the Bowery." Its frequenters were a "disgusting bunch of pigs." Fat people were objects of withering disdain because they showed so little self-control. "He's anal," acknowledged his daughter Cynthia. "Classic Freudian anal."

The "comestible army," arranged by Stephen Golden's wife, June, and Cynthia's au pair, Nina, was only one example of the playfulness that characterized the summer of 1971 at Rock Hill, a summer of unusual happiness and harmony in the Sulzberger clan. Punch, basking in the afterglow of the Pentagon Papers, felt a new confidence in his role as publisher. Even Carol was more relaxed, secure in the knowledge that her husband was no longer perceived as struggling.

In an unprecedented gesture of intimacy, she invited Stephen and June to live with them at Rock Hill for the season. She bought a player piano and didn't seem to mind when visiting teenagers smoked her cigarettes and drank her beer. Every night whichever Sulzberger cousins were in the area converged on the house for food, talk, and, on Saturday evenings, Punch's movie screenings. During a dinner party several cousins hung by their ankles from the terrace above the Rock Hill dining room, making faces at the startled guests below. Late at night, long after Iphigene had gone to bed, they skinny-dipped in the Hillandale pool, a practice that came to an end one evening when the lights were abruptly switched on and every bug in the state of Connecticut dive-bombed the water, within minutes encrusting the water with dead insects. "It was the summer of the gypsy moths," said June.

For Stephen, the time was particularly meaningful because of the connection he was able to make with Punch. After the Kent State killings in May 1970, he had dropped out of Columbia's School of General Studies to join the Movement for a New Congress, a student organization working to elect antiwar candidates. Eventually he had taken a job with the Film Society of Lincoln Center. During the summer of 1971, when Punch lived full-time at Rock Hill, the two men commuted into the city together each morning, companionably reading their newspapers in silence in the backseat of Punch's chauffeured car. They arrived back home separately, soaked in the hot tub, and shared a drink before dinner. Their unspoken closeness meant a lot to Stephen, whose troubled relationship with his late father was never far from his mind, but it also underscored the gulf that remained between Punch and Arthur Jr. "It's too bad Punch can't be as warm with his own son as he is now for the first time with Stephen," Carol confided to June, who had come to view the Sulzbergers as a female-oriented clan in which the men were really boys adrift, searching for a male bond.

Arthur Jr., however, didn't make it easy to approach him. He had worked on *The Daily Telegraph* in London early in the summer and arrived back at Rock Hill toward the end of July sporting a Carnaby Street look. His unruly curls spilled out from beneath a wide-brimmed hat, he wore loud ties and wire-rim glasses, and carried a cane. Carol had no use for Arthur Jr.'s new image, which she dismissed as a bid for attention, but she was so much at ease that particular summer that she made her feelings known in an uncharacteristically humorous way. One night she showed up for cocktails dressed exactly like her stepson, right down to the wire-rim glasses and cane, leaving the assembled group roaring with laughter.

While Arthur Jr. organized elaborate water-gun wars with his cousins on the immense Hillandale property, his sister Karen watched from the sidelines. Because she had continued to live with their mother after Arthur Jr. had moved in with Punch, the siblings were not close, and she had never spent an entire summer with the extended Sulzberger clan. She felt left out and uncertain of her place.

Recent events had only reinforced her status as an outsider. After graduating from the George School, a Quaker boarding school outside Philadelphia, Karen had gone to France for a year, returning in the summer of 1971 to find that her mother, newly divorced from David Christy, had remarried and was living in Topeka, Kansas, where her third husband, Jerry Johnson, was an administrator at the Menninger Foundation. Reluctant to spend her final summer before college in the Midwest, where she knew no one, Karen decided instead to reside with her father and stepmother at Rock Hill. Sensing her anxiety, Punch and Carol went out of their way to welcome her. "You've finally come home!" Punch had said by way of greeting when she arrived.

Karen soon found that she had at least one thing in common with her aunts, uncles, and cousins: a distaste for the antics of Arthur Jr. and Dan Cohen. "They loved each other, but they made everybody else ready to kill them," said Judy. Their talent to annoy was dramatically on display toward the end of the summer, when Arthur Jr. showed up at Michael Golden's wedding in his customary wire-rim glasses, a string tie, and a headband, while Dan appeared in a choir robe with a thick gold chain around his neck and his hair in an Afro. Michael and his bride, Anne, were highly amused; Ruth was not. "She took ten years to recover," said Dan. Arthur Jr. and Dan were delighted that they had been able to cause such a commotion. What they could not foresee was that the legacy of their Merry Prankster era would haunt them for decades to come. "No one has ever forgotten that," Dan said later. "People look at Arthur and me and have this visceral response: 'Oh, God, here they go again.'"

Arthur Jr. and Dan had entered Tufts University together in the fall of 1970. No fewer than four Sulzberger cousins — Cathy, Arthur Jr., Dan, and Karen — attended the school during the same period. With a fifth, Lynn Golden, enrolled at nearby Brandeis, the Tufts campus and its environs became a kind of mini-Hillandale, a place where the cousins shared houses, meals, vacation trips, late-night conversation, and, eventually, even girlfriends. They all insisted they had made their college decisions independently, attracted by Boston and the rave reviews of Cathy, who was a senior at Tufts when Arthur Jr. and Dan were freshmen. But as children of divorce, it was also true that these cousins, perhaps more than the others, yearned for the safety and predictability of family ties.

During their freshman year Arthur Jr. and Dan found themselves in the same co-ed dormitory, one floor apart. For Dan, Tufts was a nurturing, tolerant place where he gained confidence and discovered his social skills. He started out as a chemical engineering major, but soon found calculus detestable and boycotted the class altogether, earning an F in the subject. That pattern of intense interest followed by complete abandonment was Dan's curse. Something would capture his attention, then his mind would wander and he would lose focus. It was difficult for him even to sit through a movie without getting up and walking around. Years later, when the condition had a name, several family members would suggest that Dan suffered from attention deficit disorder, a congenital affliction that makes concentration difficult. At the time, he simply felt that he "just didn't have the discipline to stay with what was required in certain areas."

Many colleges during the early 1970s allowed students to design independent-study programs rather than fulfill the standard requirements of a conventional major. With Dan's meandering attention and his disdain for rules, Tufts' version of this plan, called the College Within, was a salvation. The subjects he chose — oceanography, theater and lighting design — may have been an eclectic mélange, but this kind of freedom made it possible for him to excel. During one of Tufts' monthlong reading periods, he consumed more than fifty books on his own.

While Dan dabbled in a variety of subjects, Arthur Jr. single-mindedly prepared himself for a newspaper career. He shunned the Tufts student paper and only began reading *The New York Times* in earnest his sophomore year, but academically he focused on fields he thought would serve him well as a journalist — political science and international relations. The summer before college, at his father's suggestion, he had worked for the *Vineyard Gazette*, the Martha's Vineyard paper owned by Scotty Reston. During his first January break at Tufts, he got his hands dirty in the pressroom of *The Boston Globe.* "There was just not a question in my mind [that I wanted to be in newspapers]," he remarked. "There wasn't even a question to ask the question."

In almost all other respects, however, Arthur Jr. was typical of most people his age. He experimented with grass and hallucinogenic drugs, read Kurt Vonnegut and Richard Brautigan, and played the music of the Grateful Dead. His love of argument, which had begun at Browning, intensified at Tufts as divisive issues such as Vietnam, race relations, and women's rights took on heightened urgency. The social and political upheaval of the era shaped him as surely as America's period of postwar peace and hegemony had shaped his father. Punch avoided confrontation at all costs; his son courted it. "I have a belief in the power of debate; I distrust the appearance of surface calm," Arthur Jr. said. "The sixties were a time when society debated itself in a very open and sometimes harsh way, and in the end we wound up in a better place for it."

For Dan, Vietnam barely cast a shadow. He attended a few SDS meetings, handed out flyers near Boston Common for a single day, then lapsed into a kind of studied apathy, rarely picking up a newspaper. Arthur Jr., on the other hand, had long considered himself a political activist. As a nine-year-old in 1960, he had sported a JFK button on his jacket; in his senior year at Browning, he had been suspended for a day for trying to help organize a shutdown of the school following the Kent State shootings. His antiwar activities sprang largely from conviction, but they were also pragmatic: he had drawn 88 in the draft lottery — a precariously low number. Washington still permitted college deferments, so although he was temporarily safe, he was in danger of being called up if the war dragged on much longer.

Arthur Jr.'s first arrest for civil disobedience took place outside Raytheon Company, a defense and space contractor. Wearing Punch's old marine jacket, he joined other demonstrators blocking the entrance to the company's gates. "That was an easy one," he said. "The cops couldn't have been nicer." The second arrest came after a much less peaceful sit-in at the Federal Building in downtown Boston. His hands bound behind him, Arthur Jr. watched as the police slammed a hand-cuffed woman up against the wall of an elevator because she had made a taunting remark.

Punch held his tongue following Arthur Jr.'s first arrest, but when he got word of the second, he flew to Boston. Over dinner at Locke-Ober, a clubby bastion of Boston Brahminism, he asked his son why he was involved in the antiwar movement and what could be expected from him in the future. Arthur Jr. assured his father that his recent familiarity with the interior of Boston police vans was not the beginning of a trend. Afterward, as the two men strolled around Boston Common, slightly tipsy, Punch posed what Arthur Jr. would later characterize as "the dumbest question I've ever heard in my life," and got "the dumbest answer." "If a young American soldier comes upon a North Vietnamese soldier," Punch said, "which do you want to see get shot?" Arthur Jr.'s answer was calculatedly provocative. "I would want to see the American get shot," he replied defiantly. "It's the other guy's country; we shouldn't be there." To Punch, such sentiments bordered on treason, and he exploded in anger. "How can you say that?" he yelled as Arthur Jr. tried to defend his position. Years later Arthur Jr. remembered those tense moments on the Common as the worst fight he and his father ever had. "It's the closest he's ever come to hitting me," he said.

By the time he reached college, Arthur Jr. had finally shot up to his full height of five foot ten and a half inches, but his face was still smooth and boyish. To appear older, he added pipes and cigars to his trademark hat and cane. In discussions on subjects ranging from the war to the environment, he hurled facts like weapons, as a way of appearing wiser and more informed.

Competition was a strong undercurrent in the friendship between Arthur Jr. and Dan. On the surface Arthur Jr. appeared the more assured of the two — superior in intellectual combat while yielding to Dan in athletics. To Dan, his cousin appeared suave and fearless with the opposite sex. His freshman year, Arthur Jr. met Jennifer Boyd, a bright, fun-loving woman who had a room three doors down the hall. Within ten days they were living together.

Dan observed Arthur Jr.'s new relationship with ill-concealed envy. By his own admission, he was "phenomenally shy" with women, capable of forming friendships, yet uncertain how to take the next step to romance. By the spring of his junior year, however, a girlfriend switch had occurred: *Dan* became involved with Jennifer Boyd, and Arthur Jr. was now at loose ends. The couple stayed together for three years. "She was the first love of my life," said Dan. "I didn't know a lot, but at least it helped me build up confidence in myself." As for sharing the same girlfriend, he and Arthur Jr. never addressed it. "We kept our friendship; I don't know how it made him feel," said Dan.

§

In late September 1972 *The New York Times* endorsed George McGovern, the Democratic presidential nominee, over the Republican incumbent, Richard Nixon, in what turned out to be one of the most polarizing electoral contests in American history. Abe Rosenthal, the *Times'* managing editor, later admitted that he didn't vote at all, explaining, "I wouldn't vote for Nixon, McGovern made me ill, and Norman Thomas wasn't around." Three months earlier, in what the White House dismissed as a third-rate burglary, five men had broken into Democratic headquarters in the Watergate hotel-and-office building. The *Times'* Washington bureau, distracted by the upcoming conventions and national election, and disorganized because of a series of absences and personnel changes, scarcely took note of the event. In the first week of what would come to be known as the Watergate scandal, *The Washington Post* published 218 column inches about the story; *The New York Times* ran just 73. It would take more than two years for the *Times* to get on top of the story — a wincing embarrassment so soon after its triumph with the Pentagon Papers.

In unusually harsh language, the *Times'* McGovern endorsement castigated Nixon for failing to keep his promise to end the Vietnam War, for widening the racial divide, and for allowing "the odor of corruption . . . and sleazy campaign practices" to permeate his organization. McGovern trailed the president in the polls; nonetheless, the *Times* said, he embodied a "vision of an American society that cares and an American democracy that works." To Nixon, the *Times'* editorial confirmed the wisdom of his decision not to submit to questions from the paper's editorial board. It *should* endorse McGovern, the president said bitterly, because he "stood for everything [the *Times*] stood for — permissiveness, a bug-out from Vietnam [and] new isolationism."

Arthur Hays Sulzberger had spent his own personal time and capital to help Eisenhower, but he had made it a rule never to give money to political campaigns. Iphigene was not similarly constrained, and in the 1972 election she donated $25,000 to McGovern. Not long after the New Hampshire primary, she had suggested that the *Times* do a story on how much Nixon was costing the taxpayers in security for his Florida and California homes, his Secret Service detail, the maintenance of Camp David, and so on. Abe Rosenthal had replied that such a feature would open the paper to accusations that it had singled out Nixon. Presidents were expensive, he said; Nixon no more so than others. "I think the thing that really bothers me is that he isn't worth his salary, let alone his travel expenses," Iphigene had shot back, suggesting good-naturedly that Rosenthal put her letter "in the shredder — in case the FBI is snooping!"

The Republicans' tightly choreographed nominating convention disgusted her. "From the way the script was written, the Republican Convention was following the example of the Supreme Soviet or the friends of Chairman Mao," she wrote in a letter to the editor published September 8, 1972. "One also wonders whether the idea of breaking into and bugging Democratic headquarters was inspired by similar Communist examples. Apparently the Republican party is not only trying to defeat the opposing candidate but also to eliminate democracy." As with all her letters to the editor, Iphigene masked her identity by signing the name of a deceased relative.

Not long after the publication of the Pentagon Papers, Nixon had ordered his vice president, Spiro T. Agnew, to investigate the feasibility of an official secrets act to restrain the press. The assignment was an apt one for Agnew, who had distinguished himself as the administration's attack dog on the media, especially what he called the "elitist Eastern Establishment press." Many *Times* readers agreed with Agnew's charges of conspiracy and bias. "The very bones of Adolph S. Ochs must be rattling in his grave at what has happened to the newspaper he founded [sic] and which has since become a prisoner of the Liberal Left establishment," one irate man wrote Punch.

Despite what its detractors said, where news was concerned, the paper's vaunted objectivity remained firmly intact. In a 1972 article titled "Is It True What They Say About *The New York Times*?" the conservative *National Review* surveyed five developing news stories, including one about Agnew, and begrudgingly concluded that the *Times* was not the "hotbed of liberalism" that its critics claimed. Still, under John Oakes, the *Times'* opinions had incontrovertibly taken a sharp turn to the left. With its stand against escalating the war, its endorsement of McGovern, and its advocacy of pollution controls and other regulations, the paper was increasingly perceived as politically liberal, antibusiness, and shrill in tone. An internal analysis conducted by a senior executive in the *Times'* marketing and sales department found that the editorial page was the principal reason a significant segment of the public had "lost confidence in the impartiality" of the paper.

The criticism worried Punch, for he, too, considered John's attitude toward business needlessly antagonistic to advertisers and frequently wrongheaded. He was hardly in favor of tailoring the *Times'* editorial opinions to benefit the paper's bottom line, but he did think it prudent not to endanger the *Times* financially without good reason. Indeed, he could be tough about the appearance of conflict of interest, especially when it involved his own family. As Marian's for-profit board member- ships had mounted, for example, including a groundbreaking seat as the first female director of the Ford Motor Company, he had demanded that she choose between them and her job as the *Times'* director of special activities; Marian decided to resign from the paper and keep her direc- torships.

With the retirement of Arthur Krock in 1966 at the age of seventy- eight, the *Times* had lost its conservative bullhorn on domestic politics. John Oakes had lobbied hard to dislodge Krock, whom he considered "not only incredibly reactionary but also frequently inaccurate." Punch agreed that, with his denunciations of the Voting Rights Act and other traditionally southern prejudices, the columnist had outlived his moment, but he also felt that for balance, the *Times* needed a commen- tator sympathetic to the right.

At a charity dinner during the 1972 election, Punch found himself seated on the dais next to William Safire, the tart-tongued speechwriter in the Nixon White House who had given Agnew his memorable denun- ciation of the press as "nattering nabobs of negativism." "Is it true you're interested in becoming a newspaper columnist?" Punch inquired. "Yeah," Safire replied, "but there's no money in the newspaper business." *The Washington Post* had recently invited Safire and Frank Mankiewicz, a McGovern adviser, to write a series of competing articles for its Op-Ed page. The editorial-page editor at the *Post* had liked what he saw and had prevailed upon the paper's publisher, Katharine Graham, to offer Safire a permanent column, but Safire considered the salary too low. He planned instead to leave the White House after the election and return to public relations.

Punch had read about the *Post*'s unusual offer and upon meeting Safire decided on the spot to pursue him. "Let's talk," Punch said. "Maybe we can make a deal that would be attractive enough for you." A week or so later Safire came to *The New York Times* to discuss terms, and within days accepted Punch's offer, which was about 20 percent higher than that of the *Post*. John Oakes, meanwhile, had heard of Punch's interest in Safire, and the idea that the *Times* was seriously considering employing a Nixon flack who had once worked for Florida governor Claude R. Kirk Jr. — a man John considered "worse than a crook" — sent him into a tailspin. He fired off a long memo entreating Punch, before he did "anything drastic," to consider more palatable alternatives such as Irving Kristol, co-editor of the *Public Interest,* or Jeffrey St. John, a journalist who several years earlier had made an unsuccessful run for a New York congressional seat on the Conservative Party ticket.

After reading the memo, Punch called his cousin to the publisher's fourteenth-floor office. "I guess I went a little further in talking to Bill Safire than I'd indicated," he told the startled John sheepishly. "I hired him." Since the publication of the Pentagon Papers, Punch no longer felt the need to establish his credentials as a champion of the press, nor was he as intellectually intimidated by his cousin as he had been in the early days of his publishership. He had also come to have some pride in his ability to judge people, and he trusted those instincts regarding Safire. "Let's just try this," he urged John. "It'll only be on a trial basis, and I'm sure that after he's been here for a year, you will tell me that he's the greatest appointment I've ever made."

When Safire came to pay his respects a few days later and to seek John's counsel on column writing, John received him with icy courtesy. "Mr. Safire, I cannot give you any advice," he said. "You must know that I was not in favor of your coming here, and if you don't know it, I have to tell you that." A few weeks later Safire returned with a peace offering: a bound volume of *Mid-Week Pictorial,* the rotogravure magazine John's father had edited in the early part of the century, which Safire had found in an old bookstore. John insisted on reimbursing Safire for the gift, and afterward made it his practice never to see or speak to the *Times'* conservative columnist unless he had to.

Shortly before Safire's first column appeared, John asked that a disclaimer appear in the paper stating that the opinions on the Op-Ed page were those of "individual writers," not of *The New York Times.* After Safire's twice-weekly column was launched, John sent Punch stacks of mail from outraged readers. "I know how you feel about him," Punch responded wearily. "Can't we now close the matter, please?"

Punch didn't flinch, not even when Safire wrote in his initial columns that Watergate was a "tempest in a Teapot Dome." "Punch took a lot of heat then, but I didn't hear a peep out of him," Safire said. "Whenever I saw him . . . he gave me the impression that I was doing what I was hired to do: run against the grain and present a different point of view." By the end of 1973, after more damning details had emerged about Nixon, Safire had the courage to write that his initial assessment of the Watergate scandal had been "grandly, gloriously, egregiously wrong." That admission, coupled with revelations that he and several other journalists had been wiretapped by the White House and the subsequent news tips that Safire generously passed along to colleagues, helped put him on the road to rehabilitation. But for many at the *Times,* Safire's real redemption occurred during a Washington bureau picnic, when he plunged into a swimming pool to rescue a *Times*man's child who had sunk to the bottom. "After that, I could go to lunch with people," he said dryly.

34

The Four-Part Miracle

I F ANYTHING GOOD HAD COME OF THE HUMILI-
ating and costly labor agreement of 1970, it was Punch and his top
executives' resolve to ensure that such a situation would never
occur again. No sooner was the ink dry on the agreement than there
were discussions of what steps to take when the contract expired in 1973
for the *Times* to be in a position to win the right to automate. The
Cowles acquisition was an important factor in that strategy because it
gave the paper outside funds to keep operating during a strike, but
equally critical was a tough-minded executive named Walter Mattson.

Mattson, a tall, blue-eyed man of Swedish descent, had fallen in love
with newspapers as a child visiting his uncle, who owned a weekly near
Pittsburgh. His first full-time newspaper job was as a Linotype operator
at the Portland (Me.) *Press Herald,* where he worked nights while attending college. He had come to the *Times* in 1960 as assistant to the production manager after working as an advertising man and newspaper
consultant, earning a graduate degree in engineering from Northeastern
University and laboring in production at the *Boston Herald Traveler.* He
soon caught the eye of assistant general manager Andy Fisher, who had
dispatched him to Los Angeles to work with the short-lived western edition. Following the disastrous 1970 agreement, Punch had promoted
Mattson to vice president in charge of production and ordered him and
his second-in-command, John Mortimer, to come up with a battle plan
to bring the printers to heel.

Mattson and Mortimer's strategy for dealing with the ITU included
an unequivocal demand for automation; forming a united front with
the *Daily News,* with which it had broken during the 1970 talks, a schism
that played into the hands of the union's wily president, Bert Powers;
and the development of a way to publish the paper in the event of a
strike. To bring the rest of *Times* management into the loop, Mattson

and John Pomfret, a labor specialist and assistant to the publisher, persuaded Punch to put himself and his top news and business people through a one-week team-planning course given by the American Management Association. "We were able to get everyone in the same room and figure out what it would take to knock off the unions," said James Goodale. "For me, the big thing was that we concluded that *we could do it*. We figured out how much money we had, what our strategy was, and how long a strike we could take and still finance [a showdown with the unions]."

Upon completion of the course, Punch reorganized the business side of The New York Times Company, creating four senior vice presidents, of which Mattson was one, with power over personnel and industrial relations. He publicly announced his determination to get the ITU's ban on automation removed, while Powers refused to reveal his position on the issue. The March 30, 1973, deadline for renewing the contract with the ITU and nine other unions came and went. No strike ensued; negotiations continued.

Mattson's role was to show Powers that this time, the *Times* actually had the will to prevail. Like Adolph, Mattson took pride in his early life as a tramp printer, and in his pocket he still carried a card identifying him as a former member of the ITU. He set up an alternative composing room at the *Times* and, along with the *Daily News*, established a super-secret training center in West Orange, New Jersey, where secretaries, editors, and other nonunion employees were taught how to run photo-composition equipment. When the rogue press operation was ready to go, Mattson housed it on the same floor as the *Times'* cafeteria so that printers coming up for a meal could not miss the security guard sitting at the end of the hall, protecting a room full of mysterious equipment.

At Powers's request, Mattson gave the ITU president a guided tour through the *Times'* mini-plant, but what affected him more, Powers said, was a visit to the nonunion composing room of *The Miami Herald*, a paper that several years earlier had fought an epic battle to rid itself of the ITU. There he saw with his own eyes how few people were really required to put out a paper with automated equipment. The *Herald* produced twice as many pages as *The New York Times* with half as many printers; in five years Powers's hosts at the *Herald* told him, they expected to cut that total in half. How could the *Times* afford to cede to union demands yet again, Powers asked himself, when the savings the paper stood to gain were so great? "I got the message then and there," he said. "[I saw] that it was in our interests to get a settlement and get it as quickly as we could."

A crucial element in the *Times'* plan was to extract promises from the other unions that their members would continue to work if the ITU struck. Because Powers had made so many enemies, that task proved to be remarkably easy. Ever since the 1962–63 strike, the press union leaders had seethed about the ITU president's patronizing arrogance, as well as his galling expectation of solidarity when he took his printers out, despite the fact that the other unions had few or no strike benefits.

By April 1974, more than a year after the contract had expired, the ITU was poised to strike. To put pressure on the other unions to join him, Powers obtained a resolution of full support from the AFL-CIO Central Labor Council. But rather than striking the *Times,* which everyone had assumed would be his target, he ordered a work slowdown at the *Daily News.* Ads and stories were not set by press time; the paper grew thinner and thinner. As it scrambled to move automated equipment from the West Orange training center to its offices on East Forty-second Street, the *Daily News* warned that it would put its independent pressroom into operation if a settlement wasn't reached by May 6.

Barely a day before the deadline, Powers asked the *Daily News* to remove its threat so that negotiations could continue. When no such concession was forthcoming, the paper ordered all the printers out of the building and the rogue press operation swung into action with the clandestine help of the nonunion people trained by the *Times.* True to their word, the other unions waded through lines of picketing ITU members and continued to work. Mattson, meanwhile, was regularly receiving information about Powers's plans from a source inside the union who went by the code name "Sam Boks," a reference to a Korean restaurant where the informant and Mattson had had their first secret meeting. When this combination of pressures failed to budge Powers, the ITU council invited Ted Kheel to bring all the participants to ITU headquarters in Colorado Springs. Shortly after the first meeting on May 20, a workable agreement began to take shape.

Mattson, Sydney Gruson, and several other executives briefed Punch on the terms as the publisher lay in bed in his Fifth Avenue apartment. Punch was well known for his psychosomatic back pain, which flared up during stressful moments, which the anxious talks with the ITU certainly were. That summer he would spend eight weeks in the hospital in traction, reading the Watergate impeachment proceedings. At the time, Gruson, one of three executive vice presidents at the paper, was also suffering from a back ailment. To make himself comfortable, he lay flat on Punch's bedroom floor as Mattson began his summary of the labor contract; every time Punch interrupted to ask a question, Gruson's voice would erupt from below, offering an insight.

Adding to Punch's distress was his decision to delay the publication of a story about the ITU negotiations written by A. H. Raskin, the same writer who had produced the exhaustive and candid analysis of the 1962–63 strike that Orvil had courageously published shortly before his death. Months earlier, as the ITU talks had dragged on, managing editor Abe Rosenthal had asked Raskin, the paper's deputy editorial-page editor, to take a similar look at the 1973–74 labor discussions. "Don't pull any punches," Rosenthal had told him, repeating the same instructions the journalist had received from Ted Bernstein more than ten years earlier.

When Raskin turned in his lengthy piece, Rosenthal declared that it "made him proud to be a newspaperman." Then, on Saturday, May 25, the day before it was scheduled to run, Punch phoned Raskin and told him that he had decided to defer publication until after the contract was ratified. He had to consider the *Times'* financial interests, he explained. If the paper publicly revealed the other unions' contempt for Powers, the ITU president could be so humiliated, he might renege on the contract. When Raskin protested that other companies' labor deals were always fair game, ratified or not, Punch asserted that the *Times* was not "any other corporation" and that its mission was far more important than that of, say, a shoe factory. Exactly right, Raskin retorted, and for that reason the paper had a moral obligation *not* to treat itself as a special case. Punch was unconvinced.

Raskin considered resigning, then thought better of it. Three days later he wrote Punch a scolding letter. "Are we to live, in reporting about ourselves, by a less exacting standard than the unbendable ones we set for everyone else?" he demanded. "And, if we do, what is left of our precious integrity?" Raskin did not mean to imply that Punch and his top executives were "evil, grasping, mercenary men," but, he wrote, "the real test of fidelity to our principles comes in just such cases of grievous potential risk, as it did in the Pentagon Papers decision." Punch was not persuaded. As far as he was concerned, he was not only protecting the

Times, he was doing precisely what Orvil had done: pledging to publish a frank account of the paper's delicate labor negotiations *after* all the unions had ratified the agreement.

On July 29, one day after formal ratification, Raskin's dramatic five-thousand-word account of the 1973–74 ITU contract talks appeared in *The New York Times* under the headline CITY PAPERS ON THRESHOLD OF FUTURE AS RESULT OF 11-YEAR AUTOMATION PACT. *Time* magazine later described the accord as a vindication of Punch's diversification strategy, but in the end, interunion politics and a desire to "get" Bert Powers had played a far more important role in bringing down the printers.

Within two months, news sent to the *Times* from its London and Washington bureaus was edited and set electronically. In early 1975, at Mattson's instigation, the paper leased an industrial building in Carlstadt, New Jersey, where, using thirty-six offset presses and automated inserting equipment, the *Times* would soon print a third of its daily paper and 70 percent of its Sunday sections. By the summer of 1978, after the *Times* had spent $35 million to build a new plant, also in Carlstadt, the entire paper would be produced using "cold type." By then, 1,700 of the nation's 1,786 dailies had switched to automated typesetting, making the *Times* one of the last papers in the country to embrace computerized technology.

Punch had little time to celebrate the *Times'* victory. In 1975, just sixteen months after the landmark ITU agreement, New York City became mired in a crippling fiscal crisis. Hundreds of thousands of jobs simply evaporated or moved out of town. The *Times*, which counted on classified advertising for 40 percent of its revenue, watched helplessly as its lucrative Help Wanted business plunged by half. To help trim expenses, Abe Rosenthal, a fierce believer in the preeminence of the newsroom, proposed an uncharacteristic sacrifice: a one-time reduction in the paper's "news hole," a move he predicted would save $130,000. But such economies made little difference, and by the end of the year the *Times'* operating profit stood at a dismal 1.9 percent, compared with 4.8 percent at *The Washington Post* and 10.5 percent at the *Los Angeles Times*. Clearly, something dramatic had to be done.

§

Late on the afternoon of Friday, April 30, 1976, Arthur Gelb, the *Times'* tall, gangly assistant managing editor, stood nervously nursing a drink in the spacious Club Room at Sardi's, waiting for the party he had organized to begin. For months he had worked with art director Lou Silverstein and editor Marvin Siegel to create Weekend, a special section of cultural features and movie and theater listings that had made its first appearance that morning. Papers such as *The Washington Post*, the *Los Angeles Times*, and *The Miami Herald* already had a set number of pages dedicated to lifestyle issues, but for the *Times*, which prided itself on comprehensive coverage of world and national events, a section with nothing in it but "soft news" was a radical departure. How would readers and advertisers respond to the "new" *New York Times*, with its uncharacteristic showcasing of leisure-time news?

Managing editor Abe Rosenthal had assigned Gelb the job of overseeing the development of Weekend, then carefully stepped aside and kept his distance, lest the project prove to be an embarrassment. The result was that as the date for the inaugural issue neared, Gelb felt uncomfortably alone. No one had volunteered to organize a launch party for the section, so he had decided to throw one himself. He had reserved the upstairs room at Sardi's, issued invitations to Punch and the paper's top executives, and spent hours on the phone persuading actors, writers, Broadway producers, and high-profile television journalists to attend. With such celebrities as guests, Gelb hoped to add a touch of glamour to the party and prove to skeptics that Weekend had been accepted by the city's cultural elite.

Walter Mattson, general manager of *The New York Times*, shared none of Gelb's apprehension. By the time he arrived at Sardi's, he was ebullient and ready for a drink. He was confident that Weekend would be a big moneymaker. The section was fat with ads, and spot checks of newsstands earlier in the day had shown the *Times* to be 50,000–60,000 copies ahead of its usual sales. "That thing took off just like that," recalled Mattson with a snap of his fingers.

Gelb's chief concern was not Weekend's circulation, but rather whether his peers and those in the literary and cultural community whose opinion he valued would feel the *Times* had sold its soul and cheapened itself. "Well, what do you think?" Gelb asked Punch as the crowd at Sardi's began to swell. Punch's answer was chillingly noncommittal: "Time will tell."

Taking their cue from the publisher, the rest of the news executives mingled awkwardly with their drinks sweating in their hands, wary of declaring themselves prematurely. Just at that moment, Mike Wallace, cohost of the CBS newsmagazine *60 Minutes* and one of the "names" Gelb had personally invited, strode into the room and planted himself in front of the lanky editor. Throwing his arms open wide, he declared Weekend to be "the best thing the *Times* has ever done." Within the hour the mood changed from one of caution to one of celebration as guests lined up to congratulate the *Times* on its stylish new addition.

Weekend was in fact only the first installment of a grand redesign of the *Times* that would prove to be every bit as revolutionary as the changes Adolph Ochs had instituted soon after acquiring the paper in 1896. Using the hard-won flexibility that had come with the right to automate, the *Times* broke out of its ninety-six-page, two-section strait-jacket and became a four-section paper. Over the next two years, four standing fronts were introduced, which, along with Weekend, added one section for each weekday: Sports Monday, Science, Living, and Home. In addition, a greatly expanded daily business section was created.

Although almost none of the innovations in the remodeled *New York Times* was truly new — many were shamelessly cribbed from Clay Felker's groundbreaking *New York* magazine — a few first took shape in the prototype of an afternoon daily that the *Times* had produced in 1967, when the demise of the *World Journal Tribune* had left New York with only one afternoon paper and the opening, theoretically, for a second. Rosenthal, then assistant managing editor, and Mattson, then production manager, had overseen the assembly of a dummy newspaper, which Rosenthal had jokingly referred to as *The Daily Phantom* and "the no-bullshit *Times*." Unshackled from Ochsian conventions, the two pilot issues — one under the name *New York Today*, the other called *The New York Forum* — were an inventive hybrid: a paper that adhered to the journalistic standards of the *Times* but included heretical touches such as a cartoon and book review on the front page and a New York Living page. After five months of study, Punch had decided against starting an afternoon paper, fearing that the money and people it would require would divert attention from "our main job on the *Times*." But, Punch said, he was sure that the "valuable ideas" that had bubbled up during the experiment would eventually "find a home in the *Times* itself."

A year later, in the fall of 1968, Punch had convened a committee of editors to debate the question of whether the *Times* should move to a four-part format. Although there was consensus that such a paper could be produced and be more than a mere elaboration of the existing two-part *Times*, Rosenthal worried that the "character" of the paper would suffer in the process. He also realized that developing a four-part paper would require him to deal more closely with the business side of the *Times*, whose values he feared would gradually come to affect decisions about how the *Times* covered and presented news.

But Punch, under the tutelage first of Andy Fisher and later of Walter Mattson, had become persuaded that the *Times* needed a major over-haul if it was to survive. As head of a public company — and one under considerable strain — he could not afford the luxury of his father's gen-teel attitude toward finance. The mission of *The New York Times*, Punch told one interviewer at the time without a hint of shame, was first to be profitable, and then to cover the news, explaining that if the paper didn't make money, "we can't have any other mission."

Times reporters may have joked that the paper should start a Dying section to complement Living, complete with ads for funeral parlors, and launch a new insert called News, but the fact was that by the early 1970s the paper was in desperate need of a makeover. Americans were turning more and more to television for breaking news. Nationally, the number of people who bought a newspaper every day had dropped 3 percent, leveling off at 61 million; in the greater New York area, only half the *Times*' target audience read the paper. When polled about what they wanted from their papers, readers said more information about homes, entertainment, health, leisure, and daily living concerns — subjects that had been traditional mainstays of women's magazines. The *Times* was out of step and paying the price for it every day in lost sub-scriptions, lost newsstand sales, and lost advertising contracts.

Rosenthal eventually relented in his opposition to the four-part paper, but only after Mattson presented him with nightmarish evidence that the *Times* was headed off a cliff without it. "I was told we were within one rise in the price of newsprint of going into the red," he recalled. Once convinced, he threw himself into the project with typical dervishlike energy.

Rosenthal was right about one thing: the development of the new sec-tions would require the news side and the business side to work together in ways they never had before. Punch had long tried to break down the company's rigid compartmentalization and encourage teamwork between the temple and the countinghouse. Now Rosenthal and Mattson were faced with a real-life test case, one in which the stakes couldn't be higher. How they handled each other — and how Punch handled them — would be critical to the success or failure of the revamped *Times*.

One of the things Punch admired most about Mattson was his remarkable ability to forge good relations with the frequently prickly newsroom. In 1970 Punch had put Mattson in charge of production precisely because he possessed "that final band of steel," as Punch called it, that made him credible with the news department. When Mattson told the managing editor that a special section absolutely had to be in the composing room by four o'clock, it wasn't an artificial deadline; he meant it and took the time to explain why. He also believed — as Punch did — that plowing money into reporting and editing was the best investment the *Times* could make in its future as a business. In short, Punch knew that Mattson embraced the values of *The New York Times*.

As an executive, Mattson fit Punch perfectly in both style and temperament. Like Punch, Mattson was a former marine who placed great store by order and precision. "You could set your clock by Walter," said Mike Ryan. "Everything was absolutely predictable and reliable." One-on-one with Punch, Mattson was straightforward and well organized. He didn't overwhelm the publisher with long lists of options, and he cheerfully took on anything Punch didn't like to do. "Walter was his right hand," said Sydney Gruson. "Any hole, any vacuum, Walter filled it immediately. Punch hates detail, really hates the nitty-gritty. Walter adores it. So anything that was around, Walter just swept in. He says, 'I'll look after that, I'll look after that.' Pretty soon, Sulzberger's plate was clean."

Unlike the volatile Amory Bradford, Mattson was even-tempered. Unlike the ambitious Andy Fisher, he kept his personal aspirations in check. He disdained the trappings of a top executive and, as general manager, chose to work in a small office on the ninth floor with a metal desk, an area rug, and a small, round conference table tucked in one corner. "I guess this is what you call 'Swedish sparse,'" Punch had joked when he saw the place for the first time. In fact, Mattson had deliberately located his office in a spot that forced subordinates to walk by his open door to reach their desks. Invariably, he would wave them in for what came to be known, with a cringe, as "Walter's pumping sessions."

Mattson had no taste or skill for cocktail-party chatter and accepted the job as general manager only after Punch swore that he would not be required to take part in what Mattson called "the city social swirl" unless there was a clear business reason to do so. At dinner parties his monosyllabic responses were legendary. "I spent several years one evening with Walter," sighed John Oakes, who once found himself seated across from Mattson by a New York hostess.

Some thought Mattson overly invested in his persona as a working-class man of the people. He delighted in shocking other executives by telling them that he bought his suits at Sears, Roebuck and Co. and that he pressed them himself on the weekends, putting in a razor-sharp crease with a Hammacher Schlemmer pants-pressing machine. Punch's wife, Carol, could not abide the *Times'* general manager, whom she considered "uncouth and uncivilized." His table manners appalled her — he held his fork like a shovel, she complained — and she and Punch rarely socialized with Mattson and his wife, Gerri. But Punch, who probably would have been just as happy as a handyman or a gardener as publisher of *The New York Times,* got along with Mattson beautifully. "Walter was fabulous in that position," said Stuart Greenspon. "He treated Punch with great respect and always gave him full credit."

Punch and Rosenthal, however, were less naturally compatible. Rosenthal — passionate, insecure, arrogant, and occasionally vainglorious — was a distinct counterpoint to Punch, who fled from emotional outbursts and was largely oblivious to the prerogatives of power. He had hoped to establish with Rosenthal the kind of confidential relationship he had once had with Turner Catledge. But when Punch had called him "Professor" — the salutation he had always used with Turner — Rosenthal had politely asked him to stop; he felt that *professor* subtly conveyed the sense that he was a retainer. Rosenthal described himself as "more of an outsider. . . . I never became a member of the court. I had good relations with Punch, but we never went traveling together as families like the Catledges and the Wickers."

If Mattson had the dependable security of a rock, Rosenthal was quicksilver — unpredictable, erratic, brilliant, animated. When Warren Hoge came to the *Times* from the *New York Post,* his first assignment, as was the custom, was to work as a reporter on the metropolitan desk. Five weeks into the job, Rosenthal called Hoge into his office and offered him a position as regional editor in the suburbs. Hoge, who had his sights set on loftier goals, graciously refused, and the two men parted after what Hoge thought was a cordial exchange. The next day in the city room,

Mike Levitas, editor of the Sunday *Book Review,* walked by Hoge, turned around, and said over his shoulder, "What you did last night is very *grave.*" Ten minutes later Arthur Gelb, looking taller than ever, loomed in front of Hoge. "Abe's hopping mad," he said. "If I were you, I'd take the damn job."

Hoge was distraught. Friends on the staff told him that after his interview the night before, Rosenthal had summoned the metropolitan desk editors to his office. "Who does Hoge think he is?" Rosenthal had demanded, pacing the floor. "This man is not *Times* material! If he realizes his mistake, then I might reconsider, but in the meantime, I don't want any of you to speak to him." Faced with a *Times* career that threatened to be only five weeks long, Hoge reluctantly resolved to accept the job in the suburbs. It took him several days to get an appointment with Rosenthal, who studiously put him off. When Hoge finally had his audience, he admitted his error and with an excess of humility asked to be reconsidered for the job in the suburbs. Rosenthal allowed as how he now questioned whether Hoge was the right man for the post and said he wanted the weekend to think it over. On Monday Rosenthal finally gave Hoge the position, but for the next six weeks didn't speak to him. "There's a really good Abe, and there's a really bad Abe," Peter Millones, a *Times* editor, told Hoge by way of comfort. "You've caught the really, really bad Abe and you'll just have to get through it."

Punch, of course, was spared such fits of pique. Rosenthal treated the publisher with great deference, tempered by a conviction that it was *The New York Times'* reporters, not its owners, who made the newspaper. "You've got the stock, but I've got the paper," he had once brashly told Punch while still a correspondent. Punch, like his father, exercised his authority over the newsroom with a light hand. He attended Rosenthal's front-page meeting most afternoons but rarely made a comment, though from time to time he bantered with the editor on the subject. "Tell me," he would say to Rosenthal, "you can put anything you want on the front page, can't you?" "Yes, not without discussion, but basically yes," Rosenthal would reply. "And when you're not here, your deputy can put anything he wants on the front page?" "Yes," Rosenthal would say, nodding. After Punch had run through practically all the names on the masthead, he would conclude with a twinkle, "Well, Abe, tell me one more time, so I understand: Why, then, would it be against the First Amendment if *I* put something on the front page?"

Because Punch was so taciturn and Rosenthal so blustery, many in the newsroom assumed the *Times* editor had the power to manipulate or even intimidate the publisher — an impression Rosenthal did little to dispel. But Punch was hardly a pushover, and through experience Rosenthal had gradually learned how to "read" his signals. "I'll think about it" was a phrase that, in Punch-speak, meant that the discussion was over, and whatever issue Rosenthal was advocating had been dismissed.

During the development of the four-part paper, Punch depended on these two very different men not only to get along but to meld as a team. That they managed to do so was attributable mostly to Mattson. "Walter turned Abe into a partner," said Kathy Darrow, then a *Times* lawyer. "[That] says a lot about his ability to deal with people." Even Rosenthal, who frequently found himself outmaneuvered at meetings with Mattson, admitted years later that the *Times'* general manager was "smarter and tougher than I was in many ways."

As managing editor, Rosenthal took pains to insulate the newsroom from the business side of the paper. He didn't allow anyone from the advertising department to deal directly with his editors. He wanted his reporters to think that he, and only he, called the shots. When Punch sent him a memo with eighteen story ideas for the new Home section, ranging from leather-bound books to fire extinguishers, Rosenthal removed the publisher's name, had his secretary retype the memo, scrambled the order of suggestions to suit his taste, and then sent it to the appropriate editor under his own signature. Mattson's victories were often repackaged to appear as though they had been Rosenthal's. If he lost a fight with the business side, as he sometimes did, he would call his people in and announce, "I have this great idea." Over the years even the invention of the four-part paper itself came to be regarded as a jewel in Rosenthal's crown, despite his having actively opposed it at first.

Mattson didn't seem to mind Rosenthal's taking the credit as long as he won the battles that mattered to him, and he consciously worked at maintaining good relations. Often, following the afternoon news conference, he would drop in on the *Times* editor in his Asian-accented office, just off the newsroom. Over glasses of scotch, Mattson would announce his latest brainstorm for linking editorial content to advertising. Invariably, Rosenthal would leap up, pace back and forth, draw furiously on his cigarette, and lecture Mattson on the integrity of the news department. Mattson would sit calmly, smoking his cigar and sipping his drink. Finally, after Rosenthal had expended himself, he would stop, whirl around on Mattson, and say, "Okay, goddamn it, what do you want?" Then the two men would sit down and work out a mutually satisfactory solution. "That must have happened a dozen times," said Mattson, laughing, "and it always ended the same way: 'Goddamn it, what do you want?'"

Rosenthal respected Mattson's backbone, his command of everything from the intricacies of printing-press technology to labor agreements and advertising rates, and especially his genuine reverence for the news values that made *The New York Times* unique in American life. Even in the 1960s, when Arthur Hays Sulzberger had had an unwritten rule discouraging people on the business side from setting foot in the newsroom, Mattson had wandered there at will, talking to the editors, getting to know their concerns. As a result, the wariness that had long characterized relations between the news and business sides of the paper began to soften. "There was trust," said Lance Primis, then a *Times* ad manager. "Abe believed we would really not do anything that would denigrate the news report."

Emblematic of this trust was that Rosenthal ultimately did not resist coordinating news with advertising as long as it was news that drove the decision. When Mattson suggested that the *Times* provide a regular education story on Wednesdays, a day when there was considerable education advertising, Rosenthal was only too happy to oblige, because the paper ran education stories virtually every day anyway. But if a writer was pressured to cover a subject simply to satisfy an advertiser, he rose like a cobra.

Rosenthal's principled concern for the honor of the *Times* was legitimate, but he also feared that his credibility with his own reporters would suffer if there was the slightest perception that he had sold out to the advertising department. By the time Sports Monday, Living, Home, and Weekend were all firmly in place, there had already been several instances in which Mattson and company had gone too far for Rosenthal's taste. It was in this atmosphere of heightened sensitivity that they squared off over what the theme should be for the fifth and final daily section. Mattson wanted fashion, a subject guaranteed to attract ads from department stores and specialty shops. Rosenthal worried that adding yet another light consumer section would tip the scales and make the paper too soft. *Penthouse* magazine had recently profiled Rosenthal under the headline SUPEREDITOR IGNORES NEW YORK'S DEMISE IN MAD SCRAMBLE TO PRINT SOUFFLÉ RECIPES, and The New York Times Company was taking a drubbing for its creation of the gossipy *US* magazine, an inferior imitation of *People* that Ruth and Iphigene hated and, privately, Punch admitted he should never have started.

Early in 1978 Rosenthal suggested to Punch that the *Times* start a science section. Science was a respectable subject, and it could claim a tradition at the *Times* dating back to the polar expeditions and daredevil flights of Adolph's day. With no obvious advertising to support it, however, Mattson was unenthusiastic and refused to earmark additional money or space to produce it.

After hearing from the advertising department, Punch, too, had come to have serious reservations about the economic viability of a science section, but he had no intention of imposing his judgment on his top editor. With Rosenthal and Mattson at loggerheads, Punch simply let the matter slide for a few months. Then Rosenthal was given a gift in the form of a pressmen's union strike against the *Times* and other New York papers, the last big labor-management dispute at the paper over the manning of the Forty-third Street presses. For eighty-eight days in the summer of 1978, the *Times* was shut down and Mattson's attention was taken up by union bargaining. With his opposition temporarily distracted, Rosenthal decided he wanted "something to welcome readers back." Knowing he had no support from the business side, he shuffled his existing allotment of pages and, without adding staff, cobbled up Science Times. Punch, with his love of aviation and technology stories, signed off on it because he had become persuaded it was "a much better product for *The New York Times* than the other." The first issue appeared November 14, 1978, eight days after the *Times* resumed publishing.

Mattson was sportsmanlike in defeat. "That was Abe's baby, one hundred percent," he said of Science Times. "We decided it wasn't going to be profitable for us but that it was a hell of a good section and would have great reader interest." Mattson had been right about one thing: there was no advertising base for a section devoted to science. It was not until the advent of the home computer in the early 1980s that the link between the readers of Science Times and a potentially lucrative advertiser became obvious. When Mattson's deputy, John Pomfret, suggested that Rosenthal start a computer column to attract ads from IBM, Apple, and other PC manufacturers, Rosenthal uncharacteristically agreed that it was a good idea because computer technology was an "interesting, expanding, and useful field which we do not now cover."

It's debatable whether the introduction of the four-part paper "saved" *The New York Times,* as some accounts later maintained, but it certainly aided in its rescue. The paper soon regained the daily circulation it had lost in the early 1970s and by the mid-1980s welcomed another 150,000 readers. A few years later annual operating profit topped $200 million.

But the four-part *Times* had an effect far beyond simply benefiting the paper's bottom line. The development process showed that the news department and the business side could, in fact, work together without endangering the essential character of the newspaper. Because Mattson, Rosenthal, and a few of their top aides had established trust and rapport, Punch had not had to referee every decision — something he had been trying to achieve from nearly the first day of his publishership. The "forest of trees," as he often called the battling fiefdoms of the *Times,* had somehow managed to grow together at the top.

The image of cooperation would prove to be an illusion, however; decades would intervene before the newsroom and the business side would work so well together again. As the *Times* became more prosperous, Rosenthal had fewer reasons to mute his suspicions of the business side, and the rivalry and competition would reassert itself. Eventually, Punch would abandon the ideal of teamwork and resign himself to the fact that both sides operated best under their autocratic leaders — Mattson and Rosenthal. The dilemma of how to break down the wall between those who produced the journalism and the people who produced the money would be a problem he would eventually bequeath his successor.

35

Getting Rid of Troublesome Priests

O**N THE MORNING OF SEPTEMBER 9, 1976, JOHN** Oakes and his family were preparing to catch the ferry from their summer home on Martha's Vineyard to the Massachusetts mainland when the phone rang, and what John later called "the worst day of my life" began. Fred Hechinger, his associate editor on the editorial page, had called at Punch's request to read John an editorial endorsing Daniel Patrick Moynihan, the former Harvard professor and mid-level official in the Nixon administration, as *The New York Times'* choice in the New York Democratic primary for U.S. senator. Hechinger had been handed the endorsement hours earlier, along with a note indicating that Punch wanted it to run in the next day's paper. "I like it the way it is," Punch had written — unusually firm language that Hechinger interpreted to mean that the publisher would permit no changes of any kind. John listened intently to the editorial, which described Moynihan as, among other things, "that rambunctious child of the sidewalks of New York." "I damn near died," he recalled. "Aside from the choice of Moynihan, it was badly written."

John immediately phoned Punch to register an outraged protest. He viewed Moynihan as "a big phony" and had never forgiven him for his authorship of the famous "benign neglect" memorandum during the Nixon years, a document Oakes felt was insensitive to blacks and a retreat from the government's social contract. John's candidate was Congresswoman Bella Abzug, Moynihan's leading rival, whom he acknowledged many thought of as a "left-wing crazy woman with a hat." Nevertheless, he felt she was a sincere advocate of "urban liberalism and social humanitarianism." Punch, however, disliked the brassy feminist, and he took comfort in the fact that men whose opinions he respected — Scotty Reston and Charles G. Bluhdorn, chairman of Gulf + Western Industries, one of Punch's closest business friends — agreed with him.

In early August, before departing on vacation, John had tried to persuade Punch to endorse Abzug, hoping that the *Times'* stamp of approval would swing wavering moderates and liberals to her side in what promised to be a close contest. When Punch refused, John changed tactics, arguing instead that, under its own rules, the *Times* did not have to back anyone in a primary. Only after he had secured what he thought was "a clear understanding" that no primary endorsement would be forthcoming did he leave for Martha's Vineyard.

Punch later said he had come away from this conversation with a far more nuanced "understanding." But even if John's memory was correct, several things had occurred while he was on vacation that had spurred Punch to take his own course. One was a grim *BusinessWeek* cover story headlined BEHIND THE PROFIT SQUEEZE AT THE NEW YORK TIMES that chronicled the breathtaking nosedive of *Times* stock, from more than $60 a share in 1969 to $13 in September 1976, and repeated the old complaint that the *Times* had become left of center and "stridently antibusiness in tone." Punch thought this was not the moment for the paper to be seen as championing an Abzug victory.

The second development was Moynihan's dangerously thin lead. In the wake of Nixon's resignation, New York Republicans were in disarray and were unlikely to win the general election. Whoever emerged as the victor in the Democratic primary was bound to be New York's next senator. In such a close race, a *Times* endorsement carried more weight than usual and might even be determinative.

Under these conditions, Punch felt a renewed urgency to support Moynihan and had decided to take advantage of John's absence to enforce his prerogative as publisher. In a highly unusual step, he had written the Moynihan endorsement himself and then shown it to his chief aide, Sydney Gruson, who, despairing of its style, had gone looking for help. He had found it in associate editor Max Frankel, who had recently sent Punch a tortured analysis of the two candidates that had concluded improbably, "If we could, we should vote for Bella Moynihan." At Gruson's urging, Frankel had reworked Punch's draft endorsement, drawing heavily on the pro-Moynihan points he had made in his memo. It was this document that Fred Hechinger read over the phone to John Oakes.

When it became clear to John that Punch was determined to publish the endorsement, he implored him at least to sign it so that it would be clear that the statement did not represent the view of the *Times*' editorial board. Punch refused. "John used to argue that [the editorial page] was the voice of the publisher, particularly on decisions about whom we were going to support," Punch said. "But when that moment of truth came, he forgot what he had been preaching in the past." As a gesture of conciliation — and in a dramatic break with precedent — Punch instead invited John to write a dissenting letter to the editor taking issue with the Moynihan endorsement. The offer put John in the awkward position of publicly disagreeing with his own editorial page, but with no other recourse left to him, he accepted.

John scribbled his thoughts on a memo pad during the forty-five-minute ferry ride to the mainland and, as soon as he reached the shore, dictated the composition to Fred Hechinger's secretary from a pay phone. What arrived in the composing room later that afternoon was a biting seven-paragraph rebuttal in which John "disassociated" himself from Punch's endorsement and described Moynihan as "charming, highly articulate and certainly intelligent, but so are many other opportunistic showmen." The letter was scheduled to run the same day as the Moynihan endorsement. As soon as it was set into type, a copy went upstairs to Punch, who killed it on the spot.

When John arrived back in the office on September 10, he had already read the Moynihan editorial in that morning's *New York Times*. With a sigh of resignation, he recast his original 450-word letter in terms that Punch found acceptable. What actually appeared in the next day's paper was a single sentence, signed by John, politely expressing "disagreement" with the endorsement. Three days later, on primary day, September 14, Moynihan won with 36 percent of the vote to Abzug's 35 percent — a difference of about nine thousand votes. The *Times*' endorsement had undoubtedly helped tip a crucial 1 percent of New York voters toward Moynihan.

During the initial phase of the Moynihan battle, John had considered resigning, even though he knew that it would have been "kind of a silly gesture." The reason was that by then he was already a lame duck, with only three months left in his term of office. Earlier that spring Punch had announced that, effective January 1, 1977, he was removing his cousin as editor of the editorial page and putting Max Frankel in his place. The swiftness of John's ouster, together with Punch's insistent endorsement of Moynihan, signaled Punch's new resolve to take control of an editorial page that John had operated with near autonomy for fifteen years and, at the same time, to shift the *Times'* politics from the left to the center. "I was ready for a change," said Punch. "I wanted to have my own person in there."

Punch's putsch, as John's removal was called in some quarters, was also an indication of how ragged relations between the two men had become in recent years. The harsh editorials that Punch considered antibusiness manifestos were only part of the problem. Punch had winced at editorials defending graffiti ("an indigenous form of painting") and thrown up his hands when John wanted to endorse a city tax for public-interest reasons, even though it had the potential to adversely affect *Times* profits.

For most of his publishership, Punch had been preoccupied with doing what was necessary to transform *The New York Times* into a modern business. His distraction in attending to these details, combined with John's often stiff-necked refusal to be crossed and Iphigene's sympathy with John's left-leaning politics, had made it more trouble than it was worth to replace him. Now, after thirteen years on the job, Punch was fifty, battle-tested, and self-assured. He still courted his mother's support for projects but did not need it the same way he had when he was a new publisher and his father was alive. Politically, as he himself recognized, he was no longer a blank slate: "John was staying liberal and I was getting older, growing more conservative," he said. "We just drifted apart."

Punch also had a personnel problem that would be neatly solved by John's departure: he needed a consolation prize for Max Frankel, who had moved from Washington to become Sunday editor three years earlier and who Punch feared would quit as a result of losing the competition for executive editorship to Abe Rosenthal. Punch had resurrected the post of executive editor, last held by Scotty Reston in 1969, because he had wanted to unify the Sunday and daily news departments under one leader. In Rosenthal, Punch was certain he had an editor with the backbone to effect such a merger. As important, Rosenthal had the support of *Times* general manager Walter Mattson.

Frankel, on the other hand, had been vocal in his distaste for the "muscular business departments," and the business-side executives who had worked with him as Sunday editor felt that he was unduly brittle. His vision for the *Times'* future was not of a large, sectioned paper — "a bloated package . . . like a supermarket," as he described it — but of a smaller, tighter publication aimed, like *The Wall Street Journal,* at the demographic elite. Scotty Reston, Frankel's patron in the Washington bureau, had heavily promoted his onetime protégé, as had Iphigene, in part because she trusted Reston's judgment and in part because she personally enjoyed Frankel's serious-minded intellectualism and knowledge of world affairs. *Time* had recently included the forty-six-year-old editor in a cover story on the country's "200 Faces for the Future." But ultimately Punch had come down on the side of Rosenthal, eight years Frankel's senior, as the better choice.

The appointment not only gave Rosenthal power over the Sunday paper but effectively eliminated the position of Sunday editor, thus putting Frankel out of a job. Punch had no desire to lose Frankel, a superb journalist who as Moscow bureau chief in the late 1950s had "discovered" the pianist Van Cliburn and, more recently, won a Pulitzer Prize for his coverage of Nixon's trip to China. Punch also admired Frankel's studied, professorial approach to problems and his moderate brand of liberalism, which, he hoped, would give the editorial page a more measured tone.

Frankel, however, feared that running the editorial page would taint him as too opinionated and prevent him from managing the news operations at a later date. "It's a dead end," he complained to Sydney Gruson in a memo. He also felt that John's uneven staff of writers put him in the untenable position of captaining a leaky vessel. He would head up the editorial page, he told Punch in so many words, only if he could purge the department, put in his own people, and really shake things up. With that understanding, Frankel accepted the job.

The only hurdle that remained was telling John Oakes, which Punch did one afternoon in late March 1976, in his fourteenth-floor office. He wasted no time on small talk. "The clock is ticking away," he told his cousin. "What do you think about stepping down from your job at the end of the year?" John was speechless. He was more than two years away from turning sixty-five, the *Times'* official retirement age and a Rubicon that had been ignored frequently at the publisher's discretion. "Punch, this is a little sudden," John stammered. "Has there been any editorial position we've taken that requires you to ask me to step down at this time?" "Absolutely not," Punch replied. "You've done a great job." The problem, Punch explained, was that he was afraid he would lose Frankel if he didn't make him editorial-page editor.

John had always assumed his successor would come from the ranks of the editorial board. Now, not only was he being pushed out with what he considered unseemly haste, but it was apparent that he was not going to have any say about who would replace him. John admired Frankel but told Punch that since Frankel had never written editorials, he needed more seasoning. Why not put off installing him for a year or so, John asked, and in the interim give him some training? Punch remained firm and gave John another shock by telling him that he expected to announce the new arrangement the following week.

That weekend, two days before the announcement, John, in a near panic, invited himself to Rock Hill to have another long talk with Punch. He was deeply concerned about his reputation, John said, certain that the suddenness of his exit would be widely interpreted as a repudiation of him, his staff, and the views they had espoused on the *Times'* editorial page. He implored Punch to push back the date of his departure from January 1, 1977, to May 1, 1978 — the month of his sixty-fifth birthday. When it became clear that Punch wouldn't budge, he retreated to January 1, 1978, and finally to the fall of 1977. Punch again refused, although he did sweeten an offer, made earlier, to keep John on as a senior editor, senior vice president, and occasional columnist. "I thought that he felt that he was buying me off, and I didn't like that one bit," said John. "And it had become clearer to me by this time that Frankel had not even wanted this post, which only added to the bitterness of the blow."

The next day John informed the editorial board of his upcoming departure and Frankel's arrival. On April 6, as planned, *The New York Times* carried a story announcing the immediate unification of the Sunday and news departments under Rosenthal and the shifts soon to take place on the editorial page. That afternoon Punch wrote John a letter marked PERSONAL AND CONFIDENTIAL. "My admiration and respect for you during this most difficult time was given a whole new life," he began. "These last two weeks, I know, have been terribly difficult not just for you, but for your family, and that, in turn, has made it difficult not only for me, but for my family, for they are one and the same. . . . You're a great gentleman and I would like to thank you for your understanding in this tough time." It was the first time during the emotionally wrenching fracas that Punch had invoked any family association.

When John had told his staff about his replacement, he was ignorant of Frankel's reorganization plan and assured them that he foresaw no policy changes. Less than two weeks after the announcement appeared in the *Times*, however, Rosenthal received a list of the writers Frankel hoped to ax from the editorial board and transfer to the newsroom. In a "strictly confidential" memo to Punch ruminating on Frankel's choices, Rosenthal commented with some astonishment that "Max has won your approval to get rid of almost everybody in the department." In fact, the plan called for eliminating two-thirds of the board — eight of its twelve members. News as explosive as that was impossible to keep secret at the *Times*, and word of the "hit list" soon reached John. In language evocative of official war correspondence, he complained to Frankel about the fact that several of his men had been "marked for forcible removal to the News Department." The next day Punch personally met with the editorial board, but his placating words had little effect. "There has been altogether too much grief for everyone in this," Frankel told John, adding that he had no idea "unthinking gossip and malicious comment would so distort the situation."

Despite the wheels that had been set irrevocably in motion, John made one last, desperate attempt to rescue the situation. In mid-May he again petitioned Punch to delay the process of turning the editorial page over to Frankel, arguing that it encouraged the notion that the "independent policies of editorial leadership that have long characterized the *Times*" were under assault. In an act of amazing bravado, he attached a memo he had drafted for Punch's signature, which stated: "I have asked [John Oakes] to defer for another year his projected retirement. . . . I want to take this occasion to reiterate that there will be no break in the *Times*'s editorial policies as they have been presented by a dedicated and extraordinarily able board of editors whose page, under Mr. Oakes' direction, has for many years given unique leadership to the public affairs of the city, state and nation." Wearily but with considerable sensitivity, Punch acknowledged the difficulty John was having accepting these "necessary, even inevitable" changes. But he did not waver on the timing of John's departure. "The die has been cast," he said.

The showdown over the Moynihan endorsement took place in this atmosphere of regret and bitterness, a showdown that John came to view as his final humiliation. But as the 1976 presidential campaign progressed, tempers grew even shorter. In July Punch called John down for using the phrase *God forbid!* in an editorial about the possibility that the Republicans might nominate Ronald Reagan. "Worse things can happen," Punch told him, to which John spat back, "What? A nuclear bomb!?" By October the editorial board was in a virtual state of rebellion, with one member "on the verge of a nervous breakdown" and John furious with Frankel, who, he said, expected "to take a cram course from me on how to put out [the] page."

Iphigene suggested that a farewell luncheon be arranged in John's honor and promised to attend if it was held, but John declined. On January 1, 1977, he retired as editor of the *Times'* editorial page and became an intermittent columnist on the Op-Ed page, from which he would expound his views on conservation and social justice for the next twelve years.

Barely a month later *Time* magazine saluted the "bright, diplomatic tone [that] has crept into the *Times'* editorial page" — an indication that Frankel had already begun to hit the less dogmatic notes Punch preferred. As a goodwill gesture, and at Iphigene's urging, Punch nominated John for a Pulitzer Prize in editorial writing, an honor that until then had eluded him — and continued to do so. The publisher and his cousin continued to spar as energetically as they ever had during John's days as editorial-page editor. When John used the word *bullshit* in a column — a quote from one of his sources — Punch expressed "dismay and astonishment" and invoked *The New York Times* stylebook, which forbade such language. "I don't like those kinds of words in *The New York Times*," he said emphatically. John retaliated by sending him a copy of an item in the paper he found to be equally objectionable — a health column written by Jane Brody. The subject: vaginitis.

§

Having rid himself of one troublesome relative, Punch turned his attention to another: Cy Sulzberger, whom he forced to retire at the end of 1977, the year Cy turned sixty-five. Like John, Cy declined to go quietly, and angrily protested that Punch was being unfair. Scotty Reston had continued to work at the *Times* at sixty-eight, he pointed out, as had seventy-two-year-old sportswriter Red Smith. Again, Punch was adamant, even gleeful, in his refusal to reconsider. Ever since Cy had snubbed him during his stint in the Paris bureau in the 1950s, Punch had been biding his time, waiting to exact revenge. "Cy mistreated him and [Punch] never got over it," said Sydney Gruson. "He was just fixated on that bastard's early behavior toward him."

His father's admiring attention toward Cy had also remained a raw wound for Punch. Since childhood he had felt helpless to compete with his erudite, better-educated, and vigorously masculine cousin. "As a boy, when he was very stupid and unable to get into a good school or college, Uncle Arthur and Aunt Iph always held me up to Punch by name as an example of what he ought to be," Cy confided in his personal diary. " 'Why can't you be like Cyrus?' From this naturally developed a hatred, which festered. It was idiotic of the poor boy's parents. I fear I may have been made to pay for their error."

Cy's characterization of himself as a victim was typical of his paradoxical personality. He was notorious for being insensitive toward others, yet was easily affronted by discourtesy. In 1958, after a special screening of the movie *Gigi* in New York, several members of the Sulzberger clan had exited the theater and climbed into private cars waiting to take them to dinner. When Cy was directed to one of the vehicles, he found his cousin Judy waiting in the backseat and decided she wasn't sufficiently grand to merit his company. "He opened the door, looked in, saw who was in it, closed the door, and walked away," Judy recalled. "That was the way he was." Cy's approach to reporting was much the same. He focused exclusively on the most powerful people in whatever country he happened to be, and eventually came to view himself as deserving the same treatment as the heads of state who filled his column. "He had the advantage of that kind of access," said Flora Lewis, a *Times* columnist based in Paris, "but he also had the disadvantage of it, because the number one person often doesn't really know what's going on."

During his years as publisher, Punch had listened impatiently to Cy's tirades about money and privilege. Even though his salary put him among the top fifteen people at the paper, he complained continually that he had been financially "screwed." "Cy was a terribly greedy man who would ask for one economic concession after another," recalled Gruson. "He never spent a penny of his own money." In 1966, two years after Punch had made Scotty Reston associate editor, a position that elevated him to the masthead, Cy had lobbied for the same title. Initially, Punch had resisted, but egged on by Iphigene, who wanted Cy appeased in the name of family harmony, he had come up with a quid pro quo. He told his cousin that the title could be his if he would agree to help strengthen the *Times'* foreign coverage. It would be especially useful,

Punch had said, if, when "we send a new correspondent abroad, you take him in hand and introduce him to people he ought to get to know." Cy had refused, haughtily dismissing Punch's offer as "too late." The real reason he turned down the title was that he had no intention of sharing his sources, nor would he tolerate any curbing of his independence. "He just was not a team player," said Punch. "Everybody [in the family] thought I was being mean to him. But I didn't think I was being very mean."

Punch's insistence on Cy's retirement, however, had a brutality to it. The order came barely a year after Cy's wife, Marina, had died suddenly at the age of fifty-seven. Taken together, the two events effectively toppled all the support pillars of Cy's life. In mid-July 1976 Marina had entered the American Hospital in Paris for a hysterectomy necessitated by cancer. One week later she suffered an embolism in her lungs and died. Cy had arrived at her room for a morning visit just in time to see his wife, her face contorted in pain, wheeled out by frenzied doctors. "I lost my darling Marina," he wrote in his diary, "and it is only when something is gone that you appreciate its true and irreplaceable value. . . . Now there is nothing but a hollow that will never be filled." That afternoon a grieving Cy went to the Paris bureau to compose Marina's obituary. When it was done, he handed it to his secretary, Linda Lamarche, to be put on the wire. Then he looked searchingly into her eyes and asked, "Shall I write my own?"

Two weeks after her death, Marina's ashes were scattered in the Aegean Sea off the island of Spetsais, where Cy and Marina had a vacation home, and Cy threw himself into his work, traveling to Plains, Georgia, in mid-August to interview Jimmy Carter. Soon he was plagued with insomnia and self-recrimination. "I realized with horror that in all my long life I had never done a single thing of which I could genuinely be proud: no act of true courage, generosity, sacrifice, or even pure kindness," he wrote. "It is appalling to contemplate." He and Marina had recently moved into an airy apartment at 25 Blvd. de Montparnasse. The home was so new that before her operation, Marina had not even had time to hang the curtains. Following her death, it remained undecorated and gradually became a desolate monument to Cy's loneliness. "This apartment is my coffin," he told friends.

Cy tried to keep up the old routines, but without Marina to smooth the way, he soon stopped receiving invitations to parties except for professional occasions. "When she died, he just fell off the map in a social sense, because no one particularly cared to see him," said Flora Lewis. His constant companion was a young dog named Christopher Beagle, which he had given Marina as a present. Under Cy's care, the dog became neurotic, urinating on the carpet and ruining the furniture. "Christopher became obsessively and disagreeably my father's crutch for the next ten years," said his son, David.

By 1977 Cy was in a state of perpetual melancholy. His gout had worsened, and his eyesight, never good, was failing. Because he was partially deaf in one ear, he took no pleasure in concerts or the theater and frequented only a few restaurants where he was known and could get a quiet corner table. He had spent so much of his life traveling and interviewing important people, that he had never really gotten to know his grown son and daughter, Marinette. Suddenly, David, living in London, had to readjust his life to take care of his father — something he both welcomed and resented.

Despite the sorry state of Cy's personal life, Punch insisted on his retirement by the end of the year. Then, in September Cy was vacationing on Spetsais, brooding about his imminent departure from the *Times,* when he received a call from Carl Bernstein, who had left *The Washington Post* after his Watergate triumph, that only added to his troubles. Bernstein was working on a story for *Rolling Stone* about journalists who had provided assistance to the Central Intelligence Agency. A CIA officer had alleged that the Agency had once given Cy a background paper about Soviet spies that Cy had put his name on and published as a column in *The New York Times.* Bernstein further asserted that Cy had been asked to sign a pledge to keep confidential any classified information the CIA shared with him. "Tommyrot," Cy replied angrily as Bernstein rattled off the accusations. He had talked to CIA operatives just as he talked to all sources, he explained, but he had never taken an assignment from them, nor had he published any Agency paper under his byline.

Bernstein's story, when it appeared, was explosive not only for what it claimed about Cy but for allegations it made about Arthur Hays Sulzberger and *The New York Times.* Bernstein reported that between 1950 and 1966, the *Times* had allowed about ten CIA employees to pose as clerks or part-time correspondents in some of its overseas bureaus. Cy was quoted as saying that Arthur had signed the Agency's confidentiality pledge, although he could not remember "with certainty" whether he had also done so himself.

The issue of the CIA's use of reporters was very much on Punch's mind at the time of the *Rolling Stone* piece. More than a year and a half earlier, *The New York Times* had published a story revealing that in the 1950s the Agency had tried unsuccessfully to recruit one of the paper's reporters. The *Times* had filed a Freedom of Information request with the CIA to obtain the names of American and foreign news organizations that had supposedly provided cover for intelligence-gathering activities since 1948, a request that the CIA had rejected. Then, in May 1976 a Soviet weekly had suggested that the *Times'* Moscow bureau chief and two other American reporters had links to the CIA. The *Times* had categorically denied the charge, citing past assurances from CIA director George Bush that the Agency had not used any *Times* staffers or employees in its operations.

Before the *Rolling Stone* allegations hit the newsstands, the *Times* preemptively published a story summarizing them, citing as a source the issue of the magazine "now going to press" and noting that Cy was "vacationing in Europe and could not be reached for comment." The section concerning Arthur prompted Iphigene to phone executive editor Abe Rosenthal and give him a statement that Rosenthal marked MUST USE, which appeared the next day in a follow-up article in the *Times*. "Mrs. Iphigene Sulzberger, widow of Arthur Hays Sulzberger, called *The New York Times* today to say that Mr. Sulzberger had told her that he had been approached by the CIA to use *The New York Times* as cover. Mrs. Sulzberger said that her husband had told her that he had refused on the grounds that it would be journalistically unethical and endanger the safety of foreign correspondents." The piece also quoted Cy, who denied he had ever worked for the CIA and characterized the suggestion that he had published an Agency report with his name on it as "a lot of baloney."

What the *Times* printed about its relations with the CIA was technically correct, but what the articles failed to spell out was that Bush's assurance that the Agency used no *Times* staffers was true only of full-time employees. At roughly the same time, *New York Times* reporter John Crewdson had received information from a source he considered reliable saying that the *Times'* stringer in Brussels had been involved with the CIA. Later Scotty Reston would say that he believed two of the

Times' Middle East correspondents had once worked for the Agency. "The CIA obviously had somebody on the paper, but we never could find out who it was," said Sydney Gruson. "George Bush said no, he wouldn't tell us who they were but he promised he would not try to enlist any other *Times* people or any new *Times* people. So they had somebody."

Though there was no hard evidence, rumors had persisted for years among the overseas press corps that Cy had Agency ties. The whispering campaign was probably attributable in part to jealousy and in part to his close relations with the CIA leadership. Cy had personally known every CIA director since 1953, when Allen Dulles took over the job, and he was unabashed about his willingness to help the Agency by providing his perspective on the countries in which he traveled. In turn, he often received information and news tips, not all of it disinterested. Cy was on friendly terms with many CIA station chiefs overseas. In cables between Chip Bohlen, U.S. ambassador to France, and Robert Amory, CIA deputy director for intelligence, Cy's codename was Fidelis ("faithful"). But it is unlikely that he ever accepted an assignment from the CIA; he was simply too cantankerous to take orders from anyone, and as he later wrote Harrison Salisbury, "It was one of the tenets of my journalistic career never to [work for the CIA] and never to hire anybody who was employed in such capacity."

It was also true that Cy's vanity, his confidence in the Agency, and his overweening desire to be on intimate terms with those in power made him an easy target to be "taken" by the CIA. In 1972, during a lunch with Richard Helms at the Hay-Adams Hotel in Washington, the then CIA director had praised Cy's ability to keep secrets. "I talk to you the way I talk to no other newspaperman," Helms had told him. "The others: well, sometimes they get so tempted by something they learn that I can't always trust their discretion. But with you, I know you've already kissed the girl before." According to Bernstein, it was Helms who in 1967 had given Cy the Agency briefing paper he had allegedly reproduced practically verbatim as a column published in *The New York Times*.

Like his uncle Arthur, Cy was a product of World War II, a time when journalists generally considered it patriotic to help the American intelligence community. Although Vietnam forever altered that relationship, the question of how a newspaper should balance national-security concerns with its responsibility to inform the public had remained a conundrum. In 1966 the *Times* had submitted a five-part series on the Agency in advance of publication to John A. McCone, the recently retired director of the CIA, who removed some elements that he regarded as sensitive. In the early 1970s, at the request of CIA director William Colby, who personally called Punch, the *Times* had held a story about the *Glomar Explorer,* a deep oceanic recovery vehicle built to harvest Soviet ICBMs from an eighteen-year-old Soviet submarine sunk in the Pacific Ocean. "In retrospect, it seems quite obvious that Colby manipulated the press," executive editor Abe Rosenthal later concluded in a memo in which he analyzed his own actions and those of Punch and other top editors at the time.

The accusations against Cy were soon amplified by *MORE* magazine, an antiestablishment journalism review, which specifically named E. Howard Hunt, a former CIA officer and paroled Watergate conspirator, as the author of the column Cy purportedly cribbed from the Agency. Cy repeated his previous denials of CIA involvement, and while he did not challenge the assertion that he had obtained information for the column from Helms, he maintained that the writing was his, as were the conclusions. In vain, he tried to persuade the *Times'* lawyers to sue on behalf of himself and the paper, and it stung all the more that no one at the *Times* rushed to his defense. "Cy felt that he was sort of left out there hanging," said Flora Lewis. "Of course, his chickens were coming home to roost."

In December 1977 Cy published his retirement column under the headline MEMORIES AND FADED DREAMS. Reflecting on his forty-four years as a journalist, he made a point of saying *not* that he was about to retire but that "I am *being* retired" — a distinction that was not lost on sympathizers within the Sulzberger clan.

On January 1, 1978, Cy's official day of retirement, the *Times'* editorial page published a short tribute titled "Reporter Extraordinaire." It noted that Cy had personally known and written about "almost every great figure in the world," and saluted his "intelligence and tenacity" but offered no words of warmth or affection. Thereafter, Cy continued to live in his Blvd. de Montparnasse apartment as what his son, David, called "a time-warp American." Cy had left the States in the 1930s and had lived virtually his entire adult life overseas. He had never voted; his image of what it meant to be an American was rooted in the past. His children, one born in Cairo, the other in Athens, both raised in Paris and British boarding schools, seemed slightly foreign to him. "He was the most baseball and baked-potato-minded American you could ever encounter," said David. "Consequently, I think he was ill at ease with these European children."

In retirement, Cy took long walks with Christopher Beagle, wrote occasional pieces as a special correspondent for *The New York Times* syndicate, and authored several books, including a biography-cum-memoir of Marina based on her letters. But his melancholy never left him. In *How I Committed Suicide: A Reverie,* he wrote of his inconsolable grief following his wife's death. In the fictional final scene, Cy shoots Christopher Beagle, then himself. "I know that he loves me," he wrote of the dog. "He is my protector and we desperately need each other." The cloying self-pity so annoyed David that one night shortly after the book's publication, he blurted out to his father, "Why don't you just do it, then, instead of writing about it?"

Iphigene, as usual, tried to make things right. She sent Cy plane fare for a visit to the United States when he became burdened with medical bills and encouraged him to accept a fellowship at Harvard, a post he turned down because he feared Christopher Beagle would be barred from his classroom and the library. As for Punch, Cy refused to have any commerce with him. Three years after his retirement, Jean Sulzberger, a cousin, organized a party for Cy during one of his periodic visits to the States. As a matter of courtesy, she invited Punch, who declined. "Don't put me on the guest list," Punch wrote Jean. "Ever since I got him to retire, he thinks I'm a villain and will not eat with me."

36

A President and a Family Counselor

I N THE SUMMER OF 1978, THE INVESTMENT FIRM
of Furman Selz Mager Dietz & Birney issued a bullish analysis of
The New York Times Company that would have been inconceivable just a few years earlier. Although the paper's 5.4 percent profit margin continued to trail that of *The Washington Post* and Times Mirror's
publishing division, it had more than doubled since 1975, the nadir of
New York City's economic decline and the year the *Times* suffered a
sharp drop in national advertising. *Times* stock was now on Wall Street's
buy lists, thanks in large part to Punch's strategy of diversification. In
1978 The New York Times Company's thirty-seven subsidiaries produced $224 million in revenue and $29 million in operating profits,
almost the same revenue and net income the company as a whole had
produced a decade before. Furman Selz attributed the dramatic
upswing to Punch and his "hand-picked team of young business- as
opposed to newspaper-oriented executives" who had developed a "radical (for the *Times*) and far-reaching program that had revamped the
paper and brought labor costs under control.

The *Times'* turnaround was certainly a welcome development, but the
good news was undermined by an enervating struggle for power going
on at the very pinnacle of the company. The conflict had begun in 1973,
when Punch had added chairman to his titles of president and publisher
and, at the same time, created three executive vice presidents: Walter
Mattson, who was the general manager of the newspaper; Sydney
Gruson, whose brief was acquisitions; and James Goodale, who oversaw
corporate headquarters operations, including legal and financial functions. Punch's intention was to observe each man closely and eventually
tap one to be the first nonfamily president of the company. For several
years this troika, collectively known as the executive committee, worked
together successfully. But by 1978 the tension of competing behind the

scenes for the presidency began to show. The men bickered openly in meetings, and gridlock set in. "They were at such loggerheads," said Mike Ryan, the company's secretary and corporate counsel. "It began to be difficult to get decisions because the struggle for power was so intense."

Sydney Gruson, the oldest of the three, was the least likely to win the contest, and he knew it. Though he was witty and well connected, Gruson's strength was his close relationship with Punch, not his business acumen. "I was a very good sounding board for him and a good companion," he said, "but I didn't have the experience to run a newspaper of that size." Although Gruson's worldly manner and savoir faire suggested a silver-spoon heritage, he was a self-invented aristocrat who had been born both poor and Jewish in Dublin. The family had later emigrated to Toronto, where in his youth Gruson earned money by setting pins in bowling alleys and working as a bellboy; after twelve years with the Canadian news agency, he joined the London bureau of the *Times* in 1944. Following a series of overseas postings, including remarkable dispatches from Poland chronicling the anti-Stalinist uprising of 1956, he had come to New York as the paper's foreign editor. Punch appreciated Gruson's bantering humor and epicurean tastes, but Turner Catledge had found his high living inappropriate for a reporter. While Gruson was serving in the Mexico City bureau, he had entertained the managing editor with several rounds of golf, afternoons at the bullfights, and long sessions at the local racetrack, where Gruson owned five horses. Turner enjoyed himself thoroughly, but as soon as he returned to New York, he recalled Gruson from the field. "It never occurred to me that Turner would think ill of me because I lived the kind of life I did," Gruson said later. "I had never missed a story."

In 1967 Gruson had skillfully negotiated the merger of the international edition of the *Times* with the *Herald Tribune*, which resulted in the creation of the *International Herald Tribune*. As a reward, Punch had promised to name him publisher of the new paper. When he failed to make good on the pledge, Gruson left the *Times* in a huff to work as associate publisher of *Newsday*, only to return at Punch's pleading eight months later as assistant to the publisher.

It was during this period that Gruson had become the man on whom Punch depended to be his facilitator, confidant, and guide to the New York social scene. His memos were voluptuously droll, full of gossip and mouth-watering details about the wine and food he had sampled while dining with business contacts ("excellent grilled Dover sole," "a 1978 Pontet-Canet, a Bordeaux of no pretensions whatsoever," "an indecent soufflé of praline of hazelnuts"). Gruson and his Swedish-born second wife, Marit, soon became two of Punch and Carol's favored traveling companions, jetting off to Israel, Europe, and Florida, where the men toured the several *Times*-owned newspapers in the area while the women took Cynthia to Disney World. For Punch, who had longed for a companion and counselor, Gruson was ideal, combining, as he did, the charm of a Noël Coward and the grit of a veteran newspaperman. "He was a good foil for Punch," said Carol. "A lot of people sell Sydney short because he makes jokes and likes to tell you something outrageous just for the sheer pleasure of watching you blow up. But underneath all that, there is a very smart, shrewd, savvy, thoughtful human being."

Punch had rapidly promoted Gruson to vice president, then senior vice president, with responsibility for the *Times'* subsidiaries and new acquisitions. It was a job for which he was ill-suited in many ways. The money-draining, journalistically déclassé *US* magazine was partly Gruson's brainchild, as was the start-up of The New York Times Music Company, which did poorly and ended up being sold. But Punch continued to value Gruson's abilities as a diplomat, sounding board, and all-round fixer. When the *Times* set its sights on acquiring *The Press Democrat* in Santa Rosa, California, Gruson did his homework and discovered that the publisher was an opera buff. When it came time to talk financials, he gave the man a rare recording of Wagner's *Ring* cycle and invited him to share box seats at the Metropolitan Opera. "Well, I thought this guy was going to burst into tears," said Mike Ryan, who witnessed the encounter. "It was the key to the deal." Successes such as that so impressed Punch that in 1975 he had informed the paper's top news and business executives that in the event of his absence or incapacitation, Gruson was to assume the responsibilities of publisher.

Despite having Punch's favor, it was apparent that Gruson was not a serious contender for the presidency, and Mattson and Goodale campaigned ever more fiercely for the spot by exploiting every possible opportunity for power. Their styles were completely different: one subtle, the other obvious. "Mattson didn't seem to be doing it, but he was trying to," said Gruson. "Jimmy was doing it in his natural ebullient, unhidden self sort of way." The atmosphere was so tense that Goodale issued an edict forbidding anyone in the *Times'* legal department to speak to

Mattson without discussing it with him first. And if they did talk to Mattson, they were to report back to him what was said.

In fact, Punch had long since decided whom he wanted to name as president: Walter Mattson. He liked Mattson's straightforward approach to problems, his encyclopedic grasp of business and production details, his stability and dedication, and his firm, decisive manner. He also knew that Mattson had the hands-on operational experience he considered essential to lead a company of growing complexity; Goodale, a Yale and University of Chicago–educated lawyer, was an excellent corporate strategist but knew little about actually putting out a newspaper.

Moreover, Goodale, while possessing a lightning-fast mind and courageous legal instincts, had a reputation for being overbearing, arrogant, and occasionally abusive. One of his own staffers — an admirer — considered him "the most uncivilized person I have ever met." He shouted during meetings, told sexist jokes in front of women, and seemed to delight in humiliating people. Goodale had once even dressed down Punch on the phone. "I don't care what fishing trip you want to go on!" he had screamed into the receiver. "You're the president and chairman of this company and you have got to attend the board meeting!"

Punch knew his own mind and could have anointed Mattson unilaterally. But he liked consensus, and given that he would be naming the first nonfamily corporate president, he also wanted outside validation, which he knew would help him sell the idea to his board of directors. He therefore hired the consulting firm McKinsey & Company in February 1978 and charged it to come up with suggestions for the future structure of The New York Times Company. The assignment sounded vague, but as far as Punch was concerned, "I knew what I wanted to do, I just wasn't sure how or the best way to do it."

Carter Bales, the McKinsey partner who took the lead on the *Times* study, originally tried to persuade Punch to look outside the paper for a president. But Punch was determined to promote from within, and as soon as Bales and Bill Kerr, a senior associate at McKinsey, began to examine the *Times*' trio of executive vice presidents, the choice became clear. Goodale, in his initial interview with the McKinsey people, came across as hubristic and patronizing. "Obviously, you guys are here to find somebody to be president of this company," he told them. "There's only one person qualified for that job, and that's me. It's not someone with a peasant background like Mattson."

Bales worried that Mattson, with his training as an engineer and his experience limited to newspapers, did not have the breadth of vision to lead the *Times*. But he readily admitted that of the three, Mattson had the best business background. Apart from one of Punch's sisters, who considered Mattson too unpolished to be president, the feeling among virtually everyone else with whom McKinsey spoke was that the "talented, tough, square-headed, stubborn, block-headed Swede," as Gruson once described his rival, was the right man, indeed the *only* man, for the job. Most important, Punch thought so, too.

McKinsey submitted its report endorsing Mattson, but Punch, reluctant to tackle Goodale, still didn't act. Then one day during a meeting of the executive committee, it became painfully apparent that it was past time to put his decision into action. The matter under discussion was an upcoming gathering of the company's top executives in the Bahamas. As Punch sat at the head of the long conference table in the *Times* boardroom, Goodale took command of the conversation and aggressively laid out exactly what had to be accomplished at the retreat, point by point.

Punch abruptly adjourned the meeting, and as the men filed out, he motioned Gruson to join him in the back sitting room that was part of his office suite. "Oh, Jesus!" he said, sinking into a chair. "Jimmy is running away with things! It just can't go on this way. We're back to square one." Although Punch had never told him so explicitly, Gruson was well aware that he wanted to name Mattson, and that it was only his distaste for confrontation that was preventing him from doing so. Punch was perfectly capable of disappointing people in the interest of *The New York Times*, even of being ruthless, but that did not mean he enjoyed it.

Gruson correctly sensed that his role was to help stiffen Punch's spine. "We're not back to square one," he said. "You want to name Mattson president of the company? Phone your sisters and tell them that's what you're going to do. Then go down and tell Mattson. Come back and tell Jimmy." Punch did exactly that, as if he were checking items off a "to do" list. One factor he had not anticipated, however, was Mattson's reluctance to take the position. Mattson's subtle campaigning for the job, as it became clear, had been mostly defensive, motivated by a desire to keep Goodale from getting it. If he had had his way, he would have kept the structure of The New York Times Company as it was. He loved being general manager and running the newspaper, for it was work he knew and was good at. Were he to become president of the entire company, *The New York Times* would necessarily be just one of a myriad of concerns. He was not certain he wanted to spend his time worrying about television, magazines, and new ventures.

To help persuade him, Punch paid a visit to Mattson's home over the Fourth of July weekend. Mattson's wife, Gerri, prepared a plate of sandwiches and then left for an appointment. Punch stayed the entire afternoon, and when Gerri returned that evening, she and Mattson discussed whether he should accept Punch's offer. "You're forty-seven," Gerri reminded him. "Maybe you should try something different before you get any older. Maybe now is the time to do it." Mattson finally agreed to take the job, but only, he added quickly, "because Punch wanted me to."

On July 23, 1979, the *Times* announced that Punch had relinquished the corporate presidency to Mattson, who had also been given the title of chief operating officer. Gruson and Goodale were both named vice chairmen, in part to avoid making them report to Mattson and in part because Mattson wanted to control the areas of the company that had previously been theirs. Stripped of his responsibility for acquisitions and subsidiaries, Gruson, ever the pragmatist, took comfort in his position-without-portfolio as Punch's alter ego. But for Goodale, who had expected to become president despite clear indications to the contrary, losing to Mattson was a devastating blow. "He collapsed psychologically for a while," said Katharine Darrow, then the assistant corporate counsel. "It was like a nervous breakdown." Within months he left the company to become a partner in the law firm of Debevoise, Plimpton, Lyons & Gates, taking a share of the newspaper's First Amendment business with him.*

As Punch had hoped, Mattson soon brought order to the corporate side of the company in much the same way that Abe Rosenthal had organized the newsroom. "The razzle-dazzle stopped, everything calmed down," said John Mortimer, who managed industrial relations and personnel. "We got into a deliberate way of thinking about things, very commonsense and one step at a time." In his first eighteen months on the job, Mattson focused on establishing control over internal operations, particularly those areas with which he was unfamiliar. He retained McKinsey & Company to study the market position of each of the *Times'* subsidiaries and went to visit the properties personally for the first time.

---

*Goodale later distinguished himself as chairman of the Committee to Protect Journalists.

Until he assumed the presidency, Mattson had never set foot in the New York offices of *Family Circle*, let alone the Microfilming Corporation of America, which was in North Carolina. Using the McKinsey study as a guide, he divested the company of twenty of its auxiliary businesses, convinced that the *Times* should shed these "never-no-mind" firms — his term for Arno Press, Teaching Resources, and other small subsidiaries — and concentrate on larger lines of business. He also sold off money-losers like *US* magazine, as well as inconsequential regional properties such as the *Zephyrhills News* in Pasco County, Florida.

Mattson was determined to learn about The New York Times Company with the same obsessive attention to detail that had characterized his knowledge of printing presses and labor contracts. With the new president's hand firmly on the corporate tiller, Punch was free to play the role he preferred: the court of last resort on strategy, the ultimate decision maker on important questions. After years of trying to encourage teamwork, he had finally given up and gratefully elevated two strongmen to run his empire on a day-to-day basis — Mattson in the corporate suite, Rosenthal in the newsroom.

Now he was able to devote himself to a new challenge, one to which he looked to Mattson for guidance: training the next generation of Sulzbergers to take over *The New York Times*. In the twelve years since Stuart Greenspon, Jackie Dryfoos's husband, had arrived as a young corporate executive, three other family members had joined the *Times,* including Punch's own son, Arthur Jr., and there were indications that others might soon follow. Adolph Ochs had had only two possible successors from within the family: his nephew and his son-in-law. Arthur Hays Sulzberger's choices were equally limited: his son-in-law Orvil and his son, Punch. Now there were thirteen great-grandchildren of Adolph Ochs; and while their interest in making a career with the company varied from nonexistent to intense, each of them felt a deep pride of stewardship in *The New York Times*. As members of the owning family, they definitely expected to be involved in the company one way or another, regardless of whether they held formal positions.

Punch knew that to maintain harmony, it would be important to treat everyone equitably, or at least to create the perception of fairness, all the more so because his own son was in the mix. Mattson soon found himself in the delicate position of career counselor for the Sulzberger cousins, an assignment to which he brought the toughness of a drill sergeant and the ambivalence and resentment of the working-class man he still considered himself to be. "Walter has a keen appreciation for the strength and stability that family ownership brings to the company," said one cousin who joined the *Times* years later. "But the notion that one of us gets promoted and moved ahead because we're a family member drives him crazy."

§

The ground rules under which the Sulzberger cousins worked at *The New York Times* in the 1970s and 1980s amounted to what one company executive called being "half pregnant." Punch decreed that being a family member entitled those who were interested only to "a leg up in getting the job." Except for that initial advantage, Sulzbergers should expect to be treated like any other employee and advance only if they merited it. The result was a kind of double-think that helped neither the company nor the family member. Because of the policy, the cousins could not be trained with the straightforward understanding that they were being groomed for big jobs. But because their colleagues assumed that the family members were headed for the top, they handled the cousins gingerly, even fearfully, but rarely with frankness. Punch was oblivious to this problem, or at least avoided it, and would say, with sincerity, that family members "have to work their butts off harder than most people if they want to go up the ladder." He felt he was freeing the *Times* from the forgiving nepotism that turned so many family-owned newspapers into employment agencies for ill-equipped children, cousins, and in-laws. Indeed, it was just such nepotism that had gotten him *his* job. Everyone knew the truth — that, barring some catastrophe, a member of the family was going to run *The New York Times* — yet not even Punch was supposed to say so out loud.

Punch's philosophy was still in the formative stage in 1967, when he had invited Stuart Greenspon to join *The New York Times*, luring him with the seductive prospect of being the "leader of the next generation." By the time Walter Mattson became president of the company in 1979, it was common knowledge that Stuart's chances of succeeding Punch were practically nil. He and Jackie had recently divorced, and despite having held various jobs in production, acquisitions, and circulation at the *Times*, Stuart had yet to be given executive responsibility for any of the company's operations. Punch, ever eager to avoid conflict, especially in the case of a family member, assured Stuart that the divorce would have no effect on his career and that he was still considered the successor. "I wanted to hear that at that time, so I believed him," Stuart recalled.

Even before the breakup with Jackie, however, Stuart's star had begun to dim. In 1972 a *New York* magazine story had appeared suggesting that Punch was not equipped to be publisher and naming Stuart as a possible replacement. The piece had come out shortly after Punch had let Andy Fisher go, and Stuart suspected that his former colleague had been the source for the speculation. Stuart had immediately gone to Punch and told him that he had nothing to do with the article and that he fully supported him as publisher. Punch had listened patiently and told Stuart not to worry about it.

But clearly Punch had been very upset by the story, which he considered "a real hatchet job." Within days he had blacklisted its author, Chris Welles, telling the *Times'* Sunday editor that he was "no longer interested in seeing [Welles's] work." Given the vehemence of his response, it was only logical that no matter how understanding Punch might have appeared to Stuart, he could never treat him quite the same again. "What you get from Punch Sulzberger is a good hearing," said Sydney Gruson. "And you may even think he's being very sympathetic to you because he tends to sit there nodding his head and being very kind and Punch-like. But to be misled by that sort of thing is a terrible mistake." For his part, Stuart acknowledged, "[The Welles article] changed my relationship with him. It caused me to back off a little bit."

Stuart's stalled career had its repercussions on Jackie, who readily admitted that if her former husband had continued to be considered "publisher material," she might have stayed in the marriage. But even without that as a factor, the union had long since begun to falter. Having married largely to satisfy what she called the "family criteria," Jackie had gradually become bored with Stuart. The death of Stuart's father in 1969 had caused him to act older than his years and had distanced him emotionally from his wife.

Shortly before the divorce decree, Stuart told Punch he longed to run something of his own. Punch asked whether he would be interested in becoming publisher of one of the *Times'* Florida newspapers. "From a professional point of view, I'd love to, but I can't at this stage of my life," Stuart replied. "I'm separated. I have two kids. I can't leave New York right now." Once again Punch assured him that he understood, but to

Stuart, the message was clear: by offering a job he knew Stuart could not accept, Punch in his own indirect, enigmatic way had signaled his soon-to-be-former in-law that he had no future at *The New York Times*. After the divorce Stuart remained at the company, uncertain whether to stay or go, but in 1981, having faced the fact that he was never going to be publisher, he decided to leave. In a letter to his sister Marian explaining Stuart's decision to leave, Punch maintained that the divorce from Jackie was only one reason: "The fact of the matter is that, while he has been doing some very competent work, he has not been doing anything very exciting."

Stuart went on to start Print Technologies Company, a firm that ran in-house copying operations for law firms, investment banks, and other businesses, and when it was eventually sold to Pitney Bowes, he became a wealthy man. But the way Punch had handled his departure from the *Times* continued to baffle Stuart, and the two men never had a candid discussion about his parting company. Punch simply felt a discomfort about Stuart that he could not express. "He didn't want to hurt me or force me out," Stuart said. "But he was happy that I left. I think he was relieved."

§

By the time Stuart had moved on, his former Sulzberger brother-in-law, Bobby Dryfoos, had been at The New York Times Company for two years. As Orvil Dryfoos's only son, Bobby had found it difficult to watch Punch's early cultivation of Stuart, but his troubled academic and personal history hardly put him in a competitive position. After dropping out of Dartmouth, Bobby had worked for several years at IBM in White Plains, New York. In 1968, at Iphigene's urging, he had gone back and earned his degree and afterward had returned to IBM and established a comfortable suburban life with his wife, Katie, and their two children. By the mid-1970s the marriage had begun to totter: Bobby, the family loner, seemed determined to remain a mystery, even to his spouse.

Bobby didn't have a conversation with Katie the first time their marriage broke up; he simply announced that he was leaving. For two and a half years, the Dryfoos children were not even aware that their father had gone. Katie told them the reason Bobby came home so infrequently was that he had a job in another town. "He was dating, and he didn't want to spend his weekends coming up to see us, so he didn't," she said.

When IBM transferred Bobby to Florida, Katie moved the family to Wellesley, Massachusetts, in order to be closer to her parents, who lived on Martha's Vineyard.

That Christmas, with a divorce pending, Bobby asked Katie if he could visit her and the children. The reunion went unusually well, and with virtually no discussion they resumed their old relationship. For six months Bobby and Katie commuted between Massachusetts and Florida. When he relocated back north, they moved into a house near White Plains. For the next year they struggled on, neither of them suggesting they seek marriage counseling. One night Bobby took Katie to a local cocktail lounge to listen to the bands. After ordering her a whiskey sour, he abruptly announced he was leaving. Katie thought he was telling her that he was going to the men's room, but he quickly explained, "I'm not happy, and I'm *leaving*." There was another woman in his life, he said, and he wanted out.

Two weeks after their divorce in 1975, Bobby remarried. The union lasted about a year — a "rebound situation," he admitted. By 1977 Bobby was living with Mary Racine, an IBM secretary. Meanwhile, Katie struggled to make ends meet; to help out, Iphigene paid for cleaning ladies and made a point of including Katie and the children in the Christmas festivities at Hillandale.

In 1979 Bobby contacted Punch about working at *The New York Times*. After years of avoiding the powerful pull of his birthright, he finally felt a desire to find out whether he had any place in the family business. Punch handed Bobby over to Mattson, who advised him to stick with his strength: computers. For about a year Bobby flew up and down the East Coast, inspecting the computer operations of *The New York Times*' subsidiaries and making recommendations for improvement. When an opportunity arose to build a computer system from scratch at the *Times*-owned *Wilmington Morning Star* in North Carolina, Bobby jumped at it.

The move led to his third marriage. Mary had turned down Bobby's earlier proposal, but practicality won out: Wilmington was deemed too conservative to tolerate a cohabiting couple. After he organized the computer system, Bobby stayed two additional years at the *Morning Star*, rotating through the major departments at the paper in what amounted to a management-training program. "I loved it down there," he admitted.

By 1983, when he agitated to come to New York after what he considered a stellar stint in Wilmington, it had become apparent that Bobby was not cut out temperamentally for the *Times*. Word had filtered back to Punch that Bobby had bragged about his connection to the owning family, implying that he was destined for great things. "That was a big failure," Judy said of Bobby's brief tenure at the company. "It didn't work because he expected he was going to shoot straight up like an arrow, and he got very arrogant about it, apparently. He thought he was going to be [a big shot], being Orv's son."

Punch informed Marian ahead of time that he was going to ask Bobby to leave. "I can't say she liked it, but she backed me up and supported it," he said. Later Bobby claimed to be happy to rejoin IBM rather than "trudging forward" at the *Times*. But at the time, he complained to his mother that he didn't feel he had been given a fair shake. Still, the experience did nothing to diminish the reverence with which Bobby, like all the Ochses and Sulzbergers, viewed the institution they had been born to own. "It's awfully easy to have pride associated with something that is perceived to be the best there is," he said.

§

In the fall of 1973, after his job at the Film Society of Lincoln Center had ended, Stephen Golden told Punch that he wanted to come back to the paper, where he had worked briefly in the mid-1960s. Punch sent him to Mattson, who, after several discussions with Stephen, came in with an unvarnished verdict. "He's not qualified to work at *The New York Times*," he told Punch. "Send him off to the bush leagues and let him get the edges rubbed off and learn more about the business, then bring him back." Stephen had had his heart set on rejoining the newsroom, but Punch took Mattson's advice and convinced his nephew that working on the business side of the company's regional newspapers was a better idea.

In February 1974 Stephen moved to Florida, where the *Times* owned *The Gainesville Sun*, and spent a year shifting from department to department. "I fell in love with the business of newspapering," he said. At the end of his training period, the *Sun* offered him the position of assistant publisher, and he decided to stay. June had remained in New York during her husband's one-year rotation, commuting back and forth on weekends. When it was clear that his job in Gainesville was permanent, she moved to Florida and set up housekeeping in a four-bedroom bungalow with a fenced backyard and a swimming pool.

After two years as assistant publisher at *The Gainesville Sun,* a publisher's position opened up at another of the *Times'* properties, and Stephen naively believed he had a chance to get it. He soon realized that Jack Harrison, head of the regional newspapers for the *Times,* had no desire to be responsible for the career of a Sulzberger family member.

In the summer of 1976 Stephen made an appointment with Punch. "I suppose he is interested in moving out of Florida and back to Fun City," Punch wrote Iphigene. During his visit Mattson invited Stephen to lunch to talk about his prospects. After they had ordered their drinks, Mattson locked his blue eyes onto Stephen's face and said slowly but deliberately, emphasizing each word for effect, "I don't like nepotism." "Me, neither," Stephen replied, "and your son better not ever ask me for a job here." They both laughed, but Mattson's meaning was clear.

Mattson started Stephen in the area closest to his heart, production. Because he worked there during the last days of hot metal type, Stephen soon found himself setting up a counseling program for printers taking company buyouts. At first he wore his family heritage with un-Sulzbergerian ostentation, grandly signing memos "Stephen A. O. Golden," to draw attention to the Ochs in his name. "Even though he had a boss to report to, he saw himself as above that," said John O'Brien, an executive with whom Stephen worked. "He knew who he was, and he let you know."

Stephen and June moved into an apartment in the East Seventies, and soon June was pregnant. David Adam Ochs Golden was born on December 12, 1978. To honor June's late father, who had awakened a desire for Jewish identity in Stephen, the Goldens decided to hold a *bris,* or ritual circumcision, in their home. Several members of the Sulzberger family refused to attend on the grounds that the ceremony was "barbaric," but Punch felt obliged to appear. He was the baby's godfather and had no excuse, since Stephen and June were observing the custom of holding the *bris* in the morning, before work. When the procedure was unexpectedly delayed for fifteen minutes, Punch had time to contemplate what it was actually all about and hastily fled, claiming that he couldn't be late for a meeting.

Once under way, the service took an unanticipated turn. *Ben* in Hebrew means "son of." Therefore, each time the *mohel* said, "David, son of Golden," the words came out, "David Ben Golden." Stephen's father's distaste for Judaism had been a continuing flashpoint between them. "We looked at each other and pictured Ben Golden spinning in the nether regions to hear his name associated with this," said June.

Within two years Stephen was working in *The New York Times'* purchasing department, buying pens and paper clips, press plates, and other supplies for the company, and his marriage had come to an end. The news was no surprise to close friends, who had long been aware of Stephen's volcanic temper — he once put his fist through a door — and of June's chronic lateness, which greatly irked her punctual husband. Years later Stephen would diplomatically assert that no one was to blame for the breakup, merely that sometimes "things just don't work out between well-meaning people." At the time, however, the divorce was painful and protracted, mainly because of June's demands for money. Negotiations ground to a halt until June's attorney decided to serve papers on Punch in the lobby of the New York Times Building demanding that, as a trustee of the Ochs Trust, Punch reveal what Stephen stood to inherit. The ploy worked. Punch was annoyed at having been dragged publicly into such an unpleasant situation and ordered Stephen to do whatever it took to bring the matter to a close. Later June phoned Punch to apologize, claiming that she had no knowledge of her lawyer's actions until it was too late. By then he had calmed down. "Okay, apology accepted," he told her. "But if it ever happens again, I want you to serve me the papers personally . . . in the nude!"

By 1981 Stephen had started dating Brenda Sanchez, the *Times'* director of personnel. It would be five years before they would marry, in part because doing so would force Brenda to resign from the *Times*. Punch felt strongly that "the personnel position (much like the company doctor) must be an independent one and cannot have a tie to the Ochs-Sulzberger family."

As for June, she, like so many of the other divorced Sulzberger in-laws, continued to enjoy Christmas with the family and occasional weekends in the country with Iphigene. "It sounds self-serving to say that Granny loved me," said June, "but I believe that. And I loved her." She never remarried, and in many respects, her life continued to revolve around the warm, nourishing sun of the Sulzbergers. "I thought she'd probably own the world by now because she has every talent going for her," said Sheila Weidenfeld, a family friend. "Life moves on. But she hasn't."

37

A *Coup de Foudre* and a Career

I N LATE NOVEMBER 1973 ARTHUR JR., A SENIOR AT
Tufts, climbed into his white Dodge maxivan and set out for
Topeka, Kansas, to spend Thanksgiving with his mother and her
third husband, Jerry Johnson. A day or so later he found himself playing
touch football in the yard of his mother's across-the-street neighbors,
the Greggs. He recognized one of the family's daughters from earlier
trips home; they hadn't liked each other much. Gail Gregg was slim,
dark-haired, and doe-eyed, with a huge, arresting smile, but what struck
Arthur Jr. this time was her manner. She was forceful and self-
assured — the very strengths he had tried to cultivate in himself, though
his way of expressing them tended to be cocky and confrontational.

Gail was the same age as Arthur Jr., but because he had repeated a
grade, she was ahead of him in school. Since graduating from Kansas
State University the previous year, she had lived in Germany, France,
and Italy, alternately working and traveling. Like Arthur Jr., Gail wanted
a career in journalism; she had worked on student newspapers since
junior high school and majored in the subject in college. The meeting
was a classic *coup de foudre* — instantaneous love. As soon as he got
back to Tufts, Arthur Jr. sent Gail an airplane ticket to come visit him,
and he stopped seeing two women with whom he had been conducting
casual relationships. She landed in Boston on January 3, 1974, moved in
with him, and never used the return portion of her ticket.

As their rapid courtship progressed, it became apparent that where
Arthur Jr. was unformed, Gail was solid and stable. She had firm beliefs
and, like Carol, was not shy about articulating them. She swore like a
stevedore and felt comfortable challenging Arthur Jr. on everything
from his political views to his wise-guy behavior. He respected her astute
intelligence and her self-confidence. Most important, he felt certain that
she loved him. "He was kind of a pain in the ass in college, thinking he

549

knew everything about everything, and we all said, 'Oh, Arthur, shut up!' " recalled Cathy. "Then Gail came along and thought he was wonderful. And she was right."

As native New Yorkers, Arthur Jr. and his cousin Dan, also a senior at Tufts, were inclined to believe that, being from Kansas, Gail was a hick, and on her first weekend in Boston, Dan planned a prank calculated to get a rise out of her. He invited Arthur Jr. and Gail to a party at his apartment. At the appointed hour, they showed up and knocked on the door, to be greeted by a crowd of male guests garishly dressed in drag. Gail barely raised an eyebrow. The next day Dan apologized. "Gail never let the laugh be at her expense," said a friend. "She always laughed with them or at them."

In Boston Gail set out to find a job while Arthur Jr. completed his studies. She so impressed the job-placement firm where she first interviewed that it hired her on the spot. Shortly after she began working, she looked up her personnel file and read that the placement counselor who had interviewed her described her as "the all-American girl." The label reflected a superficial appreciation of who Gail was, for while she may have been the head of her high school pep club, she was hardly the smiling, apple-cheeked, uncomplicated stereotype such a phrase implied.

The oldest of five children of an insurance executive, Gail was raised in a home with basic, rock-ribbed Midwestern values. When she was in high school, her brother, Tyler, who was asthmatic, had several heart attacks and became a quadriplegic. Many families would have reacted to such a tragedy with anger, self-pity, or depression. The Greggs were determined to be upbeat. "In my family, you were never allowed to say anything was wrong," Gail later told a Sulzberger cousin. She rejected her family's stiff-upper-lip attitude and resolved to be the opposite; as a result, she often came across as tough and negative.

In fact, Gail was as harsh in judging herself as she was with others. At an early age, she had decided to escape the bland complacency of her hometown and make something of her life. "Topeka is a place where getting along is more important than being good," said Arthur Jr. "You're not going to be pushed to excellence there. Gail would never have survived Topeka." Gail and Arthur shared a determination to get what they wanted: she, to leave the dullness of Kansas and enter the wider world; he, to demonstrate that he was worthy of leading the greatest newspaper in the nation. Of the two, Arthur Jr. was the more insecure in his quest, if only because, like many sons in family businesses, he had to wrestle with the self-doubt that often accompanies inherited wealth and power. "Arthur is going to go through his whole life with something to prove," said Anna Quindlen, a former *Times* columnist and close friend. "Every day he wakes up and thinks, *How can I show them today that I am the man that I want to be?*"

After Arthur Jr.'s graduation from Tufts in the summer of 1974, he and Gail headed south to Raleigh, North Carolina, where Arthur Jr. had taken a job as a general assignment reporter on *The Raleigh Times* and Gail enrolled in the graduate school of journalism at the University of North Carolina at Chapel Hill. "I suggested . . . that he do what I did, and get away from the family and go out where somebody didn't care whether he was Arthur Sulzberger [or not]," said Punch. North Carolina made sense: the state was considered a breeding ground for good journalists, and Punch knew the Daniels family, which owned the two newspapers in the capital.

The Raleigh Times, an afternoon paper with a circulation of forty thousand, was scrappier and more self-consciously local than its morning cousin, *The News & Observer.* The staff of twenty-odd reporters was young and predominantly single. Compared with his colleagues, Arthur Jr. was "absolutely, totally green," said Mike Yopp, the managing editor at the time. "We would not normally have hired someone like Arthur with zero experience. It was very much like dealing with a college intern."

If the paper's reporters and editors were apprehensive about whether Arthur Jr. would conduct himself as a person apart, they needn't have worried. "He was just like the rest of us — young, wet behind the ears, an inexperienced person who wanted to be a reporter," said Jan Johnson Elliott, a colleague. "He hung out with us. He was one of the gang." Indeed, Arthur Jr.'s two and a half years in North Carolina may have been the happiest in his life. The paper made him feel that he was a member of a team, that he belonged, that he could just be himself.

Because *The Raleigh Times* was an afternoon paper, his day started early. In order to make the first deadline of 9:00 A.M., Arthur Jr. had to arrive at the office at 7:00 A.M. By the time the final deadline rolled around at 1:00 P.M., he had conducted four or five interviews and produced forty-five or fifty inches of copy. Most days a crowd of *Times* staffers adjourned for lunch to the Mecca, an old downtown restaurant. In the afternoon there might be a meeting to cover or phone calls to make, but by 3:00 P.M. people began drifting over to the Players Retreat, a bar near North Carolina State University. On the weekends there were staff cookouts and parties with music, Southern Comfort, dope, and dancing. "It was a very social group on the paper at that time," said Yopp. "It was almost any excuse to get together."

Like every other cub reporter, Arthur Jr. made $150 a week. He rode to and from the office on a Kawasaki 900 motorcycle, and the apartment he and Gail shared in West Raleigh was decorated with hand-me-down furniture. Only his Porsche indicated that Arthur Jr. had access to a grander lifestyle than did his friends. His car notwithstanding, being perceived as wealthy was something Arthur Jr. took pains to avoid. His preference always was to portray himself as a man of the people, but his sense of what that meant reflected his privileged parentage. "It wasn't the fancy Porsche," he later said of the car he had driven in Raleigh. "It was the cheap Porsche, the one with the Volkswagen engine in the middle. It was the low end."

Arthur Jr. accompanied more experienced reporters on stories and wrote light features that, in their unedited form, were riddled with spelling mistakes. "Can you imagine anyone who can't spell *hate?*" Harold Muddiman, the city editor, laughed as he handed Yopp a page of Arthur Jr.'s copy in which *h-a-i-t* appeared several times. Still, Arthur Jr. got high marks for his perseverance and determination to learn. When he was assigned coverage of the Christmas parade — a standing joke among reporters because it always took place before Thanksgiving — he turned in an imaginative lead sentence: "It was cold enough to be December. . . . "

Shortly before Arthur Jr. had left for Raleigh, Seymour Topping, *The New York Times'* assistant managing editor, had volunteered to critique his clips. Throughout the fall of 1974, Arthur Jr. sent him stories bylined "A. O. Sulzberger, Jr.," which ran the gamut of small-town reporting: a piece about the championship horse show; an interview with The Amazing Kreskin, a magician; and a feature on a country store "where time just slides by." When, after several months, Arthur Jr. managed to produce two stories that appeared in the paper without heavy editing or overhaul, he mailed them to Topping with a note that betrayed pride in his progress. "Perhaps, if the desire ever hits you, you might throw them up to the fourteenth floor and let the old man see them," he wrote. "If not, burn them — or better yet, do you have a shredder?"

Topping especially liked one of the stories, about a new car show, and sent it on to Punch.

Like his father, who had written obituaries at *The Milwaukee Journal*, Arthur Jr. spent much of his time recording facts about the deceased. Although he was now twenty-three, his fresh-faced good looks gave him the appearance of an earnest and sympathetic teenager, and people who had lost loved ones to illness, automobile accidents, or crime found it easy to confide in him. He did so many stories of this nature that the city editor gave him a nickname that Gail used in a joking Christmas present: business cards embossed with his name and FRIEND OF THE DEAD printed underneath.

When she had gone to Boston, Gail told her parents that she was living with Arthur Jr.'s sister, Karen, also a student at Tufts. In North Carolina she came clean, prompting a puzzled letter from Gail's grandmother. "I don't know what's wrong," she wrote. "Every time I mention your name to your mother, she bursts into tears." Mrs. Gregg did not have long to weep, for Arthur Jr. proposed on October 2, 1974, Gail's twenty-third birthday and barely a month after they had arrived in Raleigh.

The wedding took place in late May 1975, in the garden of the Greggs' Victorian home in Topeka. Arthur Jr. and Gail renounced conventional gifts, and in lieu of the usual rehearsal dinner, they invited family and friends to gather on his mother's lawn the night before the wedding for an uproariously drunken game of volleyball. Arthur Jr. showed up in a long-sleeved T-shirt imprinted with a tuxedo design.

On their wedding day, it was the groom, not the bride, who wore white: white pants, white belt, and a white tuxedo shirt open at the neck — but no tie or jacket. Gail, outfitted in a simple jade green sleeveless dress that fell to mid-calf, carried no bouquet, but tucked a small bunch of flowers into her belt. The couple had wanted a judge to be their officiant (Gail was an avowed atheist) but at the last minute the judge pulled out, and a Presbyterian minister — a woman — was pressed into service.

Among the assembled guests were Arthur Jr.'s parents, stepparents, sister, and half siblings. The tangled relations made for some awkward moments, but "I didn't really give a shit," he said. "I wanted them all there, and that was the end of the story." He also didn't care that some family members disapproved of Gail keeping her name. Five months earlier Cathy had kept her name after marrying Joe Perpich, a Minnesota-born physician and lawyer — an affront to tradition that had greatly upset Carol until Joe, a psychiatrist, had persuaded her that it was important for a woman's sense of self. Gail, however, was a feminist who made no secret of her views. Because the Sulzbergers so valued patrilineal succession — and because she was marrying the publisher's only son — her decision was considered more revolutionary.

Arthur Jr. and Gail rejected the idea of a honeymoon, which they regarded as silly for two people who had been living together for a year and a half. "We fought the idea tooth and nail; we wanted to go back to Raleigh," Arthur Jr. explained. As a compromise, they took a brief trip to New Orleans, where Turner and Abby Catledge, who had retired there, hosted them for dinner. The rest of the time they lounged in their hotel room, which was "the size of a submarine cabin." After a few days Arthur Jr. and Gail picked up a Datsun Z-100 that a newspaper colleague had bought in New Orleans and, as a favor, drove it back to North Carolina. "That was the best part of the honeymoon," Arthur Jr. said. When they opened the door of their apartment, a bottle of champagne and a vase of flowers were waiting for Gail — a gift from Arthur Jr., who, before the wedding, had asked a friend to take care of the preparations as a surprise.

Gail had been awarded her master's degree in journalism shortly before the wedding and soon took a job as an intern at the Associated Press in Raleigh. That fall, she became editor of the *Western Wake Herald*, a weekly paper in nearby Apex, North Carolina, where, said Yopp, "she was forceful and scandalized the town."

Arthur Jr. spent his last six months on *The Raleigh Times* working in production and advertising. He lost his first account — an old, established men's clothing shop that "made Brooks Brothers look like cutting edge" — when he suggested that the proprietor try to "liven up the look" of his ads. In the spring of 1976, he paid a visit to his father to discuss the next step in his apprenticeship. Just as Arthur Hays Sulzberger had done twenty years earlier, Punch suggested an overseas assignment.

Gail spoke German and French, but since Arthur Jr. was abysmal at languages, Punch settled on Britain as a destination. He arranged a reporting slot for Arthur Jr. at the London bureau of the AP and a similar spot for Gail at United Press International. The first draft of his letter recommending Gail to the head of UPI betrayed doubts about his son's maturity and intelligence. "We think she is smarter than he is," Punch had dictated, but when his secretary, Nancy Finn, sat down to type the letter, she blanched. "You can't write that!" she told him. Chastened, Punch excised the offending sentence. To Finn, the incident was reminiscent of what Punch had suffered at the hands of his own father.

Arthur Jr. and Gail left for London in the fall of 1976 and moved into a flat on Lady Margaret Road in Kentish Town, two blocks from a tube stop on London's Northern Line. Like most British housing, the apartment was bone-chillingly cold. "We spent almost all our time wrapped in blankets," he recalled. Arthur Jr. soon discovered that, for all its prestige, the London bureau of the AP was a rather dull place to work. He rarely got a chance to leave the office to report a story; most of the material for his pieces came from phone interviews, British newspapers, and the internal British press wire. His colleagues were good, family-oriented people who did their work and escaped to their suburban homes. At UPI Gail enjoyed the company of a wacky Australian bureau chief named Mike Keats and reporters who bent elbows together almost every day after work at a bar on Bouverie Street. Often Arthur Jr. would join them.

In London Arthur Jr.'s eye-catching dress and deportment ripened in new directions. In lieu of an automobile, he bought a Triumph Tiger motorcycle with a covered sidecar. For Gail, who had once flown off Arthur Jr.'s bike and skinned her back, the sidecar was a decided step up, if not a paragon of comfort. Decked out in his motorcycle leathers and ubiquitous pipe during frequent visits to *The New York Times'* London bureau, Arthur Jr. came across as a hybrid of an Oxford don and James Dean. "No one viewed him as the heir," said Marion Underhill, the office manager, laughing. "He was quite confident, but he looked like such a kid." Bureau chief R. W. "Johnny" Apple Jr. appraised him more respectfully. One night he invited Arthur Jr. out to dinner. "I'm sorry, I've got night duty at the AP," Arthur Jr. explained. "Can't you trade?" Apple asked, suggesting a practice common at the wire services. "No, I'm not really in a position to do that," Arthur Jr. replied. As in Raleigh, Arthur Jr. did not want anyone to accuse him of receiving special treatment because he was a Sulzberger. "I thought that showed a lot of sensitivity," said Apple.

The highlight of Arthur Jr.'s experience abroad came in June 1977, when he traveled to Holland to cover an attack on South Moluccan gunmen who had hijacked a train and taken hostages. Having been assured by the authorities that the rescue would take place on one particular night, Arthur Jr. planted himself on a seat pulled from a Volkswagen about three-quarters of a mile from the train. Next to him was a telephone hooked up to a distant farmhouse so that he could call in his eyewitness account to the bureau chief back at the press center in Assen. All night Arthur Jr. sat there, the only reporter in the inner security perimeter, eating food given him by the Dutch army.

As dawn began to break, Arthur Jr. assumed that the attack had been called off or that the AP had been misinformed. He picked up the telephone receiver and told the bureau chief, "I guess our source was wrong." Just at that moment five Lockheed F-104 Starfighters with Dutch insignia screamed into view. The ground trembled as Dutch commandos stormed the train. "They're firing! A lot of firing! It's very concentrated," Arthur Jr. dictated excitedly into the phone. "Everybody, reporters, photographers, police, army men are ducking down behind armored personnel carriers."

The resulting story contained Arthur Jr.'s first-person account and quoted him by name. When it arrived in *The New York Times* newsroom in New York, executive editor Abe Rosenthal knew that he had to use it. A brief discussion ensued about whether Arthur Jr.'s name should be taken out of the AP story. "Look," argued Rosenthal, "if it was anybody else, we would keep the name there."

The next day the Dutch hostage story appeared on page one of *The New York Times,* quoting "Arthur O. Sulzberger, Jr." A day or two later Seymour Topping sent Arthur Jr. the clipping along with his congratulations, adding, "I am very proud to see you doing so well on the firing line." For Arthur Jr. it was a triumphal moment. He had been stationed, if only for a moment, in the equivalent of a war zone and had proved that he had the guts, reflexes, and instincts of a reporter.

In London Arthur Jr. continued to explore his Jewish identity, a quest that had started during a nine-day Outward Bound course he and Gail had taken together while in Raleigh. One day, while he and his group were out on an eight-mile run through the North Carolina hills, Arthur Jr. found himself neck and neck with a young, blond male instructor. As Arthur Jr. began to flag, he tried to come up with something that would push him on. To his astonishment, he found himself thinking, *I'm not going to let this Aryan bastard beat me.* It had been a visceral and unexpected claim to his Jewishness, and it had shocked him.

Relations were seldom comfortable between fathers and sons in the Sulzberger dynasty. Arthur had a distant relationship with Punch, who in turn found it difficult to be intimate with Arthur Jr., born in 1951. *(NYTCA)*

Punch and his second wife, Carol, aboard the *Queen Elizabeth*. Carol pushed her husband to assert himself, but her combative personality sparked conflict with his mother and sisters.

After Judy's divorce from Mattie, she married Dick Cohen, who adopted her two sons, Jace (left) and Dan, and gave them his name. The boys felt abandoned by their biological father and resented Dick.

Amory Bradford, Orvil's general manager and the *Times'* senior nonfamily executive, was proud of his arrogance and brinkmanship. When Punch succeeded Orvil in 1963, Bradford quit in a fury. *(NYTCA)*

When Punch (left) became publisher, he told one of his sisters that his first executive decision was "not to throw up." Soon, however, he was entertaining figures such as President Lyndon Johnson, who came to the paper for lunch. *(NYTCA)*

The New York Times

LATE CITY EDITION

VOL. CXX...No.41,431

NEW YORK, THURSDAY, JULY 1, 1971

15 CENTS

SUPREME COURT, 6-3, UPHOLDS NEWSPAPERS ON PUBLICATION OF THE PENTAGON REPORT; TIMES RESUMES ITS SERIES, HALTED 15 DAYS

Nixon Says Turks Agree To Ban the Opium Poppy

PRESIDENT CALLS STEEL AND LABOR TO WHITE HOUSE

He Asks Both Sides to Meet With Him Tuesday Before Contract Talks Start

Pentagon Papers: Study Reports Kennedy Made 'Gamble' Into a 'Broad Commitment'

BURGER DISSENTS

First Amendment Rule Held to Block Most Prior Restraints

Soviet Starts an Inquiry Into 3 Astronauts' Deaths

(NYTCA)

Champagne flowed when the U.S. Supreme Court ruled in favor of the *Times* in the Pentagon Papers case. At a press conference, a relieved Punch was flanked by managing editor Abe Rosenthal (left) and James Goodale, the paper's in-house counsel. (NYTCA)

Shy around strangers and afflicted with a fear of flying, Carol found the role of publisher's wife difficult at first and rarely accompanied Punch on trips. Gradually, she came to enjoy the prerogatives of his position.

Punch, shown here in the *Times*' boardroom, relied on Sydney Gruson (center) to be his sounding board and all-around fixer, and chose Walter Mattson (right), a "talented, tough, square-headed, stubborn, block-headed Swede," as the company's first nonfamily president. *(NYTCA)*

Following lunch at the White House with President Reagan, Secretary of State George Shultz (center, left), and Vice President George Bush, Punch phoned his mother to brag. Her response: "What did they want, son?" *(Official White House photograph)*

Punch thought the editorial page run by his cousin John Oakes, shown here with Hubert Humphrey, was too strident and antibusiness; in 1977 he forced Oakes to retire.

Cy Sulzberger, a crack foreign correspondent and columnist, cultivated famous personages such as Jacqueline Kennedy. Punch never forgave his cousin for snubbing him when he was a cub reporter in Paris, and forcibly retired him in 1978.
(*Courtesy of Gilbert Benno-Grazioni*)

Arthur Jr. was small and slight for his age, subdued and lacking in confidence. "I don't like to think of myself as [having been] a serious child," he said later. "I think of myself as [having been] fun-loving. But I confess [that] most of my childhood I was in a fog."

Arthur Jr. and Gail Gregg's romance was a classic *coup de foudre:* love at first sight. Their rehearsal dinner in 1975, shown here, consisted of an uproariously drunken game of volleyball on the lawn of the prospective bride's Topeka home.

After her husband's death, Iphigene surprised her family by becoming more outgoing and assertive. "She didn't have to be the wife, she could be the matriarch," explained a friend. *(NYTCA)*

The back terrace at the "new" Hillandale in Stamford, Connecticut. On summer Saturdays, Punch cooked hamburgers on a portable barbecue, a male servant standing at attention by his side holding a silver tray stacked with raw patties. *(NYTCA)*

For all the cousins, Hillandale was a touchstone and a refuge. But for the Goldens—the "long-distance cousins" from Chattanooga—it was a place of near mythical proportions. Gathered around the pool, from left: Stephen Golden, Arthur Golden, Arthur Jr., Dan Cohen, Lynn Golden, and Michael Golden.

Arthur Jr. (in headband); Stephen's wife, June; and Dan Cohen, at the wedding of Michael and Anne Golden. The newlyweds found the cousins' attire amusing, but Ruth "took ten years to recover," said Dan. Arthur Jr. and Dan "loved each other," sighed Judy, "but they made everybody else ready to kill them."

Carol considered Arthur Jr.'s mode of dress to be affected, and in the summer of 1971, as a joke she appeared for cocktails costumed just like him, with hat and cane.

After working as an assignment editor on the *Times'* metropolitan desk in New York, Arthur Jr. moved to advertising in 1982. He began with a cocky disdain for ad salesmen but soon discovered that they revered the newspaper's guiding principles no less than those in the newsroom. (New York Times *photo*)

Arthur Jr., with general manager Lance Primis at his side, speaks at a news conference during an acrimonious dispute with the drivers' and mailers' unions that cost the *Times* millions in lost sales. *(AP/Wide World/Marty Lederhandler)*

In production, Arthur Jr. worked nights for half the week and days the other. The schedule left him "feeling like a zombie." (New York Times *photo/ Angel Franco*)

Father and son share some easy words in the *Times'* boardroom on January 16, 1992, the day Arthur Jr. became publisher. *(Times History Productions/ Susan W. Dryfoos)*

A portrait of dynastic power: the official photograph of great-grandfather, father, and son that accompanied the *New York Times* story announcing Arthur Jr.'s change in status. *(NYTCA/Burke Uzzle)*

While Arthur Jr. advanced through the company, Dan remained frustrated by his lack of access to the de facto training program that had so clearly been laid out for his cousin. *(NYTCA)*

Because of his position in a secondary area of the company—forest products—and his delay in earning a college degree, Stephen Golden was not a serious contender for either of Punch's titles of chairman and CEO. *(NYTCA)*

Although she had no operational responsibilities at the *Times,* Susan Dryfoos took on the role of family historian. She later found success in film. She is shown here dressed for the 1997 Academy Awards, at which her documentary, *The Line King: The Al Hirschfeld Story,* was nominated for an Oscar. *(Morton Harris)*

In 1986, the year the
family signed a remark-
able covenant guaran-
teeing its control of the
Times well into the
twenty-first century,
Punch and his sisters
line up in their tradi-
tional childhood pose.
(NYTCA)

At the 1993 wedding of Gary Simpson and
Cynthia Sulzberger, no one would have guessed
that the mother of the bride was gravely ill.

When his first novel,
Memoirs of a Geisha,
became a bestseller
and Steven Spielberg
optioned it for a movie,
a nonplussed Arthur
Golden remarked,
"This isn't my life."
(Gerard Brewer)

Punch (left), Arthur Jr., and managing editor Joe Lelyveld surprise Max Frankel (far right) on his fifth anniversary as executive editor. Two years later Arthur Jr.'s candid critique of Frankel at a staff retreat would prove embarrassing to both of them. (New York Times *photo*)

While company president Lance Primis boosted the stock price, he saw himself as a rival to Arthur Jr. and failed to value the family's special role at the top of the *Times*. His abrupt removal in 1996 came as a shock to him. *(NYTCA)*

Arthur Jr. and Gail at the Metropolitan Museum of Art for an elaborate celebration of the family's centennial of ownership of the *Times*. (New York Times *photo*)

The new team at the *Times:* company president and CEO Russ Lewis; Punch, chairman emeritus; Arthur Jr., chairman and publisher; and Michael Golden, vice chairman and senior vice president. *(NYTCA/Fred R. Conrad)*

When Arthur Jr. asked Howell Raines, a strong-minded southerner, to be his editorial-page editor, he also invited him to be one of his top advisers and confidants. *(NYTCA/Fred R. Conrad)*

On the day Arthur Jr. was made chairman, executive editor Joe Lelyveld (far right) escorted Punch to the newsroom, where he was cheered by his editors and reporters. (New York Times *photo*)

Punch and his new wife, Allison Cowles, at a seventy-second-birthday celebration that doubled as his retirement party. Guests sipped cocktails in the arms and armor exhibit of the Metropolitan Museum of Art, where Punch had happily roamed as a child. *(NYTCA)*

A multigenerational reunion in Chattanooga in 1998. In a formal document, the family declared that preserving its role as guardian of the *Times* would always come first, well before "considerations of individual welfare." *(Jace Cohen)*

At the ceremony renaming the block in front of the Times Building "Adolph S. Ochs St." Arthur Jr. gave an emotional introduction to his father, whose respect and love he finally felt confident he had. (*New York Times photo/Paula Giannini*)

Arthur Ochs Sulzberger Jr., publisher of the newspaper and chairman of The New York Times Company. (*NYTCA/John Abbott*)

Spurred on by the experience, he read books about Judaism, talked with a Raleigh rabbi, and erratically attended services. In London he held a Passover seder in their flat; Iphigene, who happened to be in Britain at the time, came as an honored — and somewhat nonplussed — guest. Arthur Jr. realized that if he were ever to become serious about being a practicing Jew, he would have to convert, because his mother was Christian, but that did not stop him from experiencing an atavistic pull toward his heritage.* Several years later he would tell an oral historian for the American Jewish Committee, "I consider myself Jewish. No one else would, but I do."

§

In late May 1978 Arthur Jr. and Gail quit their jobs and embarked on a three-month trip from London to Japan by way of Eastern Europe, the Soviet Union, and China. Before leaving, Arthur Jr. wrote to thank Seymour Topping for helping them plan the China leg of the odyssey and to tell him that when they arrived in New York in late August, he planned to stop by the *Times* to discuss the next step in his career: Washington, D.C. His father had already agreed that the *Times'* capital bureau was the logical place for him to start at the paper, far preferable to a higher-profile position in the New York newsroom. Arthur Jr. felt ready to come home — to the States, to his family, to the newspaper that was his birthright. "I was secure in what I had done in London," he said. "It was time for me to join the *Times*."

Shortly before Arthur Jr. arrived at the Washington bureau in the fall of 1978, the pressmen struck *The New York Times*. In sympathy, the Newspaper Guild went out, too, taking most of the reporters at the bureau with it. The *Times* took advantage of their absence to move its Washington offices from Twentieth and L Streets to Connecticut Avenue and K, so that when Arthur Jr. showed up, he found himself sitting in a maze of packing boxes in a nearly deserted office. He worried that other reporters would criticize him as a strikebreaker, but as soon as the walkout was over, he discovered that they were pragmatically understanding: no one expected a reporter with the surname of Sulzberger to join the Guild or strike *The New York Times*.

---

*It wasn't until 1983 that Reform rabbis voted to recognize patrilineal descent.

In Washington, as in Raleigh, the more salient burden for Arthur Jr. was overcoming the idea that he was just a rich publisher's son. Jokes about him raced through the bureau well before his arrival, with reporters calling him "young Arthur" or "Pinch," a name he despised. "A man deserves his own nickname, and Pinch is clearly [my father's] name, twisted," he explained. No one at the bureau called him Pinch to his face, but he was aware that it was in circulation and set about to undermine it the only way he knew how: through hard work and studiously fitting in. Though only a general assignment reporter, he volunteered to substitute for other correspondents when they were away, no matter how difficult or technical their beats. If an editor asked him to call ten sources to get one quote for a story, he worked the phones late into the night. "Arthur came here knowing he had to prove something," said a former colleague in the bureau.

In Washington he traded in his motorcycle leathers and pipe for fashionable jackets, striped shirts, colorful suspenders, and cigars — a style that aped Ben Bradlee, the natty executive editor of *The Washington Post*. The change in attire was meant to telegraph his evolution to serious-minded professional, but for some, it had the opposite effect. "It was absurd," said a friend from North Carolina who observed him during those days. "It was as if he was trying to be a man, to have more weight or something. It was artificial and struck me as immature."

Several months into Arthur Jr.'s tenure, the bureau chief, Hedrick Smith, went back to reporting, dogged by complaints that he had weakened staff morale. His replacement, a folksy, charismatic Tennessean named Bill Kovach, set about to repair the damage with his characteristic directness. He set up a system under which each reporter, on his birthday, had the bureau chief all to himself for a two-hour evaluation of the reporter's strengths and weaknesses. On Fridays he hosted brown-bag lunches at which any topic was fair game: story ideas, gripes, housekeeping items. His door was always open unless he was having a private conversation; top-down management, corrosive competition, and rule by fear were things of the past. "I thought the best leadership was getting people to *want* to do what you wanted them to do," he said. For Arthur Jr., a devotee of the teamwork ethic of Outward Bound, Kovach was an ideal manager and mentor.

Before Kovach moved from New York to Washington, Punch had taken him aside and in his understated way asked him to do what he could to help Arthur Jr. After Kovach was installed in his new post, the young Sulzberger dropped by the new bureau chief's office. He was willing to do anything that was asked of him, he told his new boss — although, of course, he had his own list of preferences. Then Arthur Jr. got around to the real purpose of his visit. "There is one thing I wish you would do, if you think you can, and that is: help me understand management," he told Kovach. "From time to time, if it's okay with you, I'd like to talk to you about why you do things, how you make decisions."

Several times after that conversation, Arthur Jr. asked Kovach to deconstruct how and why he had promoted one person over another or instituted certain policies. In Arthur Jr.'s mind, if no one else's, he had moved from the status of journeyman reporter he had occupied in Raleigh and London to executive trainee. Although he was diligently preparing himself for management, his future as publisher of *The New York Times* was hardly assured. There was always the unlikely possibility that, like Bobby Dryfoos, Arthur Jr. might at some distant date be judged unsuitable. Kovach, for one, wasn't betting on that. Once, when Arthur Jr. asked him to explain his handling of an issue, Kovach replied, "Do you want me to answer you as a reporter in the bureau, or as the potential future publisher of *The New York Times*?"

Gail, who had joined UPI's Washington bureau, was well aware that others saw Arthur Jr. primarily as the scion of a great newspaper family. When *Congressional Quarterly,* a respected legislative and policy journal, offered her a job at a higher salary, she challenged her boss at UPI to match the sum in order to keep her. He looked at her incredulously and asked, "Isn't your husband making enough money?" Gail promptly resigned and took the position at *CQ,* starting out on the labor beat and moving on to economics. "Up until that point, [my name] was not an issue," said Arthur Jr. "In Washington it began to change."

Nowhere was that change more noticeable than in the Washington bureau itself, where a small clique of up-and-coming younger reporters made a point of becoming his friends. At the center of the group was Steve Rattner, a boyish-looking Brown graduate who had garnered one of Scotty Reston's prized clerkships before joining the *Times* in 1975. He quickly proved to be a gifted reporter, and executive editor Abe Rosenthal was so impressed with him that he waived the final six months of the paper's usual one-year probationary period.

Arthur Jr.'s desk faced Rattner's. Every day they listened to each other's phone calls and gibed back and forth with the same kind of wise-cracking badinage that Arthur Jr. enjoyed with his cousin Dan. Nearby sat six or seven other young reporters who, together with Arthur Jr. and Rattner, formed a kind of reportorial Brat Pack in the Washington office. Except for Arthur Jr. and a reporter named Phil Taubman, every-one in the group was single. After work they gathered for drinks or din-ner at Duke Zeibert's, an old Washington hangout. In the summers Arthur Jr. and Gail shared a house on the Eastern Shore of Maryland with Rattner and Judy Miller, a *New York Times* reporter with whom Rattner was romantically involved at the time.

Kovach warned Arthur Jr. about the dangers of consorting with such an exclusive group of friends. "I thought he was making a mistake to become too close to these people," he explained. "I told him they were going to be a problem for him the rest of his time at *The New York Times.*" Arthur Jr. listened politely, but he put no distance between him-self and his colleagues. "It's like a cancer, it can eat away at you," Arthur Jr. said of the suggestion that his friends might have more in mind than mutual affection. "Or you can say, 'Look, I like these people, I think they like me because of who I am, and I'm going to accept that fact.' " Regard-less of what Arthur Jr. believed, his friends were keenly aware that one day he was likely to be in a position to help them, and they even specu-lated about who would get what. "I remember Judy Miller telling me that Arthur Jr. was going to be publisher and Rattner would be the exec-utive editor," said Richard Burt, who covered arms control for the bureau.

Although Cathy and Karen both lived in Washington, they rarely saw Arthur Jr. "We had different circles of friends and different interests," Karen explained. At the time, Karen was also grappling with a personal crisis. Shortly before her brother moved to Washington, Jerry Johnson, Barbara Grant's third husband, had confided to her that he didn't think the marriage was going to last. "The next day I just felt like a ton of bricks had landed on me," Karen said. "I didn't want to become my mother and make those mistakes." Panic-stricken, she had called Cathy's husband, Joe Perpich, and confessed that she had been drinking too much; her life was unraveling. Joe suggested she try therapy, and soon she was undergoing five-day-a-week psychoanalysis. His support, and Cathy's, brought them all closer together at a time when Arthur Jr. and

Gail were deeply involved with their careers. And with one small child and another on the way, Cathy and Joe had different concerns.

It did not take long for Arthur Jr. to become a parent himself, however. In August 1980 Gail gave birth to a son, and although *The New York Times* had long since given up publishing birth announcements, the paper ran a short item under the headline SULZBERGERS HAVE SON. When the *New York Post* scored the *Times* for singling out a family member for special treatment, the *Times* countered that it considered the birth "news."

There was pressure to continue an unbroken line of Arthurs, but Arthur Jr. protested against making the infant Arthur Ochs Sulzberger 3rd, complaining that "a 'junior' is one thing, but when you get to third and fourth, it sounds like some kind of goddamn royalty." The couple briefly considered Arthur Hays Sulzberger Jr. but in the end struck a compromise: the little boy would be called Arthur and would get Gail's last name as his middle name, making him Arthur Gregg Sulzberger.

He had the misfortune to make his appearance during an election year, so barely a month after the child's arrival, Arthur Jr. had to leave to travel with George Bush, the Republican vice-presidential candidate. The assignment was among the most interesting he had been given during his time in the Washington bureau. As a general assignment reporter, Arthur Jr. had covered everything from the long-term impact of nuclear testing to the decisions of the Federal Trade Commission. He hadn't generated many imaginative ideas for stories, nor did Kovach consider him capable of directing a team of reporters, but he had turned in a creditable performance all the same.

For his part, Arthur Jr. had found it difficult to adjust to the *Times'* elaborate and frustrating editing process. In London he had filed stories, hit the SEND button, and watched his work appear virtually unchanged all over Europe and Africa. At the *Times,* his pieces were reworked in Washington and New York, to the point that he complained to David Binder, his editor in the bureau. Binder silenced him by telling him that *The New York Times* allowed for two kinds of writing: straightforward writing and great writing. "And he made it clear which group I fell into," said Arthur Jr.

Politically, Arthur Jr. still considered himself well left of center. An adamant arms-control advocate, he got into heated debates with his Republican colleague, Richard Burt, the bureau's defense expert, as well as with conservative columnist William Safire, who was based in Washington. "He liked to think of himself as a real liberal and an anti-establishment person," Burt remarked. "[But] how can you be antiestablishment when you're a Sulzberger?"

On election day, Arthur Jr. was in Houston with Bush, watching the returns with Michael Kramer, a like-minded magazine reporter. "We sort of clung together in desperation as the Republicans won a major landslide and Reagan came in," he said. In New York Iphigene was equally glum; she considered Reagan a "miscast, elderly juvenile." Four days later Bush sent Punch a handwritten note. "Your son is a class act," he told him. "We Republicans are all supposed to 'assail' the *Times* from time to time. But with Arthur doing his number — fair, strong reporting — it's hard to do."

Arthur Jr. stayed in Washington through the inauguration and the assassination attempt on President Reagan in March 1981. That summer he and Gail moved to New York, where they lived temporarily in Iphigene's Fifth Avenue apartment while their new residence near the Museum of Natural History underwent renovation. In the fall Arthur Jr. began work on the metropolitan desk of *The New York Times* while Gail studied business and economics as a Knight-Bagehot Fellow at Columbia University.

Arthur Jr.'s earliest goals — to work in newspapers, to join *The New York Times,* to aim for the publishership — were unfolding in a precise and well-ordered fashion. Punch gave few indications of how he viewed his son's progress and, as far as personal intimacy was concerned, remained as inaccessible as ever. One day, standing in his father's office, Arthur Jr. noticed that while there were pictures of Cynthia, Cathy, and Cathy's two children on his father's desk and credenza, there was none of Arthur Jr.'s new baby. Carol, wounded by the warmth the Sulzbergers continued to feel for Barbara Grant, had made it clear she didn't want Punch displaying any connection to that period of his life. As Arthur Jr. surveyed the photographs, Punch's secretary, Nancy Finn, saw a wistful look cross his face. "I wonder how long it will be before I see a picture of *my* child there," he told her.

38

Everyone Makes His Move

WHILE ARTHUR JR. HAD BEEN METHODICAL and disciplined in pursuit of his career, his cousin Dan had dipped in and out of a variety of fields, with only flashes of success. After graduating from Tufts with a degree in drama and biology, he had worked briefly in New York theater, then returned to Boston, where he had dabbled in graduate courses in economics at MIT and Tufts with the vague ambition of pursuing a business career. But with his unfocused background — engineering, lighting design, oceanography — he knew he would have a hard time finding a job. When he turned to the family patriarch for guidance in 1975, Punch arranged for Dan to start at *The Greenville* (S.C.) *News* in what amounted to a management-training program. Dan soon discovered that Multimedia, which owned the *News,* also ran television stations, and television intrigued him far more than newspapers. Eventually he landed a spot as a cameraman at the NBC affiliate in Orlando, Florida.

In Orlando Dan was an unexpected hit. His lucky break came one weekend when a protest broke out between a Jewish and a non-Jewish fraternity at the University of Florida. Because the news director was short-staffed, he assigned Dan to cover the story and liked what he turned in. For the next three years Dan made his way up the ranks of the newsroom as an on-air reporter. He soon proved so adept that the station assigned him to cover Orange County, the seat of Orlando's municipal government, and made him its top investigative reporter.

During long nights in dark bars, Dan chatted up city bureaucrats and disaffected cops, uncovering groundbreaking news in the process. His on-air delivery left something to be desired; he wrote poorly and his performance during live shots bordered on the incoherent. But that mattered less than the inside information he was able to unearth. His talent for ferreting out the truth soon caught the attention of a small cadre of Orlando's movers and shakers who told him they wanted to run him for mayor, an honor he politely declined.

Across town at the ABC affiliate, a newly arrived reporter named Leah Keith watched Dan's nightly coups with ill-concealed alarm. "Damn! I'm never going to make it on this beat because I'm so far behind this guy," she said to herself as she threw shoes at the TV. A tall, striking, dark-haired woman with a Phi Beta Kappa key from the University of Georgia, Leah had grown up in Little Rock in a close clan of small-town blue bloods whose roots in Arkansas stretched back six generations. Her parents were friends with Webster L. Hubbell, the future associate attorney general of the United States who would later find himself at the center of the Whitewater scandal. Her great-great-grandfather was a founder of the law firm in which the future First Lady worked.

Like her college roommate Deborah Norville, who would go on to have her own broadcasting career, Leah was a deceptive hybrid, sufficiently traditional to win a silver bowl for Best Scrapbook at her Georgia sorority, yet ambitious enough to graduate two quarters early. Soon after her arrival in Orlando, she demonstrated journalistic pluck by interviewing for jobs at local massage parlors and putting the incriminating footage on the air.

Dan and Leah started dating while they were both covering the construction of Orlando's international airport. Leah had just broken up with her live-in boyfriend, and during her first dinner with Dan, she found herself wondering why she cared so much about her lost love when the man sitting across the table seemed so warm and understanding. On a weekend together in Tampa, they ended up in a room with two single beds and a wide space in between. As they drifted off to sleep, Leah launched into a lovesick monologue about her former boyfriend. Suddenly out of the dark a pillow came flying in her direction. "Poor Dan," she said later. "I was wishy-washy about the whole thing for a long time."

That changed abruptly after Leah was raped. As a television personality, she was used to being a celebrity in Orlando, but she had no idea that one viewer had been stalking her for weeks. One evening he popped the lock on the sliding glass door of her apartment and found Leah asleep in bed with the television on. "I've been watching you," he told her before he began his attack. After the rapist fled, Leah's call for help was to Dan, who lived fifteen minutes away. He raced over to her apartment, drove

Leah to the hospital, and took on the uncomfortable responsibility of contacting her parents, whom he had never met. When she became nauseated from the injection the doctors administered to prevent pregnancy and sexually transmitted diseases, he returned home and brought back a soft silk-fringed bathrobe, gently enfolding her in it.

Leah was too frightened to return to her apartment, so for the next few weeks she stayed with Dan, who allowed her to recover at her own pace. In his other relationships with women, Dan had always been the wounded one, the one with a traumatic past. Now his troubles paled against Leah's present horror. "He didn't get to say, 'Let me tell you about my terrible father,' " she said. It was Dan who encouraged her, when enough time had passed, to find a new place to live, to return to work, to reenter the world. "You can be on the air," he told her. "You're going to be safe."

Not long after Leah went back to the station, she was offered a job at the NBC affiliate in Dallas — a larger market and a substantial advancement. She accepted it with great relief. As much as she loved Orlando and felt attached to Dan, she was haunted by the fact that the man who had raped her remained at large. Her detailed description of her attacker had proved useless; the police never arrested anyone for the crime.

On the day of her departure for Dallas, Leah climbed into her crammed car and drove off for a new life. She barely made it out of Orlando before the tears started to flow. "I cried for about eight hours," she said. For four months Leah and Dan commuted back and forth, until one weekend Dan greeted her at the Orlando airport with the news "I quit my job today. I've found a position at Warner Amex cable in Dallas."

Dan had told Leah of the close and competitive relationship he had with Arthur Jr., but she didn't meet him until the summer of 1980, when Dan and Leah took a trip back East and Arthur Jr. and Gail met them at the airport. As a rule, Dan liked to dash off planes as quickly as possible and always tried to sit near the front to expedite his escape. On this occasion, however, he let dozens of passengers stream ahead of him. Just when Arthur Jr. began to worry that his cousin had missed the flight, Dan and Leah emerged from the Jetway, sporting Groucho glasses with bushy eyebrows and big noses. It wasn't until Arthur Jr. got nearer that he noticed the bulbous nose was not a nose at all; it was in the shape of a penis. "I *have* to have a pair of these glasses!" Arthur Jr. exclaimed as they all collapsed in laughter. The humor was juvenile, but Leah didn't mind;

what impressed her more was the unusually tender sight of the two men embracing and kissing.

In June 1981 Dan wed Leah at Little Rock's St. Andrew's Roman Catholic Cathedral. The venue was an accommodation to Leah's Catholic father, who was grateful that his daughter and future son-in-law had agreed to go through Catholic marriage counseling and to raise their children in the faith. "Just cross your fingers, we'll never hold you accountable for it," Leah's Presbyterian mother had assured Dan.

As it had been at Arthur Jr.'s wedding, the gathering of the clan for Dan and Leah's marriage was riven by the strains of divorce. Though Iphigene continued to have warm relations with Dick Cohen, who had happily remarried, Judy did not welcome their forced reunion as parents of the groom. The Sulzbergers were equally uncomfortable when they realized that the reception would be held at the racially segregated Little Rock Country Club. The accumulated tension abated momentarily during the service when one of Dan's friends played a practical joke. The night before, she had stolen Dan's shoes and in bright red nail polish had written *H-E* on the sole of the left and *L-P* on the sole of the right. The next day when Dan knelt down in front of the priest, the congregation began to titter. Only later did the newlyweds discover that Dan's shoes had broadcast a scarlet SOS to the guests.

Soon after the wedding Dan left Warner Amex cable, which he thoroughly disliked, and joined Fort Worth Productions, a company that supplied films to the Public Broadcasting System and other quality outlets. It quickly became apparent that the head of the company had pursued him primarily because he assumed that Dan had money. For a while Dan cast about in Washington, D.C., looking for television jobs, but nothing clicked. He was at a dead end; except for marrying Leah, he had accomplished very little since coming to Dallas.

Coincidentally, Leah's contract at her station was up for negotiation. By then she had become disenchanted with television news and was considering law school. For both of them, it seemed a propitious moment to make a move, and for Dan in particular, the destination was obvious: *The New York Times*. After his string of defeats, the soothing safety of the family and the grandeur of its enterprise were irresistible magnets. Once again he called his uncle Punch, this time specifically requesting a spot at headquarters in New York. In January 1983 he joined the strategic-planning department.

Dan's father, still smarting from the loss of his *New York Times* board seat, expressed profound disappointment. "You're going to be just like your grandfather," Dick Cohen warned him. "How will you know when you get to the top whether you could have made it on the outside?" Judy, who had remained ambivalent toward the newspaper since childhood, was more supportive, but she suspected that her son was prompted as much by a desire to keep up with his cousin Arthur as by career considerations.

§

At the same moment that Dan joined The New York Times Company, Arthur Jr. hung up his reporter's hat and transferred to the business side of the paper. At the start of his year and a half in the New York newsroom, he had bristled at finding himself yet again on general assignment, the lowest rung on the journalistic ladder. His dream had been to come to New York as assistant metropolitan editor, but national editor Dave Jones had persuaded him that so senior a title would undermine his credibility in the newsroom. "If you spend a year as a reporter," he had told Arthur Jr. over lunch, "you'll show them what you know, and the question will never be asked about you." Arthur had let out an audible sigh. "How many times do I have to pay my dues?" he asked. "Always," Jones told him.

After several months Arthur Jr. moved to the city hall beat, where he covered New York's flamboyant mayor, Ed Koch. In early 1982 he was made assignment editor on the metropolitan desk — his first real management job. Given his workmanlike prose and creative spelling, which made him unfit to blue-pencil copy, the duties of an assignment editor — coming up with story ideas and motivating people to produce them — were more in keeping with his talents. As a reporter, he had carped about the stupidity of editors; now he had new respect for their plight. "One day you're getting your jollies from your byline," he said. "The next you're supposed to manage a group of ninety individuals and get your jollies from seeing their success — all hands-on, no training. It was the single most exhausting job I ever had."

As assignment editor, Arthur Jr. adopted the habit of walking around in his stocking feet, a fashion statement not seen at the *Times* since the arrival of an irreverent Texas import named Molly Ivins. The affectation may have seemed calculated, but in fact Arthur Jr. simply hated shoes.

Nevertheless, the image it created was of an informal and slightly rebellious regular Joe. "He was charming and enthusiastic and shoeless," said Richard Meislin, a metro reporter at the time. "If you're the publisher's son, it's exactly the right thing to do." If Arthur Jr.'s casualness helped him cajole reporters into accepting assignments they considered beneath them, his status as a Sulzberger was never far from their minds. "Well, Arthur, you know what I always say: Never argue with a Class B stockholder!" one reporter quipped after agreeing to an unwelcome task.

Arthur Jr.'s true place was conspicuously apparent during Gridiron weekend. No mere assignment editor could ever have hoped to be included in such an event, which brought the top executives and editors of the nation's major newspapers together with government leaders in Washington. Yet Arthur Jr. took his seat alongside Punch, Sydney Gruson, Seymour Topping, and Bill Kovach at a table with economist Alan Greenspan; Hannah Gray, the president of the University of Chicago; John Sirica, the granite-faced judge of Watergate fame; and other dignitaries.

It was on the metropolitan desk that Arthur Jr. came into direct contact for the first time with Abe Rosenthal, the *Times'* gifted and temperamental executive editor. He came to respect the high standards that Rosenthal set for the *Times,* even as he deplored the climate of fear the editor had created through his dictatorial and often capricious management. Sensing that he was revered but unpopular with the staff, Rosenthal occasionally lashed out like a spurned lover. He saw slights and conspiracies everywhere. Editors and reporters were afraid to challenge him lest they be sent to the journalistic equivalent of Siberia. Only deputy managing editor Arthur Gelb, with whom Rosenthal had worked closely since the early 1960s, had his complete trust. "We had the entire operation resting on the backs of two people," said Arthur Jr. "If you were to remove Abe and Arthur Gelb from the equation, the place would have been without any sense of vision."

Although Arthur Jr. never complained about the paper's top editor as other reporters did, he made little effort to endear himself to him. One day outside Rosenthal's office, a secretary caught him reading Rosenthal's telephone messages, which he had lifted from a spike on her desk. "Who the hell do you think you are?" she asked indignantly. "I'm a reporter, I've got all the instincts, I can't help it," Arthur Jr. replied, a wise-guy response that few others would have dared make. When Arthur Jr. nonchalantly showed up shoeless for a meeting with other desk editors, Rosenthal grabbed his arm and growled, "Don't you ever come to this office again without your shoes on."

Temperamentally and politically, Rosenthal was Arthur Jr.'s diametric opposite. Abe was a strong anticommunist, though an atypical one. His straitened youth had made him inherently sympathetic to the underdog, but he was disgusted when, while working as a *Times* correspondent in Poland, the Communist government had expelled him for exposing repression and brutality. During the Vietnam War era, he was an absolutist concerning the paper's obligation to do tough reporting on the war while personally he harbored deep suspicions of the radical left. Rosenthal's experience during the takeover of Columbia in 1968 and the social and political upheaval since then had made him wary of his own staff, particularly those of Arthur Jr.'s age and education. "He tended to regard [them] as being naturally left wing," said Joe Lelyveld, then a foreign correspondent. "Abe would always say, with some justice, that you have to keep your hand on the tiller and steer it to the right or it'll drift off to the left."

Rosenthal's guiding philosophy was to keep *The New York Times* "straight," by which he meant free of causes, special pleadings, and political agendas. For gay members of the staff, the word had a double meaning. "Some of the most talented people, who day after day were doing exactly what [Abe] wanted and making his product rise to the highest level, were gay men who lived in terror of him," said Anna Quindlen, a former *Times* columnist then working the metro desk. Privately Rosenthal was more ignorant of homosexuals than homophobic. In the early 1970s he had no idea that two of his news assistants were gay. Yet as an editor, he had often ordered up groundbreaking stories on the subject.

In 1963, for instance, after returning to the paper from Japan as metropolitan editor, Rosenthal had been struck by how openly affectionate gay men had become on the streets of New York, and he assigned an article on the subject. The resulting five-thousand-word piece, written by Robert Doty, ran on page one. Although its headline — GROWTH OF HOMOSEXUALITY IN CITY PROVOKES WIDE CONCERN — was derisive, as was much of the content (the piece grouped homosexuals with other "degenerates"), for the staid *New York Times,* merely devoting so much space and attention to a sexual topic of any kind was revolutionary.

Despite such milestones, when a front-page story on homosexual cruises had appeared in the travel section in 1975, Rosenthal had been apoplectic. The piece referred to homosexuals as "gays," a word that Rosenthal decreed could be used thereafter only if it was in the name of an organization or within quotes. The story had gone well beyond the mention of the *g* word. Freelance writer Cliff Jahr had painted a titillating picture of men in "black cowhide outfits trimmed with chains, zippers and metal studs" and had hinted at wild orgies belowdecks. To Rosenthal, the piece was an embarrassment and a violation of the *Times'* standards of taste, a view that he was hardly alone in holding. Iphigene had called Punch in an outrage to complain about the story and was "rabid on the subject," according to a *Times* staffer privy to the internal correspondence that crossed Rosenthal's desk at the time. It was Punch, in fact (who awkwardly joked about "queers" and felt uncomfortable viewing films such as *La Cage aux Folles*), who had ordered Rosenthal to ban the word *gay* from the paper.

By the time Arthur Jr. arrived in the newsroom in the early 1980s, Rosenthal's despotic quirks, coupled with his clear squeamishness about gays, had conspired to create an atmosphere of cowed silence among homosexual reporters. To protect their careers, they remained resolutely in the closet. Arthur Jr. found the climate disturbing and uncomfortable; like most members of his generation, he accepted sexual orientation as a matter of course. In reaction, he decided to send a signal that he didn't support this particular aspect of the Rosenthal regime.

In the course of a week, Arthur Jr. individually took the reporters on the metropolitan desk whom he suspected were homosexual out to lunch. "So," he began with each one, leaning over the table, "what is it like to be gay at *The New York Times?*" After his guest had recovered his composure, Arthur Jr. went on to say that he considered it "crazy" to work together so closely and "not have this behind us." Denying one's sexual orientation, he said, is a "silly way to live our lives." As news of Arthur Jr.'s "outing" made its way through the newsroom, the reaction among gays was one of immense relief. "It was an incredibly disarming . . . thing to do at that point," said Richard Meislin.

It turned out to be a benchmark moment for Arthur Jr. as well. Soon word filtered back to him that his colleagues had viewed his behavior not merely as a warm personal act by an assignment editor who cared about his reporters but as a bellwether of the presumed future — a brave new world with Arthur Jr. as publisher. "All of a sudden, I was being seen in a different light," he said. "That was the first time that had happened to me."

§

After the 1982 mayoral election, Arthur Jr. reluctantly agreed with his father and Walter Mattson that the time had come for him to begin learning about the company's business operations. "That was his spinach," said Dan Cohen. "He just didn't really want to spend a lot of time on the business side." His first stop was in the advertising department, where, thanks to the pro-business policies of the Reagan administration, sales were booming — "You'd have to be a moron not to make your bonus," Arthur Jr. said — and the once prevailing attitude of simply filling out orders for ads had given way to an aggressive marketing mentality. Having spent nearly all his working life in newsrooms, Arthur Jr. had the typical reporter's prejudice against ad salesmen, who he assumed were crass, money-grubbing, and intellectually thin. After a few months selling ad space to financial institutions and investment banks, he came to think otherwise.

Equally surprising was his discovery that ad executives' skills overlapped with those of reporters. Both jobs required competitiveness, the need to build relationships, a refusal to take no for an answer, and the ability to work on deadline. But that was where the similarities ended. At cocktail parties Arthur Jr. for the first time had the edifying experience of watching people drift away when he told them what he did for a living. "It took me a while before I stopped saying, 'Wait! I used to write! Come back, come back!,'" he said. The rejection sensitized him to his coworkers' feelings of inferiority. When they gingerly asked him what the newsroom thought of them, he couldn't bring himself to speak the truth — which was that reporters felt disdain — so he told a white lie: "Oh, they realize that you make the money that shows up in their paychecks."

Arthur Jr. also came to admire the strong professional values he observed at work in the advertising department. When clients pressured *Times* salesmen to promise news coverage in exchange for advertising contracts, the polite but firm answer was uniformly no. "Journalists pay lip service to [that kind of ethic], but those folks faced it every day,"

Arthur Jr. said. "And it was an issue of pride. 'This is *The New York Times.* We don't operate that way.' "

In 1984 Arthur Jr. shifted to strategic planning, where he became a member of the *Times* department that had recently been vacated by his cousin Dan, who had moved on to circulation. Despite their fraternal relationship and the fact that they lived only a few blocks apart on the Upper West Side, neither had seen much of the other since moving to New York. Arthur Jr.'s closest friends were in the newsroom; Dan's were on the business side of the company. Professionally they were no longer equal — and Dan resented it. "I hear you're doing a great job in strategic planning," Arthur Jr. had told him soon after his arrival, a remark that to Dan's ears sounded like the patronizing comment of a manager, not a colleague. Privately he complained that Arthur Jr. had cast himself as the anointed one in the family, and told friends that there was now a love/hate relationship. Dan knew that Arthur Jr. had been preparing himself for the publisher's job since childhood and that his own lack of focus and undisciplined background made any expectation that he could keep up unrealistic. Still, when an oral historian for the American Jewish Committee asked him to describe his goals at the *Times,* Dan said with considerable bravado that he thought of himself as being "able to rise to the top, being able to perhaps be the president [of The New York Times Company]."

With its young staff and broad-gauged brief — to analyze new acquisitions and ventures for the company — the strategic-planning department had been a warm, supportive point of entry for Dan. No one seemed to care that he was a member of the Sulzberger family, and he did little to draw attention to the fact. Years later Dan would insist that he felt equal to anyone in the department, but, in reality, his short attention span prevented him from succeeding at long-term projects and he had neither the training nor the experience to perform at the level of his colleagues, most of whom had MBAs. Although they had every right to resent him for not pulling his weight, Dan's affability and earnest, unassuming manner made it difficult for them to be angry. "We covered for Dan a little bit, but it was never a big deal," said his supervisor, Gordon Medenica.

Like Dan, Arthur Jr. enjoyed the company of the people in strategic planning, but professionally he considered the experience a wheel-spinning exercise and admitted, "It was my least favorite job." He disliked writing reports that seemed to go nowhere. Having no power to implement his ideas — or even to influence whether anyone else did so — made him squirm in frustration.

Arthur Jr.'s stint on the business side coincided with a period during which Walter Mattson was at the height of his powers. The *Times'* president jettisoned the inconsequential "peanut stands" bought in the 1960s and 1970s, focusing with few exceptions on newspapers, magazines, and broadcasting, and between 1980 and 1988 spent about a billion dollars on new acquisitions in an effort to diversify the company away from New York. "His has got to go down as one of the great presidencies in the newspaper business," said corporate attorney Mike Ryan. "He really kept us to our knitting."

But to those in strategic planning, that was precisely the problem. Mattson, weaned on printing presses and typesetting equipment, had no coherent strategy for buying broadcast properties, other than picking up television stations in the smallest markets because they were cheap. The company made a brief foray into the cable field, only to sell it quickly at a handsome profit. It was not that Punch or Mattson or others on the fourteenth floor were actively opposed to new lines of business; they were simply uneasy with acquisitions they didn't understand. As a consequence, they had no frame of reference for judging non-newspaper properties and held them to unrealistic standards of success. "It's easier for *The New York Times* to say yes to a twenty-million-dollar dryer for the presses than it is to say yes to twenty million dollars for a new business venture," said a former analyst in strategic planning. "They know what the dryer gives them. They don't know what the new business gives them." Mattson's other weakness was an inability to delegate. In meetings his top executives felt he made a show of soliciting their opinions, then did exactly what he originally intended. Staff members in the strategic-planning department grumbled that their carefully prepared position papers on new acquisitions and new lines of business had no effect on the fourteenth floor. "When we wanted to do something, the decision had already been made, and strategic planning was just used to justify it," said Dan Cohen.

Mattson's controlling style did have the positive effect of giving those inside and outside the *Times* confidence that there was strong leadership at the top. He led by example: no one worked harder than he did. The corporate staff privately christened the company plane *The Flying Griddle* because Mattson, once airborne, would question them mercilessly about every detail of the *Times* subsidiaries they traveled to visit. "You learned very early on not to bullshit Walter," said Medenica, who once watched Mattson "fry" a new department head who tried to bluff him. "He could be pretty brutal and cruel."

Mattson's preference for plain surroundings had not changed since he became president. His office on the fourteenth floor was painted in shades of orange and brown, and except for a beautiful desk he had lifted from a subordinate whom he had fired, the place had all the charm of a Goodwill store. Mattson's stubborn indifference to aesthetics so offended Punch's sense of proper housekeeping that while Mattson was away on a business trip, he threw out all the furniture, called in a decorator, and redid the office. On the morning of Mattson's return, Punch walked down the hall to take a bow for his handiwork. "Well, do you notice anything different?" he asked, beaming. "No," Mattson replied innocently. "What are you talking about?" The *Times* president claimed not to see the changes, but his diffidence was really a silent protest against the new decor, which didn't conform to Mattson's blue-collar self-image. "It looks like an office where a sissy sits," he told another *Times* executive with a scowl.

Unlike many at the *Times*, Arthur Jr. didn't fear the tall, taciturn company president, but there was little personal warmth between them. "He's from a different generation and has a different view of life from mine," Mattson said, "so it's highly unlikely that we would ever have had a warm and fuzzy relationship." Adding to the distance was Mattson's role — appointed by Punch — as co-architect of Arthur Jr.'s training program. Mattson's choice of assignments did not always please Arthur Jr., even when he knew they were valuable.

Harvard Business School was a prime example. "I'll never forgive him [for that]," said Arthur Jr. After listening to Mattson rhapsodize about his own experience at Harvard's program for advanced management, Arthur Jr. agreed that he needed to learn quantitative skills and broaden his outlook. After several months in strategic planning, he was accepted at, and entered, the school's Program for Management Development, and immediately loathed it. He was affronted by his class, which was predominantly white and male, and he disagreed violently with the school's conviction that maximizing shareholder wealth was the key to a soundly managed business. "I wouldn't want to work for the company they wanted me to run," he said. "They were interested in building wealth. I was interested in building value." Taking issue with the philosophy of a top-flight business school hardly seemed a sufficient reason to be wretchedly unhappy. "I think something happened to Arthur at Harvard," said a friend. "I got the sense that he got picked on and maybe isolated."

Dan Cohen had halfheartedly taken two business courses at New York University before finally giving up on an MBA because "I wasn't sure what it got me." Arthur Jr. could have done the same. He could have quit the Harvard program, come home, and put an end to his torture. He certainly wanted to. Instead, he stuck it out, doggedly learning about decision-tree analysis and return on investment. What motivated him was more than mere duty or a refusal to be defeated. For the first time, he sensed that he had a competitor within the family. Months earlier his cousin, Michael Golden, had started work at *The New York Times,* and along with a journalism degree and experience on the business side of *The Chattanooga Times,* he brought a freshly minted executive MBA from Emory University in Atlanta. "I viewed it as coming to New York with USDA GRADE A stamped on the forehead," Michael said.

39

All for One, One for All

I N 1981 THE SOUTHERN NEWSPAPER PUBLISHERS
Association held its annual meeting at the Greenbrier, an antebellum resort in the green hills of West Virginia. In the course
of the weekend, Michael Golden, vice president and treasurer of The
Chattanooga Times Printing Company, sat down with Punch, Sydney
Gruson, and his stepfather, Bill Holmberg, to discuss the status of *The
Chattanooga Times*. After fourteen years of deep losses under independent management, the paper had entered into a new joint operating
agreement in 1980 with its rival, the *Chattanooga News–Free Press*, the
second in their troubled history. The agreement reinstated the two
papers' business operations under a common management dominated
by the *Free Press*, effectively stripping Michael of any significant responsibility. Because he liked running a business and felt ready to move on to
a larger arena, he asked about the possibility of his coming to New York
and joining The New York Times Company.

Although both Punch and Gruson were receptive to the idea, Gruson
suggested an interim step first: an MBA. "The competition is a lot stiffer
in New York," Gruson cautioned him. "You should be as prepared as you
can." A few days later Michael casually told his mother that he was
thinking of getting a business degree and working at *The New York Times*.
The news made Ruth intensely unhappy, for despite *The Chattanooga
Times'* position as the perpetual underdog, she had nursed a hope that
one of her sons might one day succeed her at the paper. For her sake, as
well as his own, Holmberg tried to change his stepson's mind. "He asked
me if they named me publisher, would I stay? If I were president, would
I stay?" Michael recalled. The offers didn't tempt him; he remained firm
in his determination to leave.

After living in Rennes, France, as an English language teacher and
earning a degree in journalism at the University of Missouri — a first in

the Sulzberger family — Michael had returned to Chattanooga in the spring of 1978 with his wife, Anne, and their small daughter, Margot, with no firm purpose other than to see if they liked living and working there. Michael's ambition was to be a journalist, and for the first few months he wrote obits and covered the county courthouse as a general assignment reporter. That fall he got pulled into the paper's budget process "because the business was going so badly."

Michael was shocked at the precarious finances he found at *The Chattanooga Times*. The paper had managed to have only three profitable years since 1966, the year it had dissolved its long-standing joint operating agreement with the *Free Press* and launched the ill-fated afternoon *Chattanooga Post*. In 1970 the *Post* had died, a casualty of an antitrust lawsuit that *Free Press* owner Roy McDonald had filed against The Chattanooga Times Printing Company. With the $2.5 million McDonald had won in damages, he had purchased a color press, attracting readers and advertisers to his fat Sunday paper with splashy photographs that made the black-and-white *Chattanooga Times* look dowdy.

Despite its fiscal problems, *The Chattanooga Times* consistently took the high road, while the *Free Press* shamelessly played the role of community bulletin board. McDonald offered free death notices, ran Chattanoogans' pictures on their birthdays and anniversaries, and covered every Rotary Club and Lions Club meeting in town. *The Chattanooga Times* never feared that it might be beaten on a local political story, because the *Free Press* was often too worried about offending somebody to break such news. Only after *The Chattanooga Times* had reported some political wrongdoing would the *Free Press* follow suit, sometimes rewriting *The Chattanooga Times'* scoop and even lifting quotes from its coverage. Nevertheless, the *Free Press,* which Punch derided as a "redneck paper," was clearly what the city wanted. Its circulation figures ran well ahead of those of *The Chattanooga Times*. "I have that hillbilly touch," McDonald once said.

In the immediate aftermath of her divorce from Ben, Ruth's relationship with Michael — who was particularly close to his father — had been distant and troubled. To remedy the situation, Ruth adopted a ritual of coming home from the office, pouring herself a Jack Daniel's, offering Michael an Early Times with water, and discussing politics and the events of both their days. "It was a great time," said Michael.

"We really did get to know each other." In 1978, when he returned to Chattanooga to work at the paper, he and Anne had dinner with Ruth and Bill several nights a week. The topic was always the same: the worrisome state of *The Chattanooga Times* and the scurrilous tactics and shoddy journalism of the *Free Press*. "We'd wish for Mr. Roy to die; that was the daily prayer," said Anne sardonically, remembering their frustration.

Michael's first big project was to help write a business plan for the paper. "I read it," Punch told Bill Holmberg after the report had been sent up to New York. "I don't have to believe it." The plan forecast a rosy future — "The triumph of hope over experience," said Michael — based on a buyout in the composing room, conversion to cold type, increased circulation, and advertising growth. To obtain a more realistic picture, Punch dispatched a team from *The New York Times'* regional newspaper group to Chattanooga and ordered them to take a professional look at the situation. Michael considered the visit "the start of my real business education."

The resulting report warned that *The Chattanooga Times* was mired in "severe cash problems and needs financial assistance immediately." The analysis listed three options for the paper: shutting down entirely, going back to a joint operating agreement with the *Free Press,* or continuing to lose money. Nowhere did it find justification for the optimistic proposition put forth by Ruth, Bill, and Michael that *The Chattanooga Times* could simply grow its way out of its problems.

Punch was rather unsentimental about the Tennessee newspaper that had given his grandfather his start, but he was keenly aware that *The Chattanooga Times* was critical to his sister. When an associate suggested that he shutter the paper and make Ruth publisher of one of *The New York Times'* regional papers in the South, he refused. "You don't understand," he explained. "My sister is a major personality in that town. *The Chattanooga Times* has got to go on."

Very quickly the decision was made to try to persuade Roy McDonald to reenter a money-saving joint operating agreement. Luckily *The Chattanooga Times* and the *Free Press* had never formally dissolved The Chattanooga Times Publishing Company, the corporation that had earlier served as the papers' common umbrella. Enticing the irascible "Mr. Roy" to the bargaining table, however, proved to be a formidable task, despite the fact that he had every reason to cooperate; the *Free Press,* while dominant in terms of circulation, wasn't making money, either. But McDonald, feisty and proud, still held grudges from his previous associations with *The Chattanooga Times* and didn't want any part of a new combined business operation.

To help convince him otherwise, Punch sent his most charming and wily emissary — Sydney Gruson — to handle the negotiations. Gruson opened with a bluff: "If you don't [agree to a joint operating agreement]," he warned McDonald, "we will put all the resources of *The New York Times* behind saving *The Chattanooga Times*." The threat, however, was an empty one. The Ochs Trust, which owned *The Chattanooga Times*, had already sunk millions into the paper over the years; in a particularly low moment, Punch had called it "my Vietnam." *The New York Times* had no intention of wasting the company's money to compete with Mr. Roy.

The ploy got McDonald's attention, and talks dragged on for four or five months, until late March 1980, when the two sides reached an accord. *The Chattanooga Times* agreed to suspend its Sunday edition in return for elimination of the *Free Press* on Saturday, to print its papers in McDonald's plant, and to cede to him control of all joint business, advertising, and circulation operations. Because of McDonald's virulent anti-unionism, the news personnel at *The Chattanooga Times*, some of whom were members of the Newspaper Guild, were forbidden to set foot in the *Free Press* building. The pact, wrote a *Time* correspondent, amounted to a "surrender" on the part of *The Chattanooga Times*. "Crusty, old Roy McDonald, the out-spoken, ultra-conservative publisher of the *Chattanooga News–Free Press*, has finally put to rest the ghost of Adolph Ochs," he cabled his editor in New York.

The two papers next sought approval from the antitrust division of the U.S. Justice Department — a necessary step before the joint operating agreement could go into effect. When no decision was forthcoming by the end of April, they asked the government for temporary approval, because *The Chattanooga Times* was facing a financial crisis. On May 8 the antitrust division denied the request, setting off panic at *The Chattanooga Times*, which did not have enough funds to meet its next bimonthly payroll.

Under the Newspaper Preservation Act, the government had to agree that *The Chattanooga Times* was a "failing newspaper" before it would approve a joint operating agreement. Yet when Justice officials examined the paper's books, they saw what appeared to be a salvageable situation. Because the Ochs Trust had propped up *The Chattanooga Times* for so long, the paper was unencumbered by debt. It also had assets in its building and printing presses. With these items as collateral, Justice Department attorneys asked, why not get a loan? Bill and Michael obligingly appealed to a series of banks, but not one "would loan [them] a nickel." Their dilemma failed to sway the government. Even though the Ochs Trust had by then completely cut off *The Chattanooga Times* in order to bolster the paper's case for assistance, the Justice Department assumed that it "would support us forever," said Michael.

With cash almost gone and nowhere else to turn, Ruth made a bold, even foolhardy, decision: she defied the Justice Department and on May 12 announced that *The Chattanooga Times* was consolidating operations with the *Free Press,* effective immediately. Hundreds of *Times* employees were laid off, and the production operation went dark. "The guys at Justice went bat shit, called us up, screamed and hollered," said Michael, who had the unhappy job of defending the move. Frightened, Ruth and Bill raced to Washington to seek help from Tennessee senator Howard Baker and, on his advice, retained an influential law firm to negotiate with the Justice Department. The strategy worked: in November 1980 Attorney General Benjamin Civiletti gave final approval to the combined operations, saying the action was justified in order to keep a second independent editorial voice alive in Chattanooga. True to his mercurial nature, Roy McDonald decided not to honor his promise to close his Saturday paper, but otherwise, the merger went smoothly.

For *The Chattanooga Times,* everything but its news operation gradually disappeared. With its means of production housed in McDonald's plant, the paper no longer needed a printing press, sorting equipment, or even a separate building. The changes soon showed up in the bottom line, and by the end of fiscal year 1981, *The Chattanooga Times* boasted a small operating profit. To demonstrate her gratitude for all that he had done, Ruth sent Sydney Gruson a letter thanking him for his "caring and . . . daring on our behalf" and his "wise and patient hand." "We came from a very dark and bleak position and we still have a long way to go," she wrote. "[But] I am optimistic and no longer want to commit murder or suicide."

Ruth's buoyant outlook would prove to be premature. By 1986 the *Free Press* would have six thousand more daily subscribers than *The Chattanooga Times* and would remain the leading paper both in circulation and profit well past the death of "Mr. Roy" in 1990, proud to the last to consider himself a merchant, not a journalist. As it had since 1966, the Ochs Trust would continue to act as the paper's banker. By 1988 the amount expended by the trust to keep *The Chattanooga Times* afloat would total some $12 million.

It was *The Chattanooga Times'* uncertain future that prompted Michael to propose his coming to *The New York Times,* and that made Gruson's suggestion of an MBA appealing. In the fall of 1982, on his way to Hillandale to attend the wedding of Karen Sulzberger and writer Eric Lax, Michael stopped off in Georgia to investigate Emory's executive MBA program. He was later accepted and in January 1983 began a grueling schedule. Mondays through Thursdays he worked at *The Chattanooga Times.* On Thursday night he drove to Atlanta, attended classes at Emory on Friday and Saturday, and returned home on Saturday night. The constant pressure left him exhausted and put a complete halt to his social life.

Shortly before graduation in the summer of 1984, Michael traveled to New York to have what amounted to a rite of passage for every other Sulzberger cousin starting at *The New York Times*: a talk with Walter Mattson. Like his brother Stephen, who had recently moved from the circulation department to the company's forest products division, Michael wanted to begin his career at *The New York Times,* not at a company subsidiary, but Mattson told him there were no "real" jobs then available at the newspaper. The best opportunity, he said, was in the company's magazine group.

Michael moved his family to New York City and went to work at *Family Circle* as associate production manager. Only later would he realize that starting at the magazines instead of at *The New York Times* would handicap him in the competition to become a top executive at the company. Despite his multiple degrees and several years of experience, he accepted a $10,000 pay cut, from $45,000 to $35,000. The welcome mat had been out when Arthur Jr. came to New York. By the time Michael arrived, it seemed a bit threadbare. "They were just *delighted* to have me here," he said with unconcealed sarcasm.

§

By the mid-1980s the question of who in the "cousins' generation" would eventually succeed Punch as publisher of *The New York Times* and head of the company was omnipresent but rarely discussed. When an interviewer asked Iphigene how she envisioned the family's management of the paper twenty years hence, she joked that she had misplaced her crystal ball. "Will one of them be capable, or will they have to get someone from outside?" she asked rhetorically. "I don't know." Punch encouraged his sisters to speak up if they thought he was treating their children unfairly, and Walter Mattson took Marian, Ruth, and Judy out to lunch periodically to report on their offspring's progress. But since the culture of the family decreed it bad form to actively promote one's child at the company, they voiced few complaints.

Among the cousins themselves, however, there were signs of restiveness. "The natural assumption is that Arthur's going to be publisher, and my natural response is that that isn't quite fair," said one cousin who flirted briefly with joining the paper. Another assumption was so ingrained, it was rarely subject to comment: the next publisher would be male. Although Punch gave lip service to the proposition that every Sulzberger cousin, male or female, had an equal chance to lead the company, the reality was starkly different. "This family does not take seriously the aspirations of women," said a former *Times* executive.

No one felt that attitude more acutely than Susan Dryfoos, who by the 1980s was a divorced single mother living on lower Fifth Avenue in Greenwich Village, trying desperately to make a place for herself at *The New York Times*. Of all the Sulzberger cousins, she was the one whose wounds were most visible. As a student at Lake Erie College in the late 1960s, she was aware enough of her own emotional fragility to fear the addictive qualities of recreational drugs and alcohol; though she experimented with grass, she quickly settled on Salem cigarettes. "If I had gotten into LSD or anything harder, I would have just gone off the deep end," she said. Nevertheless, when her stepfather, Andrew Heiskell, expressed curiosity about marijuana, she accommodated him by bringing home a joint. The sight of her daughter teaching her husband how to inhale in the elegant dining room of their apartment had been too much for Marian, who burst into tears.

Shortly after college, Susan had joined *The New York Times* as a news clerk in the education and science department and soon moved to the New Jersey section as a self-described "gal Friday." When her superiors nominated her for a Publisher's Merit Award — the *Times'* way of giving its reporters a nod of recognition — their impulse to do something nice for a family member ran afoul of Punch's determination to maintain the illusion that Sulzbergers should be treated like everyone else. In the past Punch, the final authority on Merit Awards, had rarely disagreed with his editors' recommendations. When he saw Susan's name, however, he vetoed the choice, thereby creating a ticklish dilemma. Someone in the newsroom had violated the nomination's confidentiality and told Marian ahead of time that her daughter had won. Punch was furious. "If there is going to be any embarrassment on the Susan Dryfoos business, let's reinstate it," Punch told managing editor Seymour Topping. "However, in both capacities as publisher and her uncle, I do not think she really should get one at this time."

It had been brave enough that the severely dyslexic Susan had attempted to work as a reporter for *The New York Times,* but when she had announced that she was quitting the paper to write a book, the family reacted with disbelief. Her subject was a young Mormon artist who had left his religion and his home to "draw his way" across the country. For two years he and Susan traveled together while Susan chronicled the journey. In 1973, just as she was preparing to join him out West to finish the project, the young man abruptly decided he didn't want to go through with it. Marian had assumed the relationship was a love affair, but Susan insisted otherwise. "You won't believe it, Mother, but Richard and I never touched each other." "You're right," Marian replied. "I wouldn't have believed it."

Susan had next gone on to assemble tours for the Archaeological Institute of America. On the first of these trips, through France and Spain, she had met Douglas Mazonowicz, a twice-divorced Englishman close to her mother's age whose specialty was the re-creation of prehistoric art in modern forms. The Smithsonian had sponsored a cross-country tour of Mazonowicz's silk screens of cave paintings, and from time to time *The New York Times* had quoted him in its coverage of the arts. Those bona-fides meant little when Susan announced that she intended to marry him.

Marian thought Mazonowicz too old for her immature and inexperienced daughter and mounted an active campaign to scuttle the match. Iphigene took a more compassionate approach. Since Orvil's death, she had kept a watchful eye on her granddaughter. They had drawn close during their trip to China, and she knew how much the young woman longed for a home. Marrying a man only eight years younger than her father spoke for itself. With a straightforwardness that shocked Marian, Iphigene intervened, demanding, "Don't you want your daughter to be happy, at least for a while?" "If you think she's going to be happy, I'm not going to stand in the way," the nonplussed Marian replied. "I just think he's too old." The marriage took place in the fall of 1975 at High'n Dry. Almost exactly a year later — three days before Iphigene's eighty-fourth birthday — Nicholas Ochs Mazonowicz was born.

Marian had been right; the marriage was ill-advised, and in 1981 Susan and Douglas Mazonowicz were divorced. That same year Susan had realized her dream of publishing a book: Dodd, Mead & Company brought out *Iphigene: Memoirs of Iphigene Ochs Sulzberger of* The New York Times *Family.* The title page says that the memoirs were "as told to her granddaughter Susan W. Dryfoos," although many of the interviews on which the book was based had been conducted years earlier by others.

The genesis of the book stretched back to the early 1960s, when Iphigene had hired a series of interviewers to record her recollections of her father. Gradually the idea had changed from a memoir about Adolph Ochs to a first-person account of Iphigene's life. The work was still unpublished in the early 1970s when Iphigene had sat down with interviewer Frank Brunott for fourteen lengthy conversations that ranged freely and frankly over her childhood, marriage, and life as the wife of the publisher of *The New York Times.* Several years later, when Susan needed a project, Iphigene had obligingly given her blessing to the notion of resurrecting the memoir, which would be based on these earlier talks, supplemented by new ones conducted by her granddaughter. In 1979 *Iphigene: The Memoirs of Iphigene Ochs Sulzberger as told to Susan W. Dryfoos* appeared as a privately printed volume, distributed only to family members and close friends. When the commercial version came out two years later, it included an affectionate foreword by Iphigene's friend the popular historian Barbara W. Tuchman. Not surprisingly, *The New York Times Book Review* praised the work, which contained little of the candor of Iphigene's original interviews, as "a most engaging and engrossing book."

Flush from this experience, Susan established The New York Times History Project to document the paper through film and oral histories. The job came with an office at the *Times,* an assistant, and a small budget; more important, it offered her a role within the family that was as close as Susan could get to that of her grandmother, the custodian of the family's stories and myths, the guardian of its truths. "I spent a lot of time running away from the family," Susan told an interviewer three years after the publication of *Iphigene*, "and I turn out, I think, to be the embodiment of the family values."

Whatever competitive emotions Susan may have felt for her cousins, when it came to the question of sticking together for the sake of *The New York Times*, she and the rest of the younger generation were of one mind. Nowhere was that more apparent than in an extraordinary covenant the Sulzberger heirs signed in June 1986 to ensure that *The New York Times* would remain in family hands. Under the agreement, the four Sulzberger "children" — Marian, Ruth, Judy, and Punch — and their thirteen children pledged never to sell the critical voting Class B shares of company stock outside the family. Any member who wanted to redeem his or her Class B stock for cash had to offer it to the family or to The New York Times Company first. Before the stock could be sold to any outsider, it had to be converted into ordinary Class A stock. The covenant bound them to these terms until twenty-one years after the death of the longest-lived descendant of Iphigene who was alive at the time the agreement was executed.

The agreement was remarkable for a couple of reasons. First, it assured that the family would control *The New York Times* for roughly another century. But by signing it, the Sulzbergers forfeited their chance to make a killing by selling the prized Class B shares on the open market, a transaction that could have reaped hundreds of millions for each of the four branches of the family because of the high premium placed on stock that represents control of a company. When Ted Wagner, the trust and estate lawyer hired to draw up the document, told Punch and his sisters that the hypothetical windfall from selling the Class B stock could be a billion dollars or more, they weren't the least bit tempted to preserve their option to do so. "They felt if this [covenant] was going to insure peace in the future, then that's what they wanted," said Wagner.

The second unusual thing about the accord was the unanimity of family support for it. In early discussions of the agreement, Carol, Punch's wife, had asked whether there wasn't some way to maintain unencumbered control of the Class B shares without endangering family ownership, but when she was told that was impossible, she accepted the fact without argument. All thirteen cousins, even those most distant in the family orbit, signed the document willingly.

There were two reasons why Punch and his sisters felt a special urgency to take such precautions: takeovers and taxes. During the rapacious 1980s they had watched in alarm as corporate raiders gobbled up company after company, only to squeeze them for profits, lay off employees, and shed subsidiaries. At the same time, greenmail experts had made a fine art of amassing sizable quantities of a company's stock and then forcing its frightened management to pay high prices to buy back its own shares.

In 1980 the *Times* had had its own greenmail scare when Saul Steinberg, head of the Reliance Group Holdings, a Philadelphia-based insurance conglomerate, had bought up a large percentage of *The New York Times'* publicly traded Class A stock — shares that elect only a minority of the board. Whether his intention was to secure a seat as a director or simply to make money, Steinberg's actions had unsettled many at the *Times.* The unconventional financier, who had a history of targeting media companies, had earlier made hostile advances on the *Philadelphia Bulletin* and had bought up large stakes in Knight Ridder and Gannett, major newspaper chains.

Punch was sanguine about takeover; he knew there was "no way in God's green acres that [Steinberg] could do anything" because the family owned almost all of the Class B shares, which elected a majority of the board, and those shares were already in trust. But it was clear that part of Steinberg's strategy was to flush out any disgruntled family members who might want to challenge the status quo. When Steinberg's purchases hit 5 percent, Punch had been sufficiently concerned about his intentions to invite him to lunch with the aim of extracting a standstill agreement not to buy any more stock. On the appointed day Steinberg had arrived in the publisher's dining room with Henry Silverman, who ran the leveraged buyout fund at Reliance. The two men had arranged themselves around the table with Punch, Mattson, Gruson, and *Times* attorney Mike Ryan.

Ryan had carefully educated himself about Steinberg's colorful history and outsize ego, so that by the time of their meeting, he was lying in wait like an Irish boxer, eager to jab this cocky interloper and make him realize that "we were not a sleepy management; there was no fuckin' way he was going to get anything out of us." When the conversation turned combative, the excitable Ryan had blurted out, "Now, listen, Mr. Silverberg . . ." Steinberg, who by then had downed several vodkas, was sputteringly furious. Nevertheless, he stayed for the remainder of the meeting, then defiantly purchased another 350,000 shares of *Times* stock at the highest price it had been all year, increasing his holdings to 5.2 percent. His plan, he told the media, was to acquire 25 to 30 percent of *New York Times* equity.

In the legal back-and-forth that followed, Punch played the role of hard-nosed peacemaker. During a private one-on-one lunch, he convinced Steinberg to sell all his stock at the prevailing market price — a figure that resulted in a $300,000 profit to the financier. Punch had never raised his voice — he had been a gentleman throughout — but made it clear that the *Times* was not about to pay a penny in greenmail, nor was it realistic for Steinberg to think he could ever crack the solid family front. The 1986 covenant was intended to make sure that family control could be maintained, even if there was a feud at some future date.

But there was another threat to family control: inheritance taxes. Whereas Punch and his sisters would inherit their stock without tax, future generations would have to address this potentially mammoth problem. The solution was to recapitalize the company at the same time the covenant was signed, exchanging every Class B share for one new Class B share and nine Class A shares. Control of the company would reside with the new Class B shares, and the new Class A shares could be sold on the open market, when the time came, to settle inheritance taxes. In theory, there would be enough Class A shares to pay taxes for several generations.

The Sulzbergers' consensus not to sell their voting stock outside the family came just six months after the Binghams, the family that owned the Louisville *Courier-Journal* and *Times,* had imploded in a fiery feud over money and power and put their distinguished papers on the auction block. The lessons of the Bingham tragedy were certainly not lost on Punch, who had been at an out-of-town press meeting soon after the family announced it was putting an end to its sixty-eight-year-old dynasty because of divergent interests in the third generation. As the media executives buzzed about the Binghams, Punch had risen from his chair and headed toward the hall in search of a bathroom. "Where are you going?" a colleague had inquired. "To send flowers to my sisters," Punch replied with a wink.

Why the Binghams disintegrated and the Sulzbergers stayed together had a lot to do with the character of the two families. "The Binghams saw themselves as a fairy king, queen, prince, and princesses," said a journalist who knew both clans. "I don't believe that the Sulzbergers have ever seen themselves that way." Mary and Barry Bingham Sr., the family matriarch and patriarch, were dazzlingly attractive, educated at Radcliffe and Harvard, respectively, and, on Barry's side, descended from a former ambassador to Great Britain. While both families embraced an admirable ethic of noblesse oblige, their sense of obligation was different. The Binghams exuded an aura of superiority and did good works because Kentucky's most prominent newspaper belonged to them; in the case of the Sulzbergers, the family belonged to the newspaper, and its members felt they had to prove themselves worthy of the association.

That the Binghams were high WASP — Episcopalians, in fact — and the Sulzbergers were Jews also affected their behavior. When Barry Bingham Sr. died two years after the sale of *The Courier-Journal* to Gannett, a reading at his funeral from the eighth chapter of Romans summed up his conviction that he and his family were members of "God's elect." As Reform Jews, the Sulzbergers took a view more in harmony with Iphigene's favorite quotation from the book of Micah: "What doth the Lord require of thee, but to do justly, and to love mercy, and to walk humbly with thy God." Humility, modesty, staying in the background: these had been virtues of the family since the days of Adolph Ochs, who had made them his own, in part out of fear of mingling with better-educated Gentiles and in part out of fear of encouraging the stereotype of Jews as loud, grasping, and self-promoting.

The Sulzbergers also had the supreme good fortune to have Iphigene as the common figure binding together all generations of the family. She was a direct link to Adolph Ochs and had lived long enough to transmit to each of her thirteen grandchildren his core values — duty, unity, and the central importance of nurturing *The New York Times*. "There was a clear moral vision, and you knew it when you were around her," said Cathy Sulzberger. "That was her force field." Though Arthur Jr. would joke that they had all grown up with tape recorders under their pillows chanting, "You are one with the paper, you are one with the *Times*," it was true that Iphigene had somehow managed to convey to them all the conviction that the family and the newspaper were a seamless entity.

While the Binghams had lived well, though never ostentatiously, it was money and a deep-seated distrust of each other that had ultimately divided them, as it did so often in family businesses. The Sulzbergers, despite Hillandale and hovering servants, had been taught from birth never to think of themselves as rich or powerful. They had a finely tuned sense of what constituted "enough," a sense rare even among the most affluent Americans in the late twentieth century. "We were all trained that the money that was made went back into the pot to make the *Times* that much better," said Marian. Iphigene was well into her nineties before she realized that she was a fabulously wealthy woman. In 1988 her name appeared at number 273 on *Forbes'* list of the four hundred richest people in America. The magazine estimated her worth at $225 million; her income from the Ochs Trust alone was close to $10 million a year. Iphigene was so shocked that she called Andrew Heiskell and asked him how *Forbes* could possibly have arrived at such an astronomical figure. Only after this revelation did Iphigene feel comfortable enough to contribute significantly to charity. "She had been making millions, but she had a very old-fashioned view of money," said Punch. "A hundred dollars used to be a hell of a lot of money to her."

Because of his mother's critical role as the voice of moral authority in the family, Punch wanted to execute the 1986 covenant while she was alive. But he needn't have worried. Iphigene did not have to persuade her grandchildren that the pact was advisable; she had already taught them too well for that. When it came time to sign, they stood together as a unit, arms linked as a family as well as the faithful custodians of a great institution. The lessons she had imparted were like the expression of an ancient oral tradition, parables told with the promise of being carried on far into the future, just as would the family's ownership of *The New York Times,* which was now ensured by the bonds of the covenant. The grandchildren were her disciples who would carry on her mission long after she was gone — an inevitability that everyone dreaded. "Keep her going," Joe Perpich, Cathy Sulzberger's husband, wrote in his diary, almost as a prayer, after a particularly memorable weekend at Hillandale. "Keep her going."

40

A Thousand Years

AS A CHILD, PUNCH HAD BEEN A NATURAL LONER, cultivating one friend rather than many. His role as head of *The New York Times* had forced him to mingle more widely, and although he had managed to project warmth and social ease, his amiability always had the slightly stiff quality of having been studied, a trait that *Times* columnist Russell Baker described as "learned friendliness." He liked the easy fellowship of office parties and the formulaic safety of jokes. Guests in his home were sweetly shocked to find the mighty publisher of *The New York Times* taking their drink orders and mixing and serving the concoctions himself.

But even his most intimate friends got only so far with Punch before they hit an impenetrable interior wall. "He makes sure you don't come that one last step," said one associate. "He wants that separation, and those who thought they breached it find out to their great discomfort that they haven't." Some conjectured that Punch sought detachment in order to buffer himself from the pain of having to make necessary and difficult decisions affecting those he cared about. And the problem was very real: almost all of Punch's best friends were people at *The New York Times* whose careers depended on his goodwill. He and Carol spent most Sunday nights at regular haunts like "21" with executive editor Abe Rosenthal, deputy managing editor Arthur Gelb, assistant managing editor James Greenfield, and their wives. The Grusons were frequent guests at Rock Hill and family celebrations. Almost all the Sulzbergers' overseas trips were taken with people from the newspaper as well.

In 1986 Abe Rosenthal and Sydney Gruson would discover that their friendship, though important to Punch in a personal sense, was immaterial when weighed against what he perceived to be the greater good of *The New York Times*. "People who think they know him would be shocked if you used the word *ruthless* [to describe him]," said *Times* attorney Mike Ryan. "But he is a tough son of a bitch."

Punch was grateful for the transformation Rosenthal had brought about at the *Times*. As managing editor and then executive editor, he had united the daily and Sunday papers, brought the formerly freestanding Washington bureau into the fold, and maintained the news report at the highest level while helping to create the revenue-enhancing four-part paper and daily sections. His news instincts were superb, and although his tilt to the right disturbed Punch, it was not because he didn't usually agree with him but because he disliked the notion of any editor's referring to his own reporters as "left wingers" and "Commies," as Rosenthal occasionally did. At the same time, Punch valued his efforts to keep the paper "straight." "I'm a good editor," Rosenthal told *The Washington Post* with characteristic brazenness. "It's silly not to recognize that."

With his love of order, Punch also valued smooth transitions, and in this area Rosenthal had deeply disappointed him. As he approached the *Times*' mandatory retirement age of sixty-five, Rosenthal gave every indication that he would not go willingly, nor would he seriously consider grooming a successor. Some on the staff speculated that his aim was to be editor for life, like William Shawn of *The New Yorker*. In his own mind, he was indispensable and irreplaceable. "There was a kind of a permanent transubstantiation going on," said a *Times* bureau chief who knew him well. "He so personified the *Times* in his mind, he was its body and blood. It wasn't healthy."

That psychological phenomenon was not unusual at *The New York Times*, although Rosenthal was perhaps its most extreme example. For many, working for *The New York Times* was both a mission and a substitute family. Those who retired or left for other jobs made regular pilgrimages to West Forty-third Street to visit old friends, catch up on the gossip, and reconnect, if only for a moment, with something larger than themselves. In this respect, those who worked for the Sulzbergers worshiped in the same pew as the family. "I have the *Times*, that's my religion, that's what I believe in," Arthur Jr. once said, voicing a sentiment shared by many at the paper. When Punch's secretary, Nancy Finn, told her boss that he should build a nursing home for former *Times* employees so they could all be together, she was only half joking. "The *Times* is a haven for them; they just never want to leave," she said.

Punch certainly understood Rosenthal's disinclination to retire, but he also knew that, like it or not, Rosenthal was going to have to address the question of who would succeed him. Punch made his requirements clear: he wanted as executive editor someone he knew well and felt comfortable with, and he expected Rosenthal to help him identify candidates who fulfilled those conditions. Going outside the *Times* for so prominent a position was virtually unthinkable. The newspaper was a hothouse; only editors raised within the safety of its walls understood "the *Times*' way of doing things."

With a stubbornness that bordered on delusion, Rosenthal refused to recognize the reality of his situation. "Everybody who had a brain knew that Punch was the boss, [but] Abe let himself believe he was going to choose his [own] successor," said Al Siegal, one of Rosenthal's top editors. "And then he went through this imbecilic charade. . . . It was a strange interregnum." The "charade" referred to the stream of candidates Rosenthal paraded before Punch between 1983 and 1985, each of whom became the executive editor's momentary darling until the individual exhibited a fatal flaw or until Rosenthal lost interest. None of the men were people Punch knew well or came to know while Rosenthal was supposedly trying them out. As time went on, Punch could not help but conclude that Rosenthal, while appearing to honor his wishes, was in fact scuttling any attempt to find a replacement, hoping that Punch would come to his senses and keep him on as executive editor.

Rosenthal's intransigence was just one aspect of what many at the paper came to call, in retrospect, "Abe's crazy period." The *Times*' executive editor would burst into tears for no apparent reason. For long periods he simply disappeared from the office, leaving no word of his whereabouts or when he would be back. "He didn't have a nervous breakdown, but he was close to it," said Punch. "He would get so distraught that he couldn't operate well. It was a hell of a problem." The prospect of retirement — synonymous in Rosenthal's mind with his life's coming to an end — contributed to his erratic behavior, but there was also another factor: his failing marriage.

Rosenthal had married Ann Marie Burke, a Catholic girl then working at the *Times*, in 1949. As he had traveled from bureau to bureau in India, Poland, and Japan, she had dutifully followed, making a home for him and their three sons. "She kept scrapbooks of his clippings," said a *Times* staffer who knew the family. "She was like a fan." In the mid-1960s, shortly after Rosenthal returned to the States as metropolitan editor and began his meteoric rise at the *Times,* he started an affair with Katharine Balfour, an auburn-haired actress and divorcée who had created the role of Alma in Tennessee Williams's *Summer and Smoke.* Their frequently turbulent relationship would persist for the next twenty years.

In the early 1980s Rosenthal began the process of extricating himself from Balfour and moving out of the Central Park West penthouse he had shared with Ann and into a small rented apartment. By then Ann required a walker and sometimes a wheelchair to cope with the rheumatoid arthritis she had suffered for the past several decades. Under normal circumstances, Rosenthal was an emotional man; the strain of the separation drove him practically out of his mind. "You don't leave a woman you've been married to who is also partly crippled without being devastated by it," said a *Times* editor who was there at the time. "Yet he knew he had to have a new life." While Rosenthal reeled, managing editor Seymour Topping calmly decided what should appear on page one, dealt with news crises as they occurred, and basically ran the paper.

Punch, alarmed at Rosenthal's state, tried talking to him as a friend, reminding him that he wasn't the only man who had ever gone through a divorce, but it did no good. In addition, the mistrustful atmosphere Rosenthal had created made almost everyone but Topping and deputy managing editor Arthur Gelb fearful of making decisions. People began comparing Rosenthal to King Lear, and stagnation set in. "The staff had run down; the paper was all introverted and talking about itself and succession, not about the world," said Joe Lelyveld, who observed the turmoil from London.

To make matters worse, as Rosenthal was in the process of severing his ties to Balfour, he took up with a young *Times* secretary. Sunny and cheerful, the woman was hardly the striking beauty Balfour had been, but she gave Rosenthal support and maternal warmth. After he promoted her to an executive position, *Times* staff members tiptoed around her, fearful she would bad-mouth them to the boss. Punch knew nothing of the affair until a female staffer urged him to take action because she felt the relationship was damaging newsroom morale. "I don't know whether it was the shock of the divorce or what, but it was so obviously out in the open," said one of the paper's top editors.

Punch told Rosenthal the affair had to end, and for a while it apparently did. Then one weekend Rosenthal was seen buying shirts with the woman in a downtown shop. Again, Punch implored his executive editor to cut off the relationship, but although Rosenthal made an effort to comply, he didn't seem to be able to break the tie. The romance got to be "so embarrassing," said Dave Jones, a *Times* editor, "that Arthur Gelb finally screwed up his courage to tell Abe that it had [to stop]." Punch found the situation enormously frustrating. "He probably let [Abe's affair] go on too long," said an intimate, "but he wanted him to be able to get out gracefully."

As 1985 wound down, Punch's closest advisers pressed him to remove Rosenthal as soon as possible, even though he wouldn't turn sixty-five until the spring of 1987. As despondent as Punch was about the fruitless rotation of supposed candidates, it was his editor's affair at the *Times* that finally made him realize something had to be done.

Although he had been sincere in his desire for Rosenthal to orchestrate the search for his successor, Punch had had his own candidate all along: Max Frankel, whose handling of the Sunday sections and the editorial page he admired and with whom he felt a degree of personal comfort. Expelled from Germany a few days before Kristallnacht, Frankel had grown up in the Washington Heights section of New York City, home to so many German Jewish refugees that it was sometimes referred to as the Fourth Reich. Determined to learn English, lose his accent, and fit in with American society, he had worked hard in school, been accepted at Columbia University, and eventually risen to become editor of the *Spectator,* the student newspaper. After graduation in 1952 he joined *The New York Times* and, despite tempting offers over the years from the *Herald Tribune* and *The Reporter* magazine, never left. Though not as intuitive as Rosenthal, Frankel possessed a rare intellect and a steady temperament that Punch hoped would restore morale in what was by then a traumatized newsroom. He was also confident that Frankel wanted the job; that fall Frankel had taken the bold step of asking the publisher out to lunch and deftly informing him that he was available.

Despite his certainty that Frankel should be the next executive editor, Punch had actually indicated very little before offering him the job in the summer of 1986. The more daunting task was informing Rosenthal. After twenty-three years in the publisher's chair, Punch had developed a technique to cope with the pain of removing people: he would rehearse what he wanted to say with Gruson or some other close adviser, worry and sweat for several days, and finally screw up his courage and tell the person in question. Then, he said, "I would blank it all out."

To blunt the blow, Punch offered to make Rosenthal associate editor reporting to the publisher and gave him a twice-weekly column on the Op-Ed page. "There weren't any recriminations, there weren't any tears," Punch said. "I think he was so relieved that I wasn't cutting him off completely." Since the actual switch wouldn't happen until the fall, both Rosenthal and Frankel were sworn to silence, but, as was typical of the *Times,* word leaked out almost immediately.

In mid-October a story appeared in *The New York Times* announcing that Abe Rosenthal was stepping down as executive editor to make way for his successor, Max Frankel. "I read with great regret that you have decided you have reached the age to retire as Executive Editor of *The New York Times,*" Iphigene wrote Rosenthal sympathetically, never betraying the fact that Punch had advised her months before of the coming transition, as he had members of the *Times'* board of directors. On the eve of the announcement, Frankel composed a graceful handwritten letter to his former rival. "It's Friday evening and our world's about to turn and I wish at that precise moment we could properly touch, even kiss," he said, adding that he felt "oh so proud to take the chair that you have raised so high."

Within a week Rosenthal began revamping a large office on the tenth floor in preparation for his life as a columnist. As a foreign correspondent, Rosenthal had earned a reputation as a perceptive reporter and elegant writer, but even Punch had to admit that his column, "On My Mind," got off to a bumpy start with sentences rambling and thoughts drifting off, unfinished. John Oakes, predictably, found him to be "an absolute hysteric" because of his conservative views. But soon, Rosenthal won an ardent following because of his support of human rights.

By the time of his departure from the post of executive editor, Rosenthal had met the woman who would become his second wife: Shirley Lord, a thrice-married British-born author and senior editor at *Vogue* magazine. With Shirley as his guide, the notoriously unkempt Rosenthal began to sport expensively tailored suits, trendy suspenders, and well-groomed hair. Shirley was independent, socially well connected, and proud of her ample décolletage, in contrast to the sweet and mild Ann. "He's out ten nights a week," said Carol Sulzberger. "He has a whole new group of friends; some are jet-setters and some are powerful people.

He's very happy." With a remarriage, a column, and a newfound place among New York's social elite, Rosenthal's "crazy period" gradually came to an end.

As the drama of Rosenthal's exit unfolded, his allies came to view Sydney Gruson as a Iago figure, pouring poison in Punch's ear about Rosenthal and lobbying for Frankel as his replacement. But whatever satisfaction Gruson might have taken in Rosenthal's ouster was short-lived; a month after Punch named Frankel executive editor, he asked Gruson to relinquish his job as assistant to the publisher, give up the board seat he had occupied as vice chairman, and retire.

The request was eminently reasonable: Gruson was about to turn seventy, and keeping him on past the mandatory retirement age for *Times* directors would have set a bad precedent — albeit one that did not apply to Punch's sisters. But after forty-three years at the *Times* and decades of close friendship with the publisher, Gruson was so wounded by the coldness of Punch's action that he wouldn't permit him to host his seventieth birthday celebration. Instead, Gruson threw himself a small party, fled to London immediately following the board meeting at which he resigned, and spent most of the month of January 1987 in Barbados. In February he started a new job as senior adviser at the investment firm of Rothschild Inc., which had hired him to help develop clients in the communications industry.

Although the two men would remain good friends, the experience left Gruson with frayed feelings about Punch even years later. "People are close to Punch, [but] Punch doesn't feel very close to anybody," Gruson said. "He was smart enough at some point in his life to realize that people foam around the publisher of *The New York Times,* and if you're not careful, they're all biting at you or sucking at you or licking at you. It suited Punch's character and personality to remain this rigid person unto himself and never to let very much of himself out to anybody."

§

At the height of the Reagan administration, Punch was invited to a private lunch at the White House. As he made small talk with the president, he noticed with surprise a linen-draped table set for four in one corner of the Oval Office. A few minutes later the other guests drifted in: Vice President George Bush and Secretary of State George Shultz. "I had such a stiff back when I finished that lunch," Punch recalled later. "I had never sat up so straight in my life." After the meal Punch hurried back to the *Times'* Washington bureau several blocks away, got on the phone, and called his mother. "Mom, guess who I had lunch with?" he said with evident pride. Iphigene listened politely. "Oh, Punch, that's wonderful!" she exclaimed and then, with the skilled timing of a comedienne, paused for a moment before asking what, to her, was the obvious question: "What did they want, son?"

Punch understood his mother's point perfectly. The power of *The New York Times* that he, Punch Sulzberger, represented, was akin to, and certainly more long-lived, than that held by these men. In 1976, when *U.S. News & World Report* had published a cover story on the nation's top thirty leaders, headlined WHO RUNS AMERICA? President Gerald Ford had come in first, Punch at number thirteen. When the survey was repeated in 1982, Punch was still ranked thirteen, but everyone above him had changed. If the survey had been conducted when Adolph, Arthur, or Orvil had been publisher, the results would have been much the same. Presidents had their moment on the national and world stage, but *The New York Times* remained a constant, a power unto itself, year after year, decade after decade.

Punch was as conscious of this fact as his grandfather had been nearly a century earlier. "When you're before him, you know you're before the institution," said company executive John O'Brien. "Punch *is The New York Times.*" He never involved himself directly in stories and only rarely in editorials. When he read a news article that displeased him, he complained to the top editor and to him alone, never to the individual reporter. It was his way of keeping the publisher's authority in reserve, like a vast untapped store of gold bullion. Some at the *Times* likened him to the Wizard of Oz — a figure who was largely unseen and whose perceived power was all the more magnified for it. "A little mystery in the process probably doesn't hurt at all," Punch said.

By the mid-1980s Punch was finally comfortable in his job, a job that in many ways had been forced upon him by circumstance rather than as a natural outgrowth of his abilities or desires. At first, he had found it overwhelming to grapple with the business problems he had inherited, yet he had confronted them and ultimately surmounted them with a degree of success his father never had. Now, in his sixties, he began to relax. He fished in the Alaska wilderness with Mstislav Rostropovich, renowned cellist and music director of the National Symphony Orchestra, and joined in silly skits at the Bohemian Grove, the secret all-male enclave north of San Francisco where Henry Kissinger, Thomas J. Watson Jr., and other power brokers listened to lectures, drank, and relieved themselves on tree trunks. He was elected chairman of the Metropolitan Museum of Art, a prestigious position that consumed a large portion of his work week and made him, and Carol, omnipresent figures on the social circuit. He began to complain that his life consisted of either handing out awards or receiving them. "The only time I feel like a newspaperman is when I write letters to the editor," he told a friend. But his cavils were ironic, for in truth he enjoyed the accolades that had begun to come his way and even felt, with appropriate modesty, that he deserved them.

One indication of Punch's new equilibrium was the parallel life he had created for himself in London. He had come to feel so much at home there that he bought an apartment in fashionable Mayfair, where he stayed for long stretches two or three times a year. Carol had initially opposed the purchase; she preferred their usual suite at Claridge's, where the staff fussed over her like a queen. Punch, however, found the hotel too stuffy and formal, and longed for a cozy retreat where he could putter in the kitchen, curl up in the den, watch videos, and relax.

Eventually Carol came to love the flat, located at 51 Mount Street, as much as Punch did. Their trips to London were a time apart, interludes when, despite the bickering that had come to characterize their relationship, they managed to recapture the ease of their early years together. Punch and Carol's overseas routine had none of the demands that burdened them in New York. Nearly every day Carol would go shopping with Darcy Cohen, an old school friend who was married to a London-based South African lawyer, while Punch visited galleries and museums, dropped in at the bureau, or bought jackets and trousers at Burberrys and handmade shirts at Turnbull & Asser. In the evenings the Sulzbergers rarely went to the theater; but when they did, the show was usually a musical. "I hate anything with a message," Punch once told a London colleague.

Carol took it as one of her more welcome duties to oversee the decorating of the *Times*-owned apartment on Eaton Place that served as the residence of the chief of the London bureau. Her taste ran to English and American antiques, making the flat too expensive and formal to live in comfortably if one had small children. Family photos and personal art were allowed — as long as they fit in the frames she had selected and placed on the wall. When Joe Lelyveld, the first inhabitant, wanted a desk, he located a handsome reproduction and called Punch to authorize the purchase. There was an awkward pause on the line. "Joe, please, no reproductions," said Punch.

Andrew Lloyd Webber and other well-known names invited Punch and Carol to spend weekends at their country homes, but, as in the States, the Sulzbergers preferred the company of a small coterie of friends: Lord Lew Grade, a film producer and director of Euro Disney, and his wife, Kathy; Charles H. Price II, Reagan's ambassador to Great Britain, and his wife, Carol; Crown Prince Alexander of Yugoslavia and Princess Katherine, known as Clairy; Lord Rothermere, the last of the old hereditary British press barons; and the procession of carefully selected men who headed the *Times'* London bureau. "The conversation was stunningly superficial," said a guest at several such dinners. "They didn't talk about politics; they didn't talk about culture."

Punch's taste for comfort was equally apparent in his choice of food. He favored the plain fare of pubs, where he could mingle with ordinary people who had no idea who he was. "Punch has the taste of a true WASP," said R. W. "Johnny" Apple Jr., a former London bureau chief and renowned gourmand, laughing. "I'd take him to a good French restaurant and he'd say, 'I don't know why you like all this stuff with gravy on it.'" Carol, on the other hand, preferred the fawning service of private clubs such as Mosimann's or Harry's Bar, a staggeringly expensive restaurant a block from the Sulzbergers' apartment. In these exclusive venues, Carol was transported back to the cosseted milieu of her girlhood, where money guaranteed respect and she was not made to feel the irksome guilt about wealth that upper-class Europeans found so peculiar in Americans. At the same time, she was reasonably assured of running into Estée Lauder, Joan Collins, Ivana Trump, and other celebrity acquaintances from New York. "It was extraordinary," said Marion Underhill, manager of the *Times'* London bureau. "Carol seemed to know everybody."

Inspired by a Thanksgiving dinner to which Johnny Apple and his wife, Betsey, had once invited them in London, Punch and Carol began hosting their own Anglo-American holiday meal each year, and it quickly became a prized invitation for the eighty-odd guests lucky enough to attend. Though mainly American, the list included a sprinkling of international notables such as British commentator David Frost, King

Constantine II of Greece, and Lucia Flecha de Lima, wife of the Brazilian ambassador to the United States and Princess Diana's great confidante. Once or twice, Punch's closest friends from the *Times* — the Gelbs, the Grusons, the Greenfields — flew over specially for the occasion.

The routine was always the same. At 8:00 P.M. on Thanksgiving, the Sulzbergers' guests arrived at Claridge's to find a private banquet room with round tables, dramatic floral arrangements, formal place cards, and foil-wrapped chocolate turkeys that Punch brought over himself on the Concorde. After everyone was seated, Punch made a few remarks, always ending with a toast to the queen and to the American president before the platters of turkey and dressing, mashed potatoes, gravy, and cranberry sauce were served. At the conclusion of the meal, Punch invariably lit up a Montecristo #3, his favorite cigar and a brand illegal in the States because of the American embargo on Cuban goods. He would have liked to smuggle a box or two back to New York, but as publisher of *The New York Times*, he felt that he had to uphold the law. "He couldn't afford to do it, in his position," explained Lord Lew Grade.

§

Iphigene was remarkably hale for a ninety-two-year-old woman, yet it was apparent to anyone who cared to notice that her activities had gradually become circumscribed by the vicissitudes of age. She was too hard of hearing to enjoy large parties because of the distraction of background noise, preferring small gatherings where she could face people and read their lips and body language. Her phone was equipped with a hearing booster, and in recent years she had had a cataract operation and a pacemaker installed. She cheerfully insisted that she enjoyed being a white-haired matriarch and even proudly displayed a pillow embroidered with AGE ONLY MATTERS IF YOU ARE WINE, but there was no question that the indignities of senescence bothered her. "It's very annoying that when you're older and can walk across a room and finish a sentence, people think you are a phenomenon," she complained. Despite these difficulties, Iphigene resolutely maintained her routines of phone calls, letters, walks, and dressing for dinner. She had a list of regulars whom she invited to 1115 Fifth Avenue and Hillandale, where she always served the same drinks and same hors d'oeuvres and seated her guests at the same places around the table.

Most of the time, however, Iphigene ate her meals alone, a book by her plate, and visited the private quarters of her butler and cook, just to talk. Once while puttering around Hillandale's front yard, she confessed to Gino Rossi, the gardener, that she didn't care about life anymore. She was old and lonely; most of her friends were gone; her existence was boring. "But everybody needs you," Rossi insisted. "We all need you." Iphigene shrugged. She rarely indulged in self-pity, but during the long Hillandale winters, when her family was largely absent, she couldn't help feeling despondent.

The exception was Christmas, when the extended Sulzberger clan gathered at Hillandale and Rock Hill. At dusk on Christmas Eve, every-one sat around the brightly lit tree, with the stockings Carol had needle-pointed hanging from the fireplace, and prepared to indulge in a Christmas tradition Cynthia and Joe Perpich, Cathy's husband, had started: watching the classic 1947 film *The Bishop's Wife*.

Despite her advanced age, Iphigene still hosted Christmas Day lunch for the family and a variety of "strays," making sure there was a gift under the tree for each guest. When the buffet of turkey, meats, salads, and veg-etables was ready, people heaped their plates and found seats at the tables set up specially in Hillandale's broad hall and bay-windowed dining room. Afterward, if there was snow, the great-grandchildren would go sledding on the steep slopes leading to the lake. "You become overcome with hap-piness that you are with your family and you are all having such a won-derful time together," Sarah Perpich, Cathy and Joe's daughter, later wrote in a fond Christmas reminiscence that spoke for everyone.

In the spring of 1987 Susan Dryfoos was visiting her grandmother when Iphigene complained of an irregular heartbeat. Susan rushed her to the hospital, called as many relatives as she could track down, and prepared for what she feared would be a death watch. By the time Judy Sulzberger arrived at the intensive care unit, Iphigene was sitting up, nibbling toast, and able to talk. In keeping with her grandmother's desire not to use extreme measures to save her, Susan had permitted the doctors only to administer digitalis, a drug that controls heart rate. That, apparently, had stopped the arrhythmia.

A few days later Iphigene went into the bathroom at 1115 Fifth Avenue and came out confused and talking gibberish. She asked for her dead husband and didn't recognize members of her family. "I think she must have had a clot during that period when she was fibrillating [in the hospital], and it went to her brain," said Judy. The stroke didn't paralyze her, but it severely impaired her speech. After watching Arthur shuttle in and out of hospitals over the last ten years of his life, Iphigene was determined to die at home, and was restless and fretful until she was able to make it clear that she wanted to go to Hillandale. When she arrived there the next day, the family prepared for what promised to be a long, slow recovery. "Her memory came back little by little, so eventually she did know who we were," said Judy. "But she never got back to the way she was."

Iphigene's stroke hit Punch particularly hard, for he was suddenly faced with the reality that the burden of leading *The New York Times,* and the burden of leading the family, would soon be on his shoulders alone. His face looked clouded and haggard; he appeared physically to shrink. His neck became so stiff that he had to swivel his entire body around in order to see people.

When Arthur Jr. and Dan drove up to Hillandale to visit their grandmother, they found her in her bedroom, lying on a chaise longue, unable to speak. Iphigene had never allowed her grandchildren very deeply below the surface of her own emotional life. She had questioned them and prodded them and taught them and, somehow, had communicated the depth of her love while keeping every conversation at a safe distance from the sanctum in which her most intimate self was protectively sealed. Now she was mute and powerless, and for once, the younger Sulzbergers were in control. "She had lots of walls up, and we just assumed those walls were down," said Arthur Jr. "She couldn't stop us, she wasn't in a position to stop us, so we just talked to her about our feelings about her. It was a very personal conversation, as open as I guess you could get." Before they left, they wept a little. Iphigene stared back at them impassively, apparently comprehending nothing.

Soon afterward Jace Cohen left his home in Maine and came to see Iphigene. He found her as his cousins had: tuned out to her surroundings and unable to recognize him. Desperate to find a way to engage her, Jace picked up a book, sat next to her, and flipped through its pages, exclaiming over each picture as if he were reading to a child. But Iphigene ignored him. "A thousand years," she muttered. "A thousand years." "Granny, that's a millennium, isn't it?" Jace replied, hoping to find a toehold in her befuddled mind.

Jace had no way of knowing it, but Iphigene had heard a similar phrase many times before. During her trip to China in 1973, she had been honored with the salutation "ten thousand years." The blessing — *wan sui* in Chinese — is reserved for the oldest and most respected personages. On Mao Tse-tung's birthday, peasants would hail him with the greeting, which was a shortened form of "may you live ten thousand years." The blessing implied an authority and a virtue; it meant that such a person *deserved* to live ten thousand years. Iphigene had heard the words in English often when her Chinese hosts had bid her farewell; it was their way of showing respect. So why did she repeat a variation of the phrase now? Audrey Topping, who had grown up in China and served as Iphigene's traveling companion there, thought she knew: "It might have come into her mind then because she was leaving, you see."

41

A Time of Testing

I N THE FALL OF 1985, WALTER MATTSON AND Arthur Jr. lunched at one of The New York Times Company president's favorite Midtown restaurants — selected because no one else at the paper went there — and afterward walked slowly back to the office. At Mattson's insistence, Arthur Jr. had spent part of the year at the mid-level executive program at Harvard Business School, followed by several months in Sarasota, Florida, developing an expansion plan for the local newspaper, which the *Times* owned. "I wound up spending winter in Boston and summer in Florida," Arthur Jr. recalled with a cringe. "It was terrible." Now Mattson was poised to set yet another task for his charge. "Arthur," Mattson announced in his booming baritone, "it's time for you to move into the production department. *Night* production. Your hours will be seven at night till three in the morning." Arthur Jr. stopped on the sidewalk in the middle of the city bustle. "My kids are still small!" he protested, alluding to five-year-old Arthur and three-year-old Annie. "Those are terrible hours!" For fifteen minutes Arthur Jr. went through every conceivable reason why he could not — should not — be asked to oversee the paper's composing room, printing presses, and trademark white-and-blue delivery trucks. "You're not going to change your mind on this, are you?" he finally asked quietly. "Nope," said Mattson.

In the six years that he had been mapping out Arthur Jr.'s career path, Mattson was acutely aware that his charge's ultimate destination was the publisher's office. For that reason, he believed that Arthur Jr. should also understand what went on in the belly of the ship — how pressmen and drivers lived and worked, how the paper was actually manufactured and delivered each day. "It was essential that people respected him because he had some knowledge of what went on down there," Mattson said, "that he not be looked at as the prissy little boss's son who was suddenly elevated to this great position but as somebody who had earned his spurs."

Once it became clear that Mattson was immovable, Arthur Jr. accepted his lot and soldiered on. As the *Times'* production coordinator, he worked nights for half the week and days the other, a schedule that left him feeling "like a zombie" but gave him a twenty-four-hour, white- and blue-collar immersion in production and distribution procedures. He came to the experience a supporter of unions; he emerged with a conviction that the *Times* had to exert control over its production facilities, for he had seen too many pressmen and typographers sign in, leave without doing any work, and get paid anyway. At the same time, he felt enormous affection for the people in these departments, many of whom had "inherited" their jobs from their grandfathers, uncles, and fathers. It was the only place at the *Times,* he said, where he felt truly comfortable. About a month after he had started, Mattson bumped into Arthur Jr. outside the building. "How's it going?" he inquired. "Jeez, I've learned a lot," Arthur Jr. said. "I never knew you could use *fuck* as an adjective, a verb, and a noun, all in the same sentence."

After Arthur Jr. had been in production for more than a year, Punch summoned his son to his office. Arthur Jr. expected to be told that his next rotation would be in circulation, the only department in which he had not yet worked, but to his astonishment, Punch unveiled a new organizational chart with three coequal squares. In one was Max Frankel, the *Times'* executive editor. In another was Lance Primis, the former advertising chief who had recently been named the paper's executive vice president and general manager. And in the third square was Arthur Jr., who, Punch proudly informed him, was to be given the newly created title of assistant publisher. His father's purpose in moving him to the ranks of senior management, clear though unstated, was to give Arthur Jr. a taste of executive decision making without unsettling his top people. Frankel and Primis would continue to report to Punch and Mattson, respectively, while Arthur Jr. would report to both.

As head of the family as well as of *The New York Times,* Punch knew that advancing his son so far ahead of the other Sulzberger cousins was a potentially explosive act. Before he even mentioned the assistant publisher position to Arthur Jr., he had assured his sisters that he would first do something for their children. Thus, Michael Golden was made senior vice president and general manager of Retail Magazine Marketing Company, a *Times* subsidiary that handled single-copy sales of all the company's magazines, and Stephen Golden was made a director of the

Times' forest products group. Dan Cohen, who had been in circulation since 1984, was slated for a promotion within his department, but before it could even be offered, he learned of Arthur Jr.'s new job. If Arthur Jr. had been surprised by his sudden elevation, Dan was, as he described it, "caught flat-footed." Frustrated by lack of access to the training program that had so clearly been laid out for his cousin, he took matters into his own hands. Against Mattson's advice, he insisted on transferring out of circulation, where he had been doing well, and into advertising. The move — lateral, at best — would prove to be a critical career misstep.

With his boyish face and full head of curly hair, Arthur Jr. looked far younger than his thirty-five years in the photograph that accompanied the *Times'* announcement of his new position in January 1987. Privately he admitted that the job scared him. Soon after Arthur Jr. moved into an office near Lance Primis on the eleventh floor, Mattson tried to prepare him for what was to come. "You're smart, kid," he told him in his characteristic Jimmy Cagney straight-from-the-shoulder manner. "Now you're going to be dealing with people who are just as smart as you are, and that's going to be hard. It's going to demand that you raise your level of play."

Together, Mattson and Punch dreamed up an amorphous entity called the Futures Committee and made Arthur Jr. one of its leaders. With the paper determined to invest up to a billion dollars in new plant and equipment, the committee's ostensible purpose was to resolve technical issues, such as how to add new sections and color to the paper, as well as strategic problems, such as how to attract young readers weaned on MTV. But it was really a vehicle to force Arthur Jr. to confront the competing demands of news and business from a management point of view. Shrewdly, the committee's start-up was timed so that Arthur Jr. began at roughly the same moment that Abe Rosenthal retired on the news side and John Pomfret retired on the business side, opening up the posts of executive editor and general manager to new blood. Frankel, Primis, and Arthur Jr. constituted a fresh, untested triumvirate running the *Times.*

Arthur Jr. became assistant publisher during a period of unbridled optimism at *The New York Times.* Fed by the business boom of the 1980s, advertising — the lifeblood of newspapers — had grown from 104 million lines in 1983 to a record high of more than 123 million lines at the end of 1987. The *Times* was so filled with ads that it was forced to leave some out of the paper and turn down accounts. "You didn't have to be a brilliant salesman, it just poured in," said Bill Pollak, a *Times* advertising executive. "You came to work every day, your phone began ringing, and it didn't stop."

In June 1987, at the peak of the euphoria, The New York Times Company announced that it had purchased the thirty-thousand-circulation *Gwinnett Daily News* in Gwinnett County, Georgia, a rich northern suburb of Atlanta, for the astronomical price of $88.2 million. The following year it would break ground for a $40 million printing plant closer to the city. The *Times*' plan, ambitious and ultimately flawed, was to buy up other papers near Atlanta and expand the *Daily News*' reach, creating a ring around the city that would squeeze circulation from *The Atlanta Journal-Constitution,* which had grown complacent and lackluster under the ownership of the Cox family.*

A month later the *Times* announced an even more ambitious project: the construction of a highly automated color printing and distribution facility in Edison, New Jersey. The anticipated cost — $400 million — was the largest capital investment the company had ever made. The plant, which would occupy the space of twenty football fields, would enable the *Times* to use more color in its advance sections and produce bigger Sunday issues.

The physical embodiment of the company's soaring fortunes was the edition of Sunday, September 13, 1987 — at 1,602 pages, the largest in *Times* history. Then, barely a month later, "we hit the shit," as Arthur Jr. bluntly put it. The Dow Jones industrial average fell 508 points in one dizzying day. Ad sales appeared unaffected at first, causing many at the paper to consider the crash of 1987 a mere bump. In fact, it would take two years for the resulting structural changes in the economy to have their repercussions at West Forty-third Street felt. By the time they did, *The New York Times* had lost 40 percent of its ad linage, and the com-

---

*The *Times*' strategy had the effect of awakening a sleeping giant. *The Atlanta Journal-Constitution* fiercely defended its turf, hiring *New York Times* Washington bureau chief Bill Kovach as its managing editor, along with several of the paper's star reporters, and starting a special Gwinnett County edition. In 1992 the *Times* admitted defeat and closed the *Gwinnett Daily News,* selling its assets to Cox Enterprises, Inc. at a substantial loss.

pany had had its first significant drop in earnings in more than a decade. "Suddenly we were no longer talking about the Grand Plan but how to control the descent," said Arthur Jr.

On the business side, buyouts were offered to reduce payroll costs and budgets were slashed. On the news side, Max Frankel was ordered to find a million dollars in savings. "We started going after every pencil box," he recalled, as he eliminated engagement announcements as well as the stamp, coin, and bridge columns. Although it was never counted on the ledgers, he also pointed out that his reporters, in the name of austerity, continued to live in a "disgraceful slum" — the *Times'* vast newsroom, where mousetraps lay in wait for errant rodents and there was barely enough room to hang a coat or file reporters' notes. When Frankel pleaded with Punch to replace the frayed and stained carpeting, the publisher paid for it with $300,000 from his own budget.

It was a moment that underscored the significance of Sulzberger ownership. All over the nation, newspapers were coping with advertising losses by slashing costs, including news budgets, in order to keep earnings-per-share from collapsing. But at the *Times,* despite a catastrophic advertising loss, the massive news budget increased year after year. To Punch, this made good business sense because the paper's success ultimately depended on its unrivaled reputation for journalistic excellence. He ordered that every other segment of the company endure painful cuts. But not the news department. To borrow a metaphor Abe Rosenthal had used frequently during the downturn of the 1970s, the paper "put more tomatoes in the soup," hiring thirty or forty new reporters. In a direct strike at its competitors in New York, the *Times* added two pages to its sports section, six columns to the daily metro section, and twelve columns on Sunday. "That did not sell one line of advertising, nor did it produce one added reader," said Dave Jones, editor of the *Times'* national edition. "It simply undercut the competition and strengthened our hand to come out of the recession."

The crash occurred roughly a year after Max Frankel had assumed the executive editor's mantle at the *Times.* In contrast to the paranoia of the previous administration, Frankel had tried to create a collegial atmosphere. He sat on people's desks, declared that he wanted "good fun" in the newsroom, and divided Rosenthal's imperial office in half to create a conference room for the staff. When he showed up at a metro reporter's apartment for a beer following a weekend game of touch football, staffers were so stunned that they reflexively stood up as if he were visiting royalty. For gays at the paper, Frankel was a particularly welcome relief. Richard Meislin was in the midst of caring for his lover, a *Times* copyeditor who would soon die of AIDS, when he was named the paper's graphics editor. During the ritual blessing from the executive editor, Frankel, who had recently lost his wife to a brain tumor, talked to Meislin briefly about his new responsibilities and for the next twenty minutes spoke with great tenderness about how difficult it was to watch a loved one die. "Having gone through all those years of Abe Rosenthal, it was just the most amazing thing to sit across from the executive editor of *The New York Times* and listen to him express his total understanding of the situation," Meislin said.

Within the news department, Frankel was under enormous pressure; even with modest budget increases, he still had to juggle priorities and make sacrifices because, with no layoffs, contracted raises more than swallowed the additional money. The strain took its toll, and he became increasingly snappish and abrupt. He had waited his entire professional life to be executive editor of the *Times*. Now that the job was finally his, he had almost no room to maneuver. "Max gets the job in 1986 and then — whoops! — 1987 the lights went out," said Lance Primis. "The idea-generation stopped. We were defending what we had instead of a dozen years of growth."

It was in this downcast atmosphere that in April 1988 Punch promoted Arthur Jr. again — this time to deputy publisher. The title, yet another created specially for him, was a clear signal that, barring a calamitous slipup, he would soon succeed his father as publisher. The assistant publishership had been a drumroll; the deputy publishership was tantamount to a coronation. In his new role, Arthur Jr. was expected to function as a kind of publisher-in-waiting, making the final call on everything but decisions related to the editorial page. For the first time, he said, he felt that the job of publisher was his to lose.

The day the appointment was announced, Arthur Jr. boarded the bus near his Central Park West apartment for his usual ride to Times Square. A fellow passenger recognized him from his picture in that morning's *Times* and, as Arthur Jr. was getting off, touched him lightly on the arm. "We're all counting on you," he said. Arthur Jr. was so flabbergasted that later in the day he repeated the story to Dave Jones. Jones looked at Arthur Jr. with grave seriousness and assured him, "Well, we are."

Arthur Jr.'s position spelled an end to the coequal triumvirate that Punch and Mattson had so carefully engineered sixteen months earlier. Now Frankel reported to Arthur Jr., as did Lance Primis, who kept his title of general manager and, on the same day that Arthur Jr. became deputy publisher, was given the newly created post of president of *The New York Times* newspaper. Mattson had originally fashioned a job description for Arthur Jr. that would have confined him strictly to news matters, leaving the business side as entirely Mattson's domain. But much like his father, who in 1963 had refused to share power with Amory Bradford, Arthur Jr. had declared that he would not accept an empty title. In a one-on-one meeting in the *Times'* fourteenth-floor boardroom, Mattson tried to persuade Punch that if he insisted on placing Arthur Jr. over Primis, Primis might quit, an act that could color Wall Street's view of company management and have a potentially disastrous effect on the value of the stock. In the end, Punch backed his son, and Primis, four years Arthur Jr.'s senior, made no move to leave. Thereafter, Mattson called Arthur Jr. "Deputy Dawg," a nickname that, while always delivered with humor, also contained a drop of acid.

In the decade that Arthur Jr. had been at the *Times,* he had consciously kept his distance from his father, explaining that "the last thing I needed to do was to feed the perception that people could talk to me to get to him." When he became assistant publisher, he reported directly to Punch, which gave them natural reasons to come into contact. Still, they didn't begin to communicate with any ease until Arthur Jr. became deputy publisher.

Father and son shared a strong need for privacy and an air of self-protection. "Somewhere back there [Arthur Jr.] has been hurt and he's developed many, many defenses," said a *Times* executive who knew him well. "Only occasionally do you see a real person." They were also both natively optimistic and rigorously punctual. Every morning at 6:00 A.M. Arthur Jr. worked out with Steve Rattner, his old friend from the Washington bureau who had quit journalism to become an investment banker. If Rattner was as much as one minute late arriving at their Upper West Side gym, Arthur Jr. would begin without him. But that was where the stylistic similarities between father and son ended. For *Times* executives, who only began to focus seriously on Arthur Jr. as Punch's successor when he became deputy publisher, the contrast between the two men was stark.

Punch was like *The New York Times* itself: calm, low-key, deceptively strong. Arthur Jr. considered his father passive, yet *Times* columnist William Safire thought he was the strongest publisher in America, observing, "You don't have to flex your muscles if you've got the muscles." As a matter of course, Punch went to great lengths to avoid confrontation, while his son, the former high school debater, relished being in the middle of the ring. "Arthur Jr.'s participation is not stand back, look, and see," said *Times* attorney Mike Ryan. "He's one of the combatants."

Punch had a reputation as a good listener, a talent that Sydney Gruson found maddening because he tended to parrot the advice of the last person he had heard. Arthur Jr. had the opposite problem. "When you meet with Arthur, you're more likely to do the listening," sighed Howard Bishow, vice president of industrial relations. As a rule, Punch played naive and slightly absentminded, giving everyone the impression that he needed their help to get the job done. Arthur Jr., in contrast, was confident to the point of being overweening, a stance that, given his lack of experience, was a risky strategy. He lacked what is known in Yiddish as *sachel* — common sense, tact, diplomacy. Executive editor Max Frankel sometimes had to hold his tongue when the young deputy publisher made impetuous requests and comments. "I'll say this about Arthur," Frankel quipped privately to intimates. "He'll never make the same mistake three times."

The wisecracking style Arthur Jr. had perfected as an adolescent had changed little during his years at the *Times*. When people first met him, they were taken aback by his aggressive manner and rapid-fire bantering, a mode of social exchange more appropriate for a college sophomore than for a top newspaper executive. "He has a deep strain of insecurity that I'm not convinced is going to change," said a close friend. "That's why he does all that joking-around stuff." If living up to the power that seemed now finally to be within his grasp was intimidating, doing so while looking more like a copyboy than a publisher made it all the more difficult. Even Arthur Jr.'s secretary referred to him as "the kid."

Whereas Punch wore a mask of imperturbable pleasantness, Arthur Jr. found it impossible to hide his feelings. "When Arthur didn't like somebody, oohhh, you knew it," said a close friend. "It was very hard for him to cover it up." Punch's enigmatic demeanor kept him from being pinned down and gave him maneuvering room. Arthur Jr.'s inclination was to be open and direct, even though from the lofty heights of the executive ranks he soon discovered that that was not always the best way to manage.

A pointed difference between father and son was how they chose to handle friendships with people at *The New York Times*. Punch's social life revolved almost entirely around a small group of top aides and editors. If he liked someone on staff, he accepted the friendship on its own terms and didn't torture himself by questioning their motives for courting him. Arthur Jr., however, regarded his father's policy as limiting and potentially divisive. He felt that by surrounding himself with an exclusive coterie, Punch didn't get a broad enough sampling of advice. He also feared that if he were to follow his father's example, he would be accused of cronyism, and he dreaded having to go through the painful process of firing or retiring his friends, as Punch had.

Once Arthur Jr. moved to senior management, he effectively stopped seeing the friends he had made during his ascent at the paper. His rule was so hard-and-fast that he declared he would have severed ties with Steve Rattner — his closest confidant — if Rattner had still worked at the paper. Arthur Jr. claimed that his friends understood his decision, but in fact most of them were deeply hurt. Punch diplomatically made no comment; Carol, who prided herself on her total loyalty to her own friends, thought the idea absurd. "The people I've spoken to in Washington and New York can't understand why this complete cutoff," she said. "I find that a terrible mistake businesswise and I also find that you miss a great deal in your life."

Arthur Jr.'s ban extended to Gail, who at her husband's insistence also stopped seeing their *New York Times* friends socially. The accommodation was the latest in a series of sacrifices Gail had made as her husband climbed closer and closer to the publishership. During the period before their daughter, Annie — born during Gail's year as a Knight-Bagehot Fellow at Columbia University — and "little Arthur" began school, Gail had pursued freelance writing instead of full-time work. But she had quickly discovered that, even as a freelancer, being married to Arthur Ochs Sulzberger Jr. was a professional liability. Employers either fawned over her or overcompensated to prove that they weren't impressed by a famous name. "No matter how good she was, it was just not going to be possible for her to be a business writer in New York City," said her friend

Ann Pelham, who was convinced Gail would have been a star reporter on *The Wall Street Journal* had she not been married to Arthur Jr.

Writing for *The New York Times* proved to be no easier. Other *Times* spouses, such as Barbara Gelb, wife of Arthur Gelb, who had become managing editor, had published freelance articles in the paper long before their husbands held executive positions. But after Edward Klein, the editor of the Sunday magazine, accepted a story proposal Gail had submitted, he treated her as a nepotism case. "Gail was really disgusted," recalled Sunday business editor Soma Golden Behr, who had known Gail at Columbia. "I told her to tell him to go to hell." A few days later Behr and Arthur Jr. were sitting across a conference table at the *Times,* and Behr mentioned that she had advised Gail to tackle Klein. Arthur Jr. stiffened. "She can't do that," he said. "The wife of the deputy publisher can't do that."

Soon Arthur Jr., fearful that Gail's freelance employers might try to exact favorable advertising rates or other quid pro quos from the *Times* when he became publisher, asked her to give up journalism altogether. "She wished he was wrong, but ultimately she came to share Arthur's judgment on the conflicts that would be involved," said a close friend who thought Arthur Jr. had vastly overestimated the ethical dilemmas. Convinced that as a young mother, it wouldn't be possible to work full-time in any case, Gail soon turned to another passion — painting — and gamely put a positive spin on her decision. "Oh, I've *always* wanted to do art," she told acquaintances when they expressed amazement that she was no longer a journalist.

The Sulzberger family, even those in the older generation, had come to accept Gail's efforts to build an identity separate from their sometimes oppressive name. They considered her smart, focused, grounded — a woman with strong convictions and a healthy impatience with inflated egos. In short, they thought she was good for Arthur Jr. "Gail takes no shit from him . . . and she keeps him honest," said his cousin Doug Adler. She didn't hesitate to call down her husband in public when his jokes bordered on the insulting. In private she demanded that he make time for their family and not spend every minute at the office. Their marriage was one of trust, friendship, respect, political sympathy, teamwork. Unlike Punch, who never discussed business with Carol, Arthur Jr. valued Gail's counsel and freely told other executives that he ran many decisions by her.

Still, the relationship seemed emotionally cool. Gail's toughness and unswerving belief in her own vision made her something of an authority figure to Arthur Jr. and reinforced his propensity to be a loner. Like his father, he tended to retreat, hovering slightly out of reach. "I like Gail, but she's not so mothering or nurturing," said Cynthia Sulzberger. "I'm sure they love each other, but to me they have a different kind of relationship." Unlike Punch, who had contentedly spent every weekend at the family compound at Hillandale, Arthur Jr. rented a house in New Paltz, New York, far from the social demands of the Hamptons and other leisure-time venues of the moneyed and the media elite. There, he spent hours in the Shawangunk Mountains by himself or with his son, rock climbing, a sport he loved for its meditative aspects, tactical nature, and the element of fear it involved. "I think he likes the loneliness," observed Toni Goodale, wife of former *Times* executive vice president James Goodale.

Shortly after Arthur Jr. was named deputy publisher, Ruth hosted a Sulzberger family reunion in Chattanooga, during which Gail and Arthur Jr. had a dramatic fight. The day began innocently enough on a gaudy strip of highway dotted by water slides, miniature golf, and hang-gliding towers. When Vicki Dryfoos, Bobby Dryfoos's twenty-one-year-old daughter, spied people bungee jumping off an industrial crane, she challenged Arthur Jr. to join her in trying it.

Arthur Jr. didn't hesitate. Ever since his experience at Outward Bound, he had actively sought ways to prove to himself that he had physical courage. Several years earlier he had gone white-water rafting with Dan Cohen and Steve Rattner, even though racing water terrified him. Gail was livid. The bungee-jumping attraction was a jury-rigged thrill and a thoroughly risky proposition. She tried to talk him out of it, but he insisted on going, which only redoubled her annoyance. Vicki, an experienced parachutist, sailed off the crane with the grace of an Olympic diver. Arthur Jr. looked clumsy by comparison, but his cousins watching below were agreeably impressed. His safe return did nothing to lessen Gail's anger, and she didn't speak to him for several hours.

Gail was not the only one Arthur Jr. had offended. Earlier in the day he had promised Dan that they would bungee jump together. Then, while Dan accompanied his children on the alpine slide, he had impulsively decided to go with Vicki instead. "How could you possibly do that without me?" Dan demanded incredulously when he found out. Arthur Jr.

bowed and scraped, but for Dan, whose competitive feelings for Arthur Jr. were always close to the surface, it was an unforgivably insensitive act. "I've been breaking his ass about it ever since," he said.

§

Soon after Arthur Jr. became deputy publisher, he was invited to Washington to have dinner with Prince Charles. The forty-year-old heir to the British throne wanted to meet some of his American counterparts, and Arthur Jr. and Donald Graham, publisher of *The Washington Post* and son of Washington Post Company chairman Katharine Graham, were judged to be in situations roughly similar to his own. A short article in the *Times* noted that the prince talked with his dinner companions about the frustration of being a king-in-waiting and having to "invent one's job as one went along."

Arthur Jr. sympathized. There had been assistants to the publisher at *The New York Times* before — his father and grandfather were two examples — but never in the paper's history had there been an assistant publisher or a deputy publisher. The territory was virgin, and no one knew quite what to expect, including Arthur Jr. himself. That didn't prevent those in the newsroom — and attentive *Times* readers — from deconstructing his every move for clues to how he planned to conduct the paper in the future.

He soon sent signals that he intended to be far more activist and hands-on than his father, with diversity a top priority. In speeches delivered internally at first and later increasingly in public, he spoke of the economic and moral reasons why the *Times* had to hire and promote more women, blacks, Asians, and Hispanics. The demographic mix of employees and readers was changing rapidly, he told a performance-management seminar in 1989, and "we don't have much time to get our white male house in order."

A few years earlier, over lunch with former *Boston Globe* editor Tom Winship, Arthur Jr. had remarked offhandedly that *The New York Times* was "just miserable to women, miserable to blacks." As a child of the sixties, he was determined to change that. He talked about the need for parental leave, flextime, job sharing, and child care. In speeches he jolted audiences by using *she* as the pseudogeneric pronoun instead of *he*. When Anna Quindlen, the paper's star metro editor, was considering leaving the paper after her third child was born, he helped her get a column on the Op-Ed page. Quietly he let it be known that those who discriminated against gays risked losing their jobs and, with the help of executive editor Max Frankel, persuaded his father to lift his ban on the word *gay* in stories.

When he became an executive, Arthur Jr. began to joke that he was really a reporter who "got off on the wrong floor." If his natural sympathies were with news, not business, his aim was clearly to take charge of both sides of the newspaper as no publisher had since the early days of Adolph Ochs. Arthur Hays Sulzberger had had the final say on bottom-line issues while he had let Julius Adler look after the day-to-day business operations. Orvil had done the same with Amory Bradford, as Punch had with Walter Mattson. Indeed, although Punch was chief executive officer, he had structured his job so that Mattson, the president and chief operating officer, actually ran the daily affairs of The New York Times Company, including the newspaper.

Arthur Jr.'s vision was radically different. He intended to run the newspaper in every respect and had no interest in acting as the final arbiter of decisions made layers beneath him. Like Mattson, he wanted to master every gear and every bolt. "There's an anxiousness about him to prove that he deserves the job and to add value to the enterprise," said *Times* executive Gordon Medenica. "He can't just accept who he is and that he is where he is because of who he is. He wants to deserve it."

Because the business side perceived him to be a captive of the newsroom, he tried hard to demonstrate that he wasn't. He injected himself into decisions about budgets and finances in ways senior managers were completely unaccustomed to, and along with Lance Primis became deeply involved in the labor disputes that required resolution before the Edison plant could be opened. *Times* editors knew that the paper was in dire financial straits, but they had never seen a publisher so engaged in fiscal matters, and it made them nervous.

Despite his efforts to present himself as a bottom-line executive, however, he impressed *Times* business managers as doctrinairely antibusiness. In comparison with Primis, a consummate ad salesman who could adapt to anyone, Arthur Jr. was inflexible and viewed the world in black and white. Max Frankel, whom Punch had explicitly asked to "teach Arthur to be publisher," took it as one of his duties to help him distinguish shades of gray. Whenever he saw Arthur Jr. make absolute declarations, he diplomatically worked behind the scenes to rein him in.

"Max did it in a very deft fashion," said Penny Abernathy, a budget planner for the news department. "He would talk reason, Arthur would process it, and then come back with something [more moderate]."

Had Abe Rosenthal still ruled the newsroom, the combination of his own conservative politics and volatile emotions and Arthur Jr.'s liberal agenda and flip remarks would have been highly destructive for the paper. Luckily, it was Max Frankel, a man of professorial demeanor and Merlin-like patience, who was executive editor when Arthur Jr. entered the final stage of his training. Frankel believed in "the monarchy," as he called the Sulzberger family dynasty, and had an innate respect for authority. Such traits made him a forbearing, fatherly guide for Arthur Jr., much as Turner Catledge had been for Punch. "I think probably Arthur was a real pain in the behind to Max for a long time," said Soma Golden Behr. "I know they talked a lot, but he never said a disrespectful word about Arthur, at least not to me."

Frankel had attended Manhattan's High School of Music and Art and possessed an operatic-quality tenor voice. If he had not become a journalist, he said, he might have become an architect. Soon after he became executive editor of the *Times,* his artistic side manifested itself in an intense interest in larger pictures and brighter graphics. Colleagues joked about Frankel's classically Germanic love of order and predictability, and during his tenure, bureaucracy flourished. Rosenthal had had three assistant managing editors; Frankel had seven. And whereas Rosenthal had loved nothing better than chasing a hot, messy story that blew up overnight, Frankel preferred news events that stood still. He disliked random occurrences and acts of God, anything that didn't yield to cool analysis and interpretation. When a helicopter crashed outside the Lincoln Tunnel, he was against putting the story on the front page. The editors at the page-one meeting were aghast. "Jesus Christ, Max, this never happened before!" they cried. Faced with a unanimous wall of opposition, Frankel changed his mind but, he said, "I'm not happy about it."

As a correspondent in Washington, Frankel had been one of "Scotty Reston's boys" and had adopted one of the former bureau chief's key beliefs as his own: that the biggest story of all is change itself. Things didn't have to "happen" to be news. Shifts in the population and relations between the races had a longer time horizon than the daily news cycle, and by the time Frankel became executive editor, there were sound business reasons to emphasize such trend stories. Market research commissioned by the publisher's office showed that *The New York Times* had more to fear from readers' lack of interest in traditional newspapers than from its national competitors, *The Wall Street Journal* and *USA Today*, a splashy color and graphics-driven daily launched in 1982. Americans under forty now spent their time "omnidirectionally" — watching television while jogging on the treadmill or listening to the radio while driving to work. Reading a newspaper was "unidirectional"; it required single-minded attention and a commitment of time. Neither Frankel nor Arthur Jr. thought newspapers were doomed to extinction, but they shared a belief that the *Times* must become more provocative and entertaining if it was to maintain the readers and advertisers it had, and to attract more.

To make the paper user-friendly, Frankel demanded shorter stories and, in a command that would have disturbed Adolph Ochs, told reporters to give the reader interpretation as well as facts. No longer was "news" simply what happened yesterday. Now, soft features — "good reads," in the parlance of the newsroom — began to appear regularly on page one, including a piece about the resurgent popularity of country music and an article on rising hemlines. *Times* purists were appalled. When a reporter just four years Arthur Jr.'s senior expressed his misgivings, the deputy publisher dismissed him as "a prisoner of the fifties."

When he became executive editor, Max Frankel was fifty-six and Punch was sixty, which meant that if everything went according to plan, Arthur Jr. would have a long time to wait before he would be able to appoint his own top editors. But Frankel had retained Arthur Gelb, the imaginative sixty-two-year-old who had been Rosenthal's right-hand man, as his managing editor, and Gelb was approaching mandatory retirement. As a result, Arthur Jr. had the chance to make a major newsroom decision barely a year after becoming deputy publisher.

The managing-editor job had always been a key appointment; in this case it carried added weight because Frankel's age meant that whoever laid claim to the prize was likely to succeed him as executive editor. By then Arthur Jr. would be publisher, and a new era of *Times* history, with a new team in charge, would begin. Although Arthur Jr. didn't have the explicit power to name a managing editor — by tradition, the decision was the executive editor's — he could certainly veto aspirants and influence who was included in the pool. The appointment would be the first test of his judgment at the highest level of the *Times*, and how he handled himself would reveal a great deal about his fitness to be publisher.

The most obvious candidate was Joe Lelyveld, forty-nine, the lean, socially awkward, brilliant foreign editor. Lelyveld had joined *The New York Times* in 1962 after earning degrees at Harvard and Columbia's Graduate School of Journalism and spending several years in the army. A tireless and shrewd reporter on the metropolitan desk, he had caught Abe Rosenthal's eye and soon became a protégé. A stint in India followed, as well as a bitter and unhappy period as a Washington-based columnist for the Sunday magazine. Along the way, he had picked up a Polk Award for a yearlong series covering a fourth-grade class in Manhattan and a Pulitzer Prize for *Move Your Shadow: South Africa, Black and White*, a book about apartheid based on his observations during two tours as the *Times'* correspondent in South Africa.

In late 1986, at Frankel's request, Lelyveld had stepped down as London bureau chief and returned to New York as the paper's foreign editor. Unlike many at the *Times*, he claimed never to have had a driving ambition beyond his next assignment. "I guess I've neglected to build a career," he had written Rosenthal while on leave of absence writing *Move Your Shadow*. Lelyveld considered himself a writer first and an editor barely at all, yet to his surprise he found that he liked being head of the foreign desk and had had no desire to move any higher at the paper until Gelb's looming retirement raised the question of the next managing editor.

Gelb himself lobbied for Lelyveld to be his successor, but Arthur Jr. had other ideas. His own candidate was Dave Jones, the avuncular editor of the national edition. When Arthur Jr. had first returned to New York to work on the metropolitan desk, Jones had willingly played the role of counselor and, during the years the younger Sulzberger was making the rounds in advertising and corporate planning, had been one of the few editors who had kept him apprised of what was going on in the newsroom. As head of the national edition, Jones had demonstrated that he could work smoothly with the business side. Lelyveld, in contrast, was an unknown quantity with a reputation for being rebellious and uncooperative.

Frankel, however, urged Arthur Jr. to become better acquainted with Lelyveld, and in the summer of 1989 the two men traveled to Berlin to attend a meeting of the International Press Institute. Each morning they jogged together in the city's many parks, talking about the *Times*. The deputy publisher liked what he heard — and he was also frankly worried that Lelyveld might leave if he came down in favor of Jones. While changing planes in Frankfurt on his way to a vacation in Venice with Gail, he phoned Frankel and told him, "You're right: It's Joe."

Back in New York, Frankel took Lelyveld to dinner and formally invited him to be his managing editor. "I need a brother," he said warmly, reaching his arm across the table. After they left the restaurant, Frankel drove Lelyveld to his home on the Upper West Side. As Frankel navigated West End Avenue, earnestly talking about everything Lelyveld would have to learn and do, Lelyveld, overcome by the emotion of the moment, interrupted him to ask, "Well, we're going to have some fun, too, aren't we?" Frankel turned and looked at him as though he were slightly deranged. "Sure," he said noncommittally.

Like Frankel, Lelyveld was an apostle of interpretative journalism. After settling into the managing editor's office in January 1990, he sent out a memo admonishing editors not to "smother" the voice of *Times* writers. Since Adolph Ochs's day, *The New York Times* had been an editor's newspaper. It valued facts and spoke with one voice: the voice of authority, the voice of the Establishment. Turner Catledge and Abe Rosenthal had loosened up the writing considerably, but except in the case of naturally lively writers like Maureen Dowd and Francis X. Clines, examples of lyrical eloquence and unbridled creativity were still relatively rare in the paper of record. For a certain select group of correspondents, Lelyveld's edict amounted to the journalistic equivalent of glasnost. They experimented with first-person pieces and made insouciant references to movie icons, slang, and pop culture.

Arthur Jr. wholeheartedly endorsed the fresh breezes blowing through the *Times*. "People learned more about President Bush from Maureen's insights into what drove him as an individual . . . than they did from any of our reporters who stuck more clearly to the nuts and bolts of the politics," he maintained. By grooming a small stable of stars, however, Lelyveld inadvertently divided his staff into sheep and goats. Everyone wanted the same freedom reporters such as Dowd and Clines enjoyed, yet not everyone was equipped to practice it responsibly or gracefully.

The first sign that the revolution at *The New York Times* was in danger of spiraling into anarchy occurred in the spring of 1991, when Dowd wrote a story based on the galleys of Kitty Kelley's soon-to-be-released book, *Nancy Reagan: The Unauthorized Biography*. To create buzz, Simon and Schuster had held back all review copies while selectively making one available to *The New York Times*. Dowd had had less than twenty-four hours to read the material before filing her story, which, because of the quick turnaround, merely repeated much of the unsubstantiated gossip in Kelley's book, including a suggestion that Mrs. Reagan had participated in sexual trysts with Frank Sinatra at the White House. When Frankel condemned the article as "not up to *Times* standards" in a subsequent staff meeting, Dowd was furious. She felt that she had simply done what she had been asked to do — turn in a colorful story under a near impossible deadline — and she had to be talked out of resigning.

Barely ten days later the *Times* was searching its soul yet again, this time over an article that was such an egregious violation of the paper's traditional code of conduct that a story about it in *Time* magazine carried the headline TARTING UP THE GRAY LADY OF 43RD STREET. The piece under attack was a profile of the woman who claimed to have been raped by William Kennedy Smith over Easter weekend at the Kennedy family estate in Palm Beach, Florida. Not only did the article reveal that the woman's name was Patricia Bowman — a reversal of the *Times'* policy not to identify alleged rape victims going back at least to 1959 — but it offered up a number of salacious tidbits, including the fact that Bowman had had a child out of wedlock and was considered a regular on Palm Beach's barhopping circuit.

Frankel himself had ordered the profile, never intending to identify Bowman. But when he learned on April 16 that NBC News was planning to name her during that evening's broadcast, he insisted that the piece be rushed into print and, feeling that Bowman no longer had any privacy to protect, instructed the editors to include her name. Frankel expected every major news organization in the country to do likewise. The next day, however, *The New York Times* stood practically alone in its decision to identify Bowman, and *Times* staffers, especially the women, were in an uproar.

For many *Times* readers and reporters, the most shocking slip in standards wasn't the inclusion of Bowman's name but a quote from an unnamed high school classmate who described her as having "a little wild streak." Under Abe Rosenthal, anonymous quotes had been discouraged; anonymous *pejorative* quotes had been forbidden. Taken together

with the other negative details in the article, the *Times* seemed to be saying that Bowman "deserved it." Two days later, during a confrontational
assembly of three hundred staffers in the *Times*' auditorium, reporters
excoriated Frankel and his team for the smeary tone of the profile. "How
could you say that woman is a whore?" one demanded. "I think we can
trust readers to make the right judgments; I can't account for every weird
mind that reads *The New York Times*," replied national editor Soma
Golden Behr, who had overseen the piece. Reporters were stunned: the
idea that their editors were blaming the readers instead of themselves
sent many to new depths of despair and confusion.

Punch was in London when the Bowman story appeared. He read the
piece in the *International Herald Tribune* and was furious at his editors
for unilaterally reversing the *Times*' policy about naming rape victims
without even notifying him, much less asking his opinion. He had
seethed as the British press had reveled in the controversy over the story
and *still* no one called. His sisters phoned to complain, and Carol,
thrilled to have an opportunity to drive a wedge between Punch and
Arthur Jr., was shrill in her insistence that something had to be done. In
the midst of the clamor, Joe Lelyveld arrived in London on a previously
scheduled trip and was surprised to find the publisher distraught.

While Lelyveld was winging his way to London, Anna Quindlen
wrote a Sunday Op-Ed column that condemned the Bowman story as a
"mistake." Anxious readers sent Quindlen letters saying they hoped she
wouldn't lose her job. They had ample reason to worry, in fact, for
Punch was intolerant of employees who "peed" on the paper, as he put
it. In 1985 he had fired metropolitan affairs columnist Sydney Schanberg
after he had accused *The New York Times* of being "venal" in one of his
many columns on Westway, a proposed Manhattan highway project.
Arthur Jr.'s *New York Times*, however, was a kinder, gentler place. When
Quindlen bumped into Arthur Jr. in the newsroom the day after her column appeared, he put his arm around her shoulder, and said in a voice
loud enough for everyone to hear, "That was a good column yesterday."
Many interpreted the gesture to mean that he agreed with what Quindlen
had written. "[That was] one of the most misunderstood statements of
all time," Arthur Jr. said later. "I wasn't trying to say that I thought she
was right or wrong. . . . I was simply saying: 'Good for her for disagreeing, because columnists ought to feel they can disagree with the paper.' "

On April 26, nine days after the offending profile, the *Times* ran an editor's note saying that the paper had not meant to imply that it was "challenging" Bowman's account of the rape. "It remains the *Times*' practice to guard the identity of sex crime complainants," the note went on, "as long as that is possible and conforms to fair journalistic standards." Despite the furor, Frankel remained convinced that he had handled the Bowman story correctly. Even later, after Arthur Jr. and Punch had concluded that their executive editor had erred, Frankel's only regret was that he had lacked the courage to keep using Bowman's name in subsequent articles the *Times* did about the case.

But for the disillusioned news staff, something precious had been damaged: the *Times*' moral compass. Abe Rosenthal may have been suspicious and explosive, but under his leadership, reporters had been aware that they were accountable to a high and clearly enunciated standard. Now many wondered what that standard was — or whether there was one at all. "I don't know that we'll ever recapture the sensibility we had," said assistant managing editor Carolyn Lee.

In public Punch downplayed the wound inflicted by the Kitty Kelley story and the Bowman profile. Yes, the Bowman piece was "terrible" and "a slip in standards," but that didn't mean the *Times* was going to become "a gossipy paper to compete with the tabloids." In private, however, he was sufficiently concerned to demand that Frankel appear before the *Times*' board of directors to explain what had happened and why. In a show of solidarity, Arthur Jr. accompanied Frankel to the meeting and spoke briefly about the assault the executive editor had endured in the *Times*' auditorium.

The series of events taught Arthur Jr. a valuable lesson about the paper's power. It had not mattered that NBC had broadcast Bowman's name; it had mattered that the *Times* had published it. As expressed in the quote from *Othello* that seventeen-year-old Adolph Ochs had copied in his autograph book more than a hundred years earlier, the *Times*' "good name" was the well from which it drew its authority, but that well was not inexhaustible. If it was squandered, the entire enterprise would be lost forever. Like his grandfather and his father before him, Arthur Jr. would have to prove that he could be a worthy guardian of this incalculable treasure, and the Palm Beach rape incident had not helped make his case. Instead, it had put his father in precisely the position he hated most: fending off criticism from his wife, his sisters, his reporters, his readers, and his board. Since naming Arthur Jr. deputy publisher, Punch had tried not to second-guess him, a strategy that Arthur Jr. greatly appreciated. Now Arthur Jr. saw the painful side of that freedom. "[My father] has always given me the rope I needed to hang myself," he said.

42

The Sword in the Stone

A T THE SECOND WEDDING OF HER GRAND-
daughter Susan Dryfoos in the fall of 1989, Iphigene was as
fragile as a sparrow and confined to a wheelchair. Susan's first
marriage, to Douglas Mazonowicz, had so unsettled Marian and other
family members that it had involved just a modest ceremony and a
reception at High'n Dry. When she decided to remarry, Susan was determined to have what she had previously been denied: a rabbi-led ceremony at Hillandale, followed by a reception at the Rainbow Room,
sixty-five floors above New York City. "It was pretty swish," said Marian.
"She even wore my wedding dress."

The bridegroom, Daniel Mayer Selznick, was accustomed to extravagance. His late father, David O. Selznick, produced some of Hollywood's
most memorable films, including *Gone With the Wind* and *A Star Is
Born.** His grandfather, Louis B. Mayer, had been the boss of Metro-
Goldwyn-Mayer, and his mother, Irene Mayer Selznick, produced *A
Streetcar Named Desire, The Chalk Garden,* and other Broadway plays.
Despite her eighty-two years, Irene was still capable of stealing the spotlight, even at her son's wedding. In the middle of the ceremony, she began
to faint. Iphigene, who had a hard time walking or speaking, struggled
out of her wheelchair and insisted that Irene take her place. Two hours
later at the Rainbow Room, Marian glanced up from her drink and to her
amazement saw Irene dancing with the furious energy of a teenager. "She
was the last one to leave," she said. "She was quite an actress."

Despite Iphigene's heroic gesture, it was clear that, at ninety-seven,
even the indomitable Sulzberger matriarch was wearing out. "I'm just so

---

*He also produced the 1937 film *The Prisoner of Zenda,* starring Madeleine Carroll,
who subsequently became the mistress of Susan's grandfather and the second wife
of her stepfather.

tired, I wish I would die," she would sigh to her live-in caretaker. Iphigene had never been religious and didn't believe in eternal life, yet death held no terror for her. After she had attended the funeral of her friend the publisher Alfred Knopf, Seymour and Audrey Topping had taken her out to lunch. "Oh, isn't it nice to think there's nothing after this?" she had exclaimed to them, as though death were a grand reward.

In February 1990 Iphigene invited Liselotte Kahn, the widow of architect E. J. Kahn and a woman who had grown up near her grandfather Julius Ochs's hometown of Fürth, Bavaria, to join her for dinner. As Iphigene descended in the Hillandale elevator and entered the library, Liselotte was struck by how impeccably groomed she was. "How can one be so beautiful at ninety-seven?" she marveled to Iphigene in her German-accented English. Over dinner, they touched on many topics, including death. "What can be better than a deep, deep sleep?" asked Iphigene.

The following day Judy; Ruth's daughter, Lynn; and several other family members were scheduled to join Iphigene for lunch. When Judy arrived at Hillandale, she found that she was the only one there. Iphigene was too sick to leave her room and the estate's Portuguese cook had phoned everybody except Judy and asked them not to come. "Why didn't you tell me?" Judy demanded. "Why did I drive all the way out here if she wasn't feeling well?" The servant gave Judy a searching look. "We thought you might like to see her," she said.

Judy went upstairs, where despite a harsh cough, Iphigene managed to get out of bed, move to a chair, and eat lunch on a tray. "I got a phone call from Budd this morning," Judy told her mother. Judy's marriage to her third husband had been no more successful than her previous ones to Mattie Rosenschein and Dick Cohen. Budd had begun to cheat on her not long after the wedding, and although Judy had tolerated his infidelities at first, thinking that "this was something he could do on one level and be married on another — the way my father did it," when he became blatantly involved with one particular woman, Judy stormed out. They divorced in 1984. For the next five years Budd bounced from one live-in girlfriend to the next. By the time he spoke with Judy that Saturday morning in late February, he was "miserable" and desperate to see her again. "Does he want you back?" Iphigene inquired. "I don't know," replied Judy.

Iphigene was hardly crisp and alert, but she managed to conduct a reasonable conversation. When Judy rose to leave, Iphigene clung to her daughter a little. "I felt she was trying to say something," recalled Judy, who, as a doctor, was familiar with the glassiness dying patients got in their eyes. Iphigene had had that look for some time. On Sunday Judy called Hillandale, and the caretaker told her that her mother seemed better.

Early Monday morning one of the caretakers entered Iphigene's room and found her in a deep sleep. Gently she shook her arm. Iphigene came to for a second, grabbed the caretaker's hand, and stopped breathing. At 7:40 A.M. on February 26, Iphigene Ochs Sulzberger, whose life had spanned nearly the entire twentieth century, was dead of respiratory failure. Knowing that Judy had medical training, the caretaker notified her first. "Should I come out there?" Judy asked. "No," the caretaker replied. "I think it's too late." The woman reached Punch at his apartment in the city. "Mother had just gone to sleep," he said. "It was a nice way to go, without any tubes [or heroic measures]. She had said a long time ago that she wanted to die at home."

The next day the front page of *The New York Times* featured a photograph of a sixty-nine-year-old Iphigene and an accompanying article that took up more column inches than most major news stories. Later, in its "Talk of the Town" section, *The New Yorker* compared the fond, folksy recapitulation of her life to an obituary of a publisher's mother in a small-town paper. But to consider Iphigene merely the publisher's mother was to grossly understate her role in *The New York Times* and the place she held in the soul of the family. "[The writer] Paul Bowles said when he came to Tangiers forty years ago, that [the city] rang a gong in his life that resonates throughout," said Joe Perpich, Cathy Sulzberger's husband. "Granny sounded that gong and it just resonates through your life."

Stephen Golden was in Albany, New York, the morning his grandmother died. He immediately turned around, caught a plane back to the city, and went out to lunch with his wife, Brenda. Since 1987 Stephen had been enrolled in a special program at New York University, working toward the undergraduate degree that had eluded him years earlier. He was nearly forty-three and scheduled to graduate in May. "The one regret I have is that Granny never lived long enough to see me get a college diploma," he told Brenda before bursting into tears.

Such unrestrained grief was rare in the initial hours following Iphigene's death. Rationally, the Sulzbergers knew that the woman they had variously called Mother, Granny, and Great-Granny was old, frail, and ready to die. But she was also a fixture in their lives, and they found themselves unprepared to deal with her sudden absence. "Everybody was oddly emotionless," said Dan Cohen's wife, Leah. "They didn't quite know what to do. It just wasn't real."

The next evening family and friends gathered at Marian and Andrew's apartment. Sulzberger cousins flew in from around the country. New York City mayor David Dinkins, on his way to an engagement and dressed in a tuxedo, stopped by to offer his sympathy. There was half-eaten food on the tables and the kind of automatic conversation people have when they can't bring themselves to address the sad reality that has brought them together. "When did you get here?" they asked one another politely. "How long are you staying?" No one could believe that Iphigene was gone, least of all her four children, who at one point disappeared upstairs to discuss arrangements for out-of-town guests after the memorial service. Forty-five minutes later they emerged. "We've decided not to make a decision," Punch announced solemnly, at which the cousins' generation laughed knowingly. Their parents put such a premium on getting along that even something as straightforward as planning a reception totally paralyzed them. "It was difficult for them to work through," said Dan. "We finally said to them, 'You have to do it,' and they relented and did it."

Washington Post chairman Katharine Graham; James Hoge, president and publisher of the New York *Daily News;* and former New York mayors Ed Koch and John Lindsay were among the more than one thousand mourners who gathered at Temple Emanu-el on Wednesday, February 28 — Adolph and Effie's one hundred and seventh wedding anniversary — to celebrate Iphigene's life and mark its passing. Bobby Dryfoos escorted his former wife, Katie, to a pew in front, not far from the bouquets of yellow, white, and pink flowers that stood before the main altar. As she squeezed past Stuart Greenspon, Stuart whispered, "This is the 'ex-' row." Sure enough: when Katie surveyed her companions, "it was all of us [ex-spouses]."

Susan Dryfoos spoke on behalf of the family. "Dear, wonderful Granny, you've been tired these past years," she began. "You wanted to go to be with your husband, your parents, my father. You spoke of it often. You finally got your wish. You can rest peacefully. You did a good job." Then, using words that echoed Adolph's will and had been passed down in the family like divinely inspired scripture, she called *The New York Times* "a trust" and "a tradition that is far greater than any single individual." Publicly she pledged her generation to "carry on" and to "be humble." "No swelled heads," she promised her grandmother. "Our memory of you will keep us straight."

Harrison Salisbury, a retired *Times*man and author of *Without Fear or Favor,* a book about the paper, spoke of Iphigene's subtle editorial influence on the *Times* and her ability to mold her "warm, opinionated family into a band of keepers of the faith." Punch had originally asked Scotty Reston, the family's poet laureate, to perform the eulogy, as he had at Orvil's and Arthur's funerals, but Scotty had declined. Punch was grateful to Salisbury for taking over the task, but his overabundant praise and windy delivery offended his Sulzbergerian sense of propriety. "God, he went on and on," said Punch. "He made it sound like Mother was responsible for the collapse of communism. It really was a very strange speech."

The service provided a moment for family members to begin to unburden themselves. Several of them cried openly, but Punch stared straight ahead, fighting for control. "There were tears in his eyes," recalled Karen, who sat next to him. "I clutched his hand occasionally to give him a little support. It was a public moment; he didn't break down." Earlier that day — Ash Wednesday — Punch had shocked a *Times* staffer by making a joke about his mother's cremation. The staffer had appeared at work with a smudge of ash on her forehead. "Oh, dear!" Punch had quipped. "I hope that isn't Mother!"

Judy was the only one of her siblings to go to Temple Israel Cemetery for the interment of Iphigene's ashes, accompanied by an assortment of cousins and spouses. "It had nothing to do with whether I loved her more," insisted Judy. "It had to do with the ability to cope." Soon a less-than-majestic inscription would appear on the stone bench above the spot: SHE HAD LOVE AND KNOWLEDGE TO GIVE AND TIME TO SHARE IT.

Despite his public mask of reserve, Punch was devastated by his mother's death. "Now I am an orphan," he told his daughter Karen. With his parents' passing, Punch was, like every other human being, forced to face his own mortality. But Iphigene had been far more than simply a parent, for she had been his confidante, his trusted adviser, and his champion. She had also been head of the family and the symbolic head of Adolph Ochs's *New York Times,* titles and burdens that Punch suddenly inherited. "He realized that he had become his mother," said Karen's husband, Eric Lax. "Now he was the leader of the family and everybody was going to turn to him, whereas she had assumed a great deal of that over the years."

Punch didn't confide his grief and anxiety to anyone. He certainly couldn't talk to Carol, and he had never felt comfortable confessing personal problems to his sisters. With no other outlet, the tension turned inward. After his mother's stroke three years earlier, Punch had developed a pinched nerve in his neck that had never completely disappeared. Now he began to look ill — "Awful," said Judy. "Really sick."

At sixty-four, Punch had angina and high cholesterol, which he controlled through exercise and a strict diet. For the past eight years, he had faithfully appeared at 6:00 A.M. at the Cardio-Fitness Center not far from the *Times* and worked out for an hour on the treadmill and stationary bicycle. By 7:30 A.M. he could be found sitting at his desk, showered and changed, sipping tea and eating a light breakfast. The scotch and steaks that had been the steady fare of his youth had long since been supplanted by grilled fish, vegetables, wine, and beer. His one remaining vice was chocolate chip cookies. "If he were a girl, he'd be an anorexic," said his daughter Cynthia.

To ease the back pain that had plagued him during labor disputes and other high-tension moments, Punch had installed a hanging bar in one of the doorways off the company boardroom. Standing on a box, he would grasp the bar and dangle for several minutes to take pressure off his vertebrae, in full view of his grandfather Ochs, who stared at him from the László portrait that hung over the boardroom's green marble fireplace. But the real cure for his back problems had come, surprisingly, from a psychiatrist. Dr. John Sarno believed that most back pain was psychosomatic: by indulging in "aimless labor" and diverting the mind from whatever was causing anxiety, one could relieve the constricted blood vessels and nerves that were putting pressure on the back. As soon as Punch got results, however, he stopped seeing Sarno. "I think he just got too close to home for him," said Judy. "He didn't want to rock the boat [of his inner self]."

With the death of Iphigene, the Ochs Trust, which owned *The New York Times* and *The Chattanooga Times*, automatically terminated, and the Class B stock was divided among four new trusts, one each for Marian, Ruth, Judy, and Punch and their descendants. Because of the 1986 covenant, there was no danger that the family would lose control of

The New York Times or be forced to sell because of inheritance taxes. Iphigene's will also made it clear that she considered her "lawful" descendants to be only those legally adopted or "born in wedlock," an allusion to George Alexanderson, the son Punch had allegedly conceived thirty-four years earlier with Lillian Bellison. Elsewhere, she listed a series of $100,000 bequests to the charities that she had favored throughout her life: Barnard, the New York Botanical Garden, Hebrew Union College, and the Federation of Jewish Philanthropies of New York.

The dissolution of the Ochs Trust meant that suddenly Marian, Ruth, Judy, and Punch were wealthy. All their adult lives they had complained about being perceived as rich without having the bank accounts to back it up. Now, each of the four Sulzberger children came into possession of *New York Times* stock worth more than $80 million, a cache that generated dividend income of several million dollars a year. "They got along very happily for the first sixty or so years of their lives without it, and suddenly this thing hit them," said Ted Wagner, the family's trust and estate lawyer. "It was a culture shock."

Because her marriage to Ben Golden had been damaged by the resentment he had felt at the financial ties binding him to the senior Sulzbergers, Ruth was determined not to place the same burden on her children. As soon as she was able, she set up multimillion-dollar trusts for Stephen, Michael, Lynn, and Arthur, no strings attached. "I was always broke, having to borrow money and sign papers [as an adult]," she said. "I've been so happy that I've been able to give a little money to my children." Her brother and sisters declined to follow suit. "I've given my kids a little but not as much [as Ruth]," said Punch. "[I] told them they could wait a little longer."

Iphigene's death left Hillandale without an occupant. None of her four inheritors wanted to live there, and with a monthly maintenance bill of $35,000, the house and grounds were too expensive to keep merely out of sentiment. Reluctantly, Punch and his sisters decided to put the estate, including Rock Hill, up for sale. Dividing up Iphigene's personal effects was emotionally wrenching enough, but Carol added to the discomfort by quarreling over certain pieces. To avoid disputes, each of the four siblings assigned themselves different colored scraps of paper to mark the items he or she wanted. If two people claimed the same item, they drew straws to see who won the right to it.

The system worked well until both Carol and Judy wanted the same chest at Hillandale, which Judy then won in the draw. Carol, however, refused to accept defeat. It wasn't that she felt nostalgic about Hillandale, but she had already picked out the perfect spot in the Sulzbergers' apartment for the piece to go. She hounded Punch so mercilessly that with great reluctance he phoned his sister and told her, "There is a lady here who really wants that little chest." "But we had a lottery and I got it!" Judy protested. "I know," Punch said in a weary voice that made it clear he had called his sister under duress.

Punch wanted to let the matter drop, but Carol redoubled her campaign, calling Judy directly and offering to trade a table for the prized chest. Finally, after the third or fourth appeal, Judy capitulated in the interest of peace. The episode did not sit well with Ruth, who felt that as an in-law, Carol had no right to act so high-handed and proprietary. "You've gotten just about everything in this house!" she told her sharply. Given how cool relations had been between Carol and Iphigene, and how little regard she had for her mother-in-law's taste in clothes and furnishings, it was ironic that Carol should be the one to squabble over her possessions. "Mother would have been spinning," said Judy, rolling her eyes.

Arthur and Iphigene had bought Hillandale in 1949 for $125,000; forty-two years later the Sulzberger heirs listed the estate for sale at $7.2 million. By December 1991 a deal had been struck with a couple who owned a large New York–based travel agency. All that remained was for the family to assemble for one last Christmas and make their farewells. "We were just wrecks," said Cynthia. "It was the saddest thing." At the final dinner eleven-year-old Sarah Sulzberger Perpich, Joe and Cathy's daughter, stood up and in a prepared speech reminded her grandparents and aunts and uncles and cousins that Hillandale was where Eric had proposed to Karen, where Cynthia had brought her boyfriends, and where many of them had lost their first tooth. "I'm sure you're all very sad," she said, "but believe me, Hillandale and Rock Hill will never forget you." Sarah's brother, David, broke down and had to leave the table.

As Punch watched his family dissolve in tears at their final departure from Hillandale, he felt vitally connected to their grief. Although he had flirted with the idea of keeping Rock Hill, remaining on the property while strangers lived in his parents' home made him shudder. Still, striking out on his own was a totally foreign concept. In the city he lived in the same Fifth Avenue apartment building his sister and late brother-in-law, Orvil, had once inhabited, several blocks from where his parents had lived, and only a short walk from the town house in which he had grown up. In the country he had spent every weekend in a family enclave as insular and self-referential as Hyannis Port was to the Kennedys. Although he was sixty-four, he had only intermittently had the adult experience of living in a place that was completely outside his family's field of gravity. Such independence would have been incomprehensible to Adolph Ochs, for whom the family was the fulcrum of social and professional life. But times were changing. Iphigene was gone. Soon, Hillandale would be gone, too. Could the center hold without them?

§

Iphigene's death meant that for the first time, Carol was the undisputed queen bee of *The New York Times.* No longer did she have to endure weekends on her mother-in-law's estate or listen to her sermons on smoking. No longer did Punch drift up to the main house at Hillandale for private tête-à-têtes. Now, finally, Carol could emerge from behind the shadow of the revered Iphigene, with whom she had always felt competitive and not quite satisfactory. Not that Carol had any interest in slipping into Iphigene's place as the hub of the family. That role fell naturally to Ruth, to whom many in the younger generation had long turned for frank answers about everything from personal dilemmas to career advice. As far as Carol was concerned, the ownership of the company was now split several ways, the thirteen cousins and their offspring had divergent interests, and it was not her job to unify them. "You can't keep things the same forever," she told a family member.

As soon as Punch and his sisters had decided to sell Hillandale, Carol had gone shopping for a new home in the Hamptons, the most expensive and glamorous part of Long Island and the area where she had long yearned to spend her weekends. She and Punch settled on a roomy $2.5 million clapboard house not far from the beach with a rose garden, a pool, and a vast backyard. The location, on Gin Lane in Southampton, put the Sulzbergers on the toniest street in the toniest of the three Hamptons. For Carol, who once told a friend that her idea of going to the country was "looking out the window," the proximity to the A-list of society and good restaurants was eminently agreeable after the isolation of Hillandale.

The only thing threatening Carol's new sense of well-being was the ever nearer prospect of Arthur Jr.'s becoming publisher, for in her mind, his promotion meant her demotion. Over the years she had grown to like the power that accrued to the wife of the publisher of *The New York Times;* now, with Iphigene gone, that power no longer had to be shared. But what would happen to her if her husband no longer held the publisher's title? "No one will call me anymore," she fretted to intimates. "I'll lose all my friends."

As Arthur Jr. was gradually transformed in her mind from aggravating stepson to implacable enemy, she began to fight his becoming publisher every step of the way. She scoffed when others suggested that he was the best prepared of his generation for the job; he had only done what every other publisher's son had done, she protested, and besides, he had had it easy because none of the other cousins "really came around." "Believe me," she insisted, "if I were Ruth or Marian or Judy, I would have been in there." When Arthur Jr. and the publisher's office were mentioned in the same breath, she denigrated the importance of the job, saying, "If tomorrow there was a trained monkey at the head of *The New York Times,* that trained monkey would be the one invited to the White House."

If Punch was ever to name Arthur Jr. publisher, he knew it was going to have to be in defiance of Carol. He was certainly willing to accept that, but from bitter experience he knew that she would not be gracious in defeat. "Did you ever see the film, *Who's Afraid of Virginia Woolf?"* inquired a friend who knew them both well. "That's what it was like: rough, rough, rough [on both sides]. They fought like cats and dogs."

Even if Carol had been more secure, she and Arthur Jr. were too alike in certain characteristics and too dissimilar in others ever to be friends. They both made snap judgments about people — Arthur Jr. on the basis of politics, Carol on the basis of clothes, looks, and manners. Carol knew that Arthur Jr. disapproved of her love of designer clothes and her interest in European royalty. Every week, at Carol's request, the manager of the *Times'* London bureau sent her the latest copy of *Hello!,* a European-based gossip magazine, as well as the most recent books and articles on Princess Diana and other members of the British monarchy. Arthur Jr. was not mollified by Carol's being pro-choice. He sensed, correctly, that she was motivated on most partisan issues more by contrariness than by conviction and that except for abortion, his stepmother shared the social values of Reagan Republicans: she was against feminism and affirmative action, squeamish about gays, and unapologetic about her enjoyment of the luxuries wealth afforded her.

Carol, in turn, considered Arthur Jr. an arrogant phony. His insistence on taking the bus and subway everywhere and shunning three-star restaurants struck her as reverse snobbery. It annoyed her when Arthur Jr. and Gail stayed in what she called "crummy hotels" instead of Claridge's or the Ritz. "You really want to say, 'Lighten up!' or 'Get a life!'" Carol complained in exasperation. Arthur Jr. refused to buy a car; when he made his weekend treks to New Paltz, he rented from Avis. Despite the fact that he had grown up on the East Side, he disdained that part of Manhattan, which to him was little more than a gleaming ghetto of limousines, fur coats, and small yapping dogs; instead, he self-consciously chose to live on the Upper West Side, where residents valued their integrated neighborhoods and long history of social activism. Even after his close friend Steve Rattner moved across the park and into a twenty-five-room, $7 million apartment that had once belonged to a lesser Guggenheim, he refused to see the East Side as anything other than, as one intimate put it, "the place where all the people he doesn't like live." The fact that he dressed with the flair of a Beau Brummel and lived in a spacious co-op on Central Park West seemed not to tabulate. "Believe me," Rattner said, "Arthur does not live under a rock."

Beyond their stylistic differences, Carol complained that Arthur Jr. was intent on imposing his left-leaning political agenda on *The New York Times*. Her tirades on the subject became so incessant that Punch regularly found himself roaring back: "Didn't YOU ever make a mistake?" In 1963, when Punch had come to the publisher's job with far less training than Arthur Jr., he had made more than his share of missteps, and his father's angry explosions and tart blue notes had made an indelible impression. He had no desire to stand at Arthur Jr.'s elbow, critiquing his every move.

Punch often said that people who believe in orderly transitions eventually do have to transit. For him, that moment came in 1991. He had just turned sixty-five, and Arthur Jr. was increasingly vocal in his impatience to take the reins. A strong management team was in place, and Punch would still be around to help out as chairman and CEO. He believed that he had cleared every obstacle to a smooth changing of the guard, but as it turned out, he had neglected a critical constituency: his board of directors. At the November meeting he announced his intention to step aside as publisher and install Arthur Jr. in his place. To his amazement, there was palpable hesitation in the room. Few around the conference table knew Arthur Jr. well. As deputy publisher he had made only one presentation to the board, and the directors had been singularly underwhelmed. John Akers, chairman and CEO of IBM; George Shinn, former chairman and CEO of First Boston Corporation; and other CEOs and former CEOs who served as outside directors had been particularly alarmed by his seeming immaturity and lack of leadership. "We'd heard a lot of stories," said one board member. "People would say, 'I was talking to so-and-so, and he tells me Arthur's the most impossible SOB.' "

Eventually, the directors said they wanted some time to discuss the appointment. Punch and his sisters absented themselves, and Walter Mattson, the highest-ranking *Times* executive left in the room, moderated the conversation. Over and over, board members pressed Mattson for assurances that if they ratified Arthur Jr. as publisher, it would not be read as a signal that they had also tacitly ratified him as the company's eventual chief executive officer. Punch had held both titles, as well as chairman, which had worked out to everyone's satisfaction, but with Wall Street sensitive to any hint of irresponsible nepotism in family-controlled companies, the arrangement might not be advisable in the future. Nowhere was it written in stone, Mattson told them, that a family member had to be CEO of The New York Times Company, and he was certain the Sulzbergers wanted only the "very best person" for such an important job. To reinforce the point, Punch later sent a letter to the board saying that while he hoped a family member would succeed him as CEO, that would not happen unless the person was well qualified to do so.

When the directors summoned Punch and his sisters back into the boardroom, they told them that they had tabled the question of making Arthur Jr. publisher. They weren't rejecting him out of hand, they explained, but simply wanted time to learn more about him. They knew that once Arthur Jr. was anointed, they could not dislodge him without severely bruising his feelings as well as Punch's, and so wanted to proceed with particular caution. Technically, Punch had the right to ignore his directors, for he alone had the power to name the next publisher of *The New York Times*. But because he valued the concurrence and support of his board, imposing his will was out of the question.

When Arthur Jr. heard that his long-awaited promotion had been delayed, he was distraught. Punch and Mattson tried to cushion the blow by blaming themselves; they had not adequately prepared the board for two major announcements, they said. One was making Arthur Jr. publisher. The other was naming Lance Primis president of The New York Times Company, replacing Mattson, who had asked to take early retirement. The directors, who knew Primis about as well as they knew Arthur Jr., felt that senior management was railroading them into approving two key appointments at one meeting on the basis of very little information.

Arthur Jr.'s period of anxiety was brief. Over the next several months, Punch and Mattson visited board members individually, addressing their concerns about the coming transition. By January 16, 1992, when the directors assembled again in the *Times* boardroom, they had satisfied themselves that Arthur Jr. was the correct choice to be publisher. They had also accepted a reporting arrangement that made him answerable on editorial matters to his father and on business matters to Walter Mattson, who had agreed to stay on as company president until the fall, when the *Times'* new automated color printing and distribution facility in Edison, New Jersey, was scheduled to open. At the same time, Punch had refused to honor his son's request for a seat on the board of directors — an arrangement *Washington Post* publisher Donald Graham enjoyed — for fear that it would upset the cousins.

On the morning of Arthur Jr.'s anointment as publisher, he was uncharacteristically jumpy. The board's refusal to endorse him three months earlier had disquieted him, and even though he was an accomplished speaker, the presentation he had to make to the board before the formal vote left him unnerved. Adding to the pressure was Susan Dryfoos, who in her capacity as head of The New York Times History Project was poised to record the important day on film. Shortly after 9:00 A.M. Arthur Jr. strode to a lectern that had been placed at the far end of the conference table, to the left of the portrait of Adolph Ochs, as a fierce January wind rattled the heavy sash windows.

For the first time he wore gold cuff links engraved with JANUARY 16, 1992 — a gift from Gail to commemorate the occasion. Just as Punch introduced him as the man "who today is going to be named publisher of *The New York Times,*" one of the bottom windows farthest from Arthur Jr. suddenly shot upward with a loud bang. A rush of winter wind sent the curtains flying into the room, hurtling a framed photograph of the late shah of Iran from its place on a side table to the floor. Arthur Jr. paled. "The spirit of Adolph Ochs!" one board member gasped, glancing up at the László portrait. "No, no, it's the winds of change," nervously joked another. As *Times* executives raced to the window and struggled to close it, Arthur Jr. tried to regain his composure and make light of what several witnesses considered an "omen" and "an absolutely eerie thing." "I hope that's not an evaluation of my fitness to be publisher," Arthur Jr. remarked with as much savoir faire as he could muster. Had the superstitious Adolph been alive, he would no doubt have read auguries into the unlikely event. The window was so heavy that it took two hands to lift it; how could a mere gust of wind, however strong, have caused it to fly open? "It was frightening," said Mike Ryan, who had a good view from his seat by the wall. "I've been in that boardroom for thirty-five years and I've never seen anything like that." (Stranger still was what happened to the clock that hung on the outside of the Times Building, just below the fourth floor. Adolph had installed the original in 1931. After a fire in 1962, it had been replaced by a clock nearly seven feet tall and seven and a half feet wide that spelled out *Times* in Gothic lettering, and the hour and minutes in incandescent bulbs. The day that Arthur Jr. was made publisher, the bulbs blew out, and the clock went dark.)

After the board meeting Punch and Arthur Jr. held a joint press conference to announce the changes and, as tradition dictated, said a few words to the paper's reporters and editors. The next morning readers awoke to find a front-page photograph of a solemn-faced Punch dressed in his trademark single-breasted suit, white shirt, and striped tie, sitting self-consciously on the edge of the *Times'* boardroom table beneath Adolph Ochs's portrait. Beside him stood an equally sober Arthur Jr., his hands thrust casually into his pockets, looking impossibly young and sartorially splendid in a finely cut double-breasted suit.

Inside, on the editorial page, was Arthur Jr.'s statement of purpose. Entitled "From the Publisher," it misquoted Adolph's original "without fear or favor" pledge, just as every publisher had done before him, and made much of the fact that he was a member of the fourth generation of a dynasty that continued to follow the journalistic precepts laid down by his great-grandfather. Despite his invocation of enduring values, however, Arthur Jr. was categorically different from every other family member who had ever been publisher. His political views had been fired in the kiln of the 1960s, and in contrast to his predecessors, he came to his job as an activist, brimming with energy and opinions and a determination to shake things up.

What gave him the right to do so, at least in his own mind, was the long training program he had gone through. He had self-deprecatingly referred to his position of heir apparent as "a womb with a view," but the reality was that, compared with his father, his uncle, his grandfather, and even Adolph, he was the most thoroughly prepared publisher *The New York Times* had ever had.

His prolonged period as a reporter had also given him another significant credential: an identity as a journalist. His father supported journalistic values, but Punch's reportorial training had been short and privileged. Arthur Jr. had earned his stripes the old-fashioned way, and only two other members of the clan — Cy Sulzberger and John Oakes — could claim the same. At *The New York Times,* no place was more of a meritocracy than the newsroom. Arthur Hays Sulzberger may have found jobs for his mistresses in the promotion department, but it was inconceivable that he would have ever dared foist off unprepared personnel on the news-gathering apparatus of *The New York Times.*

Punch had been shockingly ill-equipped to run *The New York Times* when he was thrust into the role twenty-nine years earlier. Yet despite his poor training and seeming lack of aptitude, he had gone on to be arguably the greatest *Times* publisher since Adolph Ochs. Nearly half of the sixty-three Pulitzer prizes *The New York Times* had ever won were awarded under his leadership. He had succeeded in freeing the paper from the stranglehold of the unions, diversified the company and taken it public, and had stayed the course through the crisis of the Pentagon Papers. The result was a company that had gone from a $100 million business in 1963 to a $1.7 billion business in 1992. Whereas Arthur Hays Sulzberger had relinquished his publishership with visible pangs of regret, for Punch the transition came with a feeling of satisfaction. He may not have been able to show easy affection to Arthur Jr., but presenting him with his most precious possession — *The New York Times* — was a dramatic display of how deeply he cared.

Tributes to Punch poured in. New York senator Daniel Patrick Moynihan read a "celebration" of Punch into the *Congressional Record.* Katharine Graham, chairman of The Washington Post Company, called him an "outstanding publisher and a modest and wonderful man." And, she added, "he's really funny." Indeed, it was Punch's self-effacement and understated humor that had endeared him to so many throughout the years and had defused countless tense moments. Even his farewell memo to the staff, in which he thanked "the thousands of men and women who stood watch with me" as though he were the commanding officer of a naval destroyer, contained a light touch at the end. "P.S.," it said, "See you in the cafeteria."

Punch had sent each cousin a Federal Express letter notifying them in advance of Arthur Jr.'s ascension. None considered Arthur Jr. a poor choice for the job, but the cousins had wanted an opportunity to debate the process, something the culture of the family strongly discouraged. The inevitability of Arthur Jr.'s succession had been a forbidden topic. "It's like having a president — a good president — but who elected him?" said one cousin.

Dan, especially, found Arthur Jr.'s new status difficult to accept. Although he had long expected it, he couldn't help feeling the need to match his cousin's accomplishment. With Leah at his side, he went to his mother and proposed that she resign from the *Times*' board of directors and give him her seat. Judy was surprisingly receptive; during her eighteen years on the board, she had been ambivalent about her role. Compared with Marian and Ruth, who were well informed on journalistic issues and spoke up at meetings, "I hardly ever say anything. . . . I really feel out on the fringe." Judy would gladly have let Dan take her place had Punch not persuaded her that it would cause parity problems with the other cousins and look bad to Wall Street to have a mid-level employee who was also a family member as a company director.

During Punch's reign as publisher, his three sisters had rarely questioned his judgment. Arthur Jr. came to the publishership with three sisters and nine cousins, four of whom had their own ambitions at the company. Their parents had been taught since childhood to maintain a superficial pleasantness in the interest of family harmony, but the new generation had been raised in an era of greater openness and egalitarianism. The cousins valued consensus, but they didn't fear conflict. Already several had begun to question the received wisdom that Arthur Jr. would eventually inherit Punch's two remaining titles — chairman and chief executive officer. Didn't others in the family have as legitimate a claim on power as he did?

Dealing with this shifting dynamic within the clan would require all the wisdom and diplomacy Arthur Jr. could summon. So it seemed eerily appropriate that, several days after he became publisher, his sisters presented him with a gift from Steuben: a clear glass stone with the gold-handled sword Excalibur buried in it. Arthur Jr. had never heard of the Steuben owl that Ruth, Judy, and Punch had given Orvil when he became publisher in 1961, nor of the mysterious moment when it broke cleanly in two, so he read nothing portentous into the gift. But as events would show, the Arthurian legend would have special meaning for him beyond his first name. His time of testing was not yet over. The moment would come when he would again have to prove his worth, draw the sword from the stone, and claim his crown.

PART FOUR

The Next Generation

43

Welcome to the Revolution

T HE MOOD WAS UNCOMFORTABLE IN THE CON-
ference room as Doug Wesley, a management consultant and
professional "facilitator," tried to goad senior editors and a
smattering of lower-level department heads into speaking freely about
the climate of fear that permeated the *Times* newsroom. Arrayed around
a horseshoe-shaped Formica table, the twenty men and women were
gathered in early December 1992 for a two-day retreat at the Hyatt
Regency Hotel in Greenwich, Connecticut, at the request of the new
publisher, to draft a "mission statement" for *The New York Times* and to
talk about the need for change at the paper.

When no one made a move to speak, Wesley got specific. He wanted
to discuss the page-one conference — the meeting executive editor Max
Frankel held every afternoon to discuss which stories would appear on
the next day's front page. Despite Frankel's expressed desire to encourage
"good fun" in the *Times* newsroom, the sessions had come to resemble
the movie *The Paper Chase*, with Frankel taking the part of Professor
Kingsfield as the humiliating Socratic inquisitor, and managing editor
Joe Lelyveld playing his terrifying teaching assistant. There were days
when editors couldn't get a full sentence out before Frankel or Lelyveld
jumped on them, shooting holes in their logic or eviscerating the story
as they had proposed it.

Finally national editor Soma Golden Behr broke the ice. She had
worked for Frankel as a member of the editorial board and remembered
the discussions then as collegial and Frankel as "relaxed" and "never
snappy, never arrogant." What was it about the job of executive editor,
she wondered aloud, that now made him such an intellectual bully? "I
think of the page-one meeting as a colloquy," Frankel responded, mystified that the gathering would be considered anything but a comradely

conversation. "I've been in a lot of page-one meetings," Arthur Jr. shot back, "and the one thing I can tell you, Max, is that it ain't no colloquy!" The room fell silent.

Prior to the retreat, Frankel and Wesley had met for lunch, at which Wesley had told him the meeting was going to focus on creating a mission statement that would express the "core values" of *The New York Times.* The business side of the paper had already drafted its own version several months earlier; Greenwich was to be the newsroom's chance to revise the language before the two sides met to hammer out a final document. Instead of a constitutional convention, however, Greenwich had turned into a scathing critique of Frankel's management. He felt betrayed and mistreated, and finally he turned directly on Wesley. "You were dishonest with me," he said. "You told me this meeting was going to be about one thing, but it's all about how I manage. You set me up." As the group broke for lunch, the ashen-faced Frankel told the editor seated next to him, "I don't feel welcome here anymore. If they want me to go, this is a lousy way to tell me."

When the group reassembled in the afternoon, it was Arthur Jr., not Wesley, who assumed the role of moderator. He opened the session by apologizing to his staff; he had never intended for the meeting to devolve into an assault on the executive editor. He admired both Frankel and Lelyveld, he said, and had confidence in them as journalists. He just wanted them to be more democratic, less command-and-control. In the well-chosen phrases that characterized all his public speech, Frankel diplomatically replied that he felt fealty to the Sulzberger family and commitment to the changes Arthur Jr. had embraced. At the same time, he expressed irritation at the notion that any psychobabbling business consultant could presume to tell the *Times* newsroom how to improve. "We can do that ourselves," he said. The exchange caused editors and department heads to recoil in embarrassment. Harsh page-one meetings aside, Frankel had turned the cowed newsroom of Abe Rosenthal into a more humane place to work. Why, then, had Arthur Jr. allowed his top editor to be so singled out for abuse that these awkward public declarations were necessary?

Creating a new statement of purpose, like the retreat itself, had been Arthur Jr.'s brainchild. Adolph Ochs's stirring pledge to "give the news impartially, without fear or favor" had served *The New York Times* well for nearly one hundred years, and neither Arthur Hays Sulzberger nor Orvil nor Punch had had any inclination to change it. But it was Arthur Jr.'s view that the vow was disturbingly vague and not broad enough for a polyglot population. "As you become more diverse, you've got to be clearer about what it is you're trying to say, because the words mean different things to different people," he insisted. He also had another goal: to use the mission statement as a vehicle to "get the senior [news and business] management of this newspaper to come to grips with some of the fundamental issues that had been dividing them." He had watched his father play the role of court of last resort at the paper; he didn't want to spend the next twenty years of *his* life refereeing every conflict that came along between the newsroom and the business departments.

In the end, the meeting broke up with an agreed-upon mission statement, but with people farther apart than when they had arrived. Arthur Jr. had gathered his news executives to talk candidly about communication and change. He left having lost control of the meeting, having allowed his executive editor to be humiliated in front of his subordinates, and having gotten beaten up a bit himself. "Arthur unleashed forces he didn't fully understand," said an editor who was there.

The situation wasn't improved by a joint news and business retreat six weeks later, in mid-January 1993, again at the Greenwich Hyatt Regency, where Arthur Jr. moderated two daylong sessions meant to thrash out the differences between the news and business drafts of the mission statement. Greenwich Two, as it came to be called, ended in explosive failure. One editor estimated that it set relations between the two sides of the paper back a decade. Arthur Jr. had wanted his executives to reach consensus on their own without his interference, a process that he readily admitted was slower than top-down management but that, he was convinced, produced superior results. "If I have to make a decision, I've failed," he was fond of saying. Yet when the contentious Greenwich Two concluded with no agreement on the mission statement, Arthur Jr. could no longer avoid taking charge.

He appointed a six-person news and business negotiating committee to draft a final document and, in what the editors correctly viewed as a complete triumph for their camp, made it clear that despite his desire to bring the business and news sides of the paper closer together, the historical wall separating the "church" of the newsroom from the "state" of the advertising, circulation, and promotion departments would remain at its traditional height: no one on the business side, he proclaimed, should approach anyone from news below the level of the masthead — the uppermost reaches of the newsroom.

The issue was a heatedly emotional one at the *Times,* where the strict observation of church and state required that those who gathered the news remain insulated from the financial considerations of producing the paper. To the business staff, the "wall" was a class issue, symbolizing as it did the patronizing distrust they had long experienced at the hands of reporters and editors. Arthur Jr. had led his business executives to believe he agreed with their desire to lower the barrier; when he maintained the existing order instead, they felt betrayed and dejected — the opposite of what he had hoped to achieve. "Arthur's ambition was to make people work together, and he ended up being forced to mediate an adversary battle that was worse than what he'd started with," said Sunday magazine editor Jack Rosenthal.

Five months later, in a *New Yorker* article called "Opening Up the *Times,*" Arthur Jr. was quoted as saying he was satisfied with the rough-and-tumble encounter groups he had engineered. "We got rid of a lot of the underbrush," he declared. "We uncovered the fundamentals. We reached agreement." Even years later, and in private, he refused to acknowledge that Greenwich had been a mistake. Others were far less upbeat. In the *Times* newsroom, editors continued to be indignant on Frankel's behalf because of his orchestrated abasement. Punch would never have permitted something like that to happen, they fumed to one another.

What they did not realize, or had forgotten, was that Punch had thrown his general manager, Andy Fisher, into an equally nasty ambush twenty years earlier. Those meetings had been run by a different corporate "facilitator," Chris Argyris, and Punch had been a far more passive participant than Arthur Jr. He had never forced the news and business sides to confront each other, and their alliance, such as it was, had never been codified. That earlier exchange had come about with all the ambiguity Punch loved and Arthur Jr. hated. But despite these differences, father and son had both been motivated by the same desire: to encourage the managers of *The New York Times* to work together as a team.

§

From his first day on the job, Arthur Jr. was a publisher unlike any *The New York Times* had seen since the young Adolph Ochs. Arthur Hays

Sulzberger, intimidated by the specter of his recently deceased father-in-law, had proceeded cautiously during his early years as publisher. Orvil had been too insecure to challenge the status quo, and Punch too unprepared at first to do more than rely on the counsel of his father's aides. Indeed, at the time of their ascension, all three had made public statements reassuring readers that change was not on the agenda.

Arthur Jr. had no interest in pledging measured reform. From the moment he became publisher, he was like a silversmith, noisily banging *The New York Times* into a shape that reflected his own values, beliefs, and personality. Unlike his father, who had begun his reign with the tentativeness of a student, Arthur Jr. gave the impression that he knew all the answers. Even as a mature publisher, Punch had called meetings to order and then sat back while others managed the debate. In contrast, Arthur Jr. did his homework beforehand, actively chaired to the point of dominating the discussion, and relished stirring up controversy. Punch worked behind the scenes and didn't care who got the credit; Arthur Jr. wanted everyone to know he had the power. "Arthur feels he has to make decisions publicly, with everyone watching," said corporate attorney Mike Ryan.

His self-confident air was also deceiving, for Arthur Jr. was not nearly as fully formed as he appeared to be. One associate tartly suggested that he needed to "go back in the oven and bake a little longer." Much of his frenetic effort to transform *The New York Times* was really an attempt to define himself. Privately some editors and managers complained that he was self-indulgently figuring out who he was on their time.

Arthur Jr.'s quest for a management style had begun several years before the ill-fated Greenwich meetings, when he had first embraced the theories of Dr. W. Edwards Deming, an American business philosopher and statistician whose theology of "total quality management" had helped revitalize Japanese industry after World War II. Arthur Jr., then deputy publisher, had come across Deming's name in *The Reckoning,* David Halberstam's book about the auto industry, but he didn't focus on him until Lance Primis, the *Times'* general manager and Walter Mattson's clear successor, strode into his office one day and suggested that Deming's ideas might help them push decision making down to lower levels at the paper when the moment came for the two of them to lead.

Deming's tenets were naturally appealing to Arthur Jr. The first was to quantify the production process mathematically so that managers would rely on data rather than anecdotes when making decisions. The approach was better suited to assembly lines than to newspapers, but for Arthur Jr. it held the promise of inherently democratic decision making based on fact, not an executive's whim. By far the more important principle to Arthur Jr., however, was to create a humanistic workplace, emphasizing teams to get results. He had witnessed firsthand the tension that Abe Rosenthal's rule had instilled in editors and correspondents, and the lack of initiative Mattson's centralized authority had produced in *Times* executives. To Arthur Jr., Deming's vision was Outward Bound in a business suit, and he was eager to see if it could be applied at the *Times*.

Soon thereafter, Primis, Arthur Jr., and two deputy general managers, John O'Brien and Russ Lewis, trooped to Washington, D.C., at Deming's invitation to attend a four-day seminar he was conducting for the U.S. Department of Defense. By the end of the second day, they all agreed they had heard enough and adjourned for dinner at a local Chinese restaurant, where they continued to discuss what they had learned. For each of them, Deming meant something different. To Arthur Jr., Deming was a way to make the paper reflect his inclusive values. For Primis, O'Brien, and Lewis, all of whom had thrived at the *Times* by accommodating themselves to Walter Mattson, Deming meant freedom and a release of energy that could potentially benefit the company. "If we were to implement Deming's major ideas," O'Brien asked his companions, "what would *The New York Times* look like?" That question ignited a conversation so thrilling that by the time dessert arrived, the men did not want to leave. They asked the waiter to bring them dinner all over again. "I had duck twice," said O'Brien. "In my mind, that was the night we said [to one another], 'We're going to do [sic] change.' "

For the next year and a half, Arthur Jr. and Primis worked with members of the business side of the paper to form Deming-style "cross-functional" committees. Arthur Jr. felt that he needed Deming, at least in the beginning, to buy credibility with the paper's business types, who would never have accepted the precepts of Outward Bound — especially from a wet-behind-the-ears publisher — but who would respond to the philosophy of a perceived heavyweight in management. "Why do you embrace Deming?" newsroom budget manager Penny Abernathy asked him. "What he's saying is what you already believe in a commonsense kind of way." "Yeah," Arthur Jr. replied, "but who's going to listen to a forty-year-old who looks like he's twenty-five?" In the newsroom, however, the idea of following the dictates of a management guru was anathema. With the business side clamoring for the validation of an external authority, and the news side suspicious of that very thing, it should have surprised no one, including Arthur Jr., that his efforts to "lower the wall" at Greenwich fizzled so completely.

Following those sessions, Frankel and managing editor Joe Lelyveld obligingly tried to make the page-one meetings more collegial by drawing up a seating chart that put them at opposite ends of the table rather than huddled together like two intimidating judges at the front. They also mocked the new arrangement by unveiling it over a spread of wine, cold shrimp, and canapés. "We were told to be more civilized," Frankel announced with unconcealed sarcasm to his assembled editors. In May 1993 the much-debated mission statement was finally mailed to employees' homes. Headlined OUR COMMITMENT, it pledged those at the *Times* to produce the "best newspaper in the world" and repeated the words "without fear or favor," but the balance of it was as uninspiring as a corporate press release and quickly disappeared into filing cabinets.

Changing how the news and business sides of the paper interacted was only one aspect of Arthur Jr.'s brave new world. As deputy publisher, he had pinpointed diversity as "the single most important issue" the *Times* faced. Now, with the heft of the publisher's office behind him, he became more active and outspoken. He set up a Deming-like diversity committee of news and business people whose open-ended mandate was to look at everything from salaries to career paths. In a videotaped message to the first convention of the National Lesbian and Gay Journalists Association, he declared that he hoped to provide health insurance and other benefits to employees living in same-sex partnerships. When Bill Clinton made dropping the military's ban on gays his first major act as president, the *Times'* editorial page applauded while the news pages featured articles celebrating gay soldiers. The *Times*, exulted *The Advocate*, a gay publication, was undergoing "lavender enlightenment."

Arthur Jr. appointed Gerald Boyd assistant managing editor, making the former *Times* White House correspondent and metro editor the first black on the masthead, and hired Bob Herbert as the paper's first black columnist and Margo Jefferson as the first black critic. In one year, from

1993 to 1994, the number of women on the masthead rose from three to five. Arthur Jr. spoke at the organizing breakfast of the first Bring Our Daughters to Work Day and made sure the *Times* was listed as an official supporter. When his eleven-year-old daughter, Annie, accompanied him to work that day, she toured the building with other *Times* offspring, attended seminars on journalism, and helped produce a newspaper — *Girls' Times* — in which she revealed the appalling fact that her father actually liked airplane food.

For all of Arthur Jr.'s support of diversity, his own identity as a Jew remained tenuous. As the son of a Jewish father and Christian mother, he had "great flexibility," he said, and could define himself as one or the other, depending on the occasion. He knew he would never have had that option in Hitler's Germany, and therefore *had* to think of himself as Jewish, but as his friend Steve Rattner put it, "He doesn't embrace it. He's kind of resigned." When the *Times* published a profile of a black opponent of quotas that traced the man's attitude back to a self-hating grandmother who was prejudiced against dark-skinned blacks, Jim Sleeper, a conservative columnist for the *New York Post*, wondered in print how Arthur Jr. would like it if his attitude toward his Jewish ancestry was framed as self-hatred rather than as a legitimate, personal point of view. "We Lithuanian Jews 'know' that German Jews can be repressed, abstract and snooty . . . and that there is no greater peril to the social fabric than a guilt-ridden Episcopalian," Sleeper wrote mockingly.

Old-timers at the paper complained that Arthur Jr. was trying to establish his legacy too quickly. "I'll outlive the bastards!" he cheerily — and tastelessly — told Ken Auletta, the *New Yorker* writer who had chronicled the Greenwich meetings. As articles began to appear in other publications, with titles such as "Is *The New York Times* Too PC?" and "The Other Side of the Rainbow," some worried that the publisher's attitudes about race, gender, and sexual orientation were skewing coverage and damaging the *Times'* credibility. Others felt as many Clinton supporters did during the national uproar over gays in the military: they feared that Arthur Jr. was foolishly squandering his political capital on a side issue and that when matters more vital to the paper's survival came along, there would be little left. But Arthur Jr. saw himself as setting a moral standard for the *Times*. "He has a highly developed sense that if something is right, you do it," said Rattner. "The idea that Arthur would think about political capital is really not his [style]."

That moral streak also colored how he viewed his role outside the paper. He continued as vice chairman of the New York City Outward Bound Center and as a member of the board of the North Carolina Outward Bound School — long-standing commitments that predated his publishership. But unlike Punch, who had served for many years on the boards of Columbia and the Metropolitan Museum of Art (where in 1987 he was named chairman), Arthur Jr. declined all other invitations for participation. Only those organizations directly related to the paper, such as the Times Square Business Improvement District and the Newspaper Association of America, made the cut. Just as when he had shed his friends at the *Times*, Arthur Jr. explained that he was trying to avoid conflicts of interest. Others, however, saw his actions as a self-conscious effort to differentiate himself from his father. When Barnard College president Ellen Futter invited Arthur Jr. to serve as a trustee, following in the footsteps of his grandmother, he told her that he didn't think the publisher of *The New York Times* should sit on institutional boards. After he left the room, Futter turned to *Times* columnist Anna Quindlen, a Barnard alumna and trustee, and said, laughing, "Well, we all know what *that* was about!"

Arthur Jr. sometimes seemed to go out of his way to gore New York's Old Guard. He pointedly ignored Brooke Astor, the respected philanthropist and the city's social doyenne, when she was seated next to him at a dinner party, choosing instead to exchange shouted witticisms across the table with Georgette Mosbacher, wife of oil magnate Robert Mosbacher, secretary of commerce in the Bush administration. "There's a difference between cultivating people and going out of your way to offend them," said a horrified woman who witnessed the scene. "I could tell you ten stories like that."

Arthur Jr.'s office on the eleventh floor of the Times Building was similarly a stylistic counterpoint to his father's. Punch's complex of rooms communicated unostentatious tradition and a comfortable dowdiness; Arthur Jr.'s office conveyed modernity and informality. His desk, reached across an expanse of blue wall-to-wall carpeting, was sleek and modular; at one end stood his computer — the only terminal at the paper able to access both the news and the business operations — with an eye-popping *Star Trek* screen saver. In his small sitting area, two salmon-colored chairs and a couch surrounded a cool, dark green marble coffee table. On a side table sat an orange model motorcycle with a helmeted rider and sidecar, a reminder of the sidecar Arthur Jr. had once owned in London. Across the room, above the dark-stained wooden reading easel, was a large movie poster advertising John Wayne in *Sands of Iwo Jima* — an odd choice for a man who so consciously disdained the traditional macho stereotype. Visitors were startled to see the publisher of *The New York Times* don a headset and answer his incoming calls with a curt "Sulzberger!" or fling his leg over the arm of his chair as though he were at home watching television. Except for photos of past publishers and immediate family members, the only touch of tradition was a loudly ticking ship's clock by Seth Thomas.

Punch hated making speeches and whenever possible tried to avoid them. Arthur Jr. not only enjoyed declaiming from the podium, he was gifted at it. For an important speech, he spent several days interviewing people by phone and consulting the large clipping file he maintained for such occasions. Once he finished a draft, he rehearsed the speech out loud, often in front of his secretary, and churned out as many as ten complete revisions before settling on a final version. Unlike Punch, who painfully read his lines and disliked the unpredictability of public settings, Arthur Jr. was a born showman — quick on his feet, comfortable with extemporaneous remarks, and adept at fielding hostile questions from the floor.

A year after he was made publisher, he presided over the first of what would become annual staff meetings on the state of *The New York Times*. The number of news and business employees was now so large that he had to book the event into Town Hall, a theater on West Forty-third Street, and give the same presentation three or four times in order to accommodate the crowd, but he was determined to let everyone at the paper have a shot at him. The formal program, which included overhead slides showing advertising and circulation numbers and other trends, was part sales meeting, part tent revival, and part corporate annual report. Punch would never have made himself so vulnerable, especially in a situation that required mastery of financial detail; Arthur Jr. seemed to relish it. Once the scripted part was over, he would walk out from behind the lectern, lean on one side of it as though he were spending a casual afternoon in a bar, and field questions. The staff admired Arthur Jr.'s accessibility; they thought it showed "guts." But the same instinct that propelled him to be open also gave exposure to a surprising insensitivity. When one employee stood up to express concern about the company's

401K plan, Arthur Jr. scoffed. "How old are you?" he demanded. "Forty," the man replied. "You're too young to be worried about that," Arthur Jr. told him. "Hell, I'm forty-two and *I'm* not worried about a 401K yet." Throughout the room, eyes rolled. Arthur Jr., denizen of mass transit, patron of inexpensive Chinese restaurants, a man who had refused the car and driver that came with the publisher's office, had just betrayed himself as a rich kid.

44

A Smile, a Shoeshine, and a President

ARTHUR JR. HAD THE MISFORTUNE TO BEGIN HIS publishership during a period of severe financial constraint. The advertising boom of the expansionist 1980s had proved to be a historical anomaly; never in the following decade would the *Times* experience the extraordinary linage it had enjoyed before the crash of 1987. By 1992 the national recession pounding the country had put its own peculiar stamp on New York City. Everywhere, businesses were closing or declaring bankruptcy, among them important retailers such as Alexander's and B. Altman's, whose ads had long graced the paper's pages. The *Times* laid off fifty-five people, including six junior members of the news staff — the first forced reductions since the 1970s — and bought out more than two hundred more, while expenses for coverage of the Persian Gulf War, the Olympics, and a presidential campaign strained the budget. An acrimonious dispute with the mailers and the drivers' union, whose members bundled and sorted papers and delivered them to newsstands, street boxes, and subdistributors for home delivery, cost the *Times* millions in lost sales. At the end of Arthur Jr.'s first full year as publisher, the paper's profit had plummeted by a third; the company as a whole had a net loss of $44.7 million.

At the same time, the role of newspapers was undergoing a metamorphosis. The Internet was on the brink of becoming a revolutionizing medium, while on television, CNN delivered news instantaneously, all day and all night; cable channels like C-SPAN and Court TV dissolved the barrier between the viewer and an actual event. Increasingly, *Times* headlines conveyed news that was already familiar to many readers from other sources. Arthur Jr. figured that only 10 percent of the stories in his paper every day were reported exclusively in *The New York Times*, a change that, he said, redoubled reporters' responsibility to "add value" by explaining and interpreting the news.

But added depth didn't attract the many overworked baby boomers stretched thin for time, or Generation Xers whose lack of interest in reading had been blamed on everything from television to personal computers to the dissolution of the nuclear family. No matter how colorful or entertaining or user-friendly newspapers became, people were abandoning the habit of reading them. In 1990 barely 50 percent of Americans said they read a paper every day, down from 75 percent in 1967. In the New York metropolitan area, just one in ten households subscribed to the *Times*, a dismal performance compared with the home bases of *The Boston Globe*, the *Chicago Tribune*, and other big-city dailies.

The one constant on which *The New York Times* could depend was its quality, which continued to soar above that of other newspapers. As newspaper chains and conglomerates bought up papers, draining them of their individuality and demanding profit levels that struck at the heart of their news-gathering apparatus, *The New York Times* had come to resemble an oasis of excellence. To be sure, there were other superior papers — *The Washington Post*, the *Los Angeles Times*, *The Wall Street Journal* — but in many cities across America, papers that once proudly produced original national and foreign coverage had long since abandoned it because of the expense. The gulf between the great and the mediocre had widened, leaving *The New York Times* in an isolated splendor from which it could derive pride but little pleasure. For decades much of the paper's influence had come from its ability to inspire imitation in its journalistic brethren. Now, with some chains setting profit goals of 30 percent or higher, editors had to make their numbers. By the time Arthur Jr. became publisher, *The New York Times'* power as a shining example for other papers had been lost to the bean counters. The popular wisdom was that the *Times* might win Pulitzer Prizes, but it didn't make money. The nation's publishers admired it in the abstract and were glad it was there, but it was no longer a viable model.

Arthur Jr. appreciated full well the position *The New York Times* occupied in the constellation of American journalism. The paper had always been edited by elites for elites, and despite his desire for diversity and egalitarianism and just plain financial survival, he had no intention of changing its basic nature. He simply wanted to make the *Times* more accessible, to broaden its appeal without sacrificing its depth. Like Punch and the rest of the Sulzberger family, he considered the newspaper to be the essence of The New York Times Company. The company's magazines and television stations and regional newspapers existed to provide a steady stream of income to protect the *Times* from the harsh realities that had diminished other papers. "Yes, we make money," Arthur Jr. said, referring to the company as a whole. "But we make money to continue our search for truth." And "truth," he explained, was *The New York Times*' mission — "probably one of the greatest missions of any organization in the world."

Not everyone at the company shared Arthur Jr.'s view. For those in "corporate" — the shorthand term people used to refer to everything the company owned apart from the newspaper — preservation of *The New York Times*' independence was no longer a primary motivating force. With the disappearance of the outside threats that had plagued Punch — crippling strikes and the lack of a diversified financial base — corporate didn't feel as protective of *The New York Times* as it once did. One factor influencing the changed attitude was that the paper no longer brought in the majority of profits. Indeed, during the economic downturn in New York, the company's twenty-eight regional newspapers jointly made more than *The New York Times*.

While Walter Mattson had been president of The New York Times Company, these two camps — the newspaper and corporate — were integrated at the top for the simple reason that Mattson, having also assumed many of the functions of the publisher and the chief executive officer, dominated both. That arrangement came to an abrupt halt with Arthur Jr., whose desire to be a "complete publisher" meant that he had no interest in subcontracting out any of his authority to Walter Mattson or anyone else.

It was anticipation of his lessened power over the newspaper, among other things, that caused Mattson to take early retirement in the fall of 1992. He was also aware that his role with the Sulzberger family was about to change. Since first becoming president in 1979, he had worked with Punch to place family members in jobs at the company, charting their career paths, evaluating them, and in at least one case easing them out. Once it was certain that Arthur Jr. was going to win the publisher-ship, Mattson looked ahead and saw that he was bound to be drawn into the competition between Arthur Jr. and his cousins for the rest of the prize: Punch's titles of chairman and chief executive officer. Mattson had some physical problems and had long told colleagues he hoped to take early retirement, but left unsaid was the brutal truth: he assumed

Arthur Jr. would likewise triumph in the contest for Punch's power, and he wanted no part of it.

While Arthur Jr. was grateful for the unsparing approach Mattson had taken to his professional development, he also felt they were stylistic opposites. If Mattson had remained in place, the confrontational relationship he and Arthur Jr. already had would surely have escalated into open warfare. For that reason, Mattson decided that it was better to retire and allow Arthur Jr. to go his own way with a "new team other than me." Punch, however, vehemently wanted Mattson to stay and repeatedly tried to talk him out of his plans. "He welcomed Walter's dictatorship," said a senior executive, "but I think there was also a bond of trust there and they genuinely liked each other." Despite Punch's pleas, Mattson remained determined to retire.

Once the finality of Mattson's decision sank in, Punch felt betrayed. Not only did Mattson's departure mean that he would now have to assume more of the day-to-day management of the company than he felt comfortable with, but Mattson had given him no room to maneuver in the choice of who would follow as president. The only executive remotely prepared for the job was Mattson's handpicked successor, Lance Primis — a man not of Punch's generation whom Punch did not know well.

Mattson had had his eye on Primis as far back as 1981, when Primis was the *Times'* vice president for advertising and Mattson was general manager and president of the newspaper. Mattson found Primis "enormously creative," a "wonderful storyteller," and "fun" — in short, a personable counterpoint to the hard-driving Mattson. In essential ways, though, Primis was as much a self-made man as Mattson, with the added gloss and sheen of a salesman. Born in Brooklyn to a close-knit, middle-class family one generation removed from the villages of Russia and Eastern Europe, Primis grew up buffeted by the crosscurrents of tradition, assimilation, and upward mobility. During his childhood his family was so strictly kosher that he had to bury a "meat" utensil in the backyard because he had mistakenly put it in a bowl of sour cream. When Primis's father moved his wife, daughter, and two sons eight miles east to the predominantly Italian American town of Valley Stream, Long Island, their Brooklyn relatives considered it heresy. Yet it was precisely because of their refusal to be bound by the cultural insularity uniting the rest of the clan that Primis's branch was considered the achieving one in the family.

Primis found his talent early in life: sports. Baseball was his winning skill, and he was accepted at the University of Wisconsin at Madison on a baseball scholarship. There he joined a fraternity that had a history of not admitting Jews, majored in English with an advertising/marketing minor, and tried to find his footing during the turbulent antiwar years. When students protested the presence of Dow Chemical recruiters on campus because the company manufactured napalm, Primis, dressed in a DRAFT BEER, NOT STUDENTS T-shirt, got teargassed along with the rest, but he later admitted he did it more to be seen as a regular Joe, not because the questionable morality of the war had genuinely enraged him. "I wanted all the bases to be covered," he said. "You never know who you might need."

An injury his senior year effectively ended his chance of a baseball career while simultaneously saving him from military service. Instead of a ball club, Primis joined Scott Paper Company, selling toilet tissue up and down a territory that stretched from lower New York State to Bayonne, New Jersey. He soon learned how to josh with a store manager to get access to the order book and how to slip a few dollars to the kid who stocked shelves to put another row of his "product" facing the customer. "I was the commander of the paper aisle," he said. "I loved it." But when he asked for a promotion after only a few months on the job and was told he was in too much of a hurry, he abruptly quit, figuring that luck would somehow provide.

It did. He soon received a call from *The New York Times'* personnel director, informing him of an opening in the advertising department. (In fact, Primis had not even applied to the *Times;* the University of Wisconsin had sent the company his résumé.) In February 1969 Primis started his career taking classified ads over the phone, surrounded by gay men and older women, the mainstays of the paper's sixth-floor phone room. His self-confidence, unthreatening manner, and upbeat attitude made him a good salesman; he found it easy to persuade people to take out an ad not just for one day a week, but seven, not just for their car but for their house. The alchemy came when he opened the paper and saw the ad that he had taken, that he had typed, published in *The New York Times.* He became so enamored of the magic that during his first weeks in the phone room, he clipped out every ad he had sold and pasted it in a scrapbook.

After five months he was transferred to retail advertising, where he began his rapid rise up the ladder, becoming advertising director in 1979 at the age of thirty-three. By then he had thoroughly internalized the mystique of *The New York Times* and the strict separation between church and state. He recalled how the first time he attended a meeting in the newsroom, "I couldn't believe that some toilet-tissue salesman was roaming these halls" and felt overwhelmed to be "allowed" on the same floor with the people who actually produced the paper. Primis's awe was sincere, and it was a large part of his effectiveness as a salesman for *The New York Times*. He believed in the newspaper. But there was more than simple reverence behind his self-denigrating comments. Like Arthur Hays Sulzberger's joking about marrying the boss's daughter, Primis was always quick to say what he presumed others were thinking: that he was out of his league among the giants of journalism.

The man Mattson encountered in the early 1980s hardly appeared lacking in qualifications or confidence. During Primis's first year as ad director, the business-consulting firm of McKinsey & Company studied the advertising department and concluded that it urgently needed modernization. Later Primis would say that McKinsey taught him how to think. That was hyperbole, but what was indisputably true was that it helped him create a research-based marketing department out of what had been a collection of old-fashioned, reactive order takers. Using what he had learned from McKinsey, Primis devised the first marketing plan the newspaper had ever had. He raised ad rates 12 to 15 percent annually during the high-inflation period of the early 1980s. Then, with the onset of the Reagan years, advertising volume soared and ad revenue along with it. The humming economy was just another of Primis's lucky breaks. To Mattson, he looked like a marketing genius.

Mattson was congenitally predisposed to salespeople. He admired anyone who could speak well, make a smooth presentation, and hold a group's attention. Primis was all that and more. He had the capacity to adapt to people regardless of their station, and those who walked into his office invariably walked out feeling better, even though they couldn't quite put their finger on why. "Lance is the guy you'd want to ride across the country with, have as your college roommate, or have as your boss," said Russ Lewis, then deputy general manager. "He could be the host of *The Tonight Show*."

Mattson had overwhelmed people with his grasp of facts, whether the subject was printing presses or the demographics of New York City. Primis overwhelmed people with his glib charm. He had the ability to pick up complicated information quickly and parrot it back — not always with complete understanding. His speech was sprinkled with malapropisms and his crude locker-room patter and references to football and baseball terms made some female executives feel shut out. Once, while explaining to senior staff members how he talked retailers into buying ads, he played the part of the advertiser by tucking up his legs and spreading them, as if to say, "Come fuck me." Whereas Mattson wore his frugality like a badge of honor, Primis played golf — a game Mattson dismissed as a rich man's sport — and reveled in his red Lotus. Such ostentation in any other executive would have caused Mattson to raise an eyebrow. Instead, he was smitten. "Walter held Lance not just in high regard but liked him," said Lewis. "It was mostly a love affair."

Primis was one of the few people on the business side of the company who could tease Mattson and talk back to him. When Mattson pushed, he pushed back, a trait Mattson liked because it showed that Primis was prepared to fight for what he wanted. In meetings, Primis cleverly got his way by staging calculated bouts of silence. "I used to pout," he said. "I wouldn't say anything, and Walter hated that." The two were classic mentor and protégé, father and son, and by the late 1980s it was obvious to other *Times* executives that Mattson had chosen Primis to be his successor.

On September 17, 1992, Punch announced that Lance Primis, forty-six, would replace Walter Mattson as president of The New York Times Company and that Mattson would retire but remain involved in company affairs as vice chairman of the board. Curiously, in the official press release there was no indication of who would fill Primis's former spot as president and general manager of the newspaper. In fact, Arthur Jr. had persuaded his father that he should do the job himself for a while. He wasn't ready to name a replacement yet, he explained, and argued that working both jobs — publisher, and president and general manager — would be good experience for him. "He wanted to make the point to the business side as well as the journalistic side that he was in complete control," said former managing editor Seymour Topping.

The arrangement complicated Primis's first days as company president, and he made no secret of his annoyance. "*He's* going to be general

manager?" he sneered to associates. "May God have mercy on us!" He
needn't have worried, for within six months Arthur Jr. had had enough.
Thin and stressed by the long days and rancorous Greenwich meetings,
which had dramatically demonstrated the difficulty of wearing two
hats, he appointed deputy general manager Russ Lewis to fill the position. "He was trying on the idea of being his own president, no question
about that," said a close colleague. "[But] I never saw anyone so happy to
turn the job over."

He was now free to focus completely on being publisher, a job that
required him to report to his father on issues related to news and to
Primis on issues related to business. When Primis had been president
and general manager of the newspaper, he had reported to the publisher. Now the roles were reversed, and Arthur Jr. was answerable to
Primis, who as company president had oversight of the newspaper's
budget. The new dynamic provided fertile soil for rivalry. Arthur Jr., in
particular, felt hemmed in. "He underestimated how much of Punch's
power accrued from being both publisher and CEO," said *Times* columnist Anna Quindlen. "That made his relationship with Lance prickly
because he wants to be able to say, 'We want to do this? Fine, let's do it.'
[And he can't]." So sensitive was the power arrangement that none of
the internal organizational charts showed Arthur Jr. reporting to Primis.

In their strong speaking style and towel-snapping humor, Arthur Jr.
and Primis were alike. Even their names — Arthur and Lance — evoked
the friendship between King Arthur and his staunch knight Lancelot.
But they were different in a way that was particularly ironic. Arthur Jr.,
the scion of wealth, didn't trust luck, while Primis, the boy from Brooklyn, asked his secretary to buy him weekly lottery tickets and turned a
deaf ear to bad news. Ever the salesman, his modus operandi was to be
relentlessly upbeat whatever the circumstances, confident that he could
charm himself out of any dilemma. Once when a senior executive asked
Primis to recount his rise to the presidency, she was amazed to hear him
tell the tale as one of serendipitous good fortune — no sweat, no struggle, no clawing. "I think he genuinely believed that," she said.

The Di-Gel on his desk told a different story, as did the baseball bat
resting in the corner of his new fourteenth-floor office, located at the
opposite end of the hall from Punch. Primis was a star pitcher who had
gone on to be a star pitchman for *The New York Times*. By all rights, he
should have kept a ball and glove as a token of his talent. Why showcase

a symbol of what he couldn't do, rather than what he could? "It's a huge frustration," Primis said. "I sit here and I hold the bat and I say, 'If only I could have been a hitter.'"

He had reasons to feel inadequate. Although he was now president of an entire corporation, his expertise was almost entirely in one area: advertising. He had a chairman he barely knew, a publisher who saw him as an impediment and potential rival, a corporate staff frightened and passive after years of autocratic rule, and new constituencies in the form of directors and shareholders and Wall Street analysts, whose culture and language he didn't yet understand. "I wasn't trained for this job," he wearily told a member of the senior staff two years after being named president. She was taken aback by Primis's candor, but not by the sentiment: "I think he was letting me know that . . . it wasn't his fault things weren't going well."

45

Whispers and a Megaphone

I N THE SPRING OF 1992, WHILE ARTHUR JR. WAS
visiting Washington, D.C., for the annual Gridiron Club dinner, he
sat in on one of the bureau's brown-bag lunches. As part of his
report on the home office, he unveiled a prototype of a new section the
Times was about to launch in its Sunday edition. Called Styles of the
Times, it combined the gossipy glitz of *The Washington Post*'s well-read
Style section with edgy features on fashion, parties, and downtown
music and clubs. The aim was to lure members of the MTV generation
to the Sunday paper by trying to be something *The New York Times* had
never been before: hip. "Younger readers had better like it, because all
the older ones will drop dead when they see it," Arthur Jr. joked to the
Washington correspondents.

He was not wrong. With stories on gay rodeos, a clothing store special-
izing in lace-up "bondage trousers" for skinheads and dominatrices, and
the joys of Billy Idol and cyberpunk, Styles of the Times was Arthur Jr.'s
most visible first move as publisher — and one that, a year and a half
after its inauguration, he admitted was his first failure. It quickly became
the butt of jokes — *Time* magazine compared it to "a grandmother
squeezing into neon biking shorts after everyone else had moved on to
long black skirts"— and during its scant two years of existence, it tested
the limits of Punch's patience, outraged Carol, and increased the already
crackling tension between the news and business sides of the paper. And
most important in an era of dwindling profits, it never made money.

Like Weekend, Living, and the other sections that were created to rescue the *Times*' finances two decades earlier, Styles originated as a way to
attract advertising. Lance Primis suggested to executive editor Max
Frankel that the paper create a trendy new section with the tone and
demographics of *W,* the influential fashion-industry magazine. His goal
was to provide a place for the New York specialty shops and boutiques

that were frozen out of the first section of the *Times* because of Saks Fifth Avenue, Lord & Taylor, and other upscale, high-volume advertisers. To explore the idea, Frankel formed a committee heavily weighted toward younger staffers and, along with managing editor Joe Lelyveld, gave the dominant voice to a thirty-four-year-old consultant named Adam Moss.

Moss was the founding editor of *7 Days,* an irreverent weekly aimed at affluent young Manhattanites that had folded in the spring of 1990. That fall, at the suggestion of *Times* drama critic Frank Rich, Lelyveld had invited Moss to lunch. Good-looking and well dressed, Moss possessed downtown savvy and a passion for journalism that broke the mold. In him, Lelyveld saw the kind of plugged-in visionary the paper needed to rejuvenate its image; in Lelyveld, Moss saw an editor eager to respond to Arthur Jr.'s challenge to shake the dust of tradition off *The New York Times.* "[Joe] came on like this grand rebel and insurgent," Moss recalled. "The spirit of the conversation was 'We have to change this and we have to change that.' Everything was so full of possibilities." In March 1991 Moss agreed to join the paper as a consultant.

When Arthur Jr., Frankel, Lelyveld, and deputy general manager Russ Lewis saw the initial mock-up of Styles, they were knocked out by the giant pictures and extra-large type that set the design apart from everything else in the paper. For the debut issue, Moss and the committee gave Frankel two choices: a front page with a picture of a large red AIDS ribbon and an accompanying story about the growing backlash against wearing it, or a front page featuring a photograph of a bare human arm and fist. Underneath the headline THE ARM FETISH, the article analyzed "the body part as fashion accessory."

Frankel was against using the AIDS ribbon story; it was too newsy for Styles, he thought, and too much about death. The arm piece, however, was surprising. What he and the other senior editors were too square to realize, and what no one bothered to tell them, was that a muscular bare arm and fist was an instantly recognizable image of a specific form of sexual activity in the gay community.

The first edition of Styles of the Times appeared on Sunday, May 3, 1992. That evening Punch and Carol were dining with former *Times* correspondent Nicholas Gage and his wife when Gage volunteered that he had been startled to see "The Arm Fetish" in that day's paper because of what it meant in downtown gay circles. Punch and Carol gave each other perplexed looks. "It has to do with fist-fucking," Gage informed them helpfully. When the Sulzbergers remained bewildered, Gage was forced to give them a quick primer in gay sexual practices.

Because of his discomfort with "queers" and "dykes," nothing could have offended Punch more — except perhaps the parody of Styles that appeared several weeks later in *The Village Voice*, which featured a photograph of an aroused hunk in his underwear under the headline THE PENIS FETISH. Punch was unhappy that Arthur Jr. had publicly embarrassed him, although he knew that sons, especially those in family businesses, were inclined to do exactly that. But what really enraged him was the idea that *The New York Times* had been held up to ridicule. The "arm cover" quickly became a popular poster among New York City gays, and at Arthur Gelb's seventieth birthday party, Abe Rosenthal even made Styles part of his toast. "I knew we were in a new age when I saw the first edition of Styles of the *Times*," he said. "Not only did it give New York the finger, it gave it the whole arm." Punch, who was among the wellwishers, managed a wan smile. "It wasn't very hard to figure out [my father's discomfort]; even *I* picked up on that," said Arthur Jr., who later admitted that using the word *fetish* anywhere in Styles' maiden issue had been a mistake.

If its cover had been the section's only problem, Styles might have survived. But the gay-oriented stories kept coming, as did fashion pieces that many readers considered so cutting edge as to be incomprehensible. "Tell me, please, why is fashion only for 13-year-olds and nuts?" Russell Baker asked in his *Times* column after a Styles cover appeared featuring men's suits with the jacket sleeves worn separately from the jackets. Carol, who cared passionately about fashion and had many friends in the business, complained that the section favored Isaac Mizrahi and other designers she considered marginal and far-out while ignoring established names like Oscar de la Renta and Bill Blass. In public, at least, Arthur Jr. seemed pleased by the negative reaction. During a party at the Metropolitan Museum of Art, a dignified older man came up to him and said he thought that the jazzy new section was, well, "un*Times*ian." Arthur Jr. thanked him and later told a crowd of people that alienating older white male readers meant "we're doing something right."

Compared with the stand-alone sections created by Abe Rosenthal and Walter Mattson in the 1970s, the concept of Styles of the Times was not a radical departure. But Adam Moss was no Arthur Gelb, whose brilliance had spawned the once controversial Weekend section. Gelb had been a homegrown *Times*man, steeped in the paper's folkways and traditions, and instinctively knew how to devise something that was different but still consistent with *Times* values. Moss, on the other hand, was an outsider who wasn't familiar enough with the paper's audience to make sensitive choices. And while Rosenthal had monitored the rollout of each section in the 1970s with avid vigilance, Frankel and Lelyveld stood back from Styles, reluctant to interfere. "They said, 'Adam Moss, he's a very hip guy, he must know about this downtown scene. So, you do what you want because we're just old fogies,' " said national editor Soma Golden Behr. The result was a section that was practically an offshore operation within *The New York Times.*

The section faced practical problems as well. With very little money at its disposal, Styles was understaffed and largely reliant on freelancers. Fashion, which was presumed at first to be the section's driving force for stories as well as ads, didn't turn out to have enough news to sustain the necessary momentum. And as Styles' reputation became more and more controversial, advertisers began to withdraw, to the point that the *Times'* advertising department had to give away ads just to fill the space.

In November 1993 Punch and Arthur Jr. met with Frankel, Lelyveld, and Russ Lewis to evaluate Styles' prospects. When Punch stated in no uncertain terms that he wanted to kill the section, the editors pleaded for six months to turn it around. They got their grace period, but the business side, which had come up with the idea for Styles in the first place, abandoned the experiment. In June 1994 Styles died as a separate entity and was quietly folded into the back of the Sunday metro section. Three weeks later an item appeared on Page Six, the gossip section of the *New York Post,* claiming that Carol had been telling friends that she and Punch were upset about the direction the *Times* was taking under Arthur Jr. "Blatant baloney," Punch replied through a spokesman.

But the substance of the item was true. Styles may have been Lance Primis's idea and Arthur Jr. may have kept it going mostly to satisfy Frankel and Lelyveld, who continued to believe that all it needed was a slight rejiggering and more time and money, but he was the publisher, so it was his project. Although Punch hadn't wanted to interfere too much for fear of repeating the sins of his own father, Carol felt no such compunction. Styles had given her fresh ammunition with which to attack Arthur Jr., and she kept at it long after the section had disappeared inside the paper.*

Changes at the Sunday magazine only made matters worse. Less than a year after the launch of Styles, Adam Moss was appointed to the magazine to help modernize its look and brighten its content. Although he didn't have the top position, he wielded outsize influence because the magazine's editor, Jack Rosenthal, had little design experience. Within months the same sensibility that had shocked readers of Styles began cropping up at the magazine. A photo spread headlined LIVING DOLLS showed grown women dressed up as children, suggesting a sort of kinky child pornography, while an illustrated feature on the brisk market in Nazi memorabilia included items made out of human skin. Arthur Jr. was tolerant of such lapses in taste until the magazine ran a photograph of a naked Japanese S and M actress, bound with ropes, waiting to perform a scene for a video company called Prisoner Productions.

For one of the first times in his young publishership, he felt compelled to demonstrate that even *his* revolution had limits. He sent an outraged memo to Jack Rosenthal and instructed Frankel to run an editor's note apologizing to readers, conspicuously copying the correspondence to his father. "It was an inappropriate image for our paper," he said. "I came down with a ton of bricks on them." Moss later admitted that Arthur Jr.'s attitude took them all by surprise. "We thought the line was more flexible," he said. (Arthur Jr.'s warning apparently had little effect, for the following Sunday, one day before the Fourth of July, readers awoke to find a picture of a man with his pants bunched around his ankles, sitting on what appeared to be an outdoor latrine, waving an American flag with one hand and flashing the peace sign with the other.)

Arthur Jr.'s "line," unlike his father's, was a mixture of propriety and ideology. Both concerns came together in March 1994, when Arthur Jr. was called upon to make a quick and costly call about a Sunday magazine cover story. On its own, the feature — a debate between Floyd Abrams, the *Times'* outside counsel in the Pentagon Papers case, and feminist Catharine MacKinnon, a University of Michigan law professor, about pornography and the First Amendment — was hardly offensive. But when Bill Pollak, executive vice president for sales, walked into

---

*Several years later a more restrained version was revived as a stand-alone section called Sunday Styles.

the publisher's office and showed him the multipage gatefold ad that appeared immediately behind the cover — a promotion for Express jeans that was lurid even by contemporary advertising standards — Arthur Jr. immediately recognized the dilemma. "I could just see Catharine Mac-Kinnon standing up the next morning and saying, 'This is what *The New York Times* has done,' " he said. "She would have perceived this as being our political stance on [pornography]."

Pollak's concern was not Catharine MacKinnon; he just wanted to prevent any embarrassment for his advertiser and avoid outraged letters to the editor. The question was, With only hours before the presses began rolling, should either the story or the ad be changed? Arthur Jr. hastily summoned Pollak, Moss, and Janet Robinson, head of magazine advertising, to his office. To give himself every option, he ordered Robinson to see whether a different advertiser could be found, he asked Moss to come up with a substitute cover, and he told production to find out how much a change would cost. When the group reassembled three hours later, Moss had managed to make a new cover story out of a piece on U.S. aid to Afghan insurgents, previously scheduled inside the magazine, and Robinson had located a less provocative advertiser willing to take the multiple pages occupied by Express jeans. But change, in whatever form it took, would cost an astronomical sum.

Arthur Jr.'s anxiety perplexed Joe Lelyveld, who was sitting in as the paper's top editor while Frankel was out of town. "We run those ads," he shrugged. "Why pretend we don't?" Even when Russ Lewis, president of the newspaper, agreed that the cost outweighed the principle, Arthur Jr. remained convinced that it would not be right to let the magazine proceed as originally planned. "I felt [the *Times*] was inadvertently making a political choice," he said. "I just couldn't live with it."

That both the news side *and* the business side advised him to let the matter drop, however, gave him pause. Arthur Jr. decided to call his father, who had just arrived at his Southampton home for the weekend. "I wish you could see this," Arthur Jr. told him as he described the pornography cover story and the Express jeans ad in detail and explained why he thought one of the two had to go. Punch listened quietly. He had had his own complaints with the Sunday magazine, but offending an outspoken feminist didn't concern him. When Arthur Jr. finished, Punch offered no opinion but simply said, "Whatever you do, I'll support you." With that, Arthur Jr. ordered the cover changed from the

Abrams-MacKinnon debate to the Afghan insurgency, and he would later characterize the moment as his first real test as publisher. Moss and others considered it "a wild overreaction."

The Sunday magazine and Styles of the Times showed that Arthur Jr.'s clarion call to shake things up at *The New York Times* had been heard — sometimes too well. But such changes weren't happening in a vacuum; standards were coarsening everywhere in journalism. Even the once prim *New Yorker* sported the headline A SUITCASE FULL OF SHIT and published the word *fuck* four times on one page.

If ever there was a place that seemed impervious to the trend toward "buzz," it was the editorial page of *The New York Times*. The rise of televised political ads and professional spin doctors, along with the weakening of party affiliations, had made newspaper endorsements, even those of the mighty *New York Times,* almost beside the point. Since John Oakes's departure in 1978, the *Times'* editorial page had lost its heat and fallen into a liberal predictability that made it one of the least read parts of the paper. The *Times* educated its readers on current events, but only rarely did it stir passion. While Punch may have wanted the editorial page to reflect the institutional values of the *Times,* Arthur Jr. wanted his editorial page to have a more distinctive voice, a voice that echoed his own confrontational personality and outspoken views.

He found the person to produce such journalism in a strong-minded southerner named Howell Raines. With his curly salt-and-pepper hair, Roman nose, and incipient jowl, Raines, forty-nine, had the self-assured, slightly haughty look of a modern-day Caesar. Born in Birmingham, Alabama, and raised by a mother whose family hailed from the only pro-Union county in the state, Raines was a classic southern liberal on race. Birmingham-Southern College, the all-white institution where Raines earned his degree the same year the Civil Rights Act was passed, was just twenty blocks from the church where four young black girls had been killed in a bombing. "I wasn't protesting [during demonstrations that spring]; I was afraid," Raines said. "I lived through this great confrontation and didn't participate fully because I wasn't brave enough." The searing recognition of his own cowardice made him unusually interested in the moral questions of public life, and he determined never again to shrink from declaring his beliefs.

Raines had stayed in Alabama until he was twenty-eight, working for a variety of papers, including *The Tuscaloosa News* and *The Birmingham*

News. Three years as the political editor at *The Atlanta Constitution* and two years at the *St. Petersburg* (Fla.) *Times* followed, along with the publication of a novel and an oral history of the civil rights movement. Attracted by Raines's lilting southern style and tough political coverage, Abe Rosenthal had hired him in 1978 to report on the South from the *Times'* Atlanta bureau and cover the 1980 presidential campaign. In 1981 he went to Washington as the paper's chief political correspondent, briefly crossing paths with Arthur Jr., who was on the verge of joining the *Times* newsroom in New York. After one year as bureau chief in London — a miserable interlude because of his disintegrating marriage — Raines returned to the States to head up the Washington bureau.

Like Abe Rosenthal, Raines had only modest academic credentials. He had risen on his talent, competing with journalists who had come to the *Times* through the more common path of the Ivy League pipeline. In Washington he was a demanding taskmaster who had deliberately created a meritocracy, showering attention and plum assignments on a small lineup of stars while other reporters complained that he didn't speak to them for months. *The New York Observer,* a cheeky weekly known for its media coverage, likened his manner to that of the imperious Captain Queeg. He demanded that reporters stack books on their desks vertically instead of horizontally, and once ordered a news clerk to bring his office ficus tree out into the rain so it could be watered naturally. Privately, detractors turned his name into a verb: "to Raines" meant to have slaves and not admit it.

With his fervor for team-building and compassionate management, Arthur Jr. seemed an unlikely Howell Raines fan. But as someone who had struggled to prove that he, too, had earned his own success, Arthur Jr. found Raines beguiling. He also saw a kindred spirit: a contrarian whose values had taken shape during the sixties, who viewed the world as a moral battleground, who relished intellectual combat, and who wasn't shy about expressing his convictions in muscular, unequivocal language.

In the spring of 1992, shortly after Arthur Jr. was named publisher, Raines approached him with the idea of becoming a columnist once the presidential election was over. It was high time the paper had a Washington-based counterweight to the conservative William Safire, he argued. Arthur Jr. listened politely before making his own proposal: he wanted Raines to become his editorial-page editor. Raines had never written an editorial in his life, and the job was not on his list of things he wanted to do. "Why me?" he asked. "I want the page to have a distinctive literary voice," Arthur Jr. replied, "and you can provide that." Raines promised to think about it.

That summer, during the Democratic National Convention in New York, Raines and Arthur Jr. met for dinner. Raines expected the publisher to quiz him about his feelings on abortion, capital punishment, and other issues he was certain to confront as editorial-page editor, but instead, Arthur Jr. told him that his vision of the publisher's job was one in which the editorial-page editor and the executive editor would serve as two of his main advisers, along with the paper's general manager. What he wanted was a kind of informal executive committee that would plan the future of *The New York Times* on an ongoing basis. No publisher had ever conceived of the paper's leadership as a brain trust before. Being part of Arthur Jr.'s innermost circle gave the post of editorial-page editor an extra measure of power that appealed to Raines, and he agreed to take the job.

Raines's first days as editorial-page editor coincided with President Clinton's first days as president, and his vividly stern editorials on everything from the administration's budget strategy to its handling of the standoff with David Koresh in Waco, Texas, had Washington talking. Shortly after the inauguration, Arthur Jr. was invited to lunch at the White House with the new president. The conversation went along pleasantly enough until near the end, when Clinton asked why the *Times'* editorial page had been so hard on him. The paper had endorsed him, after all. Arthur Jr. explained that he liked to think of the *Times'* policy as "tough love." "I've seen the tough," Clinton replied. "Where's the love?"

Like Arthur Jr., Raines cherished the values of *The New York Times*, but tradition simply for tradition's sake didn't interest him. He wanted those in power to notice what the *Times* thought about local, national, and foreign policy, and under his leadership, they did. "There's not a paper in the country today where [officials] feel they have to pay attention to the editor of the editorial page because he can give you trouble," a retired Scotty Reston said five months after Raines took over. "They'll be paying attention to Howell Raines."

The Jewish community had never *stopped* paying attention to the *Times'* editorial page, regardless of who edited it. While Arthur Jr. had none of the anxieties about Jewish issues that had bedeviled his grandfather during World War II, he nonetheless had to acknowledge that a large segment of the Jewish community regarded the *Times* as hostile to Israel. Whatever satisfaction Jews may have taken from the appointment of Thomas L. Friedman as the paper's first Jewish bureau chief in Jerusalem in 1984, it was tempered by what some considered to be his hypercritical coverage of Israel and, later, by his tough columns about the Jewish state on the Op-Ed page, which Raines oversaw. Like Punch, Arthur Jr. took a hands-off approach to both news and opinion. "If someone ever screamed at Arthur Jr. or his father about me, it has never been communicated to me," said Friedman. "I feel totally insulated."

As publisher, however, Arthur Jr. could hardly escape complaints about the paper's treatment of Jewish issues — many of which came freighted with assumptions about his own background and bias. When Esther Girsberger, the incoming editor of Zurich's *Tages-Anzeiger* newspaper, paid a call on Arthur Jr. during a visit to New York, she criticized the *Times'* coverage of the hunt for Nazi gold and editorials she felt were unfair to the Swiss. The meeting turned combative when she mentioned that she was distantly related to Jews and had spent time in Israel. "Well, you know," Arthur Jr. informed her coolly, "*I'm* not Jewish." Under different provocation, of course, he was quite capable of saying he *was* Jewish.

Arthur Jr. liked the editorial page's iconoclastic style and was secretly thrilled when it made people in power furious. The change pleased even the conservative Carol, who agreed with the attacks on the Clinton administration while at the same time proclaiming Raines's stand on affirmative action to be motivated by "typical southern guilt." Not since the days of Arthur Hays Sulzberger had the publisher of *The New York Times* and its editorial-page editor been so much of one mind.

But if Arthur Jr. had learned anything from the William Kennedy Smith/Patricia Bowman rape incident two years before Raines's arrival on the editorial page, it was that *The New York Times* wielded enormous power. He had begun to realize that in order to preserve that power, he would have to use it sparingly, strategically, intelligently. So although he never disagreed with the substance of Raines's editorials, privately he came to feel that sometimes the pieces "overmade their case" or "made their case too harshly." He and Raines began to talk about shadings and nuance; gradually the page became less strident. "You don't need a megaphone from that platform; whispers carry," Arthur Jr. told two visitors in 1994, using words his father no doubt had used with him only a year or two earlier.

46

Management in a Bucket

O N A SUNNY SPRING DAY IN 1993, LANCE PRIMIS, his sleeves rolled up and his coat off, loped into the *Times'* fourteenth-floor boardroom and took a seat at the head of the long, polished conference table. The dozen vice presidents to his left and right had carefully avoided the two or three places closest to him. Primis wrapped his legs around either side of his chair and rhythmically bounced his shiny black tassel loafers on the floor like an athlete ready to perform. "I used to think it was just Walter, but I'm glad it's just the position," he quipped, a reference to his predecessor's reputation for intimidating subordinates. Two executives took the hint and moved in closer.

Primis removed his watch and placed it in front of him to monitor the time. The staff knew what was coming: the dreaded "bucket speech." Primis had made the same presentation to other groups of managers in the company. It was his version of a campaign stump speech, a call to arms for executives to "break out of the cocoon," as well as a declaration of strategy, his first as president. "I have divided the company into four buckets," Primis began, glancing at notes he had scribbled on a yellow legal pad.

Primis had spent the first eight months of his presidency trying to understand what The New York Times Company was all about. He had visited executives in every corporate department and at every subsidiary, asking them how they thought the company should position itself for the future. The question caught managers off guard. Primis was the president; wasn't it *his* job to tell *them* their direction? Certainly, that was what Mattson had done, but Primis didn't have his mentor's taste for detail, nor was he interested in doing everything himself. "If you think I'm spending my nights worrying about your operating division, forget it!" he had told one startled *Times* sales executive. "My radar screen is up here," he said, indicating a high perch, "and you don't even make my screen unless there's a problem."

In sentences thick with management jargon, Primis listed the four "buckets" that made up the company: the businesses the *Times* already owned; potential new "synergies" and "value-added" projects involving the company's regional newspapers, magazines, and broadcasting properties; new acquisitions and partnerships that would "deliver" the content of *The New York Times* and other publications to readers via fax, CD-ROM, and on-line technologies; and research and development into "businesses we don't know anything about [yet]." Managers should be ever mindful that the company's "core competency" was gathering and editing news, he explained, but warned them that "if you do what you always did, you'll get what you always got" — and that wasn't good enough anymore. Primis's mandate — from Punch, from the board — was to "grow the company," and the only way he could do that was to make the culture less "vertical" and more "horizontal."

The managers listened quietly, for a few of Primis's ideas — marketing *New York Times* stories to Hollywood filmmakers, for example — frankly shocked them. Timidity characterized the staff Primis had inherited from Walter Mattson, a staff that had grown cautious and flabby under a president who interceded to solve every crisis. They had had no experience taking risks or making independent decisions, and without Mattson's sure and dominating hand, they were virtually paralyzed.

Primis suffered from a different handicap: he had come to the presidency of The New York Times Company with little training and no coherent vision. The second half of his title was chief operating officer, but as far as many *Times* executives were concerned, Primis wasn't an operations guy and didn't understand business as Mattson had. The "bucket" speech was a stab at defining what he wanted to do, but it was little more than a pastiche of ideas cribbed from recent books on management theory. Primis was struggling, searching, and clearly at sea about what should be done with all those "buckets."

His uncertainty was on display in the months preceding the *Times'* June 1993 announcement that it planned to buy *The Boston Globe*, the largest newspaper in New England. Under normal circumstances, the New York Times Company president would have been centrally involved in the negotiations. But Primis was too inexperienced to do more than stand on the sidelines while Punch and Walter Mattson, now vice chair-

man of the board, put the agreement together. The one responsibility
Primis did have — to address the *Globe*'s directors the night before their
vote on the proposed merger — was such a disaster that the deal fell apart
completely, and it took five months to put the pieces back together.

Discussions had begun in October 1992, with a courtly overture from
Punch to William (Bill) O. Taylor, the *Globe*'s publisher and chairman
of the board of its parent company, Affiliated Publications Inc. The
Taylors and another family, the Jordans, descendants of the founder of
Jordan Marsh department stores, had controlled the *Globe* since 1873.
Two trusts — one for each family — owned a third of the stock of Affil-
iated, which had gone public in 1973. But because Affiliated, like *The
New York Times,* had two classes of stock — voting and nonvoting — the
families jointly controlled 68 percent of the votes on the Affiliated board.

The family trusts were set to expire in 1996, and with approximately
125 heirs, only a few of whom were actively involved in the business, Bill
Taylor worried that the kind of rancor that had caused the Binghams of
Louisville to sell their *Courier-Journal* and *Times* to Gannett might
infect the Taylors and the Jordans. If it did, the *Globe* would become the
object of a bidding war and could easily end up in the wrong hands. To
circumvent that horror, the family quietly let it be known that they were
seeking an owner with similar values, at a price that would keep the
heirs united.

From the *Globe*'s perspective, The New York Times Company was a
suitable match, and Walter Mattson was discreetly informed that if
the *Times* was interested, Bill Taylor would be receptive to a phone call
from Punch. Mattson and Punch were both giddy at the prospect of
acquiring *The Boston Globe,* which would provide a significant diversification away from New York City and give The New York Times Company
access to the elite Boston market, with its many universities, hospitals,
and high-tech companies. The *Globe* was one of the fifteen largest newspapers in the country, and because of the weakness of the Murdoch-
owned *Boston Herald,* it commanded most of the newspaper advertising
in its region. Besides the *Globe,* Affiliated also owned a 33 percent interest in BPI Communications, the publisher of nineteen magazines,
including *Adweek, Billboard,* and *The Hollywood Reporter.* "What we had
here was a once-in-a-lifetime chance to buy a Rembrandt," said David
Gorham, a *Times* executive. "You buy a Rembrandt or you pass it up, but
you don't get another one."

At sixty-six and sixty, respectively, Punch and Bill Taylor had been friends in the newspaper business for years, like their fathers and grandfathers before them. So when Punch made his initial approach, he didn't stand on ceremony, and by mid-November the *Times* and the *Globe* were negotiating in earnest. Once the price was settled on, however, several potential deal breakers emerged, including how much autonomy the *Globe* would have under *Times* ownership.

As time went on, Bill Taylor became increasingly nervous about the fine print that began cropping up in successive incarnations of the agreement. In late January 1993, a few days before the *Globe*'s eleven-member board was scheduled to discuss the deal and vote on it, he read the final draft and was alarmed to see that several of the red flags he and his family had raised had not been addressed as he had expected. "It feels like the *Times* is going to come in here like Napoleon conquering Russia," he fretted to one director a few days before the board meeting.

Into this strained atmosphere strode Lance Primis, who arrived at Boston's Ritz-Carlton Hotel on the evening of January 27, one day before the vote, to speak to the *Globe* board about the soon-to-be-consummated union. When Mattson had been asked which emissary he thought the *Times* should dispatch to address the *Globe* directors at this crucial moment, he had enthusiastically suggested Primis. Organizationally, it was appropriate for The New York Times Company to send its president, but more important, Primis was a skilled salesman.

Primis went into the dinner certain that his mission was "a three-foot putt," but as soon as the soup was passed, he knew he was in trouble. He had had no exposure to the *Globe* board before and had not been warned that Bill Taylor and several other *Globe* directors were having second thoughts. Moreover, because the final agreement called for Taylor to report directly to Primis — not to Punch, as one chairman to another — his youthfulness and inexperience only raised further concerns among the already agitated directors.

After the tables were cleared, Primis rose to make his speech. He consciously diluted the strength of his original remarks, but his nuts-and-bolts discussion of how the reporting arrangement would work between the *Globe* and the *Times* played directly into the directors' worst fears about its independence and local control, confirming Bill Taylor's already plentiful misgivings.

The next morning the directors voted unanimously against selling *The Boston Globe* to *The New York Times*. In New York, where the *Times* board had already voted affirmatively on the acquisition, Punch was stunned to get Taylor's call informing him of the decision. He had had every indication — from Mattson and from Taylor himself — that the sale would go forward. When he walked down the fourteenth-floor hall to tell Mattson and the other senior executives that the deal had fallen through, they didn't believe him at first. "It came apart last night," he informed them. "We didn't do our homework. We didn't have the thing under control."

That afternoon Punch called up Sherry-Lehmann, a premier New York wine merchant, and sent a case of French wine to everyone in Boston and New York who had worked on the negotiations, including the secretaries and junior associates at the investment firms advising the two companies. With each case was a card that read, "This would have tasted better with Boston baked beans." It was a typically classy Punch touch and helped defuse the tension and embarrassment.

Punch and Mattson didn't take Primis to task for his catastrophic appearance before the *Globe* board. Punch was certain that the two newspapers would eventually kiss and make up, and he was right. In March 1993 Mattson arranged to meet John Giuggio, a former *Globe* president and Affiliated director, at Giuggio's retirement home in Florida, and around the dining-room table, they drafted a revised agreement. Soon thereafter, they arranged for Punch and Bill Taylor to sit down and talk things through. Unlike the first round, this time Punch was very much in evidence, taking care to cultivate all the Taylors, including those in the younger generation. When Arthur Jr. went to Boston in April for the annual meeting of the Newspaper Association of America, he also made a point of having a meal with Ben Taylor, Bill's cousin and heir apparent. By late May the deal was back on track, with a critical provision allowing the *Globe* to remain a Massachusetts corporation and to become a subsidiary, not a division, of The New York Times Company, with its own board of directors. *Globe* management was given a five-year reprieve from changes; after that, the Taylors had a "moral commitment" from the *Times* that members of the Taylor family could continue to run the newspaper.

On June 10 the boards of *The New York Times* and *The Boston Globe* approved the merger agreement. The price — $1.1 billion, paid mostly in *New York Times* stock — was the highest ever for an American newspaper. This was "an extraordinary opportunity that we could not let pass," Punch exulted in the *New York Times* story that appeared the next day about the transaction.

Wall Street analysts, however, judged that the *Times* had paid a premium for a traditional urban newspaper in a part of the country with sluggish growth, when every other media company was investigating more dynamic investments. Shares of *Times* stock plummeted two and a half points the day the deal was announced, and would continue to drop to the lowest level in many years. When the *Times* announced on June 22 that it would spend $100 million to support the stock, *The New York Observer* expressed outrage. In a story headlined THE SULZBERGERS STICK IT TO TIMES STOCKHOLDERS, the weekly noted that the *Times* had paid forty times after-tax earnings for the *Globe* when "solid media companies" could be acquired for ten to fifteen times earnings. Moreover, said the article, the $100 million stock buyback "virtually depletes the company of its cash reserves." The latter wasn't literally correct, but over the next two years the *Times* would continue to prop up its stock, buying back a total of 22.4 million shares at a cost of hundreds of millions of dollars. "[The deal] was great for the Sulzbergers, terrible for the other stockholders," admitted Sydney Gruson. "It expanded the family's empire hugely without giving up one jot of control."

Punch was unfazed by the criticism. *The New York Times* was indeed a public company, but he and his sisters still had the majority of the votes on the board. As far as he was concerned, the *Globe* was a perfect strategic fit: a business the company knew how to run, and one that gave the *Times* a lock on the Northeast Corridor. What is more, the difficult negotiations had given him a chance to be a hero and to play the critical role of peacemaker with the Taylor family — all at the age of sixty-seven! Two days after the deal, Punch dined at Elio's, his favorite Upper East Side restaurant, where he was so excited that he could barely sit still. Normally a formal dresser and never a gadabout, he went from table to table with no tie or coat, his shirt unbuttoned at the neck, greeting friends and chatting as though he were the host at a wedding reception.

§

Lest he be accused of brownnosing, Joe Lelyveld, the *Times'* managing editor, was always quick to point out that he had acquired his weekend home in New Paltz well *before* the new publisher had. Arthur Jr. and Gail had ceased renting in the early nineties and had bought a two-story modern house surrounded by woods, with plenty of space for Gail to paint and a forty-five-foot-high rock-climbing wall in the main room for Arthur Jr. and their son, known within the family as "little Arthur," to practice belays. The Sulzbergers and the Lelyvelds were in and out of each other's homes a lot, but hardly every weekend.

So nothing seemed out of the ordinary when the two couples got together at Arthur Jr. and Gail's one afternoon in January 1994. Soon after their arrival, Arthur Jr. handed Lelyveld a mug of coffee and suggested that they all take a walk in the snow. As Gail and Lelyveld's wife, Carolyn, tramped on ahead, Arthur Jr. reminded Lelyveld that Max Frankel had asked to retire early. "I would like you to be the next executive editor," he said, drawing out each word to underscore the gravity of the invitation. Lelyveld accepted without hesitation, and for a brief moment the two embraced. Later, after the Lelyvelds had climbed into their car and started off for home, Carolyn turned to her husband. "What the hell was happening back there?" she demanded. Lelyveld said he had just agreed to become the next executive editor of *The New York Times*. He was more shaken than elated — evidence of the profound ambivalence he had felt about nearly every move he had ever made at the paper. "I was happy [about the promotion] but I didn't have any sense of triumph," he said. "It was never my dream."

Ever since Arthur Jr. had selected him as managing editor, it had been a foregone conclusion that one day Lelyveld would replace Frankel, but no one had expected Frankel to leave quite so soon. He was only sixty-three and a half, more than a year short of retirement age. Every other top editor at the *Times* had had to be shoved out the door, yet Frankel had actually requested to be relieved. He was, in fact, weary of the job, which had coincided with one of the worst economic downturns of the past several decades. In addition, the close relationship that had sprung up between Arthur Jr. and Howell Raines had generated rumors that Lelyveld might not have a clear field; to ensure that his man got the prize, Frankel decided to step aside before Raines made any further inroads. Frankel had quietly informed Arthur Jr. shortly after his humiliation at Greenwich that he planned to retire the following year. For the next eight months he had kept the news to himself, letting Lelyveld in on the secret only a week or two before Lelyveld's walk in the snow with Arthur Jr.

There were three appointments that any publisher of *The New York Times* could indisputably call his own: president of the newspaper, editorial-page editor, and executive editor. Arthur Jr. had already filled the first two slots with men of his choosing: Russ Lewis and Howell Raines. With Lelyveld's elevation, his team would be complete. But that still left Lelyveld's soon-to-be vacant post of managing editor, and while the executive editor officially made the decision, the publisher was always deeply involved. Lelyveld wanted to make an imaginative choice: someone with whom he could work easily, who would balance his strengths and weaknesses, and who would meet Arthur Jr.'s explicitly stated requirement that the next managing editor *not* be seen as the automatic successor to the executive editor.

Lelyveld sketched out a list of possibilities. Out of a sense of duty and decorum, he spoke to Howell Raines and Sunday magazine editor Jack Rosenthal. But he considered Howell too independent and headstrong to make a good deputy — "He would have had his own agenda, not mine," Lelyveld said — and Jack suffered from health problems and hadn't worked in the newsroom for over twenty years. In early March Lelyveld and his wife dined with Eugene Roberts, a onetime national editor of the *Times* and former president and executive editor of *The Philadelphia Inquirer*, who was now a member of the faculty at the University of Maryland College of Journalism. Lelyveld had first encountered Roberts, a laconic North Carolinian and protégé of Turner Catledge, while covering Ted Kennedy's appeal of the inquest in the Chappaquiddick case and was familiar with his disconcerting habit of suddenly going silent in the middle of conversations. His preternatural calm and squat frame had earned him the affectionate nickname "the Frog."

For all his quirks, Roberts was a superb editor. In 1972 when he had taken over *The Philadelphia Inquirer*, the paper was one of the worst in the country. By the time he retired in 1990, worn down by budget disputes with the owning Knight Ridder chain, the *Inquirer* had won seventeen Pulitzer Prizes under his leadership. Lelyveld respected Roberts as a newsman and as a manager; reporters would walk through fire for him, yet he had also successfully run the business side of the *Inquirer* and at one point had even been its circulation manager. Over dinner he casually asked Roberts how old he was. "Sixty-one," Roberts replied. The conversation then drifted off in other directions.

The next day Lelyveld phoned Roberts in Washington to get his counsel. How was he supposed to choose a managing editor without creating expectations that that person was his successor? he asked. "You could not have a managing editor at all," Roberts began in his slow southern drawl. "You could take two younger people and break them in with other titles and run a competition for a couple of years and then choose one of them. Or you could take an old fart who's two or three years away from retirement, appoint him, and buy some time." There was a short pause. "Well, how about *you?*" Lelyveld inquired. "Are you serious?" the stunned Roberts asked. "If you're willing to discuss it, I'll be on your doorstep tomorrow morning," Lelyveld replied. There were thorny financial details to iron out — since his retirement, Roberts had been a paid consultant to Knight Ridder, a *Times* competitor — but it was clear that he wanted the job.

When Lelyveld exuberantly told Arthur Jr. he thought he had found his managing editor, however, the publisher's reaction was muted. He was uneasy about Roberts' age and his ties to Knight Ridder. Because Arthur Jr. scarcely knew Roberts except by reputation, Lelyveld arranged a three-way lunch after the annual Gridiron Dinner in Washington. The meeting went well, and when Arthur Jr. and Lelyveld returned home, they broached the idea of Roberts's becoming managing editor with the *Times* chairman. Punch asked few questions and dismissed any potential problems regarding Roberts's financial entanglements. "If it's worth doing, let's not get hung up on details of money," he said. "Let's just find out how to do it."

Arthur Jr. remained uncertain. He knew the appointment would please old-timers at the paper who felt the *Times* had been hijacked by the Adam Mosses of the world, but was that the kind of message he wanted to send at this early stage in his publishership? His fears were allayed when word seeped out and the overwhelmingly positive reactions began to pour in. Roberts represented serious journalism and in-depth reporting, commodities that were in short supply even in what remained of the nation's great newspapers. *Times* columnist Anna Quindlen actually yelped with joy when Arthur Jr. told her the news. Bill Kovach, the *Times'* former Washington bureau chief, compared Roberts's impending arrival to London's victory over the German Blitzkrieg: "For the people who had been fighting *USA Today*–type journalism for years, the shelling has stopped." Lelyveld simply sat back and basked in the waves of approval.

One afternoon in early April, the day before the changes were announced in the newspaper, Frankel stood atop a desk in the newsroom and told the staff that Lelyveld would be succeeding him. Then Arthur Jr., his jacket off, his shirtsleeves rolled up, clambered up in Frankel's place. "We have some booze for you all over there," he said with comradely gusto at the conclusion of his remarks, waving his hand toward the champagne that had been iced down for the occasion. "Maybe the way Arthur lives, champagne and Budweiser are the same thing," one reporter commented later. "But to anybody in the newsroom, 'booze' means boiler-maker gin."

Finally it was Lelyveld's turn to climb onto the desk and make his first address to the troops as the paper's incoming executive editor. Lelyveld was a brooding, introverted, self-absorbed type and awkward at public speaking. He had turned down a speaking engagement scheduled for two days earlier because he worried that he would lose too much sleep if he accepted. Yet his talk in the newsroom that day was one of the best of his career. Despite the fact that he had rehearsed it, the speech appeared spontaneous and, for Lelyveld, was unusually emotional. As he remi-nisced about the moment five years earlier when Frankel had taken him to dinner and told him he needed "a brother," he got so choked up that he could barely continue. He saluted Frankel's leadership while at the same time alluding to the "good fun" Frankel had promised but had never quite delivered. "I want us to take ourselves less seriously and take what's going on out there more seriously," he said. When he had fin-ished, Mike Kaufman, a *Times* veteran and childhood friend, stuck out his arm to help him down. Lelyveld's hand was ice cold.

That night Lelyveld and his wife celebrated at Elio's. With them were eight close friends from the paper. As the wine flowed and a glow settled over the table, Carolyn leaned toward her dinner partner and alluded to what Arthur Gelb once described as Lelyveld's "on the one hand, on the other hand" habit of agonizing at every crossroad in his life: "I told Joe, Now that you're executive editor, I don't ever want to hear you say, 'I *think* I'm happy' again."

The remark spoke to Lelyveld's deep distrust of any emotion that hadn't first gone through the filter of his iron self-control. It wasn't that he disapproved of spontaneous behavior; he just rarely allowed himself to indulge in it. In 1971 Lelyveld, Mike Kaufman, and James Markham, another *Times* correspondent, had labored till 2:00 A.M. finishing a long piece on the Attica prison uprising. As they exited the Times Building, exhausted but elated, Markham broke into an impromptu tap dance under the streetlights of West Forty-third Street. "How I envied him!" Lelyveld said years later at Markham's funeral.

Lelyveld's background was complex. During World War II his father, Rabbi Arthur J. Lelyveld, had headed the Zionist Committee on Unity for Palestine and later helped influence President Truman's recognition of the state of Israel. In 1944 the family had moved from Omaha, Nebraska, where Rabbi Lelyveld had had a congregation, to New York City. By then his marriage was foundering, and for a year Lelyveld's parents lived apart while Joe and his younger brother bunked in with their paternal grandparents in a one-bedroom apartment on Ocean Parkway in Brooklyn. Decades later Lelyveld would weep while watching *Lost in Yonkers,* Neil Simon's play about a widower who leaves his two sons with their steely German grandmother, because it reminded him so much of the bewildering abandonment he had experienced as a child.

The family reunited in an apartment on Riverside Drive, but as national director of the Hillel Foundations, Rabbi Lelyveld was often out of town. Lelyveld's mother, an attractive, intelligent woman who had given up her dream of becoming an actress to perform her duties as a rabbi's wife, alternated between her work on a Ph.D. at Columbia and a job as a Hillel director at Hunter College, while a succession of maids cared for the boys. "After that year when we weren't together, I built up in my mind the idea that we were an unusually warm and close family, but I don't think it was true," Lelyveld later said. Eventually Lelyveld's father divorced his mother and married a younger woman with two children. His father's loyalty to his second family created a distance Lelyveld found difficult to bridge. "Joe has never been able to fully deal with that," said a friend. "He has never dealt with human failure very well."

Lelyveld's feelings about his father made him unusually rebellious toward authority, which led him to make his way at the paper on his own terms, regardless of what his superiors thought. Once when a colleague described himself as a man who had been a "good boy" during his *Times* career, Lelyveld burst into a laugh. "I've *never* been a good boy!" he said. Both he and Arthur Jr. were cockily independent, but within an extremely conventional context: *The New York Times.* Lelyveld was angrier and moodier than Arthur Jr., but they shared a tendency — obvious in Lelyveld, masked in Arthur Jr. — to be loners.

As an editor, Lelyveld was rational to the point of appearing cold, and his ambition for the paper was icily clear: simply put, he wanted it to be great. But "great" to Lelyveld meant publishing outstanding stories, period, whereas Arthur Jr. balanced his vision with the human element. "I don't think Joe thinks much about [making people happy]," said a colleague. "He thinks about what can we do to reward greatness so that more greatness happens. I don't think he worries about the run-of-the-mill reporter who's feeling bedraggled."

With such pronounced differences in priorities, some at the *Times* wondered why Arthur Jr. had put Lelyveld in charge of the paper. "All the negatives about Joe are very much at odds with all the things Arthur Jr. says he wants," said one young editor, "so he's faced with this cross-pressure: someone who is a brilliant journalist but who doesn't have the [desired] tone and temperament." Lelyveld had withering contempt for Deming, for example, an attitude that, because it came from the top, effectively stalled Arthur Jr.'s attempts to foster teamwork. Joe was all for Arthur Jr.'s efforts to promote blacks, gays, and women but was slow to release money in the newsroom budget earmarked for diversity training because he thought the approach naive and vaguely degrading.

Initially Lance Primis and others on the business side were nervous about the new executive editor. They had had few dealings with Lelyveld when he was managing editor and now feared that he harbored the conventional newsroom prejudice against the company's moneymakers. But they took comfort in the fact that Gene Roberts had used marketing research and other business tools at *The Philadelphia Inquirer* and were heartened by Lelyveld's early attempts to thaw relations. In July 1994, just a few weeks after becoming executive editor, he accompanied the paper's three top news executives, three top business executives, and Arthur Jr. to Mohonk Mountain House, a rambling nineteenth-century inn a short drive from New York City, for a mini–planning summit. It was the first time the news side and the business side had met formally since the ill-fated Greenwich conferences, and Lelyveld took pains during the weekend to strike a conciliatory tone. "They didn't all weep and reach out and touch my hand and embrace me," he recalled later. "But a couple of people said it had been a very positive thing."

47

The New "Good Son"

I N EARLY MAY 1994 ARTHUR JR. RETURNED TO HIS
office after a directors' meeting at the North Carolina Outward Bound
School to find a blistering handwritten note from his father marked
CONFIDENTIAL on his desk. While Arthur Jr. had been out of town,
Punch had read in *The New York Observer* that the *Times'* contract with
the Newspaper Guild, ratified only days earlier, provided health insurance
and other benefits for same-sex couples. "Domestic partners" benefits, the
first ever offered by a New York daily, fulfilled a promise Arthur Jr. had
made two years earlier to the National Lesbian and Gay Journalists
Association. But to Punch it was a distasteful surprise. Despite the fact
that he had been briefed numerous times on the Guild contract, he could
not recall ever having been told about this provision. Arthur Jr. certainly
hadn't mentioned it, because he was certain that if he had conscien-
tiously circled the language in red ink, his father would have vetoed it.

So instead he had deliberately gone around Punch and in the process
had embarrassed and angered him. "He has a right to be pissed at me,"
Arthur Jr. acknowledged a few days after receiving Punch's sharply
worded note. "I finagled it; I did an end run." But, he added with a tone
of moral certainty, "My father's position on [gay benefits] is wrong." If
Arthur Jr.'s actions sprang from an admirable principle, they also
revealed him as having a stereotypical son-of-the-owner sense of entitlement. Certainly no nonfamily executive would have dared flout the CEO's
firm policy on such an explosive issue.

In fact, Arthur Jr. hadn't expected his father to be blindsided quite
so completely. Through the normal chain of command, he had kept company president Lance Primis apprised of details of the Guild negotiations
as they unfolded, and had assumed that Primis, in turn, would do the
same with the chairman. But Primis would later insist that his attention

had been diverted by larger contract issues and he hadn't realized gay benefits were even part of the package. Although the publisher and the company president had differing recollections of who told whom what, they both knew that nothing infuriated Punch more than being surprised, especially by subordinates, *especially* on issues concerning homosexuality.

After he had digested the angry note, Arthur Jr. called his father to apologize. He had made a conscious decision to go around him, he admitted, but he certainly hadn't expected the news about gay benefits to catch him flat-footed. By then Punch had cooled down, though the incident left lingering doubts in his mind. In the next few years he would have to decide who should succeed him as CEO and chairman. The board of directors was pressuring him to resolve the issue, and for the first time in memory it was not a foregone conclusion that Arthur Jr. — or any family member — would inherit all of Punch's titles. Some on the board argued that the moment had come for The New York Times Company to behave like every other publicly traded corporation and appoint a professional chief executive officer, and perhaps even a non-family chairman. Although Punch was a reflexive advocate of family management, Arthur Jr.'s latest ploy momentarily sapped him of confidence in his son. The domestic-partners clause bothered him, but what disturbed him more was the devious method by which Arthur Jr. had chosen to achieve it. "Punch has to take into consideration the judgment of the person that he's appointing," said general counsel Kathy Darrow, "and that was not great judgment not to tell his father."

In the aftermath of the domestic-partners dustup, Arthur Jr. elected to be charitable about Primis's motives in the matter. The company president had been "trapped" and "in an awkward spot," he insisted. If Primis had trained a spotlight on gay benefits, Punch would surely have taken the clause out of the contract, and the president would have made an enemy of the publisher. What Arthur Jr. didn't say was that by remaining silent and letting the contract language speak for itself, Primis had also kept his own hands clean and, in the bargain, weakened Arthur Jr. as a rival for the position of CEO — a position Primis wanted for himself. "He left me hanging a bit," acknowledged Arthur Jr.

In fact, by the time the gay-benefits incident occurred, the rivalry between Primis and Arthur Jr. was already apparent. The two men met once or twice a week on issues related to the newspaper but otherwise kept their distance. When Primis urged Arthur Jr. to lunch with New

York real estate agents, to meet with theater association owners, and generally to be more visible among the movers and shakers of the city — all for the good of *The New York Times* — Arthur Jr. refused, arguing that it was wiser to stay close to home and improve the paper from within. Privately Primis complained that Arthur Jr. didn't listen to him or seek his advice. Soon Primis intimates began telling their counterparts at *The Boston Globe* that Arthur Jr. wasn't an automatic choice to inherit Punch's titles and that the young publisher didn't really count for much in the company's future. Such blatant nepotism would sink the stock price, they said, and tradition aside, the family couldn't allow that. When Joe Lelyveld heard similar murmurings during his own visit to the *Globe,* he was sufficiently alarmed to schedule a one-on-one lunch with Punch and inform him that, in his opinion, Primis's treatment of Arthur Jr. was "dangerous for the paper."

Punch had told Primis early in his presidency that an important part of his job was to "help me with my family," acting as his sounding board and counselor as he worked through the question of succession. But in the wake of Arthur Jr.'s fall from grace because of the domestic-partners clause, Punch gave Primis reason to believe that he himself was the new "good son."

Because Mattson hadn't engineered a way for his protégé to spend much time with the chairman, Primis had had almost no personal relationship with Punch prior to becoming president. The summer before Primis's promotion, the two had met only once to discuss their future together. "Well, Punch, are you ready for this?" Primis had asked toward the end. "Are *you* ready for this?" Punch had replied in the half-joking, half-truthful tone he sometimes affected. Then he made a comment that spoke to his apprehension of the twenty-year age difference between them, as well as his dismay at Mattson for leaving him with only one candidate for president: "So, I've got to train another one, huh?" In the months that followed, Punch became more actively engaged in the business. With the all-controlling Mattson in retirement, he seemed to enjoy a new sense of authority. "Finally there is someone whom Punch can really be a boss to," said his secretary, Nancy Finn, referring to Primis.

In the early months of Primis's presidency, Punch did make a point of nurturing their connection. The two would go out to Chinese restaurants and talk candidly far into the night about the company and the family. Afterward, Primis would retire to the pied-à-terre near Lincoln Center that he had bought soon after becoming president, kick off his shoes, and reflect with astonishment and delight that he, Lance Primis, a former toilet-tissue salesman, was in the incredible position of being president of The New York Times Company and a confidant of Punch Sulzberger. By the time the domestic-partners fracas happened, he felt certain that Punch was leaning away from choosing a family member as his successor — a decision that could only mean good things for Lance Primis.

But Primis had always had difficulty distinguishing between personal relationships and business ones. His position was not as strong as he thought it was, and he soon made missteps that caused Punch and others to wonder again whether he was qualified to run the company. During a day-and-a-half meeting in Southbury, Connecticut, Primis asked his top executives the same question he had asked them soon after taking over: "Tell me what our strategy should be." But this time, he didn't really care what answers came back, for he had already decided that he wanted to create a new division made up of smart outsiders "committed to getting us into businesses that expand the box." Primis knew he didn't have the background to decide which innovative new lines of business the company should pursue, nor did he feel confident that the staff he had inherited could help him.

When it became clear that Primis was manipulating his executives into agreeing that the company needed to go outside for expertise, they reacted with indignation. Between sessions, they asked one another again why *Primis* didn't have any ideas, and wondered aloud whether he knew what he was doing. They felt that Primis had as much as admitted that *he* didn't have the vision the company needed and then had pointed an accusing finger at *them* for not providing it. In fact, both statements were true. Several members of the Taylor family attended Southbury as representatives of *The Boston Globe* and appraised Primis and his team with the dispassionate clarity of outsiders. In private they confessed shock at the irresoluteness and amateurishness of *New York Times* management, at the warring camps within the company, and at the damaging competition between Primis and Arthur Jr.

At Southbury Primis floated the idea of buying the Madison Square Garden arena, the New York Knicks and New York Rangers, and the MSG cable television network from Viacom. Large media companies had recently awakened to the fact that by owning their own sports teams, they could eliminate the escalating cost of buying broadcast rights to the games. For a jock like Primis, the prospect held intrinsic appeal as well as the potential for generating huge revenues. Old hands at The New York Times Company were aghast; one executive dismissed it as a "macho strategy."

Neither Punch nor Arthur Jr. realized just how serious Primis was about acquiring Madison Square Garden until they read in the *Times* that the company was one of five prospective bidders. At the last minute Primis had scrambled to call and send faxes to *Times* directors with more details, but he couldn't reach most of them. "Punch came unglued," said an executive close to him. "He said [buying Madison Square Garden] was the stupidest thing he'd ever heard of. He basically said, 'Get out of it.' " To avoid public embarrassment, Punch told *The Wall Street Journal* and other publications that the *Times* hadn't really considered buying the Garden. The company was interested only in the MSG network, he explained, which fit in nicely with the *Times'* desire to add a video component to its portfolio. Since Viacom didn't want to break up the pieces, there was no use continuing the discussion.

The Madison Square Garden episode occurred barely a month after another incident that put Primis at odds with a powerful family member. The company announced that it was selling its women's magazines — *Family Circle, McCall's, Child,* and *Fitness* — to Gruner + Jahr, the U.S. publishing arm of Bertelsmann, Germany's media giant. Michael Golden, who had been the acting head of the women's magazine division since March, had had no inkling of the negotiations until Primis left a nervous message on his answering machine the day the board authorized the sale, asking him to drop by his office, as he had "something to discuss." The more Michael tried to dissuade Primis from selling, the clearer it became that if the buyer wasn't Gruner + Jahr, it would be some other publishing conglomerate. "He didn't care who it was, he was going to sell it," said Michael.

After the sale was announced, Michael became a family member without portfolio at the company. In an attempt to turn the situation to his advantage, he soon proposed to Primis that he take a position on the corporate staff, a change that would allow him to move from the Midtown high-rise where he had worked with the women's magazines to company headquarters on West Forty-third Street. He was determined to be a player in the looming succession battle, and he knew that he couldn't be a contender unless he got inside the New York Times Building, preferably in a post that put him on the executive floor, where he would have exposure to both Primis and Punch. When Michael had first arrived in New York from *The Chattanooga Times* in 1984, he had asked for a job at the paper but Mattson had refused, directing him instead to the company's magazine group. Michael had done as Mattson said, but soon after becoming general manager of *Child* magazine in 1988, he again lobbied Mattson and Punch for a business assignment at the *Times.* The answer once more was no, until Michael was finally made director of special sections in the paper's marketing department.

His tour at the *Times* lasted just four weeks, a period so short that Michael wryly referred to it as his "work-study program." He had barely gotten his pencils put away when the publisher of *McCall's* quit. Mattson and Bill Kerr, the former McKinsey consultant who had become president of the magazine group, had both agreed that Michael was the only executive with the experience to step in and salvage the situation. The following year, realizing that he had no chance to succeed Mattson as president of the company, Kerr himself resigned, but not before recommending Michael as his replacement. Instead, Punch and Mattson had eliminated Kerr's position, leaving the women's magazine division and the sports and leisure magazines to report to Mattson as separate entities. By then Michael had worn so many hats at the company that his eleven-year-old nephew, Sam Dolnick, who collected business cards, devoted a whole page in his scrapbook to his uncle. "I just don't understand it," he confided to his mother. "Michael can't keep a job."

Indeed, by the time the women's magazines were sold, Michael himself was wondering whether he had made the best career moves, especially in comparison with his cousin. "Here's Arthur running a billion-dollar business while I'm screwing around with a two-hundred-and-fifty-million-dollar business that's making no money," he said. "Not smart." The contrast made him all the more convinced that he had to have a big mainstream job on his résumé, but Primis wouldn't hear of it. The last thing Primis wanted was another family member in the upper ranks of the *Times* parrying for Punch's titles, and he knew that Michael had precisely those ambitions. A year earlier, in his *New Yorker* piece on the Greenwich meetings, Ken Auletta had quoted an anonymous family member as saying that both Michael and his brother Stephen saw themselves as potential candidates to be chairman.

At the time, Ruth had chastised Michael for being so public about his goals — although, as he testily pointed out to her in a heated phone call, *he* was not the "family member" quoted in the article. What bothered her was not that her son had ambitions, but his candor, which had violated one of the Sulzbergers' most rigorously observed rules: family members never *ever* overtly express any hope or expectation for a position at the company. "You do a good job and wait to be called," explained Michael, describing exactly the philosophy Ruth had followed herself at *The Chattanooga Times.* More and more, however, the cousins' generation was beginning to reject the old dogma. Why *wasn't* it all right to campaign for jobs like other professionals did? After all, Arthur Jr. had not been coy about his aspirations, and "I couldn't find where that had hurt him," said Michael.

With a post on the corporate staff out of the question, Primis made two counterproposals — naming Michael publisher of *Tennis,* a *New York Times* sports and leisure magazine based in Trumbull, Connecticut, or sending him to Atlanta, where the company's regional newspaper group was headquartered. Michael knew that Primis had raised the specter of Atlanta merely to demonstrate that he had the power to make his life miserable, but instead of giving ground, Michael called Primis's bluff, calmly informing him that if relocating turned out to be the right thing to do, that was perfectly fine with him. Primis soon dropped the subject; his real intention was to place Michael at *Tennis.* When Michael protested that he had already spent eight years at the *Times'* magazines and was ready for something new, Primis said he thought he needed more operating experience. Besides, Primis added, "I haven't seen you in the magazine business on *my* watch."

When it became apparent that Primis was prepared to go to whatever lengths necessary to block his entry to the company's control center, Michael violated yet another Sulzbergerian commandment: he enlisted his mother in his cause. When Ruth came to New York in late July to attend a board meeting, Michael spoke frankly of his frustration. He did not ask her to press on his behalf — a strategy that would have affronted her sensibilities and been counterproductive — but simply sought her advice and asked for her backing. The next day, when Ruth saw Primis at the board meeting, she treated the subject lightly, never making a direct appeal. "I've promised my grandchildren their father will have a job," she said.

When Michael informed Punch that Primis seemed determined to send him to *Tennis,* Punch expressed bafflement. He had served with his nephew on the board of *The Chattanooga Times* and considered him thoughtful and knowledgeable. "That doesn't make sense," he told Michael. "I want you here [at the *Times*]." That may have been his wish, but Primis contended that Punch had never made it clear that Michael should be groomed for bigger tasks. Without positive marching orders, he said, he had no idea what he was supposed to do to develop Michael's career, and Punch declined to press the issue.

By late August, with Michael still in limbo, Primis invited him to lunch and asked him point-blank about his long-term career goals. Michael was aware that Primis had designs on being CEO, but he didn't mince words, announcing that he himself wanted to be chairman and CEO. Primis accepted the statement with seeming equanimity, and even when Michael told him that what he needed at the moment was a post that would make him a strong candidate for the twin titles, Primis acted as though he was genuinely interested in helping him. Their only point of disagreement, Primis said, was on which job would put Michael in the most advantageous position. Michael exited the restaurant with the buoyant sense that he had broken the logjam. But he had mistaken a pleasant lunch for a promise of aid.

In the fall of 1994 Michael finally accepted the inevitable and became publisher of *Tennis,* where he ended up learning more than he expected, but continued to wage a persistent though polite campaign to come to West Forty-third Street. As for Primis, he appeared to emerge from the sale of the women's magazines a winner: The New York Times Company board of directors applauded the decision and gave him most of the credit for the deal's success.

If the episode demonstrated anything, it was that the question of who would eventually run *The New York Times,* and how that person would be chosen, was rapidly gathering urgency. Everyone on the fourteenth floor knew that the mighty edifice of the *Times* rested on the narrow shoulders of one very mortal man — sixty-eight-year-old Punch Sulzberger. What would happen if some turn of fate removed him from the scene before he could use his authority to make clear a structure and a plan for the future? "Every Sunday night when I'm driving back into the city [from my country house], I say a little prayer that Punch will get safely from [Southampton] into New York City," said Kathy Darrow. "It's truly horrifying to think of the disarray [if he dies]."

48

Growing Pains

ARTHUR JR. WAS SITTING IN THE NEW ORLEANS airport in late April 1995, tapping furiously on his laptop computer, drafting a statement on which he hoped he and executive editor Joe Lelyveld could agree. Only hours earlier, while attending the final day of the Newspaper Association of America's annual meeting, he had learned the contents of a letter that the *Times* had received from the Unabomber, the fugitive terrorist who had killed three people and injured twenty-three others with small, handmade parcel bombs in sixteen incidents since 1978. In the communication, the Unabomber said he might send a longer document if a newspaper or magazine with nationwide circulation was willing to print it. How the *Times* should respond was a question of enormous weight — the most important decision Arthur Jr. had been called upon to make since becoming publisher — and he wanted to get clear in his own mind how he felt about it. Typing helped him think.

The letter had arrived the previous day, and one of the *Times'* secretaries, recognizing the widely publicized markings of the Unabomber's communications, had wisely not opened it but brought it to the attention of Lelyveld, who had turned the envelope over to the Federal Bureau of Investigation to be examined for any forensic evidence. The Bureau had agreed to send back a photocopy of the contents within twenty-four hours, and had kept its word.

Because there was no way to communicate with the Unabomber directly, Arthur Jr.'s only recourse was to make a statement in *The New York Times* and hope that he would read it. On April 26 an article appeared in which the publisher said that while the pages of the *Times* "can't be held hostage by those who threaten violence," the paper would consider anything the Unabomber sent.

Several weeks later, in late June, the Unabomber mailed copies of his sixty-two-page, single-spaced manifesto to *The New York Times, The Washington Post,* and *Penthouse* magazine. The document, entitled "Industrial Society and Its Future," was a screed against modern technology that contained references to thinkers as diverse as Eric Hoffer and the social scientist James Q. Wilson. In the letters that accompanied the treatise, the Unabomber said that if the full manuscript was printed by one of the publications within three months and if one of them agreed to print three annual follow-ups, he would stop trying to kill people.

Arthur Jr. held off responding so that he and his team could be briefed by the FBI on what it knew about the Unabomber. The Bureau's psychological profile of the killer closely matched that painted by a private agency the paper had hired for the same purpose. The Unabomber was a man who was tired and at the end of his game; a man who respected *The New York Times* and wanted his opinions published there because he thought it would give him legitimacy; a man who would insist on being in control of how his work appeared; a man who thought in legalistic, contractual terms and therefore could probably be trusted to keep whatever bargain he struck.

By mutual agreement, the information-swapping session between the government and the *Times,* held in New York City, was off the record. The last thing the Bureau wanted was to see its confidential investigative work splashed across the pages of the country's most prominent paper, while Arthur Jr. feared fostering the perception that the *Times* was in collusion with Washington. "We walked a fine line between seeking [the Bureau's] advice and, quote, cooperating in every instance," he said.

Deciding how to respond to the 35,000-word document was a question that consumed hours of discussion at the *Times.* Initially Arthur Jr. felt that the paper should publish the complete manifesto just as the Unabomber had requested, arguing that "a human life is worth more than the cost of newsprint." Lelyveld recoiled at the idea of turning over the pages of *The New York Times* to anyone, much less a terrorist. And there was always the worry that if the *Times* printed a political tract as the result of a veiled threat, it would set off a stampede of copycats who wanted their views publicized, too.

Not long after receiving the document, Arthur Jr. and Lelyveld flew to Washington for a working lunch at FBI headquarters with Donald Graham, the publisher of *The Washington Post;* Attorney General Janet

Reno; Louis Freeh, head of the FBI; and twenty of his associates. From the first, Graham and Arthur Jr. made it clear that they had decided to work in tandem. Whatever the *Times* did, the *Post* would do, and vice versa.

Although neither paper had yet decided on a course of action, the Bureau came to the meeting with a definite plan: it wanted each paper to publish selected sections of the manifesto as a news story. Its hope was not only to provoke a response from the Unabomber but also to release a substantial portion of the document into the public domain, where someone might recognize a turn of phrase or a pattern of thought that would lead to the killer. Arthur Jr. and Graham agreed to the proposal; the Unabomber's manuscript was certainly legitimate news, and by printing only portions of the document, neither the *Times* nor the *Post* could be accused of allowing a murderer to dictate what went on its pages.

On August 2 *The New York Times* and *The Washington Post* ran front-page stories on the Unabomber's manifesto. Under the headline PATTERN EMERGES IN BOMBER'S TRACT, the *Times* recounted the Unabomber's conditions for putting a stop to the killing and quoted Arthur Jr. as saying that the paper had not yet decided whether to comply. "[The] demand that the Unabomber have access to our pages for three years is especially troubling," he said in a carefully worded statement meant to smoke out the killer. "There's no easy way to open negotiations with this person, and for the moment we're stymied." The excerpts of the document that ran in the *Times* were different from those in the *Post;* each paper had made its selection independently, without advice from the FBI. The quoted material, Arthur Jr. said, represented "the judgment of our editors as to what is newsworthy."

Meanwhile, on West Forty-third Street, the debate raged on. Everyone involved in the decision — Arthur Jr., Punch, Lelyveld, editorial-page editor Howell Raines, and Russ Lewis, president of the newspaper — agreed that the issue didn't involve First Amendment freedoms. The government had not ordered the *Times* to publish the treatise; therefore, the paper's integrity would not be compromised if it did so. The more pressing concern was what could happen if the *Times* *didn't* meet the Unabomber's demands. "I could imagine a widow on her lawn, saying, 'I wish the *Times* hadn't been so high and mighty,'" Lelyveld said. Although most newspapers professed never to deal with terrorists, there was ample precedent indicating that they had done so. When Croatian separatists hijacked a plane at Orly Airport outside Paris in the 1970s, for example, the *International Herald Tribune, The New York Times,* the *Los Angeles Times,* and *The Washington Post* had published their demands in order to secure the release of the passengers.

By mid-September the Unabomber had not responded to the excerpts, and with the three-month deadline only ten days away, Arthur Jr. and Donald Graham met again in Washington with Reno and Freeh. The FBI director told the two publishers that the government had decided it wanted them to print the full document. In fact, Arthur Jr. and Graham had already had a private discussion beforehand and had made an independent judgment to do just that.

The conversation then turned to the mechanics of printing, and it was quickly decided that only *The Washington Post* would publish the full document as a stand-alone section in one of its daily editions. The *Times* didn't have the technical capability to segregate the treatise from the rest of the paper, a method of presentation that was more journalistically palatable to both papers. But there were other, more strategic reasons to favor the *Post.* The FBI knew that the Unabomber lived somewhere in the West, a region where the *Post* was available at only a few outlets, as opposed to the *Times,* which had a national distribution network. The Bureau assumed that the Unabomber was carefully monitoring both papers and was likely to visit a store where the *Post* was sold to see if his demands had been met. By staking out the limited number of places in the West where the *Post* was available, the Bureau hoped to be able to identify and catch its man.

The time of publication was left up to Graham, who chose Tuesday, September 19, 1995. On the day the piece appeared, the *Times* ran a front-page story saying that the federal government had urged the two papers to print the manifesto "for public safety reasons" and that they were acting in unison and splitting the cost of publication. Because the killer clearly wanted to work with the *Times,* Arthur Jr. never felt that he or his staff were in serious danger of becoming targets, and the FBI had confirmed that the risk of harm was small. Still, the day before, the head of security at the paper sent a memo to the men and women whose names appeared every day on the masthead, asking them to contact him immediately if they received any suspicious packages.

Publication of the Unabomber's tract prompted a roar of criticism. William Serrin, chairman of the journalism department at New York University, accused the *Times* of "giving in to a mass murderer." Arthur Jr.

and Graham declined requests to be interviewed on television, and when ABC-TV's *Nightline* devoted an entire show to the row, it was Max Frankel who represented the *Times* — not in his role as former executive editor but as author of "Word & Image," his weekly media column in the Sunday magazine.

On April 3, 1996, the FBI arrested Ted Kaczynski at his cabin near Lincoln, Montana, after being tipped off to his identity and whereabouts by his brother, who had read the manifesto on the Internet. In January 1998, after a federal trial in which the prosecution sought the death penalty, Kaczynski pleaded guilty to thirteen of the Unabomber crimes, including the three fatal bombings; four months later he was sentenced to four consecutive life terms plus thirty years. For Arthur Jr., playing a role in the capture of the Unabomber was immensely gratifying, as was the process by which he and others at the *Times* had struggled with the journalistic and ethical issues involved. His determined effort to encourage people to disagree, to articulate their views without fear, was the way he preferred to manage. "Putting aside whether we made the right decision or the wrong decision ... we made the decision well," he said.

§

On Arthur Jr.'s forty-third birthday, Cindy Sulzberger dropped by her brother's office to offer her good wishes and to say farewell before he departed on a business trip to China the following day. When she arrived, she found her father and Arthur Jr. embracing and lightly kissing each other on the cheek — a sign of affection the men in Arthur Jr.'s generation had initiated but one that Punch was learning to feel comfortable with. "Happy birthday!" Punch told his son. "And about China — be careful, use your head." After delivering her own birthday greeting, Cindy hugged Arthur Jr. and left with her father. As she and Punch walked companionably down the long eleventh-floor corridor lined with photographs of the paper's Pulitzer Prize winners, Cindy suddenly had the feeling they were being observed. She turned around and saw Arthur Jr. leaning on the doorjamb of his office, looking at his father and sister with an expression of such longing that Cindy couldn't take her eyes off him. He continued to gaze at the pair until they disappeared around the corner leading to the elevators. "Was he jealous of my relationship with Dad, or was there something else he wanted to say to him?" Cindy wondered later. "I haven't figured it out, but it really touched me."

At the *Times,* relations between Arthur Jr. and Punch were warmer than they had been in years. Joe Lelyveld had once thought they didn't even know how to write memos to each other; now Punch signed his notes 'Dad,' and Arthur Jr. phoned his father five or six times a day to solicit advice. Socially, however, they remained in separate worlds. Punch had never gone to New Paltz to see Arthur Jr. and Gail's weekend house, and they, in turn, had visited Punch and Carol in Southampton only once since the sale of Hillandale. While Judy had tried to make up for her parental deficiencies by honoring a standing dinner date on Sunday nights with Dan, Leah, and her two grandsons, Punch repeatedly turned down similar invitations from Arthur Jr. "Carol has the final say on where they're going to have dinner on Sunday night," said Leah, "and if there's a family event, it's not going to focus on Arthur, Gail, and the kids." After several rebuffs, Arthur Jr. had simply stopped asking.

Carol's antipathy to Arthur Jr. had only heightened since he had become publisher, and began to take forms like sticking out her tongue at the photograph of Arthur Jr. that hung on the wall next to other *Times* publishers whenever she visited the London bureau. Nor had there been any détente in their political differences. After Ronald Reagan left the White House, Carol clung all the more tenaciously to her role as the family's conservative gadfly. When Punch and Carol were invited to the White House for a white-tie reception for the emperor of Japan, Carol refused to go. She considered Hillary Rodham Clinton dowdy, with "no figure for clothes," and President Clinton detestable. Cindy wanted to attend in her mother's stead, but Punch had been unwilling to risk Carol's wrath.

Not surprisingly, Carol's disapproval of Arthur Jr. also clouded her relationship with Gail. Although the two women chatted amiably enough on the phone, among intimates Gail made it clear that she didn't like her stepmother-in-law. Carol would occasionally buy clothes for Cathy and Karen or give them her designer hand-me-downs. Gail, however, was never a beneficiary, for as Carol frostily told a friend, "I don't do Gail." "Little Arthur" was another point of contention. Handsome, sweet, and solitary, he was much like his father had been at the same age. But as a young boy he had also been willful about food, consuming a diet that consisted mostly of carrot sticks, yogurt, boiled egg whites, and unsauced pasta. The family's doctor had advised his parents not to force the issue, and they hadn't. To Carol, who had been raised to eat whatever was on her plate, Arthur Jr. and Gail's permissiveness was unfathomable. Little Arthur's dietary quirks, coupled with his reserved manner, made it likewise difficult for Punch to find common ground. He thought the boy should play baseball or join a hockey team — anything to jolt him out of his self-imposed loner status. "My dad just couldn't relate to Arthur," said Cindy. "For a long time I think [Punch] was intimidated by him."

Punch and Carol's troubled relationship with Arthur Jr. and his family contrasted sharply with the easy warmth they felt for Cindy — or Cynthia, as she preferred to be called as a young woman. Despite having a half brother and two half sisters, the age gap between Cynthia and her siblings meant that she had effectively grown up as an only child. Although Cynthia had had Punch and Carol virtually to herself, she had also been born at a time when their public duties weighed on them most heavily. Many nights she had been left alone while her parents attended parties and official functions. Sometimes the tutor who had been hired to help her cope with her learning disabilities would have dinner with her. "She would stay as late as she could so that I wouldn't feel too lonely," recalled Cynthia. On the nights when the tutor wasn't there, Cynthia ate in the kitchen with the live-in couple who worked for the Sulzbergers and whom Cynthia regarded as "my surrogate parents."

Her own mother and father had never taken her to temple or seen to her religious education. Punch's attitude toward Jewish rites bordered on hostility. Every year he would dutifully attend a Passover seder at Max Frankel's home in Riverdale, cursing all the way about the congested traffic and the sweet kosher wine he feared would be served. Carol, though proud of her own Jewish heritage, was largely unobservant; her main concession to Yom Kippur, the day of fasting and atonement, was to sacrifice shopping. Nearly everything Cynthia learned about being Jewish had come from an Orthodox math and science teacher at Dalton, the private school she had attended in Manhattan. If Punch and Carol were gone on a Friday night, Cynthia would often stay overnight at the teacher's house, lighting the Sabbath candles and eating kosher food. On weekends at Hillandale, she attended Catholic mass with Gino Rossi, the estate's Italian gardener, and his family. "I loved it," she said. "I just thought church was the best."

Cynthia was the peacemaker in the family who got along with everyone. In high school, however, she had been as difficult as any teenager. She hid drugs in her sweater drawer and favored tie-dyed T-shirts and blue jeans to the understated classics Carol preferred. One summer she followed the Grateful Dead as they toured the American West. Having a Deadhead for a daughter was not exactly what Carol had bargained for, and the two went through a period of nearly nightly eruptions over clothing, hairstyles, makeup, and curfews. One evening, when yet another dinner had been ruined by the bickering, Punch had exploded so violently that Cynthia had rushed to her room in fright. Fifteen minutes later he appeared at her door to apologize.

Cynthia had wanted to go to Pitzer College in Claremont, California, but Punch and Carol, fearful that a West Coast school would be too lax, told her that if she insisted on going, she would have to pay for it herself. At the suggestion of a family friend, she decided to take a look at Duke, which proceeded to court the daughter of the publisher of *The New York Times* with unbridled eagerness. On the day Punch and Cynthia were to fly to North Carolina for their first visit, Duke president Terry Sanford was in New York and arranged to join them on the *Times* plane. While touring the university, she discovered that the Grateful Dead were scheduled to appear on campus the following month. Three weeks after returning home, tickets to the concert magically arrived at the Sulzberger apartment. She enrolled at Duke in the fall of 1982.

Cynthia's freshman roommate stayed up till 3:00 A.M. and slept till noon, a schedule that conflicted with her own early-to-bed, early-to-rise habits. As soon as she could, she moved off-campus and gradually found her footing, socially and academically, although her grades were never stellar. When she nearly flunked a test in a course on modern American diplomacy, she was so upset that she mailed the exam to her father to show him how difficult it was. Without her knowledge, Punch gave the test to Henry Kissinger, who as Nixon's secretary of state had formulated many of the policies covered in the course. Kissinger wrote Cynthia a soothing letter urging her not to feel so bad: he and his wife, Nancy, had taken the test and had failed it, too.

After graduating from Duke, Cynthia had been content to live at home for nearly a year before moving into her own apartment on the West Side, an apartment that Carol decorated because, as both mother and daughter conceded, she had better taste. At first, not knowing what else to do, she followed the traditional career path of upper-crust young women in New York, taking the American arts course at Sotheby's and working at the Guggenheim Museum in the public-relations department. Then an apprenticeship was created just for her at Home Box Office. Cynthia wasn't certain she wanted to go into television, and the idea that the job had been invented specially for a Sulzberger so rankled her that two weeks before she was to start, she politely turned down the position. Seeing that her daughter was drifting, Carol suggested that Cynthia call Dalton and ask for a job helping out in the lower grades. On the third day of school, an assistant teacher suddenly left, and Cynthia got the position. After two years of teaching, she decided to pursue a master's degree in special education at Manhattan's Bank Street College of Education — to help others cope with the learning disabilities she herself had struggled with all her life.

Cynthia cherished weekends because when she was a child, Saturday and Sunday were the only two days she could be certain the family would eat together. By the time she was in her twenties, her contemporaries relished their single lives in the city while she continued to spend her off hours in the country with her parents. On Fridays she would drive with them to Southampton, sitting in the front passenger seat next to Punch while Carol dozed in the back. Once there, Cynthia would settle into a top-floor bedroom decorated with teddy bears and Duke memorabilia, and if there were no pressing social engagements, the three would sit down to a simple supper in the little room off the kitchen or set up trays in front of the television so that Cynthia and Punch could watch *Star Trek: The Next Generation* or *Columbo* while Carol did needlepoint.

It was during one of these homey Southampton weekends in 1992 that Cynthia met the man she was to marry: Gary Simpson. She had recently broken up with Andrew Schiff, a descendant of banking magnate Jacob Schiff, and considered the New York dating scene dispiriting. When she complained to her dentist during a routine checkup, he said he thought that one of his other patients might be just the guy for her. "Well, what does he do?" Cynthia asked. "He's in construction," the dentist replied. "You're going to set me up with a construction worker?!" Cynthia gasped. The dentist explained that Gary was a construction *executive* with an MBA from New York University and that his family had owned and run Nab Construction Corporation, a general-contracting firm, for three generations. Reluctantly she agreed to let him contact Gary on her behalf.

Gary phoned Cynthia shortly before Memorial Day. They discovered that they would both be in the Hamptons over the holiday and agreed to meet there for a drink on Friday evening. For protection, Cynthia brought several friends with her and downed a few shots of tequila before Gary showed up, but to her surprise, she had a wonderful time. Tall, quiet, and clean-cut, Gary was ten years Cynthia's senior and "the first mature man I'd ever gone out with." For her birthday the following week, he brought her flowers and took her to Chanterelle, a romantic and expensive downtown restaurant. They spent a long weekend in Nantucket and "that cemented it," Cynthia said. Barely four months after they met, they were engaged.

The senior Sulzbergers were left breathless and alarmed by the speed of the courtship. Carol was pleased that Gary was Jewish, and although she was frankly disturbed at the prospect of a son-in-law in the construction trade, her skepticism dissolved once she met his parents and discovered that they were people of refinement who resided in Old Westbury, one of the toniest towns on Long Island. Punch simply felt relieved that, as a member of a family business, Gary seemed to understand the Sulzbergerian dynamics without having to be educated in them. At Nab, he was in his own succession battle with his father, and while helping Punch weed the yard behind the Southampton house or clean patio furniture, he would ask his future father-in-law for advice or bounce business ideas off him. He had the ability to keep company without being demanding — a quality Punch prized highly.

For Cynthia, Gary's chief attribute was that he made it possible for her to have a husband without altering her status in the Sulzberger family. Once they were engaged, Gary and Cynthia spent nearly every weekend with Punch and Carol, sharing the teddy bear–strewn room Cynthia had always occupied. He didn't seem to mind. "He joined my family and understood that this was important to me," said Cynthia. "So getting married didn't really change my life in the sense that I was leaving my parents."

One of the few things Punch and Carol enjoyed doing together was decorating a home, and the Southampton house was a showcase for both their tastes — comfortable and elegant, tasteful and whimsical. In front of the stairs leading to the second floor was a large "Punch" figure in a jester's hat sitting on a unicycle. To the right was a wood-paneled study with a television, bookshelves, and a video library. On a low rocking chair sat a pillow with the embroidered command FLY FIRST CLASS/ YOUR HEIRS WILL. Over the fireplace sat Arthur Hays Sulzberger's haunting self-portrait, an oil painting he had done in the 1940s on nights he couldn't sleep. In the Florida room — a bright, tiled, airy space to the left of the entrance hall — was a galloping carousel horse, a gift from a former *Times* executive, and past the bar, sparkling with tumblers and scotch glasses, a set of glass doors led to a small garden with goldfish and rosebushes.

Punch and Carol disliked eating by themselves and went to great lengths to ensure that they would always have company. Although they stayed in Southampton just two nights a week, Carol retained a live-in chef so that on a moment's notice she could host a dinner party. Often on Saturday nights she would spontaneously call Arthur and Barbara Gelb, close friends from the *Times* who owned a house in nearby Water Mill, and invite them over to share a meal. Afterward, the men would shoot pool while the women played gin rummy. That quiet sort of evening was made to order for Punch and Cynthia, the family home-bodies. For Carol and Gary, who liked nothing better than a lively party, it was congenial — but not as a steady diet. "Sometimes I feel like just sending the two of them out," sighed Cynthia.

Carol took command of her daughter's June 1993 wedding, and except for a tussle over the dress — Carol wanted Victorian, Cynthia preferred sexy and bare — the arrangements were painless, thanks in part to the diplomatic assistance of two special-events planners from the Metropolitan Museum of Art. The day of the wedding Cynthia was sequestered in an enormous suite at the Plaza Hotel, the site of the cere-mony and reception, where she devoured a huge room-service lunch and watched her favorite soap operas with friends. Punch stopped in while she was having her hair done, and at the sight of her father, Cyn-thia burst into tears. "Don't cry, don't do that," Punch admonished her gently, not knowing quite what to do.

At 6:30 P.M. more than three hundred guests gathered in the Plaza's Terrace Room to sip sparkling water and await the rites that would soon be performed one floor down. Joan Dryfoos, Orvil's sister-in-law, was dazzled by the glittering necks, ears, wrists, and fingers. "They must have rifled all their safe-deposit boxes," she recalled. "I've never seen such jewelry in my life." When Carol made her entrance in a full-length beige satin dress, she was as quietly elegant as the lush rose centerpieces that adorned the tables at the reception. As the band blared out "La Bamba," James Greenfield, a *Times* veteran, couldn't help staring at a table of small, formally clad boys and girls digging into double sundaes. The group was the next generation of Sulzbergers — the children of Arthur Jr., Dan, Michael, Stephen, and the other Sulzberger cousins. "There are the owners of *The New York Times*," he marveled, as certain that the family's possession of the newspaper would endure as if he had been observing a table of young Windsors or Plantagenets.

None of Carol's friends or family members attending the wedding would ever have guessed that she was gravely ill. She had deliberately ignored the warning signs in order to focus on the wedding plans, and only when the event was over did she consult a physician. The diagnosis was colon cancer. In August she underwent surgery, but within months her doctors informed the family that the disease had metastasized to her liver.

Carol had always cared far less about her health than her appearance. Over Iphigene's protests, she had continued to smoke, artfully arranging her collection of fruit-shaped Limoges china cigarette lighters on the side tables in the Southampton house. She was fanatical about maintaining a slim figure, yet loved to eat Dunkin' Donuts, cheese, organ meats, and other high-fat, high-cholesterol foods and showed no interest in exercise. As she had gotten older, osteoporosis had set in, giving her a slight but distinct dowager's hump. Aside from that single disfigurement, however, she remained a resolutely handsome woman. Once she became sick, she refused to go through chemotherapy, in part because she feared losing her hair. "She was very prideful of how she looked," said Punch.

Carol's illness could have provided a catalyst for her and Punch to recapture the closeness of their early marriage; instead, it thrust them more deeply into their separate worlds. Carol had always been an intensely private woman with a steely need for control, and that aspect of her didn't change simply because she was battling a life-threatening disease. She greatly admired Marietta Tree, the New York socialite and widow of British MP Ronald Tree, who had managed to keep her cancer a secret. To Punch and her children, Carol acknowledged that she had cancer but refused to divulge details; even Cynthia was kept in the dark about the prognosis. The only family member Carol took into her confidence was Joe Perpich, Cathy's husband, who was a physician. While facing down her condition showed courage, it also suggested the extent of her denial. "She felt that if people found out she was ill, that somehow that would be the beginning of the end, and she wanted to put off the end," said Karen.

The distance between Punch and Carol in their marriage had long been apparent. Intimates at the *Times* had gotten used to hearing Punch complain about Carol's tart opinions, inflexible behavior, and angry public outbursts — most of them directed at him. She treated her husband with what Sydney Gruson called "genial hostility." But if Carol was his hair shirt and his most severe critic, she was at the same time his most loyal supporter. No longer in love, they were bound by mutual dependence. Carol, shy and uncomfortable with people she didn't know, hid behind the status of Punch's position. He in turn relied on her authoritarian manner, which echoed similar qualities in his parents and which he had repeatedly sought in his top executives, most notably Walter Mattson and Abe Rosenthal. "That strength gives him a certain measure of security," said Gruson.

Observing their brother's prolonged marital unhappiness, Marian and Judy had urged Punch to have an affair. "Just stay out of it," he had snapped. "Don't complicate my life." The Lillian Bellison Alexanderson liaison had made Punch wary of entertaining such relationships again, and in any case, he knew that Carol was ferocious on the subject of fidelity. She strongly disapproved of *Times* reporters who carried on extramarital affairs, and had a hawkeye for any hint of social impropriety. Once, when an attractive blonde had playfully sat on Punch's lap at a party, Carol walked over and in frigid tones invited the woman to "get off."

Punch shrank from discussing with Carol the emptiness of their marriage, yet he couldn't bring himself to divorce. Just before Carol became ill, however, he confided to one of his children that he had decided to leave. But when he learned of her cancer, he resolved to be loyal. "I wasn't going to run away, I wasn't going to be like Newt Gingrich," he said, alluding to the Republican Speaker of the House who had served divorce papers on his wife while she lay in her hospital bed recovering from cancer surgery.

Carol's refusal to involve Punch in her illness took its toll on him. An abscess in his jaw caused him to lose weight; his skin took on a grayish cast. "People were spreading rumors that *he* had cancer, he was so gaunt," said Cynthia. To keep apprised of his wife's condition, he was reduced to surreptiously calling her doctors or quizzing his son-in-law Joe. "It was her life, and she was going to weigh the options and consult the people she thought could bring value to her [medical] decisions," he said. "She knew damn well I knew nothing about [medicine], so she just opted not to [talk with me]." All her life, Carol had reacted to pain by donning emotional armor. "She would not be the kind to reach out and say, 'I need you,' " said Karen. "There was no role for my father to play."

Although Punch was frustrated at being shut out, he was relieved as well. He was unusually squeamish around doctors; even a simple injection made him blanch. When Karen's husband, Eric Lax, had published *Life and Death on 10 West,* a chronicle of a woman pregnant for the first time who discovers she has leukemia, he had thrown a book party for him, bound the volume in leather, and sent him a collection of reviews but did not actually read it. "It's too close," he had told Eric apologetically. "I have daughters, they have babies; I just don't think I can handle it."

Despite fatigue, pain, and medication, Carol tried to maintain her normal routine, lunching with friends at Mortimer's, shopping, and going to the hairdresser. When Bobby Dryfoos turned fifty in November 1994, she and Punch made the trek to Tarrytown for the festivities, held in a Marriott ballroom. It was hardly Carol's kind of affair, for she disliked big family reunions and made a point of saying so. But she ended up dancing the night away, and even Punch joined Cynthia in an awkward version of the Twist. However, when he traveled to London for the Sulzbergers' usual fall getaway later that month, he went alone. A transatlantic trip was just too much of a strain for Carol.

By the following March she was feeling better and looked forward to celebrating her birthday in London with friends. Just before they were to leave, though, her health took a turn for the worse and she underwent an operation to freeze cancerous tissue in her liver. The doctors hoped that the procedure would restore a modicum of comfort and quality of life to the time she had remaining. On the day of her birthday, Punch threw a party in her room at Mount Sinai Hospital, with champagne, caviar, and cold shrimp. His gift was a pin from Tiffany, which he was sure Carol would send back. After nearly forty years of marriage, he had become accustomed to a demoralizing routine: he would buy Carol jewelry, and she would then find fault with it and exchange it for something else. This time, however, she not only accepted the bauble with apparent gratitude but kept it.

It was becoming obvious to everyone that Carol was mortally ill: the cancer soon spread beyond her liver to her lungs. Yet she continued to maintain a wall of silence about her future. During a visit to New York from her home in Los Angeles, Karen urged her father and stepmother to acknowledge reality, if not for themselves, then for the sake of the one person whom they both adored: Cynthia. "I know this isn't your forte, dealing with all this," she told Punch and Carol, "but you have to find a way to do it because Cindy is suffering." With that, Carol finally told Punch, her children, and her intimate friends the truth about her cancer. She wasn't going to get better. It was just a matter of time. She might have three months; she might have three years.

Even with the acknowledgment of her condition, Carol made no effort to mend fences. Her relations with Arthur Jr. remained as disagreeable as ever. When he called her hospital room one day to ask whether he and Gail could come over, Cynthia picked up the phone and, cupping her hand over the receiver, relayed the message to her mother. "I told you, I don't want visitors!" Carol yelled loud enough for Arthur Jr. to hear. After she had hung up, Cynthia begged Carol to reconsider. "But, Mom, I'm seeing him for dinner tonight. What will I say?" she pleaded. "That's your problem," Carol shot back.

Carol's rejection of Arthur Jr. was especially hard on Punch, and as compensation — and out of his own loneliness — he called Arthur Jr. and asked plaintively if he could come over for a meal. Cynthia did her part by accompanying her father to Elio's each night after their regular visit to Mount Sinai. One evening she varied the routine by taking him to a movie. Knowing that he liked action films, she chose *The Fugitive.* Punch had always taken great delight in his role as the chief projectionist at Rock Hill and later at Southampton, but he had not set foot in a public cinema in twenty-five years. His short attention span made sitting in a darkened theater where there was no escape sheer torture, and during *The Fugitive* he fidgeted, went to the bathroom, walked around the lobby, and glanced continually at his watch.

Carol spent the last spring and summer of her life completing two household projects: building an extension on the pool house at Southampton and helping Cynthia decorate the apartment she shared with Gary. The first weekend of August 1995, she invited Arthur and Barbara Gelb to join Cathy and Joe at the Southampton house for dinner. By then, her skin was yellow from jaundice, her eyes sunken, and her ankles swollen and discolored. She ate nothing but a baked potato and just picked at that. Though clearly in discomfort, she retained her edge. "She was giving Punch hell about something in the *Times,* as usual," said Arthur Gelb. Later, as she was ushering the Gelbs to the door, she told Arthur she wanted to show him something. In the study off the main entrance hall she pointed proudly to Cynthia's ribbons for horse jumping, a sport Cynthia had recently resumed, with a horse she named Fit to Print.

The following Tuesday Barbara Gelb phoned Carol at the Southampton house. "I feel lousy," she answered wearily. It was the first time Barbara could recall Carol admitting that she was not well. "We're expecting you this weekend," Carol signed off. Two days later Joe and Eric Lax drove to New York City to get morphine patches to ease their mother-in-law's pain. By the time they returned, Carol was dead. She had gone into a coma and passed away, surrounded by Punch, Cathy, Cynthia, and Karen.

Although Carol had been seriously ill for over two years, no one at the paper had been instructed to compose an obituary in advance, leaving Punch to write the piece himself. When the obit editor read the detached, factual account of her life that Punch turned in, he sent his reporters scrambling for personal comments to warm it up. In the short piece that appeared in the *Times* the next day, Sydney Gruson was quoted describing Carol as "the most direct and honest woman I have ever known." Maggie Greenfield, wife of former *Times* senior editor James Greenfield, praised her as someone who did "a lot of good works in a very quiet way."

Joe Perpich said a few words at the interment of Carol's urn in the family plot at Temple Israel Cemetery. As was the custom for husbands in such situations, Punch said nothing, and he did not speak the following day when hundreds of mourners gathered at Temple Emanu-El to pay their last respects. No doubt Carol would have been gratified by the number of famous faces in the throng, including New York City mayor Rudolph Giuliani; Senator Daniel Patrick Moynihan; Katharine Graham, chairman of The Washington Post Company; television host Barbara Walters; and columnist and author William F. Buckley, as well as the presence of old friends and traveling companions like Tom Wicker and Abby Catledge, Turner's widow. While the choir sang the Twenty-third Psalm and people fanned themselves with their programs to ward off the summer heat, the immediate family filed in, Punch with a jerky, distracted air, his neck so taut that it stuck out at an unnatural angle to his head.

Several weeks prior to her death, Carol had made her children and stepchildren promise that they would all say something at her memorial service, and they kept their vow. Cathy spoke of her mother's obsessive need to clean out closets — her children's and her own. Cynthia, her voice quavering, recalled Carol's early-morning phone calls, her love of train whistles, and the good times she and Punch had had in London. But it was Karen, dressed in a stylish black suit, who recounted the most poignant anecdote. Shortly before she had died, Karen recalled, Carol had taken each of her daughters and stepdaughters shopping for a new skirt and jacket. As they had fingered the racks and tried on sizes, Carol had diplomatically pointed out that as far as she was concerned, black was really the most useful color. Dutifully, they had all followed her advice. Only later had it dawned on Karen that the shopping expedition was Carol's way of making sure that her girls would look their best at her funeral. "Carol left nothing to chance," she said.

When it was Arthur Jr.'s turn to speak, a hush settled over the crowd. Most in the temple were aware of the unhappy relations between the *Times* publisher and his stepmother, and they also knew that Arthur Jr. had yet to tame his habit of making cutting remarks at inappropriate moments. If they expected Arthur Jr. to take a final swipe at Carol, however, they were disappointed. In a strong, clear voice, he delivered a gracious, honest memorial to the woman who had taken him in as a vulnerable fourteen-year-old and later become his adversary. Without glossing over her brutal candor, he expressed admiration for Carol's "grit" and the immutability of her beliefs. "Carol was like a martini," Arthur Jr. said. "The first sip is a bit of a shock, but by the second and third you feel quite comfortable. And by the end of the first martini, you want another." When each of his daughters returned to the family pew, Punch reached out and touched their hands. When Arthur Jr. came back to his seat, he kissed him.

The mourners spilled out onto Fifth Avenue and made their way by foot to the reception at the nearby Pierre Hotel. In the Pierre's Cotillion Room, the crowd buzzed with talk of whether Punch would remarry, and if so, how soon. When one guest protested that the question was indecent so soon after Carol's death, her comment was met with a disdainful stare. "This is a man who hasn't made his own dinner reservation in years," said her male companion. "And he *is* the most eligible bachelor in town."

Over the next several days, Punch went through Carol's clothes and personal effects with the same systematic detachment with which he had cleaned out his father's desk in 1968. Some items, he threw out. Others, he gave away, just as Iphigene had done following the death of Adolph Ochs. "Even if he had loved her deeply, he would have moved everything out immediately," explained Judy. "That's just his way."

49

Transitions

L ESS THAN A MONTH AFTER CAROL'S DEATH, AN
item appeared in Liz Smith's column in the *New York Post* that
was unseemly even by the standards of gossip columnists. "From
the tippy-tip end of Montauk Point through the Hollywood Hamptons
and on to Sneeden's Landing, Bedford Village, and for all I know the
Fulton Fish Market," Smith wrote, ". . . everybody is discussing the burgeoning eligibility of brand-new widower Punch Sulzberger. . . . Women
who haven't been so activated or agitated in years are absentmindedly
scribbling the words, 'Mrs. Punch Sulzberger,' on notepads by their
beds." While many at *The New York Times* were appalled, Punch was
amused by the speculation. "Where are they?" he joked at a meeting the
day the item appeared. "I'm sitting by the phone, and it's not ringing!"

In psychological parlance, Punch had already gone through "pre-
grieving." While Carol was struggling with her disease, he had come to
terms with the inevitability of her death and had begun to make fundamental decisions about what he wanted to do after she was gone.
The result was that despite his official status as a mourning widower,
he seemed shockingly cheerful. At Elio's he was spotted dining with Barbara Walters, Pamela Harriman, and Warnaco CEO Linda Wachner.
With the ebullience he always felt at the prospect of home renovation, he
plunged into a major redecoration of the bedrooms in his three homes.
"He's as relaxed and loose as I've seen him in years," marveled Arthur Jr.

Punch's high spirits were alarmingly apparent to Cindy and her husband, Gary, who overheard him giggling with someone on an upstairs
phone at the Southampton house several weeks after Carol's death. "You
didn't have to be a genius to guess that he wasn't talking to a man," said
Gary. In late September Punch boarded the Concorde and went to
London alone, ostensibly to confer with decorators and scour shops for
new swags and furbelows for the master bedroom at the Mount Street

flat. But the real reason for the trip was so that he could conveniently "run into" Allison Cowles, the sixty-three-year-old widow of William H. Cowles 3rd, the president and publisher of *The Spokesman-Review* and the *Spokane Chronicle* in Spokane, Washington.

Punch and Allison, who was in London for a holiday with her brother and sister-in-law, had known each other for more than thirty-five years. Punch had preceded Bill Cowles as chairman of the American Newspaper Publishers Association (ANPA), and both men had served as directors of the Associated Press. Their families had a connection stretching back to the early 1900s, when Adolph Ochs and W. H. Cowles, Bill's grandfather, had sat together on the board of the AP. Bill also shared a common ancestor with the Minneapolis Cowleses, the family from whom Punch had bought Cowles Communications in 1971, his first attempt at diversification.

During the many meetings and trips associated with ANPA and the AP board, Punch and Bill had been part of a "gang," as Punch called it, of family newspaper owners — an exclusive and close-knit club that included Katharine Graham of *The Washington Post,* Dolph Simons Jr. of the *Lawrence* (Kans.) *Journal-World,* and Frank Daniels Jr. of the Raleigh (N.C.) *News & Observer.* The group partied together, competed on the golf course and tennis court together, and played practical jokes on one another. Over the years Punch and Carol and Bill and Allison had become such good friends that during expeditions to London they had shared two-bedroom suites at Claridge's. When Bill had dropped dead of a heart attack while jogging in 1992, Punch had flown to Spokane for the funeral and, with several others, encouraged the family to take a gamble on Stacey Cowles, Allison's thirty-one-year-old son, as the next publisher and president of the papers, just as Arthur Hays Sulzberger and Iphigene had done with Punch at roughly the same age following Orvil's sudden death.

As Bill's widow, Allison had continued to take part in ANPA meetings and reunions of retired AP directors, where she ran into Punch, who was also alone because of Carol's illness. Like everyone else in the newspaper world, she knew that Carol was sick but had no inkling how grave the prognosis was. Her mother-in-law, a strict Christian Scientist, had forbade any mention of illness in the Cowles family, so she respected Punch's privacy. At the same time, she was pleased when he paid atten-

tion to her during the numerous dinners and cocktail parties and called
her in between meetings just to chat.

By the time Punch and Allison met in London, they were both widowed and free to pursue what by then was a clear mutual attraction.
Punch tumbled head over heels with a speed and intensity he hadn't
experienced since his romance with Barbara Grant, whom Allison
vaguely resembled. "She's cute, she really is," he enthused. "And very
smart." He admired that Allison was a trustee of Wellesley, her alma
mater, where she had been editor of the student paper and earned a Phi
Beta Kappa key. And he took comfort in knowing that she and his sister
Ruth had warm relations because of their service together on the board
of the Smithsonian Institution. Like Iphigene, Allison took pride in her
intelligence; in an era when few women pursued advanced degrees, she
had been accepted into a Ph.D. program at Harvard and had hoped, like
Iphigene, to become a professor of history. Instead, she had married Bill
Cowles, a Yale graduate and Harvard Law School student, returning
with him to Spokane and raising two children. There, in addition to her
domestic duties, she had become a leader in organizations concerned
with education, parks, and conservation — causes close to Iphigene's
heart. She lacked Iphigene's liberal convictions, but she shared her racial
and religious tolerance and kind heart. "There are two ways to succeed
in the world," Allison was fond of saying. "One is to be good and the
other is to be clever. There aren't many who succeed at being clever, so
it's much better to be good."

After decades as a spouse in a newspaper family, Allison effortlessly
embraced the complexities of Punch's life. He had rarely talked shop
with Carol, who had shown little interest in anything beyond finding
fault with the paper and, within the family, had generated conflict more
often than she did peace. In Allison, Punch found someone who not
only understood journalism but instinctively knew how to hold a business and a family together. When her father's English parents died, they
had THOU SHALT LOVE ONE ANOTHER inscribed on their tombstones, a
phrase that Allison said summarized "the way we were raised." Punch
especially liked that despite her natural sweetness and capacity for
affection, Allison was emotionally undemanding. She admired the self-
contained way Punch and his sisters handled their problems. "I mean,
why dump your emotional garbage on other people?" she asked.

Once back in the States, Punch confided his newfound happiness to his children, who privately joked that their father was off in "Allison Wonderland." Allison was as smitten as Punch. It was a natural match: they had so much in common, so many friends and memories, and they had always been fond of each other. Besides, she thought that Punch was "dear" and "fun." She suggested that he come to Spokane for Thanksgiving and meet her family, which she regarded as a "trial by fire." The large, rumpled affair had been going on in the same way for generations and included a session in which everyone sang hymns — which, of course, meant Christian hymns. To Allison's amazement, Punch stood next to the piano and chimed in with the others. He knew the melodies and all the words, a legacy of his miserable years at Browning, where he had sung in the choir.

Punch charmed Allison's elderly mother, who had moved to Spokane from Florida a few years earlier, teased her son and daughter, and tickled the babies. During the balance of the weekend, Allison took Punch hiking on Mount Spokane and introduced him to a Cowles summer place on Knight's Lake — a homesteader's log cabin with no phone, no electricity, and no running water. She had assumed that Punch would be put off by the family togetherness and rustic surroundings, but he left Spokane more determined than ever. "Punch was rushing to get married," Gary recalled. "He wanted to [do it] by the end of the year . . . but Allison thought that was too soon."

In fact, Allison felt a little ridiculous being giddy about a man at her age, yet she had to admit she was. "It's so amazing when you're a friend with somebody and then suddenly the whole basis of your relationship has changed and you feel physically involved and emotionally involved. In love! My God!" Punch continued his courtship by inviting her for Christmas with his children and grandchildren. He was paying for the entire brood to gather in Hawaii, he explained, and now that he had spent one holiday with the Cowleses, she in all fairness had to spend the next one with the Sulzbergers. Allison resisted. Carol had been gone barely four months, and she didn't want Punch's children to resent her. At their father's instigation, Karen, Arthur Jr., and Cynthia called to assuage her fears, and finally she agreed to join them, but only after Christmas Day so that they all could spend some time together by themselves.

In Hawaii Punch and Allison behaved like lovesick teenagers, holding hands and slipping their arms around each other at every opportunity. Cathy was shocked. "I've never seen my dad like that," she said. Before Punch had left New York, the ever alert Liz Smith had let it drop in her column that Punch was seeing "a lady who owns a newspaper in Washington State," a woman who is "said to be . . . planning to move here." Smith had excellent sources. By Christmas Punch and Allison were, in fact, ready to set a date — but, as it turned out, very different dates. Allison wanted to marry the following October so that she would have time to plan a large wedding with all their friends and to allow a respectful interval after Carol's death. Punch had other ideas. "No, darling," he told Allison firmly. "We're getting married March ninth. I've already checked, and everyone can come."

At the *Times* Punch was slow to make important decisions, but once he did, he moved quickly and firmly, and in his private life he was no different. Allison enlisted her children to lobby for October, but their efforts were in vain. "Doesn't your dad *ever* give up?" her son asked Arthur Jr. "Sometimes, if you throw your body in front of the steamroller, it will stop," Arthur Jr. replied. In the face of his unshakable resolve, Allison surrendered. By the time she arrived in New York for a visit in January 1996, she had accommodated herself to a March wedding, but she was still apprehensive about moving to Manhattan. She had lived in the Northwest a long time, and she didn't know if she could tolerate big-city life. She also worried whether Punch's friends would accept her.

At Scotty Reston's funeral in Washington in early December, Allison had confessed her fears to Katharine Graham, who had instantly made Allison her personal crusade. She called her friends in New York and ordered them to make the prospective bride feel comfortable. When Allison came to town, they held welcoming parties for her, and Graham herself flew up to ensure the proper introductions. "She said she felt like my mother, taking care of me," said Allison. "It was then I realized that it didn't matter: I could have had three eyes and five legs, and everyone would have loved me because Punch was happy." Toward the end of her stay, Punch's four children threw a seventieth-birthday party for their father at Arthur Jr.'s apartment. It was a small affair — just Punch's sisters, their husbands, and a few close friends from the *Times*. When Arthur Jr. discovered his father and Allison kissing on the couch, he couldn't resist assuming a paternal tone. "You've got to cut this out!" he said in a mock-stern voice. "The next thing you'll be asking me for is the car keys!"

Friends were frankly astounded to see Punch be so physically affectionate. Allison radiated an earthy sensuality far removed from Carol's
hauteur. "It's not puppy love, it's dog-in-heat love," observed Dan Cohen
with a grin. Allison liked to drink and after a cocktail felt no qualms
about using words like *shit, fuck,* and *asshole* — language Carol would
have considered appallingly unladylike — and her openness had a liberating effect on Punch. Shortly before the wedding, Punch told two visitors he was having a hard time concentrating on work. "I'm screwed up
for three weeks," he said solemnly before bursting into a hearty laugh at
the unintended pun.

On March 9 Punch and Allison were married at the Spokane home of
her daughter, Betsy, chairman of the Cowleses' television station and its
production company, Pinnacle Productions. Allison wore a white silk
filet suit with satin lapels that Punch had selected during a shopping trip
to Neiman Marcus in San Francisco; Arthur Jr. was his father's best man.
Two Washington State judges performed the ceremony, and an Episcopal
minister gave the blessing. When Allison had gently inquired whether he
would also like a rabbi, he had shaken his head, replying, "I don't even
know a rabbi!"

The photo above the wedding announcement in *The New York Times*
showed a smiling Punch in a striped shirt, his hands on Allison's shoulders, and the accompanying story revealed that Allison would keep her
own name. After years of battling the use of *Ms.* in *The New York Times*
(he relented only in 1986) and making barbed jokes about feminists, it
was the ultimate irony that Punch had married a woman who thought
"there wasn't much sense [at this point] in my trying to be 'Mrs.
Sulzberger,' the wife of the chairman of *The New York Times*." After a
reception at the country club and a night in Spokane, Punch and Allison
flew to London for a weeklong honeymoon.

When they returned to New York, Allison chose to start her new life
by adapting to Punch's surroundings. His handsomely appointed apartment on Fifth Avenue and the house in Southampton reflected Carol's
strong influence, yet the only alteration she made was to turn one bedroom into an office for herself. "These places are so perfect," she explained. "Besides, Punch likes it." The single discernible addition to the
household was Angus Khan, Allison's black-and-white collie derivative.
She had also wanted to include Admiral Bird in the move east, but Punch
had cringed at the prospect of cohabiting with a squawking parrot.

While Carol had rarely entertained at home, Allison liked nothing better than having a crowd for dinner. In Southampton her casualness amazed longtime residents. "She'll come for a meal in jeans and a lumberjack shirt," said one, noting that Carol had never even *owned* a pair of jeans. She took pains to befriend Cathy and Cynthia because of their intimate tie to Carol. Family friends were especially worried about Cynthia, who they correctly assumed would be the most hurt by Punch's hasty remarriage. She had just lost her mother, with whom she had spoken every day, and now she had effectively lost her father as well. But as disturbing as these turns in her life were, they actually helped free her.

Cynthia's marriage to Gary Simpson had been unhappy practically since the honeymoon. She found his colleagues in the construction business boring; he took no interest in her horseback riding; she took no interest in his passion for windsurfing and skiing. For her parents' sake, Cynthia had kept her troubles to herself during Carol's illness, but soon after her father remarried, she announced that she and Gary would be separating. "She did that all alone," said Allison. "It was very brave."

Even as her dissatisfaction with married life was on its way to a resolution, her relationship with her brother remained uneasy. Since childhood, Cynthia had felt that Arthur Jr. had dismissed and patronized her. Gradually she had come to believe that his attitude sprang from resentment and envy — resentment of her privileged upbringing, and envy of the unqualified love their father felt for her. Gary, whose relations with his own brother were distant, had urged Cynthia to try to forge a bond with Arthur Jr., but she couldn't find a way to break through the walls they had both erected. Once, she confessed some personal things to him in the hope that by baring her soul, he would reciprocate, but nothing happened. On the several occasions when she and Gary and Arthur Jr. and Gail had gone out for a meal, she had dreaded the moment she would have to talk to her brother alone. One night Gary had turned to Gail, leaving Cynthia staring dumbfoundedly at Arthur Jr. "I panicked and went to the bathroom four times," said Cynthia.

§

Because of Carol's illness, Punch had put off making critical decisions about transitions at the company, including who would eventually succeed him as chairman and CEO and who would one day replace him and his sisters on the board of directors. In the past both questions had

had simple answers: a family member had always been the publisher of *The New York Times* as well as chairman and CEO of the company, and Iphigene, Arthur, and Julius, and later Punch and his three sisters, had sat on the board while gradually more and more outsiders had been added. But since Punch had taken over in 1963, The New York Times Company had become a public corporation and Wall Street was bound to look askance if Sulzberger relatives were to occupy all the most important slots in management. As for the board, it wouldn't be feasible for every member of the "cousins' generation" to become a director, as had been the case in their parents' era. Not only would the board become ungainly, it would be overpopulated with people whose main qualification for service was a blood tie to Iphigene. Recruiting able outside directors under such circumstances would become nearly impossible.

As Punch settled into his duties after his honeymoon, he was under pressure from both the board and his own family to resolve these issues, and to resolve them quickly. He had long since designated George B. Munroe, a director of various corporations, including The New York Times Company, to take his place on an interim basis if he were ever incapacitated by illness or a sudden accident. But he had yet to come up with a comprehensive structure for the normal line of succession. When Louis V. Gerstner Jr., chairman and CEO of IBM, had come on the board in 1986, he was vocal in his desire for a written plan that he and his colleagues could consider. Punch knew his directors were entitled to hear his thinking on the matter; he just didn't know what he thought. To force himself to sit down at the drafting table, he sent the board a formal letter promising to address the topic of succession. He gave them no specific timetable, only a date by which he would deliver a status report. "I just knew that if I wrote the letter . . . it would give me an artificial deadline, and I work better when I have a deadline," he explained.

But the board was not the only group concerned about corporate governance. Arthur Jr.'s installation in the publisher's office in 1992 had aroused feelings of inequity among members of the fourth generation that simply hadn't existed in their parents' era. In 1963 Punch had had no serious rivals within the family for the post of president and publisher. Later, after his father died, he had likewise had no rivals for the title of chairman. Now there were five cousins working for The New York Times Company. If Punch decided to give Arthur Jr. all of his titles, as his father had done for him, his sisters and their offspring were sure to protest.

That would also almost certainly be the case regarding board membership. For years the five cousins who worked at the company had alternated sitting in on meetings as observers. It was not only part of their education but a way for directors to familiarize themselves with family members who might one day come before them as candidates for top positions. But this group — Arthur Jr., Dan, Susan, Stephen, and Michael — was hardly alone in its interest in eventual service on the board. Every Sulzberger cousin — even Jace, who worked on various car engines at his own auto repair shop in Maine, and Bobby, the most estranged of the lot — wanted a seat when their parents stepped down, although few were impolitic enough to acknowledge it publicly. Among Punch and the sisters, the understanding was that when they retired, each of them would designate a successor from among his or her children, a plan that put all four in the awkward position of having to favor one child over the others.

Shortly before Arthur Jr. had been made publisher, the five cousins working for the company had begun meeting periodically for breakfast. Over bagels and coffee they had speculated about what might happen when their parents passed away and they and their cousins were left as stewards and managers of *The New York Times*. They were disquieted by the fact that so little was clear about the terms of succession, both in the upper reaches of management and on the board, and that their parents had never discussed the topic openly with them. Just as Punch and Ruth had passively waited for their own parents to decide their roles at *The New York Times* and *The Chattanooga Times*, so Punch and his sisters assumed that *their* children would wait for their elders to decide who would get what in the generational changing of the guard.

"The sibs," as the five cousins called their parents, had passed on to their offspring the central tenets of the family: confrontation was to be avoided, and everyone must give the appearance of harmony even if harmony didn't exist. The price of sustaining this peaceful front was that family members were often harshly critical of one another behind the scenes. "[Since] you *had* to get along, being judgmental was the only way to cope," explained Stephen. The five worried that once "the sibs" were gone — without the binding force of Iphigene, without Hillandale as a common place to congregate — the family might drift apart or dissolve into warring camps. They wanted not only to break the taboo of silence that had traditionally limited family discussions of succession but to talk frankly about how, in the very different world they faced, they should begin to assume management of the company while keeping the family together as a unit. In short, they wanted to devise a new model for new times: a cousins' syndicate rather than a sibling partnership, and they wanted to create it in a manner everyone could embrace.

In the fall of 1992, spurred on by their earlier breakfast discussions, several of the cousins working for the company had done something completely un-Sulzbergerian. They had invited the four "sibs" to dinner at an East Side restaurant and made a bold proposal. They wished to convene all thirteen cousins, their spouses, and grown children in a series of family meetings, the purpose of which would be to discuss everything from who should sit on the board to how members of the next generation should be brought into the company. To ensure that they wouldn't avoid the most sensitive issues, they wanted to hire a facilitator to direct the conversation — and they wanted Punch and the sisters to foot the bill. Amazingly, three of the four "sibs" had reacted positively. The lone dissenter had been Marian, who disliked any discussion of giving up her board seat and the power it represented, but, typical of the consensus dynamics of the family, she had eventually relented.

It had been Ruth who suggested Craig Aronoff, the portly, bearded head of the Family Enterprise Center at Kennesaw State University outside Atlanta, to be the family's consultant and facilitator. One of his first acts was to convene a lunch in New York with Punch and his sisters, at which he asked a pivotal question: "Are you one family or are you four families?" The query spoke directly to the Sulzbergers' discomfort with having to choose one of their children to inherit their directors' seats. The table fell sheepishly silent as the Sulzbergers looked at one another. Finally Ruth spoke up: "Well, we're one family." Another pause followed as the reason Aronoff had asked the question sunk in. "But we're *acting* like four families," she exclaimed. "Not just acting like it," Craig confirmed, "*institutionalizing* it."

In May 1994, at Aronoff's urging, Punch gave a speech to the cousins' generation and their adult offspring, instructing them to make the "one family or four" question a central element of their deliberations as they debated issues such as board succession and whether or not family members should continue to fill the top executive slots in the company. With that, he and his sisters absented themselves from the process in order to avoid influencing their children's and grandchildren's thinking.

With Aronoff's help, the younger Sulzbergers split into committees on philanthropy, family governance, employment policy, trust participation, and board succession. One group also explored the establishment of a family office, a central place where family members could get help with estate planning and asset management.

The committees completed their work toward the end of 1994, and Arthur Golden, in his role as overall editor, gave the results a one-voice write-through. In early 1995 Punch and each of the sisters received a final, fifty-page bound volume entitled *Proposals for the Future: To the Third Generation of the Ochs-Sulzberger Family from the Fourth and Fifth Generations.* The preamble declared that of the family's two goals — maintaining its stewardship of *The New York Times* and preserving the unity of the family — its role as guardian of the paper "will certainly always come first . . . [taking] precedence over most considerations of individual welfare." Among the document's more than two dozen recommendations, there was none suggesting when and how Punch might choose his successor; the younger family members hadn't wanted to make him feel that he was being pushed out.

Although Lance Primis was one of the key players in the succession drama, he was not privy to the family's proposals. The only section the company president saw was on family training, and that began with a declaration that the younger generation of Sulzbergers believed the family should continue to play an important role in running the company. Performing such a function — as chairman of the board or as directors representing the family's controlling shares — was a principle with which Primis had no quarrel; he acknowledged that that was the Sulzbergers' right. But he had long been persuaded that the time had come for *The New York Times* to operate like other multibillion-dollar corporations and install professional management at the top.

What Primis had in mind was a conventional arrangement in which he would serve as CEO of The New York Times Company. In most corporations the CEO reports to the board directly and on an advisory basis to the chairman. Primis wanted comparable power: a free hand to run the company, with oversight by the owning family through its presence on the board, though no direct interference. He would have the final operating authority, not Punch or any other family member.

Primis had arrived at this conclusion after a cool appraisal of the business's situation. Everything he was hearing, from outside directors to Wall Street analysts who complained that the family treated *The New York Times* as its own personal "candy store," was that the company was long overdue for modern management. And who other than Primis was qualified to rise to the challenge? Punch wasn't capable of doing so, and Primis couldn't imagine Arthur Jr. in the role. He hadn't been trained for it and he didn't have the backing of the board, which had made its reservations about him clear in 1991 by demanding that his appointment as publisher not be interpreted as a signal that he would eventually become CEO. That gave Primis reason for hope, as did Punch's apparent willingness to entertain succession scenarios other than the traditional one. With directors like Gerstner demanding higher profits, leaner budgets, and stricter compliance with financial objectives, Primis assumed that all he had to do was prove that he was suited to the post of CEO, and the power that went with it could be his — family or no family.

Like most salesmen, Primis thought in terms of audiences. Early on in his presidency he had seen Punch as his "key account." Now he considered his main constituency — those to whom he most needed to "sell" himself — to be the board of directors. He made a special effort to ingratiate himself with Gerstner, the dominant member of the group, but had a difficult time with the others. New York Times Company stock was depressed, and it was certain to remain so unless earnings improved. Shares had plummeted from the high in 1987, the year of the crash. The decision to buy *The Boston Globe* had been judged so negatively by Wall Street that even after the company had spent $282 million repurchasing its own shares, the stock had barely risen. Selling the women's magazines had had no effect, either.

For Primis, the trough could not have come at a worse time. "Shareholder value" was the catchphrase of the moment, and to corporate analysts and even to a few members of *The New York Times'* board, the term meant only one thing: increased profits and an upwardly mobile stock price, quarter after quarter. Primis knew that the Sulzbergers' concept of "value" had almost nothing to do with short-term share price, but rather with maintaining the editorial quality of *The New York Times,* which ensured the steady growth of the company. Punch didn't even think of himself primarily as a businessman; on passport applications and immigration forms, he wrote "journalist" as his occupation.

Because the Sulzbergers owned the majority of the Class B stock — the shares that controlled the board — no outside interest, such as a large institutional investor, could demand that the company maximize "share-holder value" to the exclusion of other goals. But the very vehicle that gave the family absolute control also made them vulnerable. As the company had grown and new Class A stock had been issued, the actual percentage of the Class A shares that the family owned had shrunk from more than 50 percent when Adolph died to less than 18 percent. But their Class B shares, through which they controlled their multibillion-dollar company, amounted to less than one-half of 1 percent of the total stock outstand-ing — a tiny stake wielding very large power. As long as the Sulzbergers met their fiduciary responsibilities, they could run The New York Times Company any way they saw fit, but they also ran the risk of stockholder suits if they were perceived to be reckless or abusively nepotistic.

To boost its stock price, another prominent family-controlled, pub-licly traded media company — Times Mirror, owner of the *Los Angeles Times* — had recently installed a corporate outsider, Mark Willes, vice chairman of General Mills, as president and CEO. In his first year Willes shuttered the company's money-losing *New York Newsday,* eliminated three thousand jobs, and dumped $750 million in unprofitable or unpromising businesses. It didn't take long for the stock price, which Willes prominently displayed in the lobby of the Los Angeles Times Building, to nearly double. Three months after the hiring of Willes, there was another bellwether of change: the Walt Disney Company acquired Capital Cities/ABC, a deal that gave the Hollywood entertain-ment giant a network TV news outlet and eleven newspapers, including the *Fort Worth Star-Telegram* and *The Kansas City Star.* For decades The New York Times Company had viewed Times Mirror, Knight Ridder, and the Chicago-based Tribune Company as its main competitors. Now it felt the hot breath of behemoths such as Disney, Rupert Murdoch's News Corporation, and Microsoft — global conglomerates with vast amounts of money in nongeographical markets. Amid such Goliaths, *The New York Times* was a nervous David.

Primis watched this transformation in the media world with growing anxiety. Nearly three years into his presidency, he had yet to convince Wall Street that he had a coherent vision. In December 1994, in what was described as a "strategic shift," The New York Times Company had announced its intention to invest up to $1.5 billion in cable television programming, broadcasting, CD-ROMs, and on-line products over the next five or six years. Financial analysts had long considered the *Times* too heavily committed to print at a time when other companies were aggressively diversifying into new media, and gave Primis's plan a tepid reception. As far as they were concerned, it was too little too late, and the following day *New York Times* stock dropped a dollar and a half. Since then, Primis had continued to reiterate his self-proclaimed "big concept": that the "brand name" of *The New York Times* was an asset that should be capitalized on — always, he added, in "appropriate" ways. "You have to keep applying the brand of the *Times* to everything we wind up doing," he insisted.

In an effort to do that, Primis in 1995 launched the Popcorn Channel, a cable network devoted to movie theater listings, and acquired Video News International, a small video news production company. He made a deal with the Discovery Channel for a series based on the *Times'* science section; bought a TV station in Norfolk, Virginia; made the *Times* a small investor in Ovation, a fine-arts cable network; and toyed with the idea of producing original television programming. But even Primis admitted that these efforts, taken together, amounted to little more than appetizers. Wall Street remained unimpressed, and Primis didn't know what to do next. He slept fitfully, worried constantly. "I can't shut it off," he said. "I'm convinced Walter gave me this job so that my hair would turn gray, my eyes would fail, and my golf game would deteriorate."

Baffled by the intractability of the investment community, Primis called his old friend Jim Dowling, chairman of the advertising firm Burson-Marsteller, and over lunch asked him what to do. The result was a survey in which analysts were asked their perceptions of The New York Times Company and its senior management. Primis was sobered by the findings: Wall Street viewed the company as leaderless, with Punch and Primis huddled together in a hazy arrangement as coexecutives. Primis struck them as the consummate salesman — passionate and enthusiastic, but not presidential, not in command.

Primis's response was to get training to improve his presentation skills — "charm school," as one detractor called it. Toning down his natural ebullience "nearly killed me," but he gamely tried to change the way he answered questions, stressing facts over emotion. Primis unveiled the new, improved version of himself at a gathering of stock analysts in late April 1995. The meeting, held at the Macklowe Hotel just off Times Square, was the first the company had ever organized specifically to give information about itself to Wall Street. The presidents of each of the company's divisions — *The Boston Globe, The New York Times,* the regional newspapers, broadcast, sports and leisure — made formal presentations. Primis's role was to provide an overview of where the business was headed. His message was simple and direct — "I am promising you a different New York Times Company" — and it was enthusiastically received. The next day the stock spiked up a bit, even as some analysts chuckled that one of Primis's diversification schemes was distinctly un*Times*ian: capitalizing on the name of *Golf Digest,* a New York Times Company publication, by building golf driving ranges.

Another aspect of revamping The New York Times Company involved hiring fresh talent. A year earlier Primis had concluded that the executives he inherited from Mattson weren't capable of "thinking outside the box," and ever since then he had been searching for high-powered outsiders. One slot was reserved for what he and Punch called "Mr. Wonderful" — an expert in new ventures and electronic businesses. Another was for a chief financial officer, a job that, like everything else, Mattson had effectively done himself despite the fact that David Gorham, a former company controller, held the actual title and had continued on in that role in the Primis regime.

When Diane Baker, a forty-one-year-old former investment banker and managing director at Salomon Brothers, joined the company as its new CFO, Wall Street signaled its approval by sending *New York Times* stock up two and a half points in three days. Less than twenty-four hours after the announcement, Morgan Stanley raised its rating on *Times* shares, citing the selection of Baker, a tough-minded cost cutter, as a "very strong move." Primis had promised the board a better stock price and investment analysts a "new" company; now, with his choice of Baker, he had delivered. He was finally a "hitter." "Maybe you should go hire five more people, and we'll get [the stock price] to forty!" one *Times* director told him.

Baker, who had spent the previous five years as CFO at R. H. Macy & Company trying to help it emerge from bankruptcy, was an unusual choice for Primis, and for the company. Tall, hard-charging, and endlessly energetic, she had spent her entire professional life in corporate finance rather than in the newspaper industry, leading some to worry that she wouldn't understand the values of *The New York Times.* But Primis saw Baker's forceful personality and technical skills as pluses. She could do the operational part of the job that he disliked and wasn't good at while also acting as his pit bull, taking the first hit on unpopular ideas and generally playing bad cop to his good cop. Baker had met only two *Times* executives during the interview process: Primis and Punch. Once on the payroll, she reported to both — a highly unusual arrangement.

As Baker settled in and Punch got to know her, he was pleased to discover that she had broader interests than the typical banker and was closer to the family's way of thinking about shareholder value than he had expected. He was gratified by her willingness to meet with his sisters and walk them through the company financials. And he cheered when, within two weeks of her arrival, she announced that she was going to standardize the company's redundant and inefficient accounting practices, a change that promised huge savings. Still, he was troubled by her manner, which she herself described as "abrasive, confrontational, and difficult — a burr under the saddle." "She's very businesslike, and it's a little painful," Punch remarked. "It's probably good medicine, but you've got to be careful you don't take too much medicine. That can make you sick also."

Baker's boot-camp style was unlike anything *Times* executives had ever experienced. Within weeks word of her brutal aphorisms raced through the building. "I believe in carrying the wounded and shooting the stragglers," she announced to her staff. "And I'm going to shoot a lot more people if they don't get it." She boasted of never stabbing people in the back: "I come through the front door with a machete." Her tossed-off "fuck you!" to Primis in front of other executives was met with stunned silence. The *Times* was hardly a paragon of sophisticated financial management, but Baker's intimidation tactics ran so counter to the company's tradition of etiquette that soon after her arrival, Punch and Primis distributed a memo that, while not naming Baker specifically, made it clear that publicly insulting staff members or threatening their jobs would not be tolerated.

The New York Times Company was the first solvent firm Baker had ever worked for. At places like Chrysler and Macy's, she had kept creditors at bay while digging her clients out of debt, and it had made her an expert at finding efficiencies. When she trained her sights on *The New York Times'* newsroom, however, she ran into a wall of opposition. She and Primis had agreed that the newsroom could benefit, as several corporate departments already had, from a thorough examination by the consulting firm of McKinsey & Company. But the specter of McKinsey resurrected the old tensions over the proper height of the "wall" protecting the news operation from inappropriate financial pressure.

Shortly before Baker's arrival, the newspaper had reduced its staff by fifty; soon 190 more jobs were targeted for elimination. Newsprint prices had nearly doubled since 1994, and finding ways to offset the increases had become more and more difficult. Neither Arthur Jr. nor executive editor Joe Lelyveld was averse to saving money. They just wanted to make the painful choices themselves, not have them imposed by outsiders. Arthur Jr. was particularly distrustful of Baker; he felt her lack of media experience gave her no authority to make decisions about how the news department spent its money.

When the McKinsey proposal was rejected, the matter of cost cutting was left to Arthur Jr. and his team at the paper. After they presented their plan to Primis and Baker, Primis announced that he felt the business side of the *Times* had already been pared to the bone. Now it was the newsroom's turn: he wanted $3 million shaved from its budget. "There's no way I can give you those savings and have our readers and advertisers not notice," Lelyveld protested. Punch, who had a policy of never disagreeing with Primis in front of subordinates, sat in a corner and kept silent, but after the meeting adjourned, he conferred in private with the company president. Soon the newsroom was permitted to come back with cuts totaling only a third of what Primis wanted. The real battle — over whether a nonfamily senior officer of the company would ever control newsroom finances — was left for another day.

Primis had a freer hand at the company's two dozen or so regional papers, some of which posted profit margins as high as 25 percent, more than twice that of *The New York Times*. Despite that performance, Primis thought their news budgets could afford to be pruned. "They in essence have no competition in their markets, so [you] can do pretty much what you like," he explained. When he went before the board to present his "Challenge Plan" calling for smaller news holes and layoffs of reporters and editors, Ruth could barely conceal her disdain. As chairman and former publisher of *The Chattanooga Times,* she was offended by the suggestion that the company's smaller papers should be treated as cash cows, milked for profit at the expense of local readers. If family ownership stood for anything, she argued, it was that the same standards of journalistic excellence should be applied to all the company's news-gathering operations. She agreed with Punch, whose barometer of quality was simple: "You ought to have a paper that, when you walk into town, you can hold your head up."

To demonstrate that he was serious about budget cutting, Primis made personal visits to the affiliated papers he considered most in need of discipline. Soon disgruntled readers around the country were sending letters to Punch, complaining that their hometown papers had been eviscerated. Ruth buttonholed Primis on the subject every chance she got. Punch, typically, was more circumspect, and though he wasn't against having an efficient company, he did feel that Primis had a narrow view of the future, one entirely focused on short-term profits.

It was during this period of painful belt-cinching that Primis built a new office for himself at a cost of $1 million. Punch's secretary, Nancy Finn, called it "the Taj Mahal." While every other suite on the fourteenth floor was self-consciously conservative, Primis's office was pointedly modern and airy, with a fifteen-foot raised ceiling and two walls of windows overlooking Manhattan, one of which led to a small terrace graced by the cornets and fleurs-de-lis installed by Adolph's architect in the early 1920s. There was a private bathroom, a bar, and a conversation area with buff brown leather couches and a cocktail table. The curved cherry desk was custom made and large enough to serve as a conference table during meetings. Behind it, hidden in the ceiling, was a screen that could be electronically lowered for presentations. Primis maintained that the office was only meant to communicate that "this was going to be a different company" — more entrepreneurial, with "new ways of thinking." "I didn't intend it to be symbolic," he said. "But it was pretty clear we were trying to make changes. I wanted to show we were going to move forward."

Punch observed the banging and sawing going on down the hall without comment. Privately he thought it was "God-ghastly . . . but very important to Lance." He approved Primis's plan to build over the previously unused terrace and took an intense interest in selecting the office's art, which included a pointillist triptych of Manhattan at night. Otherwise, he kept his distance. Since Punch had made no move to stop him or modify the plans, and even led *Times* directors on a tour when the project was completed, Primis assumed Punch was not just enthusiastic but "quite proud" of what he had done. The reality was that Punch considered Primis's office an embarrassment, especially in light of the fiscal sacrifice others were having to make at the company, as well as a visible challenge to his power as chairman and CEO. To underscore the point, he made a show of knocking loudly on Primis's massive door, which had once been the original entry for the New York Times Building, asking, "Permission to enter, sir?" To anyone else, the meaning of Punch's gesture would have been unmistakable. Primis interpreted it as one more example of the chairman's understated humor.

50

Two Camps

AS PUNCH REVIEWED THE FIVE FAMILY MEMBERS who worked for the company, he saw only two realistic possibilities from which to choose his successor: his son, Arthur Jr., and his nephew Michael Golden. Susan Dryfoos had no training in business, and Stephen Golden, corporate vice president of forest products, worked in a secondary area of the company and had only recently earned his college degree.

Dan Cohen was also out of the running. In recent years he had moved from the *Times'* advertising department to circulation, then back to advertising again, all without a significant change in status. By 1994 even his wife, Leah, was urging him to quit and do something else. Instead, Dan informed Russ Lewis, president of *The New York Times* newspaper, that he wanted to be considered to head the paper's new electronic media group. Lewis had been expecting such a request and, in anticipation, had advised Arthur Jr. that he intended to be frank. "You should be thinking about a *de*motion, not a *pro*motion," he told Dan before going on to spell out in detail the precariousness of his situation. It was the first time in Dan's eleven years at the paper that anyone had told him the blunt truth about how he came across.

Stricken, Dan sought out Arthur Jr., who confirmed that his cousin's problems were, in fact, real. He suggested a management coach, paid for out of the publisher's budget, who would help Dan tone down his tendency to appear arrogant and to run roughshod over other people's ideas. For the next several months, Dan endured a series of brutal evaluations and behavior-modification exercises, after which he returned on a provisional basis to the advertising department, now run by a nurturing new director, Janet Robinson. By the summer of 1995, he was judged to have made enough progress to be promoted to vice president of

732

advertising sales — an important job, but not one that put him in line for the top posts in the company.

Unlike Susan, Stephen, and Dan, Michael Golden had the credentials to back up his ambition: a journalism degree, an MBA, management experience at *The Chattanooga Times,* and stints serving as publisher of two New York Times Company magazines, *McCall's* and *Tennis.* Of equal importance was his southern charm, warm manner, and self-deprecating humor, qualities that made him well liked and a natural diplomat.

The one gap in Michael's résumé continued to be his lack of experience at headquarters, and the one obstacle to filling it continued to be Primis. For over a year he had dutifully done what Primis had asked, working in Trumbull, Connecticut, as publisher of *Tennis* magazine. At the time, Punch had been reluctant to make a fuss about the move, for while he had been eager to have Michael on the fourteenth floor in order to observe him and train him as a possible successor, he had also wanted to give his new president a free hand. By the fall of 1995, however, Punch had begun to suspect that unless he intervened, Primis would let Michael languish at *Tennis* indefinitely.

When the draft press release announcing Diane Baker's appointment as chief financial officer made the rounds for internal comment, Punch had seen an opportunity to bring Michael to the *Times* without having to face down Primis: he had written Michael into the draft as assistant to David Gorham, the former CFO whom Baker was replacing. In the new lineup, Gorham was to be deputy chief operating officer; as his assistant, Michael would enjoy vice presidential status. When Primis learned what Punch had done, he said that the CEO didn't have the unilateral power to install Michael as a vice president, a level that the directors had to approve. Moreover, because Gorham's new position was ill defined, it was unclear what function his "assistant" might actually perform. In the face of these objections, Punch backed down. He did, however, extract a promise from Primis that by the end of the year the promotion would be put before the board and Michael would be on his way to the fourteenth floor — a pledge that Primis also made directly to Michael.

But the matter of Michael's promotion didn't show up on the board's agenda until the last meeting of 1995, and it might not have appeared even then had not Michael, worried that Primis would sabotage him yet again, asked David Gorham to make sure everything was on track. Gorham had spoken to Punch, and as Michael said a few days before the *Times* published a cryptic story about his new position, "There's no doubt in my mind that this is happening purely and simply because Punch wants it to happen. The last thing Lance wants is another family member involved in management."

Primis soon made that abundantly clear. On his first day on the four-teenth floor, Michael discovered that a consultant was using the office designated for him, and it wouldn't be vacant for several weeks. "Why don't you go back to *Tennis* until it's available," Primis suggested. After some independent scouting, Michael claimed an office that had been set aside for the yet-to-be-hired Mr. Wonderful.

Michael's newly elevated status was tough on Stephen and Dan, but the other cousins seemed to be genuinely supportive; one told him he deserved the "patience award." Punch was delighted and, during his nephew's first few weeks on the job, made sure Michael was at his side at every senior-level meeting. Primis, however, vigorously objected to putting him on the management committee, a group that included all the top executives on the fourteenth floor, and did his best to pretend Michael didn't exist. He rarely dropped by his office, and while he was cordial when Michael came to see him, he had little of substance to say.

Arthur Jr. certainly knew how it felt to be excluded by Primis; he had been experiencing it for years. During the heady days of Deming, he and Primis had been confreres, united in their determination to change the culture of the company. Now that they were rivals, Arthur Jr. found Primis impenetrable. He was always pleasant, always hail-fellow-well-met, but he seemed to have no interest in what Arthur Jr. had to say. When Arthur Jr. tried to discuss problems related to the newspaper, Primis offered up soliloquies about his own plans, his own ideas, his own vision for the future. During a vacation in Hawaii one family mem-ber asked Arthur Jr. what had gone wrong in the friendship he once had with Primis, but before he could reply, Gail answered for him. "Arthur and Lance were *never* friends," she said coldly.

Arthur Jr. had been slowly finding his way back to his father in the months following Carol's death. "We just one day started talking, and found that we liked each other more than we had known," said Punch. They began lunching regularly, and Arthur Jr. frequently either called his father to talk over problems or popped up to the fourteenth floor for quick face-to-face conferences. He had also learned to listen more and talk less, and gradually a new, more statesmanlike Arthur Jr. began to emerge. "You can appear so wise by just nodding," Punch told his son. "You don't have to have an instant response to everything that comes before you."

Not surprisingly, the budding affection between father and son only raised the stakes of Primis's competition with Arthur Jr. Primis continued to believe that Arthur Jr. had few qualifications to be the final authority at the company, lacking, as he did, experience with boards of directors, corporate governance, deal making, and complex financials. "We've got to keep Arthur at the newspaper," Primis cautioned other executives in private. "We can't let him try to influence the direction of the company." Although Primis had become convinced that Punch had already accepted the idea that the company needed professionals at the senior level, there was still the possibility that he would decide in favor of a succession plan with more family involvement rather than less, a possibility that made Arthur Jr.'s presence — and to a lesser extent, Michael's — an ongoing and potent threat. In a proposed new management scheme for *The Boston Globe,* Primis saw a way to solve two of his problems.

When The New York Times Company had acquired the *Globe* in 1993, it had agreed that the Taylor family and its executives could continue managing the paper for five years, provided that they made their numbers. By 1995, however, the *Globe* was way off its profit targets. Primis's solution was to create a new metropolitan newspaper division within the company, led by Russ Lewis, with both *The New York Times* and *The Boston Globe* under its umbrella. Under the plan, Arthur Jr. would no longer report to Primis but to Lewis, an arrangement that would encourage the perception that his standing had been diminished. Moreover, by deputizing Lewis to deal with the *Globe*'s financial problems, Primis could also remove himself from the nasty business of straightening out its operations — a job sure to antagonize the Taylors.

He laid out the details of the plan at a meeting of the management committee, asking cheerily, "Doesn't this make sense?" For several moments no one spoke, until finally Michael piped up. "I don't think it's a good idea," he said. "Organizationally, it adds a layer of management that we don't need and it pushes *The New York Times* down in the organization, which sends a bad message. It also defers dealing with *The Boston Globe*." Spirited discussion ensued, and the meeting broke up without resolution. Afterward, Michael buttonholed Punch. "That idea is a nonstarter," he insisted, visibly alarmed. Punch shrugged, and replied, "It's not going to happen. I didn't see any reason to argue with something that isn't going to happen."

§

As 1995 came to a close, Punch was in a state of dismay about his relationship with Primis. From the very first, he had made it clear to the company president that a large part of his job was to help him with his family, yet Primis had thrown roadblocks in the paths of Arthur Jr. and Michael, making enemies of them and Ruth and leaving Punch deeply distrustful. Relations between Primis and Stephen had reached the point that they could scarcely be civil to each other. Worse still, Primis had effectively refused to discuss with Punch the matter of what role the family should play in senior management in the future. What Punch wanted was a confidant with whom he could contemplate possible succession scenarios, someone who would "just listen" as Turner Catledge and Walter Mattson had done. But Primis wouldn't engage. He was too busy trying to sell Punch on the idea that the company had grown beyond the Sulzbergers.

Punch had always been a casual manager, strolling into his executives' offices with a mug of tea or chatting with them over lunch, all the while ferreting out what was going on in the company. In contrast, for all his apparent openness, Primis was guarded and remote, even with Punch. When Michael finally made it to the fourteenth floor, he was shocked at how little Primis saw of Punch — or of anyone else, for that matter. In meetings Primis always invited people to speak out, if only to prove that he wasn't an autocrat like Mattson. But his actual nature was to brood alone, with input from one or two loyal advisers, then announce a decision.

With the succession question looming ever larger, the company had separated into two camps: one betting on Primis, the other, made up mostly of members of the *Times* newsroom, betting on Arthur Jr. or another family member. Many on the business side felt Primis was on the right track. "It wasn't unusual for a family-owned business to evolve into a professionally managed one, and they appeared to be moving down that line," said John O'Brien, the paper's deputy general manager.

Punch knew that his nieces and nephews weren't averse to a professional CEO, a stance they had made clear in the bound book of recommendations they had presented to him and his sisters in early 1995. Indeed, they recognized that if Punch were to die suddenly, the board of directors would never choose any of them to replace him as chief executive officer. But their consensus was that the family should continue as the final authority, especially the final authority at the newspaper. Without that day-to-day power, the Sulzbergers would lose something precious: their ability to act as stewards of a great public trust, an identity that gave them a higher purpose and helped bind them together as a family. The company would also lose something invaluable: its stability and continuity. Indeed, the *country* would lose something many felt was priceless: the family's ability to make news decisions that ran counter to the financial pressures of the marketplace. What would happen to the scope and quality of *New York Times* reporting, the cousins asked themselves, if the company were led by an executive who felt his primary responsibility was to protect the stock price? How might history have been altered if it had been a professional manager, not Punch, who had had the power to decide whether to publish the Pentagon Papers?

Primis had told several of the cousins that he regarded himself as a bridge between their generation and Punch's. Because neither Arthur Jr. nor Michael nor any of the others was equipped to assume Punch's position, he argued, it made sense to let him step in and take on that role while they got more seasoning. His logic had convinced no one. Not only did the cousins consider it a transparent grab for power in the short term, they felt it threatened to relegate the family to a ceremonial role in the future. "If the next chairman or CEO is not a member of the family, it gets harder to reinstate that," said Michael. "Once you've lost that, it's hard to say, 'That didn't count, it's not precedent.' The hell it isn't!"

In the months since the cousins had delivered *Proposals for the Future*, Primis had been working with general counsel Sol Watson and others to prepare a corporate equivalent. "I think that unless we give him the shareholders' view . . . and what the company's responsibilities are on these issues, he won't have the full deck from which to make a decision [about succession]," he explained. "My fear is he'll make what he thinks is the right decision without that perspective."

With the delivery of Primis's document, Punch had no excuse to put off drafting a proposal about succession. He knew how sensitive the issue had become within the family, and he dreaded the hurt and dashed expectations that would inevitably occur once he made his final decision. But he had promised his directors a plan, and they were becoming impatient. Over the past several months he and Primis had taken them out to dinner, two at a time, so that they could talk about issues they might feel reluctant to raise at a full board meeting. As a group, their major concern was how the torch was going to be passed, especially on the board, where a number of directors, including Punch, were approaching the age of seventy.

Punch asked his secretary, Nancy Finn, to keep Wednesday, December 13, 1995, free of appointments. On that day he planned to sit down at his old Underwood manual typewriter and in his two-fingered fashion make a first attempt at mapping out what the future leadership of The New York Times Company would look like. The irony of using a beat-up typewriter to draft a document charting the course of the company in the twenty-first century was lost on Punch. Although he had a computer in his office, he never used it for writing; he had taken lessons, then promptly forgotten everything except how to retrieve e-mail. Whenever he had to compose a document, he pounded it out on the Underwood and gave the results to Nancy, who corrected his spelling and typed up a clean copy.

Punch produced a first draft but was fundamentally dissatisfied with it. He had found it easy to come up with a structure for the transition, but a challenge to drop specific names into the various slots because, he said, "[that] doesn't just affect that person, it affects a whole lot of other things" — an oblique allusion to the potentially divisive resentment that could arise if Arthur Jr. got everything. If Mattson were still around, Punch would have asked him for his reaction. But Mattson was long gone, and Punch didn't feel comfortable sharing such sensitive information with Primis. Instead, he gave Arthur Jr. a copy and invited him to come up to the fourteenth floor the following evening to discuss it. That act was a powerful demonstration of the new intimacy that had taken root between the men since Carol's death, and Punch himself admitted,

"I would never have dropped that paper on his desk a year ago." But it also suggested how profoundly alone Punch felt — without Mattson, without a president he could trust or in whom he could confide. He yearned for a counselor and a sympathetic ear. Who better, theoretically, than his own son? "That's the way it *should* work, and the way I'd like it to work," Punch said. "I'm trying it on for size."

51

Death of a Salesman

PUNCH WAS AGHAST WHEN HE PICKED UP HIS
Wall Street Journal on January 22, 1996. There on the front page
was a long story by Patrick M. Reilly about the struggle over who
would succeed him. "The future of The New York Times Company may
not be all in the family after all," read the provocative first sentence. The
article went on to say that no longer could it automatically be assumed
that Punch's son would inherit his job. Even Judy, the only family member quoted, suggested that it "might go to anyone." The responsibilities
could be divided up among the Sulzberger cousins, she said, or "[the top
executive] may not even be a family member." Louis V. Gerstner Jr. and
other outside directors were said to be "concerned" about the transition,
and Primis was identified as "a top prospect."

The following day *Times* stock ticked up three-eighths of a point, Wall
Street's way of signaling its approval of the prospect of nonfamily management. The Sulzbergers were taken aback, especially by the *Journal's*
suggestion, seemingly bolstered by Judy's remarks, that their clan, legendary for its harmony, was squabbling over power. Phone calls flew
from one coast to the other as family members shared their outrage and
anxiety. While Primis denied having talked with Reilly, a reporter he
knew well, most in the family suspected otherwise. "I don't know about
your copy of the *Journal,* but mine has Lance's fingerprints all over it,"
one cousin told Michael. Publicly Punch made no comment about the
story; privately he entertained, then dismissed, the notion that Primis
had been a source. "Punch doesn't think Lance did it," said a close friend.
"No one could be that stupid."

The Sulzberger most rattled by the article was Arthur Jr., whom
Reilly portrayed as unprepared and immature. "If *The Wall Street
Journal* story did anything, it shook his confidence," said John O'Brien,
the *Times'* deputy general manager. Barely a week after the piece

appeared, Arthur Jr. strode onto the stage of the newly refurbished New Victory Theater on West Forty-second Street to give his annual State of the Newspaper talk to the staff. Punch never attended such events, but he made a point of coming to this one. Arthur Jr. was startled to see him when he looked out over the audience, and he became visibly more nervous.

Was it true? one employee asked with trepidation during the Q and A. Was there, in fact, a battle going on at the highest level of the company? Arthur Jr. chose his words carefully. He had been embarrassed by Judy's remarks, but he betrayed no hint of that in his response. "My wonderful aunt Judy is absolutely right," he declared. "When the time comes, the board is going to look at what is best for this company. . . . But the idea that we are somehow all pitted against each other is false."

Then, with evident emotion, he acknowledged the presence of his father, who for many in the hall was the living embodiment of *The New York Times.* "You see my father in the elevator. You see him in the hallways," Arthur Jr. said. "He's a pretty vigorous-looking fellow, wouldn't you say? I think he still fits into his marine uniform. He's going to be around for a long time. And since I think that I have the best job in the world right now as publisher of *The New York Times,* I hope he decides to stay just where he is for a hell of a long time." The crowd broke into spontaneous applause.

The *Journal* article emboldened those who had long been unimpressed with Arthur Jr. to attack him more openly. A business reporter at the *Times* began to get calls from his Wall Street contacts inquiring why Gerstner was "trashing" the young publisher, and Diane Baker, the company's new chief financial officer, felt no compunction about telling a visitor that in her opinion Arthur Jr. had the personality of "a twenty-four-year-old geek." But for many on both the news and the business sides of the company, the article served to rally support. "The pendulum has swung back to Arthur Jr.," said a senior executive who witnessed the moment in the New Victory Theater.

The story also had the effect of bringing the Sulzbergers closer together. While the *Journal* had exposed the very real but characteristically muted disgruntlement in the family about the privileged position Arthur Jr. enjoyed in any succession scenario, raising the specter of a public fight horrified them. They buried their divisions and circled the wagons, more determined than ever to present a united front.

Inadvertently, it was Primis himself who became the catalyst for the Sulzbergers' fortified unity, for in him they now had a common enemy. Whether or not he had spoken to the *Journal* reporter was immaterial. The gist of the article had been that family management was on its way out at The New York Times Company, and good riddance to it — precisely the attitude Primis embodied. It wasn't just his thwarting of Arthur Jr. and Michael that bothered them, it was also his lack of respect for the family and what it stood for. Punch was particularly offended by Primis's unspoken assumption that family management couldn't possibly be professional.

In less than three years Primis had managed to antagonize virtually every member of the Sulzberger family. He made little effort to build relationships with any of them, he didn't listen to them, and though with others he could be ingratiating to a fault, with the Sulzbergers he gave the impression that he couldn't be bothered. It was as though he was actively trying to distance himself from them. Those in the clan who attended the periodic briefings held for family members who didn't work for the company felt that Primis treated them like dim-witted dividend collectors who couldn't possibly understand what he was explaining. "He'd come in and do his little thing and go," said Ruth's daughter, Lynn. "I don't think he ever ate lunch with us. It was just, 'Well, gotta talk to those kids.' " Although Punch himself never experienced such condescension, over time word of the family's unhappiness drifted up to him.

Primis's lifestyle and manner of dress were added irritants. At *The New York Times,* where executives typically sported conservative wardrobes from Brooks Brothers and Paul Stuart, Primis's expensive-looking suits and starched shirts that hugged his jock's frame a tad too tightly seemed salesman-slick and out of place. His habit of zooming off in the corporate jet to play golf with the heads of AT&T and Bell Atlantic smacked of country-club elitism, while his opulent office and recently acquired red Ferrari were offensive to the studiously unostentatious Sulzbergers. "He was a little too grand, a little too big for his britches," said Marian. His stylistic missteps and disregard for the family led the Sulzbergers to feel that at heart he just didn't "get" *The New York Times.* He almost never talked about the news; some wondered whether he even read the paper. "I think he looked at the ads," said Punch.

United by their mutual dissatisfaction with Primis, the Sulzbergers became uncharacteristically aggressive in their efforts to dislodge him. Ruth, who had been unhappy with him from the start, took it upon herself to hold discreet talks with George B. Munroe, Richard L. Gelb, and other outside directors, asking their opinions of Primis. That spring Michael lunched with Punch and took up the issue with more directness. "Look," he said, "I've been on the fourteenth floor for several months now and I'm convinced that Lance is not the [right] guy." He listed his reasons and then asked Punch how confident *he* was in his president. "On a scale of one to one hundred," Punch began, "my level of confidence in Lance is . . ." but he never finished the sentence, and instead cast about for encouraging things to say. It wasn't a lost cause, he told Michael; the situation could still be salvaged.

That was hardly the impression Ruth's daughter, Lynn, got when she met with Punch and the other three "sibs" in the spring of 1996 to discuss matters related to the family trust. After they had settled into their seats, her mother looked around the table. "What are we going to do about Lance?" she asked. Punch spoke first, announcing flatly, "Well, the kids don't like him." Lynn felt a surge of relief. Her uncle had been so taciturn on the issue that it had been difficult to tell what he thought, but now she knew that he had been listening to the family and had heard their complaints. After the meeting broke up, she had a clear sense that Primis's days were numbered.

§

With ironic symmetry, Primis's efforts to push the family into the background coincided with what was arguably its most significant milestone: the one-hundredth anniversary of Adolph Ochs's purchase of *The New York Times* in 1896. The Sulzbergers were hardly given to self-aggrandizement, but even they enthusiastically embraced the idea of a celebration. Several years earlier Punch had asked Susan Dryfoos, head of The New York Times History Project, and former *Times* managing editor Arthur Gelb, head of The New York Times Foundation, to cochair a centennial planning committee. They had put together a series of events, including exhibitions at four New York libraries and museums; a commissioned book, *The Paper's Papers,* based on material at *The New York Times'* archives; a movie about Adolph; and a slogan contest for *The*

New York Times on the Web — an echo of the competition a century earlier that had resulted in "All the News That's Fit to Print."

Susan, ever vigilant in matters of image, kept a watchful eye on the exhibitions as they were being assembled. Even so, Gelb insisted on one important journalistic mea culpa. At the New York Public Library, which played host to a retrospective of important stories throughout the paper's history, a two-sentence caption cited the *Times'* failures during the Holocaust: "*The New York Times* has been criticized for grossly underplaying coverage of the Holocaust. Although some reports were given prominence, this display shows that the criticism was valid." Next to the caption was a 1942 story proclaiming "1,000,000 Jews Slain by Nazis" that had appeared on page seven, and another reporting that Hitler had killed nearly 400,000 "Europeans." Only in the seventh paragraph had the word *Jew* appeared.

The family hosted a seated dinner for the paper's news and business leaders at the Pierpont Morgan Library, where letters and memorabilia from Adolph's early years were on display. (The exhibition included Adolph's handwritten draft of his "without fear or favor" credo, penned in August 1896, yet right next to it was a caption that once again misquoted what he had written.) After recounting the familiar tale of his great-grandfather's visit to Morgan in which the banker had converted his $25,000 in old *Times* stock to new, Arthur Jr. launched into a spirited defense of the newspaper's values — a salvo aimed directly at Primis. "Together . . . we have relearned what Adolph Ochs knew: that great journalism is great business; that a newspaper must be economically viable, but that it can be more than that, for a newspaper is a public trust." Then, raising his glass, Arthur Jr. toasted "all of us — the united family that is *The New York Times.*" "I was in tears," confessed one reporter who was there.

The glamorous centerpiece of the centennial year was a seated dinner for five hundred at the Metropolitan Museum of Art, the most elaborate party the family had ever thrown. Those lucky enough to be included received a card months in advance asking them to reserve the evening of June 26, which was followed by an engraved invitation from "Arthur Ochs Sulzberger and Allison Cowles." The guest list was a reflection of the family's high-powered world of society figures, writers, politicians, business leaders, advertisers, and executives, editors, and columnists at the paper. Their presence at the Met would be living testimony to the power and influence of *The New York Times* and, by extension, of the family that had prevailed as its owners and guardians for a full century.

With months of advance notice, a distinguished guest list, and the Sulzbergers as the star attraction, it was unthinkable that Primis, the company president, would decide not to attend. But he declined the invitation, explaining that he had "schedule problems." The day after the party, he was due in Paris for a meeting of the board of the *International Herald Tribune*. His wife and their two children planned to accompany him and take a week's vacation. The trip had been on their calendar for months.

Punch, typically, was the master of the oblique statement. Executives who worked with him successfully learned to read his body language because only rarely did he issue flat-out commands. When Primis announced that he would not be going to the party, Punch for once didn't mince words, and simply said, "I think you ought to be there." Primis protested. He knew that Punch and Michael Golden, who would also be attending the *IHT* meeting in Paris, planned to take the Concorde over the morning after the party in order to be there in time. "I don't want to take the Concorde," Primis told Punch. "The company's not going to pay for my kids, and I'm not going to fly them over there at those prices. I'll see you in Paris." Punch didn't press further, refusing to believe that his own president would not show up for an event that was clearly so important to the company and to the family. Surely Primis would go back to his office, think it over, and change his plans.

But Primis genuinely failed to appreciate what was at stake. He didn't think he would be missed at a "family" party where the seating chart went into the hundreds, and he did not grasp how much pride and prestige the Sulzbergers attached to the celebration. "There is no reason for me to follow a course of action that would have intentionally pissed off the family," he said. "Certainly not [Punch], my partner down the hall."

The Sulzbergers masked their annoyance during the gala itself, although Punch, with Allison at his side, was still in a state of disbelief. Walter Mattson scoured the museum's cavernous Great Hall during the cocktail hour, searching for his former protégé. Mattson and Punch had had their own falling-out the previous year, when Punch had asked him to resign as vice chairman of The New York Times Company board. By appointing him to the post when he retired in 1992, Punch had hoped that Mattson would continue to act as his personal adviser, if only on an informal basis, but Mattson had declined the role. Although

Punch had never made an issue of it, privately he had been hurt that Mattson had refused to help him. As his unhappiness with Primis had grown, he had come to feel doubly abandoned by Mattson, who had exited the company earlier than Punch would have liked and left him in the hands of a novice.

Once the black-tie crowd had settled into their seats in the soaring wing of the museum that housed the Temple of Dendur, Punch gave some welcoming remarks and introduced New York City mayor Rudolph Giuliani and New York governor George Pataki — Republicans whom the *Times* had not endorsed in the previous election. Giuliani, a glass of white wine in his hand, delivered a speech full of energy, humor, and self-deprecation. Pataki's comments had the flat, formulaic ring of boiler-plate. He fumbled Adolph's name, calling him Arthur Ochs, and when he twice referred to Arthur Jr. as "Pinch," eyebrows arched around the room. Had his staff not warned him that Arthur Jr. loathed the nick-name? "It was like being at a funeral where the priest didn't know the deceased," said a *Times* executive.

Cynthia floated through the gala in a long, airy gown that had been her mother's favorite. Carol had been alive when planning of the Met party had begun. With her love of fashion and high society, she would have considered the dinner one of the crowning pleasures of her life. Throughout the evening, guests came up to Cynthia and Cathy, clasped their hands, and told them how sorry they were that Carol wasn't there. "It was very hard on them," said Karen.

Arthur Jr. had no official role in the proceedings, yet as his father's possible successor, all eyes were on him. The previous month, *Adam Smith's Money World* had aired a segment that had posed the question of whether the moment had come for someone other than a Sulzberger to run The New York Times Company. Arthur Jr. had the "right name, but does he have the right stuff?" the show's reporter had asked, adding that among those speculating about succession, "Lance Primis gets high billing." Arthur Jr. had appeared on camera to rebut the notion that family management had outlived its usefulness at a modern media com-pany. "Great management is the key," he had insisted. "And that means not only people who care about profits but people who care about the quality of the journalism."

Dessert arrived in a dramatic procession of waiters marching through the glass-domed room, holding aloft spice cakes topped by lit sparklers. Inscribed in the white marzipan frosting was "Without Fear or Favor," Adolph's name, and the dates 1896–1996. As guests sipped champagne and unwrapped the party favors that had been placed at each setting — a small enamel box with Adolph's picture on top and seven of the *Times'* most famous front pages on its sides — the crowd began to disperse, chatting and air-kissing and slowly drifting off into the summer night. Punch and Arthur Jr. stayed till the end to accommodate the several photographers who wanted to take their picture. As the flashbulbs exploded, Arthur Jr. put his arm around his father, and Punch did likewise, smiling broadly. When the session was over, father and son were momentarily alone, surrounded by a few family members and stragglers. They said their good-bye, kissing each other warmly on the cheek.

§

August 18, 1996, was a bright, sunny day in the coolest summer on record in New York City, a day quite unlike its sweltering counterpart a century earlier when Adolph Ochs had officially become publisher of *The New York Times*. In front of the newspaper, the section of West Forty-third Street between Broadway and Eighth Avenue had been barricaded to traffic so that *Times* employees could assemble for a party to celebrate the renaming of the block Adolph S. Ochs Street. At the eastern end, near Times Square, a stage had been set up with seats strategically arranged so that cameras would be sure to capture Adolph's Times Tower looming in the background. The building's original facade had long since been sheathed in thin, rectangular blocks of creamy stone and covered with huge billboards. The news zipper, now owned by Dow Jones, swaddled the tower's lower regions.

The officeworkers and tourists surging through Times Square took little notice of the Muskrat Dixieland Jazz Band and the Golden Chordsmen, a barbershop quartet, who entertained the milling editors, reporters, columnists, and ad, circulation, and production people before the official speeches. When Arthur Jr. mounted the stage to take his seat, he faced two identical posters of a young Adolph Ochs, one tinted deep lavender, the other mustard yellow. After Mayor Giuliani had officially unveiled the new street sign, it was Arthur Jr.'s turn to say a few words, and he took full advantage of the occasion to speak for the family. He ticked off *The New York Times'* seventy-three Pulitzer Prizes and its seven-day-a-week circulation — the largest of any American newspaper. "Every day you produce a *New York Times* that the descendants of Mr. Ochs are enormously proud to help publish," he told the crowd.

The rest of his talk was familiar, much of it recycled from earlier centennial events. But when Arthur Jr. came to the end, he choked up a bit. "And finally, my father," he said, "my father . . ." He repeated the word, his voice tender and almost reverential. Punch, sitting behind him on the stage, did not take his eyes off his son. "I know I speak for everyone here today, and for the thousands of other *New York Times* men and women who have worked with you in years past, when I say thank you for leading this newspaper and company so well." When Punch rose to receive a commemoratory gift from Arthur Jr. — a box of stationery with the Adolph S. Ochs street address on it — the entire block erupted into prolonged applause. Punch seemed pleased and genuinely bewildered by the outpouring of affection, which for once in his life was for him and him alone.

Primis missed Punch's moment of glory just as he had the Met gala. August 18 was his wedding anniversary, and he was at his home in New Jersey, on vacation for two weeks. To date, he had been invited to at least five events celebrating the Sulzbergers' centennial of ownership and had managed to avoid every one. As far as Punch was concerned, Primis's repeated no-shows were not important; they were just "icing on the cake." As he pondered his various options for transition, he realized that even though he had never seriously considered Primis a candidate to succeed him as chairman or CEO — and the two men had never explicitly discussed the matter — Primis was nevertheless a large impediment blocking his path to the future. If Punch was to anoint his son, it was inconceivable that Arthur Jr. would ever be able to get along with Primis as his number two, and the same was true of Michael.

Late in the spring Punch's misgivings had quickened into a resolve to remove Primis as president of The New York Times Company. As he always did in matters of great import, he consulted his sisters first. Only Marian was surprised. She had appreciated Primis's help in connection with her local projects and philanthropies and, unlike her siblings, had no complaints about his treatment of her children. Because she didn't feel strongly enough to fight the decision, she gave Punch her backing.

Punch's next stop was his outside directors. In the weeks between the board meetings in July and September, he met confidentially with each in person and explained that he didn't feel compatible with Primis, that he had made a mistake appointing him president, and that he was considering replacing him. No one tried to dissuade Punch — despite the company's rising stock price and Primis's own efforts to win the board's favor, he had no passionate advocates on the board — but several were surprised to hear Punch's assessment. Until then, he had not made plain to them just how dissatisfied he was.

Toward the end of the summer, Punch took Arthur Jr. and Michael into his confidence, as he did Kathy Darrow, a veteran *Times* executive whom he had often turned to in the past as a sounding board. Years earlier, when she was making her way up the ladder in the legal department, he had given her an unusual gift: a framed cartoon from *Playboy* that showed a man sitting in the office of a female attorney. "Actually, I don't have a legal problem," the man says in the caption, "I have this fantasy about fucking a lady lawyer." Darrow had taken it as a joke. "He knew I wouldn't misinterpret it, and I didn't," she explained. "I thought it was hilariously funny."

Darrow's function was to help Punch think through the process. He had already decided on his candidate to be Primis's replacement — Russ Lewis, the lanky, bespectacled president and general manager of *The New York Times* newspaper — and although he had not yet informed him or the company's directors of his choice, he wanted to discuss how the transition might be handled. Should Primis be encouraged to stay on for several months so that Lewis could apprentice with him? Or should Lewis be installed immediately, but only as a temporary replacement so that the company could launch an executive search?

At first, Darrow favored a search, arguing that the company would benefit from projecting an image of seeking the best candidate. In time, however, she came to agree with Punch: the outright appointment of Lewis would resolve the matter quickly and would protect Punch from outside director Lou Gerstner, whose forceful and frequently biting comments at board meetings had offended Punch and made him uneasy. Earlier in the summer, when Punch had told Gerstner of his plans to let Primis go, Gerstner had lobbied so pugnaciously for a formal search that Punch had feared the director's real goal was to commandeer the process, maybe even head the search committee, and use it to effectively strip Punch of his power to name the top nonfamily executive of the company. Gerstner was already pressing to be included on a nominating committee for new directors that was under discussion. If he got that spot as well as a place on the search committee, he would stand a good chance of dominating the board.*

Primis returned from vacation about Labor Day and immediately began preparing for the September board meeting, which was less than three weeks away. The stock price was ticking up nicely, and the earnings forecast for the third quarter looked good. In July he had asked the directors to give him feedback on the company's business strategy, and he intended to incorporate their comments into a formal three-year plan. "Directionally, everything seemed fine," said Mattson. "He was being applauded by the strongest voices on the board. He couldn't help but feel things were going well."

A few days before the September board meeting, Punch summoned Russ Lewis to his office. Primis would soon be on his way out, he said; I want you to be the next president of The New York Times Company. "I didn't literally fall off the chair, but figuratively I did," Lewis recalled. In effect, the move put Lewis in the same spot Primis had been in in 1992: dropped into a job for which he had neither the training nor the experience. But Punch was determined. He told Lewis that he was comfortable with him; he felt in tune with his sensibilities and valued his accomplishments at the newspaper. At no time during their fifteen-minute conversation did Punch ever ask Lewis about his vision for the company or tell him what he expected of him in his new duties. All he requested was that Lewis keep the news confidential.

The afternoon before the board meeting, Primis was interviewed by two non-*Times* reporters, who found him in a confident mood. He was trimmer, calmer, and more serious, and he had abandoned the fidgety habit of bouncing his feet when he talked. He had just celebrated his fourth anniversary as president of the company, so the interview was a perfect moment to take stock. Primis was particularly proud of the three professional managers he had brought to the fourteenth floor over the past year, he said, one of whom — a senior vice president for human resources — had just arrived a month earlier. The company's strategy

---

*Gerstner had threatened to resign before, and Punch assumed he would do so again if he didn't get his way on the question of a presidential search. "This time I'll take him up on it," he told Darrow. He got his chance several months later when Gerstner did indeed offer to resign; he officially left the board in the spring of 1997.

was "tighter," and he and his team were "defining the business better." He spoke expansively of the recent ground-clearing at the *Times'* printing plant in Edison, New Jersey, where a golf driving range would soon be under construction. "Good cash-flow business," he said. "If it works after a few years, I'll build fifty of them." As for his relationship with Punch, he felt he had finally figured out how to read him and knew what the chairman's "comfort zone" was: "I've learned that a good argument, thorough, well documented, properly presented — that's what he wants to hear."

By then Primis knew that something was up. *The Boston Globe* had been scheduled to make a presentation at the September board meeting, but at Punch's request the item had abruptly been taken off the agenda. In its place he had asked to meet with his directors in executive session, a sure indication that he wanted to discuss succession. "This was the first [executive session] that didn't have me present," Primis said. "I knew that something significant would occur." The morning of the meeting, Primis confided to Diane Baker that he had guessed what was about to happen: Punch would remain as chairman and he, Primis, would be named CEO. "It's all coming together," he told her.

Primis sat nervously in his office while Punch met alone with the board. The session was supposed to end at nine-thirty, but when the hour arrived, the doors to the boardroom remained tightly shut. Inside, Punch was equally unsettled. Darrow had warned him to anticipate questions not only about who the next president of the company would be but about whom he intended to name as his own successor. Punch had been so worried that he had asked Darrow to accompany him to the meeting, only to be thwarted by Gerstner, who refused to allow her to be present. So instead, at Punch's request, Darrow spent the morning sitting in his office just off the boardroom, waiting to be summoned in the event that he needed her.

Punch reminded his directors that several weeks earlier, when he had spoken to them individually about his misgivings about Primis, he had promised to come back and tell them what he believed should be done. And what he wanted to do, he announced, was to remove Primis immediately and replace him with Russ Lewis. Several directors were shocked at Punch's haste; they had construed his earlier consultations as a courteous prelude to further debate of when and how Primis might be dismissed. There was discussion about the proposed separation agreement and how the news would be presented to the press. As Darrow had predicted, Punch was indeed asked the question he had dreaded, the one about his own successor. In anticipation of the moment, he had written out some notes that made clear his current thinking but left room for a change of heart. "I don't know," he told the board carefully, "but if I were to say today, I am leaning toward Arthur Jr."

As Punch had hoped, his directors agreed that the company president should go immediately, and the meeting broke up before lunch. All that remained was for Punch to tell Primis. In the thirty-three years since he had taken over the *Times*, Punch had had to fire people, but practice had not made it any easier. The night before, he had lain awake in bed playing out what he would say and how Primis would respond, knowing that no matter how carefully he rehearsed it, it would never go as he had planned.

After several false starts down the hall, a gaunt and somber Punch entered Primis's office and took a seat. "He was troubled and pained," said Primis. "I knew exactly what he was going to do when he walked in the door." Punch was straightforward. He had gotten his mind around succession, he said. He wanted a number two who was harmonious with him, his family, and what they wanted to do in the future. Primis wasn't working out. He and the company would have to separate — immediately. Primis insisted that he had never wanted any job other than the one he had; he would be happy to remain president forever. "Have you talked to the board?" he asked. Punch replied that the directors had already voted on the matter. "Is this a reversible situation?" Punch shook his head; it was too late for that.

Primis was spinning. He had never lost at anything, and his removal had come completely without warning or any signal from his boss that he was in jeopardy. Until that moment, he believed that Punch supported the direction in which the company was heading, which involved adding more and more professional management at its uppermost levels. And that meant that, in time, the CEO slot would be filled by a professional as well. By accomplishing what the board wanted — boosting the stock, taking care of shareholders — he assumed that he had bought protection. But in the process he had ignored the values of the company and the people who ultimately owned it.

The first thing Primis did was to ask his shaken secretary, Linda Slauderbach, to phone Mattson, but she was able only to reach his home answering machine. It would be nearly a week before the former *Times* president, vacationing in Maine, would hear the messages Slauderbach and Primis left for him. Preferring to tell his wife the news in person, Primis drove back to New Jersey in a zombielike state, practicing how he would frame it. She knew little of his life at the company; Primis wasn't one for bringing his work home. For her, the dismissal came as a bitter shock. "She couldn't understand it," he said. "She didn't have enough pieces to put the puzzle together."

Back at the *Times* the PR machinery was preparing to announce the new lineup. After firing Primis, Punch informed Diane Baker, who offered to resign on the spot. "Don't you even think of it! I'll spank you!" he said — a laughable image, since Punch was several inches shorter than the nearly six-foot-tall Baker. With Primis gone, Punch knew Wall Street would need to be reassured. If anything, Baker was a more important part of the management team now than she had been before. She immediately canceled a planned holiday and prepared to work the phones, explaining to analysts what the decision meant for the future direction of the company.

By the time Primis came to work the next day, he had hired a lawyer at Cravath, Swaine & Moore to represent him in the severance negotiations. When the draft press release announcing his "resignation" came to him for comment, he asked to make a few changes. He wanted no quotes attributed to him; he was damned if he was going to allow pleasant words to be put in his mouth. Then, as a signal to other companies that might want to hire him, he wanted to add a sentence clarifying that he was leaving because he wanted "to be free to seek a more certain opportunity to run an enterprise." About noon the press release, headlined RUSSELL T. LEWIS NAMED PRESIDENT AND COO OF THE NEW YORK TIMES COMPANY, went out with Primis's alterations incorporated.

At the midday news meeting Arthur Jr. told the *Times'* top editors that Primis was leaving. Later Arthur Jr. and Lewis attended a party to celebrate the opening of the paper's new newsroom, which had been under construction for over a year. "This is a great day for family management of *The New York Times*," Joe Lelyveld told one reporter in a barbed allusion to Primis's exit.

The *Times'* account of the shake-up appeared the following day, Saturday, September 21, on the front of the business section. Attributing its information to "industry analysts and one *Times* executive," the story reported that Primis's "unexpected resignation" had been prompted by Punch, who was "apparently unwilling to offer Mr. Primis any assurances that he might one day succeed Mr. Sulzberger as chief executive." Accompanying the article were three photographs: Lewis; Janet Robinson, senior vice president in charge of advertising, who was replacing Lewis as president and general manager of *The New York Times* newspaper; and Dan Cohen, who was succeeding Robinson. Although Primis's ouster had been all about family management, the story failed to mention that Dan was a member of the Sulzberger family.

From the moment the press release went out, Baker worked hard to reassure the investment community that the business strategy of the company would remain intact. Her efforts paid off: *New York Times* shares slipped just five-eighths of a point, to $32. In *The Wall Street Journal* Patrick M. Reilly, the journalist who had speculated nine months earlier that Primis might become the first nonfamily CEO, wrote that the Sulzbergers were moving "swiftly to reassert control of the [company]" in the wake of Primis's sudden exit. The Sulzbergers had, in fact, never lost control. Indeed, if the ouster of Primis was a demonstration of anything, it was of their enduring power to run The New York Times Company as they wished.

None of the accounts of his departure quoted Primis, who, at the suggestion of his friend Jim Dowling, a public relations expert, had made a policy of refusing to answer reporters' phone calls or e-mail messages. He spent the weekend packing up his office. As he struggled to load boxes into his son's truck, two *Times* supervisors who were on Sunday duty — one from the mailroom, one from the drivers' union — rushed to help him, having recognized him from union negotiations. "No, no, let us do it," they insisted. "You were a good adversary, you're not going to do this." On Tuesday Primis walked into Punch's office to say a final good-bye. He had seen how Punch had reacted when he had fired other people; Primis knew he was hurting at least as much as he was. "How are *you* doing?" he inquired. The two parted with a light embrace.

In the months that followed, Primis tried to make sense of what had happened to him. He received more than 150 phone calls and letters wishing him well and suggesting different career options, which left him feeling that "it's like being at your own wake, awake." He went through outplacement counseling and took tests from an organizational psychologist. But try as he might, he couldn't fathom what he had done wrong. "The stock is at a seven-year high, the earnings are at record levels," he said. "I accomplished all my goals, except I'm not there any longer."

What Primis still failed to grasp was that he hadn't been president of a company like Time Warner or Gannett. He had been president of The New York Times Company, an organization ruled by a monarchy. Although the stock price and earnings mattered, it was not to the same degree that they did at almost every other corporation in the country. "What happened to Lance?" one former *New York Times* executive had joked to another when he heard the news of his ouster. "Did he think the *Times* was a public company?"

52

Smooth Sailing

S OON AFTER PRIMIS'S DEPARTURE, HIS OFFICE
was closed up while it was transformed into a conference room.
Punch had offered it to Lewis, who had turned it down on the
grounds that it would send the wrong message. In his first months as
president, Lewis worked out of the tiny, nondescript office Punch had
occupied when he was assistant treasurer.

The forty-nine-year-old Lewis was Primis's stylistic opposite. His
white shirt always seemed to be coming out of his conservative dark
trousers. He slouched in chairs, took off his wire-rimmed glasses frequently to rub his eyes, and generally gave the impression of a loqua-
cious and unimposing college professor. "He's sort of an unmade bed in
a good hotel," said one family member approvingly. His tall, gawky
frame belied that he had been a varsity hockey player in high school and
remained a devoted athlete. He brought the same competitive intensity
to his work. As circulation manager in the early 1980s, he was renowned
for starting meetings by holding up photographs of his children. "If our
numbers weren't good, he would accuse us of taking bread out of their
mouths," said Bill Pollak, who worked under him at the time.

Lewis was the quintessential good son — a "relatively decent example
of an American success story," as he put it. His father, a Jewish immi-
grant from Britain, had never gone beyond the fourth grade. His
mother, whose family came from Russia, had gone to college and
become a teacher in the New York City public schools. Growing up in
the Bronx and Westchester, Lewis absorbed his parents' reverence for
education. After Northeastern University and the State University of
New York at Stony Brook, he had gone to Brooklyn Law School, graduating in 1973. To his parents, becoming president of The New York Times
Company was an achievement as miraculous as if he had become president of the United States.

Lewis had started at the *Times* as a copyboy and news clerk and briefly flirted with becoming a journalist. He had eventually joined the paper's legal department but kept a romantic attachment to his *Front Page* period. On his office wall he displayed a photograph of himself standing in the newsroom in 1970, surrounded by typewriters, cigarette ashes, crumpled coffee and sandwich containers, and several wizened male reporters. As a staff attorney, Lewis had played a small part in the *Times'* defense of Myron Farber, a reporter who had refused to obey a court order to turn over his confidential sources in connection with a murder trial. The case had cost the *Times* hundreds of thousands of dollars, and Farber had spent forty days in jail, but eventually it had resulted in an amendment to the New Jersey shield law that gave protection to journalists in the future. The experience made a dramatic impression on Lewis, and as he recalled, "That completed stage one of my understanding of what this newspaper is all about."

Lewis had worked as head of the circulation and production departments before becoming president of *The New York Times* newspaper in 1992. He had supported Arthur Jr.'s effort to build Deming-style teams, and unlike Primis, who had advocated collaboration but made most decisions alone, Lewis valued debate. He had curbed his once harsh tongue and learned to deal with subordinates in an up-front manner. "I've worked very hard to bare my soul to them, and that's a dangerous thing to do," he said. "There's no subterfuge, no guile." Lewis made no exception for Arthur Jr., with whom he tried to have a genuinely open and confidential relationship, much like the one Mattson had had with Punch. Indeed, as president of the newspaper, he had consciously adopted Mattson's model of how to manage the boss, lunching with Arthur Jr. regularly and taking care to keep him in the loop.

Punch did not know Lewis intimately when he chose him to replace Primis, but he felt confident in his new president's ability to get along with Arthur Jr. and was certain he valued what the family brought to the company. As important to Punch was his belief that Lewis understood the need to correct the balance between profits and the higher calling of journalism, which he felt had gotten skewed in Primis's myopic quest for "shareholder value."

While Lewis understood journalism, his business strategy differed little from Primis's. Where he parted ways with his predecessor was in how that strategy should be applied. He believed that the company needed to

focus on its "core purpose" in newspapers and television and to eliminate anything that veered from it. In short order, he canceled Primis's
plans to invest millions in a *Golf Digest* golf course in Florida; sold the
Popcorn Channel and a custom publishing unit that had produced
magazines for Four Seasons Hotels, Blockbuster Entertainment, and
other companies; and put six sports and leisure magazines on the block.

With Primis gone, Punch felt free, finally, to resolve the succession
issue that loomed as his last and most difficult task. He had long ago
decided that a Sulzberger would continue to be the ultimate authority at
The New York Times Company, but what remained to be settled was
equally problematic: Who should that person be? And how could Punch
divide the authority among the rest of the family so that there would be
a reasonable chance of peace?

The cousins had already discussed how they wanted to handle the
voting stock in the company, which would be their vehicle for owning
and controlling *The New York Times* after their parents died. Buried deep
in the book of recommendations Punch and his sisters had received
in 1995 was the cousins' stated wish to consider themselves members
of one family, not members of four "lines." From that philosophy —
Iphigene's old idea of all for one and one for all — flowed a decision
to consolidate the four separate trusts which held 85 percent of the
controlling Class B stock into a single trust in which every member of
the cousins' generation and their children stood to share equally. The
arrangement required a considerable sacrifice from Dan and Jace; since
they were the only two children in their line, as opposed to four in the
Goldens', they would have inherited more voting stock than the others
under the old setup. But the centripetal pull of the family, and the desire
to speak with one voice regarding the fate of *The New York Times*, was a
powerful incentive. "[Jace and I] have made it not an issue of wealth;
we've made it an issue of the mission of the newspaper and of the company," said Dan.

Since Iphigene's death, Punch and his sisters had served as trustees of
the four controlling trusts. With Primis's departure and the pending
consolidation of those trusts, the time seemed right to make a member
of the younger generation a fifth trustee, and in December 1996 the
cousins elected Ruth's daughter, Lynn Dolnick, to that position. Her
addition to the group prompted the four siblings, who had always conducted trustee business on the fly — catching one another after com-

pany board meetings and the like — to begin gathering formally for the first time.

Lynn's was just one of several seats of power that were gradually opening up to Punch's and his sisters' descendants. In the spring of 1997 ownership of *The Chattanooga Times* was transferred from the Sulzberger siblings to the thirteen cousins. As part of the change, Punch and Sydney Gruson, who was gravely ill, stepped down from the paper's board of directors, creating two vacancies. While Ruth, who remained as chairman, was keenly devoted to Chattanooga and to the paper, her own children had fled both, and the other cousins had never considered Adolph's initial newspaper venture integral to their identity. Nevertheless, there was spirited competition for Punch's and Gruson's seats. Even Bobby Dryfoos, then in the midst of yet another divorce, put himself forward as a candidate. The winners, Dan and Cathy, joined Michael, who had long been a member of the board.

Board membership on The New York Times Company was a far more complicated matter. As soon as the cousins decided to function as one family instead of four, the earlier scheme of filling family seats with one member from each branch ceased to be relevant. The Sulzbergers, however, were in agreement on one issue: at all times some family members should be directors. Whether the number was four or not was immaterial.

That didn't address the special situation of Sulzbergers who worked at the company and were, by virtue of their executive rank, entitled to a seat. Arthur Jr. had purposely not been made a director in 1992, when he became publisher, out of fear that it would upset his cousins. But with Primis gone and the family dealing more straightforwardly with such issues, the concern no longer applied, and in May 1997 Arthur Jr. was elected to the board. While Marian, seventy-eight, and two outside directors departed at the same time, Arthur Jr. wasn't viewed as replacing a family member — although Punch did admit that his son was in fact "doing double duty" as both publisher and a Sulzberger.

The most politically sensitive issue of all — who would follow Punch at the company — still weighed heavily on Punch's shoulders. He had two problems with the decision: he wanted Arthur Jr. to be his successor as the senior executive, a move the company's directors would have to formally approve, and he also had to satisfy everyone in the family that he had been fair. Passing on all three of his titles to his son was not an option; his sisters and their children would never stand for it.

Arthur Jr. accepted this reality, but he remained determined to inherit the final authority his father had over the company, and equally determined to continue as publisher of *The New York Times*. At two private dinners with his father — one nearly a year before Primis's ouster and one shortly before it — he had suggested that he remain publisher of the newspaper and add the title of chairman of the company, a position he was confident he could invest with the kind of power he needed as long as he had a cooperative CEO. "I knew I could be an activist chairman; I told him how it could work," Arthur Jr. recalled. "[The idea] just sat there like a big lump on the table, saying, 'Take me.' "

Punch hadn't taken it, however. In his experience it was inconceivable that a chairman could actually run a company. Typically a chairman presided over meetings of the board of directors, and as Sydney Gruson put it, "That's no job for a grown man." As far as Punch was concerned, the only way his son could wield the kind of operational authority he himself had enjoyed was to become CEO, a position for which Arthur Jr. had neither the standing nor the training. Even if he were fully equipped to be CEO, it was unrealistic to assume he could perform that function and still be a hands-on publisher; both were full-time jobs. Equally important, Arthur Jr.'s proposal was predicated on a "cooperative" CEO, and the most likely prospect at the time — Lance Primis — hardly fit that description.

Primis's departure, however, cleared the way for Arthur Jr.'s plan to be implemented; it just took time for Punch to realize that it was feasible. Following the conversations with his son, he had quietly consulted key members of the board, who had only reinforced his conviction that Arthur Jr. would have to conform to the conventional corporate model and become CEO — or chairman and CEO — if he wanted to run the company. In Punch's mind, that meant that Arthur Jr. would have to give up the publisher's job, and he halfheartedly tried to persuade him to do so, even as he told him that "it was the best job in journalism and was certainly the best job in the building."

With Arthur Jr. equally adamant about both remaining publisher and gaining control of the company, Punch in the spring of 1997 tentatively embraced a jury-rigged solution: he decided to establish an "office of the chairman" that would consist of himself, Lewis, Arthur Jr., and, eventually, Michael. As envisioned, the device would permit Arthur Jr. to remain in place as publisher while also giving him executive status on the fourteenth floor, thus promoting the perception to Wall Street that he was getting the necessary training to take over in several years when Punch retired.

Punch confided his plans to several critical members of the family, swore them to secrecy, and gave himself the rest of the summer to figure out the details. In early June he met with two consultants — Ivan Lansberg, who had been working with the family for some months on issues of transition and governance, and Jeff Heilpern, who had been working with the company — to begin discussing in earnest how an "office of the chairman" might actually operate. Lansberg and Heilpern had had experience with a wide variety of family businesses; they knew that titles such as CEO and chairman didn't have to be strait-jackets. With its two tiers of stock, The New York Times Company was already a quirky hybrid: a multibillion-dollar business controlled by a family through a handful of voting shares. Since that was the case, they told Punch, why not craft a solution for succession that acknowledged the power and abilities the players really had — in the family, in the company — regardless of how untraditional it might appear to out-siders? Gradually the two facilitators helped Punch understand that, as Punch himself put it, "you create a structure according to the problem that you're trying to solve rather than trying to jam everybody into a structure."

Once he realized he had the freedom to match titles and responsibili-ties as he saw fit, Punch scrapped the "office of the chairman" idea. "After I made up my mind what the top was going to be, the rest just fell together," he said. And what the top was going to be was an unorthodox arrangement in which Punch, at an unspecified date in the future, would make Arthur Jr. chairman, make Lewis CEO, and give Michael the title of vice chairman. To maintain Arthur Jr. as the final authority, Lewis would report to the chairman rather than to the board, a change that required a small alteration in the company bylaws. What made the scenario possible was that Lewis wasn't preoccupied with hierarchy and, unlike Primis, sincerely believed that the family's involvement was an asset, not a burden.

The beauty of the plan was that it reflected the way the company actually worked. Despite holding the title, Punch had never functioned as CEO, a job that had been performed by Mattson and later by Primis. Now Lewis would be in charge of the company's operations, and

Arthur Jr. didn't have any more inclination or training to perform those day-to-day functions than his father had.

The solution also relieved Punch of having to convince the board to appoint his son to a position for which he wasn't suited. It would be difficult for the directors to argue against giving Arthur Jr. the final authority as chairman, and his appointment was sure to sail through. At the same time, making Michael vice chairman would satisfy the family's requirement that the rewards be distributed equitably.

On July 28 Punch, Arthur Jr., Lewis, and the two consultants gathered in the boardroom to thrash out more details of the plan. The question of when it should be implemented, however, remained unsettled. Punch had promised his directors a letter in September updating them on his thoughts on succession. In Hawaii the previous Christmas he had gathered his four children together and confided that he had been diagnosed with Parkinson's disease; the disorder was in its early stages and wasn't life-threatening. Still, it made Punch eager to get on with other aspects of his life, such as traveling with Allison. He also disliked the prospect of announcing that he would retire in a year or so in favor of his son, a plan that would not only make him a lame duck but would paralyze those below him. Why bother to wait? he wondered. Why not step down now? Suddenly he felt certain that that was precisely what he should do. "The family was ready to have something happen, the company was ready to have something happen," he said. "The timing was right."

Punch simply blurted out what he had to say: the plan they had come up with was sensible, and the time was right — he wanted to put it into motion immediately. The dumbfounded Arthur Jr. had pushed for this solution — indeed, it had been he who had first floated it two years earlier — but he didn't want his father to feel that he had to leave so precipitously. "Let's not rush to judgment here," Arthur Jr. cautioned him. "People expect you to be in this role for at least another year; there's nothing wrong with that." But Punch was resolute in that same no-use-trying-to-change-his-mind way that Allison had experienced when he had decided the day and month they would be married.

Arthur Jr. was exuberant when he left the boardroom and a few days later invited his father to dinner at an Italian restaurant close to Punch's apartment where the well-spaced tables allowed for privacy. He wanted to make sure his father was comfortable with what he had decided. "Are you sure about the timing?" he asked. "How do you want to operate in the future? What do you think *your* title should be?" The latter was a question with no precedent. Punch's own father had remained chairman until he died, and before him there had never been a company chairman. Over the next few weeks Punch entertained becoming chairman of the executive committee, and chairman of the transition committee, before finally settling on the title of chairman emeritus.

As soon as he had decided on the timing, Punch brought Michael into the process and told him he wanted to make him senior vice president, reporting to Lewis as CEO, as well as vice chairman of the board, a position that automatically made him a director. Michael had always known that his campaign to be CEO and chairman was a long shot. He had been late coming to the fourteenth floor, and his largest management responsibility beforehand was the *Times'* troubled magazine group. Becoming vice chairman made him feel as though he had won the lottery, even as he acknowledged that he had gotten the prize in large part because he had consciously violated the family taboos and not sat passively by. "I think I made a serious investment in my ticket," he said.

The transition plans were still confidential in mid-September, when Punch, Arthur Jr., Michael, Lewis, and several hundred *Times* reporters, editors, advertisers, and well-wishers gathered in College Point, Queens, to show off the paper's newly completed color printing plant. The Good Gray Lady had published color advertisements in selected sections of the Sunday paper since 1993 from its Edison, New Jersey, plant. With the opening of the College Point facility, located on what had once been a parking lot for the 1964–65 World's Fair, the *Times* for the first time had the capability to publish color ads and photographs in the daily edition, push deadlines for sports and breaking news back to 11:30 P.M., produce a paper with as many as eight sections, and send it electronically to sites scattered across the country. The five high-speed presses housed in the plant's airplane hangar–like building made the old presses on West Forty-third Street obsolete. The last *New York Times* printed in Manhattan had been bundled onto the last beeping, gridlock-producing tractor-trailer the previous June.

After guests had completed their tour of the gleaming new plant, they were ushered into an adjacent white tent for drinks, Asian-inspired hors d'oeuvres, and speeches. Onstage Arthur Jr. stood in front of blown-up reproductions of several new section fronts that would soon make their debut. The one that featured food and restaurants had originally been called "Dining In and Out," but Arthur Jr. had vetoed the title because he thought "in and out" carried a sexual connotation. Instead, the section was destined to appear under "Dining In/Dining Out."

For Arthur Jr., creating a *New York Times* in color and expanding it to six sections was as revolutionary a step as the four-part paper had been for Punch in the 1970s. He began his remarks graciously, mentioning both Mattson and Primis, and observed that his father had never had the pleasure he had at that moment, of having *his* father witness his reinvention of the newspaper. "I don't know how my father learned to be a publisher," he said, "but I learned to be a publisher by watching him."

Over the next several weeks Punch told his sisters and Lynn Dolnick — his fellow trustees — his latest and last plan for succession. He then began a series of one-on-one, off-site visits to his directors. In early October he phoned each of the cousins and explained to them his thinking. As Michael had feared, his older brother, Stephen, was stricken, and a temporary chill fell over their relationship. Ever since Michael had gone to the fourteenth floor, Stephen had assumed Michael would be in line for a high-level job. He had just never expected it to be a position that would give his brother a seat on the board. "We'll get over it, but we're not there yet," said Michael.

§

Mortimer's, an East Side restaurant known for its wealthy and socially prominent clientele, had been one of Carol's favorite haunts. Over the years it was also the place where a number of *Times* journalists and Sulzberger friends celebrated the publication of their books. So it was fitting that when Arthur Golden, Ruth's youngest, published his first novel, *Memoirs of a Geisha,* Mortimer's was where the moment was commemorated. Three photographs of the author — one as a baby, one as a young boy, and one as a college student — looked down on the gathering from their position over the bar. As guests made cocktail chatter and picked at passed trays of deviled eggs and salmon on toast, Stephen beamed with pride. Over the nine years it had taken his brother to research and write his first-person account of Sayuri, a geisha in 1930s and 1940s Japan, Stephen had been his brother's critical first reader and loyal supporter. In the book's acknowledgments, he was the only family member other than his wife that Arthur had thanked by name. In the weeks to come, *Memoirs of a Geisha* would make its way onto the *New York Times* bestseller list, where it would remain for many weeks. Steven Spielberg would option it for a movie. "This doesn't feel like my life," said Arthur, who had toiled in obscurity from his house in Boston through three complete rewrites of the manuscript.

Among old-timers such as Abe Rosenthal, the buzz at Mortimer's was less about books than about change. The next day, October 16, would be the first time color photographs would appear on the front page.* Speculation about how readers would react was accompanied by speculation about Punch's plans for succession. At that point the family members knew what was about to transpire, as did a few selected friends and editors. That morning Punch had called Arthur Gelb, the paper's former managing editor and head of The New York Times Foundation, and told him that at the next day's board meeting, Arthur Jr. would be named chairman. At lunchtime Arthur Jr. had informed Lelyveld, editorial-page editor Howell Raines, and Janet Robinson, president of the newspaper.

Hovering near the entrance to Mortimer's, Arthur Jr. crackled with nervous energy. He had just returned from the Escalante region of Utah, where he and Dan had gone for one of their biennial "Rambo weekends," comradely endurance tests that echoed Outward Bound. While wading through a trout stream, they had talked through Dan's feelings about Arthur Jr.'s impending new status. "That's when all of the air was cleared," said Judy, expressing her hope as much as her certainty that it was true.

As the party wound down, Arthur Jr. made a point of grabbing two late-arriving guests and pulling them over to a corner by the bar, where in sober tones he announced his news. He was intent on making sure that everyone understood that despite Lewis's being named CEO and despite the fact that he wasn't going to inherit his father's three titles, he, Arthur Jr., was still going to be the ultimate authority. "It will be like Punch and Walter," he told them.

The next day Punch appeared at the *Times* in a white shirt, blue suit, and striped tie. Once the regular business of the board had been dispensed with, the directors went into closed session. In a matter-of-fact

---

*There was, in fact, an earlier front page in color: in 1891, to call attention to a price increase, *The New-York Times* printed its front-page borders in red, blue, and green.

voice, Punch announced that he was stepping aside and repeated the new configuration he had explained to each of them during his individual visits. He then nominated Arthur Jr. to be the company's next chairman. The board voted, and in an instant the baton was passed.

For Arthur Jr., the moment was the culmination of a long journey, a journey not only to prepare himself to follow his father as the head of *The New York Times* but to win his trust and admiration, something he now felt secure that he had. Punch motioned for his son to take over his seat at the head of the table, but Arthur Jr. declined, not wanting to appear to displace him.

The meeting adjourned to an adjacent antechamber known as the Chattanooga Room. Once everyone had been given a glass of champagne, Richard Gelb, chairman emeritus of Bristol-Myers Squibb and the outside director who had worked most closely with Punch during his period of decision, took the floor to make a toast. "Adolph Ochs is remembered as the one who founded this great enterprise," he began. "Arthur Ochs Sulzberger will be remembered as the one who secured it, renewed it, and lifted it to ever higher levels of achievement." Punch was surprised; he had had no knowledge that Gelb planned to make a speech. Ruth burst into tears.

The press release pointedly referred to Arthur Jr. as the company's "senior executive" and spelled out the unconventional reporting arrangements in detail. Lewis, the new CEO, would "work closely" with Arthur Jr. to "chart the future direction of the company" while Michael, as senior vice president, would have "corporate responsibility for the areas of human resources, communications, legal affairs and corporate development." The word *value* was repeated no fewer than six times — three times following the word *shareholder,* and three times in phrases such as *core values* and *the values that have served us well in the past.* If Wall Street failed to get the message that *The New York Times* was a family-controlled company that saw itself as having an important public mission as well as a responsibility to stockholders, it simply wasn't listening.

Earlier that morning Arthur Jr., Joe Lelyveld, Howell Raines, and Janet Robinson had gathered the news and business staffs of the newspaper in the WQXR auditorium and jointly told them the news. The symbolism of the meeting was not lost on those in the audience. In the past, momentous changes at the *Times* had always been announced in memos that were tacked on bulletin boards or stuffed into mailboxes.

Not only was this a much more personal approach, but for the first time the business side was invited as well as reporters and editors. For Arthur Jr., the moment was a vindication of his efforts to encourage collaboration that stretched as far back as the painful Greenwich meetings. Now the era he had worked so hard to establish had finally arrived. He had the power to lower the wall between news and business, and more important, he had the editors and managers with the sensibilities to make it work.

About 3:00 P.M. Joe Lelyveld called to invite Punch to visit the newsroom. Although he assumed that all he would have to do was "go down, see Joe, and shake a few hands," Punch was reluctant. "Well, I'll go with you," Arthur Jr. assured him. When the moment arrived, however, Arthur Jr. was tied up talking to stock analysts and couldn't leave. The newsroom had recently been renovated, and Punch was no longer even certain where the executive editor's office was, so he asked Lelyveld to come up and get him.

When the two men stepped off the elevator on the third floor, they were met by an applauding throng. The old hands were there — Abe Rosenthal, Arthur Gelb, James Greenfield — as well as many new people who had never seen Punch make his way through the newsroom to the afternoon news conferences as he had almost every day when he had been publisher. Lelyveld, in shirtsleeves and a loosened tie, escorted Punch to a place where everyone could see him while Susan Dryfoos followed them with a camera. "It's a day of firsts," Lelyveld said. "The first front page in color, a new chairman, and a new chairman emeritus." Standing with his back to the windows, Punch drank in the palpable respect and affection, sincerely shocked at the outpouring. "I got through with that," he said, referring to his appearance in the newsroom, "and I fled."

53

Live Long and Prosper

ARTHUR JR. DRESSED CAREFULLY FOR THE FIRST board meeting over which he would preside as chairman. His gray pinstriped suit was set off by a shirt with blue stripes and suspenders decorated with the Statue of Liberty and exploding fireworks. He put on the gold cuff links Gail had given him in 1992 when he was named publisher and, for the first time, donned the wristwatch she had presented him when he had been made chairman. Engraved on the watch were his initials —A.O.S— with a small, nearly imperceptible JR. in the middle of the o. On the back was inscribed LIVE LONG AND PROSPER, Mr. Spock's famous greeting from *Star Trek*, Arthur Jr.'s favorite television show.

When the company's directors filed into the boardroom later that day, they found the seating chart rearranged. Instead of taking his place at the head of the long table, as his father had done, Arthur Jr. sat at its middle, with Lewis roughly opposite him. He didn't deliver a windy speech about the destructiveness of hierarchical organizations but simply said that he had moved the seats around because "it's my personal style, mostly," and let it go at that.

Early that morning, while he was still at home, Arthur Jr. had written down a few thoughts he wanted to express to the board. One concerned the covenant he hoped to form with them. "My promise is not merely no surprises," he told them. "My promise is that on every step of major decisions, you will be informed, you will be involved, your insights will be asked for." He then turned the meeting over to Lewis. When he sat down, he heard Kathy Darrow hissing behind him from her position near the wall. "Arthur!" she whispered. "You forgot to get the minutes approved from the last board meeting!" Arthur Jr. was mortified. Nearly half an hour later, when he had an opportunity to interrupt, he said, "In my first bit of constructive criticism, it has been pointed out to me that I forgot to get the minutes approved."

Arthur Jr. still owned a motorcycle, still declined a car and driver, still took the bus or occasional taxi to work. But the flip, joke-cracking young man who had delighted in shocking his elders had become more subdued, self-confident, and mature. Since taking over as the final authority in the company, he had worked every weekend, something he previously tried to avoid out of deference to his family. "I'm struggling . . . I worry more," he said. "Everything's new, everything is the first time."

Five days after presiding over his first board meeting, Arthur Jr. and Gail arrived at the Fifth Avenue apartment of Steve Rattner and his wife, Maureen White, for a cocktail party in their honor. Guests had received playful cream-colored invitations asking them to join in recognizing Arthur Jr. "for clawing his way to Chairman of The New York Times Company" and Gail "for putting up with him." The crowd was small, made up predominantly of *Times* editors, reporters, and business types of Arthur Jr.'s generation and a few of his friends from outside the paper. Charles Schumer, the Democratic congressman from Brooklyn, mixed with Doug Marlette, the creator of the cartoon "Kudzu," Steve Shepard, editor in chief of *BusinessWeek,* and his wife, Lynn Povich, an executive at MSNBC.

From Adolph's time onward, the Sulzbergers had marked special occasions with skits and satires. At Adolph and Effie's fiftieth-wedding-anniversary party in 1933, Punch and Judy had dressed up as a miniature bride and groom complete with silk top hat and long veil. In Chattanooga Ruth was renowned for asking guests to compose poems for the birthday dinners she threw for family and friends. The tradition was continued that night in the ribald "This Is Your Life" review that Dan wrote for Arthur Jr., complete with computer-doctored "slides" — one of Arthur Jr. in a bustier and thigh-high stockings, another of him nearly bald like his father.

When it was his turn to speak, Arthur Jr. said a few kind words about the editorial and corporate people present, taking care to single out Michael and Lewis, who were huddled by the fireplace, telling them, "I look forward to taking my place side by side with you." Turning his attention to his friends, he began to recite what he claimed was an old Jewish proverb when the room erupted in laughter. The idea that Arthur Jr., with his lifelong ambivalence about the Jewish part of his background, would even *know* a Jewish saying seemed preposterously funny. "I looked it up!" he said mock-defensively before going on to offer the quotation: "When you choose your friends, aim high."

As Susan aimed her video camera at the well-wishers, guests sang along to lyrics that Dan, Rattner, and Steve Shepard had written specially for the occasion. The song about Arthur Jr. contained a humorous and sharp-edged chorus that referred to "His sisters and his cousins / Whom he aced out by the dozens." The ditty about Gail, sung to "Fugue for Tinhorns" from *Guys and Dolls,* was no less barbed. "He's got a wife with brains / Who's smart enough to refrain / From letting on/that she's the one / who often takes the reins / Can do / Can do / That Gail's got a high IQ."

Arthur Jr. found the songs hilarious. At forty-six he was, as one of the lyrics said, "The monarch of all I see / The ruler of the whole company," and he could afford to take a few friendly jabs. The kingdom that had recently been put in his care was larger and far more complex than the one his father had inherited. But over the course of more than a century, the magic and mission of *The New York Times* had somehow managed to last, in large part because of the ownership and guidance of one quite ordinary and quite remarkable family. The guests who were present that night felt that power. As they left, the pianist hired for the occasion was playing "There's a place where dreams are born" from the musical *Peter Pan.*

§

On February 5, 1998, two and a half months after the party for Arthur Jr., taxis and limousines pulled up in front of the Metropolitan Museum of Art and disgorged men in tuxedos and women in long dresses struggling to maintain their wraps and their composure against a roof-rattling nor'easter. Punch had refused to allow a retirement party in his honor — "too embarrassing, not my style," he explained — but he had agreed to let Arthur Jr. organize a celebration of his seventy-second birthday.

Given the venue, the occasion could easily have rivaled the family's 1996 centennial party in size and grandeur. Instead, it was surprisingly intimate. Members of the Sulzberger family — sixty-one in all, including spouses and children — composed more than a third of the guest list, with the balance made up of old friends and those working at the uppermost reaches of the newspaper and the company. Punch himself underscored the tone of the evening by sporting a red bottle-cap-shaped button with the word PUNCH on it, and a pin in the shape of a fist (a "punch").

The party's theme — subtly conveyed, never explicitly stated — was the Arthurian legend, with the Sulzbergers as the royal family passing Camelot's crown and its attendant obligations from one Arthur to another. So it was fitting that the cocktail portion of the evening took place in the Met's arms and armor exhibit, the room where Punch had spent so many happy hours as a child. Several of those navigating their way around the knights and metal-encased horses were surprised to see Diane Baker, the company's chief financial officer, chatting amiably with her colleagues. Despite her caustic style, she had gotten along well with Punch, but her relations with Arthur Jr., Lewis, and Michael — whom she described with some condescension as "the three boys" — were strained. "Diane goes after people," explained Michael. "Her preferred style of operating is one that simply doesn't fit [with us]." Rumors had begun to swirl that Baker was on the verge of resigning; indeed, in three weeks she would do just that, offering as her reason her desire to devote more time to her recently adopted child.

A trumpet fanfare summoned guests into the Engelhard Court, where a series of round tables had been set with red and champagne-colored roses and the chairs draped in burgundy velvet tied back by gold rope, an effect suggestive of royal thrones from the Middle Ages. After a meal of river trout soufflé, filet of beef, and hot chocolate vacherin filled with poached pears, Stephen Golden stepped to the lectern to welcome everyone on behalf of the family. Although the party had been Arthur Jr.'s idea, he had wisely arranged for each of the five cousins who worked at the company to have a public moment during the proceedings. Making Stephen master of ceremonies was a particularly sensitive act. Dan had been senior vice president of advertising since 1996 and Michael, as a result of the power shifts the previous fall, was now vice chairman, but so far nothing comparable had been found for Stephen, who had made his disappointment plain. "It's a problem," admitted Punch. "It's high on the list of Arthur and Russ and yours truly to see if we can find something that he really likes and wants to do."

After taking note of Punch's many grandchildren in the room and joking about the clan's inordinate fondness for the name Arthur,

Stephen introduced the evening's only nonfamily speaker, Abe Rosenthal, who told the time-honored story of how Punch had "put more tomatoes in the soup" instead of watering down the paper when times got hard in the 1970s. Arthur Jr. followed, hobbling to the front with the aid of an ebony cane. That day he had had an operation to remove an ingrown toenail, a recurrent condition that flared up every few years as a result of an earlier case of frostbite. "A few days ago my wife, Gail, asked Punch about his fantasies for the future," he began. "He had two: first, never to have another birthday party and, second, never to have to give another speech." He went on to talk about his father's new life with "the lovely Allison"; his new title; and his new, more relaxed routine. "Whereas once he arrived at the health club every morning at the stroke of six, this laid-back, take-life-as-it-comes kind of guy now saunters in at six-fifteen, sometimes six-eighteen. Once he didn't show up till six-twenty. Missing persons had already been called." After the chuckles had died down, Arthur Jr. concluded on a serious and sentimental note. Describing himself as his father's "son and student," he asked everyone to stand and raise a glass of champagne to "Dad, to Punch, to Arthur, to this wonderful Once and Future Publisher and Chairman."

No sooner had Arthur Jr. reached his seat than three figures skulked into the hall and with an exaggerated gait made their way to the dais, where a large copper cauldron stood, surrounded by three microphones. The trio, outfitted in shiny black witches' capes and pointed hats, was led by Marian, whose tireless efforts to redevelop Times Square had made her and her husband, Andrew Heiskell, two of New York City's most revered philanthropists. She was followed by Ruth, who, with the thirteen owning cousins, was at that very moment in the midst of a bidding war for *The Chattanooga News–Free Press, The Chattanooga Times'* historic rival, which was up for sale. In two months their effort would fail, and rather than continue in a joint operating agreement, the cousins would eventually sell out to the *Free Press*'s new owner, conservative publisher Walter E. Hussman Jr., chief executive of Wehco Media Inc., who would in turn merge the two papers. Last came Judy, the author of the evening's entertainment — a takeoff on the witches' scene that opens *Macbeth*.

Although Marian, Ruth, and Judy were all in their mid- to late seventies, they might as well have been back in the nursery at 5 East Eightieth Street. Stirring the pot with thin wooden paddles, they broke into giggles in mid-production and glanced frequently at their imperfectly memorized lines that mimicked the famous verse. "Add baboon's tongue and other slimes / Lead him to *The New York Times*," Judy had written, betraying yet again her lifelong ambivalence about the paper.

The witches exited the stage to resounding applause, and Stephen announced that there would now be a short movie about Punch's life, produced by his niece, Susan Dryfoos. Since the publication of *Iphigene*, Susan had become interested in film, producing two documentaries with *New York Times* themes: one about the paper's history of fashion reporting, the other about Scotty Reston. One year earlier her documentary, *The Line King: The Al Hirschfeld Story*, had been nominated for an Academy Award, and Susan had attended the ceremonies in one of Irene Selznick's dramatic gowns. Now, however, her marriage to Irene's son, Daniel, was unraveling; within ten months the two would be separated.

Her film for Punch's birthday was a pastiche of interviews and home movies that showed Iphigene cradling Punch as an infant and Adolph tossing his small grandson up in the air as though he were a basketball. When the lights went up, it was time, finally, for Punch to say a few words. He spoke of the "miracle of finding Allison to share my senior years" and of how "greatly blessed" he was to have such a loving family and "a cadre of friends who add a special zest to my life." He talked of the extraordinary privilege of serving two "remarkable institutions, *The New York Times* and the Metropolitan Museum of Art," where he would soon step down as chairman.

When he was through, Dan and Michael stepped forward to present the gift: a sixteenth-century infantry officer's iron gauntlet, made in Nuremberg, not far from Fürth, the birthplace of Adolph Ochs's father, resting on a velvet pillow. The appropriateness of the present went far beyond Punch's love of maces, flails, and medieval armament. "Those of us who have worked with Punch appreciate two things about him," Michael told the gathering. "He is very sure of what are the most important things to do, and he prefers to be very gentle in his way of accomplishing them. An iron fist in a velvet glove comes to mind." With that, everyone stood and sang "Happy Birthday." On the way out, each guest was given a small box wrapped with velvet ribbon. Inside was a miniature birthday cake in the shape of a knight's shield, with Punch's initials on top.

The occasion had been as much about the durability of the Ochs-Sulzberger family as it had been about its "shining star," *The New York*

Times, and the man who had led it for the past thirty-five years. Earlier in the evening Stephen had told the audience that "besides working hard to figure out *how* we [as a family] can get along, we actually *do* get along." What was it, in fact, that had allowed Adolph Ochs and his descendants to own and shepherd *The New York Times* for over a century while still remaining close as a family? The institution had demanded a great deal from all of them, yet it had also given them a position of influence they could never have achieved as individuals. They *were The New York Times,* and *The New York Times* was them. As the twentieth century neared its close, their stewardship and sense of noblesse oblige — and the paper's self-proclaimed quest for honesty and excellence — were all the more remarkable for the stark dearth of such qualities elsewhere in the culture. "We don't have trust in government. The Wall Street world? Forget it," said Gay Talese, whose book, *The Kingdom and the Power,* had expertly captured *The New York Times'* journalistic enterprise of an earlier era. "Where can people [go] who have values and a sense of right and wrong, of standards? . . . I think today the Sulzberger family and *The New York Times* [are] our only hope. And if they weren't there, I don't know where you would look."

With typical understatement, Punch was fond of saying that the Ochses and Sulzbergers had been successful simply because they had had luck. "The family came along and the company came along. They just met and it worked," he said with a clap of his hands, as if it had all been a matter of two random stars colliding. Arthur Jr. had grown up in a different world, and now, as head of the company, he faced an unpredictable future. He didn't trust luck. "The first hundred years, that's easy," he said. "The second hundred, now that's the bear."

EPILOGUE

WITHIN EIGHTEEN MONTHS OF HIS ASSUMING the chairmanship, the burden of the job began to show on Arthur Jr. In 1981, when he had first come to the *Times* as an editor on the metro desk, he had the unspoiled looks of a teenager and was sometimes mistaken for an overconfident copyboy. Now his face reflected the strain of a responsibility that even he may have underestimated. Though energetic and fit from his daily workouts, he exhibited the taut countenance of a man who had been entrusted by his family with the guidance and protection of their $2.9 billion company.

During his first months as chairman Arthur Jr. crisscrossed the country, visiting each of the company's many subsidiaries and branches. In his absence, his father's suite of offices was redecorated to conform to Arthur Jr.'s tastes. Punch's back sitting area became an intimate conference room with cream-striped wallpaper, and his modest bedroom a small library featuring books by *Times* writers. The poster of John Wayne in *Sands of Iwo Jima* that had been the eye-catching centerpiece of Arthur Jr.'s former domain was supplanted by a sculpture of a rock climber — a gift from North Carolina Outward Bound.

Punch moved to the eleventh floor to an office at the end of a corridor lined with photographs of the paper's many Pulitzer Prize winners. He was inordinately proud that the *Times* had won more Pulitzers than any other newspaper and years earlier had created the gallery to impress visitors, especially advertisers. The old Underwood on which he had tapped out his first draft of a succession plan came with him, as did a favorite paperweight: the ceramic upturned hindquarters of a horse. As chairman emeritus he spent most of his time traveling with Allison and had few pangs about stepping down. "Once things get decided and done, I'm the kind of person who puts it behind [me]," he said. "There are other things to worry about. Like walking the dog."

While Arthur Jr. became decidedly more sober in his new position, the playful wiseguy still managed to surface from time to time. A year after becoming chairman, he arrived at a Park Avenue Halloween party dressed as "Senator Putzhead," a reference to Republican senator Alfonse D'Amato, who had been ridiculed for using that word to describe a political rival. Arthur Jr.'s hastily assembled costume consisted of white tie and tails, and the Groucho glasses with bushy eyebrows and a penis nose that he had admired long ago on Dan and had borrowed from him for the occasion.

Less than a month later Arthur Jr. had something far more serious to discuss with his cousin. He had concluded that Dan should be removed from his job as senior vice president of advertising at *The New York Times* — an action tantamount to firing a brother. While he was clear in his own mind that the decision was right for Dan, as well as for the company, carrying it out was the most difficult personal experience of his career.

Janet Robinson, president of the newspaper and Dan's immediate superior, delivered the bad news, which came during an annual evaluation in which he had expected accolades. Under his leadership, the *Times* had generated more than $1 billion in advertising revenue in a year, a feat no publication had ever accomplished. Instead of praise, however, he was told what he termed "the same old stuff": that he appeared unfocused and impatient, that people were afraid of him. Dan knew that if he wanted to, he could stay on in some capacity, but given that this was just the latest in a series of negative assessments of his performance, he felt the time had finally come to make a complete break — a decision that left him curiously relieved.

Robinson asked if he wanted to see Arthur Jr.; when Dan said no, she replied, "Well, he wants to see you." That night the two cousins walked the forty blocks from the *Times* to Dan's home on the Upper West Side, talking through the situation. "This job wasn't making Dan happy, and it showed," Arthur Jr. explained. "This [kind of problem] wasn't susceptible to remediation." Dan didn't fault Arthur Jr. for his dismissal — a reaction that baffled his wife. "Doesn't this bother you at all?" Leah demanded. "This really pisses me off!" Her husband's response was muted. "It's the right choice," he told her.

In March 1999 Dan officially resigned to start a production company called Dan Cohen & Sons, which plans to develop TV and Internet programming based on material in the *Times* and its archives. For a man who had never forgiven his own father for abandoning him, the name he chose for his business seemed poignantly apt. "You never know," Dan wrote in a letter circulated to the family, "perhaps someday [my sons] will succeed me."

Soon thereafter, Dan and Arthur Jr. met at a steak house in Grand Central Station. With Arthur Jr. no longer constrained by his role as Dan's ultimate boss, they managed to resume the closeness they both had missed. "It's the best dinner we've had together in twelve years," exulted Dan, referring to the moment over a decade earlier when Arthur Jr. had been named assistant publisher and their professional destinies had diverged. "It was a weight lifted off."

Two months after Dan's departure, Stephen Golden announced that he, too, was leaving. At the age of fifty-two, he intended to pursue a joint law degree and master's in American Indian studies at the University of Arizona. Earlier, as a counterweight to Michael's vice chairmanship, he had been offered a position as head of The New York Times Company Foundation, which under the imaginative leadership of former managing editor Arthur Gelb had been transformed from a quiet sideline into a philanthropy with significant influence. But to the surprise of many of his cousins, Stephen had not been interested. In an effusive letter to the staff, Arthur Jr. praised "my cousin and my friend" for deciding to help Native Americans, a choice he characterized as "at the heart of the Sulzberger family tradition of public service." If Stephen felt any bitterness about being passed over, it was cloaked — which was also a family tradition.

§

The challenge of dealing with his cousins' exits paled next to a phenomenon that had emerged as the defining issue of Arthur Jr.'s era: the Internet. When Bill Gates, chairman of Microsoft, predicted that the Net would mean "the beginning of the end of newspapers as we know them," Arthur Jr. was forced to agree. "We are in a business that is being transformed by a communications revolution that is altering our basic sense of time and space," he told his employees in his annual State of the Times speech early in 1999. "I suspect we will look back at what we [have] accomplished . . . and remember it as being easy."

Like every other major paper in the country, the *Times* had a web site, as did the company's magazines and broadcast properties. But as the cyberrevolution gathered momentum, it became apparent that such efforts weren't sufficient. Nearly every day media conglomerates were forging electronic partnerships and spinning off Internet companies, creating a panicky fear throughout the industry that a new gold rush was on, with claims being staked that would determine who thrived and who starved. The New York Times Company wasn't AT&T or Disney; it didn't have the resources to become an on-line leviathan. Moreover, the company's flagship, *The New York Times* newspaper, was what in the withering jargon of Wall Street was called a "mature" product — meaning that improvement and expansion were likely to occur on the margins, if at all.

In early April 1999 CEO Russ Lewis ordered several of his senior executives to develop a plan to spin off the company's Internet operations as a separate entity, with the news generated by the *Times* as its marquee attraction. The concept was seductive: the new company would offer a small percentage of its shares to the public — a move that in the overheated market for Internet stocks practically guaranteed astronomical prices — and then use the unsold and overvalued shares in lieu of cash to buy interests in other Internet enterprises or acquire the software and personnel needed to establish the *Times* as an Internet player.

Lewis wasn't interested in establishing a "debating society" to argue whether the *Times* should create the spin-off, he told the executives; he wanted to know *how* the project could be done — and fast. To some, Russ's lack of interest in hearing opposing views violated Arthur Jr.'s philosophy that conflicting ideas, expressed without fear of reprisal, were good for the company. In earlier regimes executives faced with a similar situation would have grumbled among themselves about being railroaded and done nothing, but now they were emboldened to act. Gradually their complaints filtered up the chain of command, finally reaching Lewis, who sent an apologetic e-mail to everyone involved. For Arthur Jr., the moment was a sign that his efforts to encourage debate had borne fruit. "No one could have told Lance he made a mistake," he said. "He wouldn't have heard it."

But the issue of trust was not so easily put to rest. Those at the uppermost reaches of the newspaper still worried that Lewis was rushing a decision of critical importance, one that had the potential to put the new digital entity, rather than *The New York Times* itself, at the center of the company and compromise their ability to control journalistic standards. In a joint letter to Arthur Jr., executive editor Joe Lelyveld, editorial-page editor Howell Raines, and Janet Robinson, president of the newspaper, expressed their fears. Arthur Jr. sought to reassure them, but his response was noncommittal and lacked specifics.

In early May all the participants gathered on the fifteenth floor of the Times Building to discuss how to proceed. After some sharp exchanges between the executives at the newspaper and the corporate side, the *Times'* investment bankers, Goldman Sachs, weighed in with an opinion. Their verdict: the spin-off was a good idea, but the plan needed more work before it could be brought to market. While the battle over journalistic safeguards was temporarily deferred, the editors were not mollified. What if Goldman Sachs had gone the other way? they asked themselves. What then? "The whole experience left everybody feeling a little queasy," said one. To Arthur Jr. the meeting was an example of just the kind of management he had hoped to foster. "All the key players in that room were able to talk openly about their fears, their desires," he said. "We had to get over the hump of talking to each other about these issues."

Three weeks later the company consolidated all its Internet properties into one division — a necessary prelude to any spin-off. But precisely how *The New York Times'* values and standards will be maintained as the volatile electronic future unfolds remains to be seen. "I don't know where *there* is," said Arthur Jr., "but we'll get there together."

Despite his vaunted love of teamwork, that crucial decision — and others yet to come — will ultimately be his alone, just as similarly momentous calls had fallen to his relatives who led the *Times* in earlier decades. In each case the job exacted a physical price. Adolph Ochs sank into depressions; Arthur Hays Sulzberger suffered a heart attack, insomnia, barbiturate addiction, and a condition that practically crippled his hands. The publishership literally killed Orvil Dryfoos, while Punch was periodically in traction from back spasms brought on by nervous strain. For years Arthur Jr. had only ground his teeth, but now his wife, Gail, had begun to detect new symptoms of stress: the only time she saw his shoulders in their normal position was when she and Arthur Jr. climbed into their car and headed for their weekend home in New Paltz. "He knows how fragile it is; he knows how remarkable it is," she said, referring to *The New York Times* and all it stands for. "It's daunting. I don't think anyone quite appreciates how hard it is." One editor put it more bluntly: "Deep in Arthur's soul, he believes that if he blows this, he will burn in hell."

Arthur Jr. must reinvent the *Times* just as his great-grandfather did in 1896, using the same tools: a talent for leadership, an idealistic vision leavened by rigorous pragmatism, and the nerves of a gambler. He must draw on his grandfather's stewardship and his grandmother's tolerance and wisdom; on Orvil Dryfoos's humor and courage; and on his father's common sense and unerring instincts. He is bolstered by a family that has willingly sacrificed wealth and personal ambition for the sake of the institution that is both their obligation and their glory. Now, his task is to preserve the *Times,* and all it represents, and pass it on to yet another generation. It is the job, one might say, he was born for.

ACKNOWLEDGMENTS

DURING THE SEVEN YEARS IT HAS TAKEN US TO RESEARCH AND write this book, we have been assisted by countless individuals, none more important than our agent, Kathy Robbins, who offered us encouragement, wise counsel, and, above all, the incalculable gift of her faith and friendship. Jim Silberman, our original editor on the project, was there for the critical first stages of planning, research, and writing: our affection and respect for him cannot be measured. His talented successor, Rick Kot, deftly edited and shaped the final manuscript, and we are forever grateful for his hands-on skill, good cheer, and unflagging confidence in the project. We also want to thank our publisher, Little, Brown and Company, and its superlative staff, in particular Michael Liss, Beth Davey, Katie Long, Donna Peterson, and that most meticulous of copyeditors, Stephen Lamont.

During the initial months, we were assisted by Enid Klass, who identified manuscript collections critical to our inquiry and did archival research in New York City and Cincinnati. Albert Baime, a skilled writer in his own right, answered our queries on everything from the financial arrangements between *The New York Times* and the Equitable Life Assurance Society to Franklin Delano Roosevelt's relations with Arthur Hays Sulzberger, while Kimberly Zimmerman, a Duke graduate student, helped us plug holes in the text as we neared publication. We are indebted to media industry expert Lisa Donneson, who at our request produced a detailed financial analysis of The New York Times Company, and to Amanda George, who somehow managed to transcribe our interviews, become an advanced candidate at a New York psychoanalytic institute, *and* open her own practice as a psychotherapist all at the same time, offering us insights and affection along the way.

Charles St. Vil, manager of The New York Times Archives, and his secretary, Mary McCaffrey, were our nearly daily companions for the year and a half it took us to go through the bounty in their care; we benefited greatly from their help and expertise. Susan Dryfoos, director of Times History Productions, and Adele Riepe, special-projects manager at Times History Productions, gave us critical assistance in our efforts to locate photographs. Also of enormous help were Eden Ross Lipson, editor of *Times Talk,* and Nancy Nielson, vice president of corporate communications at The New York Times Company.

Of the many archivists and alumni directors who aided us, we want to give special thanks to Jane Lowenthal at Barnard College, Larry Lowenstein at Horace Mann, and Jackie Berry at the American Red Cross. David Sulzberger helped bring his father, Cy Sulzberger, to life by giving us access to his private papers in Paris, where we were ably assisted by Cy's former secretary, Barbara Tiesi. We are likewise appreciative of Tom Reston's efforts to arrange for us to see the papers of his father, Scotty Reston, at the University of Illinois at Urbana-Champaign.

Our treasured friend Steve Oney shared his vast knowledge of the Leo Frank case—the subject of his forthcoming book—while Susan Barnes offered us astute perceptions of the Ochses' life in Knoxville based on her extensive research. We are also thankful for Geraldo Samor's research into the first days of Watergate coverage, a project he conducted under the direction of John Ginn at the William Allen White School of Journalism at the University of Kansas. Our efforts to obtain information from the government using the Freedom of Information Act might well have gone nowhere without the intervention of former Tennessee congressman James H. Quillen, who helped accelerate what had become a stalled and discouragingly long process.

Our understanding of the Ochses' German ancestors was greatly enriched by Gisela Blume, who extracted genealogical records from the state archives in Nuremberg and personally led us to the grave of Adolph Ochs's grandfather in the Jewish cemetery in Fürth. Peter Philipp Riedl, a student in Regensburg, translated old documents in Fürth's municipal archives, deepening our knowledge of a culture and a time.

We could not have completed a project of this ambition and complexity without outside support. We are grateful to the Rockefeller Foundation for providing a one-month residency at its study and conference center in Bellagio, Italy, where we composed a narrative outline, and to the Corporation of Yaddo in Saratoga Springs, New York, where during a six-week stay Susan wrote the initial chapters of the book. The Media Studies Center in New York City awarded Alex a nine-month fellowship that provided everything an author dreams of: research help, a quiet refuge, and stimulating colleagues. We are deeply indebted to Ellen Mickiewicz, director of the De Witt Wallace Center for Communications and Journalism at Duke, for her enthusiasm and encouragement, and to the university's Sanford Institute of Public Policy for its generous research support.

We are blessed to count as a friend Bruce Davidson, one of the nation's great photographers, and are proud that he volunteered to take our author photo for the jacket. We are also grateful to George Bennett for his superb promotional photographs.

Finally, we want to thank our families, friends—and each other—for the most important elements in any endeavor: love, forbearance, and generosity of spirit.

June 1999   Susan E. Tifft
New York City   Alex S. Jones

A NOTE ON SOURCES

Much of the material in this book comes from interviews with members of the Ochs-Sulzberger family, with whom we had the same relationship any *New York Times* reporter would have with a cooperative subject: we had access, but with complete independence and no advance review of our work. Such an arrangement is consistent with the family's view of journalistic integrity, and it was honored without exception.

We also interviewed hundreds of the family's friends, acquaintances, advisers, and current and former employees. Because the interviews were so numerous, the reader should assume that unless otherwise noted the quotes attributed to individuals came from tape-recorded sessions with the authors. Except for documentary sources referenced in the Notes, the reader may also assume that whenever conversation or dialogue occurs, it is based on the recollection of at least one participant or observer, and in some cases, several such persons.

Our other primary source was The New York Times Archives, where we had unfettered access to a trove of material ranging from Adolph Ochs's earliest correspondence to financial records to summaries of confidential conversations with a succession of U.S. presidents. In addition, we consulted approximately fifty other archives, the most useful of which are included under "Selected Archives and Sources" in the list of abbreviations that follows.

We also made a point of visiting the sites where our subjects lived: Fürth, the Bavarian town where, at 79 Konigstrasse, the house in which Julius Ochs grew up still stands; Knoxville and Chattanooga, where Adolph Ochs spent his formative years; Lake George, where a stone pillar is all that remains of what was once Abenia; White Plains, New York, where the first Hillandale now houses the White Plains Board of Education; and Stamford, Connecticut, where the second Hillandale has been transformed by new owners. A chance encounter in the spring of 1993 led to a tour of the town house at 5 East Eightieth Street, where Iphigene and Arthur Sulzberger raised their four children, giving us a sense of the dwelling's grandeur as well as the everyday life that was lived there. That summer, during a visit to Temple Israel Cemetery to see Adolph Ochs's grave, we had another bit of good fortune: quite by accident, we met Fred

Maier, the man who had been superintendent of the cemetery in 1933, when Ochs was building his mausoleum, and who had been so struck by the publisher that he carried Ochs's calling card in his pocket and showed it to us the instant we mentioned his name. Maier's recollections of the "plain man" who was the taproot for generations of Ochses and Sulzbergers ended up as the basis for the opening scene of our book — an unlikely coincidence that the superstitious Adolph no doubt would have appreciated.

SELECTED INTERVIEWS

We conducted roughly 550 separate interviews for this book. The list below doesn't account for the frequent occasions when we had multiple interviews with an individual or a couple, nor does it reflect the much shorter conversations we had with scores of others or the sources who requested to remain anonymous. The men and women listed under "Other" are not necessarily described by their current position but by the role they played in relationship to the newspaper, to the company, or to members of the Ochs-Sulzberger family.

The Family (*including in-laws and ex-spouses*)

Adler, Doug
Adler, Julius Ochs, Jr.
Bayliss, Ann Palmer
Berry, Marinette Sulzberger
Cohen, Dan
Cohen, Dick
Cohen, Jace
Cowles, Allison
Dolnick, Edward
Dolnick, Lynn
Dryfoos, Bob
Dryfoos, Jackie
Dryfoos, James
Dryfoos, Joan
Dryfoos, Katie
Dryfoos, Susan
Golden, Anne
Golden, Arthur
Golden, June Tauber
Golden, Michael

Golden, Stephen
Grant, Barbara
Greenspon, Stuart
Gregg, Gail
Heiskell, Andrew
Heiskell, Marian Sulzberger
    (Dryfoos)
Holmberg, Bill
Holmberg, Ruth Sulzberger (Golden)
Katzander, Bobbie Adler
Keith, Leah
Lax, Eric
Oakes, John
Oakes, Margary
Ochs, Celia
Ochs, Martin
Ochs, Patricia
Ochs, Col. William
Perpich, Joe
Sanchez, Brenda

Simpson, Gary
Steinhardt, Jean
Straus, Ellen Sulzberger
Sulzberger, Arthur Ochs "Punch"
Sulzberger, Arthur Ochs, Jr.
Sulzberger, Carol
Sulzberger, Cathy

Sulzberger, Cynthia
Sulzberger, David
Sulzberger, Jean
Sulzberger, Judy
Sulzberger, Karen
Tucker, Diane Straus
Turpin, Anne Freeman (Adler)

THE NEW YORK TIMES NEWSPAPER AND COMPANY (*past and present*)

Abel, Elie
Abernathy, Penny
Adler, Bill
Adler, Ruth
Apple, R. W. "Johnny," Jr.
Arnold, Martin
Asbury, Edith Evans
Baker, Diane
Baker, Russell
Behr, Soma Golden
Berlinghoff, Alice Kernan
Bishow, Howard
Boyd, Gerald
Bradford, Amory
Burt, Richard
Campion, Tom (and Nardi)
Corwin, Laura
Cowan, Alison
Cutie, Jim
Daniel, Clifton
Darrow, Kathy
Durall, Helen
Faber, Doris and Hal
Finn, Nancy
Fisher, Andy (and Connie)
Frankel, Max
Freeman, Lucy Greenbaum
Gelb, Arthur (and Barbara)
Glaberson, Bill
Goldberger, Paul
Goodale, Jim (and Toni)

Gorham, Dave
Green, Monroe
Greenfield, James
Gruson, Sydney (and Marit)
Gwertzman, Bernard
Handelman, Ben
Hoge, Warren
Jones, Dave
Kaiser, Charles
Kaufman, Michael (and Rebecca)
Keller, Bill
Kerr, Bill
Kovach, Bill
Krollege, Arthur
Lee, Carolyn
Lee, John
Lelyveld, Joe (and Carolyn)
Levitas, Mike (and Gloria)
Lewis, Flora
Lewis, Russ
Linker, Erich
Mathews, Linda
Mattson, Walter (and Gerri)
Medenica, Gordon
Meislin, Richard
Messino, Karen
Miller, Judy
Millones, Peter
Mortimer, John
Moss, Adam
Nielson, Nancy

O'Brien, John
Oreskes, Mike
Pollak, Bill
Primis, Lance
Quindlen, Anna
Raines, Howell
Rampe, David
Rattner, Steve
Reston, Scotty (and Sally)
Roberts, Gene
Robinson, Janet
Rosenthal, A. M.
Rosenthal, Jack
Ryan, Mike
Safire, William
Salembier, Valerie
Salisbury, Harrison

Schneiderman, David
Schwarz, Dan
Shepard, Dick (and Trudy)
Siegal, Allan
Smith, Hedrick
Sullivan, Walter
Szulc, Tad
Talese, Gay
Topping, Seymour (and Audrey)
Underhill, Marian
Veit, Ivan
Vinocur, John
Wade, Betsy
Weisman, Steve
Wicker, Tom
Wren, Christopher (and Jackie)

The Chattanooga Times (*past and present*)

Bartlett, Charley (and Martha)
Bradley, Norman
Howe, Isabel Puckette
Neely, Paul

Popham, John
Puckette, Stephen
Sudderth, Bob

Other

Abrams, Floyd: First Amendment lawyer who argued the Pentagon Papers case before the U.S. Supreme Court

Akers, Jon F.: director, New York Times Company

Argyris, Chris: professor of organizational behavior who analyzed the *Times*, 1969–72

Aronoff, Craig: family business consultant engaged by the Sulzbergers

Bales, Carter: director, McKinsey & Company

Bayley, Ed and Monica: Punch's friends and colleagues during his stint at *The Milwaukee Journal*

Beattie, Diana: party planner, centennial dinner, Metropolitan Museum of Art, 1996

Birge, June Bingham: family friend

Carden, Dr. George A., Jr.: former family physician

Catledge, Abby: widow of former *Times* executive editor Turner Catledge

Christy, David, Jr.: son of Barbara Grant
Christy, Sarah: daughter of Barbara Grant
Cross, William: former director, New York Times Company
Cullen, Bob: former AP bureau chief, Raleigh, N.C.
Cullman, Joe: family friend
de Saint Phalle, Thibaut: Punch's former tutor
Deutsch, Armand ("Ardie"): Orvil Dryfoos's friend
Eisenberg, Steve: former publisher, *New York Newsday*
Elliott, Elly: family friend
Elliott, Jan Johnson: Arthur Jr.'s. former colleague at *The Raleigh Times*
Gelb, Richard L.: director, New York Times Company
Gilman, Sarah: family acquaintance in Chattanooga
Girsberger, Esther: editor, *Tages-Anzeiger,* Zurich, Switzerland
Golden, Richard Davis: Ben Golden relative
Grade, Lord Lew: family friend
Heilpern, Jeff: business consultant engaged by The New York Times Company
Hewitt, Luellen Bowles: Ruth's colleague in the Red Cross
Hittle, Gen. Donald: Punch's superior in Washington in 1950s
John, Betty Beaman: Ruth's colleague in the Red Cross
Kahn, Liselotte: family friend
Kanter, Rabbi Kenneth: former head of Julius and Bertha Ochs Memorial
    Temple, Chattanooga
Kelso, Iris: Turner Catledge relative
Kheel, Ted: mediator during the 1962–63 strike
Kougoucheff, Princess Catherine: Cy Sulzberger's former assistant
Lamarche, Linda: Cy Sulzberger's former assistant
Lansberg, Ivan: family business consultant engaged by the Sulzbergers
Limburg, Kathryn: family friend
Limburg, Myles: family friend
Livingood, J. W.: Chattanooga historian
Loos, Lisa: member of family sponsored by the Ochs-Sulzbergers during
    World War II
Maier, Fred J.: former superintendent, Temple Israel Cemetery
Marcus, Rabbi Jacob: professor of American Jewish history, Hebrew Union
    College, Cincinnati
May, William: former director, New York Times Company
Mayer, Margaret: member of family who escaped Germany with the help of
    the Ochs-Sulzbergers during World War II
Munroe, George: former director, New York Times Company
Pallier, Eda: Cy Sulzberger's former assistant
Pelham, Ann: Arthur Jr. and Gail's friend while in Raleigh

Powers, Bert: former president, ITU Local No. 6

Price, Dudley: Arthur Jr.'s colleague at *The Raleigh Times*

Prince Alexander and Princess Katherine of Yugoslavia: family friends

Pulbrook, Lady Susan: family friend

Rabinowitz, Alan: Punch's classmate at Loomis

Rhys, Brinley: Punch's tutor

Rossi, Gino: Hillandale gardener

Rothman, John: oversaw the initial organization of the New York Times Archives

Sanger, Eleanor: widow of WQXR president Elliott Sanger

Sarasohn, Judy: Arthur Jr.'s colleague at *The Raleigh Times*

Shinn, George L.: director, New York Times Company

Simon, Judge Caroline: family friend

Stewart, Donald M.: director, New York Times Company

Taylor, Ben: publisher, *The Boston Globe*

Taylor, Steve: executive vice president, *The Boston Globe*

Wagner, Ted: family trust and estate lawyer

Weidenfeld, Sheila and Ed: family friends

Weiskopf, Jim: Bob Dryfoos's former roommate

Winship, Tom: former editor, *The Boston Globe*

Wolff, Michael: newspaper industry expert

Vance, Cyrus, former director, New York Times Company

Yopp, Mike: former managing editor, *The Raleigh Times*

SELECTED BIBLIOGRAPHY

IT WOULD BE AN EMPTY EXERCISE TO LIST ALL THE BOOKS AND PERIODICALS we consulted in the course of researching and writing this book. The following includes only those publications cited multiple times in the Notes, using the author's name as an abbreviation for the work.

Barnes, Susan Gilbert. "The Ochs Family in Knoxville, Tennessee." Master's thesis, University of Tennessee at Knoxville, December 1980.

———. "Adolph S. Ochs." *American Newspaper Journalists, 1901–1925.* Vol. 25, *Dictionary of Literary Biography (DLB),* edited by Perry J. Ashley. Detroit: Gale Research Company, 1984.

Berger, Meyer. *The Story of The New York Times, 1851–1951.* New York: Simon & Schuster, 1951.

Buley, R. Carlyle. *The Equitable Life Assurance Society of the United States, 1859–1964.* New York: Appleton-Century-Crofts, 1967.

Catledge, Turner. *My Life and The Times.* New York: Harper & Row, 1971.

Davis, Elmer. *History of The New York Times, 1851–1921.* New York: The New York Times, 1921.

Diamond, Edwin. *Behind the Times: Inside The New York Times.* New York: Villard Books, 1994.

Dryfoos, Susan W. *Iphigene: Memoirs of Iphigene Ochs Sulzberger of The New York Times Family.* New York: Dodd, Mead & Company, 1981.

Emery, Edwin. *The Press and America: An Interpretive History of the Mass Media.* Englewood Cliffs, N.J.: Prentice-Hall, Inc., 1954.

Frankel, Max. *The Times of My Life and My Life with The Times.* New York: Random House, 1999.

Goulden, Joseph C. *Fit to Print: A. M. Rosenthal and His Times.* Secaucus, N.J.: Lyle Stuart, 1988.

Halberstam, David. *The Powers That Be.* New York: Alfred A. Knopf, 1979.

Jackson, Kenneth T., ed. *The Encyclopedia of New York City.* New Haven: Yale University Press, 1995.

Johnson, Gerald W. *An Honorable Titan: A Biographical Study of Adolph S. Ochs.* New York: Harper & Brothers, 1946.

Krock, Arthur. *Memoirs: Sixty Years on the Firing Line.* New York: Funk & Wagnalls, 1968.

Morgenthau, Henry III. *Mostly Morgenthaus: A Family History.* New York: Ticknor & Fields, 1991.

Ochs, Julius. *A Memoir of Julius Ochs: An Autobiography.* Privately printed.

Ostrander, Stephen J. "All the News That's Fit to Print: Adolph Ochs and *The New York Times.*" *Timeline* (a publication of the Ohio Historical Society) 10, no. 1 (Jan./Feb. 1993).

Reston, James. *Deadline: A Memoir.* New York: Times Books, 1991.

Rousmaniere, John. *The Life and Times of The Equitable.* New York: The Equitable Companies Incorporated, 1995.

Rudenstine, David. *The Day the Presses Stopped: A History of the Pentagon Papers Case.* Berkeley: University of California Press, 1996.

Salisbury, Harrison E. *Without Fear or Favor: An Uncompromising Look at The New York Times.* New York: Times Books, 1980.

Shepard, Richard F. *The Paper's Papers: A Reporter's Journey Through the Archives of The New York Times.* New York: Times Books, 1996.

Talese, Gay. *The Kingdom and the Power.* New York: Ivy Books, 1969

Wilson, John. *Chattanooga's Story.* Chattanooga: The Chattanooga News–Free Press, 1980.

NOTES

ABBREVIATIONS

People

AB	Amory Bradford
AG	Arthur Golden
AHS	Arthur Hays Sulzberger
AMR	Abe Rosenthal
AOS	Arthur Ochs "Punch" Sulzberger
AOSJ	Arthur Ochs Sulzberger Jr.
ASO	Adolph S. Ochs
BD	Bob Dryfoos
CLS	Cy Sulzberger
CS	Carol Sulzberger
DC	Dan Cohen
EWO	Effie Wise Ochs
GG	Gail Gregg
GWO	George Washingon Ochs-Oakes
IOS	Iphigene Ochs Sulzberger
JBO	John Bertram Oakes
JBR	James B. "Scotty" Reston
JC	Jace Cohen
JD	Jackie Dryfoos
JO	Julius Ochs
JOA	Julius Ochs Adler
JS	Judith Sulzberger
KS	Karen Sulzberger
LD	Lynn (Golden) Dolnick
MF	Max Frankel
MG	Michael Golden
MH	Marian Sulzberger (Dryfoos) Heiskell

MBO	Milton Barlow Ochs
OED	Orvil Eugene Dryfoos
RH	Ruth Sulzberger (Golden) Holmberg
SD	Susan Dryfoos
SG	Stephen Golden
TC	Turner Catledge

Selected Archives and Sources

AJA	American Jewish Archives, Hebrew Union College
AJCA	American Jewish Committee Archives
BC	Barnard College Archives
CH	Chattanooga–Hamilton County Library
CLSP	Cy Sulzberger Private Papers
CO	Columbia University Libraries
COH	Columbia University — Oral History Collection
COR	Columbia University — Rare Books and Manuscripts
CT	*Chattanooga Times*
CFP	*Chattanooga News–Free Press*
DDE	Dwight D. Eisenhower Library
EQ	Equitable Life Assurance Society Historical Collection
FDR	Franklin Delano Roosevelt Library
HBS	Harvard Business School — Special Collections
HT	*Herald Tribune*
JBOP	John Bertram Oakes Private Papers
JFK	John F. Kennedy Library
JTS	Jewish Theological Seminary
LC	Library of Congress — Manuscript Division
MZ	Archives of Mizpah Congregation, Chattanooga, Tennessee
NYHS	New-York Historical Society
NYP	*New York Post*
NYPL	New York Public Library — Rare Books Collection
NYPLJ	New York Public Library — Jewish Collection
NYT	*New York Times*
NYTA	New York Times Archives
NYTC	New York Times Company
PU	Princeton University — Rare Books and Special Collections
ST	Stanford University — Special Collections
UR	University of Rochester — Rare Books and Special Collections
UI	University of Illinois, Urbana-Champaign
UT	University of Tennessee at Knoxville — Special Collections
YI	Yivo Institute

PROLOGUE

"We are not the sort of people who feel we must have yachts": As quoted in Roger Kahn, "The House of Adolph Ochs," *Saturday Evening Post,* Oct. 9, 1965.

PART ONE: THE PATERFAMILIAS

Chapter 1. The Boy with No Childhood

Cemetery scene: Based on site visit and interview with Fred J. Maier, July 26, 1993.

Shortening Ochsenhorn to Ochs: In the birth register of the state archives in Nuremberg, Germany, Julius Ochs's name is recorded as "Joel Ochsenhorn, gennat [called] Julius." Until the Juden-Edikt of 1813 in Bavaria, Jews did not necessarily have family names. The Edikt forced them to take such names and to continue them. When a family already had a continued name but was too numerous, its members had to take variations, such as Ochsenhorn, Ochsenfusse, Ochsenknecht. It appears that Ochs was the original name, but that the family was forced, after 1813, to adopt Ochsenhorn.

JO character; Civil War; Knoxville: JO *Autobiography;* Barnes thesis; ASO papers, NYTA.

In 1862 General Ulysses S. Grant was so concerned about the "swarms of Jews and speculators" in Tennessee — torn as it was between North and South — that he issued the notorious General Order 11, expelling all Jews from the "department" of Tennessee. Lincoln quickly rescinded it.

When JO moved back to Knoxville in 1864, he led the effort to build one of the first bridges across the Tennessee River and mounted comic operas of his own composition. As head of the city's immigration bureau, he advocated limiting the immigration of German Jews to east Tennessee, not because members of that group hadn't become leading citizens there but because he concluded that the region "could take no more." See Barnes thesis.

ASO as young boy: JO *Autobiography; CT* Jubilee Souvenir Edition, July 2, 1928; Barnes, *DLB;* Dryfoos; Doris Faber, *Printer's Devil to Publisher: Adolph S. Ochs and The New York Times* (New York: Julian Messner, Inc., 1963); ASO papers, NYTA.

Chapter 2. Chattanooga Days

ASO in Louisville: JO to ASO, Jan. 5, 23 and March 8, 1876, ASO papers, NYTA.

Ochs household goods sold at auction: Barnes thesis, p. 56.

ASO in Chattanooga: ASO, AHS, and IOS papers, NYTA; Barnes, *DLB;* JO *Autobiography;* G. E. Govan and J. W. Livingood, "Adolph S. Ochs: The Boy Publisher," *The East Tennessee Historical Society* 17 (1945); Ostrander; Wilson; *CT,* June 20, 1948.

Rabbi Wise/EWO: ASO, AHS, and IOS papers, NYTA; Ostrander; Iphigene Molony Bettmann Oral History, May 13, 1964, AJA; Sam Cauman, *Jonah Bondi Wise: A Biography* (New York: Crown Publishers, 1960); Max I. Dimont, *The Jews in America: The Roots, History and Destiny of American Jews* (New York: Simon and Schuster, 1978); *Encyclopedia Judaica Jerusalem,* vol. 16. (Jerusalem: Keter Publishing House, Ltd., 1971); Eli N. Evans, *The Provincials: A Personal History of Jews in the South* (New York: Atheneum, 1973).

Birth of IOS, JOA: ASO papers, NYTA. ASO had hoped that Iphigene would be known as Gene, which she never was. See Berger.

The Dome Building: Berger; ASO and AHS papers, NYTA; Barnes, *DLB; CT,* Dec. 8, 1892.

Land boom: Ostrander; ASO and AHS papers, NYTA; Barnes, *DLB;* Wilson; *CT,* July 1, 1928.

The *Mercury*: Louis Rich, *Adolph S. Ochs* (New York: The American Jewish Committee, 1935); ASO and IOS papers, NYTA; *NYT,* April 9, 1935.

Chapter 3. A Jay Comes to Town

NYT history and ASO negotiations for the paper: Berger; Davis; Johnson; James Melvin Lee, "Ochs' Career from Printer's Devil to Famous Publisher," *Editor & Publisher,* Sept. 18. 1926; Salisbury; Talese; ASO papers, NYTA.

ASO's phony bank account: Interviews of E. Y. Chapin done for Berger book but not included therein, and undated interview of A. W. Chambliss, AHS papers, NYTA.

How ASO got $75,000: One of the likely family benefactors was Mrs. Pauline Franck, a cousin by marriage, who made ASO a $30,000 gift in 1896, a fact that came to light only after his death. With other relatives hounding him for loan repayment, he was understandably reluctant to make Franck's gesture known at the time. The $30,000 gift was included in a *HT* news story about the settlement of ASO's estate on July 14, 1939. A *NYT* story at the same time made no mention of the Franck debt.

The four-month Walter Scott loan was arranged through Scott's chief lieu-tenant, Albert L. Thomas. See ASO papers, NYTA.

In *Without Fear or Favor,* Harrison Salisbury also concludes that Hyde gave ASO the critical final sum at the last minute.

ASO's purchase: ASO actually got the *NYT* for nothing.

His $75,000 investment in bonds brought with it a bonus of 1,125 shares of stock. Schiff's gift of 250 shares of old New-York Times Publishing stock provided him an additional fifty shares, forty-five of which it appears ASO eventually sold to raise money or settle debts. Under the Ochs plan, 3,885 shares were held in escrow for him, contingent upon his earning "the fixed charges" for three consecutive years. Once that condition was satisfied, his total would be 5,015 shares, well over the absolute majority needed for control.

The $75,000 was not his money, and he knew the company would repay that amount, plus 5 percent interest, leaving him owing nothing to his benefactors. The Schiff stock was a gift, and the 3,885 shares in escrow were a reward for his labor. End result: ASO had every expectation that he would soon get *The New-York Times* for free.

ASO's celebratory feast: Judge A. W. Chambliss of Chattanooga was with ASO on that day and says the meal took place in "a famous restaurant of the time . . . Savroni's." See AHS papers, NYTA. The correct name, however, is Cafe Savarin, which at the time was second only to Delmonico's in price and cuisine. The eatery was located in the Equitable Building and was controlled by Equitable directors. In 1904 it was said to have "paid over" to the company at least $150,000. See Grace M. Mayer, *Once Upon a City* (New York: MacMillan Company, 1958).

Chapter 4. "A Stroke of Genius"

NYC in 1896: Jackson; Ernest Ingersoll, *Handy Guide to New York City,* 8th ed. (Chicago and New York: Rand, McNally & Co., 1898); "Life and Letters," *Harper's Weekly,* Feb. 1, 1896.

NYC journalism in 1896: Berger; Jackson; Jean Folkerts and Dwight L. Teeter Jr., *Voices of a Nation: A History of the Media in the United States* (New York: MacMillan Publishing, 1989); W. A. Swanberg, *Pulitzer* (New York: Charles Scribner's Sons, 1967); interview with John T. Hettrick (*NYT* reporter 1889–1900), 1949, COH. The first *NYT* under ASO management was twelve pages, organized into two sections, and cost three cents; it was published during a heat wave severe enough to prostrate nearly 1,300 horses.

First days under ASO management: Berger; ASO papers, NYTA. Concerning the slogan, ASO borrowed "All the News" from the *Philadelphia Times* and added "That's Fit to Print." See *Times Talk,* Jan. 1951.

"When you entered the newspaper business, the world lost a promising lawyer.": GWO to ASO, Aug. 20, 1900, MZ.

Ochs family life in NYC: Dryfoos; ASO and IOS papers, NYTA.

ASO's club memberships: ASO was listed as a member of the Lawyers' Club in *Club Men of New York, 1895–97* (New York: The Republic Press). By 1903 he was also in the Lotos Club, the Ohio Society, the New York Southern Society, and the Hardware Club.

At the turn of the cenutry, most private clubs, such as the Knickerbocker, the Lotos, and the Century, admitted few if any Jews, although the Knickerbocker, formed in 1871, counted two Jews among its founders — Moses Lazarus and August Belmont, Sr. See Jackson.

Lowering the price to one cent: During the period February 15 to August 15, 1898, the *NYT* carried no financial announcements whatsoever. See ASO deposition in Hearst case, Jan. 2, 1908, ASO papers, NYTA.

Davis described the one-cent move as ASO's "greatest inspiration" and his insight "pure clairvoyance." It was Johnson who called it "a stroke of genius."

Equitable's $150,000 loan: On January 12, 1899, ASO beseeched munitions millionaire Marcellus Hartley, a *Times* shareholder and Equitable director, for a $250,000 loan, secured by the controlling stock of the company. See ASO to Marcellus Hartley, Jan. 12, 1899, ASO papers, NYTA.

There is strong evidence to suggest that Hartley had already loaned the paper $100,000 the previous year to see it through a credit crisis. See Marcellus Hartley Dodge to AHS, May 4, 1955, AHS papers, NYTA, and ASO to Joseph Hartley, Nov. 30, 1903, ASO papers, NYTA.

Hartley did not make the new $250,000 loan. So on February 17, 1899, ASO approached Equitable for a smaller amount, $150,000, secured by a controlling interest in the *NYT*. See ASO to James W. Alexander, vice president, Equitable Life Assurance Society, Feb. 17, 1899, ASO papers, NYTA. Alexander's response is not in the files of the NYTA, but by July 13, it appears that the deal was concluded. See ASO to James W. Alexander, July 13, 1899, ASO papers, NYTA.

Because of a fire in 1912, many of Equitable's records no longer exist.

ASO's inventive arithmetic concerning escrowed shares: ASO had run the *NYT* for almost four years. In the first twenty-four months the paper lost about $94,000. In the third year, after the circulation gambit, it earned a few thousand dollars. But midway through the fourth year, profits soared so much that, as of July 1, 1900, the previous thirty-six months showed a $2,612 net profit if taken as a whole. On this basis, ASO claimed three years of profitability and demanded his stock.

For GWO's destruction of all ASO correspondence relating to the stock transaction, see GWO to ASO, Aug. 20, 1900, MZ.

Chapter 5. The Times' *Mystique*

New Year's Eve, 1900: Berger.

Family trips: ASO and IOS papers, NYTA; Dryfoos; Berger; Lally Weymouth, "Iphigene Sulzberger: The Hidden Power Behind the 'Times,'"*New York Magazine,* Jan. 17, 1977.

Newspaper of Record: The *NYT* first described itself as the "Newspaper of Record" in 1927 as a way to promote its rag paper edition to libraries. That same year, the paper organized a contest on the subject "The Value of The New York Times Index and Files as a Newspaper of Record."

Carr Van Anda: ASO and IOS papers, NYTA; Berger; Emery; Halberstam, pp. 212–13; Ostrander; *Times Talk,* vol. 5, no. 1, Aug./Sept. 1951.

ASO had first offered the job to Chester S. Lord, managing editor of *The Sun,* who "unto the day of his death in 1933 . . . regretted that he had not accepted the offer." See Benjamin Fine to AHS, April 29, 1935, AHS papers, NYTA.

The admiring book, *A Giant of the Press,* was written by Benjamin Fine on the occasion of Van Anda's retirement in 1932. Less than two years later, a note pasted in an inside cover of the copy of the book preserved at the NYTA said that after "consultation" with Van Anda, all copies of the volume were withdrawn and destroyed. The book was reprinted by Acme Books in 1968. See Shepard.

Peary: Berger; ASO and IOS papers, NYTA; interview with AHS, Aug. 18, 1965, COH; *Times Talk,* Sept. 1949.

A story about *Cook & Peary: The Polar Controversy, Resolved,* by Robert Bryce (Stackpole Books, 1997), published in the February 17, 1997, edition of the *NYT,* said: "Admiral Peary's financial and professional backers, including the National Geographic Society and *The New York Times,* supported his claim based on little more than his word and a cursory investigation of his records."

GWO and Paris edition: Berger; JBOP; MZ; ASO papers, NYTA; *NYT,* June 1, 1900.

Chapter 6. Sidestepping a Scandal

Design of Times Tower: Landau, Sarah Bradford, and Carl W. Condit, *Rise of the New York Skyscraper, 1865–1913* (New Haven: Yale University Press, 1996); *NYT,* Aug. 4, 1902; Oct. 25, 1903; and March 16, 1961; ASO, AHS, and IOS papers, NYTA; *Metropolis Magazine,* Sept. 1992.

Belmont and the naming of Times Square: Berger; Davis; ASO papers, NYTA; *The New York American,* April 7, 1904; *NYT,* April 9 and May 4, 1904; interview with John T. Hettrick (*NYT* reporter 1889–1900), 1949, COH; Clifton Hood, *722 Miles: The Building of the Subways and How They Transformed New York* (Baltimore: Johns Hopkins University Press, 1993).

ASO relations with Equitable and Hyde: While relations between ASO and Equitable were harmonious, relations between ASO and Henry B. Hyde soured about a year after ASO purchased the *NYT*. That is when Hyde became angry about the *NYT*'s editorial attacks on New York senator Tom Platt, the Republicans' "Easy Boss," and subsequently demanded repayment of a loan he had made to ASO. "It was then," IOS wrote much later, "that Marcellus Hartley [head of the Remington Arms Company and an Equitable director] advanced the necessary money [\$100,000] and saved the situation." Henry B. Hyde and ASO never saw each other again, but after Hyde's death in 1899, his son James Hazen Hyde told ASO that his father's last words were that he should make a friend of ASO. See IOS corrections to Berger's first draft of *History of NYT*, circa March 20, 1951, AHS papers, NYTA.

For background on James Hazen Hyde, see interview with John T. Hettrick (*NYT* reporter 1889–1900), 1949, COH; James Hazen Hyde papers, NYHS; Buley; Rousmaniere.

Hyde's editorial instructions to ASO: Hyde's letter says: "I would like the Equitable situation referred to as a compromise for the good of the Equitable, for the good of the policyholders, and for the insurance world in general, and not as a victory for Hyde, Alexander . . . or anyone else. . . . I do not wish boquets [sic], but would like this referred to as a victory for right and as an equitable compromise with concessions on the part of friends with different views. . . . As I said at a recent meeting of the Louisville Agency here in New York; 'Gentlemen, this is evolution, and not revolution. . . .'" See J. H. Hyde to ASO, March 15, 1905, ASO papers, NYTA.

The *NYT* editorial the following day says: "The compromise reached must be looked upon as having been ordered for the good of the Equitable, for the good of its policy holders, and for the benefit indirectly of insurance interests in general, and not as a victory for Mr. Hyde, Mr. Alexander . . . or for anyone else. It is a victory for right through an equitable compromise involving concessions on the part of friends with different views. . . . [The] mutualization of the Equitable is an evolution, not a revolution." See *NYT,* March 16, 1905.

Ryan's purchase of Hyde's stock: Coincidentally, three years earlier, Ryan had also purchased bonds on the new Times Tower.

Within months of selling his majority interest to Ryan, the disgraced Hyde went into self-imposed exile in France; ASO remained on good terms with him for the rest of his life, and received him warmly in his rooms at the Crillon whenever he was in Paris. He died in 1959 on the one-hundredth anniversary of Equitable's founding. Equitable president Alexander, who was ousted as a result of the investigation, suffered a nervous breakdown, entered a sanitarium, and soon died. See Rousmaniere; James Hazen Hyde papers, NYHS.

ASO's name in Henricks's report: To ASO's credit, the *NYT* published his name along with the rest, listing him as having had fifty shares of Equitable stock on January 27, 1903, and sixty-three the following day with no new purchases. (Hyde's shares during the same twenty-four-hour period went from 1,117 to 8,000; Alexander's nearly doubled, from 350 to 688.) The list was not meant to prove any single individual's wrongdoing. Rather it showed, in the words of the report, "that [the officers of the Equitable Society and its executive committee] were not solicitous for the Society's welfare, but active in promoting their own private interests." See *NYT*, June 22, 1905.

ASO not worried about $1.1 million building loan: Berger erroneously asserts that it was the building loan that caused ASO distress. But according to records in the NYTA, the building loan was kept on the books for years afterward and was secured, in any case, by the property itself. Being closely associated with Equitable in any way was no doubt an embarrassment — in 1906 Hearst publicly attacked ASO for being "indebted to the traction trust and the life insurance companies even for the building that he prints his paper in" — but the loan secured by the controlling stock in the *NYT* was a far bigger threat to his reputation.

ASO's deal with Dodge: Memorandum on Adolph S. Ochs and Marcellus Hartley, by Marcellus Hartley Dodge, April 26, 1949, AHS papers, NYTA; AHS to Dorothy Havighorst, secretary to Dr. Buley, June 28, 1961, AHS papers, NYTA.

ASO's claim that the *NYT* was independent of outside influences: In an essay published in 1921, ASO acknowledged that, in the early days, "it was no secret . . . that [the paper] was an active borrower." But he made a distinction between debt and power: "The truth is that from the day I assumed the management of *The New York Times* . . . I have been in absolute and free control." While the literal truth of his claim is debatable, the essence rings true. In 1900, when ASO applied for his majority stock, it was already in the Equitable safe and he had written EWO that "physical possession . . . is not important." Had Equitable or Dodge attempted to dictate policy to him or call the debt, he would no doubt have found yet another rich friend and moved the stock to another safe. Still, the facts surrounding his deal with Equitable and later with Dodge were sufficiently compromising that ASO never disclosed what really happened.

Chapter 7. "My Ownest Daughter and Onliest Son"

IOS's childhood and schooling: Dryfoos; Morgenthau; AHS, ASO, and IOS papers, NYTA.

Barnard professor's analysis of IOS: Clare Howard, "Iphigene Ochs Sulzberger," *Barnard College Alumnae Monthly* 26, no. 6 (March 1937), BC.

IOS and Henrietta MacDonnell: AHS and IOS papers, NYTA; Dryfoos; IOS Oral History, William E. Wiener Oral History Library of the American Jewish Committee, May 19, 1983, NYPLJ.

ASO/IOS relationship: AHS, ASO, and IOS papers, NYTA; Dryfoos. For description of the Harmonie Club, see Stephen Birmingham, "Does a Zionist Conspiracy Control the Media?" *MORE,* July/Aug. 1976.

Interview with *Titanic* wireless operator: Van Anda's original plan was to use the *NYT*'s four pier passes to get interviews with survivors and crew members as they disembarked the *Carpathia.* Twelve other reporters were assigned to wait outside and catch people as they got into cabs. Every scrap of information was then to be rushed to the nearby Strand Hotel, where Van Anda had installed rewrite men and telephones to call in the story, piecemeal, to the *NYT* newsroom.

The prize witnesses, in Van Anda's eyes, were the two surviving *Titanic* wireless operators, and he was prepared to pay them well for their stories, if he could get to them. At 7:00 P.M. the night of the *Carpathia*'s arrival, Van Anda decided, as a precaution, to secure a letter from the Marconi Company permitting the boys to sell their accounts. *NYT* reporter Isaac Russell was dispatched to the home of John Bottomley, Marconi's American manager, on West 123rd Street, where the famous inventor was having dinner. While Bottomley perused the release letter, Marconi told Russell that he had become curious to see the *Carpathia* himself; could the *NYT* get him a pier pass?

Russell telephoned the *NYT,* only to be told by Frederick Birchall, the night city editor, "We can't do anything for Marconi." Rather than confess the embarrassing truth, Russell, figuring Marconi could easily circumvent police barricades on the strength of his name, said the paper was glad to help and that he, Russell, would meet him at the Fourteenth Street el station in half an hour, after he delivered the release letter to his colleagues at the Strand.

At the dock, Russell made Marconi's presence known to police, who were "proud and delighted" to take him to his wireless boys aboard the ship. But just as a sergeant began to escort the pair onto the pier, a man in the crowd called out that he was Marconi's engineer and tried to join them, only to be restrained by an officer. Marconi vouched for his employee. Russell, showing great forethought, shoved his police press card in the engineer's hat, and the three men proceeded to the gangplank of the *Carpathia,* where a White Star guard stopped them. Russell announced he was a *NYT* reporter escorting Marconi and his engineer to the wireless room. The message was relayed up the chain of command to the guard's superior, who left his post to settle the dispute. "Marconi and the engineer can pass," he told the trio, "but not the reporter." Glancing at the police pass in the engineer's hat, the White Star officer assumed *he* was the reporter, shoved him back, and took Russell and Marconi aboard.

In the wireless room, Marconi and Russell found traumatized *Titanic* operator Harold Bride in a near catatonic state. Under Marconi's gentle questioning, the boy gradually told his account while Russell stood inconspicuously in the background, taking it all down.

Once off the ship, Russell and Marconi rushed to the *NYT,* where Russell began pounding out his story in short takes. Because he had not even been assigned to cover the *Carpathia*'s arrival, his editors were slow to take notice of it. Once Van Anda realized what he had, he played it for all it was worth, running the piece five columns across the front page. ASO was so pleased that he wrote Russell a congratulatory note and enclosed a $25 bonus. But Van Anda, frustrated that his careful planning had not been responsible for the scoop, never gave Russell a word of praise. The next day when the two men passed in the hall, Van Anda was tight-lipped. "I would have got [the story] anyhow," he said.

In 1921 Elmer Davis's *History of The New York Times* credited Van Anda with the story; Russell called the account "a gross and false lie." By then Russell was no longer a *NYT* employee. He had been fired in 1915 for writing a political story in which Van Anda charged he had reported a "conclusion, not a fact." See Isaac Russell to ASO, Sept. 24, 1921, Isaac Russell papers, ST; and C. V. Van Anda to Isaac Russell, June 1 and July 26, 1915, ASO papers, NYTA.

Louis Wiley: Dryfoos; Louis Wiley papers, UR; E. L. James papers, NYTA.

Chapter 8. A Non-Jewish Jew

ASO's role in Frank case: ASO papers, NYTA; Louis Marshall papers, AJCA; Talese; Leonard Dinnerstein, *The Leo Frank Case* (New York: Columbia University Press, 1968); *Personal Journal of Garet Garrett,* May 7, 1915–June 5, 1916, given to authors.

From May 1913 until September 1915, the *NYT* ran 194 articles and 22 editorials about the case.

Jewish immigration: In 1906, 153,748 Jews emigrated to the United States, but it was 1907, with 1,285,349 newcomers of many derivations, that was the peak year for immigration overall. See Morris U. Schappes, *A Pictorial History of the Jews in the United States* (New York: Marzani & Munsell, 1958), and Edward Robb Ellis, *The Epic of New York* (New York: Coward-McCann, 1966).

Passports in Russia: Before World War I, only Turkey and Russia required passports; most European countries did not, although the United States strongly advised tourists to have them anyway, for identification. Jacob Schiff's interest in the passport issue was long-standing: he was instrumental in the 1906 founding of the American Jewish Committee, which focused on Russian and Romanian treatment of Jews and on U.S. restrictions on immigration.

IOS at Barnard: Clare Howard, op. cit.; Weymouth, op. cit.; Dryfoos; Salisbury; *Barnard Alumnae Magazine,* Spring 1991; ASO and IOS papers, NYTA; *NYT,* Oct. 10, 1991; IOS academic transcript and yearbooks, BC; IOS Oral History, William E. Wiener Oral History Library of the American Jewish Committee, May 19, 1983, NYPLJ.

IOS took James Harvey Robinson's most popular class: History of the Intellectual Classes of Europe. The historian Charles Beard was one of Robinson's protégés. See Horace Coon, *Columbia: Colossus on the Hudson* (New York: E. P. Dutton, 1947).

In 1914, the year IOS graduated, the Barnard faculty had only two female faculty members — one in physics and one in chemistry, neither a full professor.

Outbreak and coverage of World War I: ASO papers, NYTA; Dryfoos; Berger; Davis; Talese; Halberstam; Emery; Ostrander; *NYT,* Oct. 11 and Dec. 15, 1914; April 9, 1935.

Chapter 9. War, Worry, and a Wedding

ASO attitude toward IOS beaux: Dryfoos; ASO, AHS, and IOS papers, NYTA.

AHS background: AHS, ASO, and IOS papers, NYTA; IOS Oral History, William E. Wiener Oral History Library of the American Jewish Committee, March 11, 1976, NYPLJ; *Times Talk,* vol. 13, no. 9, May 1960; Horace Mann records; Harold J. Bauld and Jerome B. Kisslinger, *Horace Mann-Barnard: The First Hundred Years* (privately published by Horace Mann School, 1986).

In addition to Cyrus Leo Sulzberger Jr. (b. Dec. 29, 1888, d. Feb. 21, 1894), the Sulzbergers had previously lost a daughter, Anna Hays Sulzberger (b. Aug. 25, 1886, d. Jan. 26, 1888). AHS was two when his brother Cyrus died, putting him in a similar position as ASO, who had lost an older brother at roughly the same age.

AHS/IOS marriage: Dryfoos; ASO, AHS, IOS, and JOA papers, NYTA; *NYT,* Oct. 30 and Nov. 18, 1917; *Times Talk,* Sept. 1949.

Ochs family in the military: In World War I, Jews had to fend off a crude stereotype of themselves as shirkers. One U.S. Army manual said, "The foreign-born, especially the Jews, are more apt to malinger than the native-born." The Anti-Defamation League protested to the White House, and President Wilson ordered the manual destroyed. See *Time,* Feb. 8, 1963.

GWO's change of name: *Autobiography by George W. Oakes,* undated, JBOP; family letters, JBOP; Dryfoos.

NYT's **Pulitzer Prize in 1918:** In its official histories and in the citation for the year 1918 displayed on the wall of the eleventh-floor corridor of the present-day NYT Building, the paper describes this particular Pulitzer as an award for its coverage of the war. It was, in fact, not for coverage but for the reprinting of official documents and speeches on both sides. See J. Douglas Bates, *The Pulitzer Prize: The Inside Story of America's Most Prestigious Award* (New York: Birch Lane Press, 1991).

Editorial on Austrian peace bid: *NYT,* Sept. 16 and 17, 1918; ASO and AHS papers, NYTA; Dryfoos; Salisbury; Talese; Halberstam; JBOP; F. Fraser Bond, *Mr. Miller of The Times* (New York: Charles Scribner's Sons, 1931); Leonard and Mark Silk, *The American Establishment* (New York: Basic Books, Inc., 1978).

JOA heroism: 25th Reunion Book, Princeton University, 1939, PU; JOA papers, PU; *Times Talk,* Sept. 1949; JOA papers, NYTA; *Evening Sun,* Oct. 21, 1918; *NYT,* Oct. 22, 1918.

AHS's first days at *NYT*: Dryfoos; AHS and IOS papers, NYTA; interview with AHS, Sept. 8, 1965, COH.

ASO's depression: There is an ongoing debate about whether the cause of manic-depression is biological — even hereditary — or environmental, or both. In ASO's case, it may have been a combination. According to one source, high achievers like ASO are likely to become depressed when their accomplishments are lost or threatened. The cause seems to be rooted in childhood, when they were only valued for what they achieved — at least, that is their perception. A person with a deprived childhood (psychologically or financially) sometimes feels he has to "carry the rest of the family's ambitions and so feels it necessary to strive extra hard and feels guilty at any setbacks." See Jenny Cozens, *Nervous Breakdown* (London: Piatkus, 1988).

Chapter 10. The Great Man

Teapot Dome: George Seldes, *Freedom of the Press* (New York: The Bobbs-Merrill Company, 1935); Lloyd Wendt, *The Wall Street Journal: The Story of Dow Jones & the Nation's Business Newspaper* (New York: Rand McNally & Co., 1982); Oswald Garrison Villard, *Some Newspapers and Newspaper-Men* (Freeport, N. Y.: Books for Libraries Press, 1923); *Time,* May 8, 1950; Roger Kahn, "The House of Adolph Ochs," *Saturday Evening Post,* Oct. 9, 1965; AHS papers, NYTA.

The birth of AOS: Dryfoos; ASO, AHS, and IOS papers, NYTA.

IOS kept the name Arthur Hays Sulzberger Jr. long enough to have received several silver baby cups engraved with it.

Family life at 5 East Eightieth Street: ASO, AHS, and IOS papers, NYTA; Dryfoos; JS Oral History, Jan. 11, 1983; and MH Oral History, Nov. 7, 1983, William E. Wiener Oral History Library of the American Jewish Committee, NYPLJ; AHS interview, Aug. 18, 1965, COH; Morgenthau.

AHS relations with ASO: Talese; Halberstam; ASO, AHS, and IOS papers, NYTA.

Lindbergh flight: Berger; Dryfoos; AHS and ASO papers, NYTA; AHS interview, Aug. 18, 1965, COH.

Chapter 11. A Good Name

Abenia: Kathryn E. O'Brien, *The Great and the Gracious on Millionaires' Row: Lake George in Its Glory* (Utica, N.Y.: North Country Books; 1978); RH Oral History, July 17, 1985, William E. Wiener Oral History Library of the American Jewish Committee, NYPLJ; JBOP.

The Crash: Berger; *Times Talk,* vol. 5, no. 1, Aug./Sept. 1951; Louis Berg, "The Americanization of Adolph S. Ochs," *Commentary,* vol. 3, no. 1, Jan. 1947.

Management of CT: JBOP; ASO papers, NYTA.

ASO kidney operation: ASO papers, AJA and NYTA.

Hillandale: ASO, AHS, and IOS papers, NYTA; JBOP; Dryfoos; *Education House: The Early Days* (White Plains, N.Y., Board of Education); inventory of Hillandale, EWO estate, June 23, 1937.

ASO's ban on letters about Hitler: In 1934 the *NYT* published four letters to the editor concerning the situation in Germany, five in 1935, twelve in 1936, and nine in 1937. Most dealt with finance or general topics, none with anti-Semitism. The one letter (in 1936) that directly addressed the issue of refugees and religious persecution spoke only of the plight of the Christians at the hands of the Nazis.

ASO and the succession dilemma: *Autobiography by George W. Oakes,* undated, JBOP; ASO, AHS, JOA, and IOS papers, NYTA; Berger; Dryfoos; Talese.

PART TWO: THE STEWARDS

Chapter 12. The Man Who Would Not Be King

AHS made publisher: Berger; Dryfoos; IOS Oral History, William E. Wiener Oral History Library of the American Jewish Committee, May 19, 1983, NYPLJ; TC interview, Oct. 23, 1972, TC papers, NYTA; AHS and IOS papers, NYTA.

FDR, AHS, and tax settlement: Dryfoos; Salisbury; IOS Oral History, William E. Wiener Oral History Library of the American Jewish Committee, April 7, 1976, NYPLJ; AHS, IOS, and TC papers, NYTA.

In 1933 AHS persuaded his father-in-law to hoard the paper's profits. By the time ASO died, cash reserves had swelled to $6.6 million, but these funds could not legally be used to pay death duties, since they belonged not to ASO but to the company.

At his death, ASO owned 5,503 shares of *NYT* common stock, which gave him absolute control. In the 1920s, at his direction, the company had issued nonvoting preferred stock paid to the owners of common stock — which meant that most of it went to ASO. Each share of the $100 preferred stock paid a high annual cash dividend of $8, and at the time of his death, he had about 87,000 of these shares.

The preferred stock not given in bequests went into ASO's estate, along with the common stock and all of his real estate. The key issue for setting the inheritance tax was what value the government would accept for the *NYT* common stock. The estate's lawyers suggested the low price of $250 per share; the government responded with a valuation almost ten times higher. In the negotiations that followed, the estate's lawyers argued, among other things, that ASO's death made the paper worth less by $200,000 per year, a figure they justified by citing the fact that Joseph Pulitzer's heirs had been permitted to deduct $100,000 for the same reason. Ultimately, the government settled on $566.06 per share, making the total tax bill $5.8 million.

Under AHS's scheme, the *NYT* purchased most of the estate's preferred stock, which provided sufficient cash to pay the tax. But as a consequence, the estate's income plunged to only about $75,000 per year, which was enough to maintain Hillandale but left little cash to spare.

Krock passed over: Arthur Krock papers, PU; AHS and JOA papers, NYTA.

Krock's views on race were so conservative that in 1935 he opposed a federal anti-lynching law on the grounds that it violated states' rights. See AHS papers, NYTA.

On the other hand, he was sensitive about any slight that could be construed as anti-Semitic. His name languished for years on the waiting list for membership in the Century Association. When it finally topped the list and nothing happened, he sought additional endorsements, only to have his candidacy passed over "without prejudice." In 1939 he finally gave up trying to join. "New York clubs are not readily open to such as me, with my liberal dash of Jewish ancestry," he wrote one of his recommenders. "That's fair enough, but the Century has a kind of immigration quota, hasn't it? A few of the inferiors are admitted now and then, aren't they?" See Arthur Krock to Thomas W. Lamont, Nov. 27, 1939, Lamont papers, HBS.

Chapter 13. Married to The New York Times

AOS Jewish education: Oral Memoir of Lester J. Waldman, Anti-Defamation League of B'nai B'rith, Oral Memoirs, vol. 5; AOS Oral History, Nov. 10, 1983, William E. Wiener Oral History Library of the American Jewish Committee, NYPLJ.

Madeleine Carroll: Gladys Hall Collection, Margaret Herrick Library, Academy of Motion Picture Arts and Sciences.

When AHS met Carroll, she was separated from her first husband, Philip Astley, a London real estate broker and friend of the Windsors. In 1939 she sued Astley for divorce, saying that their marriage had "not been one in fact" since 1936, when she came to the United States to make movies and he remained in London. See *NYT*, June 4, 1939.

NYT and the draft: Some isolationists accused the *NYT* of pushing for American intervention because the ownership was Jewish and therefore had a special interest in fighting Hitler. In its November 4, 1941, issue, *Cue* magazine sought to reassure its readers on this point, saying that "contrary to recent charges by isolationists, no *Times* editorial can be regarded as reflecting a specifically Jewish viewpoint. The Editorial Board of 12 . . . consists entirely of Christians."

OED background: ASO had known OED's grandfather well enough to be an honorary pallbearer at his funeral, along with Louis Marshall and Roger Straus. See *NYT*, Nov. 6, 1928.

Dartmouth's president during OED's college years was Dr. Ernest M. Hopkins, who, together with the school's director of admissions, E. Gordon Bill, manipulated the admissions process in the 1930s to control the percentage of Jewish students. Hopkins's belief in quotas got him into trouble in 1945, when he publicly declared Dartmouth to be "a Christian college founded for the Christianization of its students." He freely admitted that the school discriminated against Jews and defended the quota by saying it was set up to prevent resentment and thus anti-Semitism. See *Dartmouth Alumni Magazine,* Nov. 1930; Dartmouth College Archives; Alexandra J. Shepard, "Seeking a Sense of Place: Jewish Students in the Dartmouth Community, 1920–1940," history honors thesis, Dartmouth College, June 9, 1992; and *NYP,* Aug. 7, 1945.

In reaction, AHS wrote Hopkins saying that while he was "pretty much in sympathy with the plan you have outlined," he wondered whether it might be advisable to base selection on geography rather than religion. See AHS to Ernest M. Hopkins, Aug. 20, 1945, AHS papers, NYTA.

Chapter 14. Arthur's Crucible

Ruth in college and the Red Cross: *Times Talk,* vol. 13, no. 9, May 1960; AHS and E. L. James papers, NYTA; RH Oral History, July 17, 1985, William E. Wiener Oral History Library of the American Jewish Committee, NYPLJ; *NYT* Sunday magazine, March 14, 1943; *Jottings: The Junior League of America,* Nov. 1963; Red Cross Archives.

Mental illness of "A": AHS and E. L. James papers, NYTA.

CLS background: Horace Mann records; Salisbury; Cyrus L. Sulzberger, *A Long Row of Candles: Memoirs and Diaries 1934–1954* (New York: MacMillan Company, 1969); AHS papers, NYTA; CLSP.

The *NYT* and Pulitzer Prizes: There have been years, of course, when the *NYT* has received multiple Pulitzers, but in 1953 OED told CLS that, regarding that year's winner, "quite frankly, the unofficial rules are [we] only get one [Pulitzer] and this one was in the cards this year." See OED to CLS, May 8, 1953, OED papers, NYTA.

CLS won a special Pulitzer citation in 1951, which he attributed to the fact that he was "especially nice to Arthur Krock in 1950 [and] he put my name up for a special citation that year on his own hook — after the *Times'* nominations had gone in." Krock himself won a special citation in 1951. See CLS to OED, May 11, 1953, OED papers, NYTA.

NYT cooperation with government during WWII: AHS's attitude that he was fighting "to keep democracy alive" was shared by other journalists of the period.

During World War II the American press was generally more cooperative with the government than critical of it. Censorship was accepted as a condition of war, and newspapers often shared their insights and reporting with Washington. The *Times* gave the FBI and the army liberal access to its morgue — the paper's vast collection of clippings — and refrained from publishing stories it considered potentially helpful to the enemy. Four months before Pearl Harbor, Arthur had asked *Times* reporter Hilton Railey, an experienced military analyst, to conduct a survey of army morale. In making the assignment, he had explicitly told Railey that the results would appear in the paper only if morale was better than a recent story in *Life* had reported. If it was as bad or worse, the paper would "sit on the story as a public service" and turn the material over to the War Department.

Railey traveled eight thousand miles, visiting ten camps and two maneuver areas. His verdict: morale was abysmal. Soldiers had no clue as to why they were being trained; many resented being dragged into what they considered Britain's war. None of his conclusions reached readers of *The New York Times.* Instead, after familiarizing himself with Railey's report, Arthur made a presentation to President Roosevelt and General George Marshall in Washington. His recommendations eventually resulted in the establishment of the Army–Air Force Troop Information and Education Division of the Army. For this "outstanding patriotic service," he received the Army Certificate of Appreciation. See AHS papers, NYTA; AHS Oral History, Aug. 18, 1965, COH.

Madeleine Carroll in the Red Cross: In 1940 Carroll made her château near Paris available to French war orphans. When the German occupation caused her to flee France for the United States, she continued to send money for the children's welfare via the French Resistance. In 1943 she became an American citizen.

Using the name Madeleine Hamilton (the real last name of her husband at the time, Sterling Hayden), Carroll joined the Red Cross in December 1943 and in March 1944 was assigned to the Seventeenth General Hospital in Naples, Italy. From October 1944 to March 1945, she worked on hospital trains connecting the Allied front in France to base operations in Dijon, Marseilles, and other cities. See *NYT,* March 1, 1940 and March 4, 1946; *HT,* March 4, 1946, and Feb. 8, 1948; *Current Biography,* 1949.

AHS trip to Russia: Berger; Reston; Catledge; AHS papers, NYTA; FDR.

The American ambassador to Moscow, William Harrison Standley, was deeply suspicious of AHS, who, he felt, had deceived him and other U.S. officials into believing he had come to Russia strictly as a Red Cross official, not as head of *The New York Times.* At the time, he said nothing. But when his book, *Admiral Ambassador to Russia,* came out twelve years later, Standley gave vent to his anger. His comments were picked up and amplified by the columnist Westbrook Pegler, who wrote in the *Herald Tribune* that he was "sure the Russians considered they had been duped."

To set down the facts for posterity, AHS composed a memorandum for the file recounting the meetings with Roosevelt, Secretary of State Cordell Hull, and Undersecretary Sumner Welles at which his Russian trip was first explored and approved. This history, he wrote, "plainly indicate[s] I went [to Russia] as Publisher of *The New York Times* and that my Red Cross association was a convenient method whereby the President could permit me to travel and at the same time exclude some of the publishers whom he found 'indiscreet.'" In these few words, AHS acknowledged, perhaps unwittingly, his own transformation from anonymous publisher in his father-in-law's mold to a man who thought of himself as part of "the club" running America. AHS was "discreet"; other publishers were not. See AHS papers, NYTA.

Coverage of the Holocaust: The authors are indebted to Deborah E. Lipstadt for her thorough and authoritative work, *Beyond Belief: The American Press and the Coming of the Holocaust 1933–1945* (New York: The Free Press, 1986). She singles out two *NYT* correspondents, Frederick Birchall and Otto Tolischus, for their prescient coverage in the early days of the Hitler regime.

See also Yehuda Bauer, *A History of the Holocaust* (New York: Franklin Watts, 1982); Leni Yahl, *The Holocaust: The Fate of European Jewry, 1932–1945* (New York: Oxford Press, 1990); Arieh Tartakower and Kurt R. Grossmann, *The Jewish Refugee* (New York: Institute of Jewish Affairs of the American Jewish Congress and World Jewish Congress, 1944); Doris Kearns Goodwin, *No Ordinary Time: Franklin and Eleanor Roosevelt: The Home Front in World War II* (New York: Simon & Schuster, 1994); Robert S. Wistrich, *Antisemitism: The Longest Hatred* (New York: Pantheon Books, 1991); David S. Wyman, *The Abandonment of the Jews: America and the Holocaust 1941–45* (New York: Pantheon Books, 1984); Paul Johnson, *The History of the Jews* (New York: HarperPerennial, 1988); Donald Warren, *Radio Priest: Charles Coughlin, the Father of Hate Radio* (New York: The Free Press, 1996).

The Sulzbergers and refugees: In addition to AHS and IOS's sponsorship of relatives, it is important to note that AHS's brother David was vice president of the Jewish Social Service Association, chairing the Greater New York Coordinating Committee for German Refugees in 1939, and a vice president and executive committee chairman of the National Refugee Service, a resettlement agency, from 1939 to 1942. In 1945 and 1946 he went to Italy and Austria as part of a mission for the American Jewish Joint Distribution Committee and the United Nations Relief and Rehabilitation Administration (UNRRA).

As president of the New York section of the National Council of Jewish Women, Beatrice Sulzberger, the widow of AHS's other brother, Leo, helped find work for refugees. See Joseph P. Chamberlain Papers, YI.

Louis Zinn: The police records concerning Zinn's arrest were destroyed after the war. He was cremated and his ashes are now in container #14071 in the New Jewish Cemetery in Nuremberg. Information on Zinn's background and death come from the state archives in Nuremberg and interviews with relatives.

Chapter 15. Wartime Footing

AOS and hazing at Loomis: The year AOS arrived at Loomis, the school discontinued its International Schoolboy Fellowship, an exchange program under which for the previous three years it had accepted "well-screened" members of the Nazi youth movement and sent Loomis students to schools in Germany. See L. W. Fowles, *The Harvest of Our Lives: The History of the First Half-Century of The Loomis Institute* (Windsor, Ct.: The Loomis Institute, 1964).

AOS and WWII service: Talese; Catledge; Dryfoos; Arthur Krock papers, PU; Geoffrey T. Hellman, "Viewer from the 14th Floor," *New Yorker,* Jan. 18, 1969; Judith Michaelson, "He Found It Fit to Print," *NYP* magazine, June 16, 1971;

AOS Oral History, Nov. 28, 1983, William E. Wiener Oral History Library of the American Jewish Committee, NYPLJ; AHS, AOS, IOS, and JOA papers, NYTA.

In the spring of 1942, the *NYT* had offered MacArthur $250,000 to write a book about himself and his military experiences, to be published after the war, as well as $20,000 to his wife for her own story. Two cablegrams to that effect were found among the personal belongings of *NYT* war correspondent Byron Darnton, who was killed later that year by friendly fire off the coast of New Guinea. Colonel George Cocheau, head of the Army Effects Bureau in Kansas City — and coincidentally MacArthur's roommate at West Point — discovered the messages when they were routinely shipped home to the States for process-ing. He pulled them, concerned, as he later told MacArthur, that they might "be used to your very great disadvantage." MacArthur never accepted the offer and destroyed the cables. Why disclosure of these documents would have been embarrassing to MacArthur is unclear, but no doubt he was grateful to AHS for keeping their existence a secret. See AOS papers, NYTA.

The atomic bomb: Catledge; Dryfoos; Talese; William L. Laurence, *Men and Atoms* (New York: Simon & Schuster, 1946); Leslie Groves, *Now It Can Be Told: The Story of the Manhattan Project* (New York: Harper & Row, 1962); TC inter-view, Jan. 23, 1973, TC papers, NYTA; *TimesWeek*, Sept. 26, 1945; *Times Talk*, vol. 5, no. 1, Aug./Sept. 1951; AHS and IOS papers, NYTA.

Chapter 16. Fantasy and Reality

Dupuytren's contracture: There is no known cause for the condition, which is technically a contraction of the palma fascia — the top layer of the palm, fan-shaped from the wrist out to the fingers. It is thought to have some connection to coronary artery disease; surgery can halt it, and sometimes it simply stops spontaneously.

AHS eventually developed this condition in his feet as well, causing an almost egg-size swelling to appear on each instep. To relieve his discomfort, he wore rubber pads in his shoes. See AHS to Irene Manning, April 20, 1961, NYTA.

Postwar attitude toward Israel: IOS Oral History, William E. Wiener Oral His-tory Library of the American Jewish Committee, May 19, 1983; NYPLJ; JBR Papers, UI; *NYT*, April 28, 30 and May 9, 1945; AHS, IOS, and JOA papers, NYTA; Newark *Jewish News*, June 14, 1957.

For *NYT* coverage of the liberation of Dachau and Auschwitz, see James Car-roll, "Shoah in the News: Patterns and Meanings of News Coverage of the Holo-caust," Discussion Paper D-27, The Joan Shorenstein Center for Press, Politics and Public Policy, Harvard University, Oct. 1997. By the time Dachau was liber-ated, many Jewish prisoners had, in fact, been moved to camps farther east, leaving behind Communists, resisters, and POWs. But the victims at Auschwitz, which the *NYT* story identified only as "citizens" of France, the Netherlands, Italy, Hungary, and Poland, were overwhelmingly Jewish.

Although no Jews were based in Jerusalem, Sydney Gruson, who was Jewish, was sent to Israel from his regular posting in Warsaw for three months in 1948 to serve as Middle East correspondent.

Ben and Ruth in Chattanooga: *Time* dispatch, Howland to Don Bermingham, April 22, 1950, *Time* archive; Sidney Shalett, "The Cities of America: Chattanooga," *Saturday Evening Post*, July 30, 1949; RH Oral History, July 17, 1985, and AG Oral History, June 24, 1985, William E. Wiener Oral History Library of the American Jewish Committee, NYPLJ; AHS, JOA, and IOS papers, NYTA.

AHS made much of the fact that Stephen arrived nine months and ten days after the wedding. He composed a poem describing his new grandson as a "perfect gentleman" and sent his daughter ten yellow roses — "one for each day of grace."

Chapter 17. Freedom and Disillusionment

CLS in the 1950s: CLSP; Cyrus L. Sulzberger (ed.), *Marina: Letters and Diaries of Marina Sulzberger* (New York: Crown Publishers, 1978); Cyrus L. Sulzberger, *A Long Row of Candles: Memoirs and Diaries 1934–1954* (New York: MacMillan Company, 1969).

As a rejoinder to "Dopey," Marina called Cy "Porcupine."

AHS and DDE: CLSP; AHS, IOS, and TC papers, NYTA; DDE; Sulzberger (ed.), op. cit.; Stephen E. Ambrose, *Eisenhower: Soldier, General of the Army, President Elect, 1890–1952* (New York: Simon & Schuster, 1983), *Eisenhower: Volume Two — The President* (New York: Simon & Schuster, 1984), and *Eisenhower: Soldier and President* (New York: Simon & Schuster, 1990); David McCollough, *Truman* (New York: Simon & Schuster; 1992); *NYT*, Nov. 8, 1951.

Krock's highly placed source for the Truman lunch was Associate Supreme Court Justice William O'Douglas, a fact he revealed in his memoir in 1968. See Krock, p. 268.

Chapter 18. Redemption

McCarthy: Talese; AHS and TC papers, NYTA; DDE; Edwin R. Bayley, *Joe McCarthy and the Press* (Madison: University of Wisconsin Press, 1981); Neal Gabler, *Winchell: Gossip, Power and the Culture of Celebrity* (New York: Alfred A. Knopf, 1994).

After his firing, Barnet, a Harvard graduate and an army veteran of World War II, had trouble finding work. He picked oranges in Florida, served as a cook on a shrimp boat, and edited manuscripts for vanity presses before joining *The*

Medical Tribune, a journal distributed to doctors. He died in 1998. See *NYT,* June 19, 1998.

The case of Alden Whitman, one of the three *Times*men cited for contempt, was not resolved until 1962, when the U.S. Supreme Court found in his favor. At that time, he wrote AHS a letter of thanks and said that allowing him to remain on the job during the long litigation "sustained me immeasurably." AHS, by then retired as publisher, drafted a warm reply of support. "The era in which charges were brought against you was a disgrace to our country," he wrote. "I am glad that the position we took was sustained by our highest court." AHS's secretary, alarmed at the wholehearted endorsement of Whitman's position as that of the *NYT,* surreptitiously took her concerns to OED. He instructed her to draft a more noncommittal letter. The final version that was sent to Whitman said only, "Thank you for your pleasant letter. . . . It was good of you to write as you did." See AHS papers, NYTA.

JOA's death: In 1971 Babs was interred next to JOA in Arlington National Cemetery. On the day she was to be buried, Arthur Krollege, a *NYT* receptionist, was sitting behind his fourteenth-floor desk, which faced an oil portrait of JOA. The corridor was unusually quiet that day because so many executives had gone to the funeral. Suddenly, JOA's portrait appeared to leap off the wall. It fell to the floor with a loud crash. Krollege was so shaken that he recorded the hour the incident had occurred. "They put her in the ground at exactly the time I put down," he said later. Many in the family speculated it was the ghost of JOA, expressing his displeasure at the prospect of lying next to Babs for eternity.

JOA's attitude toward blacks: In the 1920s ASO invited the black singer Roland Hayes to lunch at the *NYT,* an act that so upset JOA that he left the building. "Julius had this southern approach: we love the Negroes, we must look after them but keep them in their place; they are fine as long as they stay in the kitchen," IOS told an interviewer years later. See IOS papers, NYTA.

NYT* and *Brown* v. *Board: The *NYT* editorial endorsing the Supreme Court decision carried a headline that by today's standards would be ill-considered: ALL GOD'S CHILLUN. The phrase was a reference to the Eugene O'Neill play *All God's Chillun Got Wings.* The editorial went on to reassure readers that the court was "of course . . . not talking of that sort of 'equality' which produces interracial marriage." See *NYT,* May 18, 1954.

Information about Streator comes from Catledge; E. L. James, TC, and AHS papers, NYTA. In his memoir, TC concedes that discrimination in travel and hotel accommodations in the 1940s and 1950s also made it difficult for black reporters to gather information and meet with sources.

AOS in Milwaukee: Edwin R. Bayley with former members of the *Milwaukee Journal* staff, *Ask Harvey, pls.* (Madison, Wis.: Prairie Oak Press, 1994). AHS, IOS, and AHS papers, NYTA.

Chapter 19. The Sorcerer's Apprentices

AHS's twentieth anniversary as publisher: Mattie Ochs to Fannie Ochs, May 11, 1955, Milton B. Ochs scrapbook #2, UT; Elliott M. Sanger diary, COR.

The relationship with Irene Manning continued for years, although she disappeared for long periods when she was involved with other lovers. She was a regular guest at the Sulzbergers' annual cocktail party during the convention of the American Newspaper Publishers Association and was acquainted with Iphigene. But she never mastered the spelling of her name, referring to her in letters as "Ephagene." See AHS papers, NYTA.

AOS in Paris and divorce: AHS, AOS, and IOS papers, NYTA; Robert Ross Alden papers, COR; decree of divorce, *AOS v. Barbara G. Sulzberger,* Nov. 16, 1956, in the Second Judicial District Court of the State of Nevada, in and for the County of Washoe, no. 165160, dept. no. 3.

George Alexanderson: On May 29, 1973, the Associated Press ran a story about AOS's successful fight to prevent an extension of child support. Nothing appeared in the *NYT.* Abe Rosenthal, then the paper's top editor, told the authors that AOS had never asked him to kill a story, but "I did it once without telling him . . . because I thought it would cause him great pain and it was not a great newsworthy item." James J. Kilpatrick subsequently scolded Rosenthal in print, saying he "had a tough decision to make and he blew it. . . . Perhaps it depends on whose Ochs is gored." See James J. Kilpatrick, "A Conservative View," for release Nov. 24/25, 1973, Washington Star Syndicate.

On January 13, 1982, the AP ran a story about George Alexanderson's suit for a declaratory judgment that AOS was his father. At the time, Alexanderson was living in Queens and working as a security guard for a Manhattan hotel; if his suit had been successful, he would been in a position to participate in the eventual distribution of trusts then held by IOS. The parties settled out of court; the files in the case are sealed.

The trust established for Alexanderson is acknowledged every year in the NYTC's notice of annual meeting and proxy statement. In 1999 the trust contained 28,806 shares of Class A common stock; AOS and MH are listed as trustees. See Notice of 1999 Annual Meeting and Proxy Statement, NYTC.

Chapter 20. An Owl and an Omen

AHS/IOS trip to Asia: Edward S. Greenbaum papers, PU; CLS diary, CLSP; Cyrus L. Sulzberger (ed.), op. cit.; DDE; Dryfoos; AHS, AOS, and TC papers, NYTA.

Bay of Pigs: The same day that Paul Kennedy's story arrived in the *NYT* newsroom for editing, AHS, in a display of unfathomable bad judgment, wrote a satirical editorial titled "The United States Attacks Cuba." The tongue-in-cheek column said that a flock of seagulls nesting off the Florida coast had been blown off course and landed near Havana, provoking Cuban president Fidel Castro to retaliate. Castro successfully routed the invaders with no loss of life, except for one gull who got caught in his beard and died of asphyxiation. Clearly pleased with himself, AHS told Charles Merz he would be "very happy" to see the article run the following week. Merz was aghast. "*Please* let's not run this," he told AHS. "As satire, it is too heavy-handed. As prophecy, it ignores the possibility of a Guatemala-staged invasion. I will put it in if you . . . tell me to. But I urge you not to. " AHS backed down. See AHS papers, NYTA.

On March 6, 1961, a month before Szulc's reporting from Miami, Herbert Matthews received confidential information about the Cuban exiles and the CIA's liaison with them. He warned his superiors at the *NYT* that the CIA was handling the situation "unintelligently" and that its "intervention . . . in the Cuban Revolution is bound to come out with a great explosion one of these days and perhaps result in great harm." See Memorandum, Herbert L. Matthews to the Publisher, OED, Charles Merz, TC, Lester Markel, and Emanual Freedman, March 6, 1961, JBR Papers, UI.

JBR's advice — "I wouldn't publish that story at all" — comes from TC Oral History, March 3, 1966, COH. JBR's own account differs. He later said he had only told OED and TC he thought the word *imminent* should be taken out of the story because his information was that the invasion was a week or more away. See JBR to Clifton Daniel, Oct. 21, 1991, Clifton Daniel papers, NYTA.

See also interview with JBO, March 18, 1964, COH; Salisbury; Reston; Catledge; and Pierre Salinger, *With Kennedy* (Garden City, N.Y.: Doubleday & Company, 1966).

In 1998, as the result of a Freedom of Information request by the nonprofit National Security Archive, the government released the CIA's brutally honest inquest into the invasion, which laid the blame for the fiasco squarely on the agency's institutional arrogance, ignorance, and incompetence. See *NYT*, Feb. 22, 1998.

Chapter 21. The Coach

OED as publisher: Arthur Krock papers, PU; *Times Talk,* vol. 16, no. 6, June 1963; Harry Levinson and Stuart Rosenthal, *CEO: Corporate Leadership in Action* (New York: Basic Books, 1984); Talese; Salisbury; JBOP; TC Oral History, Oct. 23, 1972, TC papers, NYTA; AHS and OED papers, NYTA.

Chapter 22. A Separate World

OED/Marian: AHS, IOS, OED, and TC papers, NYTA; *Times Talk,* vol. 16, no. 6, June 1963.

Hillandale: AHS papers, NYTA.

Chapter 23. Hapless Punch

AOS at the *NYT*: TC Oral History, March 7, 1968, TC papers, NYTA; AB, AOS, AHS, and IOS papers, NYTA.

AOS/Carol/Barbara home life: AHS, AOS, and IOS papers, NYTA.

Missile crisis: *NYT,* June 2, 1966, Dec. 7, 1995; *Time,* April 16, 1973; JBO Oral History, March 18, 1964, COH; AHS, OED, and TC papers, NYTA; Catledge; Frankel; Reston; Talese.

Death of David Sulzberger: AHS to Robert L. Duffus, Sept. 18, 1962, ST; AHS papers, NYTA; CLSP.

Chapter 24. A Quiet Leader

1962–63 strike: AHS, AOS, OED, TC, AB, and Frank Cox and A. H. Raskin papers, NYTA; AOS private papers; Elliott M. Sanger diaries, COR; *Time,* Dec. 21, 1962, and Jan. 18, 1963; *NYT,* April 1 and May 26, 28, 1963; *New York Journal-American,* May 26, 1963; Harry Levinson, op. cit.; Amory Bradford, *The Long Strike,* excerpts of unpublished manuscript given to authors by AB.

PART THREE: THE INHERITOR

Chapter 25. The Divine Right of Kings

Decision to name AOS publisher: Bradford, op. cit.; Dryfoos; Reston; Catledge; Talese; AHS, AOS, AB, IOS, and TC papers, NYTA; Weymouth, op. cit.; *Time,* June 20, 1963; IOS Oral History, March 31, 1976, AOS Oral History, Nov. 28, 1983, and RH Oral History, July 17, 1985, William E. Wiener Oral History Library of the American Jewish Committee, NYPLJ; *Times Talk,* vol. 16, no. 7, July/Aug. 1963; JBR's letter to AB given to authors by AB.

AOS first moves: Catledge; Reston; Salisbury; Dryfoos; Talese; Shepard; Levinson, op. cit.; Dick Schaap, "The Ten Most Overrated People in New York," *New York Magazine,* Jan. 17, 1972; Richard Kluger, *The Paper: The Life and Death of the New York Herald Tribune* (New York: Alfred A. Knopf, 1986).

Since 1942 newsroom employees had had the option — but not the obligation — to be represented by the Newspaper Guild. The 1965 contract required them to pay union dues, regardless of whether they formally joined the Guild.

AOS, JBO, and supersonic: JBOP; CLSP; AOS papers, NYTA; JBO Oral History, Dec. 7, 1977, COH.

AOS meeting/relations with Kennedy: Halberstam; Reston; Salisbury; James Boylan, "Declarations of Independence," *Columbia Journalism Review,* Nov./Dec. 1986; TC papers, NYTA; Anthony L. Lewis Oral History, July 23, 1970, JFK; Arthur Krock papers, PU.

Re: *Profiles in Courage:* A recently discovered letter in the Georgetown University Library archives from Jules Davids, a history professor in Georgetown's School of Foreign Service, to Rev. Brian McGrath, asserts that Professor Davids, who in 1954 lectured on political courage to a class that included Jacqueline Kennedy, did "the research and writing for five chapters" of *Profiles in Courage* and was paid $700 by then Senator Kennedy. See *NYT,* Oct. 18, 1997.

Kennedy assassination: TC Oral History, March 3, 1966, COH; Elliott M. Sanger diary, COR; JBO Oral History, April 30, 1964, COH; AOS and IOS papers, NYTA; Clifton Daniel, *Lords, Ladies and Gentleman of the Press* (New York: Arbor House, 1984); Tom Wicker, *On Press* (New York: Viking Press, 1978).

Thirty years later *The New Yorker* reassembled the reporters from Saigon in the early days who had reported critically from the start. The night before they were to have their pictures taken by Richard Avedon, the five gathered for dinner at Elio's — Mal Browne, Neil Sheehan, Peter Arnett, Horst Faas, and Halberstam. By that time, all had won the Pulitzer Prize. Across the room they spied AOS eating dinner with friends. "So because we could not have done it without him, we did what reporters have always wanted to do for publishers," said Halberstam. "We sent him a bottle of Dom Perignon." See speech by David Halberstam at the Libel Defense Resource Center's dinner honoring Punch Sulzberger and Katharine Graham, 1996.

Chapter 26. The Center Will Not Hold

Dryfoos family after OED death: AHS papers, NYTA; SD Oral History, May 23, 1984, William E. Wiener Oral History Library of the American Jewish Committee, NYPLJ; MH Oral History, June 14, 1967, Adlai Stevenson Project, COH; Andrew Heiskell, with Ralph Graves, *Outsider/Insider: An Unlikely Success Story* (New York: Marian-Darien Press, 1998); *NYT,* Feb. 27, 1943; BD activities from

Dartmouth College archives; eulogy for Anne Madeleine Heiskell, SD private papers.

Golden family: AHS, AOS, IOS, and TC papers, NYTA; RH Oral History, July 17, 1985, MG Oral History, Jan. 15, 1986, LD Oral History, June 23, 1985, SG Oral History, Jan. 22, 1985, AG Oral History, June 24, 1985, William E. Wiener Oral History Library of the American Jewish Committee, NYPLJ; *CT,* Aug. 15, 1992; MBO scrapbooks, vol. 14, CH; *Newsweek,* Nov. 29, 1993; Charley Bartlett to John F. Kennedy, May 17, 1962, JFK; *NYT,* Dec. 23, 1964.

Chapter 27. A Parallel Existence

AOS-Carol marriage: AHS and IOS papers, NYTA; *Time* dispatch by Regina Cahill, July 5, 1977, *Time* archive; Diamond.

Religious upbringing of AOSJ and KS: AOSJ Oral History, March 27, 1984, AOS Oral History, Nov. 10, 1983, William E. Wiener Oral History Library of the American Jewish Committee, NYPLJ.

Washington bureau bungle: Talese; Catledge; Reston; *Washington Post,* Feb. 9, 1968; *Editor & Publisher,* Feb. 17, 1968; *Newsweek,* Feb. 19, 1968; Geoffrey T. Hellman, op. cit.; *Ramparts Magazine,* May 1968; TC Oral History, Oct. 23, 1972, TC papers, NYTA; JBR papers, UI; AOS and TC papers, NYTA.

Chapter 28. Searching for Lost Fathers

AOSJ moves in with AOS: Browning and Loomis school records; AOS and AHS papers, NYTA; Edward Klein, "The Kingdom and the Prince," *Manhattan, Inc.,* Aug. 1988; Browning School *Grytte,* Nov. 1969.

Cohen family: Westminster School records; AHS papers, NYTA.

Chapter 29. The Age of Discontent

Columbia and 1968: AOS papers, NYTA; *Columbia Spectator,* Feb. 1, 1973; William Manchester, *The Glory and the Dream: A Narrative History of America 1932–1972* (New York: Bantam Books, 1981); *NYT,* April 24, 25, 26, 27, and 30, May 1, 2 and June 13, 1968; *NYT,* Nov. 22, 1997; *Village Voice,* May 9, 1968.

When Rev. Martin Luther King was assassinated, AOS gave employees who wanted to attend the funeral the day off with pay and advanced them the funds necessary for the airfare to Atlanta. The same policy applied to the Washington burial of Senator Robert F. Kennedy. See Memoranda, AOS to the Staff, April 8 and June 7, 1968, AOS papers, NYTA.

The *NYT* and Vietnam: AOS, AHS, IOS, and TC papers, NYTA; Arthur Krock papers, PU; *Time,* Jan. 10, 1964, July 23, 1965, and March 11, 1966; JBO Oral History, March 18, 1964, and Dec. 7, 1977, COH; Talese; Dryfoos; Salisbury; Boylan, op. cit.; Halberstam; JBOP; *NYT,* Feb. 1, 1966, and Sept. 1, 1968; John Corry, *My Times: Adventures in the News Trade* (New York: Grosset/Putnam, 1994).

There is some evidence that a sizable percentage of the public was against the war well before Tet. A poll taken in 1967 found that 50 percent of Americans believed involvement in Vietnam was a mistake. See Michael Schudson, *The Power of News* (Cambridge: Harvard University Press, 1995).

Death of AHS: AHS Oral History, Aug. 18, 1965, COH; AHS and AOS papers, NYTA; *CT* and *NYT,* Dec. 12, 1968; *NYT,* Dec. 16, 1968.

Chapter 30. The Phoenix Rises

IOS in China: Audrey Topping Oral History, 1981, COH; Dryfoos; IOS papers, NYTA; Weymouth, op. cit.; *NYT,* Sept. 25 and Nov. 25, 1973.

AOS's actions after his father's death: *Time* dispatch by Regina Cahill, July 5, 1977, *Time* archive; AOS, IOS, AMR, and JBR papers, NYTA; Goulden; Deena Yellin, "A. M. Rosenthal: Having His Say," *Lifestyles Magazine;* Robert Lenzer, "The Times, the Post and Watergate," *Boston Globe* Sunday magazine, Aug. 25, 1974; CLSP.

Chapter 31. Fits and Starts

Argyris study: Salisbury; Diamond; Chris Argyris, *Behind the Front Page: Organizational Self-Renewal at a Metropolitan Newspaper* (San Francisco: Jossey-Bass, 1974); AOS papers, NYTA; JBO Oral History, Dec. 7, 1977, COH; David M. Rubin, "Behind the Front Page," *MORE,* Nov. 1974.

Op-Ed page: JBOP; AOS and Clifton Daniel papers, NYTA.

In his diary on the day the Op-Ed page was inaugurated, JBR wrote that "it is a very good and a very old idea. I have been arguing for it for at least 16 years and some of my elders longer than that. . . . What held up a decision was the amiable tradition of the *Times* not to hurt anybody, but in the process we hurt the *Times.*" He went on to suggest that the Op-Ed page would "inevitably diminish and eventually kill" newspaper columnists, because such pages would make it possible to publish experts who could write on topics with far more authority for far less money. See JBR diary, Sept. 21, 1970, JBR papers, UI.

Resignation of Andy Fisher: Andy Fisher to AOS, Feb. 7, 1971, Fisher private papers; *NYT,* Feb. 11, 1971; Chris Welles, "Harder Times at 'The Times,'" *New York Magazine,* Jan. 17, 1972; JBO Oral History, Dec. 7, 1977, COH; AOS papers, NYTA; TC Oral History, Oct. 23, 1972, and Jan. 23, 1973, TC papers, NYTA.

Diversification and cost-cutting: *NYP,* Jan. 6, 1971; *Time,* Aug. 15, 1977; Welles, op. cit.; AOS papers, NYTA; Diamond.

JS and Budd Levinson: Budd Levinson Oral History, March 21, 1983, William E. Wiener Oral History Library of the American Jewish Committee, NYPLJ; *NYT,* Dec. 17, 1969.

Chapter 32: Betting the Enterprise

The Pentagon Papers: Rudenstine; Salisbury; Reston; Frankel; Sanford J. Unger, *The Papers and the Papers: An Account of the Legal and Political Battle over The Pentagon Papers* (New York: E.P. Dutton & Co., Inc., 1972); Frederick Schauer, *Parsing The Pentagon Papers,* May 1991, Joan Shorenstein Barone Center for Press, Politics and Public Policy, Harvard University; AOS, AMR, and JBR papers, NYTA; CLSP; *Time,* June 28, 1971; *Times Talk,* vol. 41, no. 4, July 1996; Silk, op. cit.; Manchester, op. cit.; *NYT,* June 13 and 17, 1971; *NYT,* May 3, 1996; David Wise, *The Politics of Lying: Government Deception, Secrecy, and Power* (New York: Random House, 1973); Denis Sheahan, "Punch of The Times," *W,* Jan. 25, 1974; Judith Michaelson, "He Found It Fit to Print," *NYP* magazine, June 16, 1971; AOS speech before Committee to Protect Journalists, Nov. 26, 1996; Ben Bradlee, *A Good Life: Newspapering and Other Adventures* (New York: Simon & Schuster, 1995).

Chapter 33. The Summer of the Gyspy Moths

NYT in 1972: Diamond; Salisbury; Bradlee; Geraldo Samor, "Watergate: The First Month," University of Kansas, William Allen White School of Journalism, 1994; AOS, IOS, AMR, and Seymour Topping papers, NYTA; Lenzer, op. cit.; Nixon statement as quoted in Silk, op. cit.; *Editor & Publisher,* Oct. 20, 1973; John C. Ottinger and Patrick D. Maines, "Is It True What They Say About The New York Times?" *National Review,* Sept. 15, 1972.

Hiring Safire: JBOP; AOS papers, NYTA; *Time,* Feb. 12, 1973; Marjorie Williams, "Safire and Brimstone," *Vanity Fair,* Nov. 1992; Roger Rosenblatt, "The Mysterious Ways of William Safire," *Men's Journal,* Oct. 1994.

At a private dinner in 1969, JBR sounded out Vermont Royster of *The Wall Street Journal* about how the *NYT* might go about publishing more "balanced opinion" on its pages. Later, JBR advised AOS to regard a conservative voice as a "useful corrective" to the perception that the *NYT* published only opinion that was "liberal or worse." See memorandum, JBR to AOS, Veit, and Gruson, Dec. 16, 1969, and memorandum, JBR to AOS and Bancroft, undated, JBR papers, UI.

When *The Washington Post* failed in its bid to hire Safire, it hired conservative George Will instead. See Diamond.

Chapter 34. The Four-Part Miracle

1974 strike: *BusinessWeek,* Feb. 3, 1973; *NYT,* April 11 and 22, 1974; *NYT,* May 3, 1974; *NYT,* July 29, 1974; AOS papers, NYTA; JBOP.

The four-part paper: Diamond; AOS, AMR, and TC papers, NYTA; JBO Oral History, Sept. 29, 1978, COH; *Times Talk,* Aug. 1967; *Time,* Aug. 15, 1977; Dean M. Skylar, "The Use and Application of Marketing and Research at Daily Newspapers," master's thesis, University of Missouri, May 1978; Levinson, op. cit.; Silk, op. cit.; Richard Pollak, "Abe Rosenthal Presents The New New York Times," *Penthouse,* Sept. 1977.

Chapter 35. Getting Rid of Troublesome Priests

JBO retirement: Diamond; JBOP; Richard Pollak, "Times Family Feud Sizzles," *MORE,* December 1976; Weymouth, op. cit.; Silk, op. cit.; AOS papers, NYTA; *NYT,* Jan. 1, 1977; *Time,* Feb. 7, 1977; *BusinessWeek,* Aug. 30, 1976.

A 1998 *NYT* editorial announced that although the paper had generally refrained from primary endorsements in major elections, it was changing its policy that year and anticipated "doing so in the future." The editorial listed a handful of past exceptions, including the 1976 Moynihan endorsement. See *NYT,* Sept. 6, 1998.

CLS retirement: CLSP; CLS, *Marina,* op. cit.; CLS, *How I Committed Suicide: A Reverie* (New York: Ticknor & Fields, 1982); Salisbury; AOS and AMR papers, NYTA; *NYT,* Sept. 12 and 13, 1977; *MORE,* Oct. 1977; *NYT,* Dec. 17, 1977; *NYT,* Jan. 31, 1976; *Editor & Publisher,* Dec. 31, 1977.

For a detailed analysis of how the *NYT* and other news organizations handled the *Glomar Explorer* project, see Salisbury.

Chapter 36. A President and a Family Counselor

SG marriage/work at *NYT*: SG Oral History, Jan. 22, 1985, William E. Wiener Oral History Library of the American Jewish Committee, NYPLJ; AOS papers, NYTA.

Chapter 37. A Coup de Foudre and a Career

AOSJ and GG in Raleigh: Seymour Topping papers, NYTA; *NYT,* May 25, 1975.

AOSJ and GG in London: *NYT,* June 11, 1977; Seymour Topping papers, NYTA; AOSJ Oral History, March 27, 1984, William E. Wiener Oral History Library of the American Jewish Committee, NYPLJ; GG and AOSJ, "The Long Way Home," *NYT* Sunday magazine, July 1, 1979.

AOSJ in Washington: AOSJ speech at Smithsonian Institution, Jan. 15, 1992; Seymour Topping, AOS, IOS, and AMR papers, NYTA; Edward Klein, "Paramount Player," *Vanity Fair,* Jan. 1994; Margaret Carlson, "The Times of His Life," *Time,* Aug. 17, 1992; Edward Klein, "Prince Pinch," *Manhattan, Inc.,* Aug. 1988; *NYT,* Aug. 6, 1980; *NYP,* Aug. 7, 1980.

Chapter 38. Everyone Makes His Move

DC and LK in Florida, Texas, and NYC: DC Oral History, March 10, 1983, William E. Wiener Oral History Library of the American Jewish Committee, NYPLJ.

AOSJ, AMR, and gays: Michelangelo Signorile, "Out at The New York Times, Part II," *Advocate,* May 19, 1992; Paul H. Weaver, "The New Face of The New York Times," *New York Magazine,* June 24, 1968; *Newsweek,* Nov. 29, 1965; Goulden; Ransdell Pierson, "Uptight on Gay News," *Columbia Journalism Review,* April 1982.

AMR adamantly disputes the idea that he was a homophobe and notes that he knowingly hired and promoted several gay journalists.

Chapter 39. All for One, One for All

Succession to publishership: IOS Oral History, May 19, 1983, William E. Weiner Oral History Library of the American Jewish Committee, NYPLJ; AG Oral History, June 24, 1985, William E. Wiener Oral History Library of the American Jewish Committee, NYPLJ.

SD work and remarriage: SD Oral History, May 23 and July 12, 1984, William E. Wiener Oral History Library of the American Jewish Committee, NYPLJ; AMR papers, NYTA; *NYT,* Sept. 6 and Nov. 9, 1975; *NYT,* Aug. 26, 1977; *Time,* June 5, 1978; *Cincinnati Enquirer,* Dec. 20, 1981.

Family covenant: *NYT,* June 20, 1986; *NYT,* Feb. 27, 1990; AOS papers, NYTA.

Chapter 40. A Thousand Years

Retirement of AMR: *Washington Post,* Jan. 7 and Oct. 11, 1986; *NYT,* June 10, 1987; *NYT,* April 4, 1990; *Time,* Oct. 20, 1986; AMR, AOS, and Frankel papers, NYTA; *NYT,* March 19, 1992; Barbara Matusow, "Max Frankel's Mandate: Peace in Our Times," *Washington Journalism Review,* January 1987; Goulden; Frankel.

IOS in old age: *Vanity Fair,* June 1993; Joe Perpich, "Cindy's Wedding," June 17, 1993, and David Perpich, "Childhood Experiences," Jan. 1993, and Sarah Perpich, "Seasons," Oct. 15, 1993, Sulzberger/Perpich private papers.

Chapter 41. A Time of Testing

The crash of 1987: *NYT,* July 17, 1987; Richard Shumate, "Paper Tiger," *Atlanta Magazine,* Jan. 1993; Margaret Carlson, op. cit.; *NYT,* Nov. 14, 1987; Frankel.

AOSJ as deputy publisher: Edward Klein, "Prince Pinch," *Manhattan, Inc.,* Aug. 1988; Diamond; Frankel.

William Kennedy Smith rape story: *NYT,* April 17 and 26, 1991; Carlson, op. cit.; Robert Sam Anson, "The Best of Times, the Worst of Times," *Esquire,* March 1993; Laure de Montebello, "It Was the Best of Times," *Hamptons Magazine,* Labor Day 1991; *Time,* May 6, 1991; Frankel.

In December 1959 the *NYT* published the name of a subway clerk who had been raped. When a reader complained, TC responded: "*The New York Times* does follow the practice of not mentioning the victims' names in rape cases, except where a matter of murder, robbery or some other heinous crime is jointly involved. In this particular case the name of the victim had been widely disseminated throughout the city by the AP and UPI and other news media. The judgment of the editor in charge was that this being true the readers of the *New York Times* would be best served by mentioning the name." See TC to Mrs. Frederick B. Pollock, Dec. 16, 1959, AHS papers, NYTA.

Unbeknownst to many, Behr had actually fought to keep Bowman's name out of print and had had second thoughts about certain elements of the piece before it ran.

Chapter 42. The Sword in the Stone

Death of IOS: IOS papers, NYTA; *NYT,* Feb. 27 and March 1, 1990; Ken Auletta, "Behind the Times," *New Yorker,* June 10, 1996; *Barnard Reporter,* vol. 18, no. 2 (Spring 1990).

At their mother's death, Punch and his sisters immediately came into possession of 14 million Class A shares from the Ochs Trust worth $334 million, or $83.5 million each.

In addition, all of the Class B shares in the Ochs Trust and 3.3 million additional Class A shares were divided among four separate trusts for the four siblings. All four acted as trustees of each of the trusts. The 3.3 million Class A shares were intended to pay inheritance taxes for several generations.

In 1997 the trusts for Punch and his sisters were abolished and a new joint trust was created that includes all the Class B shares and enough Class A shares from the four trusts to pay inheritance taxes at the deaths of the members of the cousins' generation. The Class A shares that were removed from the four trusts were distributed to Punch and his sisters, who have made arrangements to pay their inheritance taxes without using money from the new trust.

AOSJ made publisher: *NYT* press release, Jan. 16, 1992; Carlson, op. cit.; Ken Auletta, "Opening Up The Times," *New Yorker,* June 28, 1993; *NYT,* Jan. 17, 1992; *Washington Post,* Jan. 17, 1992; *Times Talk,* Nov. 1963; Memorandum, AOS to the Staff, Jan. 16, 1992.

PART FOUR: THE NEXT GENERATION

Chapter 43. Welcome to the Revolution

The Greenwich conferences: Ken Auletta, "Opening Up The Times," *New Yorker,* June 28, 1993; *NYP,* Dec. 8, 1992; Leon Wieseltier, "Total Quality Meaning," *New Republic,* July 19 and 26, 1993; *NYT,* Dec. 21, 1993; Jeremy Main, "The Curmudgeon Who Talks Tough on Quality," *Fortune,* June 25, 1984.

AOSJ and diversity: William McGowan, "The Other Side of the Rainbow," *Columbia Journalism Review,* Dec. 1993; *NYT,* Sept. 10, 1993; AOSJ speech to sales meeting, Sept. 15, 1992; "A Changing Times: The Diversity Newsletter of the NYT," Oct./Nov. 1994.

AOSJ's identity as a Jew: Commentary by Jim Sleeper, *NYP,* Aug. 5, 1997.

Chapter 44. A Smile, a Shoeshine, and a President

Outlook for newspapers circa 1992: "Media: A Brave New World," Alex, Brown & Sons Inc. Research Media Group, Nov. 19, 1992; *NYT,* March 29, 1993; *NYT,* Feb. 9, 1993.

Chapter 45. Whispers and a Megaphone

Styles of the *NYT*: Carlson, op. cit.; Diamond; *New York Magazine,* Nov. 16, 1992; *NYP,* July 29, 1993; *New York Observer,* Nov. 29, 1993.

Howell Raines as editorial-page editor: *NYT,* Sept. 12, 1992; *Washington Post,* May 10, 1993; *New York Observer,* July 19–26, 1993; *New Yorker,* Aug. 22–29, 1994.

Thomas L. Friedman and Jewish critics: Friedman has won two Pulitzer Prizes, both for coverage of the Middle East.

Chapter 46. Management in a Bucket

Acquisition of *The Boston Globe*: *NYT,* June 12, 13 and Aug. 16, 1993; *Boston Globe,* June 11, 12, and 13, 1993; Ron LeBrecque, "All the News Just Doesn't Fit," *Boston Magazine,* May 1996; *Wall Street Journal,* June 14, 1993; *Editor & Publisher,* June 19, 1993; *New York Observer,* June 21 and July 5, 1993; NYTC press release, Sept. 28, 1993, and Oct. 20, 1994.

Joe Lelyveld made executive editor: AMR papers, NYTA; *New Yorker,* July 11, 1994; *Times Talk,* vol. 40, no. 2, April 1994; *Editor & Publisher,* May 21, 1994; Frankel.

Chapter 47. The New "Good Son"

Domestic-partners fracas: *New York Observer,* May 9 and 13, 1994; *Union Times,* April 21, 1994; Memorandum of Agreement Between the New York Times Company and the Newspaper Guild of New York, Local 3, April 29, 1994; *Editor & Publisher,* April 30, 1994.

Prospective bid for Madison Square Garden: *NYT,* July 6, 1994; *NYP,* July 8, 1994; *Wall Street Journal,* Aug. 22, 1994.

Chapter 48. Growing Pains

The Unabomber: *NYT,* Aug. 2, 1995; *NYT* and *Washington Post,* Sept. 19, 20, and 24, 1995; *American Journalism Review,* June 1996; *NYT,* April 4, 1996; *Time,* April 15, 1996; *Newsweek,* April 15, 1996; *NYT,* May 5, 1998; William Finnegan, "Defending the Unabomber," *New Yorker,* March 16, 1998.

Cynthia Sulzberger wedding: *NYT,* Feb. 7, 1993; Sulzberger/Perpich private papers; *NYT,* June 18, 1993.

Chapter 49. Transitions

Marriage to Allison Cowles: *NYP,* Sept. 5 and Dec. 11, 1995; *NYP,* Feb. 20, 1996; *NYT,* Feb. 21 and March 10, 1996.

Family governance: Selected pages from *Proposals for the Future: To the Third Generation of the Ochs-Sulzberger Family from the Fourth and Fifth Generations,* Sulzberger family private papers; Ken Auletta, "Behind the Times," *New Yorker,* June 10, 1996; Selected issues of *The Lookout* (family newsletter), JC private papers.

Hiring Diane Baker: Morgan Stanley Research Report on NYTC, Sept. 13, 1995; Donaldson, Lufkin & Jenrette Securities Research Report on NYTC, Sept. 13, 1995; *NYT,* Sept. 13, 1995.

Chapter 50. Two Camps

MG made corporate executive: *NYT,* Dec. 29, 1995; NYTC press release, Dec. 28, 1995.

Chapter 51. Death of a Salesman

Dismissal of Primis: *Wall Street Journal,* Jan. 22 1996; *NYP,* Jan. 23, 1996; Ron LeBrecque, "All the News Just Doesn't Fit," *Boston Magazine,* May 1996; Ken Auletta, "Behind the Times," *New Yorker,* June 10, 1996; *Times Talk,* vol. 42, no.1, Jan./Feb. 1996; Transcript, *Adam Smith's Money World,* May 16, 1996; NYTC press release, Sept. 20. 1996; *NYT,* Sept. 21, 1996; *Washington Post,* Sept. 21, 1996; *Wall Street Journal,* Sept. 23, 1996.

Centennial of family ownership: *NYT,* March 18 and 24, 1996; *NYT,* June 27 and 30, 1996; *NYP,* June 30, 1996; Harold Evans, "Beyond the Scoop," *New Yorker,* July 8, 1996.

Chapter 52. Smooth Sailing

Decision to name AOSJ chairman: *NYT,* June 15, Sept. 14, Oct. 17, 1997; *Times Talk,* May/June 1997; *Time,* Sept. 29, 1997; NYTC press release, Oct. 16, 1997; *New York Observer,* Oct. 27, 1997.

Chapter 53. Live Long and Prosper

AOS's 72nd birthday party: *The Lookout,* March 1998, JC private papers; *NYT,* Feb. 27, 1998; *NYT,* Jan. 5, 1999.

In October 1998, after a formal search, The New York Times Company chose one of its own — John O'Brien — to replace Diane Baker as CFO.

Epilogue

Dismissal of DC; resignation of SG: *NYT,* March 3 and May 20, 1999.

NYT and the Internet: *NYT,* May 25, 1999.

INDEX